Reconsidering Islam in a South Asian Context

For Prof. Rutherford,
Mentor & friend —
Reza 09

Social Sciences in Asia

Edited by

Vineeta Sinha
Syed Farid Alatas
Chan Kwok-bun

VOLUME 25

Reconsidering Islam in a South Asian Context

By
M. Reza Pirbhai

BRILL

LEIDEN • BOSTON
2009

Cover illustration: Mughal Tomb in Makli Necropolis, Pakistan (Pirbhai, 2000).

This book is printed on acid-free paper.

Library of Congress Cataloging-in-Publication Data

Pirbhai, M. Reza.
  Reconsidering Islam in a South Asian context / by M. Reza Pirbhai.
    p. cm. — (Social sciences in Asia ; v. 25)
  Includes bibliographical references and index.
    ISBN 978-90-04-17758-1 (pbk. : alk. paper) 1. Islam—South Asia—History.
2. Islamic renewal—South Asia—History. 3. Muslims—South Asia—History.
I. Title. II. Series.

BP63.A37P57 2009
297.0954—dc22

2009022847

ISSN 1567-2794
ISBN 978 90 04 17758 1

Copyright 2009 by Koninklijke Brill NV, Leiden, The Netherlands.
Koninklijke Brill NV incorporates the imprints Brill, Hotei Publishing,
IDC Publishers, Martinus Nijhoff Publishers and VSP.

All rights reserved. No part of this publication may be reproduced, translated, stored in a retrieval system, or transmitted in any form or by any means, electronic, mechanical, photocopying, recording or otherwise, without prior written permission from the publisher.

Authorization to photocopy items for internal or personal use is granted by Koninklijke Brill NV provided that the appropriate fees are paid directly to The Copyright Clearance Center, 222 Rosewood Drive, Suite 910, Danvers, MA 01923, USA.
Fees are subject to change.

PRINTED IN THE NETHERLANDS

*Dedicated
to
Qamar Iqbal Pirbhai*
(1944–2005)

CONTENTS

Acknowledgements ix
Translation and Transliteration Note xi
Maps xiii
Chronology of Major Muslim States, Relations with the
   English East India Company and British Raj in South Asia,
   570–1947 xvii

Introduction 1

PART ONE
FOUNDATIONS: ISLAM AND THE MUGHALS

Chapter One: The Categories of Doctrinal Islam 19
   I. Al-Ghazali and al-Hujwiri: Categorising Islamic
      Thought 22
   II. The World of Reason 30
   III. The Other-World of Intuition 53
   Conclusion: The Fallacy in Paradigms of 'Intrusive' Islam ... 62

Chapter Two: Indicism, Intoxication and Sobriety among the
   'Great Mughals' 67
   I. Jalal al-Din Akbar and the Intoxicated Way 71
   II. Muhi al-Din Awrangzib and the Sober Path 91
   Conclusion: The Trouble with 'Unbounded' Indicism 114

PART TWO
TRANSFORMATIONS: ISLAM AND COLONIALISM

Chapter Three: Codification and a 'New' Sober Path 119
   I. Shah Wali Allah and Pre-Colonial Trends in the
      Sober Path: 1707–1765 133

II. Shah Muhammad Isma'il and the *Tariqa Muhammadiyya*: 1765–1857	148
III. Deoband and Company: 1857–1947	161
Conclusion: A 'New' Sober Path	173
Chapter Four: Anglicisation and the 'Old Islam'	177
I. Islam in a Textual Context	186
II. Islam in an Oral Context	206
Conclusion: Out with the 'Old,' In with the 'New'	218
Chapter Five: Objectification and a 'New' Intoxicated Way	223
I. Sayyid Ahmad Khan's 'Nature'	232
II. Mirza Ghulam Ahmad's 'Messiah'	248
III. Muhammad Iqbal's 'Self'	257
Conclusion: A 'New' Intoxicated Way	266
Chapter Six: Nationalism and the 'New Islam'	269
I. The 'Inner' Domain: The 'New Islam,' Gender and Community	273
II. The 'Outer' Domain: *Umma, Qawm* and Nation	291
Conclusion: From Sultanates to Nations	332
Conclusion: Towards a 'Post-Orientalist' History	337
Selected Bibliography	345
Glossary	359
Index of Persons	361
Index of Subjects	365

ACKNOWLEDGEMENTS

This book could not have been written without the liberality and support of a number of individuals and institutions over many years. Interest in the subject first germinated when I was a doctoral candidate in the stimulating environment at the University of Toronto. I must therefore begin by thanking Milton Israel, Linda Northrup and Paul Rutherford, my mentors and guides through the trials of graduate school, for encouraging me to pursue the very subject of this book, and for laying the scholastic foundations necessary to translate flighty interests into a focused work.

Just as beginning a book requires inspiration and assistance, so does bringing the project to a satisfactory end. I am indebted to many for completing this work, but none more so than my colleagues at Louisiana State University. In particular, Gaines Foster, Chair of the Department of History, has extended every facility to smooth the writing process, John Henderson and David Lindenfeld have read and tendered invaluable advice on the work in progress, and Suzanne Marchand has offered sagacious counsel on everything from research to publication. I must also thank Clifford Duplechin and Mary Lee Eggart of the Department of Geography and Anthropology for their fine work on my maps. Gratitude is also due the Office of the Dean (Arts and Sciences) and the Office of Research for their aid over the years. And finally, I must cite the Louisiana Board of Regents through the Board of Regents Support Fund (Contract # LEQSF (2008–09)-RD-ATL-06), for the generous financial support without which this book could not have been finished.

Many will have to forgive me for not mentioning them, but I could not forgive myself if I did not acknowledge the one constant through the writing process and in my life more generally. My wife and colleague, Reem Meshal, has gifted me the expertise in Islamic Studies that keeps my work honest, the home that makes work possible and the child that gives all this work meaning. I would also be remiss not to thank my sisters for putting up with my lectures, while stimulating me with their own personal and professional views on the world. My father must be recognized for supporting any and all of my pursuits, and my mother for bequeathing the sense of self that makes these endeavours possible in the first place.

Finally, I would like to thank Lee Kiat Jin, Nandita Sinha and the Social Sciences of Asia series editors at E.J. Brill Publishers, for all their efforts in bringing this work to fruition.

TRANSLATION AND TRANSLITERATION NOTE

This work's considerable reliance on Arabic, Persian and Urdu sources is both advantageous and problematic for transliteration. All three languages not only utilise a variant of the Arabic script, but Persian includes a great stock of Arabic terms and the larger part of Urdu vocabulary is Arabic and/or Persian. The advantages of this linguistic relationship may be evident, but problems stem from grammatical and phonetic differences less immediately apparent. For example, phonetic differences often lead the same word to be transliterated differently from language to language, as in the case of the Arabic '*wahy*' and the Persian/Urdu '*vahy*'. As well, differences in conjugation can render the same word unrecognisable, as in the Arabic '*aqwam*' and the Urdu '*qawmun*'. Given that this study's readers may not be familiar with all three languages, the above differences may result in confusion. Thus, all shared terms mentioned are transliterated in the Arabic form. Where differences of the latter variety occur, the Arabic singular is given with the English 's' to denote plurality. Of course, terms particular to a given language are given in the corresponding form. As well, the Persian/Urdu '*izafat*' is given as '*-i*'. The transliteration system utilised for all three languages is that of the *International Journal of Middle East Studies*. As the majority of terms transliterated are by no means obscure to those familiar with either Arabic, Persian or Urdu, diacritical markings are only included in the Glossary.

Map 1

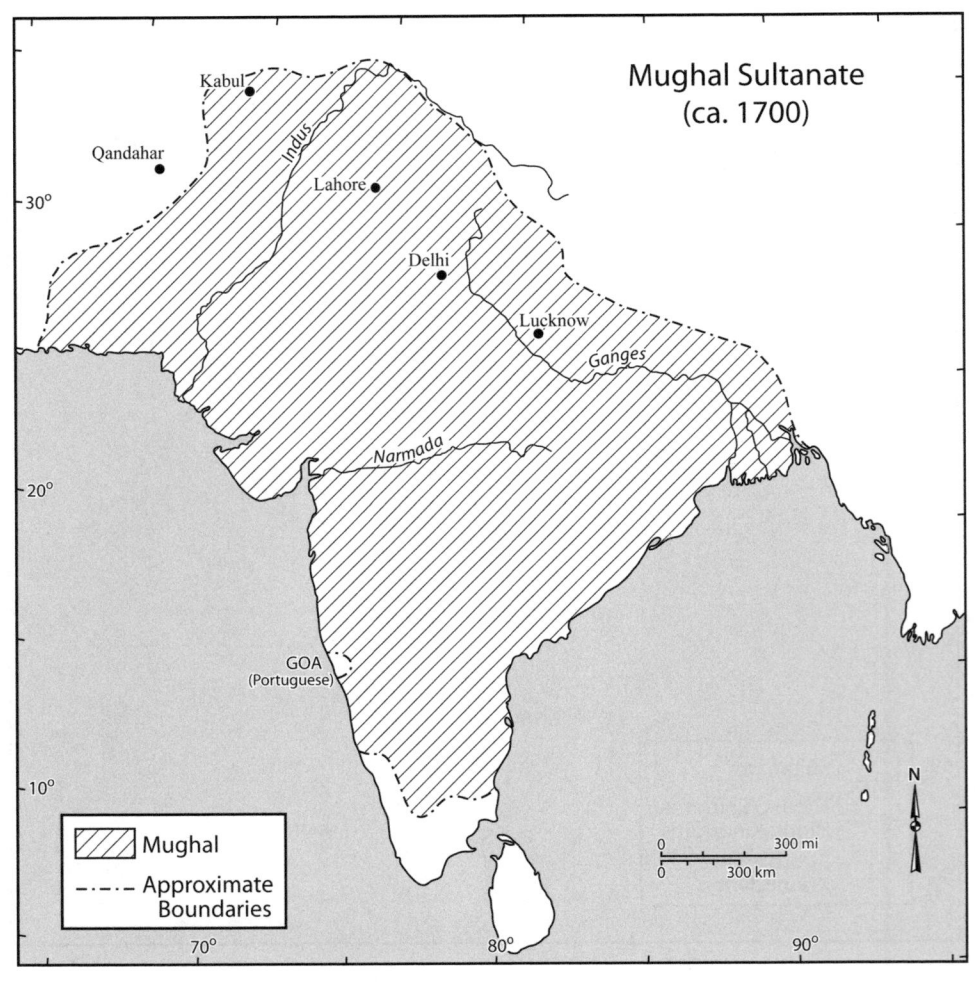

Map 2

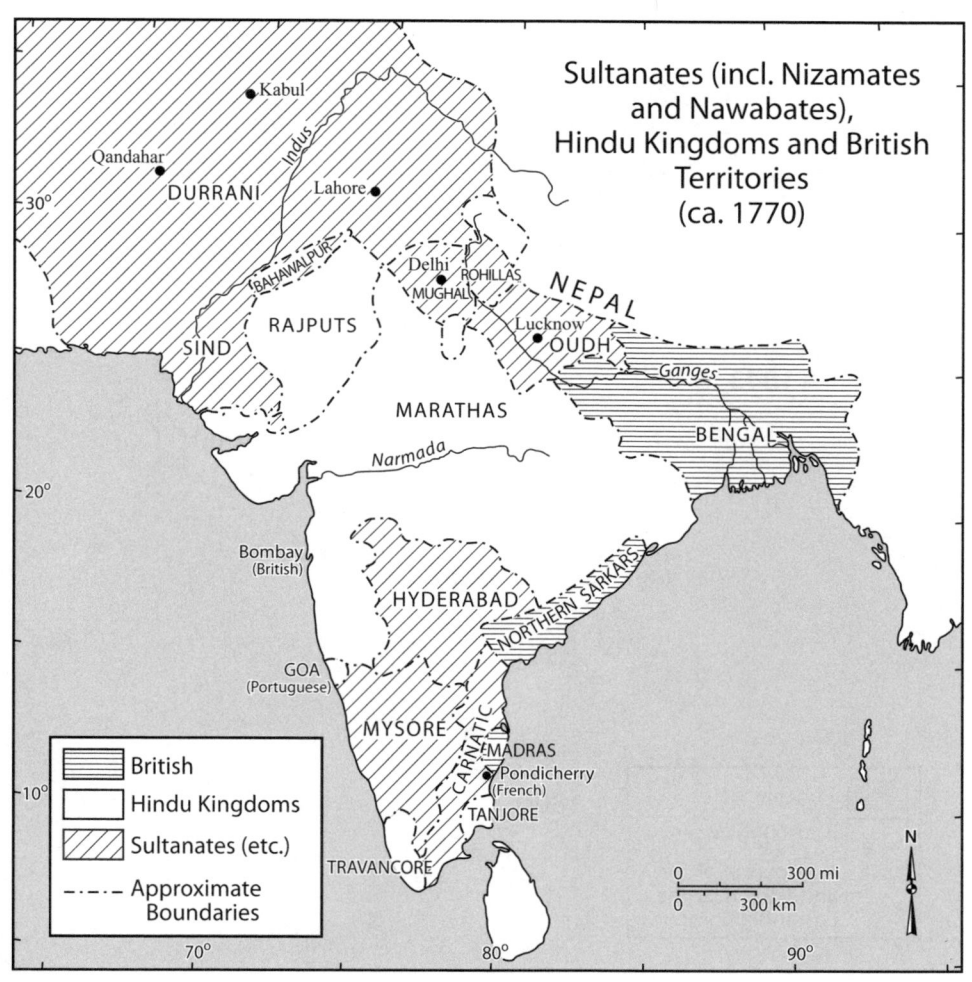

Map 3

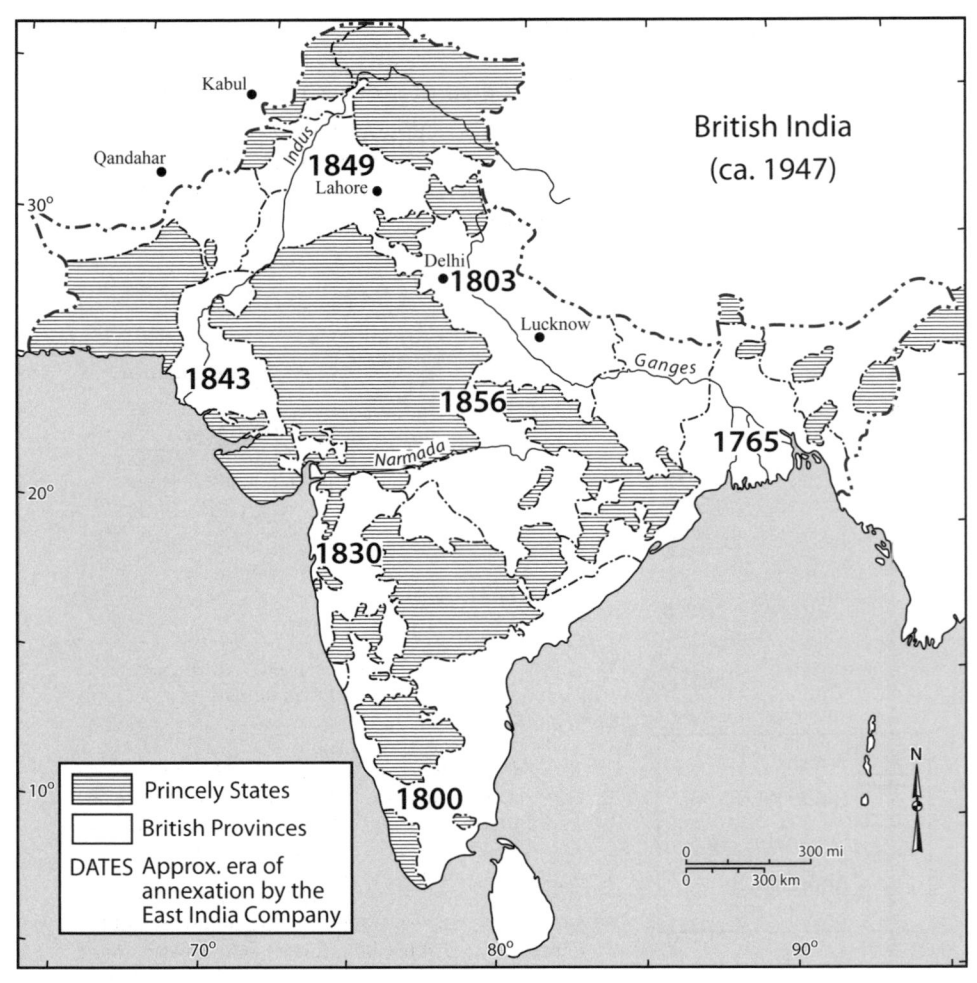

Map 4

CHRONOLOGY OF MAJOR MUSLIM STATES, RELATIONS WITH THE ENGLISH EAST INDIA COMPANY AND BRITISH RAJ IN SOUTH ASIA, 570–1947

570–632: Muhammad establishes the first Muslim state in the Hijaz (Western Arabia).

632–661: 'Elected' Medinan Caliphate of Abu Bakr (d. 634); 'Umar (d. 644); 'Uthman (d. 656); 'Ali (d. 661). Conquest of Sassanian (Irani) Empire, including 'satraps' in Afghanistan and Baluchistan.

661–750: 'Dynastic' Umayyad Caliphate. Capital: Damascus. Conquest of Afghanistan, Baluchistan, Sind/Multan.

750–1258: 'Dynastic' Abbasid Caliphate. Capital: Baghdad. Rise of 'Sultanates' (c. 900s). Establishment of independent 'Amirates' in Sind/Multan (c. 900s).
- 962–1151: Ghaznawid Sultanate: Capital: Ghazna. Conquest of Amirates of Sind/Multan and Hindu Kingdoms of Punjab. Raids into Gangetic Basin.
- 1151–1206: Ghurid Sultanate: Capital: Lahore. Annexation of Ghaznawid territories in South Asia. Conquest of Hindu Kingdoms of Gangetic Basin and Delta (including Bengal).

1206–1526: Delhi Sultanates. Capital: Delhi.
- 1206–1290: Mamluk Sultanate. Annexation of Ghurid territories in South Asia.
- 1290–1320: Khalji Sultanate. Annexation of Mamluk territories. Conquest of Hindu Kingdoms in Rajasthan and Gujarat. Raids into the 'Deccan' (Southern Peninsula, below the Narmada River). Successful defence against Mongol invasions.
- 1320–1415: Tughluq Sultanate. Annexation of Khalji territories. Conquest of the Hindu Kingdoms of the Deccan. Breakaway Sultanate of Bengal founded (1336), Bahmanid Sultanate (1347), Sultanate of Kashmir (1349), Sultanate of Khandesh (1388), Sultanate of Gujarat (1391) and Sultanate of Malwa (1401). Amir Timur, ancestor of the Mughal Sultans, loots and burns Delhi (1398).

- 1415–1451: Sayyid Sultanate. Annexation of Tughluq territories in Ganges Basin and Punjab.
- 1451–1526: Lodhi Sultanate. Annexation of Sayyid territories. Re-establishment of independent Amirates of Sind/Multan.

1347–1687: Deccan Sultanates. Various Capitals.
- 1347–1512: Bahmanid Sultanate: Capital: Ahsanabad (Gulbarga)/Muhammadabad (Bidar). Annexation of Tughluq territories in the Deccan.
- 1490–1636: Ahmadnagar Sultanate: Capital: Five at various times. Annexation of north-western Bahmanid territories. Conquest of Sultanate of Berar (1574).
- 1490–1687: Bijapur Sultanate. Capital: Bijapur. Annexation of south-western Bahmanid territories. Conquest of Sultanate of Bidar (1619). Hindu Marathas, under Shivaji, establish breakaway state (1674).

  Portuguese capture and colonise Goa (1510). French East India Company acquires Pondicherry (1674).
- 1490–1574: Berar Sultanate. Capital: Achalpur. Annexation of north-central Bahmanid territories.
- 1492–1619: Bidar Sultanate. Capital: Bidar. Annexation of south-central Bahmanid territories.
- 1512–1687: Golconda Sultanate. Capital: Golconda/Hyderabad. Annexation of eastern Bahmanid territories.

  English East India Company granted trading rights at Masulipatnam (1611). Portuguese influence in the region reduced by the arrival of other European competitors.

1526–1707: 'Great Mughal' Sultanate. Capital: Delhi/Agra/Lahore.
- 1526–1530: Zahir al-Din Babar. Defeats Sultan Ibrahim Lodhi at Panipat, outside Delhi. Lodhi territories added to Kabul and Qandahar. Conquest of Amirate of Multan (1528).
- 1530–1556: Nasir al-Din Humayun. Overthrown by Sher Shah Suri, a former official of the Sultanate of Bengal (1540). Restoration with the aid of the Safawid Sultanate of Iran (1555). Loss of Qandahar to Safawid Sultanate (c. 1556).
- 1556–1605: Jalal al-Din Akbar. Begins conquering or entering into matrimonial alliances with various Hindu Rajput Kingdoms (1562–71). 'Tributary' status for most Hindu/Tribal Kingdoms

of Orissa (1576) and Gondwana (1595). Conquest of Sultanate of Malwa (1562), Sultanate of Gujarat (1572), Amirate of Sind (1573), Sultanate of Bengal (1574), Sultanate of Kashmir (1586) and Sultanate of Khandesh (1601). Qandahar re-taken from the Safawid Sultanate (1595).
  – 1605–1627: Nur al-Din Jahangir. Defeats combined forces of the Sultanates of Ahmadnagar, Bijapur and Golconda; establishes Mughal 'suzerainty' in the Deccan. Loss of Qandahar to Safawid Sultanate (1622).
    English East India Company granted trading rights in Gujarat (1608) and Bengal (1617).
  – 1628–1658: Shihab al-Din Shah Jahan. Conquest of Sultanate of Ahmadnagar (1636). Qandahar changes hands, but is finally lost to Safawid Sultanate (1653).
    Dutch East India Company granted trading rights in Bengal (1630).
  – 1658–1707: Muhi al-Din Awrangzib (a.k.a. 'Alamgir). Conquest of Sultanate of Bijapur (1687) and Sultanate of Golconda (1687). Mughal Sultanate at its territorial zenith, but Maratha Wars in Deccan on-going (1674–1707).
    French East India Company granted trading rights in Gujarat (1668). Third Anglo-Dutch War reduces Dutch East India Company influence in the region (1674).

1707–1858: 'Lesser Mughal' Sultanate. Capital: Delhi.
  – 1707–1712: Bahadur Shah (a.k.a. Shah 'Alam)
  – 1712–1713: Jahandar Shah
  – 1713–1719: Faruq Siyar. Brought to power by the Sayyid brothers, 'Abd Allah and Husayn 'Ali, who assumed the office of *wazir* (prime minister) and *mir bakshi* (commander of the military), and reduced the Mughal Sultan to a figurehead ruler, eventually murdering Faruq Siyar for plotting against them.
    English East India Company granted duty-free trading privileges in Nizamate (Viceroyalty) of Bengal (1717).
  – 1719: Rafiʿ al-Darjat; Rafiʿ al-Dawlat (a.k.a. Shah Jahan II); Muhammad Ibrahim. All instated by the Sayyids as figureheads, Rafiʿ al-Darjat died three months after accession, Rafiʿ al-Dawlat was murdered by the Sayyids and Muhammad Ibrahim was deposed by his successor, Muhammad Shah, who was also brought to power

by the Sayyids, but managed to break their hold on power with the aid of the Nizamate of Hyderabad (Deccan). Maratha 'confederacy' expands in Deccan up to Gujarat/Malwa.
- 1719–1748: Muhammad Shah. Nizamates of Bengal, Hyderabad and Oudh begin operating independently as hereditary states that only acknowledge the nominal authority of the Mughals, but forward no revenue to Delhi. Sikh 'Barons' begin rise to power in Punjab. Nadir Shah, post-Safawid ruler of Iran, sacks Punjab and plunders Delhi, emptying the treasury (1739). Ahmad Shah Durrani (a.k.a. 'Abdali) of Qandahar sacks Lahore (1748).
- 1748–1754: Ahmad Shah. Dominated by the Nizamate of Hyderabad, and eventually murdered by his *wazir*, Ghazi al-Din, son of the Nizam. Sind ceded to Ahmad Shah Durrani (1749).
- 1754–1759: 'Alamgir II. Installed, then murdered by Ghazi al-Din. Ahmad Shah Durrani sacks Delhi (1756).
- 1759–1760: Shah Jahan III. Installed, then deposed by Ghazi al-Din. Marathas defeat Nizam of Hyderabad, annex western provinces; Maratha influence extends to Punjab/Delhi (1760).

  English East India Company deposes Nizam of Bengal (allied with French), installs rival (1757). Defeat reduces the French East India Company to a minor player in region.
- 1760–1806: Shah 'Alam II. Ahmad Shah Durrani (with local allies) defeats Marathas—Maratha 'confederacy' disintegrates into multiple states (1761). Independent 'Amirates' rise in Sind (1783). Sikh Maharaja Ranjit Singh establishes state in Punjab (1801).

  English East India Company and 'puppet' Nizam of Bengal face the combined forces of the Mughal Sultan, Nizam of Oudh and deposed Nizam of Bengal; the latter are defeated. Treaty of Allahabad: Mughal Sultan reduced to English East India Company pensioner; Nizam of Oudh cedes eastern territories to English East India Company; English East India Company declared '*diwans*' (revenue agents) of Bengal, Bihar, Orissa—first major British territorial possession (1765). First and Second Anglo-Maratha Wars (1775–82/1803–05); Marathas defeated, cede western territories and revenues to the English East India Company. Sultanate of Mysore rises to challenge English East India Company and the allied southern Maratha states and Nizamate of Hyderabad; defeated after four wars against the combined forces of the latter (1782–99); English East India Company annexes most of Mysore's territories. English East India Company captures Delhi (1803).

- 1806–1837: Akbar II. Installed and maintained by the English East India Company. Third Anglo-Maratha War (1817–18)—Maratha states reduced to English East India Company vassals; English East India Company annexes considerable territories on west coast and central areas.
- 1837–1858: Bahadur Shah II. Installed and maintained by the English East India Company. Sind (1843) and Punjab (1849) conquered by English East India Company (1843). Nizamate of Oudh annexed by English East India Company (1856). Gangetic Uprising (a.k.a. 1857 'Mutiny')—some leaders pledge restoration of Mughal sovereignty; defeated. Mughal Sultan deposed, convicted of treason and exiled. Mughal Sultanate abolished. English East India Company regime ended; British government assumes 'Direct Rule' of South Asia (1858); pledges to maintain 'subsidiary alliances' with remaining 'Princely States.'

1858–1947: British Raj. Capital: Calcutta/Delhi
- 1874: English East India Company dissolved by act of Parliament.
- 1877: Queen Victoria declared 'Empress of India.'
- 1885: 'Indian National Congress' founded.
- 1906: 'All-India Muslim League' founded.
- 1909: 'Separate Electorates' for Muslims and Hindus established by Morley-Minto Reforms.
- 1916: 'Lucknow Pact' between Muslim League and Indian National Congress agrees on separate electorates in any future Indian constitution.
- 1919–1922: Khilafat-(Gandhian) Non-Cooperation Movement bring Muslim and non-Muslim leadership together.
- 1928: 'Nehru Report' (Indian National Congress) repudiates Lucknow Pact.
- 1930: Muhammad Iqbal calls for 'separate' Muslim state in 'North-Western' provinces.
- 1940: 'Lahore Resolution' of Muslim League ratifies call for 'separate' Muslim states in Muslim majority provinces.
- 1947: British withdraw from South Asia, ending colonial rule. 'India' and 'Pakistan' respectively created out of contiguous 'Hindu' and 'Muslim' majority districts and Princely States (except Kashmir [disputed]).

INTRODUCTION

The geopolitics of the 21st century has placed Islam and Muslims under the scrutiny of global policy-makers and their media-consuming constituencies. South Asia—home of the *madrasa*s that spawned the Taliban Movement, bastion of Al-Qa'ida and, since 2001, the site of armed conflict between such 'Islamists' and US-led forces—has been thrust into the spotlight. As is usually the case when such parties and stakes are involved, however, that light is not always true, and that gaze, rarely focused. The image presented is more often than not blurred by the political, economic and cultural interests of its governmental, non-governmental and media handlers, even before passing through the tinted filters of their constituencies and consumers, non-Muslim and Muslim. The intellectual and institutional history of Islam in South Asia is one of the prime casualties.

The irony of commonly circulated perspectives—perhaps the most frequent manner in which they are blurred and filtered—is that they regularly reflect the tired perspectives of 'Orientalism'. Primarily referencing European scholarship initiated with the Enlightenment and imperial expansion, Edward Said's seminal works on the subject illustrate that with the passing of time, the assumptions and essentialisms of this discourse shaped the perspectives of European and North American intelligentsia and governing classes.[1] Although many critics have argued that this discourse was not hegemonic, the lens that Orientalism forged, often inspired by colonial exigencies, is widely acknowledged to have projected the assumption of a stark dichotomy between a rational, progressive and egalitarian 'West', and a fanatically superstitious and stagnantly despotic 'East'. This included visions of an essentially rational and benevolent Christianity versus a violently dogmatic Islam. For many privy to the discourse, Islamic doctrine was presented as rigid and inherently bigoted, where 'true believers' were portrayed as wielding scripture in one hand and a sword in the other, bent on converting or killing 'infidels'. Swap the sword for an AK-47

---

[1] See Edward Said, *Orientalism* (New York: Pantheon Books, 1978); and *Culture and Imperialism* (New York: Knopf, 1993).

and the longevity of Orientalism as discourse is clearly visible today. Granted, there are Muslims who perpetrate violence in the name of Islam, but as Said's *Covering Islam* argues, the essentialisation of Islam and Muslims on this point, without due consideration of Islam's variegated nature or the underlying, socio-political motives of its multifarious followers, is neither new nor accidental.[2] It is part of a more systemic relationship between the production of knowledge and the relations of power in the 'modern' world. In speaking of 'Islam' and the 'West', therefore, the popular mantra of yesteryear and today is the same—a 'clash of civilisations'.

As history is among the casualties of conveniently 'clashing civilisations', the manner in which academics—particularly historians, anthropologists and sociologists—apprehend and represent Islam and Muslims is crucial. Thankfully, Said is by no means alone among post-colonial academics to question past scholarship and encourage the rise of a historically grounded and multihued depiction of Islam and its believers. When post-colonial academics approach a contemporary context that includes violent Islamist movements, they find roots in the decline of longstanding 'sultanates' and beginnings of European 'colonial' rule in the 18th century, the political, economic and social reforms introduced by (or adopted from) European models throughout the 19th century, and the public adoption of the European concept of nationalism in the 20th century. In the South Asian arena, late studies of the Mughal Sultanate—which dominated the region's politics and culture from the 16th century—have cast aside biased visions of 'inclusive' Hindus finally rising against their 'intolerant' Muslim 'oppressors', to identify the sweeping structural changes overtaking South Asia, when explaining the state's decline in the 18th century. The idea that British colonial rule prospered in South Asia due to the rational, progressive and egalitarian nature of the post-Enlightenment 'West', in relation to the superstitious, stagnant and despotic ethos of the 'Orient', has also been superseded by unravelling the intricacies of trans-global participation in trade and empire building. The 'Civilising Mission' that brought legal, fiscal and educational reform to South Asia is now revealed as a means by which a predatory Empire legitimated itself, as well as being a major contributor to the transformation of the region's religious communities

---

[2] Edward Said, *Covering Islam: How the Media and the Experts Determine How We See the Rest of the World* (New York: Pantheon Books, 1981).

into primary and antagonistic identities, leading to the establishment of 'Hindu' India and 'Muslim' Pakistan in 1947, and further contributing to the radicalisation of Islam and Hinduism under the political, economic and cultural pressures of post-coloniality.

This book forges ahead with post-colonial approaches to doctrinal Islam and Muslim practice focused on South Asia. By focusing on Islam and South Asian Muslims in the transition from Mughal to post-colonial South Asia, its chapters explore the foundations of South Asian Muslim post-coloniality, while illuminating the historical roots of late trends common to the Muslim World more generally, in a manner accessible to a broad scholarly audience. I highlight the influence of Said because the prime insight stimulating late scholastic effervescence in the field of South Asian history, well articulated by Gyanendra Pandey, is that 'Orientalists' and their 'Nationalist' heirs (Indian and Pakistani) were guilty of 'the emptying out of all history—in specific variations in time, place, class, issue—from the political experience of the people, and the identification of religion, or the religious community, as the moving force of all Indian politics'.[3] By drawing attention to 'specific variations in time, place and class', and taking, as Gyan Prakash recommends, an 'interpretive position that would trace third-world identities as relational rather than essential', this book not only illustrates that religion was one among many factors shaping political life, but that even when speaking of religion alone, Muslims were, and remain, divided into a number of sects and schools of thought that render the idea of a uniform community of intent difficult to resolve.[4]

Aside from Pandey and Prakash, works on Islam and South Asian Muslims that have already followed through on Said's approach have yielded a plethora of valuable conclusions. Speaking of the Mughal period, Barbara Daly Metcalfe comments that, 'In literature, as in architecture and art, new work, rooted in diverse social and political contexts, points us beyond the static dichotomies ["Muslim" and "Hindu"] that have shaped historical narratives too long'.[5] Her meaning is illustrated

---

[3] Gyanendra Pandey, 'The Colonial Construction of "Communalism": British Writing on Banares in the 19th Century', *Subaltern Studies*, vol. 6 (Delhi: Oxford University Press, 1989), p. 132.

[4] Gyan Prakash, 'Writing Post-Orientalist Histories of the Third World: Perspectives from Indian Historiography', *Comparative Journal of Society and History* (April 1990), p. 399.

[5] Barbara Metcalfe, 'Presidential Address: Too Much, Too Little: Reflections on Muslims in the History of India', *Journal of Asian Studies* 54:4 (1995), p. 962. The type

by Richard Eaton's appraisal that, without losing their 'connectedness' to Muslims elsewhere, Indo-Muslims 'interact[ed] with, and [were] embedded within, particular sub-cultures of South Asia, such that by the end of our period [18th century] Islam had become as Indian as any other religious tradition of the subcontinent'.[6] Although this book concurs with such conclusions, it does find that the route by which they are resolved requires further elucidation. In essence, the problem is that such 'new work', including that of Said, is dependent on a dominant paradigm concerning the relationship between doctrinal Islam and Muslim practice that has not been revised in the last 30 years, and itself harbours some of the assumptions and essentialisms of 18th–19th century Orientalists and 20th century Nationalists. In particular, contemporary scholarship continues to forward Orientalism's imposition of 'Orthodoxy' and 'Heterodoxy' when defining Islamic doctrine, though the terms now used might differ. As a result, not only the fringe dwelling pushers of 'clashing civilisations', but many mainstream academics contribute to the continued prominence of the perspective that doctrinal Islam is inherently rigid and that its true followers are consummately bigoted.

Underwriting much of the historical research on the transition from the Mughal to post-colonial periods are approaches to Islam and Muslims based on writings from the 1970s and 1980s. For example, by the 1970s, the sociologist Ernest Gellner and the Islamicist Montgomery Watt had, respectively, written of 'High Islam' or 'Traditional Islam', defined as scripturalist, legalistic and exclusivist, and 'Folk Islam', defined as superstitious, hierarchical and mediationist. The European influence of the colonial period added a positivist 'Liberal Islam' in Watt's case or 'Islamic Modernism' in Gellner's writings, among those privy to 'Western' education, while prompting a reactionary 'fundamentalism' or 'puritanism' among advocates of the High/Traditional discourse.[7] With regard to Muslim practice, therefore, the anthropolo-

---

of works to which she refers include: Aditya Behl, 'The Landscape of Paradise: Malik Jayasi and the Embodied City', *9th Annual South Asia Conference* (Berkeley: University of California, 1995); and Catherine Asher, *Architecture of Mughal India* (Cambridge: Cambridge University Press, 1992).

[6] Richard Eaton, 'Introduction', *India's Islamic Traditions, 711–1750*, ed. R. Eaton (New Delhi: Oxford University Press, 2005), p. 27.

[7] See Ernest Gellner, *Muslim Societies* (Cambridge: Cambridge University Press, 1981) and *Postmodernism, Reason and Religion* (London: Routledge, 1992); and Montgomery Watt, *Islamic Fundamentalism and Modernity* (London: Routledge, 1988).

gist Clifford Geertz urged the recognition of 'Muslims' (referring to those bound to 'Islamic' scriptural authority defined largely in legalistic terms) and 'nominal Muslims' (referring to those who 'transgress' scriptural authority), in assessing the social spaces in which doctrinal Islam is active.[8] A cursory survey of the history of South Asia reveals that the core of such formulations constitutes the dominant paradigm in determining historical assessments of the South Asian Muslim's simultaneous 'connectedness' with the broader 'Muslim World', and 'embeddedness' in 'India'.

At the centre-stage of the discourse on pre-colonial South Asia stand various forms of what Metcalfe terms 'Indicism'. The basic premise of Indicism is well expressed in Bernard Cohn's writings, which resolve the 'mediationist' tendencies identified with 'Folk Islam' and 'nominal Muslims' in the thesis that 'Muslims and Hindus operated with an unbounded substantive theory of objects and persons'.[9] That is to say, Cohn's Mughal South Asia operated on 'substantive theories of objects and persons' influenced by, but transcending 'High' or 'Traditional' Islam. Therefore, Cohn describes the cultural complex of the period as an 'unconscious' collectivity, inclusive of 'a whole matrix of custom, ritual, religious symbol, [and] a textually transmitted tradition'.[10] And in what ways does 'textually transmitted tradition' intervene? Cohn's implicit response is explicitly outlined in Gautam Bhadra's caution that the type of 'mutuality of Hindu and Muslim' believed to reside in cultures that 'transgress' the 'boundaries' of 'official or formal' Hinduism and Islam does not imply 'fusion' or loss of 'separate significations'. In fact, the 'bland theory of tolerance', which he reads in some alternative versions of 'mutuality', is argued to ignore 'the acute intolerance and sectarianism that popular sects sometimes displayed towards each other'.[11] Evidently, Indicism ventures little further in defining Islam

---

[8] See Clifford Geertz, *Islam Observed* (Chicago: Chicago University Press, 1968).

[9] Bernard Cohn, 'The Command of Language and the Language of Command', *Subaltern Studies*, vol. 4 (Delhi: Oxford University Press, 1985), p. 279.

[10] Bernard Cohn, 'The Census, Social Structure and Objectification in South Asia', *An Anthropologist Among Historians and Other Essays* (New York: Oxford University Press, 1990), pp. 228–29.

[11] Gautam Bhadra, 'The Mentality of Subalternality: Kantanama or Rajdharma', *Subaltern Studies*, vol. 6 (Delhi: Oxford University Press, 1989), p. 66. For a particularly acute example of the 'bland theory of tolerance', see N.K. Wagle, 'Hindu Muslim Interactions in Medieval Maharashtra', *Hinduism Reconsidered*, eds. Gunther-Dietz Sontheimer and H. Kuke. (New Delhi: Manohar Publishers, 1997), pp. 134–52. Here, one finds Muslims uniformly referred to as *Yavanas* (foreigners) and *Mlechhas* (impure/outcastes) in league

in relation to South Asia than did Gellner et al., a fact confirmed in Bhadra's own resolution of two levels of 'Islam' in 'India': the 'formal' ('bounded' and antagonistic to 'mutuality') and the 'informal' (theoretically 'unbounded' and practically 'mutualistic'). And, in turn, this formula is little different from Orientalism's visions of Orthodoxy and Heterodoxy.

The pervasiveness of the paradigmic approach to Islam and Muslims can also be read in works that deal with more specific figures and movements in the pre-colonial period, including those in Eaton's own edited collection of essays. For example, Iqtidar Khan's representation of the Mughal Sultan Akbar's (r. 1556–1605) 'mediationism' as an 'attempt to distance himself from a pro-Islamic policy', Satish Chandra's suggestion that 'Akbar's concept of state was strikingly modern and secularist', and Harbans Mukhia's raising of Akbar to 'divinity', illustrate the commonly held view of Akbar's policies as a 'transgression' of High/Traditional Islam.[12] Meanwhile, the wide acknowledgement of Sultan Awrangzib's (r. 1658–1707) policies as 'pro-Islamic' is roundly justified by his legalism, as in John Richards' juxtaposition of Akbar's mediationism with Awrangzib's imposition of an 'Islamic character on to the political culture'.[13] Of course, these ideas extend well beyond the above specialists, to permeate general histories of South Asia, as in Burton Stein's assessment of Akbar's policies as 'practical political rationale' meant to 'blunt' the innately 'Islamic' tendency to 'place most...subjects under continuous pressure to convert'.[14] Meanwhile, Awrangzib's credentials are unflinching portrayed as 'Islamic' and simultaneously prone to 'religious bigotry', incompatible with the 'tolerance of Akbar'.[15] The entire thesis is repeated most succinctly by Sugata Bose and Ayesha Jalal, who write of Akbar's regime as a sign of 'a pragmatic streak and determination to adapt to the Indian environment', while Awrangzib's legalistic regime represents a 'reversal of the

---

with Kali ('evil') and bent on destroying *dharma*, but the author interprets the very mention of Muslims in Brahmanical works as evidence of Hindu 'tolerance'.

[12] Iqtidar Khan, 'The Nobility Under Akbar and the Development of His Religious Policy', *India's Islamic Traditions*, p. 125; Satish Chandra, 'Jizya and the State in India During the Seventeenth Century', *India's Islamic Traditions*, p. 139; and Harbans Mukhia, *The Mughals of India* (Oxford: Blackwell, 2004), p. 49.

[13] John Richards, *The Mughal Empire* (Cambridge: Cambridge University Press, 1998), p. 164.

[14] Burton Stein, *A History of India* (Oxford: Blackwell, 1998), pp. 171–73.

[15] Ibid., pp. 179–82.

politics of alliance building and religious flexibility'.[16] The point here is not to suggest that Akbar was less mediationist, or Awrangzib more so—although such revisions may be due. Rather, it is to clarify that the influence of the dominant paradigm concerning doctrinal Islam and Muslim practice not only assesses Mughal polity by excluding the details of mystical, philosophical and theological doctrines from 'Islam' to equate it with legalism, but also assumes that legalism is ultimately 'anti-mediationist', playing no role in the legitimisation of the norms and customs in Muslim praxis.

No reading between the lines is necessary to arrive at the last conclusion stated above. In Yohanan Friedmann's contribution to precisely the subject of 'Islamic Thought in Relation to the Indian Context', legalism alone is referenced as 'orthodox' and presented as '[d]iametrically opposed' to 'the attempt to find a common denominator' with local traditions.[17] Of course, the above tendency is not restricted to discussions of Mughal polity, but is extended to the definition of Muslim scholars from that era. Friedman mentions various philosophically, mystically, theologically and legally erudite scholars from the Mughal period who exhibited a wide variety of mediationist perspectives; but only in the life and work of the legalistic Naqshbandi Sufi, Shaykh Ahmad Sirhindi (d. 1624), does he find that 'Islam preserved its pristine purity and refused to make concessions to the pagan environment'.[18] Meanwhile, examples of mediationism dependent on non-legalistic doctrine 'abandons the cherished Islamic conviction that Islam is, in the eyes of Allah, the only true faith', as in the case of Awrangzib's philosophical and mystical brother and rival, Dara Shukoh (d. 1658), who argued that the 'Hindu' *Upanishads* are a 'revelation' and 'essential for understanding the less clear statements of the Qur'an'.[19] Although declaring Dara Shukoh's ideas a 'significant contribution to Islamic thought', it is important to note that Friedmann views this level of mediationism as innovative and exceptional, describing it as 'deviant enough to put Dara Shukoh beyond the pale of medieval Indian Islam'.[20]

---

[16] Sugata Bose and Ayesha Jalal, *Modern South Asia: History, Culture, Political Economy* (London: Routledge, 1999), pp. 40–41.
[17] Yohanan Friedmann, 'Islamic Thought in Relation to the Indian Context', *India's Islamic Traditions*, p. 51.
[18] Ibid., p. 61.
[19] Ibid., p. 59.
[20] Ibid., p. 58.

If this is how contemporary academics view Muslim intellectuals, no doubt the same assumption also extends beyond scholarly classes to permeate the assessment of lay individuals and groups. Ali Asani's discussion of the Khoja Isma'ilis is characteristic, citing their participation in Gujarati 'custom'—from the disinheritance of women to the use of *ginan*s (devotional songs) in prayer—as evidence of 'Indic' norms, while the Islam of the 'orthodox Muslim' is restricted to the practice of congregational prayer (*salat/namaz*) on *'Id*, the resort to *qadi*s (judges) for marriage rites, participation in Muharram processions, and so forth.[21] Similarly, David Hardiman's essay, 'From Custom to Crime: The Politics of Drinking in Colonial South Gujarat', informs the reader that the 'orthodox' Muslim, bound by legalism, did not imbibe alcohol, while those residing in the unbounded realm of Gujarati 'customary law' did with impunity.[22] That is to say, legalism is not only identified as the 'true' Islam, whether among the elite or subaltern groups, it is defined as anti-mediationist and any alternatives that make 'concessions' to the local environment are equated with the 'transgression' of 'medieval Indian Islam'. And so, 'Indicism' looms large in the historiography of pre-colonial South Asia.

The manner in which historians of South Asia define Islam and Muslims in the Mughal context has obvious repercussions on the discourse on the colonial period, particularly given that it is the manner in which 'colonial difference' represents a 'transformation' of pre-colonial norms that is at issue. As a discussion of this period constitutes the majority of this book, only a singular example will suffice here. Consider Ayesha Jalal's statement that, '[a]lthough classified as members of distinctive communities [by the British], Punjabi Muslims, Hindus and Sikhs in their everyday lives observed social customs which owed nothing to religious doctrines'.[23] Clearly, this conclusion depends on the assumption that doctrinal Islam, or 'normative' Islam to use Jalal's term, is defined as 'scriptural, legalistic and exclusivist', playing no part in legitimating those social customs. Consequently, the 'Indic' condition of Punjabi Muslims is obviously viewed through the lens of 'Folk Islam'

---

[21] Ali Asani, 'Creating Tradition Through Devotional Songs and Communal Script: The Khoja Isma'ilis of South Asia', *India's Islamic Traditions*, pp. 286–87.

[22] David Hardiman, 'From Custom to Crime: The Politics of Drinking in Colonial South Gujarat', *Subaltern Studies*, vol. 4 (Delhi: Oxford University Press, 1985), pp. 165–228.

[23] Ayesha Jalal, *Self and Sovereignty: Individual and Community in South Asian Islam Since 1850* (London: Routledge, 2000), p. 146.

and 'nominal Muslims'. Also consider Jalal's perspective of those with 'Western' educations. She identifies theology (*kalam*) and jurisprudence (*fiqh*) as central pursuits of 'revivalist' and 'reformist' endeavours arising under colonial rule. Along with co-author Sugata Bose, Jalal credits 'reformers' like Sayyid Ahmad Khan (d. 1898) and Muhammad Iqbal (d. 1938), and 'revivalists' like the scholars of *Dar al-'Ulum* Deoband and the *Jama'at-i 'Ulama'-i Hind*, with 'imaginative cultural borrowings and intellectual adaptations that consciously transgressed the frontiers between 'us' and 'them', while forwarding 'projects of internal, social regeneration and reform which, on the whole, strengthened the ability to contest Western colonial power'.[24] However, 'Saiyid Ahmed's [sic] rational approach to Islamic theology and law', write Jalal and Bose, is 'new fangled', while 'true' Islam is assigned to the 'revivalists', who are assumed to say little doctrinally 'new' beyond the anti-mediationist legal ideals of the past.[25] In other words, these 'reformers' and 'revivalists' are the same groups that Gellner et al. referred to as 'modernists' and 'fundamentalists'. Thus, Bose and Jalal echo the larger body of literature on the period by not only precluding the influence of non-theological or non-legalistic doctrines among fundamentalists/revivalists, but also by assuming pre-colonial stasis in all the disciplines involved. The influence of established schools of philosophy and mysticism on the reformer/modernist's 'rationalism' is subsumed in the dynamism created by colonial pressures or 'Western' education, just as 'concessions' in the pre-colonial period are viewed as 'transgressive', but 'pragmatic'. In the final analysis, although everyone from Friedmann to Jalal concur with Eaton that Islam is 'as Indian as any other religious tradition on the subcontinent', their dependence on the same overarching paradigm in defining Islam and Muslims, insures that none mean this to imply that various aspects of 'India' (or 'Europe') were or can be viewed as doctrinally 'Islamic'.

The essential problem with the dominant paradigm is that if such a perspective of doctrine and practice were applied to other religious traditions such as Hinduism, for example, any practice outside the bounds of *dharmashastra* (legal treatises) would have to be considered 'transgressive' of Hinduism as a whole. Thankfully, this is not the case when studying Hinduism today. It is not surprising, therefore, that

---

[24] Bose and Jalal, *Modern South Asia*, p. 112.
[25] Ibid., p. 114.

despite widespread use, criticism of aspects of the dominant paradigm concerning the relationship between doctrinal Islam and Muslim practice began almost as soon as Watt, Gellner and Geertz, to name only the architects featured here, began outlining their own versions. Nor have some of these critiques been ignored by historians of South Asia. One regarding the class-based assumptions of Gellner's 'High' and 'Folk' formulations is explicitly acknowledged in Bhadra's preference for the terms 'formal' and 'informal' Islam, but only insofar as making it clear that 'scripturalism, legalism and exclusivism', and 'hierarchy, superstition and mediation' are not class-bound. However, it is extremely rare to read the types of critiques made by Jacques Waardenburg, Marshall G.S. Hodgson and Vincent Cornell. Taking on Geertz, in particular, but by extension all of the aforementioned historians of South Asia, Waardenburg points out that the above dichotomies assume a 'core' Islam (i.e. legalism), which some Muslims follow and others do not, thus imposing themselves into the definition of what is or is not Islam, and who are or are not Muslims.[26] That such impositions are troublesome is evinced by Hodgson's contention that 'Islam', in fact, comprises no more than extant scripture (Qur'an and *hadith*), the 'Islamic' includes all disciplines, schools and sects (not merely legists) involved in that scripture's interpretation, and that a third sphere, termed 'Islamicate', involves the cultural domains in which 'Islam' and the 'Islamic' are active and in which Muslims and non-Muslims participate.[27] Regarding the relationship between the 'Islamic' and 'Islamicate', Cornell steps in with the observation, based on a detailed study of the disciplines of theology (*kalam*) and mysticism (*tasawwuf*), that each encapsulates 'theologies of hospitality' and 'theologies of hostility' towards the persons, objects, institutions and intellectualism active in the local environment.[28] Although he does not extend his analysis to legalism and philosophy, Cornell's ideas are implicitly confirmed by scholars of

---

[26] See Pieter Vrijhof and J. Waardenburg, eds. *Religion and Society* (Le Hague: W. de Gruyter, 1979).

[27] For the most complete articulation of Hodgson's ideas, see Marshall G.S. Hodgson, *The Venture of Islam*, 3 vols. (Chicago: University of Chicago Press, 1974).

[28] These are not Cornell's terms alone, but are employed by such diverse authors from the field of Religious Studies as Richard Hayes, working on Buddhism, Ashok Vohra and Vasudha Narayanan, working on Hinduism, Stephen Sykes, studying Christianity, and Alon Goshen-Gottstein and Barry Levy, writing of Judaism. For a sample of their writings, published together, see *Religion, Society and the Other: Hostility, Hospitality and the Hope of Human Flourishing* (Sevilla: Elijah Interfaith Academy Think Tank, 2003).

both those disciplines. Custom was not listed among the four 'sources' of the *shari'a* by the originators of Islamic jurisprudence in the 8th and 9th centuries, but Gideon Libson is one among many to explain that custom (*'urf/'ada*) has had a place in the *shari'a* since the inception of the schools of law.[29] As well, those concerned with Islamic philosophy routinely identify such schools of thought as the 'Ishraqis', who dominated the discipline in the era of 'Great Mughals' and their 'successors', with, in Majid Fakhry's words: (1) the guaranteed 'right of reason to probe the deepest religious mysteries'; and, (2) the 'unity' of 'religious and metaphysical truth', such that it is 'the duty of the seeker to seek truth wherever it can be found: in Greek philosophy, in ancient Persian thought, in Muslim Neo-Platonism, and in Sufism' or, one might add, the pre-Islamic intellectual and religious traditions of South Asia.[30] As historians of South Asia, bound to 30-year-old formulations, rarely take such insights into account in their definitions of what is or is not 'Islam', and who are or are not 'Muslims', the time to consider a new paradigm—particularly one that pays close attention to internally established modes by which 'cultural borrowings' and 'intellectual adaptations' have been consciously accommodated or rejected—is surely now. Thus, this book's prime contribution to post-colonial scholarship is a new paradigm cognisant of late conclusions in Islamic intellectual/cultural history, as well as its application in a reading of the copious amount of published Arabic, Persian, Urdu, Punjabi and English texts used by historians of South Asia in outlining the phases of transition from the Mughal to post-colonial periods.

The 'South Asian context' on which this book focuses is the region from Lahore to Lucknow, centred on Delhi. Although excursions into Sind, Gujarat, Bengal, Bihar and Orissa are taken where appropriate, the area of focus is predicated on the fact that this was the Mughal 'heartland' in the pre-colonial era, the font of regionally definitive doctrinal, political and cultural movements in the colonial period and, by the early 20th century, the centre of British colonial authority and

---

[29] Gideon Libson, *Jewish and Islamic Law: A Comparative Study of Custom During the Geonic Period* (Cambridge: Harvard University Press, 2003), p. 69. For custom in *fiqh* more generally, see Mohammad Zain Othman, 'The Status of 'Urf in Islamic Law', *IIUM Law Journal* 3:2 (1993): 40–51; M. al-Awa, 'The Place of Custom ('urf) in Islamic Legal Theory', *Islamic Quarterly* 17 (1973): 177–82; and "Ada', *Encyclopaedia of Islam* (Leiden: Brill, CD ROM Ed.).

[30] Majid Fakhry, *A History of Islamic Philosophy* (New York: Columbia University Press, 1983), p. 339.

indigenous nationalist movements. In Chapter One, with the aid of specialised works in each of the main disciplines of Islamic thought, I consider a host of Arabic and Persian writings, either produced within this area or acknowledged to have been widely read in it during the Mughal period, to show that approaches to Islam and Muslims that seek to end the 'emptying of all history', falter by pursuing a path that accounts for 'connectedness and embeddedness' by emptying 'India' of all but legalistic Islam. In essence, I argue that by remaining bound to the dominant paradigm outlined above, historians of South Asia fail to realise that the primary sources do not view doctrine or practice in the manner they envision. As Hodgson's concept of the 'Islamic' already suggests, the primary sources acknowledge multiple 'classes of seekers', each proposing itself as the 'best' interpretation of scripture, but few presuming to represent the 'only' possible interpretation. In fact, so many 'disciplines' and 'schools' of thought fall into these classes that any new paradigm cannot help but narrow the field to manageable categories. Waardenburg's caution about injecting as little as possible of one's self into the definition of 'true' doctrine and practice, therefore, leads me to the categories that the primary sources themselves acknowledge. I show that these internal categories are determined by the relationship that individual schools draw between Revelation (*wahy*), Reason (*'aql*) and Intuition (*kashf*) as 'sources of knowledge'. Certain schools, referenced as 'Sober' and inclusive of theological, legal and mystical doctrines, make a case to 'subordinate' knowledge gained by the exercise of Reason and/or Intuition, to that availed through Revelation. Other schools, termed 'Intoxicated' and inclusive of philosophical, theological and mystical doctrines, argue that Reason and/or Intuition are 'equivalent' to Revelation as sources of knowledge. For lay Muslims, therefore, depending on which category or school is either dominant in their domain or self-consciously chosen to represent 'Islam', a variety of attitudes towards local complexes of thought and social customs can be legitimated. The general characteristic of a 'Sober Way' is to allow for intellectual adaptations and cultural borrowings within the boundaries of defined 'religious communities', while that of the 'Intoxicated Path' ranges from the outer limits of the Sober Path to absolute antinomianism and/or latitudinarianism. In this scheme, neither category (Sober or Intoxicated) is class-bound, regionally specific, or temporally static. Rather, scholastic representatives of both in every centre of Muslim habitation provide the 'connectedness' with the broader 'Muslim World' of which Eaton speaks. As for 'embeddedness' in a locality such as 'India', applying Cornell's terms, each legitimates 'hostility' and 'hospitality' towards local complexes of thought and social customs. Carrying these insights into a discussion of the elite court and political culture of the 'Great Mughals' in Chapter Two, my reading of Persian histories, official documents and European travelogues (among other assorted works), leads me to the conclusion that Akbar is the quintessentially 'Intoxicated Muslim', while Awrangzib is a good representative of the 'Sober Muslim' in the pre-colonial context ending with the 17th century.

The non-static nature of the categories of Islamic thought and Muslim practice, including the possibility of new schools arising, implies that the stark and homogenising delineation between pre-colonial and colonial periods—one that has caused most works related to Muslims in South Asia to end or begin their appraisals in the mid-19th century with the dawn of 'direct rule' from Britain, also known as 'British Raj'—must also be open to re-examination. Chapter Three, therefore, focuses on doctrinal changes in the Sober Path arising in the early 18th century and follows them through to the late 19th century. Being focused on Delhi, the Arabic, Persian and Urdu philosophical, theological, legal and mystical writings of the 'Wali Allahi' school are juxtaposed with the consensus of historical opinion on the impact of the colonial 'Codification' of Muslim law, beginning in the 1780s. My intention is not to suggest that such colonial measures are irrelevant to the firming of religious boundaries that eventually contributed to the imagining of India and Pakistan. Rather, I aim to show that the effect of such policies must be balanced with the fact that the Wali Allahi school is part of a far broader, pre-colonial attempt (extending across the Muslim World) to activate the doctrine of *ijtihad* (independent reasoning) to codify Islamic law by explicitly negating all doctrinal legitimisation of local complexes of thought and social customs. That is to say, the Wali Allahis, their intellectual peers and heirs represent the rise of a 'new' Sober Path, not in a 'revivalist' sense or in a South Asian context alone, but as an expansive movement rising about the 18th century that forwarded a form of Islamic doctrine previously unheard of in history. To illustrate that this was not merely a trend among scholarly classes, but extended into lay domains, in Chapter Four I focus on two factors and sets of sources which suggest that among the literate elite and middle classes, the 'new' Sober Path attained an authoritative voice, while among the subaltern groups, the 'old' Sober Path increasingly challenged the influence of the Intoxicated Way by the late 19th century.

First, using British surveys of 'indigenous' educational institutions in Bengal, Bihar, Orissa, Sind and Punjab during the 19th century, I show that *madrasas*—these were once a primary vehicle by which the 'old' Sober Path was disseminated to scholars and, by means of *maktabs* and home-tutoring, to lay persons—all but collapsed wherever British rule and its policy of 'Anglicisation' spread, but were reconstituted by the late 19th century primarily to teach, or coincidently to forward, the 'new' Sober Path. Second, a consideration of Punjabi folk literature from the late 19th century suggests that by this point in time, little trace of the antinomianism once prevalent among the subaltern groups can be found. Instead, the exclusivistic and/or latitudinarian attitudes of the 'old' Sober Path are represented. Given the assumption of firm religious communities inherent in the doctrinal approaches of the Sober Path, 'old' and 'new', I, therefore, conclude that to the effect of British initiatives like Codification and Anglicisation, one must add parallel indigenous lines of influence rising to prominence before and beyond colonial mandate.

Chapter Five carries the discussion beyond Codification, Anglicisation and the 'new' Sober Path, to consider 'Objectification' and a 'new' Intoxicated Way. By focusing on the Urdu writings of Sayyid Ahmad Khan, Mirza Ghulam Ahmad (d. 1908) and Muhammad Iqbal, I show that rather than Objectifying Islam through the lens of 'Western' education, such scholars systematically engaged longstanding doctrinal mechanisms by which they either assimilated or rejected aspects of European thought. One feature that binds them all, despite great doctrinal variety in other respects, is the abandonment of 'absolute immanence' and the antinomianism/latitudinarianism that it implied, in favour of a dependence on 'transcendentalism' and the legalism it upheld. When added to their uniform appeal to *ijtihad*, it is clear that the above shift was inherited from the dominance of the 'new' Sober Path among their class by the late 19th century. In Chapter Six, the implications of this doctrinal shift in terms of notions of community are juxtaposed with the influence of 'Nationalism'. Again, appealing to a wide variety of Urdu writings by the aforementioned and others, I argue that the 'New Islam', Sober and Intoxicated, played a pivotal role, along with colonial assumptions, institutions and pressures, in pushing the rise of 'communalism', or religiously conditioned political identities. Although the variegated political and economic interests of the Muslim elite and bourgeoisie, rather than the rise of communal identities, account for divisions on the ultimate resolution of India or

Pakistan, I argue that the very fact that the only options considered were either 'composite' or 'separatist' nationalisms—both of which depend on the highlighting of religious community in their definition—cannot be explained by colonial influence or the particularities of regional Muslim interests alone. To these must be added the fact that the 'New Islam' legitimised no 'mediationist' options of the type pursued by the 'Great Mughals'.

As this outline suggests, this book is not based on new material. Its contribution to post-colonial scholarship stems from the construction of a new paradigm by which to access the relationship between doctrinal Islam and Muslim practice (whether in South Asia or elsewhere), and the original perspective this new paradigm provides in the reading of a wide variety of primary works not usually read together. By breaking free of a dominant paradigm that conceives of doctrinal Islam as statically legalistic and culturally intrusive, this reading of sources reveals an Islam that is dynamic, multifaceted and systematically hostile and/or hospitable to the local environment in which Muslims live. Hence, this is the study of an Islam that not only mediates the relationship between Muslims and non-Muslims, but also between Muslims of various sectarian, scholastic and disciplinary stripes. The implication concerning Islam and Muslims in the post-colonial context is that 'true believers' cannot be restricted by externally or internally imposed visions of rigidity or bigotry, and even those Muslims who exhibit such traits must be understood as the products of a historical process underwritten by political, economic and cultural factors. It is my most cherished hope that this book not only adds to the already large body of literature intent on expunging Orientalism's assumptions and essentialisms from the study of Islam and Muslims, but by this means also positively influences broader scholarly approaches to an otherwise much misrepresented doctrinal tradition and the history of its adherents. The latter group includes many Muslims who, being no less shaped by academic perspectives than non-Muslims, while simultaneously being sculpted by the 'New Islam', also perceive Islam and themselves in singular terms, ignoring the extensive spectrum of ideas and institutions that shaped the ages and hold the potential to reshape the future.

PART ONE

FOUNDATIONS:
ISLAM AND THE MUGHALS

CHAPTER ONE

THE CATEGORIES OF DOCTRINAL ISLAM

In 1095, after four years as an instructor at the prestigious *Madrasa al-Nizamiyya* in Baghdad, jurist and theologian Abu Hamid Muhammad al-Ghazali (d. 1111) resigned for personal reasons. In his *Munqidh min al-Dalal*, written after years of study that carried him from Baghdad to Damascus, Jerusalem, Hebron, Medina and Mecca, before returning him to his hometown of Tus (Iran), al-Ghazali wrote of the disillusionment with scholastic learning that drove him to seek an alternative approach to 'Truth'.[1] The most striking feature of his intellectual journey is that his abandonment of the Baghdad *madrasa* did not mean a turn away from doctrinal Islam, even in its legal form. Rather, he encountered and listed four 'Classes of [Muslim] Seekers' on his search, one to which he belonged while a *madrasa* instructor, two that he studied and rejected during his travels, and a last in which he found reason to end his search. In order, these are: (1) the *mutakallimun*—'exponents of thought and intellectual speculation'; (2) the *falasifa*—'exponents of logic and demonstration'; (3) the *batiniyya*—who 'derive truth from an infallible *imam* [leader]'; and, (4) the *sufiyya*—who 'possess vision and intuitive understanding'.[2]

It may seem inappropriate to begin a work on Islam in the transition from Mughal to post-colonial South Asia with the biography of an 11th century author whose travels never touched the region. Yet, al-Ghazali's works, which are still widely read across the Muslim World, best illustrate the limitations of any formula that reduces doctrinal Islam to a 'formalism' that is legalistic and judged locally intrusive, while sidelining all other disciplines as 'informal', hence, customarily accommodative. In essence, such approaches do not encapsulate doctrine or reflect the

---

[1] Abu Hamid Muhammad al-Ghazali, *Munqidh min al-Dalal*, ed. and trans. W. Montgomery Watt, *The Faith and Practice of al-Ghazali* (Lahore: Shan Muhammad Ashraf, 1963). It should be noted that there is great debate over al-Ghazali's actual motives for leaving the *madrasa* in Baghdad, ranging from a fallout with the incumbent Sultan to fear of reprisals from local Isma'ilis (i.e. the *batiniyya* he describes).
[2] Ibid., pp. 26–27.

ways in which Muslims viewed Islam, in or outside of South Asia, before or during the era of concern to this book. Thus, scholars cognisant of the scope of doctrines that shaped Muslim practice from the time of al-Ghazali until the end of the 'Great Mughal' era (1526–1707), including but by no means restricted to Jacques Waardenburg, Marshall G.S. Hodgson and Vincent Cornell, attempt to include all of the major variants of doctrine in their definitions of doctrinal Islam. From this perspective, they observe that the relationship between the 'Islamic' and the local, be the latter Semitic, Hellenic, Turkic, Persian or Indic, is not one of static antagonism or periodic intrusion upon 'unbounded theories of persons and objects', but demands frameworks of dynamic and alternating accommodation and rejection. The kernel of the above insight is important, for Cornell's notion of hospitality and hostility, in particular, most succinctly captures the complexity with which the social historian must contend in characterising the relationship between doctrinal Islam, Muslim practice and regional cultures—a far cry from the 'clashing' paradigms of Islam and Indicism employed by most contemporary historians of South Asia.

To better address the issue of the South Asian Muslim's 'connectedness' with the broader Muslim World, therefore, I return, in Section I below, to al-Ghazali's *Munqidh min al-Dalal* and add his *Ihya' 'Ulum al-Din*, comparing them with the *Kashf al-Mahjub* of his South Asian contemporary, 'Ali ibn 'Uthman al-Hujwiri (d. 1072–7), whose tomb remains a major pilgrimage site in Lahore (Pakistan). Ultimately, this comparison reveals that despite distance in time and space, both explicitly acknowledge three basic 'sources' of knowledge in Islam: reason (*'aql*), intuition (*kashf*) and revelation (*wahy*). They also implicitly divide the 'classes of seekers' into those who professedly subordinate knowledge derived by Reason and/or Intuition to Revelation, referenced as the 'Sober', and those who consider knowledge derived by Reason and/or Intuition as equivalent to that contained in Revelation, referenced as 'Intoxicated'. To further illustrate the prevalence of these concepts, while also beginning to tie their doctrinal underpinnings to 'embeddedness' in South Asian cultures and institutions, Sections II and III delve into the writings of theologians, jurists, philosophers and mystics of various schools, originating in South Asia and across the Muslim World. The selection of authors and works is based on one overriding provision: they and their writings provide a survey of the breadth of legal and mystical doctrines that defined the 'Islamic' across the Muslim World, including South Asia, from the 11th to the 17th centuries. A concentration on legal and mystical doctrines is merely necessitated by the impossibility of doing justice to more disciplines in this context, as well as because legalism plays so central a role in the dominant paradigm employed by historians of South Asia, while mysticism provides a foil.

With the above provision in mind, framed by an array of specialised secondary literature, Abu al-Hasan al-Mawardi's (d. 1058) mainstream Shafi'i perspective from Basra and Kufa, in about the time that al-Hujwiri was writing in Lahore and Ghazna (Afghanistan), is contrasted with Taqi al-Din Ahmad ibn Taymiyya's (d. 1328) more peripheral Hanbali perspective from 14th century Damascus and Cairo—peripheral not only because the latter was a Hanbali in Shafi'i/Maliki heartlands, but also because his perspective led contemporaries like Ibn Battuta (d. 1377), famed for his travelogues, to ponder whether he had a 'screw loose'.[3] Abu al-Walid Muhammad ibn Ahmad ibn Rushd's (d. 1198) inclusion, meanwhile, adds the perspectives of a noted jurist and philosopher of 12th century Cordova, and provides an introduction to Maliki and Hanafi law. Moving beyond the law to outline its connection with polity, 'Abd Allah ibn al-Muqaffa' (d. 757) rewinds the discussion to 8th century Iraq, before Nizam al-Mulk al-Tusi (d. 1092) carries it to 11th century Iran, and Diya' al-Din Barani (d. 1357) illustrates the relationship between all the above and the legal and political norms of 14th century Delhi. Muhi al-Din ibn al-'Arabi's (d. 1240) Murcian background returns the discussion to Iberia in the 13th century, but this time with an eye on the relationship between the law and Sufism that Nizam al-Din Awliya' (d. 1325) and Sharaf al-Din ibn Yahya Maneri (d. 1381) reflect in the 14th century, and Shaykh Ahmad Sirhindi (d. 1624) in the 17th century, environs of Delhi.[4] Read together with al-Ghazali's and al-Hujwiri's works, the above authors' categorical, disciplinary and doctrinal leanings contribute to the identification of two basic cultural attitudes: the 'Intoxicated Way' and the 'Sober Path'.

---

[3] See Donald P. Little, 'Does Ibn Taymiyya have a Screw Loose?' *Studia Islamica* 41 (1975): 93–111.

[4] The works read include 'Abd Allah ibn al-Muqaffa''s *Risala fi al-Sahaba*, Abu al-Hasan al-Mawardi's *Al-Ahkam al-Sultaniyya wa al-Wilayat al-Diniyya*, Nizam al-Mulk al-Tusi's *Siyasat Nama*, Abu al-Walid Muhammad ibn Ahmad ibn Rushd's *Bidayat al-Mujtahid*, Muhi al-Din ibn al-'Arabi's *Fusus al-Hikam*, Taqi al-Din Ahmad ibn Taymiyya's *Al-Siyasa al-Shar'iyya* and *Al-Hisba fi al-Islam*, Nizam al-Din Awliya's *Fawa'id al-Fuad*, Diya' al-Din Barani's *Fatawa-i Jahandari*, Sharaf al-Din ibn Yahya Maneri's *Maktubat al-Sadi*, and Shaykh Ahmad Sirhindi's *Maktubat*.

Although both exhibit hospitality and hostility towards aspects of local intellectualism and custom, the former's hospitality more firmly tends towards the dissolution of divisions dependent on religious community, based on antinomian and latitudinarian precepts, while the latter attempts to build bridges between well-defined religious communities, though latitudinarian impulses often obfuscate sectarian divides. The problem this line of inquiry poses for the dominant paradigms of Islam and Indicism is that the very examples of 'transgression' the above uphold are, in fact, legitimate in the eyes of doctrinal Islam, often including its legalistic strains.

I. *Al-Ghazali and al-Hujwiri: Categorising Islamic Thought*

The frantic pace of socio-political and intellectual change and development from the death of Prophet Muhammad (632) to the birth of al-Ghazali's and al-Hujwiri's generations is well known. Having arisen in the deserts of Western Arabia, by the time al-Ghazali and al-Hujwiri took up their pens, Islam had spread from Lahore in the east to Cordova in the west, and travelled even further with traders and missionaries. Muslim ranks had also extended beyond Arabs to begin including Syrians, Egyptians, Berbers, Ethiopians, Greeks, Persians, Turks, Pathans, Baluchis, Sindhis and Punjabis, to name only a few general groups. In the coming centuries, more peoples would be added to the fold, and with them, not only the intellectualism of their pre-Islamic pasts, but also the customs of their regional contemporaries, would be brought to bear on the definition of Islam. With such expansion and multiplicity for a backdrop, consider how al-Ghazali and al-Hujwiri sought to categorise the mass of often conflicting ideas that arose following Muhammad's death.

The four intellectual classes of which al-Ghazali spoke in *Munqidh min al-Dalal*—the *mutakallimun*, the *falasifa*, the *batiniyya*, and the *sufiyya*—revolve around distinct approaches to 'Truth'. Addressing each in turn, al-Ghazali defines the *mutakallimun* as specialists in *'ilm al-kalam*, or 'scholastic theology'. He describes the 'science' of these theologians as the use of 'systematic argumentation' to protect the 'creed received from the prophetic source' against 'heretical innovations'.[5] In so

---

[5] Al-Ghazali, *Munqidh min al-Dalal*, p. 28.

far as their methods allow, al-Ghazali charitably concludes that this class has been successful in fulfilling its objectives. However, methods based on the premises of their opponents and those which these theologians were 'compelled to admit by *taqlid* [imitation], or *ijma'* [consensus], or bare acceptance of the Qur'an and *hadith*', are the reason al-Ghazali cites for his own dissatisfaction with this class of intellectuals.[6]

The *falasifa*, on the other hand, are identified as specialists in *hikma*, or 'speculative philosophy'. Al-Ghazali divides these philosophers into three groups, labeling them: the *Dahriyun* (Materialists); the *Tabi'yun* (Naturalists); and, the *Ilahiyun* (Theists).[7] Each of these 'groups' is described as engaging in one or more of six 'philosophical sciences': Mathematics, Logic, Natural Sciences, Metaphysics, Political Science and Ethics.[8] In each of these 'sciences', al-Ghazali finds nothing inherently unacceptable. His only objection is their propensity to lead Muslims away from the 'creed received from the prophetic source', not merely as defined by the theologians, but particularly by the Ash'ari school. This school's tenets are taken up below, but its influence on al-Ghazali can be read here in his evaluation of the Materialists as '*zanadiqah*' (heretics) because they 'deny the Creator...and consider that the world has everlastingly existed'.[9] The case of the Naturalists is more subtle. They are said to acknowledge 'the Creator' through 'manifold researches into the world of nature and the marvels of animals and

---

[6] Ibid., pp. 28–29. *Taqlid, ijma'* and *hadith* are considered below. For the history of the Qur'an, see Charles J. Adams, 'Quran', *The Encyclopedia of Religion*, vol. 12 (New York: MacMillan, 1987): 156–76. For a more in-depth study displaying alternative perspectives, see Fazlur Rahman, *Major Themes of the Quran* (Minneapolis: Bibliotheca Islamica, 1994), and J. Wansborough, *Quranic Studies* (Oxford: University Press, 1977). Regarding *kalam*, see M.E. Marmura, ed. *Islamic Theology and Philosophy* (Albany: SUNY Press, 1984); M. Watt, *The Formative Period of Islamic Thought* (Edinburgh: Edinburgh University Press, 1973); and H.A. Wolfson, *The Philosophy of the Kalam* (Cambridge, MA: Harvard University Press, 1976). For the Ash'ari school in particular, see George Makdisi, 'Ash'ari and the Ash'arites in Islam Religious History', *Studia Islamica* 17 (1962): 37–80; 18 (1963): 19–39.

[7] Al-Ghazali, *Munqidh min al-Dalal*, p. 30. For an introduction to Islamic philosophy, see Henri Corbin, *History of Islamic Philosophy*, trans. L. Sherrard (London: Kegan Paul, 1993); Majid Fakhry, *A History of Islamic Philosophy* (New York: Columbia University Press, 1983).

[8] Al-Ghazali, *Munqidh min al-Dalal*, pp. 33–43. Al-Ghazali's six 'philosophical sciences' are based on al-Farabi's classification in his *Ilsa al-'Ulum*. For a discussion of this work and the 'philosophical sciences' (i.e. mathematics, astronomy, medicine, biology, etc.), see Seyyid Hossein Nasr, *Science and Civilization in Islam* (Lahore: Suhail Academy, 1999).

[9] Al-Ghazali, *Munqidh min al-Dalal*, p. 30.

plants'.¹⁰ Only those who conclude from this that the 'non-existent' cannot return to 'existence', or those who argue that 'temperament' has a role in 'constituting the power of animals', are declared 'heretical'. His argument is that such beliefs deny the omnipotence of God, not to mention the 'reward and punishment' of Heaven, Hell and the Day of Judgement.¹¹ Similarly, the Theists are attacked primarily for their metaphysics. Al-Ghazali places Socrates, Plato and Aristotle, along with such Muslim thinkers as Abu 'Ali al-Husayn ibn Sina (d. 1037) and Muhammad ibn Muhammad al-Farabi (d. 950), in this group.¹² Such Muslim thinkers are particularly condemned for their 'Aristotelian' views, which al-Ghazali believes are 'unable to satisfy the conditions of proof...in logic'.¹³ As well, concepts such as God knowing only 'universals not particulars', and 'spirit' not 'body' journeying to the afterlife, amount to the denial of the same theological propositions as in the case of the Naturalists.¹⁴

Al-Ghazali's third 'class of seekers' is the *batiniyya*, whom he describes as followers of Pythagorean metaphysics and the doctrine of 'authoritative instruction' (*ta'lim*).¹⁵ In the latter regard, al-Ghazali informs his readers that the *batiniyya* argue that in searching for the 'unseen' (*batin*)—i.e. the 'Truth'—'not every instructor is adequate, there must be an infallible instructor (*mu'allim*)'.¹⁶ Al-Ghazali's response is that on metaphysical grounds Aristotle long ago exposed the 'weak-

---

¹⁰ Ibid., p. 31.
¹¹ Ibid., p. 31.
¹² Along with Abu al-Walid ibn Rushd (d. 1098), Abu 'Ali al-Husayn ibn Sina (d. 1037) and Muhammad ibn Muhammad al-Farabi (d. 950) are among the most studied Islamic philosophers following in the peripatetic tradition. Apart from the works of Corbin, Fakhry and Marmura cited above, for Ibn Sina, also see D. Gutas, *Avicenna and the Aristotelian Tradition* (Leiden: E.J. Brill, 1988). For Al-Farabi, see J. Lameer, *Al-Farabi and Aristotelian Syllogistics* (Leiden: E.J. Brill, 1994). For Ibn Rushd, see G. Endress and J. Aertsen, *Averroes and the Aristotelian Tradition* (Leiden: E.J. Brill, 1999).
¹³ Al-Ghazali, *Munqidh min al-Dalal*, p. 37.
¹⁴ Ibid., p. 37.
¹⁵ In general, al-Ghazali's *batinyya* refers to Shi'ism, but particularly that line (Ismai'ilism) associated with the Fatimid Imamate and a group of scholars known as the 'Brethren of Purity', who held Neo-Pythagorean views. For an introduction to the subject, see S.H.M. Jafri, *The Origins and Early Development of Shi'i Islam* (London: Longman, 1979); Bernard Lewis, *The Origins of Isma'ilism* (Cambridge: W. Heffer, 1940); Majid Momen, *An Introduction to Shi'i Islam* (New Haven: Yale Press, 1985); S.M. Stern, *Studies in Early Isma'ilism* (Leiden: E.J. Brill, 1983); and I.R. Netton, *Muslim Neo-Platonists: An Introduction to the Thought of the Brethren of Purity* (London: Allen & Unwin, 1982).
¹⁶ Al-Ghazali, *Munqidh min al-Dalal*, p. 45.

ness and corruption' in Pythagorean thought.[17] On practical grounds, al-Ghazali finds the 'infallible teacher' doctrine flawed in that there is 'no demonstration' of who this person might be.[18] And, on theological grounds he argues that the only 'infallible instructor is Muhammad, no one after him'.[19]

The final class that al-Ghazali considers—the *sufiyya*—is immediately set apart from the rest in the very tone of his language.[20] In comparing the 'knowledge' gained through this and other classes, al-Ghazali gushes: 'What a difference there is between *knowing* the definition of health and satiety...and *being* healthy and satisfied'.[21] In many respects, al-Ghazali means this quite literally, knowledge in the Sufi 'way' (*tariqa*) ultimately not being 'apprehended by study', but by 'immediate experience' (*dhawq*).[22] This 'experience' is not that of 'sensory perception', which al-Ghazali in any case argues is proved to be limited by 'intellectual apprehension', or 'reason' (*'aql*).[23] This is 'supra-intellectual apprehension', or 'intuition' (*kashf*), which he contends even exposes reason's limits. In al-Ghazali's words, 'the man to whom He has granted no immediate experience at all, apprehends no more of what prophetic revelation really is than the name'.[24]

Al-Ghazali writes of two 'stages' of 'supra-intellectual apprehension'. At the first stage, by means of various exercises designed to sink 'the heart completely in the recollection of God', the individual can experience revelations and visions, and sight angels and the spirits of prophets while in a waking state.[25] In the 'higher' stage, one is said to experience 'annihilation' (*fana'*) in God. Al-Ghazali eschews the task of putting into words a 'state' (*hal*) he claims cannot be accurately articulated, but he does criticise the descriptions of *fana'* articulated by some Sufis. Those who conceive of the 'state' in terms of 'incarnation'

---

[17] Ibid., p. 53.
[18] Ibid., p. 52.
[19] Ibid., p. 46.
[20] For an introduction to Sufism, see A.J. Arberry, *Sufism: An Account of the Mystics of Islam* (New York: Harper & Row, 1970); J.S. Trimingham, *The Sufi Orders in Islam* (London: Oxford University Press, 1971); Annemarie Schimmel, *Mystical Dimensions of Islam* (Chapel Hill: University of North Carolina Press, 1975); and V. Baldick, *Mystical Islam: An Introduction to Sufism* (London: I.B. Taurus, 1989).
[21] Al-Ghazali, *Munqidh min al-Dalal*, p. 55.
[22] Ibid., pp. 54–55.
[23] Ibid., p. 24.
[24] Ibid., p. 61.
[25] Ibid., pp. 60–61.

(*hulul*), 'union' (*ittihad*) or 'connection' (*wusul*) are declared in error.²⁶ Although al-Ghazali does not explain his reasons in this particular work, one can infer that his problem is that such terms deny the theologians' understanding of God as 'transcendent', while upholding a vision of God's 'absolute immanence'—a point to be discussed further below.²⁷ Here, however, it must be stated that although al-Ghazali presents the intellectualism of his day in terms of four 'classes', it is clear that other intellectual categories can also be inferred.

To begin with, there is the division between advocates of 'reason' and advocates of 'intuition'. Further than this, there is a division within the advocates of 'intuition' on the issue of *fana*' and the implication of 'immanence' or 'transcendence'. Underlying this last division, as previously mentioned, are debates concerning the Sufis' and the theologians' reasoning on the 'creed received from the prophetic source'. The same premise is employed to divide the advocates of 'reason'. For example, al-Ghazali states:

> The man who verbally professes belief in prophecy, but equates the prescriptions of the revealed scriptures with philosophic wisdom, really disbelieves in prophecy, and believes only in a certain judge [i.e. the philosopher].²⁸

---

²⁶ Ibid., p. 61. The origin of the doctrine of *fana*' is as obscure as that of Sufism. Interestingly, the likeness between the concept and certain Hindu and Buddhist principles has prompted some to argue that the doctrine of 'annihilation in unity' (*al-fana' fi al-tawhid*) may have been introduced by the conversion of Hindus or Buddhists, such as Abu 'Ali al-Sindhi. He is reputed to have been one of Abu Yazid al-Bistami's (d. 874) teachers, the latter of whom, along with Husayn ibn Mansur al-Hallaj (d. 922), popularised the concept with declarations such as 'I am Truth' (*ana al-haqq*), an echo of the Vedantic 'That you are' (*tat tvam asi*), and similar Buddhist concepts. The most extensive arguments of this kind are made in R.C. Zaehner, *Hindu and Muslim Mysticism* (Oxford: One World, 1994); and T. Izutsu, *A Comparative Study of the Key Philosophical Concepts in Sufism and Taoism*, 2 vols. (Tokyo: KICLS, 1966–67). Islamicists such as Corbin and Fakhry may not agree with the specifics of Zaehner's arguments, pointing instead to Gnostic Christian and Hellenic influences, but they do concede the influence of Hindu and Buddhist thought in Sufism and Islamic thought in general. For example, see Fakhry, *A History of Islamic Philosophy*, p. 270.

²⁷ Al-Bistami and al-Hallaj are two of the 'originators' of the line which al-Ghazali finds in error. A seminal work on this line is L. Massignon, *La Passion de Husayn Ibn Mansur Hallaj*, 4 vols. (Paris: Gallimard, 1975). Al-Ghazali's line begins with such individuals as al-Junayd (d. 910), who promoted the concept of 'subsistence' (*baqa'*) to counter the implication of an 'immanent' divinity. See Fakhry, *A History of Islamic Philosophy*, pp. 241–56.

²⁸ Al-Ghazali, *Munqidh min al-Dalal*, p. 77. Also see pp. 72–73.

In essence, this implies that apart from the four 'classes of seekers', al-Ghazali also alludes to four 'categories of thought'. Those who 'equate' the Truth gained through independent 'reason' and/or 'intuition' with that derived from 'revelation' (*wahy*), and those who seek to place the latter—i.e. Truth derived from revelation—above conclusions reached through independent reason and/or intuition. That this is not a feature of one work alone can be confirmed by turning to al-Ghazali's voluminous *Ihya' 'Ulum al-Din*.

In the later work, al-Ghazali references the same 'categories of thought', though emphasising alternative disciplines, schools and individual thinkers. Along with the theologians, as representatives of those who employ 'systematic argumentation' to extol the creed held in scripture, the *Ihya' 'Ulum al-Din*'s third volume focuses on the *fuqaha'* (jurists) and *fiqh* (jurisprudence), described as a discipline 'mixed with some sort of proof'.[29] Firmly argued to be a necessary feature of 'faith', this legalism is favourably contrasted with the 'acquired knowledge' of the philosophers, but like theology, it is viewed as insufficient in relation to the knowledge gained by the 'friends of God', or Sufis, through 'intuition' (*kashf*).[30] Sufis are also divided, but in this instance between those who follow the *shari'a* and those antinomians who believe that 'lawful and unlawful things are the same'.[31] Given the persistence of the categories of thought implicit in al-Ghazali's writings, it is in search of these categories that one can begin the discussion of al-Hujwiri and the relationship between Muslim intellectuals of different geographic regions.

Between Ghazna and Lahore, far from the intellectual environs of West Asia that nurtured al-Ghazali, al-Hujwiri wrote *Kashf al-Mahjub* when al-Ghazali was no more than a boy. This temporal and geographic distance, not to mention financial troubles, a stint in prison as well as complaints about losing his books in Ghazna, appear to have had little bearing on the permeation of the above 'categories of thought' in al-Hujwiri's conception of doctrinal Islam, as well as the disciplines of study and schools with which al-Ghazali illustrated his views. Regarding the distinction between advocates of 'reason' and 'intuition', al-Hujwiri writes that while 'gnosis' (*ma'rifat*) among the theologians is achieved

---

[29] Al-Ghazali, *Ihya' 'Ulum al-Din*, vol. 3, trans. Fazl al-Karim (Karachi: Dar ul-Ishaat, 1993), p. 19.
[30] Ibid., pp. 18–34. Also see pp. 287–91.
[31] Ibid., p. 298.

through 'right cognition (*'ilm*) of God', among the Sufis it is achieved through 'right feeling (*hal*) towards God'.³² In the same context, he writes disapprovingly of theological schools, such as the Muʿtazila, who argue that 'gnosis is intellectual and...only a reasonable person (*'aqil*) can possibly have it'—in effect, denying 'intuition' a role.³³ Much like al-Ghazali, al-Hujwiri argues that 'reason' and 'intuition' are not mutually exclusive. In al-Hujwiri's words, 'the exoteric aspect of Truth without the esoteric is hypocrisy, and the esoteric without the exoteric is heresy'.³⁴

Beyond the basic division between 'reason' and 'intuition', al-Hujwiri also acknowledges further division in these categories that concur with al-Ghazali. In terms of 'intuition', distinctions are based on descriptions of *fana'*. According to al-Hujwiri, these fall into two categories: 'intoxication' (*sukr*) and 'sobriety' (*sahw*). In essence, the premise of the 'intoxicated' is described as one in which 'the fixity and equilibrium of human attributes' is the 'greatest veil between God and Man', and thus must be destroyed in the state of 'annihilation'.³⁵ This 'state' is described as 'the destruction of human attributes...in God, so that only those faculties survive in him that do not belong to the human genus'.³⁶ To the 'sober', the destruction of human attributes is not so absolute; rather, human attributes 'subsist' in God as if in suspension. Thus, the 'sober' describe the state as 'the vision of subsistence (*baqa'*) while the attributes are annihilated'.³⁷ Evidently, these are subtle distinctions, but they do express the same division highlighted by al-Ghazali. In effect, the 'intoxicated' are those whose ideas imply an 'absolutely immanent' Divinity, while the 'sober' maintain a basically 'transcendent' God in line with the theologians.

In the realm of 'reason', al-Hujwiri is far less specific than al-Ghazali, perhaps due to the separation he suffered from his books. Although he mentions such 'philosophical sciences' as astronomy, mathematics

---

[32] ʿAli ibn ʿUthman al-Hujwiri, *Kashf al-Mahjub*, trans. Renold A. Nicholson (Karachi: Dar ul-Ishaʿat, 1990), p. 267.

[33] Ibid., p. 268. Apart from the previously cited histories of Islamic thought, for an introduction to the Muʿtazila, see Richard Frank, *Beings and their Attributes: The Teachings of the Basran School of the Muʿtazila in the Classical Period* (Albany: SUNY Press, 1978).

[34] Ibid., p. 14.
[35] Ibid., p. 185.
[36] Ibid., p. 185.
[37] Ibid., p. 187.

and medicine, he makes no detailed study of the philosopher's metaphysics. Yet, he nowhere condemns this 'class' as a whole. The only 'school' he criticises is the 'Sophists' (*sufista'iyun*), which he believes hold that 'nothing can be known and knowledge itself does not exist'.[38] He argues against them on logical grounds, but describes them as 'heretics' rather than 'apostates'.[39] They stray from Truth, according to al-Hujwiri, because the denial of knowledge is not only the denial of revelation and prophecy, but God—one of whose 'attributes' is knowledge that 'penetrates what is hidden and comprehends what is manifest'.[40] Given al-Hujwiri's and al-Ghazali's emphasis on theology above philosophy, as well as their shared preference for Ash'ari above Mu'tazili schools of theology, one can infer that al-Hujwiri also conceived of the advocates of 'reason' in terms analogous to al-Ghazali. First, the limit of the 'Islamic', in al-Hujwiri's and al-Ghazali's opinions, is not necessarily the divide between the 'classes' of theologians and philosophers, but that between schools that deny revelation/prophecy, and those that accept them as sources of 'knowledge'. And second, just as al-Hujwiri understood 'intuition' as either 'intoxicated' or 'sober', based on the relationship between it and theological proof, it follows that he grasped 'reason' based on the same criterion. That is, divided figuratively between the 'intoxicated,' who 'equate' Truth arrived at through 'reason' and 'revelation', and the 'sober' who hold 'revelation' to be the prime source of Truth.

The startling uniformity in al-Ghazali's and al-Hujwiri's understanding of doctrinal Islam, not merely in terms of the disciplines and schools to which they refer or commonly adhere, but in respect of more abstract 'categories of thought', obviously sheds light on the question of defining the 'Islamic'. Unless one is willing to limit doctrinal Islam to the intellectual and sectarian biases inherent in any one of al-Ghazali's 'classes of seekers', the underlying 'categories of thought' in his and al-Hujwiri's work provide a less prejudicial conception of the totality of the 'Islamic'. The only limit these categories uphold is with regard to thought that denies 'revelation' (i.e. the Qur'an) and 'prophecy' (i.e. Muhammad) as sources of knowledge. Thus, by adopting these categories in this study's approach to doctrinal Islam, only al-Ghazali's

---

[38] Ibid., p. 13.
[39] Ibid., p. 15.
[40] Ibid., p. 12.

'Materialists' and al-Hujwiri's 'Sophists' would be considered 'un-Islamic', falling outside the common principle of 'sober' and 'intoxicated' intuition and/or reason. Adding that representatives of, and reference to, each category can be identified in the 'Great Mughal' context, while the specific schools mentioned by al-Ghazali and al-Hujwiri may have ceased to be, the utility of these 'categories of thought' is worthy of further consideration.

Al-Ghazali and al-Hujwiri also begin to illumine the relationship between doctrinal Islam and the intellectual traditions and social customs of South Asia. On one level, they suggest that at least among Muslim scholarly classes, the categories, disciplines and schools of thought engaged in, not to mention the idiom of discourse, is uniformly 'Islamic'. On another plane, the same works imply that geography and time do play a role, even among the scholarly class. For example, while al-Ghazali describes the doctrines of the *batiniyya* as 'Pythagorean', al-Hujwiri likens the same to 'Hindu' and 'Buddhist' ideas.[41] Furthermore, al-Ghazali writes in Arabic, while al-Hujwiri writes in Persian. Thus, to speak of these thinkers as representatives of an essential Islamic 'culture' is also not feasible. Yet, 'connectedness' on a doctrinal level is undeniable. The question this discussion ultimately raises, therefore, is one of the central topics of this book: How is intellectual 'connectedness' related to the cultural 'embeddedness' so apparent? The first step towards an answer is to further explore the doctrinal variety inherent in the categories that frame al-Ghazali's and al-Hujwiri's perspectives on Truth.

II. *The World of Reason*

In the later part of the 8th century in Baghdad, the first formal school of theology, known as the Mu'tazila, was established in opposition to the number of less formally organised interpretations of Qur'anic Truth to have arisen by that time. One of the Mu'tazila's earliest members, Wasil ibn 'Ata' (d. 748), argued:

> God is wise and just and it is impossible that evil and injustice should be referred to Him and hence it is impossible that He would make men do the opposite of what He had commanded and that he should ordain

---

[41] Ibid., pp. 262–63.

something for them then recompense them for it; it thus follows that that man is the doer of good and evil, belief and unbelief, obedience and disobedience...God has endowed him with power over all this.⁴²

As this statement suggests, the Mu'tazila were advocates of 'freewill', and the 'power' with which God had endowed humanity to differentiate 'good' from 'evil' was the capacity to Reason. Following from this basic postulate, the Mu'tazila articulated five principles that they held to be internally consistent. The first is God's 'justice' (*'adl*), expressing the idea that God would be 'unjust' if He punished a person whose sins He preordained. This leads to the second principle, 'the promise and the threat'. Montgomery Watt explains: the 'basic point was that where God in the Qur'an had promised reward or threatened punishment, He was bound to carry this out'.⁴³ What, then, of the status of the 'sinner'? In response to those who argued that such an individual was not a 'Muslim', and others who argued that belonging to the faith depended on its profession rather than specific acts, the Mu'tazila articulated the third principle of 'the intermediate position', holding that the grave sinner was neither an unbeliever (*kafir*) nor a believer (*mu'min*), but fell in between. Thus, the grave sinner could be punished, but not expelled from the community.⁴⁴ The fourth principle, 'commanding the right and forbidding the wrong', implied, in Abu al-Hasan al-Ash'ari's (d. 935–36) words, 'that it is an obligation to command the right and forbid the wrong, where there is opportunity and ability, by tongue, hand and sword'.⁴⁵ Where the individual is acting in accord with the 'right', support is incumbent, and when 'wrong' opposition is expected from the believer.

The last of the Mu'tazila's five principles is God's 'unity' (*tawhid*). On the most basic level, this is an argument for the absolute transcendence of God against associationism (*shirk*), anthropomorphism (*tashbih*) and corporealism (*tajsim*). As al-Ash'ari explained:

> The Mu'tazila agree that God is one; there is no thing like Him; He is hearing, seeing; He is not a body, not a form, not flesh and blood, not an individual, not substance nor attribute; He has no colour, taste, smell,

---

⁴² Cited in Wolfson, *The Philosophy of the Kalam*, p. 616.
⁴³ Montgomery Watt, *The Formative Period of Islamic Thought* (Edinburgh: Edinburgh University Press, 1973), p. 229.
⁴⁴ Ibid., pp. 229–30.
⁴⁵ Cited in Watt, p. 231.

feel, no heat, cold, moisture nor dryness, no length, breadth nor depth, no joining together nor separation.[46]

This unity even extended to the 'attributes' of God, such as 'knowledge', 'power' and 'life'. For the Mu'tazila, God could not have knowledge, etc., which was something eternal yet distinct from Him, for that would place something other than God in the eternal realm. Thus, in Watt's opinion, many of this school held that 'the meaning of saying that God is knowing, powerful and living is that he is not ignorant, impotent or dead'.[47] One cannot argue with Watt, for in the Mu'tazila scheme, not even the Qur'an could be seen as eternal, leading to the doctrine of the 'created' Qur'an, i.e. the idea that being on a 'preserved tablet' [85:21], the Qur'an is 'finite or limited, and that finitude is only possible in the case of what has been created'.[48]

It should be apparent that the Mu'tazila raised the role of Reason in the interpretation of the Qur'an to exalted heights. The schools of theology to rise in opposition to the Mu'tazila, in defence, for example, of 'predestination', thus employed the former's dialectical method to uphold their own views. Foremost in this field was the Ash'ari school, founded by the aforementioned al-Ash'ari, who began his scholarly life as a Mu'tazili. The gist of al-Ash'ari's repudiation, in the words of Majid Fakhry, is that 'Good is what God has prescribed, evil what He has prohibited'. Following from this strictly 'voluntarist thesis', al-Ash'ari and his followers were reluctant to attach value to knowledge attained through Reason without the aid of Revelation. Thus, according to Ash'aris, 'God's power and sovereignty are such that the very meaning of justice and injustice is bound up with His arbitrary decrees. Apart from those decrees, justice and injustice, good and evil, have no meaning whatsoever'. In other words, 'God is not compelled', as the Mu'tazila argued, 'to take note of what is fitting in regard to His creatures and to safeguard their moral or religious interests, so to speak, but is entirely free to punish the innocent and remit the sins of the wicked'.[49] Furthermore, implicit in this perspective is the Ash'ari rebuttal of the Mu'tazila dependence on freewill with the argument for God's absolute omnipotence. According to al-Ash'ari and his followers, God's

---

[46] Ibid., pp. 246–47.
[47] Ibid., p. 246.
[48] Ibid., p. 244.
[49] Fakhry, *A History of Islamic Philosophy*, p. 238.

justice is not denied by predestination, for injustice 'can only denote the transgression of what has been prescribed'.[50] With regard to God's attributes and the status of the Qur'an, therefore, the Ash'aris argued, again in Fakhry's words, 'the essential divine attributes of knowledge, power, and life are eternal and subsist in God's essence'. They are not 'identical with this essence', as the Mu'tazila claimed, nor are they 'not identical with it'.[51] The point is important because the Ash'aris' perception of the attributes of God's as eternal, meant they could also argue that the 'Word' of God was eternal; hence, their doctrine of the 'uncreated' Qur'an, the 'Eternal Word'.[52]

On the face of it, such 'principles' and polemics would appear far removed from Muslim society at large, particularly when it is noted that both Ash'aris and Mu'tazilis agreed on the transcendence of God. Such a shallow reading of these debates, however, is a mistake. First and foremost, it does not require much imagination to consider that the place accorded Reason by Mu'tazilis and Ash'aris, respectively, would profoundly influence the attitude of each school's subscribers towards other sources of knowledge, including pre-Islamic thought and the so-called 'philosophical sciences'. Consider, for example, that it was under the auspices of the overtly Mu'tazili Caliph of the Abbasid period (750–1258), al-Ma'mun (d. 833), that the famous *Bait al-Hikma* (House of Wisdom) was instituted and a 'Translation Movement' undertaken to systematically bring the knowledge of the world into the fold of Islam. As well, the role of individual principles, such as the createdness/uncreatedness of the Qur'an, is well studied in terms of the *Mihna* (Trial) begun by the same Caliph.[53] Last, but not least, it should also be recalled that as sectarian divides crystallised, aspects of Mu'tazilism became enshrined as the official theological creed of Imami Shi'ism, while Ash'arism became the dogma of Sunnism. The impact of these doctrines on cultural movements, therefore, cannot be underestimated, particularly when contemporary developments in the discipline of law are added.

---

[50] Ibid., p. 230.
[51] Ibid., p. 231.
[52] Apart from Fakhry, a detailed exposition of Mu'tazila and Ash'ari views on all the above points is also presented in Wolfson's *The Philosophy of the Kalam*.
[53] See M. Hinds, 'Mihna', *Encyclopedia of Islam* (Leiden: E.J. Brill [CD ROM Edition], 2004); and M. Rekaya, 'Al-Ma'mun', *Encyclopedia of Islam* (Leiden: E.J. Brill [CD ROM Edition], 2004).

While theologians sought to define 'right' and 'wrong' belief, others concerned themselves with 'right' or 'wrong' actions. Growing hand in hand with theology, therefore, the drive to articulate the law can also be identified as one of the earliest manifestations of Muslim intellectual life. In fact, by the time Mu'tazilis were debating with Ash'aris and others in the 9th century, four major schools (pl. *madhahib*/sing. *madhhab*) of jurisprudence (*fiqh*)—Hanafi, Maliki, Shafi'i and Hanbali—had arisen in proto-Sunni circles, while the Jafari school laid the foundations of two Imami Shi'i branches—Akhbari and Usuli—which took shape between the 11th and the 13th centuries. Theoretically, all jurists upheld the Qur'an as having 'absolute validity' as a source of the *shari'a,* the body of law produced through jurisprudence (*fiqh*).[54] According to the corpus of theory known as *usul al-fiqh* (principles of jurisprudence), however, in cases where the Qur'an was not explicit, jurists could turn to the concept of *sunna* (the 'trodden path'), referring to the example of the Prophet Muhammad and his 'Companions' (*sahaba*). Such 'examples' were drawn from the literature known to Sunni scholars as *hadith*, and Imami Shi'i scholars as *akhbar*.[55] When

---

[54] There are numerous works on *fiqh*, but two are recognised as the 'foundations' of contemporary study. These are J. Schacht, *An Introduction to Islamic Law* (Oxford: University Press, 1962); and N.J. Coulson, *A History of Islamic Law* (Edinburgh: University Press, 1964).

[55] The form of *hadith/akhbar* appears to have been influenced by the pre-Islamic Arabian preoccupation with genealogy, and derived from the genre of *khabar* (pl. *akhbar*), 'a story or an anecdote which was not so much fixed by any reference to a general timeframe as it was to a particular and unusually remarkable figure or event'. As well, for *hadith* scholars the Qur'an's reference to Muhammad's exemplary conduct meant that these were not mere historical reports, but each contained the 'silent' or 'living' tradition of the exemplar, the *sunna*, a concept mentioned in the Qur'an. Thus, a scholar could claim to have identified a number of *sunna* in each *hadith*. Furthermore, depending on the status one accorded the early Caliphs/Imams, or 'companions' of Muhammad, their *sunna* could also be sought, as could the '*sunna* of the ancients' and 'those who came before' (Qur'an, 8:38, 15:13, 17:77, 18:55, 35:43), and the '*sunna* of God' (Qur'an, 48:23, 35:43, 4:85). The Arabian literary tradition and the import placed on *sunna* in the growing field of jurisprudence is quite naturally related to the growth in the ranks of *hadith* scholars (*ahl al-hadith*) from the earliest date. By the 10th century, *hadith* had evolved into a formal 'science'. Six works—namely, those of Muhammad ibn Isma'il al-Bukhari (d. 869), Muslim ibn al-Hajjaj (d. 815), Ibn Maja (d. 887), Abu Dawud al-Sijistani (d. 889), al-Tirmidhi (d. 889) and al-Nasa'i (d. 915)—came to be acknowledged as the 'Six Books' of Sunnism, while the *Muwatta'* of Malik ibn Anas (d. 795) and the *Musnad* of Ahmad ibn Hanbal (d. 855) have also been held in high esteem. As well, the collections of al-Kulayni (d. 940), Ibn Babawayh, or 'Shaykh al-Saduq' (d. 991) and Muhammad ibn Hasan al-Tusi (d. 1067) gained similar status among the Imami Shi'a. Theoretically, the 'soundness' of a *hadith* would be tested by its *isnad* (chain of transmission; lit. 'support') and the closeness of its *matn* (text) to

sunna also failed to provide insight, the jurist moved beyond literature to 'derive' the *shari'a* by means of *ijma'* (the consensus of the learned), supplemented by *qiyas* (analogical reasoning).[56] The process of deriving law by this method was known as *ijtihad* (independent reasoning) in both sects, and the jurist qualified to engage in *ijtihad* was called a *mujtahid*. Divisions between schools were dependent upon which of the three sources beyond the Qur'an (*sunna, ijma'* or *qiyas*) was assigned a greater (or any) degree of influence in the derivation of *shari'a*. However, within sectarian bounds, and at times across them, all schools were 'regarded, and regard one another, as alternative and equally valid interpretations of the religious law of Islam'.[57]

One of the foremost contemporary historians of Islamic jurisprudence, Joseph Schacht, echoes the majority in pointing out that *ijtihad* has not been continuously employed by jurists. He writes that from the 9th century, 'the idea began to gain ground that only the great scholars of the past had the right to independent reasoning in law (*ijtihad*)'. By the 10th century, 'a consensus gradually established itself... to the effect that all future activity would have to be confined to the explanation, application, and, at the most, interpretation of the doctrine as it had been laid down once and for all (*taqlid*)'.[58] The implication is that *taqlid* (imitation), rather than *ijtihad*, was the over-riding principle of the pre-colonial period, inclusive of Mughal domains. However, *taqlid* should not be read to mean that various degrees of *ijtihad* were not called for and exercised by some, or that a rigidly 'codified law' had arisen. One must repeat the fact that as all schools held the Qur'an to be central, they also acknowledged each other's interpretations as

---

the Qur'an. See Abdul Kader al-Tayob, 'The Transformation of a Historical Tradition: From Khabar to Tarikh', *American Journal of Islamic Social Sciences* 5:2 (1988), pp. 220–26. For a broader discussion of the development of *hadith* literature, see James Robson, 'Hadith', *Encyclopaedia of Islam*, vol. 3 (Leiden: E.J. Brill, 1960), pp. 23–28. (Note: Unless otherwise indicated, all *Encyclopaedia of Islam* articles are from the 2nd Edition, first issued in 1960.)

[56] Although differences in Shi'i and Sunni *usul* are evident, as the application of *fiqh* is largely analogous, *qiyas* and *'aql* may be likened to each other in this basic context. See Momen, *An Introduction to Shi'i Islam*, pp. 185–88. For a more specialised study of Shi'i jurisprudence, see H.M. Tabataba'i, *An Introduction to Shi'i Law: A Bibliographical Study* (London: Ithaca Press, 1984).

[57] J. Schacht, 'Fikh', *Encyclopaedia of Islam*, vol. 2, pt. 2, p. 890.

[58] Ibid., p. 890. It should be noted that in the Shi'a context *ijtihad* continued among the jurists as a whole until the 18th century, when the concept of *marja' al-taqlid* arose to require that only the opinions of the *mujtahid* considered most knowledgeable should be followed. See Momen, *An Introduction to Shi'i Islam*, p. 188.

valid, and extended to the litigant the right to request decisions by any school, including those different from the one sponsored by the state.

Yet, one cannot ignore that the *shari'a* does have literary anchors. Qur'anic references, therefore, insured that despite distances in time, space and scholastic affiliation, the 11th century Shafi'i jurist of Baghdad, Abu al-Hasan al-Mawardi, and a 14th century Hanbali writing between Damascus and Cairo, Taqi al-Din Ahmad ibn Taymiyya, like all who preceded and followed them, agreed that apostasy, adultery, sodomy, fornication, intoxicants, theft and murder were 'crimes' with 'statutory', rather than 'discriminatory', punishments. However, the role of the Qur'an as a source of law was limited by the scant references it makes to legal issues. That is to say, in the case of the aforementioned issues alone were specific penalties (*hudud*) argued to be 'prescribed'. Furthermore, al-Mawardi and Ibn Taymiyya's writings show that even with respect to prescribed offences with statutory punishments, scholastic differences of opinion were commonplace. In the case of 'sodomy', Ibn Taymiyya relays that among Hanbalis opinion varied between death and lesser penalties.[59] As well, with regard to 'fornication', al-Mawardi informs his reader that Shafi'i opinion ranged from flogging to banishment.[60] Moving beyond the variety of opinion within a singular school, consideration of others only extends the ethos of variety further. Ibn Taymiyya categorically argues that flogging is due anyone who 'consumes' any intoxicant.[61] Al-Mawardi, on the other hand, not only suggests that punishment may vary from flogging to public humiliation, but adds that some scholars argue 'inebriation', rather than consumption, is the crime, while others argue that only wine, or only alcoholic beverages are banned, but inebriation is not at issue.[62] Similarly, in the case of theft, Ibn Taymiyya is unequivocal in his judgement that the right hand must be amputated for any theft above 3 dirhams, while al-Mawardi points out that there are differences

---

[59] Taqi al-Din Ahmad ibn Taymiyya, *Risala fi al-Siyasa al-Shar'iyya*, ed. and trans. Omar Farrukh, *Ibn Taymiyya on Public and Private Law in Islam* (Beirut: Khayat Book & Publishing Co., 1966), p. 118. For a more thorough discussion of legal attitudes towards homosexuality, see Louis Crompton, 'Male Love and Islamic Law in Arab Spain', *Islamic Homosexualities*, eds. S.O. Murray and W. Roscoe. (New York: University Press, 1997): 142–60.

[60] Abu al-Hasan al-Mawardi, *Al-Ahkam al Sultaniyya wa al-Wilayat al-Diniyya*, ed. and trans. W.H. Wahba, *The Ordinances of Government* (Reading: Garnet Publishers, 1996), pp. 63, 242–56.

[61] Ibn Taymiyya, *Al-Siyasa al-Shar'iyya*, p. 120.

[62] Al-Mawardi, *Al-Ahkam al-Sultaniyya*, p. 248.

of opinion on minimum amounts for amputation, the nature of the property stolen that warrants amputation, and the person due amputation if the crime is committed by a group.[63]

The import of the differences of opinion within and between the schools' laws, as well as the validity of each opinion, is only further emphasised when one moves beyond the 'prescribed' and 'statutory', to matters decided by reference to *sunna*, *ijma'* or *qiyas*. Consider, for example, the *shar'i* perspective on *al-jihad al-asghar* ('the little struggle'), as described by the 12th century Andalusian jurist, Abu al-Walid Muhammad ibn Ahmad Ibn Rushd.[64] 'Scholars [of all schools] agree,' writes Ibn Rushd, 'that the *jihad* is a collective not a personal responsibility…The obligation to participate in the *jihad* applies to adult free [Muslim] men who have the means at their disposal to go to war and who are healthy, that is, not ill or suffering from chronic diseases'.[65] Furthermore, the 'maximum number of enemies against which one is obliged to stand one's ground is twice the number [of one's own forces]'.[66] There is also general agreement on the fact that the 'aim of warfare…is two-fold: either conversion to Islam, or the payment of poll-tax [*jizya*]',[67] and that the prerequisite for war 'is that the enemy must first have heard the summons to Islam'.[68] Against whom one may declare *jihad*, and what 'rights' were accorded enemy combatants, however, is the subject of scholarly debate.

From al-Mawardi's Shafi'i perspective, bandits, apostates and heretics may be fought, but this is not termed '*jihad*', which only applies to non-Muslims living in *dar al-harb* ('land of war'), situated outside of territory governed by the *shari'a*, known as *dar al-Islam* ('land of Islam').[69] Al-Mawardi's primary justification for fighting bandits is to

---

[63] Ibn Taymiyya, *Al-Siyasa al-Shar'iyya*, pp. 112–14; Al-Mawardi, *Al-Ahkam al-Sultaniyya*, pp. 245–47.

[64] Abu al-Walid Muhammad ibn Ahmad ibn Rushd, *Bidayat al-Mujtahid*, trans. Rudolph Peters (Leiden: E.J. Brill, 1977). For a general discussion of *jihad*, see Rudolph Peters, *Jihad in Medieval and Modern Islam* (Leiden: E.J. Brill, 1977).

[65] Ibid., pp. 9–10.

[66] Ibid., p. 21.

[67] Ibid., p. 23.

[68] Ibid., p. 19.

[69] Al-Mawardi, *Al-Ahkam al Sultaniyya*, pp. 60–78, 148–53. These concepts are not found in the Qur'an, but are mentioned in the *hadith* literature. For a discussion of the development of these concepts and their ties to the theory of *jihad*, see A. Abel, 'Dar al-Harb', *Encyclopaedia of Islam*, vol. 2, pt. 1, p. 126; and 'Dar al-Islam', *Encyclopaedia of Islam*, vol. 2, pt. 1, pp. 127–28.

maintain order, while heretics and apostates are attacked for having left the 'true faith'.[70] The standard al-Mawardi applies to differentiate between the apostate/heretic is as follows. A believer pays *zakat* (alms tax), but heretics and apostates do not. Meanwhile, an apostate is distinguished from a heretic insofar as the former does not acknowledge *zakat* as a 'duty', while the latter does but chooses to violate the injunction. The punishment for the apostate is death, without the opportunity of deferment through truce, the payment of tax, the forfeiture of property, or the submission of oneself to slavery. In the case of the heretic, however, the end of fighting is to 'deter, not to kill'.[71] Thus, in opposition to the conduct deemed legitimate with apostates, the heretic cannot be attacked while retreating, the injured and captives cannot be killed, property cannot be claimed as *fay'* (i.e. for the 'benefit of all Muslims' and so administered by the state), women and children cannot be enslaved, and goods cannot be destroyed or looted.[72] Ibn Taymiyya echoes al-Mawardi's understanding of this mode of combat, but the Hanbali view also makes reference to conflict with 'apostates' and 'heretics' as *jihad*.[73] In Ibn Taymiyya's opinion, in fact, an individual who accepts the obligation of prayer (*salat*), but does not perform it after being 'ordered', can be put to death as an apostate.[74] In other words, from Ibn Taymiyya's Hanbali perspective, not only is the distinction between the heretic and apostate largely ignored, but those Muslims judged in error are largely equated with non-Muslims, and those states they rule identified as *dar al-harb*.

Distinctions between the schools do not end with definitions of the 'Muslims' to be fought, or the 'rights' accorded to the defeated party. The same can also be observed in the case of 'non-Muslims'. Recall that in the theory of *jihad*, there is agreement between schools on the stipulation that the 'enemy' must have had the opportunity either to accept conversion or the payment of *jizya* before the *mujahid* can embark on the warpath. Hanbalis and Shafi'is, like Ibn Taymiyya and al-Mawardi, respectively, extended safe conduct with the payment of *jizya* to the *ahl al-kitab* ('People of the Book'), i.e. primarily Jews and Christians. Ibn Rushd, however, illustrates that Malikis and Hanafis

---

[70] Al-Mawardi, *Al-Ahkam al Sultaniyya*, pp. 68–72.
[71] Ibid., p. 63.
[72] Ibid., pp. 65–67.
[73] Ibn Taymiyya, *Al-Siyasa al-Shar'iyya*, pp. 88–89.
[74] Ibid., pp. 143–44, 147–48.

accepted that *jizya* may be collected from 'polytheists', thus legitimising the categorisation of Hindus—along with Christians and Jews—as *dhimmis* (lit., 'the protected'; i.e. non-Muslim subjects of the *shar'i*-state).[75] Furthermore, according to juristic political philosophy in general, a *dhimmi* could seek employment in the state up to the highest ranks of the bureaucracy (*wazirat*) and military (*amirat*), as well as in the judicial arms serving non-Muslims.[76]

Beyond the fact that two of the four Sunni schools virtually equate polytheists and 'People of the Book'—at least in so far as the state's jurisdiction extends—it is important to note that:

> ...in dealing with captives, various policies are open to the *Imam* [leader]. He may pardon them, enslave them, kill them, or release them on ransom or as *dhimmis*, in which latter case the released captive is obliged to pay *jizya* [poll tax].[77]

It is further stipulated that the killing of captives is only sanctioned 'on the condition that *aman* [safe conduct] has not been granted'.[78] As well, Ibn Rushd notes that some jurists 'taught that captives may never be slain'.[79] This disagreement is restricted to the context of captives who are 'able-bodied, unbelieving males'. However, there 'is no disagreement about the rule that it is forbidden to slay women and children, provided they are not fighting'.[80] To this, Malikis and Hanafis add that 'neither the blind, nor the insane, nor hermits may be slain and that of their property not all may be carried off, but that enough should be left for them to be able to survive. Neither is it allowed...to slay the old and decrepit'.[81]

Differences between schools and individual jurists within schools on the three groups to be fought and the legal stipulations circumscribing offensive action indicate that the *shari'a* accommodates significant

---

[75] Ibn Rushd, *Bidayat al-Mujtahid*, p. 24. Literally 'the protected', *dhimmi* refers to non-Muslim subjects of an 'Islamic' state. For an introductory survey of the concept of *dhimmi* and the actual status of non-Muslims in various Muslim settings, see Claude Cahen, 'Dhimmi', *Encyclopaedia Islam*, vol. 2, pp. 227–31; also A.S. Tritton, *The Caliphs and their Non-Muslim Subjects* (London: Milford, Oxford University and Cass, 1930); and Benjamin Braude and Bernard Lewis, eds. *Christians and Jews in the Ottoman Empire*, 2 vols. (London: Holmes & Meier, 1982).
[76] For example, see, Al-Mawardi, *Al-Ahkam al-Sultaniyya*, pp. 23–29.
[77] Ibn Rushd, *Bidayat al-Mujtahid*, p. 12.
[78] Ibid., p. 13.
[79] Ibid., p. 12.
[80] Ibid., p. 15.
[81] Ibid., p. 15.

variations in, for example, the status of polytheists or the 'rights' of a captive. Consequently, it must be stated that not only concepts like *jihad*, but a variety of institutions viewed as *shar'i*, defy its definition as a 'code' or 'set of principles', even under the pall of *taqlid*. Rather, the *shari'a* is a legal 'process' that is highly accommodative of scholarly difference, from jurist to jurist, as much as from school to school. As well, even a brief overview of stipulations concerning inheritance and endowment illustrates that where scholars are in agreement over one point, there often exists an alternative approach to the question, which offers another response to the problem.

First of all, it should be clarified that upon payment of *jizya*, *dhimmi*s are provided autonomy in the realm of 'personal law', concerning norms of marriage, divorce, inheritance rights, and so on. Juristic ideals concerning inheritance, therefore, apply only to Muslims, listing every iota of a person's holdings to be distributed according to fractional stipulations derived from the Qur'an and *sunna*.[82] Although there are differences between schools, including Sunni and Shi'i varieties, by focusing on the Hanafi school—the 'official' creed of the Mughals—one gains a sense of the details involved.[83] After deductions from moveable and immoveable property to pay for funeral expenses and debts, one-third of the estate can be bequeathed by a 'will'. However, the heir may only be a family member if other familial heirs consent.[84] Regarding the remaining two-thirds of the estate, the deceased plays no role in determining heirs or the 'shares' they receive. Rather, rights to shares are accorded to relatives as distant as the descendents of uterine uncles and aunts. In the case of such distant relatives, however, receipt of a share is dependent on the absence of some or all of a primary class of heirs referred to in the Qur'an. These include husband/wife, grandfather and grandmother, father and mother, brothers and sisters, and sons and daughters (uterine and consanguine), but individual shares received depend on the particular composition of surviving heirs, as well as on the gender of the recipient (men generally receiving twice

---

[82] For a thorough introduction to the development of the laws of inheritance, see David Powers, *Studies in Qur'an and Hadith: The Formation of the Islamic Law of Inheritance* (Berkeley: University of California Press, 1971); and N.J. Coulson, *Succession in the Muslim Family* (Cambridge: Cambridge University Press, 1971).

[83] For an introduction to Hanafi and Shi'i theory on inheritance in the South Asian context, Mughal, colonial and contemporary, see Imdad Husain Minhas, *Inheritance in Islam: Hanafi and Shi'i Laws* (Lahore: Nadeem Law Book House, 1998).

[84] Ibn Rushd, *Bidayat al-Mujtahid*, pp. 20–21.

the share of women).⁸⁵ For example, the mother of the deceased must always receive a one-third share when there are no surviving brothers and sisters, children (or the children of a deceased son) or husband/wife. If any of these heirs exist, the share for a mother drops to one-sixth. Only when there is no surviving mother, on the other hand, is the maternal grandmother due a one-sixth share of the estate.⁸⁶ When there are no legitimate heirs of any class, the estate is handed to the *bayt al-mal* (state treasury) to be employed, according to the theory of *fay'*, for 'the benefit of all Muslims'.⁸⁷

Thus, by the formulations of the Hanafi school (and jurisprudence in general), the *shari'a*, not individual Muslim choice or the state, determines the manner in which the largest share of property is to be consigned upon its owner's death. However, it is also *shar'i* for the revenue from any holdings to be bequeathed in perpetuity to individuals or groups of the holder's choice through the institution of *waqf* (endowment). Therefore, in his 'The Maliki *waqf* according to Wills and *waqfiyyat*'—a study of the institution of *waqf* in North Africa—Aharon Layish notes there is not one *waqfiyya* in which the holder's mother received anything, and lists a number in which daughters were the sole recipients, quite contrary to Maliki and, by extension, all the schools' laws of inheritance.⁸⁸ In the light of this, 'inheritance' and 'family endowment' appear as mutually exclusive systems, the former imposing sanctions on the property holder, the latter circumventing them. However, recalling the theory of *fay'*, the legal avenues of inheritance and endowment—the first minimising choice while maximising familial beneficiaries, the other maximising choice while minimising at least the number of familial beneficiaries—can be argued (as jurists obviously hoped) to serve a single end: 'the benefit of all Muslims'.

Finally, it should be noted that customary law was not listed among the four 'sources' of the *shari'a*. As Gideon Libson has argued, this is due to the fact that 'custom' reflects 'human behaviour, while Muslim jurists conceived of their legal system as superhuman'.⁸⁹ Nevertheless,

---

⁸⁵ Ibid., pp. 41–56.
⁸⁶ Ibid., p. 90.
⁸⁷ Ibid., p. 29.
⁸⁸ Aharon Layish, 'The Maliki Waqf According to Wills and Waqfiyyat', *Bulletin of the School of Oriental and African Studies* XLVI (1983), pp. 9–10.
⁸⁹ Gideon Libson, *Jewish and Islamic Law: A Comparative Study of Custom During the Geonic Period* (Cambridge: Harvard University Press, 2003), p. 69. For custom in *fiqh* more generally, see Mohammad Zain Othman, 'The Status of 'Urf in Islamic

he explains that the inclusion of customary practice in the *shariʿa* has been a feature of the system from its inception, even reflected in the variegated nature of the rulings considered above. The Malikis, in particular, based many of their early rulings on Medinan custom, granting it the sanction of *sunna*, and, 'as long as the literary redaction of *hadith* literature was still in progress', custom could be accommodated without formal recognition.[90] Throughout this formative period, however, debate was ongoing and such foundational Hanafis as Abu Yusuf (d. 798) and Muhammad al-Sarakhsi (d. 1097) were strong advocates for the inclusion of custom as a fifth 'source'.[91] Not immediately winning this sanction, those in favour of its inclusion came to view custom as a 'material source'. That is to say, custom was given *de facto* recognition by means of such 'legitimate' concepts as *istihsan* and *istislah*, which empowered the jurist to show 'preference' for a particular ruling, even if not arrived at by *qiyas*, on the basis of 'public interest' or 'equity'.[92] Al-Sarakhsi defined *istihsan* as 'the renunciation of analogy and adoption of what is more fitting for people'.[93] Al-Ghazali, writing on the concept of *istislah*, described it as allowing the jurist to bring into consideration 'what is aimed at for mankind in law'.[94] The apparent need to accommodate custom, as well as the influence of such thinkers, was so strong that by the Mughal period, Libson concludes, 'custom had become a virtually independent source in Hanafi legal thought'.[95]

Law', *IIUM Law Journal* 3:2 (1993): 40–51; M. al-Awa, 'The Place of Custom ('urf) in Islamic Legal Theory', *Islamic Quarterly* 17 (1973): 177–82; and "Ada', *Encyclopaedia of Islam* (CD-ROM Ed., 2004).

[90] Libson, *Jewish and Islamic Law*, p. 71.

[91] Ibid., pp. 70–71. Also see B. Johansen, 'Coutumes locales et coutumes universelles aux sources de regles juridiques endroite musulman hanafite', *Annales Islamologiques* 27 (1993): 29–35. Also N. Calder, 'Al-Sarakhsi', *Encyclopaedia of Islam* (CD-ROM Ed., 2004); and J. Schacht, 'Abu Yusuf', *Encyclopaedia of Islam* (CD-ROM Ed., 2004).

[92] For an introductory discussion of 'juristic preference', see R. Paret, 'Istihsan and Istislah', *Encyclopaedia of Islam*, vol. 4, pt. 1, p. 257. For more detailed discussion, see John Makdisi, 'Legal Logic and Equity in Islamic Law', *American Journal of Comparative Law* 33 (1985): 63–92; Ahmad Hassan, 'The Principle of Istihsan in Islamic Jurisprudence', *Islamic Studies* 16 (1977): 347–62; Husain Kassim, 'Sarakhsi's Doctrine of Juristic Preference (Istihsan) as a Methodological Approach toward World Affairs', *American Journal of Islamic Social Sciences* 5 (1899): 181–204; and W.B. Hallaq, *A History of Islamic Legal Theories: An Introduction to Sunni Usul al-Fiqh* (Cambridge: University Press, 1997), pp. 107–33.

[93] Cited in Libson, *Jewish and Islamic Law*, p. 77.

[94] Cited in R. Paret, 'Istihsan and Istislah', p. 257.

[95] Libson, *Jewish and Islamic Law*, p. 71.

Custom also played a role in juristic political philosophy. Ibn Taymiyya acknowledges that in the post-Caliphal Islamic state, 'those in command are of two classes... the *'ulama'* (jurists/theologians) and the *umara'* (governors).[96] The relationship between these 'classes' most 'in accord with the *sunna*' is when the *umara'* 'has no jurisdiction whatever, its function being merely to execute decrees of the *fuqaha'*'.[97] His reasoning in this regard is clear. The 'Islamic' state is to be governed according to the precepts of the Qur'an and *sunna*. However, the 'responsibility [to govern] is collective', and 'the measure of obligation is ability, and every man is responsible to the extent of his ability'.[98] Therefore, those best 'able' to interpret the 'sources' are also best suited to legislation. Not surprisingly for a jurist, this means that the Islamic state is ideally governed by the jurists and their *shari'a*. Yet, Ibn Taymiyya is not oblivious to ground realities. He argues that the Muslim community (*umma*) is made up of three types of Muslims: (1) 'Those who live entirely by their own capricious whims'; (2) 'Those who live according to sound religious principles'; and, (3) 'Those in whom both of the above co-exist'.[99] It is the last group that he believes to 'constitute the majority of the believers... They sometimes go this way, sometimes that, and mix right action with wrong'.[100] This being the inclination of the community, he argues that the ideal *shar'i*-state, one in which judicial autonomy is sacrosanct, cannot be, for '[t]he affairs of men in this world can be kept in order with a certain connivance in sin, better than with pious tyranny'.[101] That is to say, the *sultan* (ruler)—governing by 'fear' and 'agreement'—is necessary, for without leadership, neither religious nor worldly order can be established.[102] Thus, although Ibn Taymiyya declares 'despotism' a 'sin', he

---

[96] Taqi al-Din Ahmad ibn Taymiyya, *Al-Hisba fi al-Islam*, trans. M. Holland (Leicester: The Islamic Foundation, 1985), p. 116.

[97] Ibid., p. 25.

[98] Ibid., p. 23.

[99] Ibid., pp. 97–98. The term '*umma*' (lit. 'community') is found in the Qur'an, employed with a range of meanings, particularly in reference to religious communities. In *hadith* literature, however, the term is used to refer more specifically to the 'Muslim community', ideally without bars of race, gender or the individual Muslim's place of abode. A Muslim in *dar al-Islam* or in *dar al-Harb* is a member of the *umma*, the only condition, according to the *fuqaha'*, being adherence to the *shari'a*. For an introduction to the concept, see F.M. Denny, 'Umma', *Encyclopaedia of Islam*, vol. 10, pp. 859–63.

[100] Ibid., p. 98.

[101] Ibid., p. 95.

[102] Ibn Taymiyya, *Al-Siyasa al-Shar'iyya*, pp. 29, 187.

categorically states that '60 years of a despotic ruler are better than a single night without a ruler'.[103]

Considering the leeway for Sultanic legislative authority even legitimated by Ibn Taymiyya, it is no wonder that the bureaucrats who wrote 'Mirrors for Princes' institutionalised the idea in various ways.[104] A prime example of such literature is the *Siyasat Nama*, written by the same *wazir* of the Seljuq Sultanate (1040–1157), Nizam al-Mulk al-Tusi, who not only founded the Madrasa al-Nizamiyya at which al-Ghazali taught, but was also involved in hiring him. It is clear that al-Tusi's line of political thought has roots in the Sassanian political tradition, an observation amply confirmed in the writings of his forerunner, one of the Abbasid Caliphate's most renowned authors and translators, 'Abd Allah ibn al-Muqaffa'. Writing in the first decade of the Abbasid Caliphate, Ibn al-Muqaffa' borrowed from Persian political philosophy to present the Caliph as divinely appointed, arguing that God endows rightful rulers with 'pure intentions'.[105] This is due to the fact that a person with 'a good disposition to accomplish important acts' is necessary '[for the profit] of the elite and the masses' of the *umma*.[106] Nevertheless, Ibn al-Muqaffa' concedes that the 'religious sciences' and 'personal opinion' (*ra'y*) must also play a role in state.[107] Given that the ruler's power of 'reason' is god-given, however, Ibn al-Muqaffa' argues that when there is difference in religious opinion among the *mujtahids*, the ruler has the acuity and power to decide among them.[108] In other words, the Caliph is the ultimate political and religious authority. Thus, the Caliph may be removed only if he fails to enforce 'specifics' (e.g. *hudud*) that can be identified, not vague notions of rectitude.[109] In most other regards, Ibn al-Muqaffa' maintains the vision of the jurists of his day, but it is his highly centralised vision of power that carries forward into the era of Sultans. Thus, in al-Tusi's *Siyasat Nama*, written at a time in which Caliphal power had waned before the rise of Sultans, the Caliph's 'god-given' right to rule is transferred to the Sultan. Al-Tusi

---

[103] Ibid., p. 188.
[104] For an introduction to 'Mirrors for Princes', see E.I.J. Rosenthal, *Medieval Islamic Political Philosophy* (Cambridge: Cambridge University Press, 1958).
[105] 'Abd Allah ibn al-Muqaffa', *Risala fi al-Sahaba*, ed. and trans. Charles Pellat (Paris: Maisonneuve et Larose, 1976), p. 20.
[106] Ibid., p. 22.
[107] Ibid., pp. 28–30.
[108] Ibid., pp. 42–43.
[109] Ibid., pp. 25–26.

acknowledges God's sovereignty, represented by the supremacy of the *shari'a*, but argues that '[i]n every age and time God (be He exulted) chooses one member of the human race and, having endowed him with goodly virtues, entrusts him with the interests of the world and the well-being of His servants'.[110] This is the Sultan, and in matters of state al-Tusi declares that the latter has 'no need of any counsellor or guide'.[111] In other words, 'political' legislation is 'outside' the legislative capacity of the jurists, but sanctioned by God nonetheless. As for 'religious' legislation, al-Tusi concedes '[i]t is incumbent upon the king to inquire into religious matters, to be acquainted with divine precepts and prohibitions and put them into practice', such that 'kingship and religion are like two brothers'.[112] The question is: What specifically separates the 'political' and the 'religious'?

The realm of 'political' authority reserved for Sultans by al-Tusi and other writers of this genre is also described by Diya' al-Din Barani, a 14th century historian and political philosopher in the court of the Delhi Sultanate.[113] His definition of the Sultan's political authority is important for three reasons. First, Barani echoes al-Tusi's views on the dimensions of the ruler's legislative authority. Second, the difference in Barani's and al-Tusi's reasonings illustrates that the genre of 'Mirrors' literature in which both wrote is not without a variety of opinions. And third, Barani suggests that the South Asian Muslim political elite, like the scholarly elite represented by al-Hujwiri, were 'educated' in the same doctrinal Islam, in all its variety, as Muslims in other regions.

Regarding the ruler's legislative authority, Barani refers to the Sultan's legislative domain as '*dawabit*', or 'state laws', a widely used term. He

---

[110] Nizam ul-Mulk al-Tusi, *Siyasat Nama*, trans. H. Darke (London: Routledge & Kegan Paul, 1978), p. 2. For an introduction to the Seljuq state, in which al-Tusi served as *wazir*, see A.K.S. Lambton, 'The Internal Structure of the Seljuq Period', *Cambridge History of Islam*, vol. 5 (Cambridge: Cambridge University Press, 1968).

[111] Ibid., p. 11.

[112] Ibid., pp. 59–60.

[113] Diya' al-Din Barani, *Fatawa-i Jahandari*, trans. Afsar Khan and ed. Mohammad Habib, *The Political Theory of the Delhi Sultanate* (Delhi: Kitab Mahal, 1962). Barani was intellectually active during the period of the Tughluqs—the third of five dynasties to rule from Delhi between 1206–1526. For a political history of the five dynasties (Mamluk, Khalji, Tughluq, Sayyid and Lodhi) known as the 'Delhi Sultanates', see Peter A. Jackson, *The Delhi Sultanate: A Political and Military History* (New York: Cambridge University Press, 1999). For more a more social history, see Hamida Naqvi, *Agricultural, Industrial and Urban Dynamism under the Sultans of Delhi, 1206–1555* (Delhi: Munshiram Manoharlal Publishers, 1986).

considers *dawabit* in the Delhi Sultanate to be concerned with three issues: (1) court etiquette and conduct, where 'customary' practices prevail; (2) appointment of state officers; and, (3) apprehension and prosecution of 'rebels' and 'conspirators' against the state.[114] More like Ibn Taymiyya than al-Tusi, however, Barani assigns this legislative authority to the Sultan on the grounds of necessity. Sultanate, in Barani's estimation, is 'royal government', or government following the ways and means of pre-Islamic Persian emperors. He argues: 'Now, between the *sunna* of the Prophet...and the customs of the Persian emperors...there is complete contradiction and total opposition'.[115] The only reason Sultanate exists in Barani's world is:

> ...just as the eating of carrion, though prohibited, is yet permitted in time of dire need, similarly the customs and traditions of the pagan emperors of Iran...should from the viewpoint of truth and correct faith, be considered like the eating of carrion in time of dire need.[116]

In other words, echoing Ibn Taymiyya's views, Barani's Sultanate and its legislative authority is 'connivance in sin' out of practical necessity. The necessity itself is born of Barani's recognition that character, education, age and class divisions in society imply that 'there can be no stability in the affairs of men without justice'.[117] As '[r]eligion and justice are twins', the explicit need of society is to enforce the *shari'a*, which Barani deems impossible without Sultanate for one reason: the call of the 'religious scholars' does not move the people, while 'fear of the Sultan, his terror and power, and his blood-shedding sword' does.[118] He attempts to resolve the contradiction by arguing:

> ...[t]he policy of the state is distinct from the personal life of the king; it would, of course, be appropriate for kings to set the example of obeying the laws they impose on others, but the fact that they are themselves falling into sinfulness is irrelevant to the functioning of their governments.[119]

When legalism in Islam is analysed even as briefly as above, it becomes clear that neither the limit of four 'sources' (Qur'an, *sunna*, *ijma'* and *qiyas*), nor the preponderance of *taqlid*, can be seen to reduce the

---

[114] Barani, *Fatawa-i Jahandari*, pp. 64–65.
[115] Ibid., p. 39.
[116] Ibid., p. 40.
[117] Ibid., p. 16.
[118] Ibid., pp. 16, 40.
[119] Ibid., p. 3.

shariʿa to a code or abstract it into a set of principles. Differences between schools even on issues 'prescribed' in the Qurʾan, the acceptance of a multiplicity of opinion even within one school, as well as the acknowledgement of mutually exclusive systems such as inheritance and endowment, reflect the fact that Islamic jurisprudence is explicitly constructed as a legal process—one that is aware of and accommodating towards social variety and change. The aspects of legal theory that ultimately negate the notions of 'transgression' and 'intrusion' so common among historians of South Asia, however, resides in the obliquely central role 'custom' (*ʿurf*/*ʿada*) is also afforded, as well as the degree of legislative autonomy provided the Sultan. Furthermore, the breadth of attitudes towards legalism cannot be completely considered, unless one also acknowledges that even Sober Sufis like al-Ghazali and al-Hujwiri viewed *shariʿa* as no more than the 'exoteric' aspect of Islam. As al-Hujwiri put it, '*Shariʿa* cannot possibly be maintained without the existence of *haqiqa* (Truth), and *haqiqa* cannot be maintained without observance of *shariʿa*'—a relationship that led many jurists to study mysticism, and many mystics to study jurisprudence.[120] Thus, when considering the *shariʿa*, one must also take into account the legal attitudes of scholars who couple the law with their 'esoteric' pursuits.

A brief introduction to five prominent 'legalistic' Sufi orders in South Asia is sufficient to illustrate the variety of 'ways' available to the initiate.[121] These orders are the Chishtiyya, Qadiriyya, Shattariyya, Suhrawardiyya and Naqshbandiyya, all active in the Mughal context.[122]

---

[120] Al-Hujwiri, *Kashf al-Mahjub*, p. 383.

[121] A number of Sunni Sufi orders have been open to or tended towards Shiʿism, at least in terms of the usage of common terminology and the veneration of the Imams, particularly ʿAli. However, there have also been Shiʿi orders such as the Nurbakhshiyya, which spread from Iran to Kashmir. The Niʿmatullahiyya also spread from Iran to South Asia, where it flourished under the Southern Bahmanid Sultanate (1347–1528), while suffering reversals in Iran only to be revived there by Maʿsum ʿAli Shah Deccani. The latter may be considered 'intoxicated' orders, while the 'sober' brand of mysticism in Shiʿism is known as *ʿirfan* (gnosis). As Momen states: 'It includes many of the ideas and much of the technical vocabulary of Sufism but divests itself of the features which the 'ulama' find most objectionable: the formal structure of orders, initiation, the murshid-murid relationship, dhikr, concepts such as wahdat 'l-wujud, etc... Typical works in the field of 'irfan deal with bringing out the inner, esoteric meaning of the Quran based on the process of ta'wil (bringing out the spiritual meaning) rather than tafsir (technical commentary) of the verses.' See Momen, *An Introduction to Shiʿi Islam*, pp. 208–16.

[122] It should also be noted that the descriptions given here are time-specific, and that in the eras before and after that of the Great Mughals, the orientations of some of these orders was different. A case in point is the Suhrawardiyya. Early saints of this order

Beginning with the Chishtiyya, it is noteworthy that members eschewed the accumulation of wealth and association with the state, encouraged incantation (*dhikr*), allowed devotional music (*sama'*), legitimated the Hindu practice of breathing exercises and, at times, even adopted the Buddhist practice of employing a begging bowl.[123] The Shattariyya resembled the Chishtiyya in legitimating much Hindu and Buddhist practice, but eschewed the former's austerities to allow for the accumulation of wealth.[124] The Suhrawardiyya, on the other hand, grew to discourage *sama'* and overtly Hindu and Buddhist practices, while accepting wealth and patronage under the pretext that this allowed their moral influence to be felt in state.[125] The Qadiriyya resembled the Suhrawardiyya in their approach to mysticism, but unlike the former—who organised in *khanqah*s (hospices)—they led solitary lives of wandering the countryside.[126] Finally, the Naqshbandiyya were most resolute in the belief that the *shari'a*, as defined by Hanafi jurists, was the lynch-pin of the Sufi way.[127] Thus, only in the Naqshbandiyya was performing daily prayer, fasting, paying of *zakat* and refraining from *sama'* promoted by all initiates. Among the others, however, a range of legal attitudes prevailed.

---

are noted for highly 'syncretic' approach to practice, while by the Mughal era, they largely discouraged this movement, as noted below. Furthermore, individual Sufis were more often than not initiates of more than one order, though the orientation of these orders was usually similar. A number of works address the activities of these orders, including Annemarie Schimmel, *Islam in the Indian Subcontinent* (Leiden: E.J. Brill, 1980); and Carl Ernst, *Eternal Garden* (Albany: SUNY Press, 1992). However, none provides a more encyclopaedic introduction to the orders, their practical orientation, and the lives and works of their members than S.A.A. Rizvi, *A History of Sufism in India*, 2 vols. (Delhi: Munshiram Manoharlal, 1983).

[123] See K.A. Nizami, 'Chishtiyya', *Encyclopaedia of Islam*, vol. 2, pt. 1, pp. 50–56; and Rizvi, *A History of Sufism in India*, vol. 1, pp. 114–89, vol. 2, pp. 264–320.

[124] See K.A. Nizami, 'Shattariyya', *Encyclopaedia of Islam*, vol. 9, pp. 369–70; and Rizvi, *A History of Sufism in India*, vol. 2, pp. 151–73.

[125] See F. Sobieroj, 'Suhrawardiyya', *Encyclopaedia of Islam*, vol. 9, pp. 784–86; and Rizvi, *A History of Sufism in India*, vol. 1, pp. 190–240.

[126] See D.S. Margoliouth, 'Kadariyya', *Encyclopaedia of Islam*, vol. 4, pt. 1, pp. 380–84; and Rizvi, *A History of Sufism in India*, vol. 2, pp. 55–150.

[127] See K.A. Nizami, 'Nakshbandiyya', *Encyclopaedia of Islam*, vol. 7, pp. 934–39; and Rizvi, *A History of Sufism in India*, vol. 2, pp. 174–263. For the development, spread and practices of the Naqshbandiyya—an order central to the discussion of this book—see M. Gaborieau, A. Popovic and T. Zarione, *Naqshbandis: Cheminements et situation actuelle d'un order mystique musulman* (Istanbul-Paris: Editions Isis, 1990).

THE CATEGORIES OF DOCTRINAL ISLAM 49

A case in point is Sharaf al-Din ibn Yahya Maneri, a 14th century mystic of the less prominent, but scholastically influential, Firdawsiyya.[128] In his *Maktubat al-Sadi*, note a characteristic letter addressed to a disciple who was also a *qadi* (judge), listing three classes of 'sins'. The first is the abandonment of *fara'id* ('duties' of prayer, fasting, etc.). In this matter, in stark contrast to the jurists and their Naqshbandi supporters, who tend to advocate punitive measures against such transgressions, Maneri writes that people 'ought' to perform these duties to the 'maximum extent possible'.[129] In other words, persuasion, rather than punishment, is the appropriate course of action to be taken by the 'upright', while the individual's failure to comply is also considered in the light of circumstantial 'possibility'. The second class of sins consists of acts deemed between 'creature' and God. These include alcohol consumption, usury and music, which Maneri suggests the sinner must 'strive' to avoid.[130] In this case, not only is punishment absent, but such sins are deemed to be between humanity and God, thus overtly beyond the jurisdiction of the jurists. The last class of sins involves the acts of individuals towards others. These include property disputes, violations of the 'body' (from rape to backbiting) and leading people 'astray' in faith. In each of these cases, the onus is placed on the sinner to make amends, rather than on the legal authorities to seek restitution.[131] The overall tenor of Maneri's work is that 'repentance' and making peace with the aggrieved (man or god) is more important than punishment.

Maneri is by no means alone in exhibiting this attitude towards the *shari'a*. Nizam al-Din Awliya'—one of Maneri's most influential contemporaries, though of the Chishtiyya—puts the above dictate most succinctly as follows: 'The penitent is equivalent to the upright'.[132] The longstanding nature and geographic 'connectedness' of this attitude among Sufis is best illustrated by the fact that al-Ghazali devotes a

---

[128] For background on this influential and widely read author, see Paul Jackson, *The Way of the Sufi: Sharaf al-Din Maneri* (Delhi: Idara-i Adabiyat-i Delhi, 1987).
[129] Sharaf al-Din Maneri, *Maktubat al-Sadi*, ed. and trans. Syed Hasan Askari (New York: Paulist Press, 1980, p. 18.
[130] Ibid., p. 18.
[131] Ibid., pp. 18–19.
[132] See Nizam al-Din Awliya', *Fawa'id al-Fuad*, ed. and trans. B.B. Lawrence, *Morals of the Heart* (New York: Paulist Press, 1992), p. 81. For an introduction to the author's life and work, see Muhammad Habib, *Hazrat Nizam al-Din Awliya': hayat aur ta'limat* (Delhi: Shu'bah-i Urdu, Delhi University, 1972).

chapter to the subject of 'repentance' (*tawba*) in the fourth volume of his *Ihya' 'Ulum al-Din*.[133] Hence, these attitudes towards 'sin' confirm that although certain Sufi orders view the law as essential, they reduce the distinctions between classes of Muslims which many jurists construct. 'Heresy' is acknowledged, as in the work of al-Hujwiri, but 'apostasy' is virtually absent from the discourse when the thinker, school or sect acknowledges revelation (Qur'an) and prophecy (Muhammad). As well, with regard to non-Muslims, the recognition of all religious communities as 'People of the Book' is commonplace. For example, even in the writings of the Naqshbandi Mirza Jan-i Jahan (d. 1781), the argument presented is that Hindus should not be considered '*kafirs*' as their '*Vedas*' are revelationary. Furthermore, Jan-i Jahan clarifies that the ritual use of 'idols' by Hindus is akin to Sufi meditation rather than the 'worship' of idols practised in pre-Islamic Arabia.[134] Although none of these ideas is alien to jurists, in relation to the body of juristic approaches, the above attitude implies that among Sufis who promoted the law, far less emphasis was placed on the collective enforcement of the *shari'a*, than on the individual 'striving' to live by the meaning of the *shari'a*.

Apart from legalistic Sufis, this discussion of legalism, not to mention the world of Reason more generally, would be incomplete without mention of the philosophers. This need is driven home by the fact that the aforementioned legist, Ibn Rushd, was also a philosopher of such note that he became known in the Latin world of the Renaissance as 'Averroes'. So numerous are the philosophers and so varied their ideas that it is impossible to construct a succinct yet meaningful exposition. Even their classification by the likes of al-Ghazali and al-Hujwiri as 'Naturalists', 'Theists', 'Sophists' and so on, is inadvisable as such terms do not provide any definition of the manner in which individual thinkers combined and developed, say, Platonic and Aristotilean ideas (not to mention Hindu and Buddhist ideas) to construct specifically 'Islamic' doctrine. Thus, one must be content with the notion that such diverse opinions—as Abu Bakr Muhammad al-Razi's (d. 925 or 932) arguments for the transmigration of souls, al-Farabi's linking of

---

[133] Abu Hamid Muhammad al-Ghazali, *Ihya 'Ulum al-Din*, vol. 4, trans. Fazl al-Karim (Karachi: Dar al-Isha'at, 1993), pp. 8–60.
[134] See Rizvi, *History of Sufism in India*, vol. 2, pp. 390–432.

the immortality of the soul to the wisdom it has acquired, and Ibn Sina's argument for the unity of the Soul—are all aspects of Islamic philosophical inquiry.[135] The point at which all these early philosophers may be said to agree, however, is that Reason is an 'equivalent' source of knowledge to Revelation.

As one might expect, such speculative philosophy did not proceed without objections from the very schools of thought disenfranchised by it. This culminated in al-Ghazali's now classic refutation considered above, a sense of which can be gleaned from the previously cited adage concerning the 'difference between knowing the definition of health and satiety', and 'being healthy and satisfied'. So compelling have his ideas been judged by some contemporary scholars that many have argued al-Ghazali effectively smothered the urge for philosophical inquiry among Muslim intellectuals. However, in keeping with Henri Corbin's perspective, it is more accurate to conclude that rather than extinguish that flame, scholars like al-Ghazali and al-Hujwiri redirected it. On one level, they helped to create a bridge between the theologians, jurists and mystics. On another level, they prompted peripatetic philosophers such as Ibn Rushd to argue for the unity of Truth, whether gained by Revelation or Reason; the former providing the 'external' (*zahir*) aspect (including the 'law') and the latter providing it its 'inner' (*batin*) meaning.[136] On a third level, scholars like al-Ghazali also provided the impetus for those who held Reason to be an independent source of knowledge to form bridges with those who argued the same for Intuition. Thus, as will be shown in the context of Intuitive learning below, Muhi al-Din ibn al-'Arabi, also known as *Ibn Aflatun* (the Son of Plato), defended Sufi doctrine in Neo-Platonic terms. As well, Shihab al-Din Yahya al-Suhrawardi (d. 1191), without questioning the 'right of reason to probe the deepest religious mysteries', vindicated 'the unity of religious and metaphysical truth and the duty of the seeker to seek truth wherever it can be found: in Greek philosophy, in ancient Persian thought, in Muslim Neo-Platonism, and in Sufism'.[137] This was the view of the Illuminationist (*Ishraqi*) school, whose influence continued to be felt well into the 19th century in the form of the followers of the

---

[135] Fakhry, *A History of Islamic Philosophy*, pp. 112–83. Also see fn. 10, above.
[136] Ibid., p. 309.
[137] Ibid., p. 339. Also Corbin, *History of Islamic Philosophy*, pp. 205–20.

Hikmat-i Ilahi (Divine Philosophy) of Sadr al-Din al-Shirazi (d. 1641), also known as Mulla Sadra.[138]

The philosophers cannot be said to have had the kind of direct influence on Muslim society which, for example, the jurists can be shown to have wielded. Al-Farabi's commentary on Plato's 'Republic' cannot be argued to have led to states headed by philosophers. However, their indirect influence is irrefutable. Traces of Platonic thought, for example, can be read in juristic political philosophy. Furthermore, the philosophers' arguments for Reason as a source of knowledge deeply permeated theology. It will also be shown below that many of the philosophers' ideas were well and truly incorporated into Sufism. As a 'class of seekers', therefore, the philosophers shaped the schools of thought which would impact social developments more directly.

By way of summation, the above survey should illustrate the breadth of doctrines included in the world of Reason inherited by Mughal elites, while also hinting at the variety of cultural orientations they would imply for the individual Muslim. Even focusing on no more than legalism, an understanding of the *shari'a* as the evolving end of an intellectual process dependent on various sources beside 'scripture', including local custom, is essential to grasp the connections between doctrinal Islam and local practice. Simultaneously, however, it is clear that the schools of thought mentioned above fall into two camps with regard to the relationship between Revelation and Reason. The philosophers and Mu'tazila theologians unquestionably promote Reason as an independent source of knowledge, while jurists, Ash'ari theologians and legalistic Sufis, much like al-Ghazali, profess to limit the role of Reason before the more literal dictates of Revelation. Even in the latter cases, however, there are instances in which Revelation is overridden by Reason, as not only illustrated by the juristic use of *qiyas*, but also by the construction of concepts of 'juristic preference' and 'equity' that side-step specific injunctions of scripture in favour of custom. That is to say, although overlaps occur and bridges are built, the world of Reason is divisible into two subsets, with the former representing an 'Intoxicated' approach and the latter reflecting 'Sobriety'. The cultural orientations attached to each subset are discussed further below, but first, the picture of doctrinal Islam cannot be completed without the added colour of knowledge rooted in Intuition.

---

[138] For Sadr al-Din Shirazi, see James W. Morris, *The Wisdom of the Throne: An Introduction to the Philosophy of Mulla Sadra* (Princeton: Princeton University Press, 1981).

III. *The Other-World of Intuition*

Scholars of Sufism never underestimate the importance of doctrinal variety. The scope of difference is, in fact, very well highlighted by M.A.H. Ansari, who draws attention to one of the hundreds of letters penned by the Naqshbandi Shaykh Ahmad Sirhindi (d. 1624), who wrote of his early life:

> I was informed of the profoundest ideas of Shaykh Muhi al-Din ibn al-'Arabi's philosophy... which the author of the Fusus [re: *Fusus al-Hikam*] had said to be the culmination of spiritual ascent... I was so much engrossed in that *tawhid* [unity] and intoxicated with it that... I wrote the following two couplets which were the product of sheer intoxication (*sukr*).
>
> This *shari'a* is, alas, the way of the blind.
> Our way is the way of infidels and fire-worshippers.
> Infidelity and faith are the lock and the face of that beauty.
> In our way infidelity and faith are one.[139]

Sirhindi does not claim 'intoxication' as his permanent 'way', however, as he explained in another letter:

> After a period I had a new vision of things which dominated my consciousness... [I]t happened that God... carried me beyond that stage [intoxication]... I regretted my earlier experiences, turned to God and begged for His mercy. Had I not been guided in this manner and shown the greatness of one stage after the other, I would have remained at the stage of *tawhid* because in my view there was no stage higher than that.[140]

Sirhindi's imagery reconfirms that two general paths defined the way of Sufism by the 17th century: the first already identified as 'intoxication' (*sukr*) in the work of al-Hujwiri, in which 'infidelity and faith are one', and the second being 'sobriety' (*sahw*), in which the above interpretation of *tawhid* is false, meaning 'Our way' and the way of 'infidels' differ. Following al-Hujwiri's and Sirhindi's lead, therefore, the development of Sufi doctrine can be approached from the perspective of the split outlined above.

---

[139] Shaykh Ahmad Sirhindi, *Maktubat Imam Rabbani*, ed. Nur Muhammad (Lahore: Nur Muhammad, 1964), vol. I:31, p. 102. The translation is from M.A.H. Ansari, *Sufism and Shariah* (London: Islamic Foundation, 1986), p. 14. For further reading on Sirhindi, also see Yohanan Friedmann, *Shaykh Ahmad Sirhindi* (Montreal: McGill-Queen's University Press, 1971).

[140] Sirhindi, *Maktubat*, vol. I:160, pp. 338–30; Ansari, *Sufism and Shariah*, p. 15.

It is widely held that Islamic mysticism in general, and Sufism in particular, evolved from the urge in some quarters to emphasise the 'Other-Worldly' strains in the Qur'an and the example of Muhammad's life. Thus, as Fakhry puts it, 'we hear of many an early pious Muslim, such as Abu Dharr al-Ghifari (d. 652) and Hudhayfa (d. 657), both companions of the Prophet, who chose the hard ascetic life at a time when most of their contemporaries had chosen the softer life'.[141] Within 50 years, Hasan al-Basri (d. 728) would carry this impulse to propose a spiritual 'method' which consisted of 'reflection (*fikr*), self-examination (*muhasabah*), and total submission to the will of God, resulting ultimately in a state of inner contentment (*rida*)'.[142] In the following half century, al-Basri's influence was felt in many circles. However, Rabi'a al-'Adawiya (d. 801) is credited with not only following al-Basri's lead, but developing out of the concept of yearning (*shawq*) for God, her own idea of the love (*hubb*) of God, i.e. in words attributed to her, 'a love of passion and a love prompted by Thine worthiness as an object of love'.[143]

Sufi organisation and instruction at this early stage involved informal gatherings for religious discussions called 'circles' (*halaqa*). *Dhikr*, the repetition of a Qur'anic verse or other significant phrases, represented the major meditative method and could be practised anywhere, including mosques. Thus, as late as the 9th century, Sufi practice was not regarded as a challenge to theology or law. The situation changed only once theology and law themselves began to crystallise, and Muslim ascetics further developed their own concepts of self and divinity, concepts that would, as Fakhry explains, 'go beyond the ritual aspect of the religious law ... to reach out to a reality (*haqiqa*) that thoroughly transcends it'.[144] At the forefront of this movement were Abu Yazid al-Bistami (d. 874) and Husayn ibn Mansur al-Hallaj (d. 918). Al-Bistami introduced the doctrine of 'annihilation' (*fana'*), which the likes of al-Ghazali would later critique, leading him to declare, 'Glory be to me', 'I am Thou', or 'I am I'.[145] Although there are differences in al-Bistami's and al-Hallaj's notions of the relationship between self and divinity based on the latter's concept of God's inherence in the individual soul,

---

[141] Fakhry, *A History of Islamic Philosophy*, p. 263.
[142] Ibid., p. 264.
[143] Ibid., p. 264.
[144] Ibid., p. 270.
[145] Ibid., pp. 272–73.

in the case of al-Hallaj, the statement 'I am God' provided the pretext upon which he was most horribly put to death by order of a juristic tribunal.[146] Al-Hallaj's death, therefore, provides a convenient indicator of when Sufism branched off from other disciplines, while also defining a split between the Intoxicated, such as himself and al-Bistami, and the Sober strands of mystical thought and practice that already existed and would follow.

In this early period, among the thinkers who sought to counter the Intoxication of such thinkers as al-Bistami and al-Hallaj, some outlined the concept of 'subsistence' or 'survival' (*baqa'*) to counter al-Bistami's doctrine of 'annihilation'. Abu al-Qasim al-Junayd (d. 911), meanwhile, went further by arguing that theology has priority over gnosis (*ma'rifa*). This opened the way for latter-day Sober Sufis, such as al-Hujwiri, to rally behind theologians and jurists, seeking synthesis of the two modes of thinking, culminating in al-Ghazali's argument that annihilation was not identity with God (*ittihad*), but 'no more than the recognition of God's unity (*tawhid*)'.[147]

Moving on from the period in the development of Islamic thought that ended with al-Ghazali's successful fusion of the Sober brands of Reason and Intuition, the 13th century work of Ibn al-'Arabi, which Sirhindi eventually found so objectionable, may be identified as an attempt to systematise Intoxicated Sufism, while also synthesising it and the emanationist thought of 'Theistic' philosophy. Yet, it is interesting and important to note that despite the above differences of opinion, by the time the Mughals entered the scene, all Sufi orders, including the legalistic ones noted above, upheld Ibn al-'Arabi's doctrine of *wahdat al-wujud* (Unity of Being) as affirmation of either the Intoxicated concept of *fana'* (annihilation), or the Sober concept of *baqa'* (subsistence).[148] It appears that all could agree (to the extent they did) because Ibn al-'Arabi's philosophy provided a compelling alternative to the theologians' transcendentalism, while still leaving interpretative room

---

[146] For the most thorough consideration of al-Hallaj's ideas, see Louis Massignon, *The Passion of al-Hallaj*, 4 vols., trans. Herbet Mason (Princeton: Princeton University Press, 1982).

[147] Fakhry, *A History of Islamic Philosophy*, p. 280.

[148] For a discussion of the influence of *wahdat al-wujud* in South Asia, see W.C. Chittick, 'Notes on Ibn al-'Arabi's Influence in India', *Muslim World* 82 (1992): 218–41. The one exception to this rule, of course, is the Naqshbandiyya-Mujaddidiyya of Ahmad Sirhindi, which came to follow his alternative doctrine of *wahdat al-shuhud*, discussed below.

for the concept of subsistence. Illustrating the first aspect mentioned, anti-transcendentalism, in his *Fusus al-Hikam*, Ibn al-'Arabi wrote:

> For those who truly know the divine Realities, the doctrine of transcendence imposes a restriction and a limitation [on the Reality], for he who asserts that God is [purely] transcendental is either a fool or a rogue.[149]

In the same breath, however, leaving room for the concept of subsistence, he declared:

> It is similar in the case of one who professes comparability of God without taking into consideration His incomparability, so that he also restricts and limits Him.[150]

The 'truth' for Ibn al-'Arabi, therefore, was that:

> The Reality is manifest in every created being and in every concept, while he is [at the same time] hidden from all understanding.[151]

Thus, this concept of 'Reality', at once 'manifest' and 'hidden', clarifies why Sober and Intoxicated Sufis argued that Ibn al-'Arabi was their supporter.

Weighing into this debate, contemporary scholars of Islam suggest that Ibn al-'Arabi allows the concept of transcendence to be inherent in his concept of immanence, but as a 'lower' level of understanding. Considering the above concept of 'Reality' more closely, note that Ibn al-'Arabi begins the *Fusus al-Hikam* with the following statement about 'creation' and the universe:

> The Reality wanted to see the essences of His Most Beautiful Names, or to put it another way, to see his own Essence, in an all-inclusive object encompassing the whole [Divine] Command, which, qualified by existence, would reveal to Him His own mystery.[152]

That is to say, the Reality consists of two parts, the 'Divine Essence' and the 'all-inclusive object...qualified by existence', or the 'Cosmos'.

---

[149] Muhi al-Din ibn al-'Arabi, *Fusus al-Hikam*, ed. and trans. R.W.J. Austin, *The Bezels of Wisdom* (New Pork: Paulist Press, 1980), p. 73. For Ibn al-'Arabi, see, William C. Chittick, *The Sufi Path to Knowledge: Ibn al-Arabi's Metaphysics of Imagination* (Albany: SUNY Press, 1989); Henry Corbin, *L'Imagination creatrice dans le soufisme de Ibn Arabi* (Paris: Flaumarion, 1988); and Alexander Knysh, *Ibn al-'Arabi in the Later Islamic Tradition* (Albany: SUNY Press, 1999).
[150] Ibn al-'Arabi, *Fusus al-Hikam*, p. 74.
[151] Ibid., p. 73.
[152] Ibid., p. 50.

This transcendence, however, is described as that between a person and his shadow, the latter having no objective existence of its own.[153] Furthermore, this contingency is like that of all numbers to the number 'one', wherein all 'numbers derive from the one...Thus, the one makes number possible, and number deploys the one'.[154] At a 'higher' level of knowing, therefore, 'the transcendent Reality is the relative creature...All this is One Essence...There is naught but He'.[155]

In the relationship between the Divine Essence and the 'illusionary' Cosmos, Ibn al-'Arabi assigns humanity a distinct place. It is only in humanity that the above polarity is united, thus it is only humanity that can be aware of Reality as it 'truly' is.[156] Not even 'angels' are so 'elevated', comprehending only 'those Divine names peculiar to them'.[157] Within humanity, however, 'elevation' is a matter of degree, each aware of only that which is revealed to him or her. Ibn al-'Arabi refers to the 'most elevated of existing beings' as *insan al-kamil*, the 'Perfect Human'. Such an individual 'integrates in himself all Cosmic realities and their individual [manifestation]'.[158] The first of this kind was Adam—'that singular spiritual essence from which humanity was created'—and a prime example is Muhammad, 'Seal of Prophets'.

Muhammad's distinction as *insan al-kamil* is not a function of his 'prophethood'. In fact, an 'apostle' (*rasul*), as the bringer of a new 'book', and a 'prophet' (*nabi*), as the renewer of a previous book's message, are both dependent on 'revelation' and are thus portrayed as 'simple from the intellectual point of view'. Furthermore, these functions are largely 'legislative' and come to an end with Muhammad, the 'Seal'.[159] Thus, Muhammad derives his distinction as *insan al-kamil* from his share in 'sainthood' (*waliyat*), that 'all-inclusive and universal function that never comes to an end'.[160] Interestingly, Ibn al-'Arabi leaves the concept of 'sainthood' rather vaguely defined in this work, but one can

---

[153] Ibid., p. 123.
[154] Ibid., p. 86.
[155] Ibid., p. 87. A thorough discussion of this aspect of Ibn al-'Arabi's cosmology can be read in W.C. Chittick, *The Self Disclosure of God: Principles of Ibn al-'Arabi's Cosmology* (Albany: SUNY Press, 1998).
[156] Ibn al-'Arabi, *Fusus al-Hikam*, p. 56.
[157] Ibid., pp. 51–52.
[158] Ibid., pp. 55, 85. Also see Masataka Takeshita, *Ibn al-Arabi's Theory of the Perfect Man and its Place in the History of Islamic Thought* (Tokyo: ISCAA, 1987).
[159] Ibn al-'Arabi, *Fusus al-Hikam*, pp. 165–68.
[160] Ibid., p. 168.

infer that while knowledge is 'revealed' to prophets, saints are those who acquire 'perfect' knowledge through 'direct experience'.

When all Reality is knowable as 'One', the jurists' and theologians' 'believers', 'non-believers', and shades in between, would appear difficult to maintain. Ibn al-'Arabi confirms this hypothesis throughout his *Fusus al-Hikam*, but nowhere more succinctly than in the following lines:

> Men may be divided into two groups. The first travel a way they know... which is their Straight Path. The second group travel a way they do not know...which is their Straight Path.[161]

Ibn al-'Arabi applies this principle to established religions by placing them in two categories: 'the religion of God' and the 'religion of created beings'. Both are presented as 'in harmony with divine dispensation' on the rationale that 'religion might be called or interpreted as a custom ['ada], since there befalls [the servant] only that which his own state demands and necessitates'.[162] To the mystic, therefore, there is no singular 'Path'. As Ibn al-'Arabi puts it:

> The perfect gnostic is one who regards every object of worship as a manifestation of God in which He is worshipped. They call it a god, although its proper name might be stone, wood, animal, man, star or angel. Although that might be its particular name, Divinity presents a level [of reality] that causes the worshipper to imagine that it is his object of worship.[163]

Ibn al-'Arabi's assertion that 'all religion is for God' certainly contravenes the tendency of the jurists and theologians to judge all others from the standpoint of their own schools and disciplines. Nevertheless, Ibn al-'Arabi does not dispense with the view of society as made up of 'religious' communities. Furthermore, these communities are effectively graded on a 'spiritual' scale, with the Muslim *umma* ranked highest thanks to its acceptance of Qur'an and *sunna*, i.e. the knowledge necessary to fulfil the spiritual needs of the community on both an exoteric and an esoteric level.[164] Thus, in the final analysis, the *shari'a* is not abolished. In fact, it is promoted as the 'highest' manifestation of prophetic legislation. However, this distinction is subordinate to the idea that the *shari'a*'s provisions only represent the exoteric aspect of

---

[161] Ibid., p. 132.
[162] Ibid., pp. 113–16.
[163] Ibid., p. 247.
[164] Ibid., p. 165.

Reality, and in this respect charts only one 'path' among many 'which God acknowledges'.[165] As a result, for many including the youthful Sirhindi, adherence to the *shari'a* was not necessary, it being interpreted as 'custom' (*'ada*) equivalent to the legalisms of other communities.

The eventual reticence to accept Ibn al-'Arabi's doctrine noted in Sirhindi's late 16th/early 17th century context dates back to the works of such Sufis as 'Ala' al-Dawlah al-Simnani (d. 1336), who ranks among the most prominent of Ibn al-'Arabi's early critics. However, Sirhindi is to Sober Sufism what Ibn al-'Arabi was to the Intoxicated—a systemiser. In Sirhindi's case, it is the bond between Sufis, jurists and theologians that his doctrine of *wahdat al-shuhud* (Unity of Witness) seeks to cement. Put most succinctly, rather than quibbling about *fana'* and *baqa'*, Sirhindi turned Ibn al-'Arabi's doctrine on its head, acknowledging the detection of immanence as a lower form of gnosis, but raising the recognition of transcendence to the highest stage of knowing. Thus, in Sirhindi's estimation, the Cosmos is a manifestation of the Divine Essence, but 'the world cannot be identified with God, and there is no mutual predication between them. The shadow cannot be identified with the Real. The difference between them is objective and real; like the difference between any two different objects'.[166] Given the nature of Sirhindi's critique, he countered Ibn al-'Arabi's implication that 'All is He' (Pers.: *hama 'ust*) with the maxim that 'All is from Him' (*hama as 'ust*).[167] By substituting transcendence for immanence as the highest level of gnosis, of course, Sirhindi reasserted the subordination of sainthood to prophethood, and so, of Intuition to Revelation. In so arguing, he not only echoed the theological notion of a transcendent divinity, but defended the methods and conclusions of theology above those of Sufis in a manner that al-Ghazali, for example, had not. As Sirhindi stated in one characteristic letter:

---

[165] Ibid., p. 113.

[166] Sirhindi, *Maktubat*, vol. II:1, pp. 853–60. The translation is from 'Selections from the Letters of Shaykh Ahmad Sirhindi', ed. and trans. M.A.H. Ansari, *Sufism and Shariah*, p. 269. On *fana'* and *baqa'*, Sirhindi argued that both are experiential (*shuhudi*) not existential (*wujudi*), and their purpose is wonder (*hayrat*) and conviction (*yaqin*), not knowledge. See *Maktubat*, vol. I:97, p. 240; I:240, pp. 503–4; I:266, p. 589; I:272, pp. 654; vol. II:99, p. 1172.

[167] Sirhindi, *Maktubat*, vol. II:1, pp. 853–60. The translation is from 'Selections from the Letters of Shaykh Ahmad Sirhindi', p. 268.

One must know that the final beliefs of a Sufi which he comes to after completing all stages of *suluk* [in this case represented by *Shuhudism*] and reaching the highest degree of saintship (*wilayat*) are the same as the beliefs of the theologians... The theologians arrive at them through scriptural text or reason, and the Sufis arrive at them through *kashf* [Intuition] or inspiration... One of the Sufi doctrines that conflicts with theological beliefs is the doctrine of One Being (*wahdat al-wujud*)... On account of this they [*Wujudis*] have denounced the doctrine of the theologians regarding the existence of the attributes [of God]; and dubbed it as infidelity and dualism. May God save us from such wrong denunciations...! It is incumbent on the Sufi that before he reaches the ultimate truth, he should follow the doctrines of the theologians even if they conflict with his *kashf* or inspiration. He should believe that the theologians are right and that he is wrong. For the doctrine of the theologians is based on the infallible words of the prophets who are guided by revelation (*wahy*), which is above doubt. Hence his *kashf* and inspiration which conflict with the doctrines that are derived from *wahy*, are wrong. To consider one's *kashf* superior to the views of the theologians, is in fact to consider it superior to the absolute truths of revelation. This is erroneous and disastrous.[168]

Sirhindi's defence of theology makes it quite clear that he was obviously not opposed to the *shari'a*, as were some Intoxicated interpreters of Ibn al-'Arabi's thought. However, Sirhindi even went beyond earlier Sober Sufis, including al-Hujwiri, writing in another of his letters that 'Some Sufis have said that the *shari'a* is the outer shell of the *haqiqa* and the *haqiqa* is the inner essence of the *shari'a*. Such words indicate that the speaker does not have right experiences'.[169] When 'right experience' is held, he argued:

The *shari'a* and *haqiqa* are one; neither is different from the other. Their difference is a difference of principle and its elucidation, of reason and intuition, of faith and vision, of effortful obedience and spontaneous submission... Disparity with the *shari'a* is... a clear proof that the Sufi has not reached the ultimate truth.[170]

---

[168] Sirhindi, *Maktubat*, vol. I:286, pp. 697–99. The translation is from 'Selections from the Letters of Shaikh Ahmad Sirhindi', pp. 260–62. For a more specific reference to the superiority of prophethood and revelation in relation to sainthood and intuition, also see *Maktubat*, vol. I:95, pp. 236–38; I:268, pp. 629–32; I:302, pp. 795–801; I:313, pp. 826–27; vol. II:55, p. 1041.
[169] Sirhindi, *Maktubat*, vol. I:84, p. 227. The translation is from 'Selections from the Letters of Shaikh Ahmad Sirhindi', p. 224.
[170] Ibid., p. 224.

That is to say, according to Sirhindi and his doctrine of *wahdat al-shuhud*, the notion that 'infidelity and faith are one' could not and should never be upheld. Subsequently, a final observation to be drawn from Sirhindi's perspective is that his formulations most forcefully advocated a turn from the 'other-worldly' orientation of Sufism, towards the 'this worldly' attitude of the jurists. 'Right belief' was not sufficient; to 'obey the *shari'a*', the perfect Sufi had to engage in 'action', promoting right conduct in the interests of community.[171]

In essence, the distance between the most Intoxicated interpretation of Ibn al-'Arabi's *wahdat al-wujud* and Sirhindi's ultra-Sober *wahdat al-shuhud* runs the gamut of Sufi doctrine in the 'Great Mughal' era. However, it should also be noted that apart from metaphysical reasons that discouraged the observance of *shari'a*, practical ones were also posited that affected legalistic schools. Prime examples are the Malamati movement and Qalandari order, with the former even influencing the conduct of individual *pirs/shaykhs* in the Naqshbandiyya. The essence of Malamati thinking, which arose about 9th century Iran and seems to have been influenced by Hellenic 'Cynicism' and/or Syrian Christianity, is that 'all outward appearance of piety or religiosity... is ostentation', being intended for personal gratification or divine reward. Thus, let alone abiding by the minutiae of the *shari'a*, offering prayers (*salat*), engaging in any other public acts of ritual, or even doing 'good deeds', should all be avoided to draw society's 'blame' (*malam*)—the ultimate proof of sanctity.[172] The Qalandariyya, also arising in 9th century Iran and Turan, evinces the influence of Buddhist ascetic practices. The core difference is that in the Qalandari view, 'the avoidance of all display' was a sign of 'contempt for the transient world and everything in it'.[173] A secondary difference is that while the Malamatiyya was a movement that influenced orders in various locales beyond Iran, by the 13th century, the Qalandariyya was an order in its own right and claimed adherents from South Asia to North Africa.

The Qalandariyya's systematic antinomianism carries the discussion back to Sirhindi and his will to strengthen the bond between legalistic

---

[171] Ibid., vol. I:22, pp. 71–76; I:36, p. 115; I:71, pp. 200–01; I:73, pp. 205–06; I:272, pp. 648–49; vol. II:57, pp. 1047–48; II:93, p. 1133; and, vol. III:54, p. 1341.
[172] See Hamid Algar, 'Malamatiyya', *Encyclopaedia of Islam* (CD ROM Ed., 2004).
[173] See Tahsin Yazici, 'Kalandariyya', *Encyclopaedia of Islam* (CD ROM Ed., 2004).

Sufis and jurists, as well as theologians. However, they also most poignantly raise the issue of whether these doctrines and practices, Sober or Intoxicated, shaped the social attitudes of their followers. Studying their impact on Sufi scholars in the South Asian context, S.A.A. Rizvi has already suggested a connection between doctrine and practice that bears repeating:

> The effects of the Wujudiyya and Shuhudiyya conflicts were not only felt in the ideological spheres but had serious repercussions on the ethico-social world-views of their followers as well. The Wujudiyyas were unable to support existing religious differences and disputes and did not even object to idol worship or polytheism, so long as the object of worship was God himself. The Shuhudiyyas, on the other hand, did not hesitate to assert militantly the superiority of Sunnism, not only over Shi'ism but over all religious communities.[174]

Although Rizvi concentrates on 'wujudi' and 'shuhudi' divides, one must be cognisant of the broader categories of Sobriety, in which Intuition is subordinate to Revelation, and Intoxication, wherein Intuition enjoys equivalence with Revelation, particularly given that all 'wujudis' were not anti-*shar'i*. When this complexity is sorted out, however, and it is added that every scholar of pre-colonial Muslim societies asserts that Sufism represents the prime form of popular Muslim worship, Rizvi's conclusion takes on great urgency for social historians.

Conclusion: The Fallacy in Paradigms of 'Intrusive' Islam

When al-Ghazali withdrew from his Baghdad *madrasa* to eventually write his *Munqidh min al-Dalal*, he could not have known the 'deliverance from error' he would provide contemporary scholars of pre-colonial Islam in South Asia or elsewhere. Implicit in his 'Classes of Muslim Seekers' is a spirit that upheld all the routes to Truth he travelled as ultimately 'Islamic', even though he would chose one over all others. Furthermore, in confirming the connectedness of his West Asian experience to those of South Asians like al-Hujwiri, both thinkers also illustrated the widespread appreciation of the categories in Islamic thought upon which they formulated their evaluations. Based on the sources of knowledge they acknowledged, Reason and Intuition emerged as the basic avenues towards Truth, while Sobriety and Intoxication,

---

[174] S.A.A. Rizvi, *A History of Sufism in India*, vol. 1, pp. 460–61.

respectively, defined those who professed knowledge derived through Revelation as closer to Truth than that based on Reason or Intuition, and those who equated knowledge derived by means of Reason and/or Intuition with that supplied by Revelation. When the individual disciplines and schools bound by these categories of thought were also drawn into the picture by turning to thinkers from Iberia to South Asia, not only was connectedness further revealed, but it suggested that there is no cause to transform al-Ghazali's Arabic and al-Hujwiri's Persian, or their linking of certain schools to Hellenic or Indic ideas, respectively, into regional or ethnic 'Islams', whether Arab, Persian or Indian. The major disciplines of Islamic doctrine—theology, jurisprudence, philosophy and mysticism—were uniformly acknowledged and studied wherever Muslim polity and/or large concentrations of Muslims were present. Regionality and ethnicity are only reflected in the specific schools representing each of these disciplines, as well as the manner in which they are hospitable or hostile towards local intellectualism and social customs.

As scant a survey of the 'World of Reason' and the 'Other-World of Intuition' as this renders any paradigms that seek to limit 'formal' Islam to legalism, while declaring all else 'informal' an absolute misrepresentation of the doctrinal variety that is Islam in the pre-colonial period. The formulations of the jurists, theologians, philosophers and mystics presented above represent no more than a sliver of Islamic thought, and barely an introduction to the disciplines, schools or scholars covered; yet it clarifies that incredible doctrinal distance separates all of the above. Furthermore, when referencing any of the above disciplines, schools and scholars, it is clear that their views not only acknowledge, but legitimise non-scriptural knowledge and customary practice. Furthermore, there are differences that extend beyond the basic categories of Reason and Intuition. The philosophers, Mu'tazila theologians and extreme 'wujudi' mystics routinely declared Reason and/or Intuition sources of knowledge equivalent to Revelation, while the jurists, Ash'ari theolgians, some 'wujudi' and all 'shuhudi' mystics professed in theory, if not in practice, the primacy of Revelation over Reason and/or Intuition. That is to say, two major attitudes towards knowledge umbrella the above multiplicity, and each corresponds with particular socio-ethical worldviews that I refer to as the 'Sober Path' and the 'Intoxicated Way'.

It is important to acknowledge that jurists and those among the theologians and mystics who considered the law paramount generally divided the world into two religious groups: 'Muslims' and 'non-Muslims'.

Such scholarly classes further divided Muslims into 'believers', 'heretics' and 'apostates', the first class belonging firmly to the Muslim community, the last falling firmly outside it, while the place of heretics was clearly debated, with al-Mawardi refraining from declaring *jihad* legitimate against them, and Ibn Taymiyya not hesitating to do the opposite. Meanwhile, the legalistic Sufi acknowledged 'believers' and 'heretics', but scarcely mentioned 'apostasy'. As well, among all of the above, non-Muslims were also divided, but into 'People of the Book' (*ahl al-kitab*) and 'Infidels' (*kafirs*), the latter group further categorised as 'idol-worshippers', 'polytheists', and so on. Among the jurists, al-Mawardi included Jews, Christians, Sabians and Samaritans as 'People of the Book', all being followers of the Abrahamic tradition in his view.[175] The very description of the '*kafir*' as 'polytheist', among other things, defined the term while also suggesting that by the standard of the jurists, Hindus would be considered '*kafirs*'. However, as noted by Ibn Rushd, Hanafis and Malikis regarded 'People of the Book' and 'polytheists' as *dhimmis* if they remitted the appropriate taxes. This did not necessarily mean that 'polytheists' were no longer considered '*kafirs*' by some, but it did allow for the consideration of Hindus as 'People of the Book' by others. In either case, however, acknowledgement as *dhimmis* held the advantage of being declared virtually autonomous in the case of 'personal law', while employment by the state was legitimated up to the highest ranks. Thus, it can be said that although adherents of the Abrahamic and Hindu traditions were theoretically set apart as 'monotheists' and 'polytheists', they were not practically distinguishable outside the realm of personal law. Read as a whole, therefore, the 'Sober Path' is a blend of hospitality and hostility towards the people, objects, institutions and intellectualism active in any locality, rather than a rigid, intrusive creed averse to alliance building.

The 'Intoxicated Way' also represents a range of possibilities, but with an antinomian and/or latitudinarian potentiality that is nowhere evident in the 'Sober Path'. On an intellectual plane, the philosophers' attitude towards Reason could result in the absolute dissolution of boundaries between different systems of knowledge, whether Hellenic, Indic, or otherwise. Socially speaking, the virtual equivalence that some 'wujudi' Sufis argued to exist between the *shari'a* and the 'customs' of other religious communities exhibited the potential to legitimate as

---

[175] Al-Mawardi, *Al-Ahkam al-Sultaniyya*, pp. 159–60.

'Islamic' virtually any local institution, at times extending to the elimination of the division of individuals or groups in the name of a specific religious community. Therefore, can it be said that doctrinal Islam was 'transgressed'? Clearly not, unless one seeks to reduce 'formal' Islam to legalism—a value judgement imposed on the above multiplicity, to say the least. In addition, given that even the Sober Path has the capacity to legitimate local customs, it would be incorrect to equate the former with Cornell's 'theologies of hostility', while touting the Intoxicated Way as 'theologies of hospitality'. Rather, hostility and hospitality reside in both attitudes, although the terms of hospitality and hostility differ. Such specifics are further illustrated in the next chapter by applying the categories of Islamic thought and the socio-ethical attitudes they imply in assessing the initiatives of Akbar and Awrangzib, i.e. by considering theory in practice.

CHAPTER TWO

INDICISM, INTOXICATION AND SOBRIETY
AMONG THE 'GREAT MUGHALS'

You already know that the fame of the two longest-ruling Mughal Sultans, Akbar (r. 1556–1605) and his great-grandson, Awrangzib (r. 1658–1707), is not merely based on the extraordinary duration of each individual's political tenure, or even the successes and failures of their expansionist policies. Their prominence is equally dependent on the apparently oppositional nature of their regimes, at least on an ideological plane. Akbar is noted for the promotion of non-Muslims to exalted heights in state employ, while Awrangzib is distinguished by the restrictions he placed on the employment of non-Muslims in various ranks. Akbar has won renown for lifting curbs on temple-building, scraping a tax on Hindu pilgrims and abolishing the collection of *jizya* (poll-tax on non-Muslims). Awrangzib has garnered notoriety for ordering prohibitions on non-Muslim and Shi'i festivals, curtailing the construction of some temples while demolishing others, re-imposing *jizya* and adding a tiered system of duty on merchants (2.5% Muslim/5% non-Muslim). Akbar extended patronage to non-Muslim artists on a grand scale, while also inviting Hindu, Jain, Zoroastrian, Christian and Jewish scholars to present their views and engage in debate against each other and Muslim scholars from the earliest days of his rule, eventually establishing a space devoted to such pursuits known as the *'Ibadat Khana* (Hall of Worship). He even initiated a 'translation movement', which rendered such Sanskrit classics as the *Mahabharata* into Urdu and Persian, through the joint efforts of Muslim and non-Muslim scholars. Such intellectual ferment led to a movement called the *Tawhid-i Ilahi* (Divine Unity), which drew much from the earlier decades of comparative study. The rites enjoined included vegetarianism and cremation, and involved a move, in 1584, from the lunar Hijri (Islamic) calendar to the solar-based *Tarikh-i Ilahi* (Divine Era). Awrangzib, meanwhile, discontinued the celebration of the Zoroastrian *nauroz* (new year) and the practice of *darshan* (appearing before the masses daily in the fashion of Hindu monarchs), dismissed astrologers from state service, and banned alcohol, gambling, prostitution and music at court.

As for the Tawhid-i Ilahi, you might recall that Awrangzib's primary competition for power was his older brother, Dara Shukoh (d. 1658), an active member of this movement and the preferred heir of Shah Jahan (r. 1630–1658). Even before Dara's defeat and execution, Awrangzib's assault was legitimised on the grounds that Dara had disgraced 'Islam' by following 'heretics' who declared Islamic and non-Islamic belief to be 'equivalent'. Upon assuming the reins of state, therefore, one of Awrangzib's first acts was to abolish the solar Tarikh-i Ilahi in favour of the lunar Hijri calendar.

The apparent differences between Akbar and Awrangzib best illustrate the difficulties faced by historians, not merely of the Mughal or South Asian context, but more broadly traversing the space and time in which doctrinal Islam has been present, for neither individual nor regime is unique. Although Akbar may represent an extreme case, his elevation of non-Muslims to high ranks, support of non-Muslim institutions, scholars and artists, involvement in the translation of pre-Islamic literary works, and even favour of state laws (*dawabit/qanun*) over *shar'i* injunctions, have been observed across the Muslim World. Similarly, Awrangzib's criticism of Sufis and Shi'as, aloofness from non-Muslims and attempts to enforce certain *shar'i* political, fiscal and cultural norms, places him in the company of many who came before and have followed him. Indeed, it is the 'normative' aspect of Akbar's and Awrangzib's political regimes and personal proclivities that poses a dilemma for scholars. Essentially, if this is the typical range of conduct observable among the elite, formally educated Muslims, what is the role and scope a historian should afford doctrinal Islam in considering society at large?

According to most historians of South Asia, considering the answer through the lens of a dominant paradigm that equates doctrinal Islam with a static and culturally intrusive legalism, Awrangzib's 'Muslim' credentials are confirmed, while Akbar's 'nominality' is set in various terms, including Asani's 'heterodoxy', Chandra's 'secularism', Mukhia's 'divinity' and Cohn's 'unconsciousness'. More specifically, when extending the dominant paradigm to the ideological and institutional framework of the Mughals, the consensus is that Akbar's regime laid the foundations of the dynasty by significantly breaking with the ideological and institutional forms of his Indo-Muslim predecessors. Consensus extends to the observation that Akbar raised himself and his successors above the aforementioned fray by making the sanctity of the dynasty, rather than 'Islam', the cornerstone of its sovereignty.[1] In J.F. Richards' opinion, the sanctification of the Mughals' 'Timurid' lineage is argued to have been employed by state ideologues to endow Akbar and his successors with religio-political authority greater than the jurists, Sufis and awaited Mahdi, allowing Akbar to legitimate control over the 'orthodox' clerical classes, while incorporating 'heterodox' and 'free-thinking' Muslims, as well as non-Muslims and their institutions, without being subject to *shar'i* 'inflexibilities'.[2] The 'heretical' sources of authority endowed by

---

[1] The range of contemporary opinion can be read in the works of J.F. Richards and D.E. Streusand. While agreeing with each other (and the authors mentioned in the Introduction to this book) on the general outlines of Mughal ideology, contemporary scholarship primarily differs on the exact institutional nature of the Mughal regime initiated by Akbar. Richards basically explains the Mughals' political successes by arguing that their ideology aided the establishment of a 'patrimonial-bureaucracy'. While agreeing with the notion of a 'dynastic ideology' tied to bureaucratic institutions, Streusand lays greater stress on the development of a 'sovereign cult' that distanced the Mughals from 'Islam', than on the patrimonial relationship it constructed between the ruler and the ruled. See J.F. Richards, *The Mughal Empire* (Cambridge: Cambridge University Press, 1993); and D.E. Streusand, *The Formation of the Mughal Empire* (Delhi: Oxford University Press, 1989).

[2] Richards, *The Mughal Empire*, p. 37. Streusand is more attentive to the difficulties with 'orthodox/heterodox' categorisations of Islam, but as previously mentioned, he concurs with Richards insofar that the Mughal regime depended on a 'constitution' that placed the ruler 'above sectarian conflict and equipped [him] with independent spiritual insight'. Streusand, *The Formation of the Mughal Empire*, pp. 137–38. Regarding 'Timurid' lineage, this is a reference to Mughal descent from Amir Timur (d. 1405), best known in the English-speaking world as 'Tamerlane'. Timur, of course, is remembered for an outstandingly bloody tenure in power (even given the norms of the era) beginning as the Amir of a Chaghatay Mongol, but establishing himself as ruler in Balkh (Badakhshan in contemporary Afghanistan) in 1370. From here began a brutal campaign against largely Muslim states to his east and west. With much of Central Asia under his command by 1380, Timur turned south to Khurasan and Sistan, then on to Shiraz and Isfahan, perpetrating general massacres in various cites, reaching as far west as Baghdad. In the 1390s, he carried his raids northward, devastating the Caucasus on his way to doing the same to Moscow. In 1398, however, Timur turned east, destroying the western cities and towns of the Delhi Sultans, before laying Delhi to waste as well. 1400 ushered in conflict with the Ottomans and Egyptian Mamluks, winning the latter's 'alliance', but virtually destroying the Ottoman's grip on Anatolia before it burgeoned into an 'empire'. Damascus, Baghdad, Bursa, Ankara and Izmir were sacked along the way. By 1404, Timur turned his sights to China, but died before he could leave his mark. His successors were largely unable to maintain central authority over the domains that Timur had conquered, but the descendents of his son Shahrukh (d. 1447) were able to maintain control of much of Khurasan and Transoxania until Babar (d. 1530), ruler of no more than the piece of Transoxania known as Farghana, lost even that, but went on to gain Kabul, the Punjab and Delhi, establishing the Mughal state. An extremely informative and contextually rich discussion of Timur and his descendents leading up to Babur can be read in M.G.S. Hodgson, *The Venture of Islam*, 3 vols. (Chicago: University of Chicago Press, 1974), vol. 2, pp. 428–36, 490–93.

the house of Timur are identified as loosely following from the ideas of Chishtiyya Sufis and philosophers of the Ishraqi (Illuminationist) line.[3] Although later Mughals, beginning with Shah Jahan, are noted to have tempered the 'heretical' elements of Akbar's claims to authority, it is widely accepted that this 'Timurid dynastic ideology', in Richards' terms, or 'Akbari constitution' in D.E. Streusand's words, was heavily relied upon until Awrangzib began dismantling it by turning back to the jurists, and the 18th century ushered the collapse of the Mughal state in response to structural changes.[4]

Together, the above perspectives represent an attempt to avoid what Streusand succinctly terms the 'present-minded approaches' that extend from Hindu, Muslim and 'secular' projections of 'national kingship'.[5] Yet, Richards' and Streusand's views on the content of Mughal statecraft not only echo each other, but also the 'present-minded' scholarship they aim to displace insofar as they argue that Akbar constructed a dynastic ideology that 'transcended' Islam, while Awrangzib's regime alone is a representation of 'true' Islam. In the light of the many variants of doctrinal Islam and their hospitality and/or hostility towards intellectual and cultural aspects of the local environment, not to mention the 'normative' aspect of both Akar's and Awrangzib's general dispositions, can one consider Awrangzib the only 'pro-Islamic' figure on accord of his legalism, and does this equate to an intrusiveness that shuns the 'Indic'? As well, has Akbar 'transgressed' Islam by flaunting *shar'i* dictates, and does this mean his mediationism is best represented as 'Indic'? Answers to such questions are obviously necessary if one seeks to unravel how South Asian Muslims were both 'connected' with Islam and the broader Muslim World, while also 'embedded' in pre-colonial South Asia. Furthermore, as the terms of connectedness and embeddedness were transformed by the colonial regime, it is with Indicism

---

[3] Richards, *The Mughal Empire*, pp. 44–49; Streusand, *The Formation of the Mughal Empire*, pp. 89–91, 130–33.

[4] Richards, *The Mughal Empire*, pp. 171–77, 290–97; Streusand, *The Formation of the Mughal Empire*, pp. 23–36. For a thorough work more specifically on Mughal political decline, see A. Hintze, *The Mughal Empire and its Decline* (Aldershot: Ashgate, 1997).

[5] For prime examples of 'present-minded approaches', see J.N. Sarkar, *History of Aurangzeb* (Bombay: Orient Longman, 1974); A.L. Srivastava, *Akbar the Great* (Agra: Shiva Lal Agarwala, 1972); and I.H. Qureishi, *The Muslim Community of the Indo-Pakistan Subcontinent* (Karachi: Ma'ref, 1971).

and Mughal culture, rather than British interventions, that a discussion of colonial era transformations must necessarily begin.

In the sections below, I assess elite Mughal culture by substituting established paradigms concerning Islam and Indicism with the idea of Sober and Intoxicated Islam and Muslims, drawing from various genres of Persian histories and European letters and travelogues. The point here is not to suggest the 'piety' of Mughal elites, but to illustrate that the scope of doctrinal Islam was broad enough to play a dominant role in the legitimisation of interests, including the institutions of non-Muslims and/or their intellectualism and customs. That is to say, at least in the elite circles of the Mughal court, 'embeddedness' was a function of 'connectedness', and not an expression of 'transgression'.

I. *Jalal al-Din Akbar and the Intoxicated Way*

Debate on Akbar's religious credentials dates back to his contemporaries. Among the historians of Akbar's day, 'Abd al-Qadir Bada'uni—a professional secretary and one of the more reluctant Muslim translators of the *Mahabharata*—writes in his *Muntakhab al-Tawarikh* that by the early 1580s a number of prominent jurists, including Akbar's own Sunni *qadi al-qudat* (chief judge) of Bengal and an influential Shi'i *qadi* (judge) of Jaunpur, had issued *fatawa* (legal opinions) declaring Akbar an 'apostate'. This led to their executions. Such *fatawa* also emboldened segments of Akbar's administrative and military elite to compel Mirza (prince) Hakim, Akbar's half-brother and governor of Kabul, to attempt to overthrow Akbar on 'religious' grounds, obviously without success. Bada'uni himself refrains from comment on the validity of their claims, but one can easily gauge from the tone of his writing that he was as disapproving of Akbar and his supporters as the executed *qadi*s he takes pains to mention.[6]

In stark contrast to Bada'uni and his *qadi*s, Muhammad 'Arif Qandahari—a mid-level administrator in the offices of Akbar's *wakil* (regent) Bayram Khan and *wazir* (prime minister) Muzaffar Khan—portrays Akbar as the model Islamic ruler in his *Tarikh-i Akbari*. Although

---

[6] 'Abd al-Qadir Bada'uni, *Muntakhab al-Tawarikh*, 3 vols., trans. G.S.A. Ranking [I], W.H. Lowe [II], W. Haig [III] (Delhi: Idara-i Adabiyat-i Delli, 1973), vol. 2, pp. 277–320.

Qandahari's narrative ends in 1580, with his voluntary retirement before the above *fatawa* were issued, Bada'uni tells us that enough had occurred by that date for the questioning of Akbar's credentials to begin. Yet, Qandahari lauds Akbar's piety by mentioning such acts as the construction of a mosque at Fatehpur Sikri, the sponsoring of large *hajj* parties, and the dispatch of generous gifts to the '*sharifs*' (guardians of the Ka'ba) and the poor of Mecca and Medina, as well as by extremely frequent visits to the tombs of Chishtiyya saints in Ajmir, including that of Nizam al-Din Awliya'.[7] The discrepancy between Bada'uni and Qandahari's views of Akbar can be explained in two ways: either Akbar's ideas and actions became more extreme with the passage of time, or Qandahari, a Sober Sufi, did not see Akbar from the same perspective as Bada'uni the jurist. In fact, Akbar's ideas did veer further from the Sober Path, Sufi and juristic, with time, but it is also clear that the categorical divide between Bada'uni and Qandahari plays a role in their final assessments. For example, Bada'uni writes of all the scholars whom Akbar patronised and included in the 'Ibadat Khana discussions—excepting certain jurists and theologians—with utter scorn, declaring many to be *kafirs* and apostates or heretics.[8] Qandahari, on the other hand, uses the same activities to illustrate Akbar's piety, writing that 'scholars and righteous persons of all sects and beliefs engage in debate' so that the 'laws of *shari'a* as well as of reason' may be known.[9] Thus, whatever the changes in Akbar's ideas and actions after 1580, or the personal motivations of Bada'uni and Qandahari to view him as they did, one must also consider whether these authors' penchant for the disciplines and schools of one or another category of doctrinal Islam ultimately legitimated or delegitimated Akbar as

---

[7] For mosques and *hajj*, see Muhammad 'Arif Qandahari, *Tarikh-i Akbari*, trans. Tasneem Ahmad (Delhi: Pragati Publishers, 1993), pp. 276–80. There is mention of many trips to Ajmir, but the most telling account is of Akbar's journey on foot from Fatehpur Sikri, ibid., pp. 160–62. For a broader discussion of Akbar and the Mughal state's involvement with the *hajj* and the Chishtiyya shrines and scholars at Ajmir, see M.N. Pearson, 'The Mughals and the Hajj', *Journal of the Oriental Society of Australia* 18–19 (1986-1987): 164–79, and Rafat Bilgrami, 'The Ajmir Waqf Under the Mughals', *Islamic Culture* 52 (1978): 97–103. For background on the saints whose shrines are located at Ajmir, as well as the beginning of their inclusion as sites of pilgrimage by members of the upper classes, see Simon Digby, 'Early Pilgrimages to the Graves of Mu'in al-Din Sijzi and other Indian Chishti Shaykhs', *Islamic Society and Culture*, eds. Milton Israel and N. Wagle (New Delhi: Manohar Publishers, 1983), pp. 95–100.

[8] Al-Bada'uni, *Muntakhab al-Tawarikh*, vol. 2, pp. 316–17, 327–28.

[9] Qandahari, *Tarikh-i Akbari*, p. 89.

Muslim, heretic or apostate in their minds. In particular, one must ask how those inclined towards Intoxicated thought viewed Akbar, even if Bada'uni and his Sunni/Shi'i *qadis* saw him as an apostate. To begin with, however, it is appropriate to outline the ways in which Akbar's policies were in conformity with the generally Sober Path.

Much of Akbar's policy concerning non-Muslims was legitimated by the legal and political ideals of the jurists. It was mentioned in the earlier discussion on law that according to Hanafi jurisprudence—the official school of the Mughal state—a 'polytheist' could be counted as a *dhimmi*. In fact, Hindus, Buddhists and Jains had been categorised as *dhimmi* since 714, when Muhammad ibn Qasim (d. 716) was appointed the Umayyad governor of Sind, and many thinkers even classified them as 'People of Book', judging their scriptures as 'revealed'.[10] In addition, according to juristic political philosophy, it was legitimate for *dhimmis* to serve the state in any position up to the rank of *wazir al-tanfidh*, and the induction of non-Muslims in the apparatus of various Sultanates in South Asia and beyond is not rare. Even Qandahari offers nothing other than *hadiths* in favour of Akbar's induction of Hindu Rajputs into the administration, while non-Muslim officers of the state are nowhere referred to as '*kafirs*', the latter term only being raised in such contexts as the '*jihads*' waged against the Rajput forts of Rathambhore and Chitaur, i.e. in the context of non-Muslims outside the realm of *dar al-Islam*.[11] Furthermore, according to much political philosophy, *dawabit* (state laws), not *shari'a*, ruled life at court, thus legitimating practices such as *darshan*. As for marriage to non-Muslim women without conversion, it was part of juristic opinion that this was legitimate so long as

---

[10] Muhammad Tariq Awan is one among many historians to note that Arabic sources from the 8th–10th centuries refer to Sindhi Hindus and Buddhists as '*dhimmis*', not '*kafirs*'. Furthermore, the same sources make it clear that this was not merely a literary trope. The following quote, making this point, is attributed to al-Hajjaj, Governor of Iraq under the Umayyads, responding to a query from Muhammad ibn Qasim: 'As they [the Hindus and Buddhists] have made submission and agreed to pay taxes to the Caliph, nothing more can be properly required of them. They have been taken under our protection and we cannot, in any way, stretch our hands upon their lives or property. Permission is given to them to worship their gods. Nobody must be forbidden or prevented from following his own religion'. Cited in Muhammad Tariq Awan, *The History of India and Pakistan*, vol. 1, (Lahore: Ferozesons, 1991), p. 25. For a discussion of Hindus and Buddhists as 'People of the Book', beginning as early as the 8th century, see Aziz Ahmad, *Studies in Islamic Culture in the Indian Environment* (Delhi: Oxford University Press, 1999), pp. 109–14. Also see Andre Wink, *Al-Hind—the Making of the Indo-Islamic World*, vol. 1 (Leiden: E.J. Brill, 1990).

[11] Qandahari, *Tarikh-i Akbari*, pp. 66, 148–54.

the women belonged to a community whose scriptures were judged to be 'revealed'—a provision extended to Hindu scriptures long before Akbar.[12] In addition, various classes of *dhimmi*, including non-Muslim scholars, could be exempted from certain taxes, including *jizya*, and this had also been the practice among previous Muslim states. And finally, the patronage of non-Muslim scholars and artists, including the translation of their works, is commonly known to have been the practice among Muslim states in and beyond South Asia, before and during this period, so much so, that Qandahari includes Akbar's patronage of painting and music as evidence of the ruler's piety.[13] Thus, Akbar's association with non-Muslims is innovative only with respect to the identity of the parties and the scope of their involvement, rather than in regard to permissibility according to the current theory of the jurists and Sober Sufis, or the general practice of contemporary Sultanates. The sum of such activities may have raised the ire of Muslims who felt that their positions or their privileges were threatened, but their objections could not be legitimated by the Sober Path, as illustrated by an incident in 1577, of which even Bada'uni writes approvingly.

Bada'uni reports that in that year, the state-appointed *qadi* of Mathura laid a complaint before the *sadr al-sudur*, Shaykh 'Abd al-Nabi, to the effect that a wealthy '*brahmin*' had carried off materials, which the *qadi* had collected to build a mosque, and used them to build a temple.[14] Furthermore, when the *qadi* attempted to thwart the

---

[12] See Jean Boyd, 'Nikah', *Encyclopaedia of Islam* (CD ROM Ed., 2004).

[13] Qandahari, *Tarikh-i Akbari*, pp. 64–65, 178–79. The translation of Sanskrit works and the employment of *brahmin*s in the courts of various Abbasid Caliphs are well documented. In South Asia more specifically, the Bahmamid and Lodhi Sultanates provide a clear example of the patronage of non-Muslim scholars, artists and administrators before the Mughals. However, these latecomers are more the exception than the rule. That these states directly precede the Mughals, while the patronage of non-Muslims appears the rule among Mughal contemporaries (e.g. Golconda), suggests that the 15th–16th centuries witnessed a breakthrough in relations between these communities. For details of the states mentioned, see M.T. Awan, *History of India and Pakistan*, vol. 1, pp. 355–86, 467–84, 693–717. For Sanskrit/Pali works (including medicine, astronomy, mathematics, logic, ethics, theology/mysticism and literature) translated into Arabic during Abbasid times, see Ahmad, *Studies in Islamic Culture in the Indian Environment*, pp. 108–10.

[14] Bada'uni, *Muntakhab al-Tawarikh*, vol. 3, pp. 127–30. The office in question is defined in the *Encyclopaedia of Islam* as follows: 'The *sadr al-sudur* was a central minister, who was given this title when the empire was divided in *subah*s [provinces] by Akbar in 988/1580. Besides controlling land grants (*madad-i ma'ash*) and cash grants (*wazifa*), the *sadr al-sudur* also recommended appointments of *qadi*s or judges and *mufti*s [jurisconsults] or interpreters of law and customs, though he himself had no

brahmin's actions, the latter had, in the presence of witnesses, cursed Muhammad and shown contempt for Islam. In response, the *sadr al-sudur* had dispatched a summons to the accused, but he did not appear. Thus, Akbar ordered that the accused be seized and brought before the *sadr al-sudur*. In the proceedings that followed, Bada'uni reports that the issue of contention was not the guilt of the accused on the charge of blasphemy (which had been established by previous testimony), but the appropriate punishment. It appears the presiding *qadi*s were divided into two camps: one favouring the death penalty, the other public humiliation and a fine. The latter camp's arguments rested on *hadith*s calling for lenience in capital cases, as well as a specific injunction of the Hanafi school arguing that:

> ...the cursing of the Prophet by unbelievers who have submitted to the rule of Islam gives no ground for any breach of agreement by Muslims, and in no way absolves Muslims from their obligation to safeguard infidel subjects.[15]

Although Bada'uni does not outline any of the arguments of the opposing camp, he does suggest that the above doctrines do not apply to the Malikis, and that even *hadith* calling for lenience in capital cases can be ignored if the purpose of the death penalty is the 'closing of sedition and the uprooting of the germs of insolence from the minds of the common people'.[16]

The arguments seem to have been lengthy, and the case to have drawn much attention, for Bada'uni writes that Akbar's Hindu wives pleaded directly to Akbar for leniency, and non-Muslim courtiers complained that the '*mullas*' (i.e. the jurists) were thoroughly pampered and eager to display their own authority by calling for death without Akbar's order.[17] In one of the few instances in which Bada'uni writes approvingly of Akbar, he relates that when the *sadr al-sudur* asked Akbar's opinion, the

---

judicial function. The provincial *sadr*s were his subordinates, and below them were local *sadr*s (*sadr-i juzw*) and *muttawali*s (managers of land-grants)'. A. Athar Ali, 'Sadr', Encyclopaedia of Islam, vol. 8 (Leiden: E.J. Brill, 1985), p. 751. Given that al-Bada'uni presents a case in which the *sadr al-sudur*, Shaykh 'Abd al-Nabi, did perform a judicial function, it is clear that the total responsibilities of this office were not constant. For an in depth study of this office and the judiciary more generally through its *insha'* documents from Babar's (r. 1526–1530) to Shah Jahan's reigns, see M. Mohiuddin, *The Chancellery and Persian Epistolography under the Mughals* (Calcutta: Iran Society, 1971).

[15] Bada'uni, *Muntakhab al-Tawarikh*, vol. 3, p. 129.
[16] Ibid., p. 130.
[17] Ibid., p. 129.

latter replied that punishments for offences against the *shari'a* fall within the jurisdiction of the jurists.[18] Although the *sadr al-sudur* continued to be swayed by both camps a while longer, he finally issued the order to execute the accused without consulting Akbar. In other words, in this case, Akbar acted in a manner that would have satisfied even Ibn Taymiyya, relinquishing legislative authority entirely to the judiciary, despite personal and political pressure to act otherwise. However, Bada'uni does conclude this episode by suggesting that when Akbar later learned that death was not viewed as unanimously necessary, the future decline of the presiding *sadr al-sudur* became imminent.[19]

Shaykh 'Abd al-Nabi's decline came in the form of his virtual expulsion to Mecca as head of a *hajj* expedition, upon return from which he died. His ruling in the above case, however, underscored the need for greater authority over the judiciary as a whole if a regime seeking to incorporate the Hindu Rajputs, and other non-Muslim groups, was to be maintained. In response to Akbar's perceived need, a declaration was drawn up, in consultation with the leading theologians and jurists of the court, and promulgated in 1579. It is reproduced by Bada'uni, and a portion reads as follows:

> Abu al-Fath Jalal al-Din Muhammad Akbar, Badshah Ghazi (whose kingdom may God perpetuate), is a most just, most wise, and a most God-fearing king. Should, therefore, in future, a religious question come up, regarding which the opinions of the *mujtahid*s are at variance, and his majesty, in his penetrating understanding and clear wisdom, be inclined to adopt, for the benefit of the community and as a political expedient, any of the conflicting opinions which exist on that point, and issue a decree to that effect, we do hereby agree that such a decree shall be binding on us and on the whole community.
>
> Further, we declare that, should his majesty think it fit to issue a new order, we and the community shall likewise be bound by it, provided always that such order be not only in accordance with some verse of the Qur'an, but also of real benefit to the community; and further, that

---

[18] Ibid., p. 128. A later work by another author, *Dhakhirat al-Khawanin*, also writes approvingly of Akbar for a similar action of compliance before the *sadr* at an earlier date. See Shaykh Farid Bhakkari, *Dhakhirat al-Khawanin*, vol. 1, trans. Z.A. Desai (Delhi: Idara-i Adabiyat-i Delli, 1993), pp. 49–50.

[19] Bada'uni, *Muntakhab al-Tawarikh*, vol. 3, pp. 130–31. It should be noted that although this was the last time the *sadr* would run afoul of Akbar, it appears that it was by no means the first. In fact, it is reported elsewhere that once Shaykh 'Abd al-Nabi practically struck Akbar for partaking in a local custom on his birthday, the latter not responding on the intercession of his mother, who considered the Shaykh a man of 'learning'. See Bhakkari, *Dhakhirat al-Khawanin*, vol. 1, pp. 49–50.

any opposition on the part of his subjects to such an order passed by his majesty, shall involve damnation in the world to come, and loss of property and religious privileges in this.[20]

The implication of this declaration in terms of the above case of blasphemy is clear. In future, it is not the head of the judiciary, but the head of state that makes the ultimate judgment in such cases. There are two juristic avenues to a Muslim ruler claiming such authority. The first is a jurisdictional division between '*Huquq al-Adamiyya*' (Rights of Man), covering 'civil' law in which jurists have the right to act, and '*Huquq Allah*' (Rights of God), encompassing proscribed offences with statutory punishments in which the Sultan's discretion is paramount. The latter certainly applies to the case of blasphemy, but it is also clear that the above decree extends Akbar's jurisdiction to all cases and endows him with the authority to promulgate 'new laws'. In other words, the declaration makes Akbar the 'supreme *mujtahid*', the ultimate legislative authority in the land. The only juristically sanctioned ruler to wield such authority is a Caliph. Thus, it is most significant that in the wake of this decree, Akbar added the title of 'Caliph' to that of Sultan. There are extant examples of Akbar's correspondence with officers and state decrees (*faramin*) in which he is referred to as Caliph.[21] Both Qandahari and Bada'uni refer to Akbar as Caliph quite commonly in their *Tarikh-i Akbari* and *Muntakhab al-Tawarikh*, respectively.[22] Other historical works from the period, not as yet mentioned, also refer to Akbar as Caliph, including Rafi' al-Din al-Shirazi's *Tazkirat al-Muluk*, Nizam al-Din Ahmad's *Tabaqat-i Akbari*, and Abu al-Fadl ibn Mubarak's

---

[20] Bada'uni, *Muntakhab al-Tawarikh*, vol. 2, pp. 279–80. Another copy is included in Abu al-Fadl's *Akbar Nama*, which dates it at 1564, but K.A. Nizami and Streusand convincingly argue that Abu al-Fadl most likely pushed the date back for 'official' reasons. See K.A. Nizami, *On History and Historians in Medieval India* (Delhi: Munshiram Manoharlal, 1983), pp. 158–59; and, Streusand, *The Formation of the Mughal Empire*, pp. 114–22.

[21] Abu al-Fadl ibn Mubarak, *Makatabat-i 'Allami, daftar* I, ed. and trans. Mansura Haidar (Delhi: Munshiram Manoharlal Publishers, 1998) includes examples of such correspondence and *faramin*. Two letters to 'Abd al-Rahim ibn Bayram Khan, dated 1586, reference Akbar as Caliph (pp. 19–24, 27–30). Also, a lengthy *dastur al-'amal*, or order to administrators (*ummal* and *mutasaddi*s), dated 1594, references Akbar as Caliph (pp. 79–87).

[22] For example, in his opening address on Akbar, Bada'uni refers to him as 'Caliph of the Age'. See Bada'uni, *Muntakhab al-Tawarikh*, vol. 2, p. 1. Qandahari's association of Caliphate with Akbar begins with his description of Akbar's birth. Qandahari, *Tarikh-i Akbari*, p. 24.

Akbar Nama and *A'in-i Akbari*.²³ The frequency of such references only confirms that, in taking up Caliphal titles, Akbar was again following established practice among Sultans, Barani having already confirmed as much in the 14th century.²⁴ That Bada'uni is among those who acknowledge Akbar's claims to Caliphal titles, however, adds that although the above decree might have troubled him and the *qadi*s, such authority limiting the autonomy of the judiciary, it did not raise them in open opposition as it remained within the scope of certain strains of juristic thought. Indeed, it was not until 1582, three years after being declared supreme *mujtahid*—when Akbar employed his power to abolish *jizya* and end funding of *hajj* expeditions, then initiated his 'Divine Era', the *Tarikh-i Ilahi*, in 1584—that juristic opposition rose. Interestingly, all of these later initiatives were also legitimated by appeals to doctrinal Islam, though not of the Sober variety.

---

²³ Nizam al-Din Ahmad, *Tabaqat-i Akbari*, 3 vols., trans. Brajendranath De (Calcutta: Royal Asiatic Society, 1939), vol. 1, pp. i–xii; Rafiʿ al-Din al-Shirazi, *Tazkirat al-Muluk* (British Library, Add. 23883). A portion of the latter work (ff. 172b–174b) is included in Shireen Moosvi, ed. and trans. *Episodes in the Life of Akbar: Contemporary Records and Reminiscences* (New Delhi: National Book Trust, 1994), pp. 28–31. Also, Abu al-Fadl ibn Mubarak, *Akbar Nama*, 3 vols., trans. H. Beveridge (Calcutta: Asiatic Society of Bengal, 1907), vol. 1, p. 57; vol. 3, p. 526; and *A'in-i Akbari*, 3 vols., trans. H. Blochmann (Calcutta: Asiatic Society of Bengal, 1927), vol. 1, pp. 170–75.

²⁴ There is some debate in the secondary literature over the exact rank of 'Caliph' to which Akbar aspired. Nizami and Andre Wink argue that Akbar claimed 'Universal Caliphate' of the type held by the Abbasids and Umayyads. D.E. Streusand, however, represents the consensus of opinion by disagreeing on the basis that as Akbar flouted the *shariʿa*, this was only a momentary appeal to 'Islamic' legitimisation—an obvious influence of the dominant paradigm on Islam in his approach. The latter also adds that Akbar's appeal was no more than a reflection of the devolution of Caliphal titles to Sultans, as in Barani's 14th century writings. An intermediate perspective is forwarded by Halil Inalcik, whose readings of Ottoman claims to Universal Caliphate in the 18th century suggests they were based on a 16th–18th century shift in juristic thought towards the legitimisation of more than one 'Universal Caliphal', if a sea or enemy territory, stands between the claimants' domains. He, therefore, argues that Ottomans and Mughals legitimated claims to Universal Caliphate. As I am critical of the dominant paradigm informing Streusand's perspectives, I tend to concur with Wink's reasoning and consider Inalcik's approach to the Ottomans as a stepping-stone to further research on Mughal usage. This being a rather peripheral issue in this context—both 'universal' and local claimants exercising the authority of 'supreme *mujtahids*'—I have not read far into the issue to offer a conclusive argument, so have hesitantly deferred to the consensus of opinion in the historiography of South Asia. See K.A. Nizami, *Akbar and Religion* (Delhi: Idara-i Adab-i Delli, 1989), pp. 177–78; Andre Wink, *Land and Sovereignty in India* (Chicago: University of Chicago Press, 1974), pp. 29–33; Streusand, *The Formation of the Mughal Empire*, pp. 26–35, 117–22; Halil Inalcik, 'The Rise of the Ottoman Empire', *Cambridge History of Islam*, vol. 1A, eds. P.M. Holt, A.K.S. Lambton and B. Lewis (Cambridge: Cambridge University Press, 1995), pp. 321–23.

Although Akbar's rule began in the mid-16th century, by the Hijri calendar, his rule closes the first millennium of the Muslim Era. As one might expect, there was an air of anticipation at the time and millennial movements were beginning to crop up, including a Mahdist movement in South Asia having particular appeal among townspeople and low-ranking soldiers—a movement familiar to Akbar and his ideologues.[25] Furthermore, Bada'uni reports that in 1581:

> ...low and mean fellows, who pretended to be learned, but were in reality fools, collected evidence that his majesty was the *Sahib-i Zaman* (Lord of the Age), who would remove all differences of opinion among the 72 sects of Islam and the Hindus. Sharif (Amuli) brought proofs from the writings of Mahmud of Basakhwan, that he had said that in the year 990 [1582] a certain person would abolish lies, and how he had specified all sorts of interpretations of the expression 'professor of the true religion', which came to the sum total 990. And Khwaja Mawlana of Shiraj, the heretic of Jafrdan, came with a pamphlet by some of the Sharifs of Mecca, in which a tradition (*hadith*) was quoted to the effect that the earth would exist for 7,000 years, and as that time was now over the promised appearance of a Mahdi would immediately take place...The Shi'a mentioned similar nonsense connected with 'Ali, and quoted the following *ruba'i*, which is said to have been composed by Nasir-i Khusrau, or according to some by another poet:
> In 989, according to the decree of fate,
> The stars from all sides shall meet together.
> In the year of Leo, the month of Leo, the day of Leo,
> The Lion of God shall stand forth from behind the veil.[26]

---

[25] This is a reference to the Mahdawi movement of Sayyid Muhammad Jaunpuri, who claimed to be the Mahdi. On this movement, M.G.S. Hodgson writes: '[Sayyid Muhammad] taught that among the Muslims a special band should be dedicated actively to upholding the Shari'ah law, not as ordinary amirs, nor even as regular muftis and qadis, but as preachers...To be free to fulfill this function, the elite should be bound to absolute poverty...From this detached perspective they could look on the amir and the humblest Muslim soldier or craftsman as equals...It was perhaps the most thoroughgoing attempt, since the Khariji movement of Marwani [Umayyad] times, to place Islamic social responsibility squarely on the shoulders of plain Muslim believers and to strike down all the social distortions introduced by wealth and descent'. As Hodgson goes on to say, in relation to the *shar'i*-mindedness of the Mahdawis—who were active throughout South Asia from the time of Sayyid Muhammad's mission in the late 15th century through the period of Babar, Humayun and Akbar's regimes—'Akbar was more moved by the universalist' line of thought current at the time. However, the activities of the Mahdawis, in particular, illustrate that the turn of a new millennium was indeed a time in which movements promising social and religious revolution under 'inspired leadership' were rife. See M.G.S. Hodgson, *The Venture of Islam*, vol. 3, pp. 67–71.

[26] Bada'uni, *Muntakhab al-Tawarikh*, vol. 2, p. 295. The present author was not the first to speak disparagingly of Sharif Amuli and the other scholars mentioned.

Bada'uni goes on to state that while such murmurings were ongoing, the Tarikh-i Ilahi was publicly announced and stamped on coins.[27] As well, he states that Akbar ordered that a history of 'all the kings of Islam' be written to mark the millennium, 'and employed seven persons to undertake the compilation from the date of the death of the last of the Prophets [i.e. Muhammad]...up to the present day and to mention therein the events of the whole world'.[28] Despite Sober criticism, it is quite apparent that among Intoxicated thinkers there was an air of anticipation among various schools and sects, and Akbar's initiation of the Tarikh-i Ilahi represents, at the very least, his regime's ideological capitalisation on this intellectual atmosphere. Even the Sober Sufi Qandahari argued in recognition of Akbar as the *Sahib-i Zaman*, stating that Akbar's paternal side represents a line of rulers stretching back to Adam and 'chosen' by God to rule, while his maternal side links him to a renowned Sufi of Nishapur, Ahmad al-Jami (d. 1141).[29] The most recent scion of the paternal line to make his mark, according to Qandahari, is Amir Timur, from whom Akbar is separated by seven generations. Thus, he declares: 'In this is enshrined a mystery of God', for He has also 'created' seven 'heavens', seven planets, seven seas, seven days in a week, a Qur'an in seven parts (*lughats*), seven circumambulations of the *ka'ba* at *hajj*, and so on.[30] He concludes: 'By all this my object

---

Sharif Amuli had been expelled from his native Amul on the Oxus, as well as Balkh and then the Deccan, before finding the likes of Bada'uni in Akbar's regime, where he began service in 1577. According to Abu al-Fadl, by 1586, he was appointed *sadr* of Kabul, and by 1591, *sadr* and *qadi* of Bengal. Nizam al-Din Ahmad describes him as a '*muwahhid*' (unitarian) and a Sufi adept. Similarly, Bhakkari writes: 'He possessed a good share of knowledge...He was one of the unitarians and had a way and flair for mysticism; he reached a stage where he used to call everything Allah—All is He'. He appears to have died peacefully on his *jagir* near Lucknow, which Jahangir (r. 1605–1628), Akbar's son and successor, maintained and where they conversed after Akbar's death. See Abu al-Fadl, *Akbar Nama*, vol. 3, p. 718; Ahmad, *Tabaqat-i Akbari*, p. 451; Bhakkari, *Dhakhirat al-Khawanin*, vol. 1, pp. 141–42. For a broader discussion of this circle of intellectuals, see S.A.A. Rizvi, *Religious and Intellectual History of the Muslims in Akbar's Reign* (Delhi: Munshiram Manoharlal, 1975), pp. 418–37. As for Mahmud of Basakhwan, he is often identified as the founder of the Nuqtawi 'sect' in Iran, which was routed by Shah Abbas in the 1590s, but had raised enough ire to lead many like Sharif Amuli to seek greener pastures elsewhere. Their doctrines are obscure, but as the above quotes suggest, they shared something of the Intoxicated Sufi and philosophers' antinomianism and latitudinarianism. See Awan, *History of India and Pakistan*, vol. 2, pp. 251–52.

[27] Bada'uni, *Muntakhab al-Tawarikh*, vol. 2, p. 316.
[28] Ibid., pp. 316, 327–8.
[29] Qandahari, *Tarikh-i Akbari*, pp. 12–14.
[30] Ibid., pp. 14–15.

is to convey that the personality of... Akbar is endowed with infinite superiority'.[31]

Corresponding with the above millenarianism, Akbar also initiated the Tawhid-i Ilahi (Divine Unity) circle of scholars and followers in 1582. This issue can begin to be addressed by recalling that when certain jurists and theologians drafted and signed the declaration of 1579, they wrote that Akbar could enact 'new laws', provided that they were in accordance with 'some verse of the Qur'an' or of 'benefit to the community'. The significance is that this suggests that as 'supreme *mujtahid*', Akbar did not merely seek the right to rule over *qadi*s, or even to personally exercise *ijtihad* within the principles of jurisprudence. He sought 'absolute *ijtihad*', i.e. the free reign of Reason or Intuition in the interpretation of Revelation for the purposes of legislation. Although this study goes on to cite many examples of Akbar's concept of *ijtihad*, none better encapsulates the degree to which he sought intellectual autonomy than the following correspondence, included in Abu al-Fadl's *Akbar Nama*. One of Akbar's sons, Mirza Murad, wrote to his father from his governorship in Malwa (1591), requesting that books be dispatched that 'might promote intellect and discourage *taqlid* [imitation]'. Akbar replied:

> In the marshy land of tradition such a book is rarely to be found. But out of regard for him [Murad], the translation of the *Mahabharata*, which is a strange tale, just now become available, has been sent.[32]

Akbar's response illustrates that at times he ignored the doctrinal ideals of the Sober Path, including those of theology, jurisprudence and mysticism. However, from the perspective of the Intoxicated Way—those that give Reason and/or Intuition 'equal' standing with Revelation in the pursuit of 'Truth'—Akbar's response may be considered 'ideal'. This is because Akbar is not only the supreme *mujtahid* according to the decree of leading theologians and jurists, nor merely 'endowed with infinite superiority', as suggested by Qandahari, but in the more formal terms of Abu al-Fadl's *Akbar Nama*, Akbar is presented as an individual who has 'perfect knowledge of God'.[33] Or, as Abu al-Fadl puts it in a state

---

[31] Ibid., p. 15.
[32] This correspondence is not included in the version of the *Akbar Nama* translated by Beveridge, and used elsewhere. It is found in *Akbar Nama* (British Library, Add. 27247). A portion (ff. 401b–404b) is found in Shireen Moosvi, ed. and trans. *Episodes in the Life of Akbar*, pp. 94–95.
[33] Ibn Mubarak, *Akbar Nama*, vol. 1, p. 16.

letter to an official, Akbar is Ibn al-'Arabi's 'Perfect Human' (*insan al-kamil*).³⁴ It is in this context that the Tawhid-i Ilahi—a 'theosophical society' very much like a Sufi order, but enjoining rites on its initiates such as vegetarianism and cremation, more usually related to Hinduism—is best approached.³⁵

The discussion of Akbar's Intoxication began with Qandahari's mention of the former's association with Sufis through genealogy and fervent patronage of the Chishtiyya. It is well known that Fatehpur Sikri is built on the site of Shaykh Salim Chishti's (d. 1572) burial place—a saint to whom Akbar 'successfully' appealed for intercession in favour of bearing an heir—and his tomb is a central structure of the palace complex, directly facing the 'Ibadat Khana, where the Tawhid-i Ilahi initiates would meet.³⁶ The symbolic connection drawn between Akbar's regime and Sufism through the architecture of Fatehpur Sikri is quite literally reaffirmed by the body of historians considered here. Qandahari and Abu al-Fadl, for example, refer to a particular event in 1578, a year before Akbar's public declaration of himself as supreme *mujtahid* and his invitations to Hindu, Jain, Zoroastrian, Christian and other non-Muslim scholars to debate at the 'Ibadat Khana.³⁷ In early summer that year, Akbar and his highest-ranking officers were on a hunt in the Salt Range on the border of Baluchistan and Sind.³⁸ They were joined by local Baluchi chiefs and tribesmen to form a large 'hunting ring', but

---

³⁴ Ibn Mubarak, *Makatabat-i 'Allami*, p. xxiii.

³⁵ Among Orientalists and contemporary scholars like Mukhia, who read Akbar's initiatives as a sign he had abandoned Islam, the Tawhid-i Ilahi is perhaps the most-cited example, arguing that it was Akbar's attempt to construct a 'new religion' for 'Indians'. For a review of the Tawhid-i Ilahi from the 'new religion' perspective, see Mukhia, *The Mughals of India*, p. 47. The alternative view, quite standard in more contemporary works, is that the Tawhid-i Ilahi is an elite 'cult' born of Akbar's lack of interest in (or outright contempt for) established faiths, as well as his inclination towards 'pantheistic' philosophies. See M.A. Ali, 'Akbar and Islam (1581–1605)', *Islamic Society and Culture*, pp. 123–34.

³⁶ For further reading on the architectural plan of Fatehpur Sikri, see Sheila Blair and Jonathan Bloom, *The Art and Architecture of Islam, 1250–1800* (New Haven: Yale University Press, 1995).

³⁷ Qandahari, *Tarikh-i Akbari*, p. 272. The most detailed account is given in Ibn Mubarak, *Akbar Nama* (Br. Lib., 27247), the appropriate portion (f. 2949) of which is reproduced in Shireen Moosvi, ed. and trans. *Episodes in the Life of Akbar*, pp. 70–73. Translated quotes attributed to Abu al-Fadl in this regard are taken from the latter work.

³⁸ The hunt was a central, thus highly ritualised part of Mughal leisurely activities. See Muhammad A. Ansari, 'The Hunt of the Great Mughals', *Islamic Culture* 34 (1960): 19–23.

with all preparations complete, the order to commence the hunt never came. Instead, an order was issued to break the ring so that 'no one should be guilty of killing a sparrow'. Pondering Akbar's motives, the hunting party agreed that he had received a 'divine flash', but different parties offered different explanations of how it came to pass. One group argued that Akbar had received 'the light of truth' from the wandering ascetics of the forest. Another speculated that Akbar had encountered 'invisible beings', such as angels or *jinn*. Yet another proposed that 'the speechless animals had in an unspoken tongue or in conventional speech conveyed to him divine secrets'. A final group, with which the Sufi Qandahari most closely agreed,[39] argued that Akbar had 'had a session with his own enlightened heart, the seat of the manifestation of divine light'. Abu al-Fadl's final word is:

> How can its significance be grasped by traditional ones of narrow vision when those who have the capacity of perceiving spiritual ecstasy can comprehend only little of that condition?[40]

Whether or not all would agree with the assessments of the elite on the hunt, it is clear that the Mughal political elite was open to the idea of knowledge through 'direct experience' (*dhawq*), and Akbar and his regime drew much ideological mileage from such beliefs.

The influence of Intoxicated Sufism, more specifically, is apparent in the actions that followed the above event. Some six months later, in December 1578, Akbar wrote to the Portuguese at Goa, requesting that they dispatch scholars knowledgeable in Christianity.[41] The accounts

---

[39] Qandahari, *Tarikh-i Akbari*, p. 272.
[40] Ibn Mubarak, *Akbar Nama* (Br. Lib., Add. 27247, f. 2949), trans. Moosvi, *Episodes in the Life of Akbar*, p. 71.
[41] Although Christianity is said to have been first brought to South Asia by St. Thomas in the early centuries CE, the religion's influence was largely restricted to a southerly portion of the region. In fact, the arrival of the Portuguese mariner, Vasco da Gama in 1498, marks the advent of Christian influence across South Asia, facilitated by European trade and imperialism. Throughout the 16th century, the Portuguese would establish various trading posts under rights granted by various local states, or by conquest, with Goa as their administrative head under a 'Viceroy'. In their political, economic and religious interests, Portuguese representatives have been cited for engaging in piracy, extortion and persecution, particularly of the Muslims under their rule, but with the effect that Indian Ocean trade came to be dominated by the arms of Portuguese fleets. Missionaries did not arrive until 1542, but the Spanish Inquisition followed soon after. It is in this context that Akbar invited the Jesuits to Fatehpur Sikri. British, Dutch and French traders, imperialists and missionaries followed and routed the Portuguese over the latter half of the century, but no major impact is felt among the Mughals until the 1600s. See Blair B. Kling and Pearson, M.N., eds. *The Age of Partnership: Europeans*

of the Jesuit ambassadors who journeyed north soon after make for interesting reading.[42] Beginning with a description of the journey from Goa north through Gujarat and Rajputana to Fatehpur Sikri, Father Antonius Monserrate described a land in which various faiths are practised, but where 'Islam' and 'Hinduism' predominate. He says that countless Sufi shrines—sites of 'vain superstition'—are strewn across the land as the 'religious zeal' of earlier Muslims destroyed the 'Hindu' temples of the north. However, the 'carelessness' of current generations 'allowed sacrifices to be publicly performed...either among the ruins of these old temples or everywhere any fragment of an idol is to be found'.[43] He admonished Akbar for his tolerance of the 'Hindu' practice of *sati* (widow immolation), but was struck by the honour Akbar and his supporters extended the Jesuits, including polemical support in debates against Muslim scholars, the accommodation of a chapel and school in Fatehpur Sikri, and Akbar's kissing an icon of Jesus on a public occasion.[44]

Such observations clearly led Monserrate and his Jesuit colleagues to conclude that Akbar and his supporters, including Abu al-Fadl, his brother Abu al-Faydi and their father Shaykh Mubarak, had rejected the Qu'ran and the prophethood of Muhammad. However, Monserrate records a rather different explanation spoken by Akbar. In a conversation between the two, in which Akbar asks Monserrate to kiss the feet of the Catholic Pope in his stead and requests that the Pope dispatch theses on the nature of God, Monserrate is taken aback by Akbar's openness. Akbar responds that he is a follower of the '*Sauphii*' (Sufis), who call upon 'one God alone with no rival'. This implies, as Akbar is said to have explained, that:

---

in Asia before Dominion (Honolulu: University of Hawaii, 1979); M.N. Pearson, *The Portuguese in India* (Cambridge: Cambridge University Press, 1987).

[42] The principal accounts considered here are Antonious Monserrate, *The Commentary of Father Monserrate*, trans. J.S. Hoyland (Calcutta: Oxford University Press, 1922), written in the 1590s; and the correspondence of other Jesuit ambassadors accompanying Monserrate, published as, John Correia-Afonso, ed. and trans. *Letters from the Mughal Court: 1580–1583* (Anand: Gujarat Sahitya Prakash, 1980).

[43] Monserrate, *The Commentary of Father Monserrate*, p. 27.

[44] For 'sati', see ibid., p. 61. Also Correia-Afonso, *Letters from the Mughal Court: 1580–1583*, p. 69. For 'polemical support', see Monserrate, *The Commentary of Father Monserrate*, pp. 37–40, 53, 65, 100–01. For the 'chapel-school', pp. 51–53. For the 'icon', pp. 138, 176.

> ...[n]othing...should prevent his [Akbar] accepting the (Christian) Law if he should learn anything which touched his heart and mind, either from the Pope, or from the General of the Society [i.e. Jesuits], or from the two priests before him, or from any other man, however poor and humble.[45]

Although such utterances had raised Monserrate's hopes of winning Akbar's conversion to Christianity, Akbar signalled his rejection of this option at the last 'Ibadat Khana discussion that the Jesuit embassy attended in 1583. On this occasion, Monserrate quotes Akbar as saying:

> I perceive that there are varying customs and beliefs of varying religious paths. For the teachings of the Hindus, the Musalmans [Muslims], Jazdini [Zoroastrians], the Jews and the Christians are all different. But the followers of each religion regard the institutions of their own religion as better than those of any other. Not only so, but they strive to convert the rest to their own way of belief. If these refuse to be converted, they not only despise them, but also regard them for this very reason as their enemies. And this causes me to feel many serious doubts and scruples.[46]

Monserrate's response to this statement was to leave the court, suspecting that Akbar 'was intending to found a new religion, with matter taken from all the existing systems'[47]—a line which later Orientalists (and some contemporary historians) would echo into the 20th century in reference to the aforementioned Tawhid-i Ilahi. This institution is taken up below, but on the subject of the influence of Intoxicated Sufism on Akbar's cultural initiatives, it must be said that not only do Akbar's ideologues relate him to Sufis by birth, patronage and formal education, but that the very idiom in which this association is made echoes that of Ibn Arabi's *Fusus al-Hikam*—from the general identification of Akbar as the 'Perfect Human' by Abu al-Fadl, to such specifics as the equation of religious 'Law' with 'custom'. In other words, his 'transgression' of the *shari'a* and the ire of the theologians and jurists (not to mention the Jesuits) is in itself evidence of Akbar's education in, and preference for, Intoxicated Sufism, at least as an ideological tool.

Bada'uni also berates the Intoxicated Sufis of Akbar's court at one point in his history, whom he blames for leading Akbar 'astray', before turning to another segment of the scholarly elite he considers rife with

---

[45] Monserrate, *The Commentary of Father Monserrate*, p. 173.
[46] Ibid., p. 182.
[47] Ibid., p. 184.

influential 'kafirs'. This is the group of 'physicians' (hukama'), the 'kafirs' being those who indulge in the contemporary metaphysics of the philosophers. On this matter, Bada'uni wrote, 'man's reason, not tradition, was acknowledged as the only basis of religion'.[48] Elsewhere he states that rather than pursuing the Sober disciplines of *tafsir*, *hadith* and *fiqh*, 'astronomy, physics, medicine, mathematics, poetry, history and novels were cultivated and thought necessary'.[49] As far as Abu al-Fadl's opinion on this matter is concerned, one need say no more than that in the *Akbar Nama*, he refers to Akbar as 'Socrates in wisdom, Plato in perception'.[50]

The *Makatabat-i 'Allami* contains a letter to the Sharifs of Mecca, dated 1582, in which Akbar defends the Islamic credentials of a philosopher, Mu'in al-Din Hashmi of Shiraz, now attached to the Mughals but under the attack of certain scholars in Mecca. The same work also contains a letter to one Chelebi Beg of Shiraz—a reputed philosopher of that city—whom Akbar bids to his court and promises patronage, along with any others he cares to bring along, in 1596.[51] Abu al-Fadl records that the philosopher arrived in 1597, as had many others in the years before.[52] Bada'uni mentions 26 influential philosophers at court, while Abu al-Fadl's *A'in-i Akbari* mentions 15, though both are agreed that the majority are originally from Isfahan or Shiraz.[53] As to the intellectual schools these philosophers partook in, an elegy composed by Abu al-Faydi for one of their ranks, Fath Allah al-Shirazi, is instructive. It includes the lines:

> Two Hundred al-Farabis and Ibn Sinas have come and gone, until he appeared; otherwise, fate has many shops of this kind of haberdashery.
>
> At times, he would traverse the world in the company of the *mashshai*s; at other times, he would rise into the sky with the cavalcade of the *ishraqi*s.[54]

The origins of these scholars, together with the mention of the Ishraqi (Illuminationist) school of philosophy, is exceedingly significant as the most prominent school of philosophy in the late 16th century Shiraz and

---

[48] Bada'uni, *Muntakhab al-Tawarikh*, vol. 2, p. 215.
[49] Ibid., p. 316; also see pp. 203–06.
[50] Ibn Mubarak, *Akbar Nama*, vol. 1, p. 22.
[51] Ibn Mubarak, *Makatabat-i 'Allami*, p. 113.
[52] Ibn Mubarak, *Akbar Nama*, vol. 3, p. 1116.
[53] Ibn Mubarak, *A'in-i Akbari*, vol. 3, pp. 611–13.
[54] The poem is cited in Bhakkari, *Dhakhirat al-Khawanin*, vol. 1, pp. 142–43.

Isfahan was rooted in the work of Shihab al-Din al-Suhrawardi (d. 1191), the 'founder' of the Ishraqi school. At the dawn of the 17th century, perhaps no more than two decades after the initiation of the Tarikh-i Ilahi and Tawhid-i Ilahi at Akbar's court, a follower of the Ishraqis, Sadr al-Din al-Shirazi (d. 1641), would carry the line forward with a movement called the *Hikmat-i Ilahi* (Divine Philosophy). This does not mean that Akbar's initiatives influenced Sadr al-Din al-Shirazi, but it does confirm that Ishraqism, among other philosophical schools arising in Shiraz and Isfahan, was quite influential at Fatehpur Sikri.[55]

As mentioned in Chapter One, one of the greatest contributions which historians of doctrinal Islam made to this discussion of Intoxicated thought at Akbar's court is that Ishraqis defended the philosopher's 'right of reason to probe the deepest religious mysteries', and argued that religious and metaphysical truth are 'united' such that it is 'the duty of the seeker to seek truth wherever it can be found: in Greek philosophy, in ancient Persian thought, in Muslim Neo-Platonism, and in Sufism'. In this light, and recalling the identification of the influence of such specific doctrines as the Sufis' *wahdat al-wujud* and the sectarian influences of Shi'is, Nuqtawis and so on, the institution of Tawhid-i Ilahi appears in a rather different form than that cast by Monserrate, Bada'uni and the *qadis*, as well as later Orientalists and some contemporary historians. Whether the invitations to representatives of various schools, sects and faiths, the translation of Sanskrit works, or the mixing of Hindu, Zoroastrian, Jain and Sufi intellectualism and rites in its perspectives—in short, all that contemporary historians of South Asia would term 'Indic' or 'transgressive' about the Tawhid-i Ilahi—is legitimized by an education in the Intoxicated Way. In fact, it appears clear that the Tawhid-i Ilahi draws its primary inspiration from the 'Unity' (*Tawhid*) of the Sufis and the 'Theism' (*Ilahi*) of the philosophers. Furthermore, even in Akbar's day, at the peak of its activities, most of the initiates of the Tawhid-i Ilahi were Muslims of the highest rank, with the exception of Hindu wives and a few influential

---

[55] For a general discussion of Safawid influence in South Asia, see Agha Ahdi Husain, 'Cultural Influence of Safavid Iran over the Indo-Pakistan Subcontinent under the Mughals', *Journal of the Regional Culture Institute* 1:4 (1968): 24–34. For the study of Ishraqi and other philosophical schools from Iran in Akbar's day, see Riazul Islam, 'Akbar's Intellectual Contacts with Iran', *Islamic Society and Culture*, pp. 351–74; and Rizvi, *Religious and Intellectual History of Muslims in Akbar's Reign*, in its entirety.

courtiers.⁵⁶ Outside such elite circles, however, it is noteworthy that in a *dartur al-'amal* (guide on administrative conduct), Akbar enjoins his officers to draw insight primarily from al-Ghazali's *Ihya 'Ulum al-Din*, and other such works, not from any work produced by those in the Tawhid-i Ilahi circle.⁵⁷ In this regard, the Tawhid-i Ilahi also continues the philosophical/mystical tradition of intellectual elitism. Furthermore, laws issuing from the state still often reflected juristic attitudes. For example, late in his reign, Akbar convened a meeting with state officers for no reason other than 'grants of favours and acts of welfare'.⁵⁸ He began the meeting by emancipating all his 'thousands' of slaves, saying, 'it is beyond the realm of justice and good conduct for me to consider as my slaves those whom I have captured by force'.⁵⁹ When recommendations from the attendant *wazirs, amirs* and so on, were requested, they included a minimum age for marriage of 12 years for boys and girls; the appointment of officers to assess the needs of the 'indigent' and make them known to the state; price controls at markets; the building of hospitals and *serais* (inns); and, the abolishment of the governor's right to impose the death penalty without 'full inquiry' and the endorsement of the head of state.⁶⁰ All these suggestions were

---

⁵⁶ Bada'uni, for example, directs his criticism at high-ranking Muslims whom he views as the main instigators. Apart from Sharif Amuli, these include Shaykh Mubarak and his sons, Akbar's foster-brother, 'Aziz Kukaltash, and such *hakims* as Mulla Shah Muhammad and the historian and poet, Asaf Khan Qazwini. Bada'uni's attitudes, along with those of other nobles, scholars and Sufis of a Sober persuasion, as well as a less 'paradigmically' constrained understanding of such thinkers and state officials' religious inclinations, are excellently surveyed in Rizvi, *Religious and Intellectual History of Muslims in Akbar's Reign*, pp. 418–54.

⁵⁷ Ibn Mubarak, *Makatabat-i 'Allami*, pp. 79–88.

⁵⁸ Ibn Mubarak, *Akbar Nama*, vol. 2, pp. 379–80. A fuller account, from which I draw, is found in *Akbar Nama* (British Library, 27, 247/ff. 327b), a portion of which is included in Moosvi, *Episodes in the Like of Akbar*, pp. 87–89.

⁵⁹ Ibid., p. 87.

⁶⁰ Ibid., pp. 87–89. Aside from the previously outlined provision that the leader of a *jihad* has the right to decide the fate of his captives, for Sober ideals concerning slavery and the favour accrued by the remission of slaves, see R. Brunschvig, "Abd', *Encyclopaedia of Islam*, vol. 1, pp. 24–40. Positive attitudes towards price controls can be read in any of Barani, Ibn Taymiyya, al-Mawardi, Ibn Muqaffa' or Nizam al-Mulk al-Tusi's works cited in Chapter One. For the construction of hospitals, inns, and so on, as well as the way in which they were funded, see the discussion of *waqf* in Chapter One. As for marriage according to jurists, although no age limit was placed on 'betrothal', the formal writing of the '*niqah*', or contract, and consummation could not take place until boys reached 12 and girls 9 years of age. See Jean Boyd, 'Nikah', *Encyclopaedia of Islam* (CD ROM Ed., 2004). For more on Mughal attitudes, also see below, fn. 127.

passed into law.⁶¹ As all of these attitudes reflect juristic thought, when they are added to the above discussion of Akbar's regime as a whole, the Tawhid-i Ilahi appears as no more a 'new religion' than Akbar's actions as Sultan appear a 'new polity'. That is to say, the Tawhid-i Ilahi is the intellectual expression of the Intoxicated Way of the Sufis and philosophers, just as the Mughal Sultanate is largely the political expression of the Sober Path of the jurists and theologians. The link, however, is that as the *Sahib-i Zaman*, or the 'Perfect Human', Akbar could move beyond the limits imposed by legal doctrine, to employ absolute *ijtihad* in legitimating such actions as the abolition of *jizya*. To the Intoxicated, as Abu al-Fadl's support suggests, in so doing there was no doctrinal contradiction between Akbar's policies and doctrinal Islam. To the Sober, as Bada'uni's admonition confirms, Akbar and Abu al-Fadl were the 'heretical' or even 'apostolic' products of the exercise of absolute *ijtihad* by the unqualified.

This discussion so far confirms, first and foremost, that unless one is prepared to essentialise 'Islam' in terms of the doctrines of the jurists—as Monserrate, later Orientalists and supporters of the dominant paradigm in contemporary history are apt to do—Akbar's political and intellectual initiatives, including the assumption of the jurisprudential privileges of Caliphs, the abolition of *jizya*, the establishment and practices of the Tawhid-i Ilahi and the promulgation of the Tarikh-i Ilahi, reflect his deployment of doctrinal Islam. As the 'Perfect Human', the above are not representative of 'anti-Islamic' policies, but are manifestations of Akbar's 'perfect knowledge' of Islam. That is to say, Mughal political culture was conducted in a variety of idioms, including those 'connected' with the broader Muslim World (i.e. Sultanate, etc.) and those 'embedded' in the local (e.g. *darshan, nauroz,* etc.), but both were legitimated by 'Islamic' thought. In this light, the very 'dynastic ideology' or 'Akbari constitution' that historians view as a 'transgression' of Islam, is revealed to be rooted in Islamic legal, theological, philosophical and mystical thought and institutions. Rather than an 'Islam' transgressed for 'India', Akbar and the Intoxicated thought he employed illustrates a South Asia systematically embraced as 'Islamic'.

By the same token, it must also be acknowledged that for all its hospitality towards local custom, Akbar's regime did not dissolve communitarian divides. For example, in Akbar's regime, the Rajputs alone

---

⁶¹ Ibn Mubarak, *Akbar Nama*, vol. 2, pp. 379–80.

rose to the highest ranks, and even then were outnumbered 4 to 1 by Muslims. However, the limits of hospitality can be most succinctly illustrated by looking at the attitudes of the scholarly and political elite towards Europeans and Christianity. As suggested by the presence of the Portuguese in the region even before the Mughals arrived, the elite was generally open to dealing with Europeans, but while Intoxicated thinkers such as Akbar and Abu al-Fadl were enthusiastic to learn about Christianity, the Sober of the court were more interested in the polemical delegitimation of Jesuit theology. At the same time, however, the 'religious' and 'non-religious' activities of the Portuguese—including extortion, piracy and Inquisition—drew sharp criticism from both sides of the intellectual divide. In a letter to 'Abd Allah Khan Uzbek of Turan (1586), Akbar wrote of his intent to launch a *jihad* and 'undertake the extermination of the *farangi kafir*s [lit., infidel Franks] who...had created unrest and were harassing and oppressing traders and pilgrims' to Mecca.[62] In a letter to Burhan Nizam al-Mulk of Ahmadnagar, written five years later (1591), Akbar reiterated the call, arguing that an alliance between the Mughals and the Sultans of Bijapur and Golconda 'would result in a united effort and subsequent victory over the territories of the *farangis* (*farangistan*) and their ports'.[63] Although these campaigns were never launched, it is clear that Akbar was not merely speaking rhetorically, given that two campaigns against Portuguese forts in Gujarat had taken place while the Jesuits were at court (1580–1583).[64]

In the final analysis, it appears that the activities of the Portuguese, though noted in both positive and negative light, were low on the list of Akbar's priorities. As for the expansion of European influence in general, an incident described in the *Waqa'i'* of Asad Beg al-Qazwini seems to best symbolise the open, yet cautious, attitudes of Akbar's regime.[65] The subject of discussion was the recently introduced item of tobacco, brought to South Asia (directly or indirectly) by the Europeans. Al-Qazwini returned to court with tobacco and a *hookah* from the Sultanate of Bijapur where he had been on a diplomatic mission in 1604. Akbar's foster-brother, 'Aziz Kukaltash, informed him that tobacco was widely smoked in Mecca and Medina, and that some 'physicians'

---

[62] Ibn Mubarak, *Makatabat-i 'Allami*, p. 44.
[63] Ibid., p. 65.
[64] Ibn Mubarak, *Akbar Nama*, vol. 2, pp. 280–81.
[65] Asad Beg al-Qazwini, *Waqa'i'* (MS, British Library, Or. 1996). A portion (f.21a–b) is reproduced in Shireen Moosvi, ed. *Episodes in the Life of Akbar*, pp. 106–08.

(*hukama'*) consider it medicinal. The pharmacist at court added that the European physicians had written much about tobacco. Al-Qazwini defended the European physicians, naively saying:

> Without having tried it and found out all its qualities, how would they prescribe it for [their] rulers, kings and men, low and high? They must have judged its good or bad qualities; otherwise they would not have acted thus.[66]

However, Akbar's physician, Hakim 'Ali, argued against Akbar smoking. He stated:

> It is not necessary for us to follow the Europeans, and adopt a custom, which is not sanctioned by our own wise men, without experiment or trial.[67]

Al-Qazwini retorted that every 'custom' is new at some point in time, that they often spread without the prior examination of the learned, and the qualities of a thing cannot always be determined unless it is tried.

Akbar is reported to have been greatly impressed by al-Qazwini's argument, responding with the words, 'Truly, we must not reject a thing that has been adopted by the people of the world, merely because we cannot find it in our books, or how shall we progress?'[68] In the end, Akbar smoked, but although al-Qazwini tells us that tobacco subsequently became a widely traded commodity and 'addiction spread everywhere', he concludes the episode by stating that Akbar never smoked again. What this episode ultimately illustrates, therefore, is that just as in the case of South Asian customs, it is with the tools of doctrinal Islam, Sober and Intoxicated, that European influence was assessed and legitimated or rejected.

II. *Muhi al-Din Awrangzib and the Sober Path*

Although there is no debate among contemporary scholars about Awrangzib's 'Islamic' credentials, all equating his Islam with legalism, there was apparently some debate in Awrangzib's day. An incident related by Muhammad Khafi Khan—a mid-level administrator and

---

[66] Ibid., p. 107.
[67] Ibid., p. 107.
[68] Ibid., p. 108.

historian in Awrangzib's regime—illustrates the point. One Friday, a Sufi was arrested when he attempted to demolish the steps of the *jama' masjid* in Delhi, where Awrangzib was due for prayers. When the Sultan arrived and the matter was brought to his attention, he asked why a man 'professing to serve God' would endeavour to destroy a mosque. The Sufi replied his actions were intended to draw Awrangzib's attention to the fact that he took notice of 'minute trifles', but acted unjustly towards his father, brothers and subjects. Awrangzib responded by asking the *qadi* in attendance for a ruling on the Sufi's punishment. The *qadi* ruled death for wanting to destroy the entrance to a mosque and for the manner in which he spoke to the 'image of God on earth' (i.e. Awrangzib). The Sufi was undeterred, questioning the ruling by stating that though the steps of the mosque could be rebuilt, the *qadi* knew not how to restore the life he intended to take. Before the *qadi* could respond, Awrangzib ended the discussion by releasing the Sufi, saying, 'Withdraw; each man has to render his own account for himself'.[69]

Without questioning Awrangzib's legalism, what such incidents relate is that opposition to the point of destroying the steps of a mosque was not unanimously viewed as 'un-Islamic'. Rather, as in the case of the above Sufi, it was a 'pious' act. Apart from such 'internal' protests and fissures, however, Awrangzib faced a host of others from decidedly better-empowered quarters. As previously mentioned, Awrangzib's primary opponent in the struggle for power was his older brother, Dara Shukoh, an active member of the Tawhid-i Ilahi circle of scholars and the preferred heir of Shah Jahan. In such cases, Awrangzib was not as lenient. Even before his defeat, Dara's intellectual orientation was raised as grounds for execution because in Khafi Khan's words, he had 'brought disgrace to *tasawwuf* [mysticism] by following some heretics who posed as Sufis, and declared Islam and unbelief to be twin brothers, on which subject he had written treatises'.[70] Thus, the same source is one among many from the period to relate that one of Awrangzib's first acts was to abolish the Tawhid-i Ilahi circle of scholars, as well as the solar Tarikh-i Ilahi calendar in favour of the lunar Hijri. From there

---

[69] Muhammad Khafi Khan, *Muntakhab al-Lubab*, ed. and trans., S. Moinul Haq, *Khafi Khan's History of Alamgir* (Karachi: Pakistan Historical Society Journal, 1975), pp. 254–55.
[70] Among Dara's works is the *Sirr-i Asrar*, a Persian translation of 50 Sanskrit '*Upanisads*'. See Ibid., pp. 5; 92.

Awrangzib went on to dismantle more of the cornerstones of Akbar's regime, as previously mentioned. Given such sweeping changes, it is no surprise that historians have long contrasted the two rulers. But why the change in the state's orientation, and how different was the ideological and institutional regime which resulted, particularly with regard to the patronage and employment of Shi'is and non-Muslims? By way of an answer to the first part of this question, it is worth beginning with a brief description of the intervening period between Akbar's and Awrangzib's rule, the latter's ideological and institutional regime being broadly tied to a series of new political factors.

Although Akbar's son, Jahangir (r. 1605–1630), ascended to power through the 'designation' of his father, as had Akbar's predecessors, Jahangir's son, Shah Jahan won his father's titles after a brutal 'war of succession' between him and his brothers, passing that legacy to Awrangzib and his brothers. The rise of 'wars of succession' as a means to power, of course, reflects the tenuous relations with external and internal powers upon which the Mughal regime was based. On the 'external' front, Jahangir's and Shah Jahan's grants of trading and territorial privileges to Portuguese 'viceroys', as well as Dutch, French and British 'companies' (not to mention those granted by other states in the region), had established the Europeans as integral features of the economic, though not as yet political, landscape.[71] At the same time,

---

[71] Dutch ships were the first to run the Portuguese blockade of Indian Ocean trade, during the closing years of the 16th century, but in concentrating their efforts on South East Asia, contact with the Mughals came after that of the British, who arrived at Surat (Gujarat) in 1608, after founding the 'East India Company' in 1600. Dutch influence would also be handicapped by the fact that by 1620, the British had displaced Portuguese power in the western Arabian Sea and Persian Gulf, and won rights from Jahangir to build a 'factory' (trading post) at Surat. The future site of Madras (Tamil Nadu) was granted by the local official of the Sultanate of Golconda in 1639, Bombay would be gained from the Portuguese in 1668, and the right to a factory at Hugli (near the future site of Calcutta, Bengal) would be granted by Shah Jahan in 1651, establishing the British at all three major coastal areas, western, eastern and southern, as well as the future 'presidencies'. By the time of Awrangzib's reign, beginning in 1658, the British had in fact built approximately 20 factories, including a few inland. Although the Dutch also gained trading rights, it was the late-coming French, who arrived in Surat in 1668, winning trading rights against the objections of the Dutch, who would most forcefully challenge British influence until the late 18th century. See Blair B. Kling and M.N. Pearson, eds. *The Age of Partnership: Europeans in Asia before Dominion* (Honolulu: University of Hawaii, 1979); Om Prakash, *The Dutch East India Company and the Economy of Bengal, 1630–1720* (Delhi: Oxford University Press, 1988); and Colin Mitchell, *Sir Thomas Roe and the Mughal Empire* (Karachi: Area Studies Centre for Europe, 2000).

the animosities stirred by the Portuguese disruption of 'trade and pilgrimage' under Akbar are echoed in Jahangir's glee at the sinking of a Portuguese fleet in Surat by British (*angrez*) force of arms in 1614/15.[72] Troubles with the Portuguese are also evident in Shah Jahan's '*jihad*' against the '*kafirs*' at Hugli in 1632, for erecting 'forts', taking control of surrounding villages, 'kidnapping' people as slaves, and 'converting the inhabitants...to Christianity'.[73] However, Jahangir's maintenance of Jesuits, like Shah Jahan's grant of a 'factory' (trading post) at Hugli to the British, proves that, as in the times of Akbar, the problem was neither with Europeans nor Christianity, but with the peripheral yet reverberating impact their activities were having on the economic and cultural regimes of the Mughal state.

As well, the Shi'i Safawid regime's annexation of Qandahar (1622) during Jahangir's watch, like the failed attempts (1649–1652) to recapture it by Shah Jahan's regime, indicates a clear shift in relations with the powers across the western border. Before the fall of Qandahar, Jahangir received embassies from Shah Abbas Safawi in 1611, 1615, 1616 and 1620.[74] After Shah Abbas captured Qandahar, relations appear to have been further strained by Shah Jahan's tussle with the Safawids for repossession of the province from 1638 to 1653, although embassies continued to be exchanged throughout the period. Awrangzib abandoned Qandahar for good, but one can see the resounding effect of earlier Mughal defeats in his description of Shah Husayn Safawi as the 'demon of the forest' as late as 1703.[75] In addition, campaigns against the southern Shi'i Sultanates of Golconda, Bijapur and Ahmadnagar, among others—beginning with Jahangir but continuing into Shah Jahan's regime—confirm that relations with states across the southern border were also strained. Jahangir's *Tuzuk-i Jahangiri* is littered with references to troubles in the south, coming to his attention by 1609 in the form of ongoing campaigns in Ahmadnagar, brought under nominal Mughal

---

[72] Jahangir, *Tuzuk-i Jahangiri*, trans. H.M. Elliot (Lahore: Islamic Book Service, 1987), pp. 96–97.
[73] 'Inayat Khan, *Shah Jahan Nama*, trans. A.R. Fuller, eds. W.E. Begle and Z.A. Desai (Delhi: Oxford University Press, 1990), pp. 87, 117.
[74] Ibid., p. 364.
[75] This remark is drawn from a letter included in a large collection that combines those collected by Awrangzib's principal secretaries, 'Inayat Allah (*Raqa'at-i 'Alamgiri*); 'Abd Al-Karim (*Raqa'im-i Kara'im*); Raja Aya Mal (*Dastur al-'Amal Aghahi*); and the anonymous, *Adab-i 'Alamgiri*. They are published as, Aurangzeb 'Alamgir, *Ruqa'at-i 'Alamgiri*, ed. and trans. J.H. Bilimoria (Delhi: Idara-i Adabiyat-i Delli, 1972), p. 95.

authority by Akbar in 1600, then spilling into Bijapur and Golconda under Shah Jahan, all of which would be passed on to Awrangzib.[76] Attesting to the growing consternation attached to the power of these overtly Shi'i competitors, in contrast to Akbar's professed willingness to send troops in defence of the Safawids against the Sunni Ottomans, Jahangir received the first letter from an Ottoman Sultan to a Mughal on the heels of Qandahar's fall, addressing the dangers of their common 'rivals', and initiating a policy of cordial relations that Shah Jahan continued by exchanging embassies in 1640 and again in 1654.[77]

As for 'internal' fissures, although various local revolts, even arising within the dynastic order, were features of Jahangir's and Shah Jahan's regimes, by Awrangzib's reign, the growing autonomy of high-ranking officials (Muslim and non-Muslim), as well as the rise of newly empowered players on the scene (Uzbeks, Ethiopians and a host of South Asian ethnicities), both driven by the rise of landed and commercial elites with sub-regional cultural ties, played a larger role in threatening and, in Awrangzib's wake, dismantling central authority.[78] Among these, the

---

[76] Virtually upon Akbar's death, the displaced Sultanate of Ahmadnagar was restored by its widely respected Ethiopian general and statesman, Malik Ambar (d. 1629). Jahangir's campaigns led to a treaty in 1616, agreeing to the nominal authority of the Mughals, but no more; the Nizam Shahi dynasty remained instituted. After the deaths of Sultan Malik Ambar and Jahangir, a power struggle between Malik Ambar's son, Fateh Khan, and the new Sultan of Ahmadnagar led to Mughal intervention on behalf of Fateh Khan, and the extinction of the Nizam Shahi dynasty in 1632. The Sultan of Bijapur's subsequent attempts to revive the Nizam Shahi dynasty led to an attack against them, followed by a more prolonged and devastating campaign in 1635. It was at this point that Awrangzib was appointed 'viceroy' of the Deccan provinces for his first stint, the second ending when he successfully staked his claim to the throne in 1657. Along the way, the Sultanate of Golconda would be dragged in by coming to the aid of Bijapur and the Maratha Bhonsles. See Awan, *History of India and Pakistan*, vol. 2, pp. 363, 381–84; also Jahangir, *Tuzuk-i Jahangiri*, pp. 74–80, 170–79, 188–89, 192–224.

[77] Of course, Ottoman relations with other South Asian Sultanates, like that of the Safawids, predate contact with the Mughals. The Bahmanids were the first to exchange embassies in the 15th century. With Portuguese attempts to capture Indian Ocean trade in the early 16th century, diplomatic relations extended to military alliances. This began with the joint naval attack of the Egyptian Mamluk Sultans and the Sultans of Gujarat (1507–1509). The Ottoman conquest of Egypt in 1517, however, diverted alliances to their regime, leading to joint operations by the Sultans of Gujarat and the Ottomans in the 1530s and the 1550s. See Awan, *History of India and Pakistan*, vol. 2, pp. 1001–03. For Mughal-Ottoman relations, also see 'Inayat Khan, *Shah Jahan Nama*, pp. 267, 270, 274, 452, 460–61, 465, 494, 496–97, 499–500.

[78] See Richards, *The Mughal Empire*, pp. 171–77, 290–97; and Streusand, *The Formation of the Mughal Empire*, pp. 23–36. For a thorough work more specifically on Mughal political decline, see A. Hintze, *The Mughal Empire and its Decline* (Aldershot: Ashgate, 1997). Also see Chapter Three in this work.

Hindu Marathas, a faction of whom Awrangzib pursued through his entire public life, beginning in the era of Shah Jahan, are first encountered in Jahangir's memoirs in 1612.[79] Although they had served in various functions in the Bahminid, Ahmadnagar, Bijapur and Golconda Sultanates since the 15th century, Jahangir notes only Maratha military services to the Nizam Shahi Sultans of Ahmadnagar.[80] Reflecting their growing power, by Shah Jahan's first years in office, Marathas such as Gheloji, Maloji and Shahuji Bhonsle were being conferred ranks in Mughal service that were previously reserved for Rajputs.[81] However, this was insufficient to prevent Shahuji from joining the Sultanate of Bijapur in a failed attempt to restore the Sultanate of Ahmadnagar after its annexation by the Mughals, only three years after being conferred a Mughal rank. Even this act of 'rebellion' and the subsequent defeat of Bijapur did not dissuade the Mughals from restoring patronage to Shahuji, as *jagirdar* of a cowed Bijapur.[82] Finally, making it abundantly clear that neither Mughal lenience nor ranks could abate the ambitions of the Bhonsles, Shahuji's son, Shivaji, went on to practically consume the Sultanate of Bijapur from within by the time Awrangzib ascended the Mughal throne, contributing to action against that state.[83] Such external and internal pressures confirm that Awrangzib inherited a state under serious pressure.

In response to the above political and socio-economic changes, Jahangir's and Shah Jahan's regimes largely stayed the general ideological course set by Akbar, from the Tarikh-i Ilahi down to deployment of Caliphal rhetoric.[84] However, it is also apparent that growing conflict with Shi'i and non-Muslim competitors meant that some tinkering was already underway by the time Awrangzib took office, e.g. Jahangir's inclusion of a ban on the production and sale of 'wine' and 'intoxicating

---

[79] Jahangir, *Tuzuk-i Jahangiri*, p. 89.
[80] Ibid., p. 89. For further reading on the Marathas, see Stewart Gordon, *Marathas, Marauders and State Formation in 18th Century India* (Delhi: Oxford University Press, 1994).
[81] 'Inayat Khan, *Shah Jahan Nama*, pp. 26, 42, 46.
[82] Ibid., pp. 97, 129, 167–70, 194–200.
[83] Awan, *History of India and Pakistan*, vol. 2, pp. 507–26.
[84] For use of Caliphal titles in the literature of Jahangir's and Shah Jahan's reigns, see Mutribi Asamm Samarqandi, *Nuskha-i Zeba-i Jahangiri*, trans. R.C. Foltz, *Conversations with Emperor Jahangir* (Costa Mesa: Mazda Publishers, 1998), pp. 26, 33, 44, 53, 55; Bhakkari, *Dhakhirat al-Khawanin*, pp. 4, 10, 15, 53; and 'Inayat Khan, *Shah Jahan Nama*, pp. 2, 4, 13, 17–18, 23.

liquors', and Shah Jahan's ban on 'prostration' (*sijda*) and his order to destroy newly erected Hindu temples between 1633–1636, which were all obvious attempts to strengthen a legalistic facade.[85] When such developments are acknowledged in the run-up to Awrangzib's rule, social historians appear quite correct in suggesting that more than 'religious bigotry' precipitated Awrangzib's strategies. The need to placate the jurists, theologians, Sober Sufis and their supporters among the new groups in the state's upper echelons, as well as to promote an ideology that more thoroughly drew lines between the Mughals and their Shi'i and non-Muslim competitors cannot be ignored. Furthermore, legalism implied that the tiered duties on merchants, as well as the re-imposition of *jizya* could provide, as Sugata Bose and Ayesha Jalal argue, 'a means of taxing the commercial wealth of Hindus and Jains'.[86] Without denying the influence of personal beliefs, that is to say if Akbar's Intoxicated Way had been a means to secure power in the socio-political context of the late 16th century, Awrangzib's Sober Path was intended to maintain that power in the late 17th century. Considering that the state continued to expand under Awrangzib's watch, it can be said that the strategy was successful. However, the spectacular collapse of the state following Awrangzib's death reveals that the institutional legacy he inherited and the leadership he exercised, more than his Sober Path, account for the successes on record. As for failures, social historians have long established that Awrangzib's initiatives were either ineffectual or ignored by underlings, with the effect that the autonomy of various ethnic groups (Muslim and non-Muslim), driven by the rise of landed and commercial elites with sub-regional cultural ties, thoroughly eroded central authority, leaving only the shell of a state by Awrangzib's death. The best evidence that the Sober Path's legalism and supposed cultural 'intrusiveness' was not a contributor to this decline is the ideological and institutional continuity it afforded, particularly with regard to the patronage and employment of non-legalistic Islam, Sufis, Shi'is and non-Muslims.

While Awrangzib's reforms were far-reaching, it should be recalled that the Sober Path is not restricted to legalism, i.e. legalism alone did not define Awrangzib's ideology. Sufism also played a prominent role.

---

[85] Jahangir, *Tuzuk-i Jahangiri*, p. 37; 'Inayat Khan, *Shah Jahan Nama*, pp. 18, 70–71, 89–90, 161.
[86] Sugata Bose and Jalal, A. *Modern South Asia* (London: Routledge, 1999), p. 41.

Just as Akbar was regarded to be privy to 'superior' spiritual insight, so, too, was Awrangzib. Niccolao Manucci, an Italian artillery-man in the Mughal army, noted that the most commonly used titles in Awrangzib's reign, which were intended to reflect his 'inspired radiance and knowledge', are: *qibla-i din wa dunya* (centre of religion and the world) and *qibla-i du jahanan* (centre of the two worlds).[87] As well, in a typical letter from Mirza Muazzam (Awrangzib's son and successor as Bahadar Shah (r. 1707–1712)), Awrangzib is addressed as the 'Centre of Faith and the *Ka'ba*', while a high-ranking officer addresses his letter to the 'saint and spiritual guide of the world'.[88] In other words, Awrangzib retained the designation of 'Perfect Human', and expressed such through the same Caliphal titles and powers assumed by Akbar and bequeathed to him through Jahangir and Shah Jahan.[89] Sufism, therefore, was employed in much the same way as in Akbar's regime, i.e. to legitimate Akbar's style of ascension to power and mode of rule. However, it is also clear that Awrangzib's 'hidden inclination' (*iradat-i batini*), as Khafi Khan termed it, did have an alternative impact on the state's mode of rule.[90] With which type of Sufism is Awrangzib officially associated? Of the seven mystics Khafi Khan suggests were influential at court, most are explicitly identified as masters of *hadith* and Qur'anic exegesis (*tafsir*), and all are identified as respectful of the *shari'a* to the extent that *sama'* (devotional music) is only mentioned in the context of one scholar, while two are said to be firmly anti-*sama'*.[91] Further reflecting this ultra-Sober emphasis, Manucci tells of how Awrangzib called to court 12 prominent Sufis who claimed they could perform miracles and intercede with God on behalf of devotees, in the process soliciting sexual favours from women seeking their 'spiritual' services. Awrangzib sardonically gave each man three days to perform a miracle in his presence; should they fail, the Sufis would be imprisoned or banished, but promised restitution should they be able to perform a miracle in the

---

[87] Niccolao Manucci, *Storia do Mogor*, 4 vols., trans. W. Irvine (Calcutta: Editions Indian, 1966), vol. 3, p. 323.

[88] Such letters are included in Hamid al-Din Khan Bahadur, *Ahkam-i 'Alamgiri*, trans. J.N. Sarkar, *Anecdotes of Aurangzeb* (Calcutta: Sarkar and Sons, 1963), pp. 51, 88.

[89] Apart from the aforementioned works from Awrangzib's era, for Caliphal titles, see Ishwardas Nagar, *Futuhat-i 'Alamgiri*, trans. T. Ahmad (Delhi: Idara-i Adabiyat-i Delli, 1978), pp. 4, 10, 21–24, 61, 71, 206, 220, 243; and 'Aqil Khan Razi, *Waqi'at-i 'Alamgiri* (Delhi: Mercantile Printing Press, 1946), p. 7.

[90] Khafi Khan, *Muntakhab al-Lubab*, p. 13.

[91] Khafi Khan, *Muntakhab al-Lubab*, pp. 541–55.

future.⁹² Evidently, Awrangzib did not deny the miraculous powers of 'saints', but objected strongly to the idea of 'saintly' intercession—an echo of ultra-Sober Sufi ideals of piety. Of course, such attitudes did exert an influence on Awrangzib's own exercise of 'hidden inclinations', at least ideologically. It was shown above that the crux of Akbar's power over the judiciary came from his claim to act as 'supreme *mujtahid*', exercising 'absolute *ijtihad*'. In the historical writings of Awrangzib's contemporaries, there are many examples of Awrangzib's exercise of a form of this 'right'. A telling example is a case that arose during the siege of a fort in 1700, during his southern campaigns. The issue was the punishment of four Muslim and nine Hindu enemy soldiers captured outside the fort. Awrangzib summoned the *qadi al-qudat* to investigate and, with the help of *mufti*s, report their findings. The *qadi* returned with a *fatwa* that the Muslims should be imprisoned for three years, while the '*kafirs*' may be offered the choice of conversion and release, or death. Before returning the *fatwa* to the *qadi*, Awrangzib wrote across the top:

> This decision [is] according to the Hanafi school...Ours is not the rigid Shi'a creed, that there should be only one tree in an entire village. Praise to God! There are four schools [of Sunni *fiqh*] based on truth, [each] according to a particular age and time.⁹³

When the *qadi* returned with multiple *fatawa* based on the methods of various schools, Awrangzib chose a ruling for the execution of all prisoners, Hindu and Muslim, 'as a deterrent'. What did he intend to deter? The answer stated is loss of 'control' over the state. In other words, the execution of all served the state better than the execution of only the Hindus. Clearly Awrangzib acted as 'supreme *mujtahid*'; but was the degree of his *ijtihad* 'absolute' as had been the case under Akbar? On this occasion, Khafi Khan provides cases confirming that Awrangzib followed in his forefathers' footsteps only to a point. He wrote that before the deposition of the Shi'i Sultan of Golconda, Abu al-Hasan, Awrangzib sought the *qadi al-qudat*'s legal opinion, but was denied the legitimisation he sought by the *qadi*'s resignation.⁹⁴ The next *qadi al-qudat* was also approached, but he declared openly in court that the Sultan was a 'Muslim', that the war was costing many Muslim lives

---

⁹² Manucci, *Storia do Mogor*, vol. 2, pp. 9–10.
⁹³ Hamid al-Din Khan, *Ahkam-i 'Alamgiri*, p. 126.
⁹⁴ Khafi Khan, *Muntakhab al-Lubab*, p. 345.

'on both sides', and that the *shari'a* enjoined 'peace' and 'mercy'.⁹⁵ With this *qadi*'s banishment from court, Awrangzib's *jihad* continued and the Sultan was deposed on the pretext that: (1) he appointed 'tyrannical infidels' to posts they were not entitled by the *shari'a*; and (2) he made 'no distinction between infidelity and Islam' by forging an alliance with the chief South Asian threat to Awrangzib's regime—the Hindu Marathas led by the Bhonsle house.⁹⁶ By ignoring the *fatawa* of two successive *qadi al-qudat*s, Awrangzib clearly went beyond the choice of opinions considered above, to declare his own opinion on the matter of Abu al-Hasan's 'Islamic' credentials. However, his choice of charges against the Sultan suggests that Awrangzib's *ijtihad* remained within the theoretical bounds of jurisprudence (*fiqh*), while Akbar's extended well beyond the principles of that discipline. Thus, Awrangzib's *ijtihad* may not have been 'absolute', but it did represent absolute legislative authority in relation to the jurists. Evidently, Awrangzib's style of legislative authority is ideologically different from Akbar's, but in the institutional sense of the head of state's authority over the judiciary, it is identical.

The degree of legislative scope Awrangzib lost by limiting his absolute *ijtihad* to the bounds of jurisprudence, he gained tenfold in terms of circumscribing the juridical independence of his fractious military and bureaucratic underlings, whether by direct decree or through his judicial officers. That political need—rather than personal preference—underwrote a policy of balancing the judicial and bureaucratic/military wings of government, is at least partly evinced by the changing ethnic and class composition of the judicial classes vis-à-vis the relatively stagnant Irani and Turkic officers in the upper echelons of other wings. Khafi Khan observed the same and illustrated his point with the following episode from Lahore. Although the author says no more of *qadi* Akbar 'Ali's parentage than that he is 'a man of the east', this is enough to suggest that he was of local stock in contrast to the 'western' pedigree of bureaucrats and military officers.⁹⁷ The episode relates how Akbar 'Ali

---

⁹⁵ Ibid., p. 345.
⁹⁶ Ibid., p. 300. The post in question is al-Mawardi's *wazir al-tafwid*, which confers sweeping civil powers upon the holder upon the 'delegation' of authority by the 'Caliph', and must be held by a Muslim, as opposed to *wazir al-tanfidh*, which restricts action to the 'implementation' of the Caliph's orders, and can be held by a non-Muslim. See Chapter One.
⁹⁷ Ibid., pp. 260–62.

had fallen out with the 'high'-born governor of Lahore for presuming to act 'on terms of equality', despite his 'lower' status as a *qadi* and a local. After many verbal exchanges, the governor ordered the *qadi*'s arrest for not appearing before him when summoned, dispatching the *kotwal* (commissar) to fetch him at once. The *qadi* resisted arrest and, in the ensuing melee, he and some of his household were killed by the *kotwal*'s men. When news of the *qadi*'s death spread through the city, Khafi Khan reports, 'the learned, the illiterate, the weavers and other artisans assembled (to demonstrate) against the *subahdar*'.[98] The demonstrations, calling for the trial of the 'murderers', continued for days and are reported to have reached such a pitch that not even the governor's servants were able to walk the streets and markets. When news reached Delhi, Awrangzib ordered the immediate transfer of the governor, and the trial of the *kotwal*. While the latter was speedily found guilty and sentenced according to the aggrieved family's request of *qisas* (right of retribution), the governor's departure was blockaded by the masses, allowing the *qadi*'s family time to lodge a request for *qisas* against him in Delhi. A trial was agreed upon, but was apparently drawn out long enough for the governor to die before a verdict was reached.[99] In other words, the case of *qadi* Akbar 'Ali and the governor suggests that 'low'-born 'local' Muslim men were filling the posts of district and city-*qadi*, and that such figures not only had influence among the people, they could have their active support.[100]

As for Awrangzib's personal intervention in favour of the judiciary as a counterweight to officers in other wings of government, the number of examples is an embarrassment of riches, so two letters should suffice to illustrate the point. In one addressed to his *wazir*, Asad Khan,

---

[98] Ibid., p. 260.
[99] Ibid., pp. 261–62.
[100] Another incident of this kind also illustrates the involvement of Sufis and dates back to Shah Jahan's reign. The city is Burhanpur and, on this occasion, the governor was killed by one of his clerks. Fleeing the scene, the clerk ran to his brother, a Sufi, and explained that he killed the governor to prevent him from committing a heinous crime, which the author neglected to record. Upon hearing his brother's account, the Sufi rallied other 'fakirs' [sic] and townspeople to march to the governor's mansion and demand that the governor not be accorded the burial rites of a Muslim. After days of protest, the crowd was quieted only when reminded that the governor was a relative of Shah Jahan, and that the clerk would receive another posting, which he did (at Shah Jahan's order) after the public outcry was voluntarily subdued. See Jean Baptiste Tavernier, *Les Six Voyages*, 2 vols., trans. V. Ball (London: Oxford University Press, 1925), vol. 1, pp. 43–44.

concerning an ongoing case over which the bureaucrat was presiding, Awrangzib ordered:

> It is irreligious to imprison the plaintiff. Both the plaintiff and the defendant must be made free from the power of this suit. You should refer this case to *qadi al-qudat* so that he may decide it according to the brilliant Muslim law and there is no oppression practised on and partiality shown to either of them. God be praised, that our *qadi* is honest, good and pious; he does not look on this man or that, and in deciding the cases he considers the true facts.[101]

Another typical letter was dispatched when his son, Mirza Muhammad 'Azam, conspired to have a lower officer's *jagir* transferred to himself by complaining that the man 'drinks wine' and engages in many other 'kinds of *bid'a*'. Awrangzib responded by reminding his son that the offices of a *mirza* and a *subahdar* did not extend into the jurisdiction of a *muhtasib* (public censor). He then advised his son to inform the *sadr al-sudur* to ask the local *muhtasib* to investigate.[102] When not ordering bureaucrats, etc., to consult the judiciary, Awrangzib empowered the latter wing of the government by personally upholding their methods and sources in his dealings with officers. The *Ahkam-i 'Alamgiri* reports that when a high-ranking official descended from a Sufi of Samarqand used the phrase 'by the *karamat buniad* (miraculous/grace-laden) command' in his official orders, Awrangzib ended the practice by writing that neither his high rank nor his descent from a *pir* meant the officer possessed *karamat*.[103] Another choice example again concerns his self-serving son, Mirza Muhammad 'Azam, to whom Awrangzib wrote on another occasion:

> In order to please...[another official]...you have not dismissed the tyrant, Hasan Beg of Chakleh Kura. The people there are lamenting and bewailing and are much distressed. They say [verse]: 'If you will not give us justice, there is the Day of Judgement for our justice'. The real accountants record the tyranny of the officers in your and my accounts. Know well for compensating these actions and enquire into the condition of the inhabitants of that place, otherwise the *jagir* will be taken away from you and you will have no recompense.[104]

---

[101] 'Inayat Allah, *Ruqa'at-i 'Alamgiri*, p. 117.
[102] Hamid al-Din Khan, *Ahkam-i 'Alamgiri*, pp. 62–63.
[103] Ibid., pp. 81–82.
[104] 'Inayat Allah, *Ruqa'at-i 'Alamgiri*, pp. 19–20.

Advising the *wazir*, Asad Khan, in the matter of a local governor's misconduct, Awrangzib suggests the governor be admonished with the following words: 'The horse merchants and others are complaining. There is a true tradition [*hadith*] that "Oppression will cause darkness on the Day of Judgement." Why did you not remember this tradition?'[105] In the latter instance as well as in other such correspondence, Awrangzib's choice of words and general attitude clearly indicate his appeal to jurisprudential literature.

The last case is not the only way in which the empowerment of jurisprudence and the judiciary impacted (or were meant to impact) the lives of the subaltern classes. Although famed in contemporary scholarship for his re-imposition of *jizya*, Awrangzib is not widely recognised for having remitted more than 80 customary taxes early in his reign, in Khafi Khan's words, to 'alleviate suffering' caused the people by war and drought.[106] Awrangzib judged most taxes to be 'un-*shar'i*' and, when one considers the examples of the taxes mentioned, it is clear that they were 'tax-breaks' for herdsmen, cultivators, artisans and petty traders. They included *rahdari* (road-toll), *pandari* (on commercial real estate, from the street vendor to the banker), *buz-shumari* (on goats), *bargadi wa charai* (on grazing), *banjarah* (on petty grain merchants), and *tawanah* (on Sufi *'urs* and Hindu *jatra* festivities). Furthermore, in direct response to hunger caused by the ravages of war in his early years, Awrangzib endowed 10 'soup-kitchens' (*langar khana*) in Delhi, and 12 more in surrounding towns; he also urged state officers of all ranks to follow his example, within their respective means, and in the provinces in which they served.[107] Echoing Khafi Khan, the author of the *Ma'athir-i 'Alamgiri* states that Awrangzib paid *zakat* and besides:

> ...used to spend so much money in religious alms (*khairat*), beneficent public works, like the building of public inns (*mubarrat*), and pensions (*idrarat*), that the expenditure of former rulers had not reached even a hundredth part of it. In the blessed month of Ramzan (*Ramadhan*) he used to distribute among the needy 60,000 rupees and in other months smaller amounts than that. Numerous free kitchens (*balghur khana* or *langar khana*) for feeding weak and the poor were established in Delhi

---

[105] Ibid., p. 91.
[106] Khafi Khan, *Muntakhab al-Lubab*, pp. 93–95.
[107] Ibid., p. 131.

and other provinces; wherever there was no inn or *serai* for accommodation of travellers before, they were built.[108]

As well, the *Futuhat-i 'Alamgiri* states that when Awrangzib was informed that the people of Hyderabad (Deccan) 'on account of their poverty, were unable to pay *jizya*', he ordered that *jizya* and other taxes 'be not collected from them and that they be asked to remain in their villages and districts (*mahals*) and engage themselves in cultivation and their professions'.[109] And finally, the author of the *Ahkam-i 'Alamgiri* wrote that when the *amin* (collector) of *jizya* for Jaunpur was reported to have misappropriated Rs 40,000 and given it to charity, Awrangzib ordered the provincial *diwan* (revenue officer) not to seek restitution as the collector's act was ultimately pious.[110]

Given that such tax-breaks applied to all subjects, irrespective of religion, while *zakat* was levied on Muslims alone, fiscal policies are, in fact, a prime indicator of the politics of 'alliance building' under the ideals of the Sober Path. At the top ranks of the state, in keeping with juristic political philosophy, non-Muslim officers were exempt from *jizya*.[111] Furthermore, the *wazirat* continued to function as previously, Awrangzib's first *wazir* being the Hindu Raja Ragunath Khatri, followed by three Shi'i *wazirs* in succession, each dying in office.[112] One incident, recorded in the *Ahkam-i 'Alamgiri*, is sufficient to confirm that the same attitude of inclusiveness can be extended beyond the above appointments to the general complexion of state. When a Sunni Turani officer conspired to usurp a Shi'i Irani officer's post by accusing him of being a 'heretic', Awrangzib responded:

> What connection have worldly affairs with religion? What right have matters of religion to enter into bigotry? 'For you is your religion and for me is mine' [Quranic quote]. If this rule [of excluding 'heretics'] were to be established, it would be my duty to extricate all the [Hindu] Rajas

---

[108] Saqi Musta'idd Khan, *Ma'athir-i 'Alamgiri*, trans. J.N. Sarkar (Calcutta: Royal Asiatic Society, 1947), p. 315.

[109] Nagar, *Futuhat-i 'Alamgiri*, p. 184. Khafi Khan also reports that certain taxes on agricultural produce, such as corn, 'permitted by the Shar'...were remitted as a relief measure to lessen the hardships caused by the rising prices of grain'. Khafi Khan, *Muntakhab al-Lubab*, pp. 93–94.

[110] Hamid al-Din Khan, *Ahkam-i 'Alamgiri*, p. 93.

[111] See R.C. Hallisey, *The Rajput Rebellion Under Aurangzeb* (Columbia: University of Missouri Press, 1977).

[112] See C.M. Agrawal, *Wazirs of Aurangzeb* (Bodh-Gaya: Kauchan Publications, 1978); Laiq Ahmad, *The Prime Ministers of Aurangzeb* (Allahabad: Chugh Publications, 1976).

and their followers. Wise men disapprove of the removal from office of able officers.[113]

This is no more a 'secular' statement than it is an Intoxicated one, but clearly resorts to 'Islamic' political philosophy, particularly the notions that non-Muslims are legally permitted to serve the state to the rank of *wazir al-tanfid*, and that the appointment of officers is under the jurisdiction of *dawabit*. That this was not an isolated case is best illustrated by a statistical analysis of the *Ma'athir al-'Umara*—this recorded the names and designations of state officers—which shows that while 22.5% of Akbar's officers were Hindu, in Awrangzib's case the figure had risen to 31.6%.[114]

Aside from the employment of Shi'is and non-Muslims at the highest ranks, formal state institutions legitimated by Awrangzib's Sober Path allowed more general initiatives by which to follow the same inclusive pattern. Four types of 'under-privileged' recipients were extended 'grants' known as *soyurghal*, which has been calculated to have represented 2%–6% of the gross revenue collected by the regime under each of the 'Great Mughals', including Awrangzib.[115] The figure is echoed in studies of *taqsim* (tax receipts) for various *pargana*s (districts) and villages of Rajputana; these documents add that down to the level of villages in these *pargana*s, 1%–5% of the land was generally *'ayma*, enjoying tax-exemption.[116] Although historians such as Irfan Habib

---

[113] Hamid al-Din Khan, *Ahkam-i 'Alamgiri*, p. 88.
[114] See M. Athar Ali, *The Mughal Nobility Under Aurangzeb* (London: Asia House Publishing, 1966). Also Shah Nawaz Khan, *Ma'athir al-'Umara*, trans. H. Beveridge (Patna: Janaki Prakashan, 1979).
[115] Rafat Bilgrami, 'Women Grantees in the Mughal Empire', *Journal of the Pakistan Historical Society* 36:3 (1988): 207–14. Also see Irfan Habib, *The Agrarian System of Mughal India* (Bombay: n.p., 1963), p. 314.
[116] S.P. Gupta and S.H. Khan have published all the extant *taqsim* (tax receipts) down to the village level, of various *pargana*s in Rajputana under the *jagirdari* of Mahahraja Jaswant Singh, one of Awrangzib's highest-ranking Rajput officials. For the *pargana* of Udehi, *taqsim* survived in 1650–1800. It shows that for this entire period, the *pargana* extended about 380,000 *bigha*s (of various standards), and included approximately 130 villages (*basti*s) and 2–3 *qasaba*s. The average area declared a village, including forests, wastelands, field, etc., ranged from 1,000–2,500 *bigha*s, while *qasaba*s with villages attached cover 15,000–20,000 *bigha*s. *Pargana* Udehi realised approximately Rs. 35,000 in taxes levied on *kharif* and *rabi* crops, until sharp increases began in the 18th century. At 330,000 *bigha*s of cultivable land, however, this was a rather high-yielding *pargana*. At the elevated rates of the 18th century, extant documents reveal that the average annual payment/village, ranged from Rs. 1,000–2,000, with some villages paying as little as Rs. 1,000 and others forking out Rs. 3,500, dependent on the productivity of the land and season. In most cases, the revenue realised was considerably less than the

have argued that *'ayma* lands, and the *madad-i ma'ash* grant by which they were conferred, extended only to Muslims, others have clearly illustrated that grants (*inam*) and endowments (*waqf*) administered by the *sadr al-sudur* continued on the whole as previously—old grants and endowments being renewed, and new ones being issued to Hindus, Jains and Zoroastrians.[117] Furthermore, B.N. Goswamy and J.S. Grewal's unique collection of *madad-i ma'ash*, pertaining to one family of 'Jogis' and their 'shrine' at Jakhbar in Punjab, provides documentation to confirm that from Akbar's initial grant at the end of the 16th century, these Hindu clerics received *madad-i ma'ash* throughout and beyond Awrangzib's reign.[118] As well, the only criterion of eligibility for the *musammati* type of grant (reserved for women) was that the woman had no means of livelihood.[119] In cases where the grantee died, all of the above sources illustrate that the grant was renewed in favour of the deceased's family members.[120] In addition, elaborate rules were drawn up under Awrangzib's regime that generally favoured women heirs in the case of grants to women.[121] Although the *sadr al-sudur* was the officer ultimately in charge of endowments and grants, in Jahangir's regime an officer known as the *sadr-i inath* was appointed specifically

---

revenue assessed (*jama'*). See S.P. Gupta and S.H. Khan, *Mughal Documents: Taqsim* (Jaipur: Publication scheme, 1996), p. 23.

[117] See I. Habib, *The Agrarian System of Mughal India*, pp. 310–12; and M.L. Bhatia, *Administrative History of Medieval India* (Delhi: Radha Publications, 1992).

[118] B.N. Goswamy and J.S. Grewal. *The Mughals and the Jogis of Jakhbar* (Simla: Indian Institute of Advanced Study, 1967).

[119] Bilgrami, 'Women Grantees in the Mughal Empire', p. 208.

[120] The *madad-i ma'ash* documents pertaining to the Jogis of Jakhbar bear this out well, covering many generations and relations. Incidentally, explaining the discrepancy between Habib and Bhatia, they also show that with respect to *madad-i ma'ash*, and clearly reflecting the idea among some of the judiciary that such grants were meant for Muslims alone, the grant was revoked about 1673, as part of a general order by Awrangzib. However, the same lands were instituted in the name of the current Jogis as *jama'-i istimrar* ('fixed revenue') at the paltry rate of Rs. 107. This remission was also forwarded to heirs upon the death of the Jogi to whom it was issued, while the designation of *madad-i ma'ash* was restored in the time of Awrangzib's successor, Bahadur Shah. In other words, this was clearly an administrative shuffle, more than the cancellation of assistance to non-Muslims. For the pertinent documents, see Goswamy and Grewal, *The Mughals and the Jogis of Jakhbar*, pp. 47–193.

[121] The idea of a woman's property more generally passing to female heirs appears to have been a wider phenomenon than Awrangzib's measures for *musammati* grants. In the *Shah Jahan Nama*, 'Inayat Khan reports that upon Mumtaz Mahal's death, half her personal effects, in the amount of Rs. 10,000,000, were given to her daughter Jahanara Begum, while the other half was distributed among the other six heirs (four boys and two girls). 'Inayat Khan, *Shah Jahan Nama*, p. 71. The issue clearly deserves further study.

to consider the needs of women, and that office was maintained and held by women through Awrangzib's reign.[122] And finally, if difficulties arose in these or other matters, the Sultan himself was not exempt from judicial review, Khafi Khan recording that Awrangzib appointed *shar'i wakils*, officers seated at every provincial capital to hear from 'anybody having a legal claim against the Badshah [emperor]'.[123]

Although many more examples of continuity on the level of state institutions can be cited, which incidentally reconfirm even Akbar's heavy reliance on modes of government legitimated by the Sober Path, it is clear that there is a difference. Awrangzib's regime does not rest on an ideology in which the '72 sects of Islam and Hindus' may be dissolved, but is dependent on an acute distinction between the '72 sects of Islam and Hindus'. Regarding the specific issue of non-Muslim worship, it has already been mentioned that temple destructions took place during the reign of Shah Jahan, and studies on the issue have revealed that restrictions on non-Muslim worship in that time (as in Awrangzib's), including the demolition of temples, applied to particular localities and times in which rebellions were under way, rather than being general orders pertinent to all temples at all times.[124] Otherwise, the most obvious example of non-Muslim autonomy in personal religious conduct is illustrated by attitudes towards *sati* (widow immolation), female infanticide and child marriage—customs largely specific to the northern regions of the subcontinent, but practised by certain classes of non-Muslims and Muslims. Backtracking for a moment, it was mentioned that Akbar had sought to place a lower limit on the marriageable age to at least 12 years old, for both boys and girls, and it can be added that Monserrate mentions that Akbar banned *sati* upon

---

[122] Bilgrami, 'Women Grantees in the Mughal Empire', pp. 207–11.
[123] The circumstances of the decision to introduce *shar'i wakils* are also important in suggesting the state's responsiveness to the need for orderly administration, particularly in dealings between the state and the influential merchants of such port cities as Surat in the province of Gujarat. Khafi Khan writes that in the late stages of Shah Jahan's reign, when one of Awrangzib's rivals (Murad Bakhsh) had declared his independence in Gujarat, the governor had exacted a Rs. 500,000 loan from two Muslim merchants. Upon Awrangzib's assumption of power, the funds and promissory notes were forwarded to the Mughal treasury, which acknowledged the debt on the basis of a Hanafi ruling. Khafi Khan concludes that *shar'i wakils* were henceforth appointed to sit with the *qadis* of 'every city, subah [province] and the neighbouring territories' to ensure that such cases were dealt with judiciously. Khafi Khan, *Muntakhab al-Lubab*, pp. 251–55.
[124] See Z. Faruqi, *Aurangzeb and His Times* (Delhi: Idara-i Adabiyat-i Delli, 1972).

his insistence.[125] Yet, none of the other primary sources read here mention an actual ban on *sati*, and even if it had been issued, it and the limits on child marriage were apparently quite ineffectual as Jahangir wrote with fascination on these 'customs', suggesting they continued to be practised among non-Muslim and Muslim subaltern groups.[126] Regarding such practices among Muslims, Jahangir wrote:

> The people of Rajaur [in Kashmir] were originally Hindus. Sultan Firoz converted them. Nevertheless, their chiefs are still styled *rajas*. Practices which prevailed during the times of their ignorance are still observed among them. Thus, wives immolate themselves alive on the funeral pyres of their husbands, and bury themselves alive in their graves. It was reported that, only a few days ago, a girl of 12 years old had buried herself with her husband. Indigent parents strangle their female offspring immediately after birth. They associate and intermarry with Hindus—giving and taking daughters. As for taking, it does not so much matter, but as for giving their own daughters—heaven protect us. Orders were issued prohibiting these practices for the future, and punishments enjoined for their infraction.[127]

While Jahangir was outraged by Muslim participation, Jean Baptiste Tavernier—a French merchant trading in the region during Shah Jahan's and Awrangzib's reigns—reports that the Muslims he met informed him that *sati*, etc., could not be banned among non-Muslims as, from the perspective of the jurists, such rites belonged to the domain of 'personal law'.[128] Nevertheless, Tavernier observed that by Awrangzib's regime it had been ordered that at least with regard to *sati*, a non-Muslim woman needed her provincial governor's permission. Tavernier states

---

[125] Monserrate, *The Commentary of Father Monserrate*, p. 61. Also see Correia-Afonso, *Letters from the Mughal Court*, p. 69.

[126] Jahangir, *Tuzuk-i Jahangiri*, p. 72.

[127] Ibid., p. 135. Regarding the issue of intermarriage between Hindus and Muslims, it is worth adding that Jahangir specifically states the case of Muslim men and unconverted women 'does not so much matter', only non-Muslim husbands with Muslim wives being problematic from the standpoint of the *shari'a*. In Shah Jahan's time as well, 'Inayat Khan reports that when travelling between Kashmir and Lahore, Shah Jahan was approached by local 'sayyids and shaykhs' in Bhimbar and Gujrat (Punjab) with complaints of Hindu men married to Muslim women, and vice versa. However, the *firman* that Shah Jahan issued called only for the conversion of non-Muslim husbands, upon threat of summary divorce and fine. The *firman* is said to have led to thousands of conversions, the raising of two temples, the 'release' of 70 women and slaves from their non-Muslim 'captors', and the appointment of scholars to educate the new converts. In other words, there is no mention of the Muslim men of the region having to formally convert or divorce their wives. See 'Inayat Khan, *Shah Jahan Nama*, pp. 139–40.

[128] Tavernier, *Les Six Voyages*, vol. 2, pp. 306–07.

that where governors were Hindu, the practice continued unabated, but that Muslim governors commonly 'reason' and make 'enticing promises' to the women, even sending the latter to their own wives and daughters so 'that the effect of their remonstrations may be tried'.[129]

There were also changes at court, including the aforementioned retirement of the Tawhid-i Ilahi and Tarikh-i Ilahi, as well as bans on alcohol, gambling, prostitution and music at court, and the dismissal of astrologers from state service. When read in the context of Chapter One's discussion of legal thought, it is quite apparent that Awrangzib adopted an extreme position on the latter issues. However, even his Sober Path cannot be read to imply that Intoxicated thought was effaced under his rule, only that its place was again circumscribed by the attitudes exhibited by al-Ghazali, al-Hujwiri and their Sober heirs previously mentioned to have won Awrangzib's favour. Manucci lists 24 'physicians' at Awrangzib's court, all of Irani stock. Their titles include *Aflatun al-zaman* (Plato of the Age), *Aristu al-zaman* (Aristotle of the Age), *Jalinu al-zaman* (Galen of the Age), *Buqrat al-zaman* (Hippocrates of the Age) and *Bu 'Ali al-zaman* (Ibn Sina of the Age).[130] Francois Bernier, a French physician employed as a secretary by one of these figures, Hakim al-Mulk Danishmand Khan (a.k.a. Mulla Shafi'i), serving as the governor of Delhi in the 1660s, writes that 'astronomy, geography and anatomy are his [Danishmand Khan's] favourite pursuits'.[131] In this regard, Bernier explained William Harvey's and Jean Pequet's works on anatomy to his employer.[132] Danishmand Khan is also identified as being 'acquainted with the doctrines of the *Soufys*'.[133] Following from these metaphysical interests, Bernier translated the philosophical works of Pierre Gassendi and Rene Descartes, while his fellow secretary, a Hindu *pandit* formerly in the employ of Dara, taught his employer Vedantic philosophy.[134] In other words, although philosophy continued to be patronised, it was increasingly restricted to 'Theistic' strains, while emphasis was placed on physical sciences, as further illustrated below.

---

[129] Ibid., pp. 306–07.
[130] Manucci, *Storia do Mogor*, vol. 2, pp. 332–34.
[131] Francois Bernier, *Travels in the Mughal Empire*, trans. Archibald Constable (Delhi: S. Chand & Co., 1972), p. 353.
[132] Ibid., pp. 323–25.
[133] Ibid., p. 320.
[134] Ibid., pp. 323–25.

Interesting accounts of Awrangzib's personal attitude are also provided by Manucci and Bernier.[135] Upon his ascension to power, Awrangzib's former tutor, Mulla Salih, came to court hoping to gain advancement. Instead, he received a verbal flaying and a summary dismissal from Awrangzib's presence. The problem was the education Awrangzib had received from the '*Mulla*'. By both accounts, this included Arabic grammar, jurisprudence, theology and philosophy, but was found deficient by Awrangzib for a number of reasons. First, theology and philosophy are dismissed as 'idle and foolish propositions' in Bernier's account, and 'ornaments in talking to learned men' in Manucci's version.[136] Found lacking, according to Awrangzib, were world history, geography, political philosophy and the military arts, i.e. an education to promote the value of 'reason' and 'sound argumentation'.[137] Furthermore, Awrangzib is reported in both accounts, though in Manucci's words, to have declared:

> All your purpose and effort was to turn me into a good Arab, making me waste my time over a language which demands from 10 to 12 years to obtain a little proficiency. Meanwhile, my youth and my capacity for lofty things had vanished.[138]

Both authors add that Awrangzib concluded one would be better served if not only education, but also the practice of 'prayers', 'law' and the 'sciences', were conducted in his 'mother tongue'.[139] Awrangzib's criticism of theology and philosophy, and his praise of physical sciences while 'adhering' to the *shari'a*, again echoes the attitudes of al-Ghazali and al-Hujwiri, but illustrates how a layman with extra-scholastic concerns read their implications. The ethos this bred concerning ethnic and regional variety, as well as relations between Muslims of various sects and non-Muslims, is summed up in Awrangzib's last will and testament.

---

[135] Bernier, *Travels*, pp. 154–62; Manucci, *Storia do Mogor*, vol. 2, pp. 26–29. Interestingly, the Muslim authors of the period do not mention this incident. One may thus speculate that the incident did not but occur, but is an attempt by European authors to place European Renaissance critiques of Muslim clerics in the mouth of the 'Caliph'. However, this can be questioned as Bernier reports that he was told the tale by Danishmand Khan, who was present for the exchange (Bernier, pp. 154–55). Manucci also relates the tale second-hand (Manucci, pp. 154–55.) Thus, it appears more likely that the Muslim authors are exercising self-censorship, probably in an attempt to ensure that Awrangzib's Sober credentials are not challenged.
[136] Bernier, p. 160; Manucci, vol. 2, p. 27.
[137] Bernier, p. 160; Manucci, vol. 2, p. 29.
[138] Manucci, vol. 2, p. 29.
[139] Bernier, pp. 158–59; Manucci, vol. 2, pp. 28–29.

When advising his sons on statecraft, Awrangzib wrote that 'Iranis', though extremely haughty by nature, make the best administrators (*mutasaddis*). 'Turks', on the other hand, make the best soldiers as it is in their character to know when to retreat, unlike the 'crass stupidity of the Hindustanis, who would part with their heads but not leave their positions'.[140] A comparison is also drawn between Iranis and Hindustanis, whether Muslim or non-Muslim, in a letter to the governor of Kabul, which draws from astrology even though astrologers had been banned from court. In this letter, Awrangzib claimed that as 'the Sun is the guardian planet' of the Iranis, their 'intellectual keenness' is 'four times' that of Hindustanis, 'whose tutelary planet is Saturn'.[141] The defect in the Iranis is that by reason of the Sun's frequent 'conjunction with Venus', they are prone to 'ease-loving'. The distinction of the Hindustanis is that being 'governed by Saturn [they] are accustomed to toil'. As well, by pointing out that Saturn is more frequently in conjunction with Jupiter than Venus, Awrangzib suggested that Hindustanis, both Muslim and non-Muslim, are more adept at war than Iranis. Furthermore, Hindustan does not refer to all of South Asia, and the same cross-religious attitude is applied within South Asia, as in the distinction between Hindustan and the 'Deccan', most of which was not formally annexed until Awrangzib's regime. For example, echoing the rhetoric of Akbar's, Jahangir's and Shah Jahan's reigns, Khafi Khan refers to Awrangzib's defeat of the Sultanate of Golconda as that of the 'Deccani army', and that state's officers, irrespective of religious persuasion, as 'the Deccanis'.[142] That is to say, whatever one's religion, ethnicity or class, those born in Iran, Hindustan or the Deccan, are born under that regions' respective 'stars', Awrangzib included.[143]

---

[140] Awrangzib's will is included in Hamid al-Din Khan, *Ahkam-i 'Alamgiri*, pp. 47–48.

[141] Ibid., p. 105.

[142] This trend was already established in Mughal writings about the time of Akbar's reign, as attested by the earlier reference to Qandahari's work. For Awrangzib, an example can be seen in Khafi Khan, *Muntakhab al-Lubab*, pp. 305–09.

[143] This sense of 'being' Hindustani is also reflected in the writings of Akbar's, Jahangir's and Shah Jahan's reign. For example, Jahangir writes of being 'brought up in Hindustan', while 'Inayat Khan, writing at the beginning of Awrangzib's reign, speaks of goods 'manufactured in Hindustan' without reference to particular localities. Furthermore, the distinction between 'Hindustan' and the 'Deccan' is very strongly asserted. See Jahangir, *Tuzuk-i Jahangiri*, pp. 52, 69, 76, 78, 82, 100, 103; 'Inayat Khan, *Shah Jahan Nama*, pp. 26, 61–62, 166–67, 245.

All of the above instances of Awrangzib's rule, whether concerned with the patronage of non-legalistic scholarship or the specifics of his fiscal policies and state expenditures, illustrate that while Awrangzib shifted the state, ideologically and institutionally, from the Intoxicated Way to the Sober Path, his Sobriety, like Akbar's Intoxication, remained sufficient to legitimate a great degree of inclusiveness, while exhibiting a 'pragmatic streak'. The ultimate ethos this shift, in fact, represents is one from antinomianism and latitudinarianism to a regard for legalistic doctrines. Nevertheless, this cannot be read as inherently 'anti-Hindu', placing most subjects under continuous 'pressure to convert' and contrary to the 'politics of alliance', given the broadly 'hospitable' aspect of the Sober Path. Recalling that both Akbar and Awrangzib were representatives of an education in an 'Islam' that ventured far beyond legalism, that legalism itself accommodated great latitude with regard to custom, and that both their regimes could be argued to have benefited the longevity of the state, both appear best depicted as inclusive of and responsive to the 'India' of their day, within the limits and from the perspectives of the Intoxicated Way and Sober Path, respectively. Just compare their attitudes towards European influence as a concluding example. First, in Awrangzib's regime, merchants like Tavernier, artillery-men like Manucci, and physicians such as Bernier were far more common than in Akbar's time. Furthermore, while Monserrate attested that Akbar invited the Portuguese to send embassies, Bernier recorded that Awrangzib received French, Dutch and British embassies. Clearly, as the number of Europeans and their further entanglement in the economic and socio-cultural regimes of South Asia grew, the Sober Path did not imply opposition to their presence or employment. Furthermore, as mention of Manucci's profession suggests, there is also evidence that interest had extended beyond intellectual and mercantile interests to acquiring European technology.[144] However, conflict had also ventured past clashes due to the Portuguese maritime activities that troubled Akbar. During his reign, Awrangzib launched raids against Portuguese and British 'factories' providing supplies to his nemesis Shivaji Bhonsle,

---

[144] A more direct reference to interest in European technology is shown by a daily register (*roznamacha*) issued by the commander of a Deccani fort in 1669, which not only verifies the posting of English gunners at the fort, but also the inspection of their equipment. See Y.H. Khan, ed. *Selected Documents from Aurangzeb's Reign, 1659–1706* (Hyderabad: Central Records Office, 1958), p. 68.

illustrating the growing influence of European traders in South Asian politics by the late 17th century.[145] Ultimately, however, the cautious yet open approach to the Europeans exhibited by Akbar's regime, is no less open and no more cautious under Awrangzib. The greater scale of European influences, however, cannot be discounted from raising alarm in some quarters. Once again, this can be best symbolised by Awrangzib's favoured scholars and their attitudes towards tobacco.

In Khafi Khan's list of prominent Sufis of the day, he includes one Mir Murtada Wa'iz Multani, whose ultra-Sober credentials can be established by the fact that he did not view even *sama'* as legal, although most Sober Sufis outside the Naqshbandiyya did.[146] Multani came to the attention of the *qadis* of Awrangabad because he had been stressing the unlawfulness of tobacco in his preaching, and criticising state officials, including *qadis*, who indulged in the habit. Eventually Multani was summoned to argue his case before an assembly of *qadis*. His followers are reported to have wanted to mob the *qadis* and insult them, but their '*pir*' persuaded them not to. In the debate that followed the *qadis* argued that Multani spoke about 'the prohibition of the use of tobacco in highly exaggerated terms', and without the citation of 'standard works' or the *fatawa* of '*mujtahids*'.[147] Multani only responded by humouring the *qadis*, much to the delight of the 'thousands' of followers who had accompanied him to the mosque in which the meeting was held.[148] Needless to say, the debate ended without resolution, but the fact that it took place raises awareness of the reality that physicians were no longer alone in viewing tobacco as a 'custom' unsanctioned by the 'wise'.

---

[145] For example, an entry from the register (*siyaha huzur*) from 1690, calls for the blockade of the 'Portuguese and British' (*farang wa angrez*) ports supplying Shivaji's forts. Also, in 1686, after the British attempted to blockade trade to win concession, Awrangzib raided various British trading posts, only re-establishing British rights to trade after due submission was paid. See Khan, ed. *Selected Documents from Aurangzeb's Reign, 1659–1706*, pp. 220–21.
[146] Khafi Khan, *Muntakhab al-Lubab*, pp. 553–54.
[147] Ibid., pp. 553–54.
[148] Ibid., p. 554.

Conclusion: The Trouble with 'Unbounded' Indicism

Practice does not exactly match theory, whether speaking of the world of Mughal elites and the complex of thought that was doctrinal Islam in their day, or Mughal sources and the dominant paradigm about 'Islam' and 'India' through which contemporary historians read them. But whereas the bounds of hospitality and hostility towards the 'Indic' practices exhibited by Mughal elites approximated the rich and varied set of ideas and institutions that was doctrinal Islam in the 16th and 17th centuries, contemporary historians who approach doctrine as statically legalistic and culturally intrusive fall far shorter of accurately resolving the relationship between Mughal 'connectedness' with the Muslim World and 'embeddedness' in South Asia depicted in the sources available to them. This is nowhere better illustrated than by the false dichotomy contemporary historians commonly draw between Akbar's 'anti-Islamic' hospitality towards 'India,' and Awrangzib's 'pro-Islamic' hostility to the world that surrounded him. Their intellectual proclivities, as well as their ideological and institutional regimes, in fact, resolve as a rather different reflection of theory in practice when viewed through the lens of an alternative paradigm. Akbar, Awrangzib and their supporters were clearly well educated in the Intoxicated Way and Sober Path. When confronted with governing a region defined by multiple traditions and identities, therefore, Akbar knew that Caliphal authority, Sufi, Ishraqi and other philosophies would serve himself and his supporters. When bequeathed the same multiplicity, although aligned in rather different ways, Awrangzib knew that continuity in terms of Caliphal authority would be sagacious, but that alternative forms of Sufism, philosophy, etc., were the order of his day. They could afford these tactics, because neither Paths and Ways were 'transgressions' of the complex of thought and institutions that is doctrinal Islam; rather, both provided 'Islamic' solutions for the accommodation of the 'Indic' diversity in which they lived and sought to rule.

Doctrinal Islam's 'hospitality', in the context of elite Mughal culture, ranges from no more than the legitimisation of thought and institutions also legitimated by the non-Islamic, to the synthesis of Islamic and non-Islamic scriptures. These are precisely the relations drawn by many of the philosophers, the knowledge of all communities being 'equivalent'. This is exactly the relationship represented by the 'wujudi' Sufis' declaration that the *shari'a* of Muslims and the laws of non-Muslims are equal as 'custom'. And these are the specific thrusts of Akbar's intellectual and political initiatives. All of the above Intoxicated ideas promote the 'equivalence' of Islamic and non-Islamic thought and institutions, i.e. the end of the '72 sects of Islam and the Hindus' in exchange for the relatively free reign of class, vocational, tribal and ethnic 'customs'. The term 'hostility' also has its value. Cases have, after all, been cited of the destruction of non-Muslim sacred spaces in the name of Islam. Furthermore, the theologians not only viewed non-Abrahamic scriptures as unsound, but argued that any 'Islamic' doctrine that interprets the Qur'an to imply an 'absolutely immanent' divinity is *bid'a, shirk* or *kufr*. The jurists viewed any individual or community that did not live within the legal gambit of acknowledged 'schools' in similar light, and the stated ideal of some 'wujudi' and all 'shuhudi' Sufis was the equation of *tariqa* and *shari'a*. The latter are undoubtedly the thrusts of Awrangzib's political and intellectual initiatives, and they promoted cultures that reign in class, vocational, tribal and ethnic customs while highlighting firm borders between individual sects among the '72'.

However, it has also been shown that the Intoxicated Way is not entirely hospitable, nor the Sober Path resolutely hostile to locality. The distinction which Ibn al-'Arabi makes between the 'religion of God' and the 'religion of created beings' illustrates that Intoxicated Sufis and philosophers could be theoretically hostile to certain practices, while the broad acknowledgement of customary law by the jurists shows that they could be hospitable to many practices. As a result, in the context of Akbar, smoking tobacco was approached as a 'custom' foreign to the works of Muslim 'wise men' and so subject to the evaluation of various 'Islamic' scholars. Meanwhile, by the time of Awrangzib, *mufti*s and *qadi*s had apparently argued that smoking tobacco was a custom acceptable to the *shari'a*, telling their Sufi opponent that he could cite no reputed juristic works against smoking. In other words, the absolute distinction implied by hospitality and hostility cannot be readily transferred to the Intoxicated Way or the Sober Path. Rather, one must conclude that reflecting the Intoxicated Way and the Sober Path, both Akbar's and Awrangzib's regimes represent practical and adaptive measures open to building alliances and religious flexibility, in neither case by 'transgressing' Islam, but by invoking various aspects of Islamic thought, ideologically and institutionally. The difference is the terms on which each is inclusive or exclusive; the Intoxicated Way by means of a 'melting pot' with regard to religion, the Sober Path by means of 'multi-culturalism'. In both respects, however, 'embeddedness' is a function of 'connectedness'.

Ultimately, the trouble that the above approach poses the concept of Indicism (and, for that matter, similar conceptions of Arabism, Persianism, Turkism, Africanism, etc.) is that Islam is not only embedded in 'India', but India is embedded in 'Islam'. Furthermore, given the attitudes exhibited towards growing European political and cultural influence, Islam is not connected to Europe, but Europe is being connected to Islam. Any consideration of the transformation of Islamic thought and institutions in colonial South Asia, therefore, cannot rest on the assumptions of Indicism, or be merely interpreted in the light of the influence of 'Western' education upon an otherwise stagnant, legalistic tradition. Rather, the categories of Islamic thought, the disciplines and/or schools that inhere in each, and the dynamism of the cultural attitudes embodied in the Intoxicated Way and the Sober Path must be given due recognition. These are signifiers of knowledge for those educated in them, just as the dominant paradigm of Islamic legalism and exclusivity reflects the knowledge of so many contemporary historians still educated in the ethos of Orientalism, even if change over time is apparent.

PART TWO

TRANSFORMATIONS:
ISLAM AND COLONIALISM

CHAPTER THREE

CODIFICATION AND A 'NEW' SOBER PATH

Two hundred and forty years after Awrangzib's death, the 'nation-states' of India and Pakistan appeared on the South Asian scene, born of a host of new political and socio-economic factors, but legitimated in the name of old religions. In the 60 years that have elapsed since, the legacy and further development of those new conditions remain evident in the continuous use of religious affiliations as primary signifiers of difference, most succinctly illustrated by the names given to the longest-range missiles that India and Pakistan have targeted at each other: India's 'Agni' and 'Surya', named after Hindu gods, and Pakistan's 'Ghaznawi' and 'Ghuri', referencing the 10th–12th century Sultanates that expanded Muslim rule beyond Sind. It will require the remaining chapters of this book to unravel the multifarious influences that account for such deadly rhetoric, but the turns taken by those following the Sober Path in the wake of Awrangzib's reign provides a convenient starting point.

In the post-colonial context, four organisations have come to dominate the representation of the Sober Path: *Jama'at-i 'Ulama'-i Hind* (f. 1919), *Jama'at-i 'Ulama'-i Islam* (f. 1945), *Jama'at-i Islami* (f. 1941) and *Tablighi Jama'at* (f. 1927). That 'connectedness' with the Muslim World and 'embeddedness' in South Asia was not effaced in the centuries after Awrangzib's death, is best evinced by the fact that the influence of political fragmentation and cultural regionalisation throughout the 18th century, overlapped with British imperial expansion under the auspices of the English East India Company (1765–1857), followed by the 'direct rule' of the 'Crown' in the period of the British Raj (1858–1947), did not discourage the scholars of the Jama'at-i 'Ulama'-i Hind to work closely with Mohandas K. Gandhi (d. 1948) and the Indian National Congress (f. 1885) in seeking to secure 'Indian' independence. Although schism is apparent in the Jama'at-i Islami's less-motivated support for Congress, the Jama'at-i 'Ulama'-i Islam's formation in support of the Pakistan movement, and the Tablighi Jama'at's political quietude, the most striking feature of these organisations is that they are intellectually connected to one *madrasa* which was founded in 1867 outside Delhi: *Dar al-'Ulum* at Deoband.¹

Barbara Metcalfe has produced the most authoritative work on the Deobandi *madrasa*, but the overwhelming influence of this body's line of thinking is amply suggested by a singular statistic: by 1900, at least 40 *madrasa*s had been modelled on that at Deoband, and by 1967, it had spawned 9,000 institutional clones across South Asia.² In other words, an exposition of the ideas taught at Deoband is essential to any endeavour seeking to trace doctrinal Islam in the transition from Mughal to post-colonial periods. As the differences of opinion concerning nationalism suggest, however, the echoes of Deoband in contemporary South Asia cannot minimise the fact that doctrinal considerations alone do not cover the scope of change observed since Awrangzib's death. In fact, political, economic and broader cultural upheaval is the overriding condition of the entire period from Awrangzib's death to the present. The question is how changing doctrine and society are, or should be, connected in contemporary scholarship?

Speaking of the 18th century alone, Burton Stein echoes the views of most others in the historiography of modern South Asia, when he suggests that the success of 'Great Mughal' policies contributed to the 'the most transforming element of all that led to the ultimate downfall of the Mughals and shaped the era that succeeded'—the rise of a 'new class' in South Asia, 'an indigenous capitalist class'.³ Adding more detail, Chris Bayly has shown that by the 18th century, two social groups,

---

¹ See Barbara D. Metcalfe, 'Living Hadith in the Tablighi Jama'at', *Journal of Asian Studies* 52:3 (1993): 584–608; and 'Traditionalist Islamic Activism: Deoband, Tablighis and Talibs', *Social Science Research Council* (November 2004). The latter is available on-line at http://www.ssrc.org/sept11/essays/metcalf.htm. Also see Seyyid Vali Nasr, *The Vanguard of the Islamic Revolution: The Jama'at-i Islami of Pakistan* (Berkeley: University of California Press, 1994); and Yohanan Friedmann, 'The Attitude of the Jamiyyat-i Ulama-i Hind to the Indian National Movement and the Establishment of Pakistan', *The Ulama in Modern History*, ed. Gabriel Baer (Jerusalem: Israeli Oriental Society, Asian and African Studies, 1971), pp. 157–83. For the personalities and politics of these movements in the colonial era, including their perspectives on nationalism, see Chapter Six.

² See Barbara D. Metcalfe, *Islamic Revival in British India: Deoband, 1860–1900* (Princeton: Princeton University Press, 1982).

³ Burton Stein, *A History of India* (Oxford: Blackwell, 1998), p. 202. Also note that portions of this chapter have been previously published as M. Reza Pirbhai, 'British Indian Reform and Pre-Colonial Trends in Islamic Jurisprudence', *Journal of Asian History* 42:1 (2008): 36–63.

outside the ranks of state officials, held capital.[4] The first was a 'landed gentry' (including tribal and caste heads), whose wealth and status were dependent on hereditary ownership of property and commodity production. The second was a commercial class of bankers and merchants who had been enriched by growth in domestic and intercontinental trade. These 'capitalists' rivalled the fiscal importance of cultivators by the late 17th century and, as attested to by Awrangzib's perpetual campaigning, whether landlords, merchants or bankers, they were less susceptible to state control. Thus, Mughal power having been eroded by the state's inability to harness the revenue derived from new segments of the tax-base, the state's highest officers yielded to the demand for capital by fragmenting into more local political entities by the 1720s, entities in which the capitalist played a larger role.[5] An example of this new accommodation of power is provided by the fact that the Mughals' 'successor states' responded to the lack of *jagirs* (land grants) arising in Awrangzib's reign, by turning to 'tax-farming' as the prime mode of revenue collection, an institution dependent on bankers and entrepreneurs.[6] Such 'innovative' measures account for the longevity of latter-day regimes.

---

[4] For example, see C. Bayly, *Indian Society and the Making of the British Empire* (Cambridge: Cambridge University Press, 1988). Also, C. Bayly, *Rulers, Townsmen and Bazaars: North Indian Society in the Age of British Expansion, 1770-1870* (Cambridge: Cambridge University Press, 1983). Further perspectives can be gleaned from such works as David Washbrook, 'South Asia, the World System and World Capitalism', *South Asia and World Capitalism*, ed. S. Bose (Delhi: Oxford University Press, 1990); Eric Stokes, *The Peasant and the Raj* (Cambridge: Cambridge University Press, 1978); Sugata Bose, *Peasant Labour and Colonial Capital* (Cambridge: Cambridge University Press, 1993).

[5] For a primary work covering the 18th century, see Ghulam Husayn Khan, *Siyar al-Muta'kharin*, trans. Haji Mustapha (Calcutta: J. White, 1790). This is a particularly pertinent work, though by no means the only history by a Muslim of the period, because it was one of the earliest works translated into English by a South Asian Muslim soon after it was written. Secondary works include: Muzaffar Alam, *The Crisis of Empire in Mughal North India, 1707-48* (Delhi: Oxford University Press, 1993); Satish Chandra, *Parties and Politics at the Mughal Court, 1707-1740* (Aligarh: Muslim University Press, 1959); and R.B. Barnett, *North India Between Empires: Awadh, the Mughals and the British, 1720-1801* (Berkeley: University of California Press, 1980). Also see Z.U. Malik, 'Religious Perceptions and Attitudes of Later Mughals', *Journal of Objective Studies* 6:2 (1994); 50-68; Z. Malik, 'The Subah of Kashmir Under the Later Mughals', *Medieval India* 2 (1972): 249-62; and B.S. Singh, 'The North-West Frontier Under the Later Mughals', *Quarterly Review of Historical Studies* 11 (1971-72): 41-45.

[6] For a study of the early use of tax farming by the British, see E.F. Irschick, 'Order and Disorder in Colonial South India', *Modern Asian Studies* 23:3 (1989): 459-92. For the early use of tax farming among South Asians, Muslim and non-Muslim, see Andre Wink, *Land and Sovereignty in India* (Cambridge: Cambridge University Press,

The demise of latter-day Muslim polities has its own logic, representing the 'most transformative element' in the history of the 19th and 20th centuries—colonialism. The measures taken by successor states to adjust to capitalisation only hastened the development of the capitalist classes as the bankers and entrepreneurs involved in tax-farming not only gained capital, but reinvested it in manufacturing and property.[7] As well, Stein observes that 'scribal groups' and 'ideologues', represented by 'educated and cultivated' Muslims, provided the administrative skills and legitimated 'new rulerships'.[8] Both are significant because Bayly and others go on to establish that 'many of these elements later provided capital, knowledge and support for the East India Company, thus becoming its uneasy collaborators in the creation of colonial India'.[9] In the final analysis, therefore, again in Bayly's words, the East India Company achieved political power by doing 'what local Indian rulers had been doing for the last century'.[10] Others, such as Ranajit Guha and Partha Chatterjee, may take issue with the particulars of Bayly's argument for the rise of British colonialism, but none (including myself) challenge the notion that the regime which Britain and its 'capitalist' collaborators instituted ushered in far-reaching change in the political, economic and cultural norms that had previously defined the region.

Tracing the transformation of South Asia's intellectual and cultural regimes, beginning in the pre-colonial context of the 18th century, Francis Robinson echoes the views of a host of historians in writing that, despite political regionalisation, 'there continued to be enough patronage and creativity' for some to compare the period 'with the late Renaissance in Italy, the golden age of Spain and the era of French

---

1986); and Noman Ahmad Siddiqqi, *Land Revenue Administration under the Mughals, 1700–50* (Bombay: Aligarh Muslim University, 1970).

[7] For an insightful glimpse of the relationship between capitalist classes and the Muslim successor states in a singular context, see K. Chatterjee, 'Trade and Darbar Politics in Bengal Subah, 1733–1757', *Modern Asian Studies* 26:2 (1992): 233–73.

[8] Stein, *A History of India*, p. 202.

[9] Bayly, *Indian Society and the Making of the British Empire*, p. 4. For the East India Company, see John Keay, *The Honorable Company* (London: Harper & Collins, 1991); I.E. Roberts, *History of British India under the Company and the Crown* (London: Oxford University Press, 1983); and P.J. Marshall, *Bengal: The British Bridgehead* (Cambridge: Cambridge University Press, 1988). For an Orientalist perspective on the role of the British in South Asia written early in the 19th century, see James Mill, *History of British India* (London: Baldwin, Cradock & Joy, 1817).

[10] Bayly, *Indian Society and the Making of the British Empire*, p. 6.

rococo'.[11] *Maktab*s had carried Persian literacy 'outside the ashraf [aristocratic] class' where literary activity was booming, 'rational sciences' continued to be transmitted through *madrasa*s equipped with a new 'curriculum' (*dars-i nizamiyya*), 'mystical traditions' were furthered by numerous Sufi orders, and Shi'i scholarship and institutions were firmly planted.[12] A number of 'new' cultural trends are also noteworthy, including the flowering of regional vernaculars, such as Bengali, Punjabi, Sindhi and Urdu, a growth in *hadith* scholarship, and an assault on established mystical and Shi'i traditions by certain Sunni schools and Sufi orders.[13] If the rise of the capitalist classes was the driving force behind political and socio-economic change, however, the same historians largely argue that the rise of British authority accounts for intellectual and cultural transformations of more significant varieties. Consider, for example, the discussion of legal transformations heralded by the onset of British rule.

Historians of British legal reform unanimously declare that from the moment the East India Company gained footholds in South Asia at Madras, Calcutta, Bombay and Surat, 'Royal Charters' insured that English civil and criminal law would play a role in future administration.[14] A.C. Banerjee's study has shown that the Charter of 1726 is important: it not only empowered the East India Company with legislative rights in terms of 'bye-laws, rules and ordinances for...government', but

---

[11] Francis Robinson, *The 'Ulama of Farangi Mahall* (Delhi: Permanent Black, 2001), p. 20. Robinson's presentation in this regard echoes a long list of previous scholarship, beginning with such works as H. Goetz, *The Crisis of Indian Civilization in the Eighteenth and Early Nineteenth Centuries* (Calcutta: University of Calcutta Press, 1938).

[12] Robinson, *The 'Ulama of Farangi Mahall*, pp. 20–27. It should be noted that in the South Asian context, '*ashraf*' refers to all Muslim ruling classes, rather than merely '*sayyids*' (Qurayshi/Arab descent). See I. Ahmad, *Caste and Social Stratification Among the Muslims* (Delhi: Manohar, 1973). The '*dars-i nizamiyya*' is taken up in the following chapter.

[13] Robinson, *The 'Ulama of Farangi Mahall*, pp. 27–31.

[14] Given the import of the topic, much has been written on the legal reforms implemented by the British colonial regime, whether under the East India Company or the Crown. For general overviews of the British legal regime, see A.C. Banerjee, *English Law in India* (Delhi: Abhinav Publications, 1984); and Abdul Hamid, *A Chronicle of British Indian Legal History* (Jaipur: RBSA Publishers, 1991). For a work specifically concerned with the decline of indigenous systems of law, Muslim and Hindu, see Marc Galanter, 'The Displacement of Traditional Law in Modern India', *Law and Society in Modern India* (Delhi: Oxford University Press, 1989), pp. 15–36. For works on Islamic law under colonial rule in particular, see K.P. Saksena, *Muslim Law as Administered in India and Pakistan* (Lucknow: Eastern Book Co., 1963); and M.R. Anderson, 'Islamic Law and the Colonial Encounter in British India', *Institutions and Ideologies*, D. Arnold and P. Robb, eds. (London: Curzon Press, 1993). Further works are cited below.

also set up a 'Mayor's Court', presided over by a British government-assigned judge, as the highest court of appeal. With this Charter, the British government formally entered the legal processes of South Asia.[15] At the same time, the Mughal Shah 'Alam's (r. 1748–1806) *farman* of 1765—the document by which the East India Company gained the *diwani* (revenue administration) of Bengal, Bihar and Orissa—called for Muslim and Hindu subjects to be governed according to Islamic and Hindu law, respectively.[16] The eventual result of this jurisprudential meeting was the Hastings Plan of 1772.

According to the Hastings Plan, drafted by then Governor-General Warren Hastings and adopted as policy in 1780, Islamic law was recognised in the realm of personal matters alone. Section 27 of the 1780 regulation states: 'In all suits regarding, Inheritance, Succession, Marriage...and Other religious usages or institutions, the laws of the Quran with respect to Muhammadans...shall be invariably adhered to'.[17] As well, criminal law was added when, by the late 1770s, a number of petitions and letters from the officers of the East India Company expressed the opinion that English penal law would not be well received and was, in one author's opinion, 'a matter of the most serious importance, and big with consequences most alarming to the natives of India'.[18] In Banerjee's words, the result was that 'the territorial jurisdiction of the Supreme Court [formerly Mayor's Court] was cut up into two distinct sectors. In territories outside Calcutta it would determine only "actions for wrongs and trespass"—obviously according to English Law. In Calcutta it would determine all civil and criminal actions according to English Law, subject to the condition that in suits relating to inheritance, succession and contract it would apply Muslim Law to the Muslims and Hindu Law to the Hindus'.[19] In addition, the Charter of 1781 stipulated that Parliament reserved the 'power to define the extent to which native law and usage should be given usage recognition'.[20] Except in criminal and personal matters, therefore, *muftis, qadi*s

---

[15] Banerjee, *English Law in India*, p. 11.
[16] For a discussion of East India Company motives, see A.K. Dutta, 'Why did the East India Company Recognise Hindu and Muslim Law?' *Western Colonial Policy*, N.R. Ray, ed. (Calcutta: Institute of Historical Studies, 1981), pp. 173–82.
[17] This Section of the 1780 Regulation is cited in K.P. Saksena, *Muslim Law as Administered in India and Pakistan*, p. 41.
[18] Cited in Banerjee, *English Law in India*, p. 24.
[19] Ibid., p. 25.
[20] Cited in Saksena, *Muslim Law as Administered in India and Pakistan*, p. 41.

and the very discipline of Islamic jurisprudence (*fiqh*) would play no part under East India Company governance.

The term applied to the system of jurisprudence fostered by Hastings Plan is 'Anglo-Muhammadan Law'. Betraying her adherence to the dominant approach to Islamic thought, Ayesha Jalal chimes a common note in suggesting that 'the bulging corpus of Anglo-Muhammadan law testifies to the fact that Muslim personal law, far from falling into disuse, received its greatest boost under British colonialism'.[21] What such historians fail to appreciate is that Anglo-Muhammadan law differs from Islamic jurisprudence of old in a variety of substantive ways that makes it anything but 'Islamic' in the sense so far considered. A noted scholar of Islamic jurisprudence, Joseph Schacht, describes this creation as a 'symbiosis', a 'new' jurisprudence, 'the aim of which, in contrast with Islamic jurisprudence... is not to evaluate a given body of legal raw material from the Islamic angle, but to apply, inspired by modern English jurisprudence, autonomous juridical principles' to the 'definition' of the *shari'a*.[22] Applying Weberian concepts, Scott A. Kugle argues that the shift was from a 'substantively rational' method of jurisprudence to a 'formally rational' system, such that 'case law' was substituted for 'codes'.[23] He goes on to describe two types of codification—'conceptual' and 'textual'—both of which require deeper consideration. Regarding the conceptual side of codification, Kugle writes, 'the British viewed the whole of Islamic law as a code. They imagined it to have been already completely codified [in an authoritative text] in the remote past and ready to be applied'.[24] But British judicial officers also held other conceptual biases, leading them to textual codification. Almost as soon as the system was instituted, debate arose regarding the efficacy of including 'native judges'. As early as 1788, the prime criticism issued by the likes of Indologist and judge in the Supreme Court of Bengal in Hastings' days, William Jones, was that as British judges were not learned in Arabic, they relied on the opinions of 'native lawyers and scholars', by whom the British judge could be 'misled'.[25] That is to say, race and colonial expediency were also 'conceptual'

---

[21] Ayesha Jalal, *Self and Sovereignty* (London: Routledge, 2000), p. 150.
[22] J. Schacht, *Introduction to Islamic Law* (Oxford: Oxford University Press, 1962), p. 96.
[23] Scott Alan Kugle, 'Framed, Blamed and Renamed: The Recasting of Islamic Jurisprudence in Colonial South Asia', *Modern Asian Studies* 35:2 (January 2001): 257–313.
[24] Ibid., pp. 270–71.
[25] Banerjee, *English Law in India*, pp. 31–32.

features of the tendency to codify.²⁶ Either way, Jones' remedy was to prepare legal digests that would eliminate the need for 'corrupt native lawyers'. The influence of all the above conceptualisations can be read in the fact that among the earliest published translations from Arabic or Persian to English, works on personal law feature prominently. 'One text, the *Hedaya* [sic]', writes Kugle, 'forms the foundation of Anglo-Muhammadan law'.²⁷

The paucity of works, not to repeat the intent of eliminating non-British judges, illustrates that by the turn of the 19th century, the end of one of the cornerstones of the Sober Path—*fiqh*—was set. Furthermore, treatises on law such as Neil Baillie's *The Muhammadan Law of Inheritance*, first published in 1832, would even replace the text mentioned above.²⁸ As an 1815 publication penned by Alexander Tytler attests, underlying such moves remained the mantra of 'universally corrupt' and unduly powerful 'native' officers, as well as, in Tytler's words, the hope:

> That the time is fast approaching when we shall have justice administered by Europeans only, as Circuit judges, and when the Mussulman [i.e. Muslim] Law, in criminal cases, shall be altogether disregarded.²⁹

---

²⁶ For a valuable consideration of the systemically racist nature of colonial rule, see R. Ross, ed. *Racism and Colonialism* (Leiden: E.J. Brill, 1982).

²⁷ *Al-Hidaya*, by Burhan al-Din 'Ali Marghinani (d. 1196) was translated by Charles Hamilton at Warren Hastings' request and, as Kugle continues, 'Hastings did not just find a text. [In translation] He created one. It may generally be seen to belong to the genre of *fatawa* literature. Along with this text, the *Fatawa-i 'Alamgiri* was also translated, and like the *Hedaya*, was transformed in various ways. For example, in the case of the *Hedaya*, the translator could not understand why students' opinions could differ from those of their teacher. Thus, he only included the opinions of Abu Hanifa.' Kugle, 'Framed, Blamed and Renamed', p. 272. The *Hidaya* not commenting on inheritance, a handful of supplementary works was also translated. The earliest examples are William Jones' translation of Siraj al-Din Muhammad Sajawandi's (d. 1411) *Fara'id al-Sajawandi*, published as W. Jones, trans. *Al-Sirajiyyah* (Calcutta, 1792). Also, a work by 'Ali al-Rahbi's (d. 1183) was published as W. Jones, trans. *The Mahomedan Law of Succession* (London: C. Dilly, 1782). A translation of *Mi'rat al-Masa'il* (author not given) was also published as F. Gladwin, trans. *An Epitome of Muhammadan Law* (Calcutta: W. Mackay, 1786).

²⁸ Neil Baillie, *The Muhammadan Law of Inheritance According to Abu Hanifa and his Followers* (Calcutta: 1832).

²⁹ Alexander F. Tytler, *Considerations on the Present Political State of India* (London: Black, Parry & Co., 1815), pp. 114–15. Also see R. Grant, *A Sketch of the History of the East India Company from its Formation to the Regulation Act of 1773* (London: Black, Parry & Co., 1813).

By the 1850s, reports from British judicial officers in South Asia confirm that English law and personal codes had begun to beat out the 'native lawyer' and his jurisprudential methodology.[30] As previously mentioned, Kugle is one among many contemporary historians to argue that the effect of the above developments was a turn from a 'substantively rational' (Islamic) to a 'formally rational' (English) jurisprudential method. The result of this turn is also quite universally argued to have been the rigidification of religious and sectarian boundaries. For example, K. Prior has illustrated this by means of East India Company intervention in religious disputes, M. Mines with transformations of notions of the 'self' before the law, and S. Frietag with regard to the application of criminal law.[31] In other words, there can be no doubt that British legal reforms hastened the rise of religiously defined communitarian identities, usually referenced as 'communalism', not by 'boosting' Muslim personal law, as Jalal contends, but by not, insofar as colonial jurisprudential theory eliminated variety of opinion and allowances for customary law in Islamic jurisprudence.

Yet there is also room for a critique of Kugle, Prior, *et al.*, for such characterisations of 'colonial difference' do not adequately address two critical factors. The first is an obvious distance between British legal theory and practice. As Jalal has noted, 'confronted with a welter of regionally and locally specific social arrangements...colonial officials

---

[30] This was not an even transition, but one that occurred at different rates in each of the 'Presidencies'. As one official recorded in 1852, in Bombay, where criminal law was concerned, 'all reference to Mohammedan Law has long since been abrogated' in favour of 'one extensive Regulation enacted in 1827'. In Bengal and Madras, the process was more gradual. In 1802, 'mutilation' was abolished as a form of punishment. In 1818, *fiqh* rules of evidence were pushed aside when the highest East India Company court (Sudder Court) gained the power to over-rule acquittals by *fatwa*, and in 1829, the same power was granted the lower court judges (Session Court). The author declares that as a result, since 1829, 'English law of evidence is now the guide of the courts in the trial of criminal cases'. See *The Judicial System of British India* (London: Pelham Richardson, 1852), pp. 22–23, 25–27. Also see *Proposal of a Plan for Remodelling the Government of India* (London: Smith, Elder & Co., 1853); J.S. Buckingham, *Plan for the Future Government of India of India* (London: Partridge & Oakey, 1853); A. Annand, *A Brief Outline of the Existing System for the Government of India* (London: Saunders & Benning, 1832); and J.S. Mill, *Memorandum of the Improvements in the Administration of India During the Last 30 Years* (London: W.H. Allen, 1858).

[31] See S. Freitag, 'Crime in the Social Order of Colonial North India', *Modern Asian Studies* 25:2 (1991): 227–61; M. Mines, 'Courts of Law and Styles of Self in Eighteenth-Century Bengal: From Hybrid to Colonial Self', *Modern Asian Studies* 35:1 (2001): 33–74; K. Prior, 'Making History: The State's Intervention in Urban Religious Disputes in the North-Western Provinces in the Early Nineteenth Century', *Modern Asian Studies* 27:1 (1993): 179–203.

pragmatically accommodated customary deviations', making 'no move to replace custom' until the Shariat Act of 1937.³² Although she provides an example of litigation from Punjab, it is worth highlighting the writings of Erskine Perry, who was a Supreme Court Justice in the 1840s and 1850s, to clarify the modes of adjudication employed, Perry's cases serving as the precedent upon which later cases concerning the disinheritance of daughters were decided. Perry noted that a number of cases involving Muslim women suing for a share in inheritance arose in the Bombay Presidency during his tenure, two of which reached his court in 1847. The first involved women from the Khoja community and the second, women from the Memon community of Gujarat.³³ In both cases, the women claimed that as 'Muslims', the Qur'an guaranteed them a share in their fathers' estates, while the defendants pleaded that in their communities a 'custom' disinheriting daughters had long been upheld. Perry's first order in deciding these cases was to verify the existence of such a custom by means of each community's testimony. Thus, it was established that Khojas and Memons converted from Hinduism under the influence of Isma'ili and Sunni *pirs*, respectively. The Khojas claimed to be followers of the Agha Khan—lately established 'Imam' of an Isma'ili branch—but Perry noted that community members were not educated in Arabic or Persian, and had no translations of the Qu'ran in Gujarati. They referred instead to works such as the *Das Avatar*, the highly Intoxicated work of a 15th century Isma'ili *pir* named Sadr al-Din.³⁴ The Memons were noted to be far richer than the Khojas,

---

³² Jalal, *Self and Sovereignty*, pp. 142–53.

³³ Perry refers to more than 50 cases tried in his capacity as Supreme Court Justice in Erskine Perry, *Cases Illustrative of Oriental Life: the Application of English Law to India* (New Delhi: Asian Educational Services, 1988), first published in 1854. Those of interest here are *Hirbae and Gungbae vs. Sonabae*, and *Rahimatbae vs. Hadji Jussap and Others*. Also see *Telegraph and Courier* (Bombay Edition) 1:148 (24 June 1847) and 1:174 (5 August 1847). For a thorough study of succession and inheritance in Khoja, Memon and Bohra communities, see Carissa Hickling, *Disinheriting Daughters: Applying Hindu Laws of Inheritance to the Khoja Communty in Western India, 1847–1937* (Winnipeg: University of Manitoba [unpublished MA thesis], 1998). For Khojas, Bohras and Memons more generally, see Asghar Ali Engineer, *The Muslim Communities of Gujarat: An Exploration of the Bohras, Khojas and Memons* (Delhi: Ajanta Publishers, 1989).

³⁴ In general, the description of the Khojas and Memons provided by Perry's witnesses concurs with that of contemporary historians. These communities, along with the Bohras, constitute largely mercantile Muslim groups from Gujarat. They were tribal groups adhering to Hindu or Buddhist beliefs before the advent of Islam in the region, although exact dates of conversion are obscure. Like the Khojas, the Bohras are also Isma'ilis, the rise of which is attributed to: (1) the activities of Isma'ili *dais* (mission-

in numbers, finances and, from Perry's perspective, 'Islamic' learning. He noted that some in this community even uphold a daughter's right to inheritance, but concluded that in both communities the custom of disinheriting daughters did overwhelmingly exist.

Having established the custom, Perry's next questions suggest most about the process that replaced Islamic jurisprudence. First, he inquired after the place of custom in English jurisprudence. He concluded that a custom can be recognised as 'law' if the 'majority' of a community has recognised the practice beyond memory, if it was 'reasonable', or 'not injurious to the public interests', and if it did not conflict with the laws of the 'ruling power'.[35] The first condition already established, Perry dismissed the second by writing that the disinheriting of daughters was not 'unreasonable' or 'injurious' in the eyes of English law as it accorded with 'universal custom'.[36] In order to determine the laws of the ruling power, Perry next considered the place of 'divine law' in English jurisprudence, and the role ascribed to the Qur'an by the East India Company Charter. In the first matter, he concluded:

> A jurist *qua* jurist has only to deal with human laws: he recognises the existence of divine laws, and their validity in *foro conscientiae* with those to whom they are addressed, or who believe in the revelation contained in them; but he does not recognise them as enforceable in Courts of justice any further than the secular power has ordained.[37]

---

aries) following the rise of Fatimid suzereignty among the Amirs of Sind about the 10th–11th century; and, (2) the move eastward of Isma'ili *dais* following the conquest of the area by Sunni state's such as the Ghaznawids and Ghurids between the 11th–12th centuries. The affiliation between Khojas, Bohras and the Agha Khanate, however, is more recent, beginning in the 17th–18th century, when a member of the Safawid elite acknowledged by some (Nizaris) as the Isma'ili Imam, began to gain influence among earlier converts, while also gaining new ones. When one of this line of Imams was driven from Iran to Sind, having fallen foul of the Qajar state that replaced the Safawid in the 1720s, eventually settling in Bombay by the 1850s, as the Agha Khan I, he won much influence among the Isma'ilis of the region, though many Khojas would convert to Sunnism or Imami Shi'ism when the Agha Khan began to demand payment of *zakat* to the Imamate. For Pir Sadr al-Din and the activities of Isma'ili pirs in Sind and Gujarat between the 12th–15th century, see Sarah Ansari, *Sufi Saints and State Power* (Lahore: Vanguard Books Ltd., 1992), pp. 13–17. For the Agha Khan, see Willi Frischauer, *The Aga Khans* (London: Bodley Head, 1970); and see Azim Nanji, *The Ismaili Tradition in the Indo-Pakistan Subcontinent* (New York: Caravan Books, 1978). Also see Chapter One, fn. 14.

[35] Perry, *Cases Illustrative of Oriental Life*, p. 121.
[36] Ibid., p. 120.
[37] Ibid., p. 122.

The East India Company being the 'secular power' of the day, Perry then faithfully addressed the issue of charters providing for Islamic law in the personal realm. In this matter, he concluded:

> The effect of the clause in the charter is not to adopt the text of the Koran [sic] as law, any further than it has been adopted in the laws and usages of the Mohamedans [sic] who came under our sway; and if any class of Mohamedans [sic]—Mohamedan [sic] dissenters, as they may be called—are found to be in possession of any usage which is otherwise valid as a legal custom, and which does not conflict with any express law of the English Government, they are as much entitled to the protection of this clause as the most orthodox Sunniy [sic] who can come before Court.[38]

On all these grounds, Perry not only dismissed the women's cases, but added:

> I think that the attempt of these young women to disturb the course of succession which has prevailed among their ancestors for many hundred years has failed, and, as a price for unsuccessful experiment, that their bills must be dismissed with costs, so far as the defendants seek to recover them.[39]

It is surely not an overstatement to say that the jurisprudence of the 'old' Sober Path played virtually no role in East India Company legislation by the mid-19th century, not because the Qur'an could be overruled by custom in the highest courts of the land, but because this was justified on the grounds of English jurisprudence, even though the cases mentioned are concerned with Muslim personal law. The absence of reference to Anglo-Muhammadan codes, Muslim scholars and their jurisprudential schools (including the Agha Khan in the case of Isma'ilis), adds that no attempt was even made to ascertain the 'Islamic' position. Furthermore, as the above case of the Sunni Memon women confirms, 'dissenters' from the 'code' could include Sunnis, when their customs differed from it. This leads to the second problem with the emphasis on British attempts at codification in explaining the rigidification of religious boundaries: the impact of Deobandi thought, including its antecedents and heirs.

The reason for this second oversight, I argue, stems from the dominant paradigm by which social historians assess the role of doctrinal Islam. In this case, my objection is not merely the legalistic and intrusive

---

[38] Ibid., pp. 124–25.
[39] Ibid., p. 129.

nature attributed to doctrinal Islam, but the stagnancy that underwrites both. Note, for example, that in his assessment of Islamic and colonial legal theory, Kugle assumes that all Islamic jurisprudence is 'substantively rational', not considering whether change has ever occurred outside of British influence. Not even works like those of Robinson and Mercalfe, which acknowledge the rise of 'revivalist' movements in the early 18th century and connect them to Deoband, take into account the codification which Uriel Heyd and Colin Imber have separately shown to have driven legal reforms in the Ottoman and/or Mughal domains.[40] Rather, their growing influence is categorised as reactionary 'traditionalism', prompted by a need to address or counter British initiatives. By way of contrast, Heyd in particular comments that already under Awrangzib, Mughal policy echoed the contemporary Ottoman drive to codify criminal and other aspects of law by drawing together *shar'i* and customary stipulations in their *siyasat* (state) regulations, lessening the authority of administrative figures to rule independently, while also producing a redacted Hanafi jurisprudential work, the *Fatawa-i 'Alamgiri*, intended to have the same effect among jurists.[41] In the light of such activities, it must be asked whether the growth of *hadith* scholarship and the assaults on established mystical traditions beginning in the early 18th century, were not more significant than they are thought to have been, providing further evidence that before the onset of colonial rule, certain jurists progressively theorised and promoted a 'formal' law that rejected fundamentals of the 'substantive' jurisprudence which most Muslim jurists theorised and practised to that point. Furthermore, given the era and place in which such intellectual activities were undertaken, the above angle of approach to law adds credence to Ernest Gellner's and James Tamney's theses that the 'puritanism' inherent in such Islamic movements, like Christian 'protestantism', is less a 'reaction' to 'Westernisation' than a feature of 'Modernisation', including 'capitalisation'—'Modernity' predisposing the scholarly elite and opening room for capitalists to be educated in the new puritanisms under colonial rule.[42] The same movements that profoundly influenced

---

[40] See Colin Imber, *Ebu's-Su'ud: The Islamic Legal Tradition* (Stanford: Stanford University Press, 1997); and Uriel Heyd, *Studies in Old Ottoman Criminal Law* (Oxford: Clarendon Press, 1973).
[41] Heyd, *Studies*, pp. 2–3, 317–18.
[42] See Ernst Gellner, *Muslim Society* (Cambridge: Cambridge University Press, 1981); and James B. Tamney, 'Modernization and Religious Purification: Islam in Indonesia', *Review of Religious Research* 22:2 (1980).

the intellectualism of Deobandi scholars also raise the possibility that colonial codes were influenced in some part by locally generated trends. At the very least, if representing change by means of legal reforms that included codification, one must allow for the possibility of parallel movements, one issuing from and institutionalised by the colonial state, and another already active in Muslim legal discourse, in explaining the firming of religious and sectarian boundaries.

Although there can be no doubt that British legal reforms were extensive, the problem with a historiography that places the brunt of emphasis on the role of British reforms in explaining the delineation of religious boundaries, is that it relies on a chronology that implies social norms (particularly among the Muslim elite and capitalist classes) were transformed in the space of a few decades beginning in the mid to late 19th century. Even if some argue that the colonial discourse had achieved hegemony among some classes by the 20th century, the codifying thrust of British reforms cannot be projected back. If, on the other hand, it is shown that doctrinal corollaries and/or indigenous intellectual contributors existed before and outside of British spheres of influence, the scope of change is more easily explained. In this chapter, therefore, I explore exactly the indigenous trends that complemented British initiatives to ensure that the rigidification of religious boundaries was the direct result of the vast socio-economic and political shifts occurring during the 18th and 19th centuries. While the activities of so many Muslim intellectuals (including Deobandis) during the early 20th century speak eloquently of continued 'connectedness' with the broader Muslim World and 'embeddedness' in South Asia, one cannot assume that the variables in that equation remained constant from the death of Awrangzib, even without the influence of British reforms. Therefore, this part of the discussion draws from available sources to paint a clearer picture of the Sober Path from the early 18th to early 20th centuries, focusing attention on the issue of legal codification. This aspect of the discussion is brought to light by the writings of the Wali Allahi family of scholars, who were a prominent line of Naqshbandi Sufis and jurists active in Delhi from the time of Awrangzib until the mid-19th century. With the aid of the *Fatawa-i 'Alamgiri* and multiple Arabic, Persian and Urdu works by Shah Wali Allah (d. 1763), Shah 'Abd al-'Aziz (d. 1820) and Muhammad Isma'il (d. 1831), I argue that not only was doctrinal change a major feature of early 18th century writings, but that in the Wali Allahi line one finds a definitive move towards legal codification that Deobandis inherited and promoted.

Furthermore, using the Urdu writings of Deobandi scholars, including Muhammad Qasim Nanawtawi (d. 1877), Imdad Allah Thanawi (d. 1899), Rashid Ahmad Gangohi (d. 1905), Sayyid Mumtaz 'Ali (d. 1935) and Ashraf 'Ali Thanawi (d. 1943), I make the case that by the late 19th century, a new breed of Muslim scholars with largely legalistic orientations emerged, not bound by the 'substantive' approaches of old, but much more in line with the 'formalism' of such thinkers as the Wali Allahis. These ideas were further boosted by a host of other movements, including the Wahhabiyya, Ahl-i Hadith and Ahl-i Sunnat, whose origins are rooted in the same socio-economic and political conditions as the Wali Allahis, and whose writings I also consider. Although I leave the exact chronology of change for the next chapter, all the expressions of doctrine considered here amount to the conclusion that the very aspects of the Sober Path that legitimated local custom began losing ground among the elite and capitalist classes from the early 18th century, to be progressively replaced by a 'new' Sober Path defined by 'formal' law in the 20th century. In general, therefore, the nature of the 'connectedness' with the Muslim World and 'embeddedness' in South Asia that Muslims of the British Raj period so obviously upheld, was not merely altered by British efforts to codify the law, but also reflects a shift from an 'old' to a 'new' Sober Path that echoes elements of British reforms, but is itself not doctrinally informed by them.

I. *Shah Wali Allah and Pre-Colonial Trends in the Sober Path: 1707–1765*

When Awrangzib was still in power, the leading jurists of Delhi and Lahore were gathered to work on a definitive work of Hanafi legal opinion at great expense to the state treasury. The work that resulted was the *Fatawa-i 'Alamgiri*; among the jurists who contributed to its compilation one notes Shaykh 'Abd al-Rida (d. 1690) and his brother, Shah 'Abd al-Rahim (d. 1719), both of whom were luminaries of the legalistic Naqshbandi Sufi order that believed at no stage on the mystic's path could the *shari'a* be neglected.[43] The life and work of 'Abd al-Rahim

---

[43] S.A.A. Rizvi, *A History of Sufism in India*, vol. 2 (Delhi: Munshiram Manoharlal, 1983), p. 251; Annemarie Schimmel, *Islam on the Indian Subcontinent* (Leiden: E.J. Brill, 1980), p. 153; and A. Guenther, 'Hanafi Fiqh in Mughal India: The Fatawa-i

attests that his knowledge of and adherence to the methods and rulings of the Hanafi school was unmoving. Furthermore, as a Sufi, he numbered among the scholars reticent to enter the employ of the Mughal state. Despite being forbidden by his mentor to take up employment on the state-sponsored *Fatawa-i 'Alamgiri*, however, 'Abd al-Rahim was ultimately persuaded. The involvement of 'Abd al-Rahim in this work is significant for a number of reasons. First, regarding the 'textual' codification that Kugle associates with the British, the *Fatawa-i 'Alamgiri* is itself largely based on the works later translated and employed by the British, including *al-Hidaya*, as stated in its 'Introduction'.[44] More importantly, on the 'conceptual' plane, it is noteworthy that the same introduction chastises contemporary jurists for excessive devotion to works concerned with differing opinions (*ikhtilaf*) and scholastic discussions of jurisprudential hypotheticals. This is argued to have led to the accumulation of a dizzying array of opinion by which the 'light of the *sunna*' had been lost to scholars and laypersons.[45] Contrary to *al-Hidaya*, therefore, the *Fatawa-i 'Alamgiri* was touted as 'a book inclusive of the narratives on which there is general agreement' among the jurists.[46] Methodologically speaking, the compilers continued that this work extracted the 'essence from the materials of *fiqh* and its canon of *fara'id* (religious duties)'.[47] Although not the Anglo-Muhammadan 'code', the *Fatawa-i 'Alamgiri* is itself indicative of a rising trend among Muslim jurists to reduce the scope of opinion and custom permitted as *shar'i*.[48] That this was an enduring trend is best suggested by the writings of 'Abd al-Rahim's son and intellectual successor, Shah Wali Allah.

'Alamgiri', *India's Islamic Traditions*, 711–1750, ed. R. Eaton (Delhi: Oxford University Press, 2003), p. 214.

[44] The Arabic edition used here is *Fatawa al-'Alamgiriyya* (Karachi: Qadimi Kutub Khana, n.d.). The 'Introduction' covers pages 3–4 of the first volume.

[45] Ibid., p. 3.

[46] Ibid., p. 3.

[47] Ibid., p. 3.

[48] It should be noted that such *fatawa* literature was not new, examples were found in South Asia as early as in the 13th century. The import of the *Fatawa-i 'Alamgiri*, further reflecting the tendency to 'reconcile' differences of opinion, is the emphasis its chapters give to the standardisation of procedures, including documentation. The *Fatawa-i 'Alamgiri* is also more comprehensive than earlier works, bringing together 124 separate works. Thus, as Guenther suggests, though not a 'code', the unifying intent and 'influence on the formation of laws...cannot be denied'. Guenther, 'Hanafi Fiqh', p. 225.

Although the father lived in an era of Mughal expansion, the son watched the Mughals' fall.[49] Attesting to the fact that the Mughal state's downward spiral did not equate to general socio-economic or cultural decline, by the time that Wali Allah performed *hajj* in 1730, at the age of 27, he had studied major works on *hadith*, jurisprudence, the principles of jurisprudence, theology, rhetoric (*balagha*), medicine (*tibb*), Ishraqi philosophy and Sufi mysticism at the well-endowed *Madrasa-i Rahimiyya*, which was founded by his father in Delhi.[50] In Mecca and Medina, he pursued these studies further under a host of stellar scholars and, upon his return to Delhi, devoted himself to writing more than 40 works on most of the above disciplines, as well as on political and social theory. The 'decline' he nevertheless perceived is stamped on many of these works, particularly as some of his ideas are as 'new' to doctrinal Islam as those of the British were in the region.[51] Most prominent are jurisprudential, theological, philosophical and mystical reforms building upon the 'unifying' ideals expressed in the compilation of the *Fatawa-i 'Alamgiri*.

When reviewing his writings on the aforementioned disciplines, all scholars agree that Wali Allah sought to bring divergent doctrines into 'agreement', even if they disagree on the author's intent and the nature of the outcome. For example, regarding the raging Sufi controversy over Ibn al-'Arabi's doctrine of *wahdat al-wujud* and Shaykh Ahmad Sirhindi's *wahdat al-shuhud*, M. Mujeeb maintains that Wali Allah tried to show that these doctrines were not 'in conflict with each other, but stages on the road to spiritual knowledge, *wahdat al-wujud* being an earlier and *wahdat al-shuhud* a later and more advanced stage'.[52] S.A.A. Rizvi disagrees. To Sirhindi, writes Rizvi, 'the *wahdat al-wujud* was only a preliminary stage of sufic development, but to Shah Wali Allah it was

---

[49] There are a number of thorough works specific to Wali Allah, including, S.A.A. Rizvi, *Shah Wali Allah and His Times* (Canberra: Ma'rifat Press, 1980); and J.M.S. Baljon, *Religion and Thought of Shah Wali Allah Dihlawi* (Leiden: E.J. Brill, 1986).

[50] Baljon, *Religion*, p. 4. For a useful bibliography of Wali Allah's writings, also see K. Khan, 'A Select Bibliography of Writings by and about Shah Wali Allah Dihalvi in English and Urdu', *Muslim World Book Review* 7:1 (1986): 56–65.

[51] A more direct statement of Wali Allah's concern at the fragmentation of Mughal polity are the letters he wrote to various regional rulers of his day, urging the maintenance of centralised authority, whether under the Mughals or more ascendant ruling houses of the day. Selections of these letters are published as K.A. Nizami, ed. *Shah Wali Allah ke Siyasi Maktubat* (Aligarh: n.p., 1951).

[52] M. Mujeeb, *The Indian Muslims* (Montreal: McGill University Press, 1967), p. 280.

the final stage'.⁵³ As Mujeeb does not reference the work upon which he bases his view, one must turn to Rizvi's source, Wali Allah's *Lamahat*. Here, the author articulated his theory of 'Being' as follows:

> You see both 'Zaid' and 'Amar', you abstract man from them, and by so doing you prove the existence of man in both of them. And just as you see the man and the horse and abstract animal from them... you take notice of all the essences in general and abstract Being from them.⁵⁴

In addition, Wali Allah argued that the 'one' Being was related to the apparent multiplicity of the universe as the number 'one' is related to higher numbers. He wrote:

> Is it not a fact that a mathematician when desired can bring the cardinal numbers in his imagination. Thus, he derives from one, one and one by his reconsideration, and this is how two takes place. Again, when he derives from it one and one and one by the repetition of his reconsideration, three is formed. In this way, he derives one number after another, and this is how the units and tens, hundreds and thousands are made... Now let us take this chain which we have invented as a mirror for knowing the case of the numerical nature and its inclusion in the one. From this it becomes clear that this numerical chain implies a hidden secret in the one, so that, it (the one) may agree to it (the numerical chain) in all its parts.⁵⁵

Both of the above examples suggest that Wali Allah's works are affirmations of Sufi monism, but they do not address the pivotal issue of the final 'stage'. This is most succinctly articulated in the *Sata'at*. Wali Allah wrote:

> In my opinion, what is established and confirmed is that by the real object [of gnosis] is meant, the attainment of a certain part of the plane of the Holy Fold which the Divine powers have fixed for him. The path to this real object requires a change of the bestial qualities, so that, the annihilation of the dark existence and the survival by the spiritual existence could be achieved. If the man is one of the select saints, another change besides this one, is also desired in this case, so that, the annihilation of the spiritual existence and the survival by the reality of Divinity which

---

⁵³ Rizvi, *A History of Sufism*, vol. 2, p. 257.
⁵⁴ Shah Wali Allah, *Lamahat*, trans. G.N. Jalbani (Hyderabad: Shah Wali Allah Academy, 1970), p. 6. For clarity of language, the above translation is taken from Saeeda Iqbal, *Islamic Rationalism in the Subcontinent* (Lahore: Islamic Book Service, 1984), pp. 70–71.
⁵⁵ Wali Allah, *Lamahat*, pp. 10–11.

means the prevalence of the existence of the Real (God) upon your existence, is achieved.[56]

The import of this passage is that the final stage is neither described as the 'annihilation' associated with the doctrine of *wahdat al-wujud*, nor the 'survival' defended by the doctrine of *wahdat al-shuhud*, but a state of annihilation and survival simultaneously. As J.M.S. Baljon suggests, this is because Wali Allah viewed the differences between *wahdat al-wujud* and *wahdat al-shuhud* to have arisen as a result of three factors: (1) the misinterpretation of Ibn al-'Arabi by the likes of his disciple, Sadr al-Din al-Qunawi (d. 1274); (2) difference in the terminology used by Ibn al-'Arabi and Ahmad Sirhindi; and, (3) lack of recognition that each doctrine articulates 'direct experience' of different parts of the same whole.[57] The point of this discussion of legalism is first suggested by the resulting attitude towards staple 'creeds' of theology.

In each of the works considered here, Wali Allah explicitly reaffirms the 'truth' of miracles, angels, genies, Judgement Day, and so on. So resolute were Wali Allah's convictions in these matters that Saeeda Iqbal argues for Wali Allah's 'affinity to Ibn Taymiyya'.[58] However, this conclusion cannot be accepted without qualification. In the *Ta'wil al-Ahadith*, Wali Allah clearly argued that the 'miraculous' is no more than the 'ordinary'. He wrote:

> Some happenings take place sparingly, they are therefore named as extraordinary. As a matter of fact all that is named extraordinary is ordinary, but because their causes take place rarely, they appear rarely, people do not usually expect them and name them extraordinary when they occur.[59]

In essence, this passage illustrates that Wali Allah's understanding of miracles is at least as heavily influenced by the 'immanent monism' of the Sufis and philosophers as it is by the 'transcendental monotheism' of the theologians. Miracles are 'ordinary' rather than 'extraordinary'

---

[56] Shah Wali Allah, *Sata'at*, trans. G.N. Jalbani (Hyderabad: Shah Wali Allah Academy, 1970), p. 38.
[57] Baljon, *Religion*, pp. 62–63. Incidentally, al-Qunawi's interpretation of *wahdat al-wujud* is also considered the root of later Sufi views in the previously cited works by Chittick and Kynch.
[58] Iqbal, *Islamic Rationalism*, pp. 64–65.
[59] Shah Wali Allah, *Ta'wil al-Ahadith*, trans. G.N. Jalbani (Lahore: Shan Muhammad Ashraf, 1973), pp. 42–43.

events in the same manner that all numbers are knowable by means of the 'hidden secret in the one'. Every event, like every number, is an 'emanation' of the One, even if some manifestations are frequent and others rare.

The influence of immanent monism is also apparent in Wali Allah's understanding of Judgement Day, not to mention Heaven and Hell. He viewed the individual's life as a circle whose beginning and end is 'pure intellect'.[60] Considering only the arc from death back to the 'beginning', Wali Allah stated that the individual enters an 'Intermediary World' (*'alam barzakh*), in which the body is lost, but where one retains 'the knowledge, the states and the faculties' of the individual.[61] However, in a state of consciousness approximating a 'dream', the 'natural disposition' of the individual is turned from the 'visible world' towards the 'Similitudinary World (*'alam al-mithal*)'.[62] Depending on the 'capability of an individual', this consciousness allows levels of understanding corresponding to the 'various stages of the Similitude'.[63] By Judgement Day, the individual will have gone through these stages, thus being prepared for the 'Similitudinary faculties' to replace those of the 'visible world', allowing clear vision of individual 'deeds and character' still 'perceived'.[64] At this point, the 'Great Manifestation' will appear in a 'Similitudinary form...worthy of its rank'.[65] In addition, 'all the necessary things of life, like eating, drinking and having intercourse with a woman will take certain forms...[and] they [the dead] will find pleasure in each of them', every sensation corresponding to a 'certain act of goodness' in life.[66] However, this is only the first stage of the Similitude, and these 'happy' (*sa'da*) souls will undergo many more changes in states leading to them finally 'losing themselves in Pure light', or 'disappearing in this Manifestation'.[67] On the other hand, 'unhappy' (*shaqiyya*) souls, ignorant of the 'Origin of the universe', will have gone through much confusion while in the stages of the Similitude, and 'be put in a strange perplexity'.[68]

---

[60] Wali Allah, *Sata'at*, p. 25.
[61] Ibid., p. 25.
[62] Ibid., p. 26.
[63] Ibid., pp. 26–27.
[64] Ibid., p. 27.
[65] Ibid., p. 27.
[66] Ibid., p. 27.
[67] Ibid., pp. 30–31.
[68] Ibid., p. 32.

Recalling that 'disappearing in this Manifestation' does not imply absolute 'annihilation' in Wali Allah's opinion, the above discussion of *barzakh* illustrates that the 'agreement' which Wali Allah sought to construct between philosophy, theology and mysticism, ultimately depended on two factors: (1) curbing the Sufi and philosopher's immanent monism to the degree that he could rationalise the theologian's notions of miracles, bodily resurrection on Judgement Day, and the corporeal pleasures and intellectual tortures of Heaven and Hell, respectively; and, (2) challenging the theologian and jurist's transcendent monotheism, but only slightly less than in Sirhindi's doctrinal perspective. The impact of such a formulation on philosophy and Sufism, given the relationship between theology and jurisprudence discussed below, is that monistic thinkers are provided less room to challenge the necessity of the *shari'a* based on textual sources. Thus, it is of the greatest importance that Wali Allah's approach to law was no less synthetically innovative.

In the domain of jurisprudence, Wali Allah categorically argued for *ijtihad* (independent reasoning).[69] For example, in *Hujjat Allah al-Baligha*, he stated that one of the causes behind the 'distortion' he observes in the *shari'a* as it is practised is *taqlid* (imitation).[70] Aziz Ahmad adds that, by means of *ijtihad*, Wali Allah 'developed an inter-juristic eclecticism recommending that on any point of doctrine or ritual a [Sunni] Muslim could follow the rulings of any one of the four principal juristic schools'.[71] Putting aside the point of 'inter-juristic eclecticism' momentarily, Ahmad's argument that this is expressed by allowing for the rulings of any of the four Sunni schools is misleading, this being less an innovation than a restatement of established juristic theory. Rather, Baljon's argument that Wali Allah's 'inter-juristic eclecticism' went no further than recommending the juristic tool of *talfiq*, i.e. 'piecing together' the doctrines of more than one school, appears more correct.[72] As Wali Allah himself stated in the *Hujjat Allah al-Baligha*,

---

[69] See Shah Wali Allah, *'Iqd al-Jid fi Ahkam al-Ijtihad wa al-Taqlid*, ed. and trans. M.D. Rahbar, 'Shah Wali Allah and Ijtihad', *The Muslim World* 44 (1955): 346. For background on Wali Allah's approach to *ijtihad*, also see M.A. Ali, 'A Critical Evaluation of Shah Wali Allah's Attitude to Ijtihad vis-à-vis the Views of the Other Jurists', *Hamdard Islamicus* 20:1 (1997): 19–26.

[70] Shah Wali Allah, *Hujjat Allah al-Baligha*, trans. M.K. Hermansen (Leiden: E.J. Brill, 1996), p. 351.

[71] Aziz Ahmad, *An Intellectual History of Islam in India* (Edinburgh: Edinburgh University Press, 1969), p. 8.

[72] Baljon, *Religion*, p. 167.

the 'decline' of Muslim polity suggests that the best course of action is to 'synthesise' the schools of Abu Hanifa and al-Shafi'i.[73] Ultimately, Wali Allah's *ijtihad* was employed to collapse the four schools of Sunni jurisprudence into one.

Explaining Wali Allah's reasoning, both Baljon and Ahmad agree that he conceived of an 'evolutionary' *shari'a* that would keep pace with changing social conditions.[74] Baljon suggests that Wali Allah justified his call for *ijtihad* by arguing that 'every age has its own countless and specific problems', reflecting a sense that the *shari'a* is not a static concept.[75] Rather, notions of 'right' and 'wrong' articulated by the Qur'an and *sunna* are timeless, but *shar'i* rulings differ with time and place. The latter 'rulings', whether expressed by Abraham or the latter-day prophets, including Muhammad, have always been cognisant of local environmental conditions and social customs.[76] The image that Wali Allah employs is that of a pure rain (the unadulterated *shari'a*) falling to earth and mixing with the local soil. Thus, the question to be tackled here is: How did he intend *ijtihad* and *talfiq* to resolve a *shari'a* best suited to his Muslim contemporaries?

Returning to the *Hujjat Allah al-Baligha*, one notes that Wali Allah argues that while certain pre-Islamic Arabian practices were banned by Muhammad (e.g. *riba* (usury)), mainstays of the *shari'a* such as regulations concerning marriage, divorce, prayer (*salah*), fasting (*sawm*), pilgrimage (*hajj*), ablution (*wudu'*) and so on, are modified versions of pre-Islamic Arabian 'custom' (*'urf*).[77] His point is that the Prophet relied on local customary law because, in the Arabian context, it was acknowledged as a corrupted form of Abraham's initial *shari'a*.[78] Therefore, Wali Allah argued that Arabs follow the *shari'a* because of their belief in the Prophet and the proximity of his *shari'a* to their 'custom'. Yet, he acknowledged that Arab Muslims have been enjoined by the faith to carry this *shari'a* to the rest of the world. Thus, the non-Arab's acceptance of this 'Arabian' *shari'a* is dependent in part on its recognition as the 'natural religion (*al-madhhab al-tabi'i*) of the civilised

---

[73] Wali Allah, *Hujjat Allah al-Baligha*, pp. 427–36, 451–78.
[74] For example, Baljon, *Religion*, pp. 127–30.
[75] Ibid., p. 167.
[76] Ibid., pp. 160–61.
[77] Wali Allah, *Hujjat Allah al-Baligha*, pp. 303–09.
[78] Miraj Muhammad, 'Shah Wali Allah's Concept of the Shari'ah', eds. Ahmad, Khurshid and Z.I. Ansari, *Islamic Perspectives* (Jeddah: Saudi Publishing House, 1979), pp. 343–58.

world (*al-aqalim al-salihah*)'.⁷⁹ He, therefore, urged that even if this is not recognised and such legislation is difficult, it is necessary as:

> There is no way to consider the condition of every people, and deal with each one of them, so that for each a divine law would be made; since encompassing their customs and condition according to the differences in their cities and the disparity in their religions is something impossible.⁸⁰

When it is acknowledged that 'there is no way to consider the condition of every people,' it becomes clear that Wali Allah ultimately believed that 7th century Arab 'custom', not the contemporary local customary practices of Muslims, must define the model *shariʿa* of the age.

In light of the above, Wali Allah's *ijtihad* does not imply the unrestricted use of Reason to derive new rulings for a new age, as Ahmad in particular seems to imply. On the contrary, Wali Allah's 'evolutionary' step is to limit the *shariʿa* to 'prophetic practice' (i.e. Arabian 'custom' as modified by Muhammad), overruling past juristic opinion based on non-textual sources when a clear stipulation is mentioned in the textual sources of law. In pursuit of this goal, Wali Allah went as far as to argue, 'The origins of Islam are the Qur'an and the *hadith*. There is no other source. *Ijtihad* is permissible in deciding about worldly affairs, [but] if such an affair was decided about before, the decision cannot be changed. There is not *qiyas* [analogical reasoning] or *ijmaʿ* [consensus] in the knowledge of Islam'.⁸¹ Furthermore, given that even *qiyas* and *ijmaʿ*, two of the four sources of law acknowledged by Hanafis, are frowned upon, it should come as no surprise that in Wali Allah's opinion the use of *istislah* (public utility) and *istihsan* (juristic preference) by jurists, the very jurisprudential tools employed to include non-Arab/local custom in the *shariʿa*, must be abolished.⁸² The emphasis on textual sources can be further attested by Wali Allah's approach to *hadith* (prophetic traditions)—the textual source of prophetic practice (*sunna*). It has long been noted that eight of Wali Allah's major works are devoted to the subject.⁸³ The chapters concerned with this subject in *Hujjat Allah al-Baligha* outline five ranks of *hadith*. In the top rank, one in which most individual *hadith* are judged 'sound' (*sahih*), he includes Malik's

---

⁷⁹ Wali Allah, *Hujjat Allah al-Baligha*, pp. 341–43.
⁸⁰ Ibid., p. 341.
⁸¹ Shah Wali Allah, *Al-Tafhimat al-Ilahiyya*, vol. II. (n.p., 1967), p. 142.
⁸² Wali Allah, *Hujjat Allah al-Baligha*, pp. 349, 435–36.
⁸³ For titles of works, see Khan, 'A Select Bibliography', pp. 56–65.

Muwatta', Bukhari's *Sahih* and Muslim's *Sahih* in their entirety.[84] When such enthusiasm for *hadith* is placed beside his dismay at the use of *istihsan*, etc., Wali Allah's 'inter-juristic eclecticism' and 'evolutionary' *shari'a*, like his ideas on theology, philosophy and mysticism, resolves as one privileging the letter of textual sources (Qur'an and *hadith*, but particularly the later) above established or future formulations based on the non-textual sources, especially local custom (*'urf*) in the case of jurisprudence.

While Wali Allah is not the first thinker to seek the reform of various Islamic disciplines and much of his thought conforms to that of earlier periods, departure in various disciplines is evident, nowhere more so than in jurisprudence. In particular, although identifying himself as a Hanafi, Wali Allah's jurisprudential ideals echo those of Hanbalis in the degree to which he circumscribed the use of *qiyas* and *ijma'*, let alone such subordinate conceptual tools as *istihsan* and *istislah*. In relation to previous articulations of Hanafi jurisprudence, therefore, the combination of doctrines as well as their focus must lead to the identification of Wali Allah's thought as a 'new' variant of juristic Islam that collapses the established schools—setting him apart from even his father, 'Abd al-Rahim. But can 'Abd al-Rahim and Wali Allah's jurisprudential thoughts be described as a progressive shift from a 'substantive' to a 'formal' system? I offer a positive response based on one significant trend upheld by both authors. The *Fatawa-i 'Alamgiri*—on which 'Abd al-Rahim and a host of South Asia's most reputed jurists worked—explicitly breaks with previous works in the genre by including only those Hanafi 'narratives on which there is general agreement' in seeking to arrive at 'prophetic practice'. This exact sentiment is reflected in Wali Allah's more drastic attempt to find 'agreement' between Hanafi and Shafi'i opinion, his favourable attitude towards the textual sources of law above the non-textual, and his drive to reduce the role of non-Arab custom in the definition of the *shari'a*. In seeking 'agreement', rather than upholding diversity of opinion in the law, it must be concluded that 'Abd al-Rahim and Wali Allah were participating in a movement towards codification, also describable as a continuous and developing movement away from substantive and towards formal legal rationalism prior to the rise of East India Company rule.

---

[84] Wali Allah, *Hujjat Allah al-Baligha*, pp. 387–95.

The last question this part of the discussion raises is: Why would such a movement towards codification arise in the late 17th and early 18th centuries? As previously mentioned, this period is broadly described as one of capitalisation, political and cultural regionalisation, as well as the apex of literacy in Persian. One can directly connect Wali Allah's broader agenda to the above time and place by drawing in his perspective on the Qur'an. Wali Allah is well known for his Persian translation of the Qur'an, which he defended against the arguments of 'traditionalists' who held that the Qur'an should not be translated.[85] As Baljon suggests, Wali Allah's understanding of the Qur'an was historically based, grounded in the time and place of the revelation, yet also relevant to latter-day Muslims of non-Arab background.[86] In making this point, Baljon cites the following passage from Wali Allah's *al-Fawz al-Kabir fi Usul al-Tafsir*:

> You should be aware that the Quran was sent down for the correction of Arabs as well as non-Arabs, for townspeople as well as inhabitants of the desert. Hence divine wisdom required that...what was said about God's Attributes and Names...should be understandable without a training in metaphysics and scholastics.[87]

In other words, Wali Allah's translation ultimately depends on the argument that Qur'anic narratives 'speak for themselves' and are knowable, on some level, irrespective of ethnicity, class and level of education beyond literacy. Thus, it is reasonable to assume that his translation was ultimately meant to be used by any groups literate in Persian. Furthermore, there is some evidence to suggest that there was a demand for such translations by the late-17th century. As already noted, Awrangzib lambasted his primary teacher for wasting his time with the study of Arabic, urging that one would be better served if not only education, but also the practice of 'prayers', 'law' and the 'sciences', were conducted in Persian. In addition, the profusion of short-tract literature on law and matters of conduct (*fara'id*) and doctrine (*'aqa'id*) produced and consumed by the early 19th century South Asian elite and capitalist classes, in Persian and local vernaculars, has been commented upon in histories of South Asia (and will be discussed further

---

[85] Baljon, *Religion*, pp. 8–14.
[86] Ibid., p. 137.
[87] The edition consulted here is Shah Wali Allah, *Fawz al-Kabir fi Usul al-Tafsir*, trans. G.N. Jalbani (Islamabad: National Hijra Council, 1985). This quote is translated in Baljon, *Religion*, p. 137.

in the next chapter), while Nelly Hanna has attached growth in other types of short literary works to the demand of the same classes in a 17th–18th century Ottoman context.[88] Certainly, these are not proofs of Wali Allah's intent in translating the Qur'an, but such observations provide a promising avenue for research.

Returning to the issue of codification, the assumption underlying Wali Allah's position on Qur'anic translations, as in the case of his and 'Abd al-Rahim's legal attitudes, is that a 'unitary', textual approach, bridging ethnic, class and other social barriers, is not only desirable, but possible. In the era of a centralised and sympathetic Mughal state, particularly under Awrangzib's stewardship, the route taken to fulfil the agenda of 'agreement' was the compilation of works such as the *Fatawa-i 'Alamgiri*, which would be applied by state and non-state jurists. In the absence of central authority by the mid-18th century, however, the same tactic was less possible, but clearly more desirable to some. Indeed, Wali Allah's stark initiative to remove the influence of all earlier doctrines that legitimated local custom, including variation between and within the schools of law, suggests that rather than accepting the political and cultural regionalisation of the day, he sought to counter cultural regionalism among Muslims with a package of reforms that required uniformity in doctrine and practice, at least among the elite and growing classes of literate capitalist groups, while allowing for regionalism on other levels, such as the use of 'vernacular' languages and an allowance for sub-regional states—the last aspect of Wali Allah's thought it is appropriate to address here.

In his *Hujjat Allah al-Baligha*, Wali Allah most directly laid out his views on the ideal socio-political structure for Muslims in particular and humanity in general. He wrote that 'social institutions' (*irtifaqat*) are universal and their principles agreed upon despite 'variations in the pattern and ramifications of *irtifaqat*'.[89] The primary reason for social institutions is the sustenance and propagation of humanity, but Wali Allah added that humanity is set apart from other creatures by its God-given 'comprehensive outlook' (*al-ra'y al-kulli*) and 'aesthetic sensibility' (*zarafa*), allowing humans to become aware of the 'appropriate supports

---

[88] In Hanna's case, the literary genre is 'history' and the context is Egypt. See N. Hanna, 'The Chroniclers of Ottoman-Egypt: History or Entertainment?' *The Historiography of Islamic Egypt*, ed. H. Kennedy (Leiden: E.J. Brill, 2001).
[89] Wali Allah, *Hujjat Allah al-Baligha*, p. 140.

of *irtifaqat* by means of 'acquired experience' and 'revealed sciences'.⁹⁰ The four 'supports' that humanity can identify are the nomadic and village life, the urban life, the city-state and finally, the state that unifies a number of city-states under one polity.

According to Wali Allah, the first support of *irtifaqat* is determined by the rise of agriculture, but is politically basic (i.e. tribal). Once agriculture and association led to urbanisation, however, more complex problems and a diversity of opinion on how social transactions should be conducted made it necessary to 'set up' a leader and cabinet to arbitrate between competing interests within the urban centre, thus giving rise to the 'city-state' (*madina*).⁹¹ One can infer that different experiences (i.e. that which is 'acquired') and religions (i.e. that which is 'revealed') give rise to variations in the complexion of city-states. As well, competing interests imply that conflict between city-states will arise. Thus, Wali Allah argued that the last support of *irtifaqat* is what one may call, generically, the 'imperial' state. Imperial states arise when the ruler of a city-state obtains 'so much power [over other city-states] that it is seen to be impossible that another man could dispossess him of his kingdom except after many gatherings and the spending of much wealth—an occurrence which during long periods of time only one may find possible'.⁹² As in the case of the city-state, variations between 'empires' are based on that which is perceived and that which is revealed to its leadership; hence, 'nations of superior virtues' are possible within the confines of these 'universal' supports of *irtifaqat*, Islam providing humanity a path to 'superior virtues'.⁹³

Clearly, the general framework of Wali Allah's above arguments and conceptions of civilisation and social order echo those of Ibn Sina and other philosophers writing before him.⁹⁴ However, given the 'new' ideas discussed above, it is in the stipulation that 'superior virtues' are derived from 'Islam' that one must note Wali Allah's response to the

---

⁹⁰ Ibid., pp. 115–17.
⁹¹ Ibid., p. 117.
⁹² Ibid., p. 118.
⁹³ Ibid., p. 118. Also see Abdur Rashid Bhat, 'Shah Wali Allah's Political Thought in the Context of his Irtifaqat', *Journal of Objective Studies* 3:i (1991): 67–78.
⁹⁴ Baljon, *Religion*, p. 192. Also Abdul Azim Islahi, 'Shah Wali Allah's concept of al-irtifaqat (stages of socio-economic development)', *Journal of Objective Studies* 2:i (1990): 46–53; and Muhammad al-Ghazali, 'Universal Social Culture: An Empirico-Revelational Paradigm of Shah Wali Allah', *American Journal of Islamic Social Sciences* 11:i (1994): 13–24.

political fragmentation around him. In his 'Islamic' vision of 'social institutions', Wali Allah describes states, 'city' and 'imperial', in which judicial positions are filled by those educated in 'Islamic' jurisprudence and the best means by which to promote social order is the *shari'a*. Thus, the greatest harmony is achieved when the 'emperor' is not an emperor at all (i.e. one whose authority is based on immovable coercive power), but a 'Caliph' who applies the *shari'a*. However, accord is also arrived at when the 'leader' is an 'Imam'. In describing the qualifications and duties of the Imam, Wali Allah repeats every stipulation attached to the Caliph in Sunni, juristic political philosophy, except for the necessity of the office-holder to be of Quraysh descent. The Imam must be male, learned in jurisprudence, theology and so on, and capable of undertaking *jihad*—the latter being a central part of Wali Allah's programme for 'rejuvenation'.[95] The main difference between the Imam and Caliph is that 'among the principles upon which the Imam must act is...the establishment of the universal Caliphate'.[96] In other words, there may be many 'Imams', but only one 'Caliph' over them all.

At first glance, Wali Allah's Caliphs and Imams may appear no different than the Caliphs and Sultans so far discussed. However, by equating the Imam with the Caliph in all respects but one—Quraysh descent—Wali Allah apparently sought to apply the ideal of a religio-political head of state to local states. Although Wali Allah acknowledged the Mughals' claims to religio-political leadership, he obviously did not legitimate Mughal or Ottoman claims to Caliphate, stipulating that Caliphs must be Quraysh. In fact, Wali Allah envisioned three classes of Caliphs to have arisen in history: (1) *khass* (illustrious), implying the first four '*Rashidun*' Caliphs whom the author holds were all 'designated' (*nass*) by the Prophet; (2) *amm* (ordinary), those 'elected' (as symbolised by *bay'a*) by the people, in which category the author places certain Umayyad and Abbasid Caliphs; and, (3) *jabir* (despotic), those who seize power or who, once elected, act in a tyrannical manner, in which group he places some Arab and most *'ajami* (non-Arab) claimants to Caliphal titles and powers.[97] Thus, Wali Allah wrote that the 'decline' of Muslim polity in his lifetime was due to illegal customary practices, e.g. heavy taxation, prohibition of divorce and widow remarriage, over-

---

[95] Wali Allah, *Hujjat Allah al-Baligha*, pp. 132–36, 343–45.
[96] Ibid., p. 343.
[97] Baljon, *Religion*, p. 125.

indulgence in ritual, misrepresentation of Islam by unscrupulous Sufis, and the sloth of various sections of the society—all practices which an *amm* Caliph would prohibit, but which *jabir* Caliphs had allowed.[98] On the other hand, Wali Allah wrote approvingly of the 'convention of having coins stamped with the name of the caliph [i.e. the Mughal] in this time'.[99] His challenge to incumbent leadership, therefore, is not a negation of religio-political leadership by Sultans like the Mughals. Rather, the claim of religio-political headship as Caliphs is replaced, in keeping with the 18th century Ottoman sources brought to light by Halil Inalcik, with the term 'Imam'.[100] In this light, his contemporary Mughals' illegitimacy as religio-political heads stems not from their lack of Quraysh pedigree, but their '*jabir*' conduct.

Although Wali Allah's ideas on Caliphate have been read as a 'revivalist' tendency, his ideas also need to be read in conjunction with the rapidly waning ability of the Mughals to maintain the authority and autonomy which Wali Allah believed to be vital to the functioning of a religio-political head of state.[101] In response, he sought to delegitimate Sultani claims to Caliphate by calling for its 'establishment', and searched for political renewal from the level of the 'city-state' up to the '*umma*', by adopting the concept of 'Imams', i.e. 'leaders' who could legitimately wage *jihad* on a local level, while striving to establish 'universal' Caliphate in accord with his 'new' Sober Path. In this light, what Wali Allah's ideas on social and political theory add to Islamic thought and the political culture of the Mughals is the crucially particular manner in which the term 'Imam' is employed, and the central place afforded a religious community under the charge of the ideal Imam, even if his domain is merely local.

Although the Wali Allahis are not specifically mentioned by Imber and Heyd, this reading of Wali Allahi activities extends the codifying trends in Ottoman and Mughal state settings on which the latter

---

[98] Wali Allah, *Hujjat Allah al-Baligha*, p. 153. For further reading on Wali Allah's political writings, see Mahmood Ghazi, 'Political Letters of Shah Wali Allah: A Critical Review', *Journal of the Pakistan Historical Society* 30 (1982): 86–108.

[99] Ibid., p. 139.

[100] See Halil Inalcik, 'The Rise of the Ottoman Empire', *Cambridge History of Islam* 1A, eds. P.M. Holt, A.K.S. Lambton and B. Lewis (Cambridge: Cambridge University Press, 1995).

[101] For a prominent example of the 'revivalist' assessment by an author who wrote prolifically on Shah Wali Allah, see Aziz Ahmad, *Studies in Islamic Culture in the Indian Environment* (Delhi: Oxford University Press, 1999), pp. 206–07.

comment, to the activities of independent scholars in the wake of the 'Great Mughals'. Furthermore, Wali Allahis fit well into Gellner's and Tamney's theses that the socio-economic particularities of the time and/or region, such as the capitalisation of the economy and Muslim political fragmentation, played a pivotal role in driving such jurisprudential revisions aimed at 'purification' before colonial rule could carry the law in its own directions. Obviously, 'Abd al-Rahim and Wali Allah's inspirations and motives require much further study, just as aspects of Gellner's approach have been appropriately critiqued.[102] However, based on the nature of Wali Allahi legal reforms, it seems likely that changing socio-economic conditions played a significant part in prompting their systematic attempt to reign in certain aspects of political fragmentation and cultural regionalism by modifying doctrine in a manner promoting 'agreement', laying the first stones of a 'new' Sober Path in the process.

II. *Shah Muhammad Isma'il and the* Tariqa Muhammadiyya: 1765–1857

If the thought and activities of one family in Delhi is considered insufficient to have exerted the type of influence necessary to initiate the scope of 'codifying' reform mentioned, with or without the added institutions of colonialism, one must be reminded that the Wali Allahis were not alone. First, they were part of a broader reformist trend among South Asian Sufis that extended beyond the Sober Naqshbandiyya to include the Qadiriyya, Suhrahwardiyya and, most significantly, the Chishtiyya, known for its Intoxicated leaning in the past. The leading figures of this movement were Shah Kalim Allah (d. 1729) and Mawlana Fakhr al-Din

---

[102] For critiques of Gellner, Tamney and other 'socio-anthropologists' from the perspective of those who argue for the greatest degree of 'colonial difference', see V. Das, 'For a Folk-Theology and Theological Anthropology of Islam', *Contributions to Indian Sociology* 18:2 (1984): 293–300; and G. Prakash, 'Writing Post-Orientalist Histories of the Third World: Perspective from Indian Historiography', *Comparative Studies in Society and History* 32:2 (1990): 383–408. The basic point of contention is the formers' 'civilisational' approach, which dwells on scholastic ('High') Islam, to the determent of the lived ('Low') Islam of most Muslims. The point here, however, is that the Wali Allahis suggest that so-called 'High' Islam is seeking to reform itself and the so-called 'Low' variants before the onset of colonial rule. In effect, such movements are seeking to close the gap.

(d. 1785).¹⁰³ Both maintained belief in *wahdat al-wujud* and continued to practice and propagate *samaʿ*, controlled breathing (*habs-i nafs*) and a number of Yogic ascetic practices despite criticism from the Sober camp. However, the complexion of the order was changed as practices, which were once admittedly derived from Hindu sources, were now justified by Islamic precedents. For example, Kalim Allah claimed that breathing exercises could be traced from the well-respected Sufi, Khwaja ʿAbd al-Khaliq Ghujduwani (d. 1220), to the mythic originator of Sufism, Khwaja Khidr.¹⁰⁴ Furthermore, there emerged a deeper interest in the *shariʿa*. In other words, former advocates of the Intoxicated Way began tending towards the Sober Path, at least in the realm of public conduct. As well, there were others in South Asia and farther afield whose uniformity extended beyond practice to doctrinal approach. Many of these movements adopted the name *Tariqa Muhammadiyya* ('The Way of Muhammad'), reflecting their doctrinal dependence on prophetic '*sunna*' and the *hadith* literature from which it is derived. In South Asia, the term was employed by two of Wali Allah's contemporaries, Khwaja Andalib (d. 1759) and his son, Khwaja Mir Dard (d. 1785). They were also Naqshbandi Sufis but of Sirhindi's 'shuhudi' line, who sought to reform Sufi ideas and envisaged a puritanical emphasis on the practice of the Prophet that aimed at reconciling exoteric and esoteric Islam by opening the gates of *ijtihad*.¹⁰⁵ Farther away, a prominent example of a movement termed *Tariqa Muhammadiyya* was founded by Wali Allah's Qadiri contemporaries in West Africa, who also called for a return to the textual sources of Islamic jurisprudence (Qur'an and *hadith*) as the means to enliven the 'practice of the prophet'. Their strategy also entailed the rejection of adherence to one school of law in favour of the rejuvenation of *ijtihad*, and provided the doctrinal foundations for further movements across West Africa.¹⁰⁶

---

[103] Rizvi, *A History of Sufism*, vol. 2, pp. 302–07.

[104] Ibid., p. 302. In the larger Islamic context, Khidr refers to the Biblical prophet Ilyas (Elijah). In Sufism, he is not only held up an exemplary 'saint', but is said to be an immortal and ever-present figure. In the South Asian context, he also became revered by Hindus due to the activities of Bhaktis, who associated him with the worship of the Indus River. See Schimmel, *Islam in the Indian Subcontinent*, p. 5.

[105] For the most complete review of the life and work of Khwaja Mir Dard, see Annemarie Schimmel, *Pain and Grace: A Study of Two Mystical Writers of 18th Century Muslim India* (Leiden: E.J. Brill, 1976).

[106] For Qadiri developments in Africa, see N. Levitzion, 'The Eighteenth Century Background to the Islamic Revolutions in West Africa', *Eighteenth Century Renewal and Reform in Islam*, eds. N. Levitzion and J. Voll (Syracuse: Syracuse University Press,

Moving from the so-called 'peripheries' of 'Islamdom' (South Asia and Africa) to its 'heartlands', one cannot fail to add Muhammad ibn 'Abd al-Wahhab's (d. 1787) movement on the Arabian peninsula, also calling itself *Tariqa Muhammadiyya*. Describing 'Abd al-Wahhab's ideals, Smith writes that this movement 'rejected the corruption and laxity of the contemporary decline' and with it 'the introvert warmth and other-worldly piety of the mystical way', 'the alien intellectualism not only of philosophy but also of theology', as well as 'all dissensions, even the now well-established Shi'a'. That is to say, the Islam against which this movement was fighting was 'that which had become dominant', and in its place the Wahabiyya 'insisted solely on the Law... in its straightest, most rigid, Hanbali version, stripped of all innovations through the intervening centuries' not 'literally' found in textual sources, particularly *hadith*.[107] Thus, one finds great similarities between the writings of the South Asian Naqshbandi, African Qadiri and Arabian Wahhabi movements, save for one outstanding difference. 'Abd al-Wahhab's outright rejection of Sufism is obviously not echoed in the works of Sufi scholars. Rather, as Wali Allah's writings have already illustrated, such scholars defended monistic doctrines and other Sufi approaches to knowledge. These are hardly insignificant differences, but when approaches to jurisprudence are compared, the distinctions between the social ideals of such movements amount to very little. For example, 'Abd al-Wahhab also called for *ijtihad* and, as illustrated in his *Kitab al-Tawhid*, applied it to construct a singular school of jurisprudence out of the multiplicity that validated customary practice. Thus, when defining *shirk* (associationism), 'Abd al-Wahhab included the use of amulets and talismans, sacrifice in the name of any but Allah, saintly or any other form of intercession, the visitation of graves, and so on.[108] Furthermore, for having allowed such acts to occur, 'Abd al-Wahhab admonished his contemporaries, Sufis, jurists and theologians

---

1987), pp. 21–39. It should be noted, however, that the Qadiris were not the only order to indulge in such reform, or adopt the same name in Africa. For example, by the early 19th century, the Idrisi order had spawned the Rashidi movement in Algeria, the Sanusi movement in Libya and the Amir Ghani movement in Sudan.

[107] W.C. Smith, *Islam in Modern History* (New York: Mentor Books, 1963), pp. 49–50. Also see M. Cook, 'On the Origins of Wahhabism', *Journal of the Royal Asiatic Society* 2:2 (1992): 191–201.

[108] The edition employed here is Muhammad ibn 'Abd al-Wahhab, *Kitab al-Tawhid*, trans. A.M. Mujahid (Riyadh: Dar al-Salam Publications, 1996). For passages on the types of *shirk* mentioned, see pp. 32–34, 46–57, 71–82.

alike, 'for forbidding what Allah has made permissible and permitting what Allah has forbidden', accusing them of having made themselves into objects of worship.[109] The legal implication of these similarities is that a shift in the direction of codification was not a regional phenomenon, while the social goal of religio-cultural uniformity in the face of cultural regionalism does not appear coincidental. It must be stressed that the idea presented here is not that Wahhabism rose in Arabia and spread to other regions, giving rise to the similarities noted above. On the contrary, 'Abd al-Wahhab and some of the African 'leaders' were instructed in *hadith*, a central discipline in all these movements, by a prominent, early 18th century South Asian Naqshbandi family, the al-Sindhis.[110] As John Voll and Louis Brenner have suggested, such scholarly links illustrate a developing and multi-faceted discourse, rather than the influence of one regional movement on the rest.[111] It is in the context of such broad, discursive changes, therefore, that one must place the thought and activities of not only Wali Allah and his forefathers, but also his descendents.

Following Shah Wali Allah's death, his sons, grandsons and students essentially continued his doctrinal approach,[112] i.e. they forwarded the basic agenda of 'agreement' that began with 'Abd al-Rahim. Two of Wali Allah's sons, Shah Rafi' al-Din (d. 1818) and Shah 'Abd al-Qadir (d. 1813), furthered their father's approach to the Qur'an by each rendering it into Urdu. Nor did they fail to promote similar interpretations of text, whether among scholars or laypersons, as evinced by the *fatawa* (legal rulings) of another son, Shah 'Abd al-'Aziz (d. 1824), which particularly avoided the use of provisions for custom when specific injunctions were available in textual sources, as in the case of inheritance, divorce and matrimony.[113] Furthermore, soon after the British arrived in Delhi to

---

[109] Ibid., pp. 130–32.

[110] John Voll, 'Linking Groups In the Networks of 18th Century Revivalist Schools', *Eighteenth Century Renewal*, pp. 77–78. Also see Aziz Ahmad, 'Political and Religious Ideas of Shah Wali Allah of Delhi' *The Muslim World* 52:1 (1962): 22–30.

[111] See Voll, 'Linking Groups', p. 91; and Louis Brenner, 'Muslim Thought in 18th Century West Africa', *Eighteenth Century Renewal*, p. 61.

[112] For the most thorough considerations of the latter-day Wali Allahis' doctrinal approaches, two of Rizvi's works are most informative. First, his previously cited, *A History of Sufism*, vol. 2, pp. 250–90; and S.A.A. Rizvi, *Shah 'Abd al-'Aziz* (Canberra: Ma'rifat Press, 1982).

[113] Rizvi's close reading of 'Abd al-'Aziz's *fatawa* leads him to conclude that the 'purifying' element of Wali Allah's ideas received the greatest emphasis in the works of his followers. See Rizvi, *Shah 'Abd al-'Aziz*, pp. 211–241. For three examples of the

stay (1803), Shah 'Abd al-'Aziz and the students of his generation were among the first to print short tracts that outlined Wali Allahi ideals of Muslim conduct in local vernaculars, particularly in Urdu.[114] One such scholar was Shah Muhammad Isma'il (d. 1831), Wali Allah's grandson by Wali Allah's fourth son, Shah 'Abd al-Ghani. His *Taqwiyat al-Iman*, written around the 1820s and soon after becoming one of the first works printed in Urdu, is still in wide circulation today and worth closer consideration to gauge the 'substantive' or 'formal' legal rationality of latter-day Wali Allahis and those who refer to themselves as members of the 'universal' *Tariqa Muhammadiyya*.

In essence, Muhammad Isma'il's work is a scathing critique of Islam's contemporary advocates, be they philosophers, theologians, jurists or Sufis, stated in virtually the same terms outlined in 'Abd al-Wahhab's *Kitab al-Tawhid*. It explicitly speaks to the literate Urdu-speaking classes, declaring that all the 'customs' that the so-called scholars of Islam had legitimised were equivalent to *bid'a* (innovation) and *shirk* (associationism). In his introduction, Muhammad Isma'il lamented the present condition of Islamic scholarship, which he saw as steeped in the 'false methodologies' of the Sufis and the 'free-reasoning' of the theologians and philosophers. Rather than follow such thinkers, he urged that all Muslims were obliged to seek knowledge of the teachings of the Qur'an and the Prophet, make an effort to understand them and endeavour to mould one's life within their framework.[115] In typically Wali Allahi fashion, he dismissed the idea that the Qur'an and *hadith* could only be understood by scholars, and argued that all one has to do is read these sources and accept those scholarly opinions and local customs that conform to them, while rejecting those that do not.[116]

A crucial piece of advice that Muhammad Isma'il added in his introduction identifies the *Taqwiyat al-Iman* as the work of a Wali

---

fatawa considered, also see Shah 'Abd al-'Aziz, *Fatawa-i Shah 'Abd al-'Aziz* (Delhi: n.p., 1893–94), vol. 1, pp. 51–52, 115; vol. 2, p. 23.

[114] The first printed works in Urdu began appearing in the 1820s and 1830s. For a thorough discussion of the issues keeping Muslims from adopting print until the 19th century, as well as the effects of print on religious change, see Francis Robinson, 'Islam and the Impact of Print in South Asia', *Islam and Muslim History in South Asia* (New Delhi: Oxford University Press, 2001).

[115] Shah Muhammad Isma'il, *Taqwiyat al-Iman* (Karachi: Nur Muhammad Asah al-Matabi' wa Karkhanah Tijarat Kutub, 1958), p. 11. Also see Shah Muhammad Isma'il, *Sirat al-Mustaqim* (Deoband: Kutub-i Ashrafiyya Rashid, 1960); and *Darajat-i Imanat* (Delhi: Farangi Press, 1899).

[116] Ibid., pp. 9–10.

Allahi, directing the reader towards an understanding of the Qur'an and *hadith* that echoes that line's legal vision of 'agreement'. To avoid falling into the 'false methodologies' and 'free reasoning' of the scholars, Muhammad Isma'il reminded his readers that *iman* (faith) has two parts: recognition of God and recognition of His prophets' missions. In his opinion, the first part pointed to the concept of '*tawhid*' (Unity) and the second to the '*sunna*', derived from *hadith*. These, Muhammad Isma'il argued, must be the sole guides as they are at the heart of the 'faith'. Thus, as the opposite of *tawhid* is *shirk* and the antonym of *sunna* is *bid'a*, Muhammad Isma'il painted the latter as the greatest threat to the faith. He implored his readers, unfettered by the false methodologies and free reasoning of the scholars, to believe that any actions not literally in the Qur'an and *hadith* are *shirk* and *bid'a*. In the chapters of the *Taqwiyat al-Iman*, Muhammad Isma'il further guided his readers on the Wali Allahi path by outlining the *shirk* in the methodologies of the scholars, and the resulting *bid'a* in the practices of South Asian Muslim society at large.

In the introduction to his first volume, Muhammad Isma'il argued that God has no equal.[117] Yet, he found that *shirk*—the 'association' of people with God's powers—was rampant in society because people:

> ...have left the word of God [Qur'an] and the Prophet [Sunna] to exercise their own reason (*'aql*), and follow myths and erroneous customs (*rasum*), even when faced with the word of God and the Prophet.[118]

In the following chapters, the author goes on to identify two types of *shirk*. He refers to *shirk* concerned with God's powers as '*shirk* in disposing' (*tassaruf*) and '*shirk* in knowledge' (*'ilm*), and that concerned with human behaviour as '*shirk* in worship' (*'ibada*) and '*shirk* in customs' (*'ada*).[119] God's power to 'dispose', discussed in Chapters One and Two, includes everything from creating and ordering the universe, to issuing individual rewards and punishment.[120] So complete is God's power that there can be no intercession (*shafa'a*), either by saints or prophets. The idea that someone can intercede with God on one's behalf is argued in Chapter Three to be tantamount to making a slave the master, or the master's partner or believing that the slave has influence over the

---

[117] Ibid., pp. 11–19.
[118] Ibid., p. 13.
[119] Ibid., p. 19.
[120] Ibid., pp. 20–34.

master.¹²¹ In other words, God's power to 'dispose' is His and His alone. His power to 'know' is similarly comprehensive, but not as exclusive. In Chapter Two, God's 'knowledge' is argued to cover the 'seen' and the 'unseen' (*ghayb*).¹²² Humanity is granted a share in knowledge of the seen, by virtue of God-given senses, but none of God's power over it. Similarly, humanity is granted a glimpse of the unseen but no power in that realm either. No human has, for example, knowledge of the future, despite what astrologers and soothsayers claim. However, a person can have knowledge of the unseen when it is granted through Revelation. The prophet's sole distinction is this gift of revelation (*wahy*), and any prophet, saint, leader, astrologer or clairvoyant who claims knowledge of the unseen, independent of revelation, is described as a 'liar' (*jhuta*). The main thrust of Muhammad Isma'il's discussion of 'disposing' and 'knowledge' is then made clear. As the Qur'an is for all and not meant to be wrapped in scholarly platitudes, any leader, jurisconsult (*mujtahid*), saint (*qutub/pir*) or cleric (*'alim*) claiming knowledge, and any ideas and methodologies devised by them to gain knowledge not 'literally' upheld by the Qur'an and *hadith*, are 'polytheists' (*mushrik*).

Having eliminated the authority of any non-Wali Allahi scholar's opinions, not to mention the indirect limitations thus imposed on the use of Reason and Intuition in the interpretation of the Qur'an and *hadith*, Muhammad Isma'il turned to the two types of *shirk* having to do with human behaviour. If the cultural implications of Wali Allah's anti-custom *shari'a* were not apparent in the discussion of his scholastic writings, they are laid bare by his grandson. With regard to '*shirk* in worship', prescriptions range from pilgrimages to any place but the *Ka'ba*, including the graves of loved ones or the tombs of prophets and saints, to sacrifice in the name of any but Allah and prostration before any but He. Graves, coffins, flags, relics, the seats of saints, and the raised platforms of leaders (*imams*) are listed as 'idols' (*wathan*).¹²³ '*Shirk* in customs' extends further into the cultural norms of South Asian Muslims. Dedicating one's animals or portions of a harvest to saints is *bid'a*. So are prohibitions against widow remarriage, various customs surrounding marriage and death, and a number of dietary restrictions assigned according to class, gender or occupation.¹²⁴ In other words, not

---

[121] Ibid., pp. 35–43.
[122] Ibid., pp. 27–34.
[123] Ibid., pp. 44–52.
[124] Ibid., pp. 52–74.

only are the scholars and doctrines that support local custom declared *mushrik*, but the very fabric of Muslim society legitimated by pre-Wali Allahi Islam is found to be *bid'a*.

Muhammad Isma'il's presentation of *tawhid, sunna, shirk* and *bid'a* illustrates that although the Wali Allahis sought to free the Qur'an and *hadith* from the scholastic closet and bring it to the layperson, they did not mean that the layperson is free to exercise either his/her Reason or Intuition in textual interpretation. Rather, they sought to expunge customs extraneous to the literal word. This was a double-edged sword. For example, on the one hand, it granted women divorce, inheritance and property rights that had been overruled by custom in much of South Asia. On the other hand, it sought to undermine the very basis on which religio-cultural hospitality between Muslim and non-Muslim had been legitimised, i.e. the allowance for shared customs. In the final analysis, therefore, the *Taqwiyat al-Iman* confirms that Wali Allahis, whether or not under East India Company rule, sought and promoted forms of religio-cultural 'separatism', the route to which was a clear drive to 'codify' in a manner textually and conceptually akin to the 'formally rational' jurisprudence the British did not even partially bring into effect until the late 19th century.

While continuity between the Wali Allahis is recognisable, it must also be acknowledged that latter-day Wali Allahis would have been influenced by changed social conditions, political, economic and cultural. That is to say, scholars like 'Abd al-'Aziz and Muhammad Isma'il cannot be argued to have been oblivious or immune to the colonial state. Their response, however, appears to have taken separate routes, neither of which can be ignored in assessing the spread of Wali Allahi ideals. The first is legitimisation of the colonial state. When the British initially took Delhi at the dawn of the 19th century, 'Abd al-'Aziz issued the following *fatwa* in 1803:

> According to the *Kafi* [by Hakim al-Shahid (d. 945)], those territories (*bilad*) where the orders of the Imams were obeyed and which were under their control were called *dar ul-Islam*. In this city (Delhi), the Muslim's *Imam al-Muslimin* [i.e. the incumbent Mughal] is unable to enforce his orders; instead the Christian officers' orders are openly carried out. The implementation of the infidels' orders means that they are in full control of administrative matters. They govern the people, collect *kharaj, baj* (road toll), *ushr* (tithe) on commercial goods, punish thieves and robbers and decide lawsuits according to their own regulations. They (the Christian rulers) do not interfere with some Islamic ordinances such as those on Friday prayers, congregational prayers of the two *eids, adhan*

and cow sacrifice only because they do not value the basic principles of these practices to which they are indifferent. They unhesitatingly demolish mosques. No Muslim or *dhimmi* can enter this city or its suburbs without seeking their protection. In their own interests they do not prohibit the entry of common visitors, but eminent people…cannot enter without their specific permission…[125]

The issuance of such *fatawa* beginning in the early 19th century is not the prerogative of just 'Abd al-'Aziz, and it is for this reason that his attitude is important. First, it illustrates that by the beginning of the 19th century, at least among the Wali Allahis, the incumbent Mughal had been demoted to the *de jure* 'Imam', not Caliph, thus forwarding Wali Allah's political philosophy. More importantly, however, the Imam is portrayed as vanquished, and lands under British rule declared *dar al-harb*. British rule is nonetheless to be accepted. A number of *fatawa* suggest that 'Abd al-'Aziz did not advocate *hijra* (migration from *dar al-harb*) or *jihad* under the conditions he describes in the above *fatwa*.[126] In Rizvi's words, the 'Shah wrote that *hijra* was imperative only from a *dar al-harb* in which infidel rulers prohibited their Muslim subjects from preaching Islam, observing fasts and *namaz* [*salat*], and performing congregational and Friday prayers, *adhan* and circumcision'.[127] That is to say, as long as autonomy in 'personal law' was upheld, *hijra* and *jihad* was argued to be unnecessary. Thus, another of Wali Allah's grandsons, 'Abd al-Hayy (d. 1828), served as a *mufti* in the East India Company judiciary with 'Abd al-'Aziz's blessing, during the formative phase of Anglo-Muhammadan law.[128] Given that he was one of many from the 'scribal classes' acknowledged to have participated in the East India Company judiciary as 'expounders of the law' before the 1820s, one must allow for the influence of 'Abd al-Hayy and others of his jurisprudential bent on their British colleagues. In the light of Wali Allahi ideas, in fact, one cannot assume that the 'conceptualisation' of Islamic Law as a code contained in some text was merely an assumption carried to South Asia from Europe. Rather, the conceptual and textual overlaps between the Wali Allahis and the British suggest that the rigidification of religious and sectarian boundaries noted to have been

---

[125] Shah 'Abd al-'Aziz, *Fatawa-i Shah 'Abd al-'Aziz*, vol. 1, p. 115. The translation is from Rizvi, *Shah 'Abd al-'Aziz*, p. 227.
[126] For example, see 'Abd al-'Aziz, *Fatawa-i Shah 'Abd al-'Aziz*, vol. 1, pp. 51–52.
[127] Rizvi, *Shah 'Abd al-'Aziz*, p. 236.
[128] Ibid. pp. 239–40.

occurring during this period is only partially explained by British legal assumptions and institutions. The influence of independently evolving Islamic jurisprudential ideals must also be explored, given that certain schools of Islamic thought not only employed every means (including print) to promote a codified *shari'a* independent of East India Company institutions, but as a result of 'Abd al-'Aziz's legitimising *fatawa*, they also participated in the shaping of the colonial judiciary during its formative phase.

The second route was quite the opposite of that pursued by 'Abd al-'Aziz, for Muhammad Isma'il became the chief ideologue of a *jihad* movement led by fellow student at the Madrasa-i Rahimiyya, Sayyid Ahmad Barelwi (d. 1831)—a fateful decision that cost both men their lives. Much has been written on this movement, but a few points bear repeating in the interest of this chapter's broader discussion. First, this was by no means the only *jihad* movement of the early 19th century, nor even the only one led by scholars.[129] Second, this movement, like its contemporaries, was primarily fuelled by socio-economic and political factors, ranging from the loss of political authority among the elites, the suspension of endowments, etc., for the scholarly, and a host of other reasons, including heavy taxation and price hikes adversely affecting urban and rural subaltern groups. In fact, the strongest evidence that doctrine was not the driving force is, ironically, reconfirmed by the observation that segments of both pro- and anti-colonial scholarly camps adhered to the basic legal doctrines of the 'new' Sober Path. The third point of import is that *jihad* itself, whether undertaken by Ahmad Barelwi and Muhammad Isma'il or their contemporaries, represents a route not broadly followed, either by scholars or lay Muslims. Nevertheless, the Barelwi *jihad* began in 1818, when its leaders took to preaching Wali Allahi and *Tariqa Muhammadiyya* doctrine across the Ganges region.[130] After 'Abd al-'Aziz's death in 1820 and a sojourn for

---

[129] In 1802, Mapilla cultivators launched a *jihad* against Hindu landlords and East India Company backers that would sporadically continue until the 1850s. 1806 witnessed a *jihad* among elements of the Madras Army, as well as a separate movement against grain monopolists, in Vellore and Madras, respectively. Between 1808 and the 1820s, three movements led by Bengali scholars rallied weavers, cultivators, petty landlords and/or tribal peoples against Hindu landlords and their British supporters. For these and further movements, see S.H. Chaudhuri, *Civil Disturbances During British Rule in India, 1765-1857* (Calcutta: World Press, 1955); and K.K. Datta, *Anti-British Plots and Movements Before 1857* (Meerut: Meenakshi Prkashan, 1970).

[130] Although a great deal has been written on Ahmad Barelwi and the *jihad* he launched with Muhammad Isma'il, Muhammad Hedayetullah's, *Sayyid Ahmad* (Lahore:

hajj, preparations began for an armed struggle in 1824. Two years later, in 1826, leading disciples were dispatched to Bengal and other parts of South Asia to preach and to rally support for the cause against the British. Meanwhile, Ahmad Barelwi and Muhammad Isma'il, among others, began a *hijra* to Durrani territory in Afghanistan, after Barelwi, in keeping with Wali Allahi political philosophy, was endowed with the Caliphal title *Amir al-Mu'minin*, though referenced as an 'Imam'.[131] Thus, this movement and other contemporary *jihad*s represent the first 'modern' instances in which scholars entered the political arena as alternatives to the established political elite. It is no wonder then that, on their way to Afghanistan, in Sind and Baluchistan, the Barelwi *mujahidin* were cordially received, but local political elites did not show any enthusiasm for their cause. Among the Sufis of Sind, however, the cause won somewhat more substantial support. For example, the influential Qadiriyya line of 'Pir Pagaro' even dispatched a number of their own militia, the *Hurrs*, who were usually sworn to protect only the founding *pir*'s revered descendents.[132] The same pattern of scholarly recruitment (scant as it was) continued in Afghanistan, with 270 *'ulama'* joining the cause in Qandahar, while the Durranis of Ghazna pledged no troops.

Shan Muhammad Ashraf, 1970) remains an outstanding singular source on Ahmad Barelwi's intellectual background and orientation. For a consideration of Ahmad Barelwi's specific relationship with Shah Wali Allah's thought, however, see Ghulam Muhammad Jaffar, 'Teachings of Shah Wali Allah and the Movement of Sayyid Ahmad Shahid of Bareilly', *Hamdard Islamicus* 16:4 (1993): 69–80.

[131] There has been some debate about whether Ahmad Barelwi et al. directed their *jihad* at the British, mostly caused by the apologetics of late 19th and early 20th century Muslim authors. In the next chapter, this point is highlighted by such authors as Sayyid Ahmad Khan and Siddiq Hasan Khan, who argued that the *jihad* was merely against the Sikhs primarily to lessen the blows of British reprisals for the 1857 Uprising. A thorough discussion of the issue is available in a series of articles by Shafi Ali Khan, 'The Nationalist 'Ulama's Interpretation of Shah Wali Allah's Thought and Movement', *Journal of the Pakistan Historical Society* 37:3 (1989): 209–48; 'The Nationalist 'Ulama's Interpretation of Shah Wali Allah's Thought and Movement: the Post-Jihad Period', *Journal of the Pakistan Historical Society* 38:1 (1990): 35–75; and 'The Nationalist 'Ulama's Interpretation of Shah Wali Allah's Thought and Movement: Some Ideological and Intellectual Deviations of Deoband Dar ul-Ulam from the Fundamentals of Wali Allahi Philosophy', *Journal of the Pakistan Historical Society* 38:3 (1990): 192–219.

[132] For the line of Qadiriyya *pirs* known as the Pagaros, who were one of the most influential figures in Sind's religious and political life since the early 19th century, see Sarah Ansari, *Sufi Saints and State Power* (Lahore: Vangaurd Books, 1992). For a primary account of the *mujahidin*'s visit to Sind, see J. Burnes, *A Visit to the Court of Sinde* [sic] (Bombay: n.p., 1829).

The Sikh state in Punjab was the movement's first target. Sikhs were branded 'polytheists', but local Hindus were invited to make common cause with the *mujahidin* and limited numbers are known to have responded affirmatively.[133] That the movement was ultimately directed against the British, however, is validated by a number of factors, beginning with the recognition that a disciple, Mir Nithar 'Ali (d. 1831), was killed by British forces in Bengal in the same year that the leaders of the movement were slain at the other end of South Asia in Punjab.[134] Furthermore, before his death, Ahmad Barelwi dispatched letters (in vain) to various Amirs in Central Asia, stating that the 'wicked Christians... harass the Muslims in general and their leaders in particular. They have extended their hands of tyranny over the mosques and Islamic places of worship. The *shari'a* laws have been obliterated and the laws of infidelity introduced'.[135] The movement also remained active well beyond its founders' lifetimes. In Peshawar, the death of its founders led another disciple named Shaykh Wali Muhammad to receive *bay'a* as the new *Amir al-Mu'minin*, and in Patna, the struggle was continued by Mawlawi Wilayat 'Ali (d. 1858), running into the more general Uprising (a.k.a. 'Mutiny') of 1857.[136] The movement's ideals also spread to various figures not directly related to its founders and played an important part in the rhetoric of the 1857 Uprising, even if this Uprising, like those before it, was ultimately driven by socioeconomic and political factors.[137]

For example, among the incendiary literature circulating in 1857, there is a tract attributed to a *mawlawi* (preacher) Ahmad Allah (d. 1858).[138] It outlines the arguments of jurists and theologians on the issue of Caliphate in a decided Wali Allahi manner, but legitimates a

---

[133] S.A. Khan, 'The Nationalist Ulama's Interpretation Of Shah Wali Allah's Thought and Movement: The Post-Jihad Period', p. 37.

[134] Mir Zohair Husain, 'Three Preeminent Islamic Revivalists in 19th Century Bengal: Titu Mir, Haji Shari'at Allah and Dudu Mian', *Journal of the Pakistan Historical Society* 34:3 (1986), 216.

[135] Sayyid Ahmad Barelwi, *Makatib-i Sayyid Ahmad* (Lahore: Photolitho., n.d.), f. 18a. The translation is from Rizvi, *Shah 'Abd al-'Aziz*, p. 491. For the movement's insistence on the legality of *jihad*, which entirely follows Wali Allah's logic, see Shah Muhammad Isma'il, *Sirat al-Mustaqim*, cited above.

[136] S.A. Khan, 'The Nationalist Ulama's Interpretation of Shah Wali Allah's Thought and Movement: The Post-Jihad Period', pp. 38–39.

[137] See C.A. Bayly, ed. *The Peasant Armed: Indian Revolt of 1857* (Oxford; Clarendon, 1986).

[138] For accounts of Mawlawi Ahmad Allah's life, see S.B. Chaudhuri, *Theories of Indian Mutiny* (Calcutta: World Press, 1965); S.N. Chanda, *1857: Some Untold Stories* (Delhi:

non-Qurayshi religio-political head. Having explained the arguments for Quraysh descent, the author of the tract argued:

> ...if at the time when infidels become paramount in power, a Koreshee [sic] be not found, any Mahomedan [sic] Chief endowed even with a few of the qualities of a leader and observing the tenets of Mahomedan [sic] Law can, as a matter of necessity, be selected as Chief. This leader will be called Imam-i Akbar and great benefits will be derived from him in the cause of our faith...In short, it is held lawful, even by the religious books, that the order of a Mahomedan [sic] Chief, of whatever description he may be, should be obeyed. Common sense and a regard for faith point out that servitude under the Mahomedan [sic] Chiefs and such [Hindu] Rajahs as are dependents of the Mahomedan [sic] Kings is infinitely better than that under the infidel Victoria and the English, the enemies of our faith.[139]

As well, by 1857, the rhetoric of Caliphs and Imams was spread by preaching at mosques, touring villages, writing letters and publishing books and pamphlets in local vernaculars. One such Bengali language work is co-authored by two *mawlawi*s from Dacca and presents its subject in verse. The authors provide a history of Ahmad Barelwi and Muhammad Isma'il's *jihad*, acknowledging the former's successor as the 'Imam' of the age. Thus, obedience to Ahmad Barelwi's vision is enjoined and the colonial state argued to be the work of *'kafirs'*. *Jihad* and *hijra* are declared incumbent on all Muslims, and (confirming that scholars were by no means unanimously supportive) the 'saints and teachers' who preach otherwise are labelled 'enemies of the *sunna*'.[140] In other words, while 'Abd al-'Aziz delegitimated *jihad* for many with vested interests in the growing colonial order on the basis that it upheld personal law, some of his contemporaries, students and latter-day followers provided cover for the disenfranchised by arguing that even this realm (e.g. mosques) had been violated. The 'new' Sober Path, therefore,

---

Sterling Publishers, 1976); and G. Bhadra, 'Four Rebels of 1857', *Selected Subaltern Studies*, eds. R. Guha and G. Spivak (New York: Oxford University Press, 1988).

[139] The tract, titled *'Fateh-i Islam'*, is published in full in Salim al-Din Quraishi, ed. *Cry for Freedom: Proclamations of Muslim Revolutionaries of 1857* (Lahore: Sang-i Meel, 1997), pp. 117–20.

[140] A translated extract from the work, titled *'Tutwa'*, is included as 'Appendix B' in 'From J. O'Kinealy, Esq., Officiating Magistrate of Maldah, to the Officiating Under–Secretary to the Government of Bengal' (20 October 1868), *Selections from Bengal Government Records on Wahhabi Trials* (1863–1870), ed. M. Ahmad Khan (Dacca: Asiatic Society of Pakistan, 1961), pp. 301–303. For evidence of scholarly arguments against *jihad*, see pp. 281, 294.

offered two 'legitimate' courses of action to lay Muslims. Not surprisingly, such doctrinal subtleties, not to mention the socio-economic and political factors that ultimately drove Muslims to revolt or to declare loyalty, were lost or ignored by British commentators who, particularly after the 1857 Uprising, labelled any and all remotely associated with the Barelwi *jihad* as long-conspiring 'fanatical Wahhabis'. Furthermore, in a series of prosecutions known as the 'Wahhabi Trials', the British either transported or executed the accused during the 1860s.[141] Despite the misrepresentation of these Wali Allahis as 'Wahhabis' and the invested hyperbole of 'fanaticism', such British commentators confirm that whether by means of their employ, or as a result of facing such forces on the battlefield, by the mid-19th century the general doctrinal approach of the 'new' Sober Path had made itself known in indigenous and colonial circles.

III. *Deoband and Company: 1857–1947*

Moving into the period of the British Raj, all of the doctrinal redactions observed in the pre-colonial and East India Company periods—from the curtailment of metaphysics and other rational sciences to a concentration on law and *hadith*—can be found in the intellectual approach of the late 19th century's model *madrasa*: the *Dar al-'Ulum* at Deoband (outside Delhi). Established in 1867 under the pall of the 'Wahhabi Trials', the backgrounds of the founding coterie of the *madrasa* at Deoband speak volumes of their interests and the school's agenda, both of which also contribute towards understanding the school's popularity. Muhammad Qasim Nanawtawi, Rashid Ahmad Gangohi and Imdad Allah Thanawi hailed from the Upper Doab's scholarly families, travelling to Delhi for further education when of age.[142] Their

---

[141] For an example of the typical *mawlawi* prosecuted, see the depositions of Mawlawi Khan, a 'chaplain' in the Madras Army accused of 'preaching sedition', who argued in decidedly Wali Allahi fashion that he did nothing other than preach 'against the corruption of the faith prevalent among the Muslim races in general, and the loose manners of the Bidatee [sic]'. *Selections from Bengal Government Records on Wahhabi Trials*, pp. 140–48.

[142] For background reading on the founders of Deoband, apart from Metcalfe's *Islamic Revival in British India*, also see A.S. Khan, 'A Critical Appraisal of Dar ul-Ulum Deoband and its Leadership', *Journal of the Research Society of Pakistan* 31:4 (1994): 21–28; and S.H.H. Nadvi, 'The Role of Resurgent Ulama and Sufi-Sheikhs in the

familial and scholarly pedigrees are intimately connected with the Wali Allahis. Muhammad Qasim's biography illustrates the point. He was the nephew of Mamluk 'Ali (d. 1850), a scholar of the Wali Allahi line. At the latter's arrangement, Muhammad Qasim was a student at British Delhi College (f. 1829), where he studied geometry and arithmetic, but did not write the annual exams.[143] He also continued his study of philosophy, logic and theology under Mamluk 'Ali, and took up *hadith* studies under 'Abd al-Ghani, the incumbent principle of the Wali Allahi Madrasa-i Rahimiyya.[144] It was in this period that Muhammad Qasim met Rashid Ahmad, another of Mamluk 'Ali's students from a family long associated with the Wali Allahis. Both also studied Sufi principles and practice under Imdad Allah, another student of Mamluk 'Ali and of Shah Rafi' al-Din's grandson, the successor of Ahmad Barelwi as Imam of the *mujahidin*. When Muhammad Qasim completed his studies around 1850, he took up employment at the Matba'-i Ahmadi Press, established about 1845 by another of Mamluk 'Ali's students with the express intent of publishing *hadith* collections. Before Muhammad Qasim joined the press, al-Tirmizi's collection had already been rendered in print, the maiden printed rendition of *hadith* in South Asia. The *Sahih Bukhari* (1853) and *Mishkat al-Masabih* (1854) were published with Muhammad Qasim's participation.[145] In other words, following the lead of earlier Wali Allahis, the use of printed material represents one of the main innovations of the new *madrasa* established by these figures, an innovation with obviously broad implications in explaining its success.

There is some debate about the participation of this coterie of scholars in the conflagration of 1857. Metcalfe argues that neither of the three was involved, and that mention of their involvement is only made in post-1920 biographies published by Deobandi supporters of Indian nationalism. Based on her analysis, all that can be concluded is that Muhammad Qasim was never arrested, Rashid Ahmad was arrested but released after six months, and Imdad Allah was in Mecca at the time.[146]

Reconstruction of Islamic Education: the Foundation of Deoband (1867) and Nadwa (1893)', *Muslim Education Quarterly* 3:2 (1986): 37–56.

[143] Muhammad Yaqub Nanawtawi, *Sawahn-i Qasimi* (Delhi: Mujtaba-i Press, 1894), p. 4.

[144] Sayyid Mahbub Rizvi, *Tarikh-i Dar al-'Ulum Deoband* (Delhi: Idara-i Ihtemam, 1980), p. 80.

[145] Ibid., fn. 2 and 3, p. 80.

[146] Metcalfe, *Islamic Revival in British India*, p. 82.

This appears to be validated in the case of Muhammad Qasim by a more recent 'official' history that makes no mention of involvement in the conflict. Rather, it points out that the Matba'-i Ahmadi was relocated to Meerut by 1859, leaving Muhammad Qasim to find employment at the Matba'-i Mujtabai, which was relocated from Meerut to Delhi at the same time. Muhammad Qasim, the employee of one influential press, became an editor at another that would publish the Qur'an, the works of Wali Allahi scholars and some of the texts of the *dars-i nizamiyya*.[147] Rashid Ahmad and Imdad Allah, however, are said to have fought against the British at Shamli, as in the case of the 'nationalist' biographies mentioned by Metcalfe, based on the former's arrest and the latter's earlier return from Mecca.[148] Nevertheless, it can be argued that the exclusion of these scholars from mention of participation in the 1857 Uprising in pre-1920 biographies may provide less evidence of the Deobandi distance from the Uprising, than of promoting the perception of distance in its bloody wake. This point is addressed further below, beginning with an exploration of these scholars' disciplinary orientations.

Late scholars from Deoband accredit the founding of their school to the inspiration of Imdad Allah, whose purpose was to protect the Muslims of South Asia against the 'atheist' worldviews introduced by the British.[149] The eight principles upon which the *madrasa* was to run were articulated by Muhammad Qasim.[150] As Metcalfe has shown, these principles also illustrate the manner in which the new *madrasa* differed from those of the past. First, the majority of principles are concerned with securing funding in the absence of the Muslim political elite and their *waqfs* (endowments), without having to rely on the colonial state. The solution was to employ a network of private annual donations, which could include cash grants, books, food and furnishings. To persuade the people to donate, as the first principle stipulates, their convenience was assured by use of the colonial postal service and money orders, while gratification was provided by the printed lists of donors, no matter the size of their donation.[151]

---

[147] S.M. Rizvi, *Tarikh-i Dar al-'Ulum Deoband*, fn. 2, p. 83.
[148] Ibid., p. 97.
[149] Muhammad Tayyib, 'Introduction', *Tarikh-i Dar al-'Ulum Deoband*, p. 28.
[150] These principles are reprinted in S.M. Rizvi, *Tarikh-i Dar al-'Ulum Deoband*, pp. 116–17.
[151] Metcalfe, *Islamic Revival In British India*, p. 97.

Muhammad Qasim's principles also touch upon the administration of the *madrasa*, again suggesting a substantive change from the past. Apart from the post of *sarparast* (rector), *muhtamim* (chancellor) and *sadr mudarris* (principle), a *Majlis-i Shura* (Consultative Council) was established. Muhammad Qasim's principles enunciated that the administration could not act without the consent of the Majlis, and that it was this body, not the individual administrator or instructor, that decided the course of study to be followed in each class.[152] As Metcalfe concludes, the aim of the founders in agreeing to these terms was to avoid position or seniority determining the future course of administration and instruction.[153]

With these principles in mind, the first class was offered at a local mosque in 1866 and 21 students attended.[154] What is most clear about the institution that grew from there is the influence of European institutions of higher learning on its founders through their association with Delhi College. Most pertinent to our discussion, however, is that the fixed curriculum they prescribed, the annual exams they required of students for accreditation, the mass convocations at which they awarded graduates, and the affiliated *madrasa*s that followed their lead were designed for the propagation of the 'new' Sober Path. Another is the fact that aside from using printed material, much of the writing produced by this set of scholars was in a vernacular language, Urdu, as illustrated by the works considered in the following discussion of the Deobandis' intellectual orientation.

Although the Deobandis are justifiably noted for their Wali Allahi backgrounds, it must be clarified that there is only one major discipline in which the Deobandis are identical to Wali Allah. The discipline is mysticism (*tasawwuf*), and for this continuity one must credit the senior partner of the trio, Imdad Allah. His *Tahqiq-i Wahdat al-Wujud wa al-Shuhud* perfectly continues Wali Allah's propensity to consider the distinctions between 'wujudi' and 'shuhudi' doctrines and their authors to be a matter of terminology or approach, rather than the conclusion that *fana'* is absolute, or *baqa'* a 'lower' stage of consciousness,

---

[152] See 'Principles 3, 4 and 5', in S.M. Rizvi, *Tarikh-i Dar al-'Ulum Deoband*, pp. 116–17.
[153] Metcalfe, *Islamic Revival In British India*, p. 96.
[154] 'Rudad-i Sal-i Awwal', 1283 AH, in S.M. Rizvi, *Tarikh-i Dar al-'Ulum Deoband*, pp. 120–22.

as Intoxicated 'wujudis' argued.¹⁵⁵ He also upholds the more general Naqshbandiyya notion of equating *tariqa* with *shari'a*, nowhere more stridently than in his *Faysala-i Haft Mas'ala*.¹⁵⁶

The first point of dissonance between Deobandis and earlier Wali Allahis is this: whereas Wali Allah and his sons simultaneously inclined towards philosophy, theology, the principles of jurisprudence and other disciplines employing Reason, Imdad Allah's students and co-founders of Deoband followed Muhammad Isma'il's lead to further restrict their study. In fact, Muhammad Qasim neglected courses on logic, and all philosophy was later excluded from the curriculum by Rashid Ahmad.¹⁵⁷ This lack of interest in propagating philosophy and its adjunct disciplines is echoed in the writings of the most philosophically inclined of the above scholars. At Muhammad Qasim's most 'metaphysical', one finds little beyond polemical works like the *Qibla Numa*, which is a detailed response to the charge that Muslims are 'idolaters' (*but parast*) as they 'worship' (*sajada*) the *Ka'ba*, which he attaches to Swami Dayananda (d. 1883), founder of the influential Hindu 'revivalist' Arya Samaj (f. 1875).¹⁵⁸ It employs the arguments of the theologians associated with the 'old' Sober Path to define the metaphysical plane

---

¹⁵⁵ Imdad Allah Thanawi, *Tahqiq-i Wahdat al-Wujud wa al-Shuhud* (Karachi: Pak-i Akademi, 1963). For other instances of Imdad Allah's views on *wahdat al-wujud* and *tasawwuf* in Urdu, see his *Ziya' al-Qulub* (Delhi: Matba'-i Mujtaba'i, 1877). For compilations of Imdad Allah's pertinent writings, see *Kulliyat-i Imdadiyya* (Kanpur: Matba'-i Qayyumi, 1943); and *Marqumat-i Imdadiyya* (Delhi: Maktaba-i Burhan, 1979).
¹⁵⁶ Imdad Allah Thanawi, *Faysala-i Haft Mas'ala* (Kanpur: Matba'-i Majidi, 1960).
¹⁵⁷ I.H. Siddiqi, 'Muslim Educational Movements in North India', *Journal of the Institute of Islamic Studies* 9 (1972), 121.
¹⁵⁸ Muhammad Qasim Nanawtawi, *Qibla Numa* (Deoband: Majlis Ma'arif al-Qur'an, 1969), p. 30. Swami Dayananda Saraswati (d. 1883) and his Arya Samaj, or 'Society of Aryans' (f. 1875), have been hugely influential in contributing to the militancy of Hindu nationalism. The founder is termed a 'revivalist' for his firm conviction that the only 'true' faith is that contained in the four *Vedas* and practices of the Vedic Aryans. Theologically, Swami Dayananda argued that the *Vedas* did not sanction image-worship, caste, child marriage or the subjugation of women. Politically, this 'revivalism' involved a pro-active campaign to reform 'Hindu' society, while also 'protecting' it from the abuses of others, particularly Muslims. Apart from leading to vigorous debate with representatives of Brahmanical Hinduism, the Arya Samaj's aims involved the organisation in various campaigns that would put them at odds with Muslims, including 'cow protection', which sought to restrict the slaughter of cows by Muslims, particular on *'id al-adha*, and *shuddi*, which aggressively endeavoured to 're-convert' Muslims to Hinduism, both contributing to Hindu-Muslim violence from the 1880s on. For an introduction to Dayananda's ideas, see Swami Dayananda Saraswati, *Autobiography of Swami Dayanand Saraswati*, ed. K.C. Yadav (New Delhi: Manohar, 1976); and *The Light of Truth*, trans. G.P. Upadhyaya (Allahabad: Kala Press, 1960). Also see Kenneth W.

represented by the *Ka'ba* in the concept of '*Qibla*'.[159] As for Muhammad Qasim's attitude towards contemporary European thought, one need not step further than his *Tahdhir al-Nass*, another polemical work, on this occasion defending a geocentric conception of the universe against post-Copernican developments in European astronomy. It begins with a *hadith* which states that God created seven 'earths' (*ardin*), each with its own Adam, Noah and Abraham.[160] This, Muhammad Qasim declares, is sufficient for him to believe that there are seven celestial 'stratum' (*tabaqat*), each 'created' (*mukhluq*) by God. It is this belief, he ends, that determines the difference between *ahl-i sunna wa jama'a* (Sunni Muslims) and *kafirs, fasiqs* (heretics) and *kharijis* (apostates).[161]

Muhammad Qasim's ultimate reference to *hadith* is also reflected in Rashid Ahmad's intellectual strength, although the latter most often expressed this tendency through jurisprudence and the *fatwa*. This leads

---

Jones, *Arya Dharm: Hindu Consciousness in 19th Century Punjab* (Berkeley: University of California Press, 1976).

[159] The *Qibla* is the direction in which Muslims orient themselves during prayer, i.e. the direction of the Ka'ba in Mecca. This direction was set during Muhammad's time, shifting the previous orientation of his followers towards Jerusalem. As Muhammad Qasim's work suggests, however, the concept is also understood on a metaphysical plane. See C. Schoy, 'Kibla', *Encyclopeadia of Islam*, vol. 2 (Leiden: E.J. Brill, 1st Edition), pp. 985–89. Muhammad Qasim makes many explicit references to Muslim philosophers and theologians, as well as to 'Greek' (Yunani) philosophy, drawing from this large body of thought what makes his point that the concept of 'Qibla' is not 'idolatrous'. In other words, where 'metaphysics' plays a part, it is largely Neo-Platonic in orientation, but only as far as Wali Allah's notions of transcendence allow.

[160] Muhammad Qasim Nanawtawi, *Tahdhir al-Nass* (Delhi: Matba'-i Mujtaba'i 1891), p. 1. Other Urdu works by Muhammad Qasim that suggest the same intellectual orientation as the *Qibla Numa* and *Tadhzir al-Nass*, including the polemical mode of discourse, are: *Manazara-i Ajiba* (Muradabad: Matba'-i Gulzar-i Ibrahim, 1890); and *Tafsiyat al-Aqa'id* (Delhi: Matba'-i Mujtaba'i, reprint 1934).

[161] The same reliance on geocentric astronomy is found in the 'theological' writings of Rashid Ahmad. For example, in his *Luta'if-i Rashidiyya*, the author's *tafsir* of a Qur'anic verse (18:86) that mentions the sun setting in a pool of hot water, takes as a starting point the understanding of the cosmos in terms of 'seven skies' (*sathun asman*). *Luta'if-i Rashidiyya* is published with passages from other works as Rashid Ahmad Gangohi, *Tafsir-i Rashidi* (Bijnaur: Madani Dar al-Talif, 1970). The cited discussion is on pp. 56–57. Both Gangohi and Qasim illustrate the abiding influence of Ptolemaic astronomy in Islamic theology and metaphysics. Although Hellenic and Hindu heliocentric models had been known to Muslim astronomers since the 8th century, and Nasir al-Din al-Tusi (d. 1274), Mu'ayyad al-Din al-'Urdi (d. 1266) and Ibn Shatir (d. 1375) number among the Muslim astronomers to develop mathematical models that significantly advanced astronomy, the full implications of their ideas were not incorporated into the theology and metaphysics of their days. The ultimate irony is that the mathematical concepts they developed played an important role in equipping Copernicus to forward a geocentric model.

to the second difference between the Deobandis and Wali Allah and his sons. In terms of legalism, the Wali Allahis passionately pleaded for *ijtihad*, but Deobandi *fatawa* literature makes clear the school's insistence on *taqlid* in Hanafi *fiqh*. As Rashid Ahmad states in one *fatwa*, '*taqlid* is confirmed by the Qur'an'.[162] In another *fatwa*, when asked what the proof of the necessity for *taqlid* is, Rashid Ahmad responds that only *taqlid* can insure the 'peoples' organisation (*intizam*)'.[163] However, when confronted with the question of Muhammad Isma'il's legal method, Rashid Ahmad betrays his familiarity by quite accurately describing the approach of the *Tariqa Muhammadiyya*, stating that when the former scholar found 'sound' *hadith* that contradict Hanafi rulings, he practised the letter of *hadith*. When no such *hadith* was available, he practised *taqlid* in Hanafi *fiqh*.[164] Compared with Rashid Ahmad's own approach, one finds that the method of ruling is identical. Asked about the permissibility of *dhikr jahr* (spoken incantation) in Hanafi rites, Rashid Ahmad admits that there are discordant opinions on the subject, and adds that the reason behind contrary opinions cannot be decided. Rather than admit ambiguity on the subject, or argue for permissibility on the basis of Intuition (which he acknowledges as valid in the *fatwa*), he concludes that the proof of permissibility is in certain Qur'anic verses that call for the spoken.[165] In other words, Muhammad Isma'il's *ijtihad* and Rashid Ahmad's *taqlid* are virtually identical in their preferred dependence on literal readings of Qur'an and *hadith* above the opinions of scholars of the Hanafi school. That is to say, Rashid Ahmad's '*taqlid* in Hanafi *fiqh*' is more accurately described as *ijtihad* in the *Tariqa Muhammadiyya*, a type of 'new' jurisprudence.

The theological and jurisprudential perspective of Deobandis has obvious consequences in terms of the school's cultural outlook, the ultimate manner in which they differ from Wali Allah and his sons. If the Wali Allahis were anti-custom, the Deobandis—by neglecting philosophy and theology outright, while promoting the *Tariqa Muhammadiyya* jurisprudential method as the '*shari'a*' that complemented '*tariqa*'—took the trend up a notch. The proof is in the types of customs the Deobandis

---

[162] Rashid Ahmad Gangohi, *Fatawa-i Rashidiyya*, no. 1020 (Karachi: Saeed Company, reprint 1967), p. 508. For a secondary study of Deobandi legal opinion, see M.K. Masud, 'Trends in the Interpretation of Islamic Law in the Fatawa Literature of Deoband School', (MA Thesis, Institute of Islamic Studies, McGill, 1969), pp. 26–27, 79.
[163] Rashid Ahmad, *Fatawa-i Rashidiyya*, no. 1019, p. 508.
[164] Ibid., no. 1028, p. 511.
[165] Ibid., no. 1042, p. 523.

believed were *shirk* and *bid'a*. Like the Wali Allahis, Rashid Ahmad and Imdad Allah declared staple aspects of the Muslim ritual to date, such as the celebration of *milad al-nabi* and the *'urs* (death anniversaries) of *pirs*—let alone regional festivals like *Shab-i Barat* or *Shi'i Muharram* festivals—beyond the *shari'a*.[166] Their students and successors as leaders of Deoband went further. In his hugely influential *Bihishti Zewar*, the second generation Deobandi, Ashraf 'Ali Thanawi (d. 1943), went far beyond the reform of Muslim 'worship' in line with the privileging of the Qur'an and *hadith*, to generally view what is not mentioned in these texts as either wasteful, unnecessary or distracting, and thus a 'sin' (*guna*). In this light, mere participation in Hindu festivals like Diwali and Holi, in song or dance, in the keeping of dogs as pets, the decorating of one's home with pictures, playing card games or chess, and flying kites or setting off fireworks, were viewed as *bid'a*.[167] According to the Deobandi version of *taqlid* in Hanafi *fiqh*, therefore, customs not regarded as *bid'a* even in Wali Allahi thought, let alone that of the 'old' Sober Path, were added to the list of the un-*shar'i*.

The *Bihisthi Zewar* is also an excellent work to consider in this context, as it addressed to women in particular. Metcalfe and others observe that this represents a new genre that aims to plant women in 'domesticity' in a coherently Deobandi manner.[168] One cannot help but agree about the emphasis on domesticity, large portions of the work being devoted to nothing more 'public' than making mango pickles.[169] However, given Ashraf 'Ali's views on *purda* (segregation), he proceeds

---

[166] For Imdad Allah's views on *milad al-nabi*, which he terms '*mawlid sharif*', as well as on Sufi *'urs*, see his *Faisala-i Haft Mas'ala* (Kanpur: Matba'-i Majidi, 1960). For Rashid Ahmad's views on *bid'a* as it pertains to *milad al-nabi*, see his *Fatawa-i Rashidiyya* (Karachi: Saeed Co., 1967), pp. 409–29. For Rashid Ahmad's views on the Shi'a, see *Hidayat al-Shi'a* (Karachi: Kutub Khana-i Haqqaniyya, 1963).

[167] Ashraf 'Ali Thanawi, *Bihishti Zewar* (Karachi: Karkhana-i Tirajat-i Kutub, reprint 1914), chap. 6, pp. 3–7. For a similar discourse by Ashraf 'Ali, see his *Hayat al-Muslimin* (Delhi: Ilmi Kitab Khana, reprint 1962), though the latter work focuses less on the status of women.

[168] B.D. Metcalfe, 'Islamic Reform and Islamic Woman: Maulana Thanawi's Jewelry of Paradise', *Moral Conduct and Moral Authority in South Asian Islam* (Berkley: University of California Press, 1984), pp. 184–95.

[169] Chapter 10 of the *Bihishti Zewar* is particularly devoted to household tips and recipes. Among them is reference to the making of 'English Ink' (p. 28), but otherwise there is little evidence of European influence. Chapter 9, also littered with household tips, concentrates on medical treatments that make as little reference to European medicine, as there was reference to European physics in the works of the founders of Deoband.

further than his juristic predecessors in defining boundaries. As part of his condemnation of various modes of religious gathering, a persistent theme is Ashraf 'Ali's dismay at the social 'visiting' that goes on between women, whether it be in the context of weddings, births, funerals, *'ids*, *milad*s or any other of the festive occasions declared *bid'a*. One reason for his objection to these occasions is that, as a result, women were given more opportunity to consort with non-household men, thus breaking *purda*. So stern was Ashraf 'Ali's concept of *purda*, that even women gathering on specific nights in *Ramadan* in the company of a *hafiz* to hear Qur'anic recitation was viewed as a violation. The key, however, is that all this 'visiting' led women to take out loans for luxuries such as brocades and jewellery, and spend too much on betel-nut and tobacco, all of which were judged to be un-*shar'i* in the 'new' Sober Path.[170] That is to say, Ashraf 'Ali's perspective on women entirely followed the agenda of *Tariqa Muhammadiyya* reformers, even if obviously responding to colonial critiques of 'tradition'.

Ashraf 'Ali's emphasis on *purda* did not mean that women were to be deprived of education or a 'public' role in society—'novelties' again judged by historians of South Asia to arise under colonial aegis. The *Bihishti Zewar* argues that women may secure their economic independence through a number of occupations outside the household responsibilities of marriage (but not at their expense). These occupations fall into three classes related to artisanship, commerce and scholarship. Chapter 5 of the *Bihishti Zewar* is wholly devoted to such matters as sale and purchase of lands and commodities, partnerships and loans, wages and contracts, and the trading of manufactured goods. Of course, 'interest' (*sud*) was emphatically discouraged in all dealings.[171] In terms of scholarship, literacy was obviously required to read the *Bihishti Zewar* itself, but letter writing, arithmetic and accounting were also identified as the minimum requirements of women's education for the proper management of domestic responsibilities, as well as business and property. The final option was to study Persian and Arabic 'like men' and become *mawlawi*s providing primary education, or *qadi*s offering legal services, to the women of the community.[172] As in the case of *purda*, therefore, the concern to guarantee women a share in 'public'

---

[170] Ibid., Chap. 6, pp. 13–62.
[171] Ibid., Chap. 5, pp. 16–22.
[172] Ibid., pp. 357, 375.

life quite clearly issued in part from colonial discourses, but the space afforded fits entirely into a larger set of 18th century reforms.

Even given the limitations Ashraf 'Ali placed on women, the ideal of domesticity implied the need for more mobility than Ashraf 'Ali's strictures on *purda* seemed to allow. This contradiction is taken up by a Deobandi 'graduate', Sayyid Mumtaz 'Ali (d. 1935), in his *Huquq al-Niswan*.[173] The author argues that to engage the limited types of 'public' roles afforded women by other Deobandis, including going to the market, and so on, mobility should be afforded under the cloak of a '*burqa*' (shroud).[174] This is not new, but Mumtaz 'Ali goes on to say that a woman's face and hands may be uncovered, as opposed to the general attitude of the school that the *burqa* should cover all bodily features.[175] Thus, it is important to note that despite irrefutable engagement of colonial critiques, Deobandi views on gender ultimately relied on 'old' ideals, but shorn of most allowances for local custom according to the 'new' Sober Path.[176] Only Mumtaz 'Ali offered something particular to the late 19th century in positing his unpopularly 'revealing' mode of *burqa* (in our contemporary vernacular referred to as *hijab*), but one cannot say that the 'mobility' it was meant to afford is other than that circumscribed by Ashraf 'Ali.

It must also be stressed that Deobandi scholars were no more alone in promoting their vision of Islam in the period of British Raj, than the earlier Wali Allahis were isolated in their times. On one side of their doctrinal stance stood the Wahhabiyya, considered below, and on the other formed the *Ahl-i Sunnat*, centred on the writings of Ahmad Rida Barelwi (d. 1921). Ahmad Rida was born into a scholarly family. His father was a respected jurist and Qadiriyya Sufi, as was his grandfather. In and around Bareilly, the very town from which Sayyid Ahmad Barelwi travelled to Delhi to study under the Wali Allahis, before

---

[173] Gail Minault, 'Sayyid Mumtaz 'Ali and "Huquq un-Niswan": An Advocate of Women's Rights in Islam in the Late Nineteenth Century', *Modern Asian Studies* 24:1 (1990): 147–72.

[174] Sayyid Mumtaz 'Ali, *Huquq al-Niswan* (Lahore: Dar al-Isha'at-i Punjab, 1898), pp. 102–42.

[175] Minault, 'Sayyid Mumtaz 'Ali and "Huquq un-Niswan"', pp. 147–72.

[176] The types of customs that Mumtaz 'Ali wished to see removed can be gauged through his discussion of marriage. Apart from those mentioned by Ashraf 'Ali, one notes the restriction of child marriages, non-consensual marriages, practices concerning trousseaus (*mahr*) and dowries, and well as many aspects of nuptial ceremonies. See Sayyid Mumtaz 'Ali, *Huquq al-Niswan*, pp. 102–42. Also see Minault, 'Sayyid Mumtaz 'Ali and "Huquq un-Niswan"', pp. 163–67.

going on to launch his *jihad* with Muhammad Isma'il, Ahmad Rida's and other scholarly families had fostered the study of jurisprudence, theology, metaphysics and adjunct disciplines, and had debated with the followers of the *Tariqa Muhammadiyya* on the condemnation of practices such as the celebration of *milad al-nabi*.[177] Ahmad Rida did not veer from this path. Although he adopted Wali Allahi metaphysics and, as part of the Sober Qadiriyya, valued law above other disciplines, his stress on the import of *taqlid* in Hanafi *fiqh*, unlike the Deobandis, for whom this meant virtually the same as *ijtihad* did for the *Tariqa Muhammadiyya*, was grounded in the argument that there were no qualified *mujtahid*s (jurisconsults) in this time and that, thus, *ijtihad* was impossible. In the case of the Ahl-i Sunnat, therefore, *taqlid* meant binding one's self to the opinions derived by the 'old' jurisprudential methodology, and not merely the Qur'an and *hadith*. Thus, the Ahl-i Sunnat legitimated 'custom' on a relatively larger scale, accepting prophetic and saintly 'intercession' in a manner that allowed aspects of shrine-based worship that the Deobandis unanimously condemned as *shirk* or *bid'a*.[178] No work better illustrates the degree to which this separated the Ahl-i Sunnat from their 'new' Sober rivals than Ahmad Rida's *Husam al-Haramayn*. First published in Arabic and Urdu in 1906, this work included the *fatawa* of 33 Hanafi, Maliki and Shafi'i jurists in Mecca and Medina, finding all of the theological and jurisprudential ideals of the Deobandis and the Wahhabis to constitute *shirk, bid'a*, or outright apostasy.[179]

On the other side of the Deobandis stood the Wahhabiyya. This branch of the 'new' Sober Path had been transplanted from Arabia during the early 19th century, and was represented by groups such as the Fara'idi movement in Bengal, which had also waged a *jihad* against the British. Being from the landed segment of the capitalist classes, its leadership gained popularity among the cultivators, weavers and petty

---

[177] Usha Sanyal, *Devotional Islam and Politics in British India* (New York: Oxford University Press, 1996), pp. 51, 55, 69–72.

[178] For examples of *fatawa* on the issue, see Ahmad Rida Khan, *Al-Ataya li-Nabawiyya fi al-Fatawa al-Rizwiyya*, vol. 6 (Mubarakpur: Sunni Dar al-Isha'at, 1981). Also see Ahmad Rida Khan, *Malfuzat-i 'Ala' Hazrat*, 4 vols. (Gujarat: Fazl-i Academy, n.d.).

[179] See Ahmad Rida Khan, *Husam al-Haramayn 'ala Manhar al-Kufr wa al-Mayn* (Lahore: Maktaba Nabawiyya, 1985). For a secondary discussion, see 'Are Wahhabis Kafirs? Ahmad Riza Khan Barelwi and His Sword of the Haramayn', *Islamic Legal Interpretation: Muftis and Their Fatwas*, eds. M.K. Masud, B. Messick and D. Powers (Cambridge: Harvard University Press, 1996).

landlords of east Bengal, and would continue to exert an influence into the 1850s under a second generation, led by Muhsin al-Din Ahmad (d. 1860).[180] Also from the capitalist classes, though on a more 'aristocratic' level, Wahhabi-inspired thinkers coalesced into a school known as the Ahl-i Hadith in the late 19th century. Ahl-i Hadith scholars such as Sayyid Nazir Husayn (d. 1902) and Siddiq Hasan Khan (d. 1890) were from landed families associated with the Mughals and their successor states; however, they claimed the intellectual pedigree and attempted to live up to a number of aspects of Wahhabi thought. They called for absolute *ijtihad* and, unlike jurists of the 'old' Sober Path, emphasised *hadith* while abandoning *qiyas* in the derivation of law, just as *Tariqa Muhammadiyya* and the Deobandi scholars did. Their Wahhabi pedigree and greatest distinction from the Deobandis and Ahl-i Sunnat, however, is their total rejection of Sufism.[181]

When it is added that similarly 'codifying' trends had been arising among Shi'a schools from the 18th century, works from Wali Allah to the Deobandis, Ahl-i Sunnat and Ahl-i Hadith run the gamut of the 'new' Sober Path pursued in the era of British Raj. The Deobandi version, however, represents the backbone of the doctrinal ideals represented by the Jama'at-i 'Ulama'-i Hind, Jama'at-i 'Ulama'-i Islam, Jama'at-i Islami and Tablighi Jama'at, carrying this discussion into the post-colonial period. Nevertheless, just as Deobandi ideals represented an innovative variant of Wali Allahi ideas, one cannot assume that later thinkers also did not innovate. After all, the Jama'at-i Islami and Jama'at-i 'Ulama'-i Hind legitimated Indian nationalism, Jama'at-i 'Ulama'-i Islam split from the 'Hind' group and joined with a band of Ahl-i Sunnat scholars to legitimate Pakistani nationalism, and the Tablighi Jama'at concerned itself with ostensibly apolitical grass-roots activism. Furthermore, in the post-colonial period, leaders and followers of all four groups were shaped by an entirely distinct set of socio-political and economic circumstances, leading to the 'Hind' group's political quietism within Indian borders; the 'Islami' and 'Islam' lot to political activism and, at times, militancy in Pakistan, Afghanistan and further afield; and the Tablighi's conversion into a global missionary outfit.

---

[180] See Husain, 'Three Preeminent Islamic Revivalists in 19th Century Bengal', pp. 215–20.

[181] B. Metcalfe, *Islamic Revival in British India*, pp. 268–96. Also, for insight on the Ahl-i Hadith's contemporary influence, see Khaled Ahmad, 'The Power of the Ahle Hadith', *The Friday Times* (17 July 2002).

Such post-colonial conditions and responses are, of course, beyond the scope of this book, although perspectives on nationalism in the colonial context are revisited in the final chapter. All that remains to be said here, however, is that in the ideas represented by the Deoband school, one does not read a perspective adequately described as 'traditionalist' or 'revivalist', but one that embodies the ideals of a 'new' Sober Path that is incontestably 'modern' insofar as its 'codifying' bent arose in the late 17th and early 18th centuries in response to 'capitalisation' and other related factors, while its popularity was intimately bound to the effects of colonialism.

Conclusion: A 'New' Sober Path

By following a dominant paradigm that pays little heed to variation and change over time in doctrinal Islam, social historians (and many intellectual historians) of South Asia neglect to appreciate the significance of the move from 'substantive' to 'formal' legalism that began to arise about the late 17th century. In fact, the coincidence of goals and the networks linking scholars involved in the movements surveyed above displays that neither 'conceptual' nor 'textual' codification was carried to South Asia from Britain. Segments of the 'Muslim World' were moving in such jurisprudential directions with the decline of central authority and/or the rise of locally oriented capitalist classes, as all of the above movements suggest. As for the impact of these movements on cultural reorientation, Wali Allahi and *Tariqa Muhammadiyya* legal ideals, as well as their frequent and trans-continental echoes, provide strong reason to pay closer attention to developments in Islamic legal history when assessing the period directly prior to, and the spaces contemporaneously outside of, colonial reach. In essence, if codification is important in accounting for the rigidification of religious boundaries in the case of colonial reforms, one cannot deny the same in the case of indigenous trends, particularly when custom still had a role in British courts well into the 20th century.

The Wali Allahis, *Tariqa Muhammadiyya*, Deobandis, Ahl-i Sunnat, Ahl-i Hadith and the intellectual heirs that reach into the present in the form of the Jama'at-i 'Ulama'-i Hind, Jama'at-i 'Ulama'-i Islam, Jama'at-i Islami and Tablighi Jama'at, not only insist on a version of 'Islam' that is conceptually textual and legally prone to 'agreement', they also represent a vision of the *shari'a* that progressively narrowed over time. 'Abd al-Rahim's work on the *Fatawa-i 'Alamgiri* illustrates that by the late 17th century, the Wali Allahis and others were participating in the Mughal state-sponsored redaction of law, which Heyd and others have referred to as 'codification'. In the early 18th century, Wali Allah followed up not merely by seeking 'agreement' between past opinions, but by calling for the rejection of all opinion based on non-textual sources, when mere reference could be found in the Qur'an and the vast body of *hadith*. Furthermore, while the *Fatawa-i 'Alamgiri* was obviously intended for jurists, Wali Allah's translation of the Qur'an from Arabic to Persian, and his sons' and grandsons' extensive use of Urdu, print and genres of literature expressly intended for laypersons, suggest that political fragmentation and cultural regionalism were met with attempts to curb a 'substantively rational' system that allowed for local cultural affinities through case law, while favouring a 'formally rational' system that stifled variation through codification. By the early 19th century, therefore, Muhammad Isma'il even abandoned Wali Allah's acceptance of Hanafi and Shafi'i opinion, restricting himself to past Hanafi opinion alone, when the Qur'an and an uncritical use of *hadith* was not informative. In the face of political fragmentation, cultural regionalism and, in Muhammad Isma'il's and the Deobandis' cases, colonialism, the uniformity of a 'code' crystallised as the main way that scholars could conceive of fostering the bonds between Muslims necessary to give the 'religious' community (and their class of scholars) a prominent place in the rapidly evolving order.

With regard to 'colonial difference', the above trends in Islamic jurisprudence, as well as Perry's cases tried by British jurisprudence, call into question the absolute distinction between colonial and pre-colonial legal regimes that Kugle and others assert. Although the 'new' Sober Path and the above movements were far from mainstream until the 19th century, recognising the pressure exerted by such movements on scholarly classes from Indonesia to Nigeria, one cannot underestimate the reconditioning in favour of textually based legalism that these movements bred, even if they remained peripheral in practice throughout the 18th century. Furthermore, by placing these movements within the framework of 'codification', conceptual similarities between the Wali Allahis and British codifiers lend themselves to hypothesising that theoretical congruence plays a part in explaining why so broad a base of 'scribal classes' and 'ideologues' could legitimately offer their support to the East India Company, not to mention the possibility of influencing British conceptions of Anglo-Muhammadan Law. Even British sources from the mid-19th century suggest that as late as the 1850s, in all Presidencies, the option of calling for a *fatwa* was 'rarely exercised' in higher courts, but in lower courts *mufti*s and *qadi*s remained in the capacity of 'assessors rather than of expounders of the law'.[182] Regarding the degree of 'colonial difference', therefore, it appears that the East India Company not only did what 'local Indian kings' had been doing for the last century, as Bayly, Stein and others have asserted, it may also have forwarded aspects of what Muslim 'codifiers' had been doing. At the very least, the relatively late diversions from codes evident in British policy were indirectly compensated for by large sections of the Muslim juristic community insisting on them before or outside the colonial sphere. At the same time, however, the progressive redaction of law prior to or outside the colonial regime, itself new to the region and the broader Muslim World, confirms that the rise of capitalists, political fragmentation, cultural regionalism and colonialism (i.e. the 'modern' condition) provoked a response that increasingly involved the articulation of 'puritanism', as Gellner, Tamney and others have long argued. In the final analysis, the primary sources consulted above offer little on the chronology of structural change in legal practice from pre-colonial to colonial periods, but suggest that jurisprudential aspects of the order otherwise wholly attributed to British influence were beginning to be articulated by the late 17th century and were formulated with greater vigour and variety in the centuries that followed. To appreciate the import and identify the specific chronology and extent of change from 'old' to 'new' doctrines among extra-colonial actors, therefore, one must venture away from British jurisprudential institutions to consider the very *madrasas*, *maktab*s, home tutors and vernacular schools that had been the venue for the cultural effervescence characteristic of the 18th century, and ask what they were offering in the 19th century—a task taken up in the following chapter.

---

[182] *The Judicial System of British India* (London: Pelham Richardson, 1852), pp. 23, 28.

CHAPTER FOUR

ANGLICISATION AND THE 'OLD ISLAM'

On the outskirts of Karachi, Pakistan's most populous city, stands the shrine of the 13th century Suhrawardi 'saint', Pir Haji Mango. Frequented by thousands of devotees—Muslims and non-Muslims, men and women—from the working-class neighbourhoods that now surround the shrine to the pilgrims from as far away as Punjab and Gujarat during the annual *'urs*, the shrine is a centre of prayer, song and dance, healing and, in some cases, the consumption of large quantities of hashish.[1] Apart from circumambulating the *pir*'s grave in the main shrine, the most striking feature of worship is that *barakat* (grace) and *manat* (wishes) can be gained by feeding the scores of crocodiles that live in ponds within the complex—obviously a remnant of the area's pre-Islamic past. Yet, none of the accounts of the shrine attendants and worshippers I gathered upon my visit make this connection. Instead, like the Chishtiyya reformers who linked obviously Yogic practices to Sufi figures, the sanctity of these crocodiles is invariably linked to the miraculous powers of Haji Mango, who is credited with converting local inhabitants to Islam.

No matter how peculiar the 'cult of crocodiles' may be, this shrine is no more than an example of hundreds of others dotted across Sind, Punjab and beyond with similarly 'hospitable' practices. It, therefore, emphasises the fact that neither the 'codifying' exertions of Deobandis, Wahhabis and the British, nor the socio-economic and political changes that mark the period under discussion in this book, have succeeded in eradicating latitudinarianism in Sufism, so far as the accommodation of local custom is concerned. This is largely due to the efforts of individual institutions, such as the shrine of Pir Haji Mango itself, however, and the antinomianism of the 'Intoxicated Way' is rare even in such contexts. The largely subaltern character of the place, therefore, only confirms that the sheer number of institutions affiliated with Deoband,

---

[1] This account is based on a visit to Pir Haji Mango's shrine, among others of similar ilk in Sind and Punjab, in November 2000. For background on the Suhrawardiyya in Sind, see Sarah Ansari, *Sufi Saints and State Power* (Lahore: Vanguard, 1992).

Ahl-i Hadith and Ahl-i Sunnat, the modes of funding and methods of administration and instruction employed in their *madrasas*, as well as their early and prolific use of short-tract literature, vernacular languages and print, have thoroughly discredited antinomian and/or latitudinarian doctrines in the religious consciousness of elite and capitalist classes. A similarly impactful competitor for the Intoxicated Way, has been the rise of English education under the auspices of the colonial state.

Given that the 'Old Islam' noted to have carried largely unchallenged into the early 18th century, was dependent on the continued patronage of such institutions as *maktabs* and *madrasas*, any diversion of funding or deflection of interest would obviously alter the complexion of doctrine. Of course, such diversions and deflections are exactly what the rise of British authority constituted. British intervention has, in fact, been well documented for some time. The earliest institutions patronised by the East India Company or its officers were known as 'Oriental Colleges', the first being the 'Muhammadan College of Calcutta', inaugurated by 1781.[2] As the reference to Muslims suggests, this college was opened when former Muslim elites and scholars from the region approached the East India Company to open a *madrasa*, being unable to finance it themselves. As Hastings wrote at the time:

> After the take-over of Muslim rule in India [i.e. Bengal] by the British, the condition of Muslims in general beggars [sic] description. They have gone to such a lower ebb that they cannot afford to send their children to schools.[3]

Hastings was moved enough to fund the *madrasa* himself, but very little official interest was shown in these early years. The British government did not become involved until the Charter of 1813, in which a paltry Rs. 100,000 was allotted to education.[4] A 'Committee for Public Instruction' was, however, established in 1823, but as late as 1838, one of the East India Company's prime educational reformers, Charles Edward

---

[2] Histories of the East India Company educational regime include M.A. Greaves, *Education in British India, 1698–1947* (London: University of London, 1967); S.N. Sen, *Scientific and Technical Education in India, 1781–1900* (New Delhi: Indian National Scientific Academy, 1991); and S.C. Dutta, *History of Adult Education in India* (New Delhi: Indian Adult Education Association, 1986).

[3] Cited in Mujibur Rahman, *History of Madrasa Education* (Calcutta: Rais Anwar Rahman, 1977), p. 78. Also see Lynn Zastoupil and M. Moir, eds. *The Great Indian Education Debate* (Richmond: Curzon Press, 1999), pp. 73–76.

[4] For a copy of the pertinent sections of the act, see *The Great Indian Education Debate*, pp. 90–92.

Trevelyan, reported that only 40 'colleges' had been opened under the East India Company, most by then teaching European learning in English, but including some 'oriental' works to meet judicial needs.[5]

The paucity of institutions and funding did not mean lack of debate on the future form of education in the East India Company's ever-expanding South Asian possessions. The sole defenders of the 'Oriental Colleges' were Indologists, such as William Jones, who may have wanted Islamic jurisprudence and its 'native' scholars out of the judicial process, but hoped local learning would continue to inform government in general through translation.[6] Furthermore, Horace Hayman Wilson, Secretary of the Committee for Public Instruction (1823–1832), himself a Sanskritist, added that without the support of 'Oriental' learning, particularly languages, the British could not win the support of South Asia's elite intellectuals, nor create the necessary conditions for bringing European learning (in translation) to the population in general.[7] In opposition to the funding of the Oriental colleges espoused by Indologists stood those informed by Utilitarian and Evangelical ideas. For Utilitarians, the issue hinged on the introduction of 'useful knowledge', as expressed in a report dated December 1831 and mentioned by Trevelyan.[8] Thus, in the absence of a judicial or administrative need for local learning or languages, the premise that Islamic learning was 'useful' could not easily be defended.[9] On the other hand, the idea that European learning was 'useful' could be argued from the Utilitarian and Evangelical perspectives, as well as by certain South Asians with a vested interest. Utilitarians such as Trevelyan, therefore, took pains to present Islamic learning as equivalent to that of Europe before Galileo, Copernicus and Bacon. Its metaphysics was that of Plato, its logic that

---

[5] C.E. Trevelyan, *On the Education of the People of India* (London: Longman, 1838), p. 17. A fascinating account of the cultural platitudes inhabiting the minds of such officers as Trevelyan, Wilson and others can be read in K. Prior, L. Brennan and R. Haines, 'Bad Language: The Role of English, Persian and Other Esoteric Tongues in the Dismissal of Sir Edward Colebrooke as Resident of Delhi in 1829', *Modern Asian Studies* 35:1 (2001): 75–112.

[6] W. Jones was mentioned in the last chapter for his translations of Muslim juridical works. That this did not mean Jones advocated the end of Persian literature is illustrated by the fact that the translation of a work on Persian grammar numbers among his earliest endeavours. See W. Jones, *A Grammar of the Persian Language* (1771) (Menston: Scolar Press, 1969).

[7] H.H. Wilson, 'Education of the Natives of India', *The Asiatic Journal* 19 (Jan.–Apr. 1836): 1–16.

[8] Trevelyan, *On the Education of the People of India*, p. 4.

[9] Ibid., pp. 1–3.

of Aristotle, its astronomy that of Ptolemy and its medicine that of Galen—that is to say, it was outdated.[10] At any rate, it was with this understanding of Islam and Utilitarian ideals in mind that Thomas Babington Macaulay, a member of the East India Company's 'Supreme Council of India' in the 1830s, declared the now-infamous line that a 'single shelf of a good European library was worth the whole native literature of India and Arabia'.[11]

Echoing Trevelyan and Macaulay in his condemnation of 'native learning' into the 1860s, the Evangelist and author John Murdoch, compiled the ideas of many other educators of his ideological leaning to suggest that, 'It is difficult to conceive any education less adapted to produce a beneficial effect than that imparted by the indigenous schools of India'.[12] Of course, the concerns of such Evangelicals differed from the Utilitarians in their focus on the 'moral' aspect of the indigenous system, rather than its 'scientific' accomplishment. Thus, Murdoch opined that the books used locally contain 'maxims which are absurd and grovelling; some books sanction vice of the worst character; and all indicate the most debasing superstition'.[13] Thus, as far as this group was generally concerned, 'useful knowledge' was European Christianity, particularly of the Protestant variety.

Support for English education also came from South Asians, one of the first organised expressions of which was the Bengali Hindu reformer Ram Mohan Roy's (d. 1833) *Brahmo Samaj* (f. 1828).[14] Himself

---

[10] Ibid., pp. 57–58.

[11] T.B. Macaulay, 'Minute on Indian Education (Feb. 2, 1835)', *Imperialism and Orientalism: A Documentary Source Book*, eds. B. Harlow and M. Carter (Oxford: Blackwell, 1999), p. 58.

[12] J. Murdoch, *Hints on Education in India with Special Reference to Vernacular Schools* (Madras: Scottish Press, 1860), p. ix. Also see *Thoughts on Education in India* (Allahabad: 1856); *General Association of Bengal Missionaries* (Calcutta: Baptist Mission Press, 1831); and *Christian Missionaries and Government Education in India* (London: Seeley, 1858).

[13] Murdoch, *Hints on Education in India with Special Reference to Vernacular Schools*, p. x.

[14] A letter (1823) from Ram Mohan Roy pressing the East India Company administration for English education after the first meeting of Committee for Public Instruction is included in Trevelyan's *On the Education of the People of India*, pp. 65–71, as well as in *The Great Indian Education Debate*, pp. 110–14. In Indian nationalist circles, Ram Mohan Roy is often referred to as the 'Father of Modern India'. Born into an elite Bengali *brahmin* family, he worked in the East India Company revenue service while dabbling in real estate and finance, until wealthy enough to retire in his early 40s. At this point, in Calcutta, Roy began work towards the reform of Hinduism, such that Hindu scriptures were interpreted in a monotheistic vein, image-based worship was

a Bengali *brahmin* who criticised Brahmanism, Roy borrowed from Christianity and promoted the study of European languages and sciences directly. Together, the influence of such attitudes is witnessed in the fact that although the Committee for Public Instruction was first constituted and run by Indologists like Wilson, its resolution to open new 'Oriental Colleges' in Delhi and Agra, and continue translations, was never fulfilled. When Delhi College did open its doors to students in 1829, Trevelyan declared triumphantly that it was in the interests of 'Western learning'.[15] In fact, Macaulay's 'minute' was made policy when the Governor General's Resolution of March 1835 required that all funds go towards 'English education', that no support be provided to students of existing 'Oriental education', and that funding should be withdrawn from the translation and publishing of Arabic works.[16] That same year, English replaced Persian as the language of state. By 1838, of the 6,000 students attending the 40 schools under the control of the East India Company Committee for Public Instruction, fewer than 200 were learning Arabic.[17] By the 1840s, talk had already begun of charging a fee for the study of Arabic and Persian where they continued to be taught. For example, in his report to Henry Bartle Edward Frere, Commissioner of Sind in the 1850s, his field-agent wrote that Persian should be confined to 'those who acquire it as an accomplishment', while Arabic should continue to be taught so as not to offend Muslim sensibilities, but should be restricted to only three district schools in Sind—a recommendation which Frere, like many others, passed on to his superiors at the centre.[18]

While Islamic learning and the primary languages in which it was written (Arabic and Persian) were being pushed aside by English,

---

eschewed, as were *sati* (widow immolation) and other practices. He also worked to promote European learning among South Asians. The *Brahmo Samaj* became Roy's prime vehicle for the reformist agenda he articulated, remaining a prominent vehicle for Hindu reform to the dawn of the 20th century. Fittingly, Roy was also among the earliest of South Asians to journey to Britain, dying in Bristol in 1833. Much has been written on Ram Mohan Roy and the intellectual climate in which he worked, but for an introduction, see B.M. Sankhdher, *Ram Moham Roy: The Apostle of Indian Awakening* (New Delhi: Navarang Press, 1989).

[15] Trevelyan, *On the Education of the People of India*, p. 4.
[16] Ibid., pp. 13–14.
[17] Ibid., pp. 17, 103.
[18] H.B.E. Frere, 'Education in Sind', *Education in Sind Before the British Conquest and the Educational Policies of the British Government* (Hyderabad: University of Sind, 1971), p. 26.

English was not to be the lone language of either education or administration. In place of Persian, local vernaculars increasingly served as the language of lower administration and education. This was not an easy choice, there being so many languages with which to contend. More constraining yet was the fact that none were formalised languages, at least from the British perspective. This meant that works on grammar, dictionaries and so forth, were not usually available. To this one can add an observation shared by Richard Burton and Frere in the region of Sind, but which applies more broadly: the vernaculars lacked a standardised script and many Muslims used the Arabic script, while many Hindus used as many as eight Sanskrit-based scripts.[19] In response, by the early 19th century, grammar manuals and dictionaries would become an industry in themselves, a long list of vernacular works peppering the period in which East India Company dominion extended inward from the coastal Presidencies. Furthermore, Trevelyan numbers among those who floated the idea that vernacular language should be written in the Roman script.[20] Despite the obvious difficulties that official recognition of the vernacular represented, all the sources cited here considered this the best, if not the only, option. For most, the reason is that it was impossible to teach everyone English in an instant, but it was possible to manage the work necessary to use vernacular languages for administration, while disseminating European learning through English to a select class of 'intermediary' locals. Thus, the education system that the East India Company patronised was as alien to the environment as the judicial system discussed in the previous chapter.

The promotion of English and vernacular education obviously had negative effects on indigenous institutions employing Arabic and Persian sources of instruction. In essence, the *maktabs* and *madrasas* necessary to maintain the intellectualism of the early 18th century are

---

[19] Richard Burton, 'Muslim Education at Schools and Colleges under the Native Rulers and Our Government', *Education in Sind Before the British Conquest and the Educational Policies of the British Government* (Hyderabad: University of Sind, 1971), pp. 60–61; Frere, 'Education in Sind', p. 16.

[20] *The Nineteenth Century: Linguistics Specialist Collection* (Chadwyk-Healey, 1986-Present) microfilm collection contains no less than 30 grammars, dictionaries and instruction manuals published before 1860, covering Bengali, Brahui, Baluchi, Gujarati, Hindi, Karnata, Malayalam, Marathi, Naga, Oriya, Punjabi, Pushtu, Tamil, Telugu and Urdu. Also see *The Application of the Roman Alphabet to All the Oriental Languages, Contained in a Series of Papers Written by Messrs Trevelyan and Tytler, Rev. A Duff and Mr. H.T. Prinsep; and Published in various Calcutta Periodicals in the Year 1834* (Calcutta: Serampore Press, 1836).

noted to have declined under East India Company rule due to: (1) the disruption of endowments of various types and grades supporting indigenous institutions which had survived the political fragmentation of the 18th century, but succumbed by the mid-19th century, as Gail Minault puts it, to the 'more watchful eye' of the British; and, (2) the investment of funds towards English instruction, diverting local patrons and students further from Islamic institutions once the British dropped Persian as the language of state in the 1830s.[21] Furthermore, as English institutions taught 'European' rational sciences, Francis Robinson is one among others to conclude that the very institutions supporting 'Islamic' rational sciences were severely curtailed wherever the East India Company gained authority during 19th century. Even the *Madrasa-i Farangi Mahal*, once a great bastion of rational sciences in Lucknow, dropped related courses by the late 19th century, leaving contemporary scholars to conclude that the formulations of the 18th century's indigenous 'thrust for reform' came to the fore by the early 20th century.[22]

Yet, a more thorough consideration of the process, particularly what *madrasa*s beyond the great scholastic centres of Delhi, Lahore and Lucknow were teaching and to whom in the 19th century, as well as how they evolved into institutions supporting reformist ideas, can certainly clarify when and where corresponding cultural attitudes began to change, at least among the elite and capitalist classes. Considering the links between doctrinal Islam and the cultural attitudes of Muslims established in the previous chapters—i.e. the Intoxicated Way and the Sober Path—the question is more than an academic curiosity. Indeed, when coupled with evidence that the same indigenous movements sought to alter legal doctrine in favour of codification, if it happens that the remaining *madrasa*s of the 19th century even incidentally strengthened reformist trends, cultural ramifications may be argued to represent as transformative a paradigmic shift as the introduction of

---

[21] Gail Minault, *Secluded Scholars: Women's Education and Muslim Social Reform in Colonial India* (Delhi: Oxford University Press, 1998), p. 22. Also see Joseph DiBona, ed. *One Teacher, One School* (Delhi: Biblia Impex Ltd., 1983); Aparna Basu, 'The Indigenous System of Education in the Early Nineteenth Century and its Decline', *Essays in the History of Indian Education* (Delhi: Concept Publishers, 1982), pp. 28–38; and Gregory Kozlowski, *Muslim Endowments and Society in British India* (Cambridge: Cambridge University Press, 1985).

[22] Francis Robinson, *The 'Ulama of Farangi Mahall* (London: Hurst and Co., 2001), pp. 36–37.

English legal and educational regimes by a colonial state, occuring earlier than currently thought. Thus, in this chapter, I focus attention on British studies of indigenous institutions in Bengal, Bihar, Orissa, Sind and Punjab, conducted between the 1830s and the 1880s.[23] Using the *dars-i nizamiyya*, articulated by Mulla Nizam al-Din (d. 1748) of the Madrasa-i Farangi Mahal in Lucknow, and used by Robinson and others to establish the intellectual vibrancy of the 18th century, I evaluate instruction in the institutions mentioned in such sources, facilitating a somewhat broader-based portrait of Islamic education in this period than currently available, one that is regionally and chronologically comparative, focusing on the number of different types of schools, their sources of funding, the subjects taught and the students who attended classes. Although Robinson cautions that too much emphasis 'should not be given the actual number of books in each subject', pedagogical approaches of pre-colonial *madrasa*s not based on a set curriculum, but on the individual preferences of instructors and commitment of students before Deobandi-style reforms became the vogue, the absence or presence of the works mentioned in the *dars-i nizamiyya* is an indicator of the type and level of instruction available.[24] As well, acknowledging Seyyed Hossein Nasr's caution that the 'oral tradition transformed the written book from the definitive text which was the sole basis of the ideas to be understood to the gate to a whole living world for which the book became the point of departure', I also access R.C. Temple's voluminous collection of Punjabi folk literature, recorded in the original language and forms recited by bards and performers in the 1870s and 1880s.[25]

---

[23] These include G.W. Leitner, *History of Indigenous Education in the Punjab* (Calcutta: Government Printing Press, 1883); W. Adam, *Reports on the State of Education in Bengal* (1835–38), ed. A. Basu (Calcutta: University of Calcutta Press, 1941); R. Burton, 'Muslim Education at Schools and Colleges under the Native Rulers and Our Government' (1851), and H.B.E. Frere, 'Education in Sind' (1854), in *Education in Sind Before the British Conquest and the Educational Policies of the British Government* (Hyderabad: University of Sind, 1971); and Edwin Arnold, *Education in India* (London: Bell & Daldy, 1860). Also consulted, 30 pertinent documents included in Lynn Zastoupil and M. Moir, eds., *The Great Indian Education Debate* (Richmond: Curzon Press, 1999).
[24] Robinson, *The 'Ulama of Farangi Mahall*, p. 46.
[25] To fully appreciate Nasr's point, it is important to add the example he provides. He goes on to write: 'We recall once when studying *al-Insan al-Kamil* of 'Abd al-Karim al-Jili with the late Mahdi Ilahi Qumsha'i, he read the Arabic text and then gave a long discourse on divine love and its manifestations which seemed to have little connection with the outward meaning of al-Jili's words. When asked how these words conveyed such meanings, he answered that one should look at these words as signs to the spiritual and not in their usual literal meaning and as concepts closed in upon themselves. He

Read together, the details that this consideration adds begin with the observation that East India Company rule in Bengal, Bihar and Orissa in the 1830s, and in Sind during the 1850s, had already reduced *madrasa*s to shadows of their former selves. Many in such local centres of learning as Murshidabad, former capital of the Nizamate of Bengal, Bihar and Orissa, and Thatta, former capital of the Mirs of Sind, were already closed, while those that remained offered nothing approximating the *dars-i nizamiyya* upon which the 'old' Sober Path depended. Furthermore, a survey of Punjab's *madrasa*s in the 1880s suggests that although a resurgence of *madrasa*s arising from new modes of funding, identical to those employed at Deoband, was underway, the scholars produced by such institutions could have been no more than echoes of their antecedents a century earlier, themselves instructed and providing instruction in a mere handful of texts at best. Although not necessarily advocates of the 'new' Sober Path, the absence of training in the rational sciences (including metaphysics, logic, rhetoric, astronomy, mathematics and other disciplines) and a dearth of religious sciences (including theology and the principles of jurisprudence) implies that the new breed of scholar could have forwarded only a redacted version of the Sober Path. Simultaneously, the relative longevity of patronage and the study of Arabic and Persian by the Muslim elite and capitalist classes well into the late 19th century, as well as the promotion of vernacular languages by the British, meant that, apart from the old texts still used as tools in language instruction at *maktab*s, those seeking knowledge of doctrinal Islam outside scholarly circles were increasingly dependent on the short tracts on *'aqa'id* (doctrine) and *fara'id* (ritual) produced by either the degraded scholars churned out by the types of 'fallen' *madrasa*s mentioned above, or by advocates of the 'new' Sober Path at the forefront of reconstituted *madrasa*s such as Deoband. The cultural effect is clearly audible in the oral literature of Punjab, which bears little trace of the antinomianism of the Intoxicated Way, instead resting on the degree of latitudinarianism afforded by the 'old' Sober Path, extending no further than that still observed at shrines such as that of Pir Haji Mango in Sind.

---

added that only by becoming familiar with these words through understanding the traditional oral commentary upon them would one be able to fly with their help from the earth of literalism to the heaven of symbolism... In a sense the spoken word makes possible the full understanding and correct "reading" of the written text'. See Seyyed Hossein Nasr, 'Oral Transmission and the Book in Islamic education', *The Book in the Islamic World*, ed. George Atiyah (Albany: SUNY, 1995), pp. 57–70.

I. *Islam in a Textual Context*

Given that 'useful', European knowledge could only be imparted gradually due to the language barrier and a need for no more than a small class of indigenous go-betweens, vernacular education was all that was judged necessary to fulfil the needs of lower administrative offices. In fact, the 'India Office Records' held at the British Library, London, are heavy with colonial directives translated into vernaculars by native employees, outlining the minutia of landholding, fiscal and other policies introduced by British rule.[26] Under such circumstances, field surveys to assess the state of 'indigenous' educational institutions became necessary to facilitate, if nothing else, the expropriation of funds when such institutions proved 'un-useful' to the above agenda. So it was that in the 1830s, a missionary and part-time clerk in the office of the Governor of Bengal, William Adam, found himself at a *madrasa* in the Rajshahi District of Bengal, aiming to add it to his report. He judged the institution 'typical' of the 8 *madrasa*s found in the 19 districts (*zillahs/parganas*) of Bengal, Bihar and Orissa surveyed.[27] Adam's Rajshahi *madrasa* was first endowed by the Mughal Shah Jahan (r. 1628–1658), officially yielding Rs. 8,000 annually, although a reduction of Rs. 872 was ordered by an unnamed Bengali *nawab* in the 18th century, while British assessors valued the estate at Rs. 30,000 per annum.[28] At any rate, the endowment was to be applied to the maintenance of the recipient's descendents, a mosque, a hospice for mendicants and a school.[29] The current *nazim* (trustee) of the endowment estimated his expenditure on education to be Rs. 2,000 per annum, employing two Muslim instructors at a total annual salary of Rs. 576 (plus food and lodging), while tutoring, lodging, feeding and clothing 53 students, all boys, from surrounding villages.[30] Although teaching Arabic to 5 students and Persian to 48, the subjects of study did not extend past Persian literature and histories. In comparison with the *dars-i nizamiyya*—which included 12 books on

---

[26] For example, in the case of Punjab, one might refer to various directives issued in 1850, less than a year after the region was seized, presented as *dastur al-'amal* in Urdu. See 'Vernacular Tracts 138' India Office Records, British Library.

[27] See Adam, 'First Report', 55–73, 92–94; 'Second Report', 160–66; and, 'Third Report', 287. From here on, each report is referenced by the numerals I–III, respectively.

[28] Adam, Report II, pp. 161–62.

[29] Ibid., pp. 162–63.

[30] Ibid., pp. 163, 165.

Arabic grammar and syntax (*sarf/nahw*); 2 on rhetoric (*balaghat*); 2 on jurisprudence (*fiqh*); 3 on the principles of jurisprudence (*usul al-fiqh*); 1 on traditions (*hadith*); 2 on exegesis (*tafsir*); 11 on logic (*mantiq*); 3 on metaphysics (*hikma*); 2 on theology (*kalam*); and 5 on astronomy and mathematics (*riyaziyya*)—the Rajshahi *madrasa* offered little to nothing, including only a handful of the latter's recommendations in Arabic grammar and syntax.[31] As the purpose of the *dars-i nizamiyya* was to 'sharpen the rational faculties' and create scholars 'with better-trained minds and better-formed judgement', the Rajshahi *madrasa* could not have been accomplishing anything of the sort.[32]

Taking into account the other seven institutions identified as *madrasas*, Adam's assessment of the Rajshahi example as typical is easy to confirm. Only two large institutions in the Burdwan District (Bengal) and one in the South Bihar District (Bihar) offer anything more substantive. The Burdwan *madrasas*—each of which is endowed together with a Sufi shrine, a mosque and a hospital valued at Rs. 15,000 and Rs. 50,000, respectively—teach logic, law, theology, *hadith*, metaphysics and astrology, but only employ 1–5 books for each field, most represented in the *dars-i nizamiyya*.[33] Few details are available concerning the South Bihar *madrasa*, except that logic, rhetoric, law, metaphysics and mathematics were taught using texts included in the *dars-i nizamiyya*, though

---

[31] Two versions of the *dars-i nizamiyya* are referenced in Robinson, *The 'Ulama of Farangi Mahall*, pp. 48–50, 249–51.

[32] Robinson, *The 'Ulama of Farangi Mahall*, p. 53.

[33] Without clarifying what is taught in which institution, Adam notes the following texts included in the *dars-i nizamiyya*. On Arabic grammar and syntax: *Sarf Mir* by Jurjani (d. 1413); *Sharh-i Mi'at 'Amil and Hidayat al-Nahw* by Ibn Tawqani (d. 1520); *Kafiyya* by Ibn Hajib (d. 1248); and *Sharh-i Mulla Jami* by al-Jami (d. 1492). Five other books are mentioned that do not conform to the *dars-i nizamiyya*, but including them, that is two books less than in the *dars* between two *madrasas*. On logic, four of six books are from the *dars*. These are: *Tahdhib* by al-Taftazani (d. 1389); *Mulla Jalal* by al-Harawi (d. 1699); and *Qutbi* and *Mir Qutbi* by al-Razi (d. 1354). Counting all six works, that is five less than the *dars* total. On law (including *fiqh* and *usul-i fiqh*), three of four works mentioned are from the *dars*, but this is two books fewer in comparison. The books included are: *Sharh-i Wiqaya* by Ibn Musud (d. 1346); *al-Hidaya* by al-Marghinani (d. 1196); and *Nur al-Anwar* by Nulla Jawan (d. 1718). On *hadith*, the only work taught is the sole book included in the *dars*: *Mishkat al-Masabih* by al-Khatib (n.d.). On metaphysics and theology, three of six works are included in the *dars*: *Mir Zahid* by al-Harawi; *Shams al-Bazigha* by Jawnpuri (d. 1652) and *Sadra* by Mulla Sadr (d. 1641). Including all works on metaphysics, six are equivalent to the number of books on metaphysics in the *dars*. In the field of astronomy and mathematics, the one work taught is included in the *dars*, but the number of books is four less. The work is: *Sharh-i Chaghmini* by Husayn Khwarazmi (n.d.). Rhetoric and exegesis are not taught at all. See Adam, Report III, pp. 283–84.

employing no more than 1–3 texts in each of the fields mentioned.[34] Although staff and student body of such institutions was entirely Muslim and male, and their sources of funding and the physical dimensions of these *madrasa*s may be typical of pre-colonial institutions in general, one detail this institutional paucity confirms is that anything approximating the *dars-i nizamiyya* was economically dependent on large, land revenue-based endowments and, if present, few were being applied to education in Bengal, Bihar and Orissa during the 1830s. Furthermore, regarding accessibility, it must be added that these *madrasa*s were not necessarily located in areas with the greatest Muslim populations. The aforementioned Rajshahi and Burdwan, for example, are estimated to have less than 30% and 20% Muslim residents, respectively, but host major institutions. The four districts listed with an estimated majority Muslim population—Chittagong, Mymunsing, Rangpur and Dinajpur (all in Bengal)—do not include a single institution that one might label a *madrasa*.[35] As well, Murshidabad, the former capital of the Nizamate of Bengal, Bihar and Orissa, and a city that Robinson and others name among the late, great centres of learning (Sunni and Shi'i) during the 18th century, does not host a single institution. In addition, based on British sources from the early decades of the 19th century, as well as older endowments, Adam provides evidence of former *madrasa*s at Midnapore and Cuttack (Orissa), and Burdwan, Nuddea and Chittagong (Bengal), places also without *madrasa*s during his survey in the 1830s. In the final analysis, although distant from the majority of Muslims, higher education was extended to, and availed of by, various classes of men training for employment in the remaining indigenous institutions, but lacked any semblance of the breadth, diversity and intellectual rigour which extended into the late 18th century. The only conclusion possible, therefore, is that a generation after Wali Allah, 'Abd al-Wahhab and other architects of the 'new' Sober Path, the alternatives to that strain were on the verge of falling into short supply, at least where British rule had extended. Meanwhile, as in the case of Muhammad Isma'il's *Taqwiyat al-Iman*, short tracts in Persian and vernacular languages were a prime medium for the expression of new ideas and, as discussed below, these were exactly the languages and media through which the 'graduates' of *madrasa*s would educate their 'capitalist' clientele.

---

[34] Ibid., p. 287.
[35] Adam, Report I, pp. 87–90, 91–92, 104–14.

As mentioned, the rise of East India Company authority, beginning in the late 18th century, resulted in the double blow of disrupting endowments of various types and grades supporting indigenous institutions, as well as the investment of funds in English instruction, diverting local patrons and students from Islamic institutions, particularly after Persian was dropped as the language of state in the 1830s. In fact, Adam drew the same conclusion, even echoing Macaulay's attitude in the process. Honing in on the 'four distinct purposes' that the endowment of the Rajshahi *madrasa* rested upon, Adam argued that the support of family, hospitality for the needy, and prayer as 'personal and religious', should be separated from the 'promotion of learning', which is 'public'. The latter funds, he suggested, should be brought 'under control of Government'—the type of policy which took root in the coming years.[36] Yet, one cannot assume that the 'decline' inherent in the above changes translates into a deathblow. Rather, as Kozlowski has shown, the use of endowments, particularly as tax shelters, actually increased under British rule, not drawing the action of 'regulators' until the late 19th century.[37] Furthermore, British sources from the period illustrate that in comparison with Hindus from the classes of patrons and attendees, Muslims clung to indigenous institutions in proportionally greater numbers until the late 19th century. In 1835, when news of the discontinuation of 'Oriental learning' reached the Muslim supporters of the Calcutta *madrasa*, first endowed by Hastings in 1781, H.H. Wilson, once Secretary of the Committee for Public Instruction, observed:

> The Mohammedans [sic], to use their own words, 'were confounded and beside themselves at the intelligence'; anticipating, in the suppression of the Madressa [sic], not only the extinction of their classical literature, but a preliminary step to an authoritative interference with their religion. They accordingly addressed a petition to government, signed by above eight thousand persons, including all the talent and respectability of the Mohammedan [sic] community, in which they stated their fears, in the most forcible language they could devise, and prayed the Government, 'from motives of justice, philanthropy, and general benevolence, and to *ensure its own stability*', to give orders for the continuance of the Madressa [sic].[38]

---

[36] Adam, Report II, p. 165.
[37] Kozlowski, *Muslim Endowments*, pp. 32–78.
[38] [42] Wilson, 'Education of the Natives of India', *The Asiatic Journal*, pp. 1–2. The petition can be found in *The Great Indian Education Debate*, pp. 189–93.

In the light of this petition, Trevelyan stated the obvious in 1838, when he complained that the East India Company's institutions had not succeeded in creating among their students the 'disposition to preach a crusade against the systems under which they had been brought up'.[39] In 1851, Richard Burton noted that in Sind, Muslims generally stood aloof from colonial institutions, stating that 'people subscribe to the schools of their princes'.[40] And, as late as 1860, the educator Edwin Arnold would confirm that Muslims still showed 'proud contempt' for colonial institutions, stating that when he was principal of Poona College, of 50 students only one was Muslim. He concluded, 'The cultivated native…resents the insult which has ignored his knowledge'.[41] The point here is not to suggest that cultural factors kept Muslims from British institutions any more or less than Hindus. Whatever myriad socio-economic reasons stand behind Muslim 'aloofness' and 'resentment', in the absence of colonial institutions, it was the lower-grade *maktab*s on which non-scholars yearning for formal learning depended, given that funding could be drawn from small endowments and the donations/stipends of local *zamindar*s and village-heads in rural areas, or merchants, traders and artisans in towns, rather than being hitched to the large endowments necessary for *madrasa*s. As a result, there is scarcely a sub-district (*thana*) in the 19 districts mentioned above that was not host to at least one *maktab* teaching Persian, with some *thana*s having up to 70 schools, and some districts close to 300 institutions.[42] Dropping to the village level, and noting that each was predominantly populated by Muslims or non-Muslims, the concentration of Persian *maktab*s was in 'Muslim' villages.[43] The venues of instruction varied greatly, including the verandas of patrons, independent schoolhouses

---

[39] Trevelyan, *On the Education of the People of India*, p. 131.
[40] Burton, 'Muslim Education at Schools and Colleges under the Native Rulers and Our Government', pp. 59–60.
[41] Arnold, *Education in India*, pp. 16, 38.
[42] From the *thana*s for which data is provided, the highest is Sahibgunge in South Bihar (70 Persian *maktab*s), the lowest is no *maktab*s, the highest incidence of which occurs in the *thana*s of Murshidabad (10 of 20 *thana*s have no Persian *maktab*s). See Adam, Report III, pp. 221–26.
[43] Both population demographics and the incidence of *maktab*s on a village level are available for one Bengali *thana*: Nattore. Of the 485 villages in this *thana*, the vast majority are largely populated by Muslim or non-Muslim families, while some are exclusively of one or the other community. All Arabic/Persian *maktab*s are located in villages with largely Muslim populations, while vernacular and Sanskrit schools are in villages where there is a large non-Muslim presence. See Adam, 'Second Report', Table I, in Di Bona, ed. *One Teacher, One School*, pp. 106–33.

and mosques, but the course of instruction was remarkably uniform: Persian language; the poetry of Hafiz (d. 1391), Firdawsi (d. 1020) and others; histories and prose; and short-tracts on *'aqa'id* and *fara'id* in Persian.[44] The majority of patrons and teachers were Muslims, although not as exclusively as in the case of *madrasa*s. For example, in Murshidabad (Bengal), 1 of 17 *maktab*s was supported by a non-Muslim of the area, while in Burdwan, 7 of 93 Persian teachers were non-Muslim.[45] In rural areas, patrons ranged from petty landlords to village-heads, men and women, while in towns and cities, merchants, traders and artisans contributed. Teachers were paid an average of Rs. 8 per month in cash, food and/or gifts.[46] With regard to students, when non-Muslims formed the majority of the area, most of the students were non-Muslims, as in Murshidabad, Beerbhoom, Burdwan, South Bihar and Tirhoot.[47] Whether Muslim or non-Muslim, tuition was largely gratuitous. However, there was no evidence of girls studying with boys, nor is there any mention of separate girls' *maktab*s.

Every district was also the site of *maktab*s teaching Arabic, although numbers are far fewer than Persian institutions, ranging from 17 Persian: 2 Arabic in Murshidabad to 279 Persian: 12 Arabic in South Bihar.[48] Sites of instruction echoed those of Persian *maktab*s in demographics and variety of locales, while the course of instruction ranged from Qur'an reading to Arabic language instruction, and short tracts on *'aqa'id* and *fara'id*.[49] Teachers were recompensed at the same rates

---

[44] Although many other poets are mentioned, reference to Firdawsi and Hafiz alone is sufficient to establish that reflections of Muslim persons and places, not to mention forms, themes and motifs, far broader than those of South Asia were within the reach of *maktab* students. Firdawsi's *Shah Nama* and Hafiz's *Diwan*, after all, respectively relate the histories and ethos of Islam in the Turko-Iranian context. For translated excerpts from each of the above works, as well as samples of the writings of Sa'di (d. 1292) and Rumi (d. 1273)—also mentioned to have been studied in *maktab*s—see Johan D. Yohannan, ed. *A Treasury of Asian Literature* (New York: John Day, 1956). Beyond spelling books, and so forth, books included in Persian instruction most often centre on (but are not restricted to) the writings of Sa'di, Firdawsi, Hafiz and Abu al-Fadl ibn Mubarak, including epic poetry and prose, letters and annals. See Adam, Report III, pp. 277–90. For a description of settings and pedagogy, see Adam, Report II, pp. 148–52; Adam, Report III, pp. 278, 281.

[45] Adam, Report III, pp. 278, 281.
[46] Ibid., p. 278.
[47] Ibid., pp. 279–90.
[48] Ibid., pp. 277, 284.
[49] Three works of the latter type, two on *'aqa'id* and one on *hadith*, are mentioned in the context of Tirhoot's Arabic *maktab*s: Adam, Report III, pp. 283, 290. For the diffusion of short-tract literature in late 19th century Bengal, also see Rafiuddin Ahmad,

as Persian teachers, but patrons and teachers were quite exclusively Muslim.[50] A select few also introduced students to logic, astronomy, mathematics and law.[51] There were some non-Muslim students learning the language, although numbers were small and scattered, the highest ratio of 51 Muslim: 4 non-Muslim recorded in Burdwan.[52] Tuition was again free, but girls were once again absent.

In contrast to *madrasas*, it is clear that *maktabs* were numerous and maintained high educational standards into the 1830s, providing Persian and/or Arabic instruction. Yet, the majority of patrons being Muslim, the distribution of *maktabs* and Muslims studying Persian and/or Arabic is not related to the overall number of Muslims in a district, but to the presence of Muslim patron classes. Thus, Murshidabad, for example, which is estimated to have a population of 10,000 Muslim boys and girls of school-going age (i.e. 4–15 years old), accommodates only 19 *maktabs* with a total of 47 Muslim students, while Beerbhoom, with approximately 10,000 Muslim boys and girls, accommodates 73 *maktabs* with 240 Muslim students.[53] On a village level, however, the pattern of settlement being related to religious affiliation, the presence of *maktabs* correlates with the presence of Muslims with sufficient means or educations to forward Persian and/or Arabic instruction. Contrary to the negligible access noted for *madrasas*, therefore, one finds relatively larger numbers, extending to cultivators and artisans, receiving formal instruction in Persian and Arabic at *maktabs*. In all, however, whether concerned with the class of patrons or students, one is largely speaking of the 'capitalist' classes. The same can be said for the scholars providing education.

The majority of scholars in the region teaching in both *madrasas* and *maktabs* are classified as *mawlawis* by Adam, but (echoing local Bengali usage) *mullas* are mentioned as specialists in the Qur'an and *fara'id*. The scholars at *madrasas* are counted as the highest grade of *mawlawi*, but are not given an alternative title. For the sake of clarity in this discussion, therefore, those with higher educations in the 'religious' and 'rational sciences' are referenced as '*mawlanas*', while

---

The Bengal Muslims, 1871–1906: A Quest for Identity (Delhi: Oxford University Press, 1981), pp. 84–97.

[50] For example, see Adam, Report III, p. 293.
[51] Adam, Report II, pp. 69–74; Report III, pp. 247–55.
[52] Adam, Report III, p. 283.
[53] Ibid., pp. 279–80, 313–15.

mawlawi is only used to reference the mid-rank scholar, and *mulla* the least formally educated. In these terms, Adam's works suggest that all the *mawlana*s in any given district were not engaged in teaching. For example, in the context of South Bihar, Adam mentions two authors: one a specialist in arithmetic, geometry, astronomy and other 'rational sciences' patronised by a Muslim '*raja*' of the area, and the other an author of works on Arabic syntax, logic and a 12-page Arabic tract on *fara'id*.[54] Tirhoot is also named as a district hosting two noteworthy authors, with one writing on arithmetic, astronomy, theology, *hadith* and mysticism, and the other on law. Importantly, both also wrote short tracts on *fara'id* and '*aqa'id*.[55] The latter scholars were brothers and are said to have possessed considerable property of their own. Recalling the count of *madrasa*s, therefore, one can say that the number of *mawlana*s in Bengal, Bihar and Orissa was small, but like the more numerous *mawlawi*s, hailed from the 'capitalist' class. *Mulla*s, on the other hand, a category of scholar not necessarily associated with an institution of learning and representative of the 'lowest degree of [scholarly] attainment', were available in large numbers, according to Adam. *Mulla*s taught formal Qur'an reading and ritual (*salat*, etc.), but otherwise earned their livelihoods by presiding over marriages, funerals, and so on.[56]

Home-tutoring by all three of the above classes of scholars provided an alternative means of instruction to the institutions discussed above, but *mawlawi*s, the rank of instructors found at *maktab*s, were the most prominent instructors employed. Adam wrote that home-tutoring was provided to the children of petty landlords and their agents, as well as to those of shopkeepers and traders, in every *thana* of every district.[57] A sense of the instruction involved can be gleaned from the example of Mawlawi Ghulam Muktidar and his employer, Dost Muhammad Khan Chaudhuri, a landlord in Rajshahi District.[58] The *mawlawi* was the tutor of the landlord's son, a teenager already literate in Persian,

---

[54] Ibid., p. 286.
[55] One is credited with a 36-page Arabic tract on *hadith*, a 40-page work on theology and an 18-page work on mysticism. The second is accredited a 48-page Persian work on '*aqa'id* and another of 44 pages on inheritance law, as well as shorter Arabic works on the same subjects. Ibid., p. 289.
[56] Adam, Report II, pp. 152–53.
[57] Ibid., p. 158.
[58] Ibid., p. 69.

then learning Arabic and being introduced to treatises on logic, law and *fara'id*.

By Adam's admittedly incomplete investigation, it would appear that 10%–20% of a district's Muslim students were tutored at home. An example of the highest grade of education provided is documented in the case of a Muslim *zamindar* in Rajshahi and his son, echoing the books taught and the recompense for teachers at Persian and Arabic *maktab*s.[59] Even in this context, however, the instruction of girls by non-family members seems to be rare, restricted to the wealthier landlords.[60] However, when home-tutoring is added to education through *maktab*s, the number of Muslim boys studying Persian and/or Arabic rises to approximately 1,250 of 5,000 boys (20%–30%) in Murshidabad, and an estimated 600 of 5,000 boys (8%–12%) in Bheerbhoom.[61] Evidently, while Persian still played a part in the British regime (even if on its way out), Persian skills, in particular, were sought after by Muslims and non-Muslims of the classes mentioned.

Finally, although *madrasa*s, *maktab*s and home-tutoring by *mawlawi*s provided the only avenues to a formal 'Islamic' education, they were not the only means to gain literacy. In virtually every *thana* of every district in Bengal, the number of schools teaching Bengali outnumbers all others, often by huge margins. For example, in the Murshidabad District there were 62 Bengali: 17 Persian, in Beerbhoom 407 Bengali: 71 Persian, and in Burdwan 629 Bengali: 93 Persian.[62] However, the number of Muslim teachers and patrons of these institutions is negligible. Regarding teachers in Murshidabad, 1 of 67 is Muslim, in Beerbhoom 4 of 412, and in Burdwan 9 of 629.[63] There is no reference to Muslim patrons of such institutions, all instances pointing to non-Muslims of the classes supporting *maktab*s, or European missionaries.[64] The number of Muslim students in such institutions, on the other hand, is small relative to non-Muslims, but roughly equivalent to those Muslims studying Persian and/or Arabic. It is also exclusively male. Beginning with students in Murshidabad, 82 of 1,080 are Muslims, in Beerbhoom 232 of 6,383, and in Burdwan 769 of 13,190.[65] When added to the numbers

---

[59] Ibid., p. 160.
[60] Ibid., pp. 187–88.
[61] Adam, Report III, p. 324.
[62] Ibid., pp. 223–25.
[63] Ibid., pp. 227–28, 234, 238–39.
[64] For example, Ibid., pp. 238–42.
[65] Ibid., pp. 230, 236, 240–41.

studying Persian and/or Arabic at *maktabs* or at home, this implies that figures on Muslim boys receiving some form of formal education do not change significantly in Murshidabad (20%–30%), but in Beerbhoom the number rises to 832 of 5,000 (15%–20%). At the lowest end of the scale in Bengal, one notes Burdwan with approximately 2,300 of 30,000 (5%–10%) school-age Muslim boys receiving some formal instruction. It should be noted, however, that the highest incidence of Muslims studying at vernacular schools relative to Arabic/Persian *maktabs* is in districts where non-Muslims form the overwhelming bulk of the population, such as Beerbhoom and Burdwan.

Although Sanskrit schools were also plentiful, they were not attended by Muslim patrons, teachers or students in any *thana* of any district, just as non-Muslims were not generally associated with *madrasas* or Arabic *maktabs*. English schools, however, did find Muslim patrons, teachers and students, although at rates as negligible as the accessibility of *maktabs*, vernacular schools and home tuition to girls. Not counting colonial institutions, but including those of European missionaries, the number is paltry in relation to the institutions mentioned above. A solitary English school is reported in Midnapore District (Orissa), one in Murshidabad, two in Beerbhoom, three in Burdwan, one in South Bihar (Bihar) and none elsewhere. Of these eight institutions, five were run by missionaries and three by locals. In the former category, there was one Muslim teacher, eight Muslim boys studying English, and one Muslim girl studying Bengali.[66] Of the three in the latter category, one patron was a Hindu *raja*, one a wealthy Hindu associated with Roy's *Brahmo Samaj*, and one a Muslim *raja*.[67] The latter is the same *raja* in South Bihar mentioned above to maintain a *mawlana* specialising in the 'rational sciences'. The English teacher in his employ was a local convert to Christianity and taught at an Arabic/Persian *maktab* that the *raja* also maintained.[68] The total number of Muslim students was three boys, all at the last institution. Therefore, after 60 years of East India Company rule in Bengal, Bihar and Orissa, English language, learning and institutions appear not to have penetrated Muslim society beyond a handful of the region's most affluent representatives. With the exception of vernacular instruction in districts with small Muslim

---

[66] Ibid., pp. 302–305.
[67] Ibid., pp. 301–302.
[68] Ibid., pp. 306–307.

populations relative to non-Muslims, in fact, in the very decade that Persian was retired in colonial administration, Persian and Arabic were overwhelmingly patronised, taught and sought by Muslims, particularly by those of the capitalist classes. Taking all languages into account, however, and recalling that *madrasa*s teaching anything approximating the *dars-i nizamiyya* were in short supply, it is clear that a major portion of the literary representations of 'Islam' written and read by the 1830s in Bengal, Bihar and Orissa, were the short tracts on *fara'id* and *'aqa'id* mentioned above, i.e. works closely related in tone and content to the anti-customary literature of reformers like the Wali Allahis. This trend continued throughout the 19th century, and extended wherever British rule reached, as illustrated by the following survey of formal education in Sind and Punjab during the 1850s and the 1880s, respectively. Furthermore, although *madrasa*s evidently made a comeback in some areas by the late 19th century, the manner in which they were reconstituted only added to the proliferation of a 'new' Sober Path.

Concerning the declining trend in the number and quality of *madrasa*s, eight years after annexation, letters between H.B.E. Frere, Commissioner in Sind, and Claudius James Erskine, Director of Public Instruction, as well as a report by the adventurer and captain in the East India Company Army, Richard Burton, suggest that the 'indigenous' institutions of Sind were also in dire straits by the 1850s. As Burton noted, when Alexander Hamilton travelled and traded through the region in the early 18th century, he reported 400 *maktab*s and *madrasa*s in the capital district of Thatta alone.[69] Burton, on the other hand, writing in 1851, compared Hamilton's observation with the six *madrasa*s in all of Sind that he could identify.[70] Furthermore, the quality of education in the remaining *madrasa*s was nowhere near that provided in the *dars-i nizamiyya*, only extending to a few books on logic, rhetoric, law and *hadith*.[71] Even religious sciences, such as exegesis, theology and the principles of jurisprudence were largely absent, while nowhere does one find such 'rational sciences' as metaphysics, mathematics or

---

[69] Burton refers to this individual as 'Captain Hamilton', providing no other details. I assume he is referring to Captain Alexander Hamilton, one of the few Englishmen to have ventured into Sind during this time. The only reference I have found to this individual is in J. Talboys Wheeler, *History of India from the Earliest Ages*, vol. 4, pt. 2 (London: Trubner & Co., 1881).

[70] Burton, 'Muslim Education', pp. 49–50. Also see Frere, 'Education in Sind', pp. 9–31.

[71] For example, see Burton, 'Muslim Education', p. 50.

astronomy. On the other hand, also as in Bengal, Bihar and Orissa during the 1830s, *maktab*s were still running in relative terms. Frere recorded 643 schools of various types (Arabic, Persian, Sindhi, Sanskrit) attended by 7,443 students (6,750 male/693 female).[72] Of these schools, 278 with 1,906 students taught Arabic; 275 with 4,252 students taught Arabic and Persian; 56 with 321 students taught Persian; 23 with 803 students taught Sindhi; and 10 with 85 students taught Sanskrit.[73] Despite paltry numbers relative to Bengal, such institutions otherwise followed the same patterns. They are reported to have had as many as 50–100 students at times, and are said to have been 'scattered all over the country, not always in the most populous and best-known towns, but often in remote villages, where the preceptor, having acquired a name by his skill in teaching, or reputation for superior learning, has gathered together students from distant districts'.[74] At the other end of the spectrum, Frere reported schools of just one or two students studying the Qur'an and Arabic, with the tutor teaching 'in charity' or for a 'pittance in grain or money'.[75] He draws the attention of the reader to two schools in particular, 'one where a boy and two girls are taught Arabic and Persian gratuitously by the wife of a *mochee* (cobbler)', and another in which 'two boys are instructed in the Koran [sic] by a blind woman'.[76] Burton further reflects that the books used for Arabic and Persian instruction were the same as in Bengal, Bihar and Orissa. The greatest difference between the eastern provinces and Sind, in fact, is the higher proportion of girls attending *maktab*s in the west, where not a single colonial institution existed until 1855, and that, too, was an English-medium boys' school.[77]

Moving up the Indus River and forward 30 years, Gottlieb William Leitner, principal of Government College in Lahore during the 1860s and 1870s, and co-founder of numerous other educational institutions, including the *Anjuman-i Punjab*, provides copious information on most of the districts of Punjab in the 1880s, but the six central and most populous districts of Lahore, Amritsar, Sialkot, Gurdaspur, Ferozpur and Gujranwala are sufficient to gauge the state of 'indigenous'

---

[72] Frere, 'Education in Sind', p. 31.
[73] Ibid., p. 31.
[74] Ibid., p. 9.
[75] Ibid., p. 9.
[76] Ibid., p. 11.
[77] *Gazetteer of the Province of Sind* (Karachi District), vol. 1 (1919), p. 37.

education.[78] As in Bengal, Bihar, Orissa and Sind, *maktab*s teaching Persian and/or Arabic were the most plentiful institutions patronised and attended by Punjab's Muslims. In Amritsar, there were 118 *maktab*s with 1,258 students (Muslim and non-Muslim).[79] In Sialkot, the corresponding statistics are 455 *maktab*s with 5,355 students; in Gurdaspur, 131 *maktab*s with 1,165 students; in Lahore, 280 *maktab*s with 3,847 students; in Gujranwala, 197 *maktab*s with 2,433 students; and in Ferozpur, 137 *maktab*s with 1,345 students.[80] The curriculum of the *maktab*s also echoes those in other contexts, extending from syntax and grammar books to works of literature and history. The backgrounds of patrons, teachers and students, the venues of instruction and size of the student-body also echo previous encounters. However, there are a few significant differences between the *maktab*s of Punjab and those of Bengal, Bihar, Orissa and Sind that require attention.

First, with few exceptions, the *maktab*s of the Punjabi districts mentioned teach Persian and Qur'an reading, Persian and Arabic, or just Arabic. The exceptions teach all of the above or just one of the aforementioned, including Qur'an reading. Second, large numbers of *maktab*s are associated with mosques and there are no non-Muslim teachers, although there is often more than one Muslim. Third, as in Sind, but not the eastern provinces, there is mention of at least one *maktab* for girls with a Muslim woman teacher/patron.[81] And finally, the above circumstances suggest that the majority of students were Muslim, and the frequency of *maktab*s was dependent on the presence in an area of the appropriate classes of Muslims alone. Evidently, the immediate effect of the ban on Persian as the language of state was that non-Muslims stopped studying it. On the other hand, as Leitner does not provide the appropriate demographic information, it is not possible to say what percentage of the school-age Muslim population availed of *maktab*s, but the numbers of institutions and students suggest that the proportion

---

[78] Leitner's *Indigenous Education* is divided into parts, each paginated separately. Parts are referenced here with the numerals I–II, followed by page numbers as they appear in the original 1883 edition. The import of *anjuman*s (literary societies) to the promotion of education has been roundly validated in such works as T. Aftab, 'Reform Societies and Women's Education in Northern India', *Journal of the Pakistan Historical Society* 35:2 (1987). Their role is discussed further in Chapter Six.
[79] *Indigenous Education* II, p. 52.
[80] Ibid., pp. 60, 71, 93, 120, 128.
[81] Ibid., p. 55.

is much higher than in the previous contexts considered, particularly with reference to Arabic literacy.

The broadest body of scholars in Leitner's terminology is *mawlawis*, but he includes Adam's 'low-ranking' *mullas* in the former body, while himself applying the terms *mulla* to this study's *mawlanas* (as in the colloquial usage of Punjab). Although Adam and Leitner are reflecting regional differences in usages, to avoid confusion in this context, this study's usage of *mullas* (low-ranking), *mawlawis* (mid-ranking) and *mawlanas* (high-ranking) is also imposed on Leitner. In these terms, as in Bengal, all *mawlanas* are not engaged in teaching, but by way of contrast can be found in every district of Punjab. In Lahore, however, Leitner finds more eminent scholars than in any other district of Punjab, or that I have noted in any other region. His list includes 23 scholars of various fields (two Sunni *qadis* and the regional *mujtahid* of the Shi'i), 18 'authors' in various fields and 34 'poets'.[82] Adding the number of *mawlanas* teaching at *madrasas*, therefore, Punjab in the 1880s was a greater centre of 'higher' Islamic learning than Bengal, Bihar and Orissa in the 1830s, or Sind in the 1850s. At the other end of the scale, Punjab had no shortage of *mullas* teaching no more than Qur'anic recitation, although Leitner provides no information on additional functions.

Leitner does mention the employment of *mawlawis* by the 'wealthy' to teach their sons and daughters, also suggesting that men educated their wives, but again provides none of Adam's detail.[83] However, evidence of recourse to *maktabs* in the 1880s suggests that Persian and Arabic skills were also sought after by Punjabi Muslims (but not non-Muslims) of the classes privy to home instruction. The vernacular languages taught in Punjab included Punjabi and Urdu-Hindi, but were written in various forms of Arabic and Sanskrit scripts reflecting sub-regional dialects. In the six districts of focus in this study, these vernaculars are broadly studied, but the institutions involved in teaching Sanskritic scripts are obviously most dependent on non-Muslim patronage, teachers and students. In Amritsar, for example, there is no mention of Muslim patrons, and one finds only three Muslim teachers at the '*mahajani*' (accounting) institutions listed. The only vernacular taught by Muslims with frequency is Urdu in the Arabic script, usually

---

[82] Ibid., pp. 93–94.
[83] *Indigenous Education* I, p. i.

in Arabic/Persian *maktab*s.[84] Leitner does not provide any details on the class or community backgrounds of students, but it is clear that community demographics again played a role in the study of the vernacular by Muslims. For example, in Amritsar (with a high portion of non-Muslims), the total for various vernacular and Sanskrit schools is 152 with 3,510 students, much higher than the 118 Persian/Arabic *maktab*s with 1,258 students listed.[85] By contrast, in Gurdaspur (with a high portion of Muslims), the total for vernacular/Sanskrit schools is 23 with 322 students, much fewer than the 131 Persian/Arabic *maktab*s with 1,165 students.[86] And finally, in Lahore, where some 'wealthy' Muslims lived with proportionally larger communities of non-Muslims, non-Urdu vernacular and Sanskrit schools, as well as their students, amount to only 30% of the numbers involved in *maktab*s.[87] All three cases suggest that the choice of Arabic/Persian or vernacular patronage, instruction and study was primarily influenced by 'religious' affiliation, with the vernacular losing out to Arabic and Persian among Muslims.

The lack of interest in promoting the vernacular can be explained by considering that colonial institutions offering vernacular instruction, particularly Urdu, were also available. In stark contrast to the paucity of colonial vernacular schools in the other regions considered, in all the districts of Punjab, Leitner notes 1,211 schools with 55,065 students.[88] In addition, 325 girls' schools (9,695 students) and 550 non-governmental vernacular schools received some support from the colonial state. At an all-Punjab level, the number of students is virtually equivalent to the 4,662 'indigenous' schools 'ascertained' to date, providing instruction to approximately 53,000 students, although the percentage of girls in the latter case would be decidedly lower. Although Leitner does not provide further details on student backgrounds, etc., recalling that the majority of the latter institutions with Muslim patrons, teachers and students were Arabic/Persian *maktab*s, it is clear that continued study in the vernaculars among Muslims was overwhelmingly dependent on colonial designs, or the patronage of non-Muslims. That does not mean interest was wanting. Indeed, as Leitner confirms, colonial vernacular schools had won the favour of 'the more needy in the community and

---

[84] *Indigenous Education* II, pp. 53–59.
[85] Ibid., p. 52.
[86] Ibid., p. 71; also see pp. 60, 120.
[87] Ibid., p. 93.
[88] *Indigenous Education* I, pp. 5–6.

those [of the "trading classes"] who wished to ingratiate themselves with the government'.[89] Rather, it suggests that Muslims were not interested in duplicating colonial or non-Muslim offerings. The same can also be said for the preference to study English to Persian, although this was so only among the landed and commercial elites.[90] After 50 years of Utilitarian policies and three decades of British rule in Punjab, in fact, Muslims were by no means immune to, or unenthusiastic about, colonial institutions, English and vernacular, but the high number of Persian/Arabic *maktab*s clarifies this was not generally expected to come at the expense of Persian or Arabic. That the vernaculars were also studied in large numbers, however, adds to the evidence that literate classes were further exposed to the anti-customary bent of the 'new' Sober Path. As mentioned above, works like Muhammad Isma'il's *Taqwiyat al-Iman* had been available in print for approximately 50 years. Furthermore, the scholars of the area had not only translated the Qur'an into Urdu by the 18th century and into Punjabi by the 19th century, a plethora of Punjabi short-tract literature had followed, including *tafsir* (exegesis), *hikaya* (anecdotes of the Prophet), *jang nama* (Shi'a eulogies), *bara maha* (elegies of Caliphs, etc.), *ma'ani-i namaz* (expositions on the meaning of prayer), *tawhid nama* (expositions on God's 'unity'), *nur nama* (expositions on God's 'light'), *naza'a nama* (expositions on 'death'), and *akhbarat al-akhirat* (expositions on the 'Last Judgement'), all representative of literature on *'aqa'id* and *fara'id*. Clearly, if there was any vernacular-speaking population among whom any reformer's orientation could have reached the vernacular literature of the capitalist and lower orders, the Muslims of the Punjab must number among them. This last point is best substantiated by turning to the *madrasa*s of Punjab—the institution exhibiting the greatest degree of change since the examples considered in Bengal, etc., of the 1830s and 1850s.

According to Leitner, there were 30 *madrasa*s in the six districts under consideration: 1 in Ferozepur, 14 in Amritsar and 15 in Lahore.[91] The largest of these institutions was in Amritsar; recently established, it was maintained by a Muslim merchant of the city, employing 6 teachers, supporting 200 students and teaching Persian, Arabic and various 'branches of Arabic learning'.[92] In Lahore, the larger institutions

---

[89] Ibid., p. ii.
[90] Ibid., pp. ii–iv.
[91] *Indigenous Education* I, p. 130; II, pp. 52–3, 93–7.
[92] *Indigenous Education* II, p. 52.

mentioned were patronised by Muslim landlords and were oriented towards Sunni or Shi'i perspectives, but little detail is provided on the courses offered except that law is a specialty.[93] The number of teachers in the *madrasa*s of Amritsar, Lahore and Ferozepur hovers at 3–6 individuals, each earning Rs. 5–25 per month according to rank, with the administrator and head teacher of one Shi'i *madrasa* earning Rs. 150 per month. In Amritsar, the number of students at each institution is 4–200, the median at 30–35 students with 537 total; in Lahore the corresponding figures are 8–40 students, the median at 20 with a total of approximately 400; and the sole *madrasa* in Ferozepur has 100 students.[94] All were studying gratis and were men. At the institutions of Amritsar, the 'branches of Arabic learning' taught included *hadith*, law, logic and medicine.[95] In Lahore, the fields taught included mathematics, logic, medicine, law and *hadith*.[96] In Ferozepur, it is confirmed that logic, law and Qur'anic exegesis (*tafsir*) are taught.[97] That is to say, as in the case of Bengal, Bihar, Orissa and Sind, the emphasis that *dars-i nizamiyya* places on theology and the 'rational sciences' is forsaken, with philosophy and metaphysics being the prime casualties, while the 'new' Sober Path's inclination towards law and *hadith* is reinforced.

Unfortunately, Leitner does not provide any detail on the books used but, relative to the other contexts surveyed, Punjab appears to have offered *madrasa*s in greater quantity. Furthermore, as opposed to the Bengali *madrasa*s—previously noted to have been dependent on large endowments—it is significant that many Punjabi *madrasa*s were maintained by donations from '*anjumans*' (literary societies), generally involving local petty landlords, commercial elites and colonial officers like Leitner himself.[98] For example, the largest *madrasa* mentioned above was only recently established and maintained by a Muslim merchant of Amritsar. This innovation accounts for the quantity of Punjab's *madrasa*s.

---

[93] Ibid., p. 94.
[94] Ibid., pp. 52–53, 94–96; *Indigenous Education* I, p. 130.
[95] *Indigenous Education* II, p. 53.
[96] Ibid., p. 96.
[97] *Indigenous Education* I, p. 130.
[98] For example, the largest *madrasa* in Amritsar, mentioned above, is attached to a mosque named after its builder and the entire complex's prime patron is a local Muslim merchant, supplemented by the Anjuman-i Islamiyya. The latter organisation also supports a *madrasa* attached to the Badshahi mosque in Lahore. Leitner's Anjuman-i Punjab also undertook such works. See *Indigenous Education* II, pp. 52–53, 94.

Thus, although Leitner does not provide the demographic details present in Adam's reports, it can be concluded that 'higher' Islamic education was far more accessible and availed of in Punjab during the 1880s, than was noted in Bengal and Sind earlier in the century, not because British policy had changed, but because new modes and sources of funding had emerged. Meanwhile, changes in the demographics of patrons and the form of funding also partially explain the dearth of subjects taught, new *madrasas* being unable to maintain the number of qualified persons necessary for a selection of subjects more closely related to the *dar-i nizamiyya*. While offering greater quantity, therefore, the quality of *madrasa* education was uniformly redacted from region to region across the 19th century.

In sum, no area or period considered in this appraisal offered any institutions that taught anything approximating the entire spectrum of disciplines and books included in the *dar-i nizamiyya*. Rather, the only common thread is emphasis on *hadith* and law, this too dependent on only one or two works, while the principles of jurisprudence and theology are largely absent. So, too, are virtually all of the disciplines associated with 'rational sciences'. Of course, the sources consulted here are insufficient to conclude that such disciplines were ever taught at these peripheral institutions, but the fact that books used for whatever is offered are drawn from the *dar-i nizamiyya*, does confirm that the ideal was widely known. Furthermore, it is apparent that the number of institutions had significantly decreased with the spread of British rule, given that such former centres of learning as Murshidabad (Bengal) and Thatta (Sind), among others mentioned in these regions, host no *madrasas*. As well, the scholars active in these regional and temporal contexts do not seem to be producing the voluminous commentaries of old, concentrating instead on the writing of Arabic, Persian and vernacular short-tract literature outlining *'aqa'id* and *fara'id*. The immediate reasons for this fall in the number of schools and quality of scholarship largely conform to the conclusions already available in the secondary literature, but it is also evident that different regional and temporal contexts involve locally specific factors. In Bengal, Bihar and Orissa during the 1830s—a time when the shift from Indological to Utilitarian ideals in colonial circles was just beginning to occur—Anglicisation cannot be counted among the pressures acting on indigenous institutions. Rather, it is clear that the disruption of sources of funding must be held accountable, whether by means of the reduction to penury of segments of the Muslim landed elite or direct East India Company intervention in endowments. Furthermore, there is at least some cause to consider that pre-colonial regionalisation led to some deprivations, as in the case of a portion of the revenue endowed to the Rajshahi *madrasa* being withdrawn by a ruling *nawab*. In Sind during the 1850s, in fact, having been under British rule for less than a decade, this last factor alone can account for the drop in the number of *madrasa*s from Hamilton's survey in 1744 (400 *madrasa*s and *maktab*s in Thatta alone) to those conducted almost immediately following British annexation in the 1840s (6 *madrasa*s in all of Sind). Finally, for Punjab during the 1880s, the application of alternative sources of funding to large land endowments, similar to that employed at Deoband, explains a healthier coterie of schools, but Anglicisation on its own accounts for the reduction of disciplines taught, English institutions teaching European rational sciences (three colleges existed by this time) and attracting local students of the upper classes.

It is also evident that *maktab*s, vernacular schools and home-tutoring fared better than *madrasa*s, and in this case, too, courses of instruction follow identical patterns across region and time. However, it is equally important to note that although large numbers of Muslims availed themselves of vernacular instruction in every context, institutions teaching vernacular languages in Bengal, Bihar, Orissa and Sind were largely dependent on non-Muslim patronage and teachers; meanwhile in Punjab, Urdu was included in *maktab* instruction, but the vernacular was more thoroughly propagated by non-Muslim and British initiative. Muslim patrons and teachers, on the other hand, were largely involved with instruction in Arabic and Persian in every context. As well, when Muslims did study vernacular languages, they stuck to instruction in variants of the Arabic script, while non-Muslims sought Sanskritic variants. In each case, however, girls' *maktab*s were rare although nowhere more so than in the eastern provinces. There is some evidence, nonetheless, that home-tutoring was undertaken for the instruction of women and girls of every region's elite and capitalist classes. Whether speaking of *madrasa*s or *maktab*s, the greatest number of patrons, instructors and students were from the capitalist classes, whether commercial or landed, although some segments of the subaltern classes were also engaged. As for instruction, little information is available about books used in vernacular schools, but for Arabic and Persian *maktab*s, *dars-i nizamiyya* works on Arabic syntax and grammar were employed, while old standards of Persian poetry and prose continued to be uniformly taught across region and time. The only new addition to the roster of works, in fact, is short-tract literature on *'aqa'id* and *fara'id*.

When coupled with the dissemination of the 'new' Sober Path discussed in the previous chapter—involving a turn to the *fatwa*, short-tract literature, print, the reconstitution of *madrasas* and, in some cases, the rhetoric and activism of *jihad*—the state of indigenous education described above must be seen to have had a profound effect on the cultural orientation of those involved, whether as patrons, teachers or students. In fact, as a consequence of these two factors—the articulation of the 'new' Sober Path and the qualitative decline of *madrasas*—even in the virtual absence of the influence of Anglicisation promoting Orientalist assumptions and essentialisms, before British administrative categorisations and legal reforms in favour of Codification had begun to reshape society to any great extent, the hospitality towards rational sciences and forms of legalism accommodative of local custom extended by the 'old' Sober Path was being withdrawn from the consciousness of scholarly and non-scholarly elite and capitalist Muslim classes. Subsequently, with the introduction of English instruction, including European rational sciences and British legal codification, a hefty wedge was ready and able to be inserted between 'Islamic' thought and 'rationalism', as well as between 'Islamic' institutions and 'custom'.

Of course, such hostility does not mean hostility towards non-Muslims, already illustrated by Shah 'Abd al-'Aziz's *fatawa*, which not only legitimated British rule, but also encouraged Muslim jurists like his nephew, 'Abd al-Hayy, to take up employment in the East India Company judiciary, as well as Sayyid Ahmad Barelwi's and Muhammad Isma'il's calls for Hindus to join the battle against the Sikhs and the British. What an anti-customary orientation does imply, however, is that the influence of British legal reforms and English education were not acting alone in guiding the terms of alliances with non-Muslims. A deeper education in the 'new' Sober Path, or even the degraded form of the 'old' disseminated through the educational institutions considered above, meant that when 'Islam' was employed as a legitimating agent, the terms of the alliances between Muslims and non-Muslims would almost necessarily be dependent on shared political and economic ends, rather than on collective cultural norms. It is this final point that a consideration of Punjab's oral literature confirms below.

II. Islam in an Oral Context

If the 'new' Sober Path, directly or by means of the decay of the 'old', increasingly defined the Islam of the literate capitalist classes during the 19th century, one must also ponder how far beyond this socio-economic group the cultural attitudes associated with it were able to penetrate. Not only does the oral transmission of Islam in general, as explained by Nasr above, dictate such consideration, but British surveys of vernacular presses initiated as a means of control after the 1857 Uprising reveal that the material produced was widely 'heard'. This is particularly so for the type of short-tract literature already mentioned. Early surveys reveal that popular prints were peddled across the countryside by innumerable peasants seeking to supplement their incomes in the off-season, others were posted on the walls of towns and villages for anyone to read, and readers were also commonly employed by various classes, in keeping with longstanding practice, to service illiterate men and women.[99] Also embodying pre-colonial practice, a variety of travelling musicians, story-tellers, theatrical players and village bards brought ideas otherwise held in literature to the illiterate. What was the cultural effect of such activities? The greatest problem in addressing such a question, as is the case with most issues concerning urban and rural subaltern groups, is a dearth of appropriate sources. Yet, thanks to the efforts of an Indologist, R.C. Temple, a glimpse of exactly this segment of society is available for consideration. In the 1870s, Temple compiled the poems, songs and plays performed across the Punjab, committing to paper (in their original Punjabi vernacular) the 'legends' relayed by the various types of bards mentioned above. His work was first published in three volumes as, *The Legends of the Punjab*, in 1885.[100] Reflecting his interest in 'universal' and 'Indian' themes and motifs, Temple divided the tales he collected into three categories: epic, heroic and hagiographic. Although he recognises 'Muslim', 'Hindu' and 'Sikh' hagiographies, Temple's epic and heroic categories do not consider literary variations dependent on the performer's personal background, that

---

[99] For a thorough study of British reports on vernacular presses and the modes by which their products were disseminated, see Robert Darnton, 'Book Production in British India, 1850–1900', *Book History* 5 (2002): pp. 239–62.

[100] This work has recently been reprinted, including the Punjabi original and English translations, as R.C. Temple, ed. and trans., *The Legends of the Punjab*, 3 vols. (Islamabad: Institute of Folk Heritage, 1981). All citations that follow are from this edition, thus only titles, volume and story numbers and pages are given below.

of his/her audience, or the underlying ramifications of these variations in terms of identity. In fact, Temple commented that, in general, 'the tenets of the Hindus, the Mussalmans [i.e. Muslims] and the Sikhs are thrown together in the most hopeless confusion, and the monotheism taught by the medieval [Bhakti] reformers underlies all their superstitions'.[101] In other words, this 19th century 'Orientalist' states what so many contemporary historians still accept at face value: that the culture of the majority 'transcended' Hindu, Muslim and Sikh categorisation, resting on local variants of an 'Indic' culture. Of course, historians of South Asian Muslims are less likely to leave out entirely the influence of doctrinal Islam, but when the dominant paradigm of a statically legalistic and intrusive Islam is present, their works often distort the picture nonetheless. A case in point is Ayesha Jalal, who surveys not just Punjabi, but also Urdu, Sindhi and Bengali folk tales and poetry, on the way to concluding that doctrinal Islam had a 'remarkable capacity to influence as well as blend into multifarious regional settings which in large part explains Islam's appeal for Muslims in various class, regional, linguistic and sectarian denominations'.[102] I could not agree more. The problem, however, is the terms on which 'influence' and 'blending' are described. Reflecting a statically legalistic view of Islam, her account includes 13th–19th century poets without any consideration of change, and the only variety addressed is the general influence of 'Sufism', with no mention of the influence (hostile or hospitable) of variation within that camp concerning legalism. Furthermore, particularly reflexive of the idea that legalistic thought is normative and intrusive, Jalal writes that regional and linguistic identities have 'absorbed the Islamic impact'.[103] There is hardly any mention of the ways in which doctrinal Islam has accommodated regional and linguistic identities. To be fair, Jalal is only broaching the subject to begin considering late 19th century developments, but herein lies the additional problem of a periodisation that so thoroughly separates the late 19th and early 20th centuries from all that preceded. Yet, when one revisits Temple's collection with the recognition that doctrinal Islam included a Sober Path and an Intoxicated Way that was in flux, particularly from the late 17th century, adding that each had its own modes of hostility and

---

[101] Ibid., p. 529.
[102] Ayesha Jalal, *Self and Sovereignty* (London: Routledge, 2000), pp. 10–26.
[103] Ibid., p. 26.

hospitality towards local custom, the artisans and cultivators who sang and heard these tales are revealed to have not only been quite conscious of religious community, but 'connected' to the broader Muslim World and 'embedded' in India in ways that directly relate to the influence of varied and changing doctrinal ideals.

Beginning with the 'epic' category, it is striking to note virtually no evidence of Islam or Muslims beyond the use of Arabic and Persian vocabulary standard in Punjabi or Urdu. All tales are drawn from 'classical' Sanskrit literature, particularly the *Mahabharata* and *Puranas*, reflecting Brahmanical themes and motifs, whether played in Ambala, sung in Jalandhar or recited in Merath.[104] Only two of the 10 'epics' include any Islamic motifs, both told by 'non-professional' bards: one an 'inhabitant' of a village and the other a 'scavenger' about a rural town.[105] In the first case, passing reference is made to Sufi icon Khwaja Khidr, as the 'god of water'.[106] In the second, Khidr is mentioned in similar vein, the Qur'an is mentioned in the context of sacred works, and a Muslim character is anachronistically included in an otherwise uniformly 'pre-Islamic' literary environment.[107] In both cases, therefore, Islamic motifs are employed to forward the original pre-Islamic themes. That even such 'hospitality' is in the statistical minority suggests that the epics were largely understood by reciters and their audiences as Brahmanical/Hindu works set in a pre-Islamic era, whether recited and heard by Muslims or non-Muslims.

The widespread recognition of religious differences in terms of historical periodisation is further confirmed by the 'heroic' category. Numbering among the mainstays of Punjabi literature are the series

---

[104] *Puranas* (lit., 'ancient lore') refers to a body of epic tales of gods and heroes following, historically and in literary stature, the two great Brahmanical epics, the *Mahabharata* and *Ramayana*. Generally thought to have been written between the 1st–6th centuries, the *Puranas* fall into two classes: (1) *Mahapuranas* ('Great *Puranas*'), of which there are 18; and, (2) *Upapuranas* ('Minor *Puranas*'), which are considerably more numerous. See Catrina Conio, 'Puranas', *Encyclopaedia of Religion*, vol. 17, pp. 86–90. There are 10 tales of this genre in vol. 1: 'The Legend of Safidon' (XV), pp. 414–17; and 'Princess Niwal Dai' (XVI), pp. 418–528. In vol. 2: 'Raja Gopi Chand' (XVIII), pp. 1–77; 'Raja Chandarbhan' (XIX), pp. 78–98; and 'Raja Nal' (XXX), pp. 204–75. In vol. 3: 'Hari Chand' (XLII), pp. 53–88; 'Raja Dhru' (XLVI), pp. 126–57; 'Sispal and Parduman' (LVI), pp. 332–47; 'Sispal and Krishna' (LVII), pp. 349–63; and 'Banasur' (LVIII), pp. 364–84.
[105] 'The Legend of Safidon' (XV), vol. 1, pp. 414–17; and 'Princess Niwal Dai' (XVI), vol. 1, pp. 418–528.
[106] 'The Legend of Safidon' (XV), vol. 1, p. 416.
[107] 'Princess Niwal Dai' (XVI), vol. 1, pp. 449–50, 485, 519.

of tales from the cycle of Raja Rasalu, a pre-Islamic 'king' of Sialkot. In four of the six tales, no Islamic motif or mention of Muslims is utilised.[108] Most significantly, one of the bards identified as Muslim numbers among those making no reference to Islam. In two of the six, however, much the same type of hospitality noted in the case of the epics can be read. One bard makes a passing reference to Khwaja Khidr, this time in relation to a specific river.[109] Another makes literary allusion to the 13th century Isma'ili *pir*, Shams al-Din Tabriz (a.k.a. al-Sabzawari), associated with Multan, and the 'four *pirs*' (*Chaun Biran*), i.e. four illustrious Suhrawardiyya figures regarded as the 'founders' of Sufism in the region.[110] With the exception of a passing reference and a literary allusion, therefore, Raja Rasalu and his cast of characters are as firmly rooted in the pre-Islamic 'history' of the Punjab, as the heroes and heroines of the epics are rooted in the same era of South Asian history.

Turning to tales with Muslim characters one finds a vastly altered literary landscape, both thematically and in motif. 'Hir and Ranjha', 'Mirza and Sahiban' and 'Sassi and Pannun'—standards of Indus Valley vernacular literatures—are thematically related in that they involve Muslims whose love for each other transcends tribal/ethnic lines.[111] Not only does this theme echo a genre known more widely in Islamic literature, it is directly tied to Islam by the bards reciting them in Punjab. For example, in 'The Marriage of Hir and Ranjha', their liaison is sanctioned not merely by the '*faqir*' under whom Ranjha studies, but mystically by the holiness of 'Mecca and Medina'.[112] In fact, their marriage across tribal bounds is so meritorious that it earns a 'saintship' for both.[113] In 'Mirza and Sahiban', the hero and heroine, while

---

[108] In vol. 1: 'Princess Adhik Anup Dai' (IX), pp. 225–42; and 'The Legend of Sila Dai' (X), pp. 243–366. In vol. 3: 'Two Songs about Raja Rasalu' (XLVIII), pp. 218–226; and 'The Legend of Rani Kokilan' (XLIX), pp. 227–41.

[109] 'The Adventures of Raja Rasalu', vol. 1, p. 41.

[110] 'Puran Bhagat' (XXXIV), vol. 2, pp. 377, 404.

[111] In vol. 2: 'The Marriage of Hir and Ranjha' (XXXVIII), pp. 507–80. In vol. 3: 'Mirza and Sahiban' (XXXIX), pp. 1–23; and 'Sassi and Punnun' (XL), pp. 24–37.

[112] 'The Marriage of Hir and Ranjha', vol. 2, p. 554.

[113] Ibid., p. 554. As well, there are tales of individual piety related to the saintship of Hir and Ranjha. In each, pilgrimage to their tombs, or their appearance in a dream, lead to the main character's spiritual or material fulfillment. See vol. 2: 'Abd Allah Shah of Samin' (XXVIII), pp. 177–82; 'Isma'il Khan's Grandmother' (XXXVI), pp. 494–98; and 'The Bracelet Maker of Jhang' (XXXVII), pp. 499–506.

eloping, are slain by members of both their tribes. Sahiban's last words to her dying beloved are:

> Mirza, harken to my prayer.
> Fate came on the prophets (*pagambaran*): fate hath come on thee.
> The brethren Hasan and Husayn, sons of 'Ali,
> Were destroyed in fights with the Jew.
> At the door wept Bibi Fatima: 'They will come not back to me'.
> Mirza, when [fate] slew such prophets, shalt thou escape?[114]

And finally, in 'Sassi and Pannun', the heroine, Sassi, dies in the company of a herder in the desert while en route to finding Pannun. The story she tells the latter of how she came to be wandering in the wastes in search of Pannun prompts the man to leave 'his goods, his daughters, his sons and his home. Seeing Sassi's beauty he became a *faqir*'.[115] The only words he shares with Pannun upon the hero's arrival, before relating the death of Sassi are, 'One thing I know—the world is perishable'.[116]

The above 'heroic' romances show that not only Islamic themes (e.g. anti-tribalism) are advanced, but that these themes are most often expressed with Islamic motifs, ranging from the sanctity of Mecca and Medina, to the battle at Karbala, to the process of becoming a *faqir*. The infusion of such motifs, in fact, goes much further. In 'Hir and Ranjha', the reciter invokes Prophet Muhammad, Caliph/Imam 'Ali, the Prophet's daughter and 'Ali's wife, Fatima, their sons and Shi'i Imams, Hasan and Husayn, as well as the famous Sufis al-Hallaj and Shams al-Din Tabriz. Besides this, Islamic institutions are incorporated. A discussion between Ranjha, himself a potential 'saint', and a qualified *qadi* even illustrates the antipathy between the Sober Path and the Intoxicated Way. In 'Mirza and Sahiban', Moses, Fatima, 'Ali, Hasan and Husayn are referenced, while it is said that the heroic pair of Mirza and Sahiban first fell in love while studying together as children at a mosque *maktab*, their teacher described as a stern and unforgiving *qadi*. 'Sassi and Pannun' also makes reference to 'prophetic' figures, including 'Noah' (Nuh).[117] Such references imply that accounts of the deeds of Noah and Muhammad, 'Ali and al-Hallaj, were also well known to the bards and their audiences. Furthermore, the 'anti-*qadi*'/'pro-*faqir*' bias

---

[114] 'Mirza and Sahiban', vol. 3, p. 22.
[115] 'Sassi and Pannun', vol. 3, p. 37.
[116] Ibid., p. 37.
[117] Ibid., p. 34.

of the tales clearly illustrates that Sufism provided much of the average Punjabi's 'education' in Islam.

When Sufism figures prominently, it has been observed that cultural hospitality accompanies education. This is reconfirmed by the very tales considered above. In 'Hir and Ranjha', the concept of transmigration, Rama and Sita (hero and heroine of the *Ramayana*), Brahma and Durga (Hindu gods), *pandit*s and Bhakti *guru*s are employed as literary devices or invoked as features of a multi-faith environment. However, transmigration is only employed in a metaphor of Ranjha's 'eternal' love for Hir, while Hir's troubles are likened to those of Rama and Sita. Furthermore, following local custom, a *brahmin* astrologer is engaged at Hir's marriage, but a *qadi* is employed to perform the rites. As well, Guru Gorakhnath (a renowned 15th century Bhakti thinker) is acknowledged as a 'saintly' figure, but his level of saintship is below that gained by Hir and Ranjha on account of their relationship, a 'love' one must recall that is sanctioned directly by the grace of 'Mecca and Medina'. Thus, the tale cautions that the inclusion of the non-Islamic does not necessarily imply the sublimation of the 'Islamic', 'Hindu' or 'Sikh'. Rather, it employs the non-Islamic in the service of larger Islamic themes, much as some of the epics mentioned above employ the Islamic in the service of Brahmanical themes. When confronted with a work involving Muslim and non-Muslim motifs, therefore, one must be aware of grades of hospitality, each reflecting the graded attitudes of Sufi *tariqa*s active in the region. The point is driven home by the version of 'Sassi and Pannun' told by a bard at Hoshiarpur. In comparison with the above rendition of 'Hir and Ranjha', this version of 'Sassi and Pannun' relays less hospitality than hostility towards local customs. A solitary literary allusion is made to the non-Islamic, and that only involving figures who, had they been present, could not have saved Sassi from a fate likened to 'Noah's deluge'. Thus, if there is evidence of Sufism's Intoxicated Way in these tales, the same can certainly be said for its Sober Path.

A gradation in hospitable elements, as well as evidence of hostility, can be further noted in Temple's 'hagiographic' category of tales. The majority of works in this category involve the lives of Sufis, particularly the 13th century *pir*, Sayyid Ahmad ibn Zain al-'Abidin, revered across Punjab as 'Sakhi Sarwar'.[118] In a song related by bards in Jalandhar, the

---

[118] There are six hagiographic tales associated with Sakhi Sarwar. In vol. 1: 'Sakhi Sarwar and Dani Jatti' (II), pp. 66–81; and 'Three Fragments about Sakhi Sarwar'

audience is provided a stunningly detailed account of this figure's early life. Sarwar's story begins in the Arabic-speaking lands (*mulk arab*) of the late 4th/early 5th century A.H. (10th/11th century CE), accurately described as a time of '*fitna*' and general upheaval. Under these conditions, Sarwar's father, a 'Husayni Sayyid', emigrated to Shahkot, near Multan, where he married one of his daughters to the '*muqaddam*', a *brahmin* named Pheru, and the other into the local 'Khor' (*Khokhar*) tribe. His son Sarwar, however, travelled west again, to Baghdad, where he is said to have studied under Shihab al-Din Suhrawardi (d. 1232) and Mawdud Chishti (d. 1153).[119] Despite the inaccuracies inherent in the dates mentioned, all of the above figures and tropes identify Sarwar with the Suhrawardiyya and Chishtiyya orders so prominent in Punjab, the land to which he returned to win renown as a miracle-working *pir*.

In keeping with this pedigree, in 'The Marriage of Sakhi Sarwar', one is immersed in a thoroughly Islamic literary environment through the mention of such concepts as '*umma*' directly, and figures such as 'Adam and Hawa [Eve]', besides various Sufi *pirs* of Punjab. Furthermore, the people of Multan are described as either 'Hindu' or 'Muslim', and their festivals are acknowledged as different. In the same tale, however, concessions are made to 'Hindu Gods', placing them on a par with 'Muslim Saints'.[120] Bhairon and Hanuman (Hindu gods) are incorporated in the action, joining one of the 'fours *pirs*', Shaykh Farid al-Din Ganj-i Shakar (d. 1265–1266), among other prominent Sufis, in Sarwar's wedding procession, but unlike the latter, the former are described as 'children', eating during *Ramadan* and on the Brahmanical *ekadshi* (turn of the moon).[121] And finally, the marriage itself is officiated by a *qadi*, but the ceremony is imbued with acts drawn from marriages among Hindus, including placing 'the red spot on the forehead', circling a cup of water around the heads of the betrothed and drinking it, 'putting the ring into milk and water', and holding boiled millet in 'their kerchiefs'.[122] Thus, the manner in which Islamic and customary elements are incorporated in the above tale confirms that even hospitality is circumscribed by

---

(IV), pp. 91–97. In vol. 2: 'Sarwar and Jatti' (XXI), pp. 104–15; and 'The Marriage of Sakhi Sarwar' (XXII), pp. 116–82. In vol. 3: 'The Miracles of Sakhi Sarwar' (LIII), pp. 301–26.

[119] 'The Miracles of Sakhi Sarwar', vol. 3, pp. 302–21.
[120] 'The Marriage of Sakhi Sarwar', vol. 2, p. 127.
[121] Ibid., p. 127.
[122] Ibid., p. 131.

doctrines particular to Chishtiyya and Suhrawardiyya orders. First, non-Islamic deities are not incorporated as facets or equivalents of Allah, neither are they excluded. Rather, they are only acknowledged as *pirs*. Second, the elements of customary ritual incorporated in Sarwar's wedding do not exceed what is allowed by *fiqh* and its provisions for custom (*'urf*), while representing exactly the *bid'a* (innovation) which the 'new' Sober Path of the era wished to eliminate.

The stamp of the 'old' Sober Path is on all of the 11 songs and tales concerning Sarwar. Furthermore, grades along that path, again reflecting doctrinal influence are also present. A less hospitable perspective is found in 'A Hymn to 'Abd al-Qadir al-Jilani' (d. 1166), 'founder' of the *shar'i*-minded Qadiriyya, as well as in 'Jalali, the Blacksmith's Daughter', involving a Punjabi devotee of al-Jilani.[123] The latter is set in Baghdad and bears no trace of non-Islamic literary themes or motifs, let alone the imposition of local customary practices on the non-Punjabi characters portrayed. In the former, there is again no infusion of non-Islamic motifs, except for the inadvertent mention of local marriage customs, as in 'The Marriage of Sakhi Sarwar'. Together, the above song and tale represent the firmest evidence that various permutations of the Sober Path were, indeed, represented in the oral literature of the Punjab, and that its advocates and adherents understood their cultural ideal as 'Islamic'.[124]

The entire spectrum of cultural ideals—from the absolute antinomianism and latitudinarianism encountered in some representations of the Intoxicated Way, to the well-defined relationship between religious communities found in the Sober Path—is not merely identifiable in works involving widely acknowledged *pirs* from established *tariqas*. In the case of Lal Beg—a figure of great obscurity venerated by the 'scavenger caste' of eastern Punjab—the gamut is run in relation to one figure. Temple includes four 'genealogies' of Lal Beg, told by various individuals in the Ambala and Karnal districts.[125] The first in the series represents Lal Beg's intellectual legacy by outlining the lineage of his '*guru*', named as 'Balnik' and identified by Temple as Valmiki,

---

[123] Both are in vol. 2. 'A Hymn to Abd al-Qadir Jilani' (XXVI), pp. 153–62; and 'Jalali, the Blacksmith's Daughter' (XXVII), pp. 163–76.

[124] In vol. 3, also see 'The Saints of Jalandhar' (XLVII), pp. 158–217; 'Basti Shiekh Darvesh' (LIV), pp. 322–26; and 'Sayyid Asmun' (LV), pp. 327–31.

[125] 'Genealogies of Lal Beg' (XVII), vol. 1, pp. 529–44.

the traditionally ascribed author of the *Ramayana*.[126] The previous '10 incarnations' (*das avatar*) of Balnik given include none but Brahmanical figures, including 'Mahadeo' (Shiva) and characters from the *Puranas*.[127] In stark contrast to this 'Hindu' work, the second genealogy includes no mention of any Brahmanical figure. Instead, Muhammad and such figures as 'Isa (Jesus), Khwaja Khidr, Idris (Enoch) and Jibra'il (Gabriel), not to mention the concept of '*umma*', are invoked in the context of Lal Beg's birth.[128] Putting the third genealogy aside for the moment, the fourth differs from both the above in that Islamic and customary motifs are employed. However, it is clear that the Islamic references are far more numerous than the customary, and that the relationship between them echoes something of the Sarwar cycle's ideals. 'Gaurja' (wife of Shiva) is said to have placed a 'robe and cap' on Lal Beg at his birth, thus being interjected in the action alongside a host of Sufi *pirs*. Otherwise, only literary reference is made to the 'Golden Age' (*krita yuga*) as well as to two figures from Sanskrit literature.[129] The third genealogy is the only one exhibiting 'Indicism's' purported cultural 'transcendence'. Here, the motifs do not match those of any strain in the broader literature of the region, relying on local figures, or very local terms for more widely recognisable entities. Temple speculates that 'Kumba' is Mecca, and 'Gordhan' is Gautama (Buddha), but with any certainty one can only note the inclusion of Valmiki, Ganesha (Hindu god) and Khwaja Khidr.[130] Hence, this tale alone is a reflection of the most extreme grade of the Intoxicated Way, the sole example in which all traditions are sublimated in a very local 'cult' of Lal Beg.

The weighted representation of various grades of Intoxicated and Sober cultural attitudes based on religious affiliations does not mean that other modes of identity did not intersect the religious. Indeed, the strong anti-tribal rhetoric of certain 'heroic' tales itself suggests the importance placed on clan and tribal affiliations. Among the heroic tales not yet mentioned, some convey no more than the honour of one or another side in an inter-clan or tribal feud. A point of additional interest is that many other tales honour local '*rajas*' (kings). This is particularly well represented by four tales from Kyonthal, near Simla in eastern

---

[126] Ibid., p. 529.
[127] Ibid., pp. 530–31.
[128] Ibid., pp. 531–33.
[129] Ibid., pp. 535–44.
[130] Ibid., pp. 533–34.

Punjab.[131] All are recorded in Junga, capital of the Kyonthali Rajas, and attributed to 'inhabitants' identified as members of the 'Koli' (weaver) community.[132] The first tells of a conflict between the Raja of Kyonthal and the neighbouring state of Sarmor; the next of the battles and feuding that followed a local *jagirdar*'s assertion of 'independence' from the Kyonthali state; the third is a love song whose hero is a Kyonthali military commander (*negi*); and, the fourth relates the virtual 'press-ganging' of a local '*sardar*' into the military service of the Kyonthali state. In each case, the 'hero' is the Raja of Kyonthal's opponent, be he *raja, jagirdar, negi* or *sardar*. In other words, from the perspective of the Koli bards, it is not the 'elites' in general, but specifically the Kyonthali state that is unsympathetically portrayed.

While the Koli bards did not identify with the local state, other bards promoted the identification of locals with local governmental institutions. In the ballad of 'Sansar Chand of Kangra', another of the hill-states around Simla, the professional bards (*mirasis*) are decidedly partisan towards Kangra in its battle with neighbouring Sarmor.[133] In 'Raja Jagat Singh of Nurpur', the *raja* is lauded for his military feats and economic successes.[134] The same tale, told in prose and verse by *mirasi*s, illustrates another means by which local bards aggrandised local authorities, attaching them to the personages of larger governmental structures, such as '*badshahs*'. In particular, favour of the Mughal state is employed as a means by which to further exalt the stature of its hero. The same is the case in the ballad of 'Raja Jagdeo', recorded from bards in Montgomery District, as well as 'The Adventures of Mir Chakur'.[135] The same effect—of exalting local rulers by drawing in the Mughals—is also apparent in other tales, but with a different spin. In these cases, the Mughals are the 'greater' authority defied or degraded by the local 'hero', as discussed below. Taken as a whole, tales related to local rulers suggest that the artisans and cultivators who told or heard them, recognised and resisted local states and rulers on a communitarian basis, but consistently viewed the system of *rajas, jagirdar*s

---

[131] All are found in vol. 1. 'Raja Mahi Prakash of Sarmor' (XI), pp. 367–79; 'The Story of Syama' (XII), pp. 380–99; 'The Song of Negi Bahadur' (XIII), pp. 400–3; and 'Madana the Brave' (XIV), pp. 404–13.
[132] Ibid., p. 367.
[133] 'Sansar Chand of Kangra' (XXIV), vol. 2, pp. 144–47.
[134] 'Raja Jagat Singh of Nurpur' (XXV), pp. 148–53.
[135] 'Raja Jagdeo' (XXIX), vol. 2, pp. 183–204; and 'The Adventures of Mir Chakur' (XXXV), vol. 2, pp. 457–94.

and *badshah*s as the legitimate mode of government, whether Muslim or non-Muslim.

Given that local *raja*s dating back 2,000 years to Raja Rasalu are current in this body of late 19th century oral literature, it is striking that of the myriad 'empires' that engulfed local states over that time, only the Mughals find significant mention, with the Delhi Sultans coming in second. Interestingly, although there is reference to a '*farangi*' character in one tale, the 'British Empire' is barely represented at all.[136] Beyond this, in one of the six tales from the Raja Rasalu cycle, a bard from Rawalpindi specifies that the action relayed took place in 'the year of Christ 80'.[137] This lack of British inclusion is true for Hindu, Sikh and Muslim bards, but their assessments of the Mughals are not identical. While Muslims paint their *badshah*s in largely complimentary light, both Hindu and Sikh bards are as prone to employ the Mughal motif in a complimentary as in the negative sense. It is significant, however, that in the case of the negative, the Mughals and the Delhi Sultans do not merely represent a generic 'external' aggressor, but a specific 'Muslim' other against whom any mode of dissension is of 'religious' merit. Worthy of note is 'Raja Rattan Sain of Chittaur [sic]', a bardic version of Rajput Chitaur's fall to Sultan 'Ala' al-Din Khalji in the 14th century.[138] In this 'Hindu' vision, the driving theme is the need for caste propriety and female sacrifice in the face of conquest. The conquest itself is symbolised by the call to prayer (*adhan*), forcing millions of Chitaur's 'guardian goddesses' (*deota*) from a city fallen primarily due to the treachery of a '*baniya*' (lit., 'merchant'), or 'low-caste' *wazir*.[139] In 'Raja Amar Singh of Garh Mehta in Bikaner', and 'Raja Pirthi Singh of Jodhpur', the Mughals Shah Jahan and Awrangzib are, respectively, characterised in much the same light as 'Ala' al-Din Khalji.[140] The first tale is related by a bard from Kapurthala state and the latter in Ambala cantonment, but both involve a Hindu Rajput family that served at

---

[136] 'Three Versions of Sarwan and Farijan' (XXXIII), vol. 2, pp. 365–74. These stories, told widely in eastern Punjab by the mid-19th century, are decidedly anti-British in tone. They concern the assassination of the East India Company Resident at Delhi, William Fraser (Farijan) by a *nawab* in 1835, and the *nawab*'s subsequent execution. Although the substance of the affair is cloudy, in these studies, the assassination is portrayed as a reprisal for Fraser's indiscretions with a *zamindar*'s wife.

[137] 'The Adventures of Raja Rasalu' (I), vol. 1, p. 1.

[138] 'Raja Rattan Sain of Chittaur' (XXXII), vol. 2, pp. 350–65.

[139] Ibid., pp. 363–65.

[140] 'Raja Amar Singh of Garh Mehta in Bikaner' (L), vol. 3, pp. 242–51; and 'Raja Pirthi Singh of Jodhpur' (LI), vol. 3, pp. 252–60.

the highest ranks of the Mughal state during the tenure of the aforementioned. The focus of both stories is the 'minor' members of this family. Amar Singh, for example, was the brother of Jaswant Singh (one of Shah Jahan's and Awrangzib's highest-ranking officers). Amar Singh, however, was skipped in succession and banished from his own homeland by the nobles of Marwar. In this bardic version, Amar Singh is characterised as contemplative, trusting, faithful to 'Ram' and a 'great warrior'. His wife is the self-sacrificing ideal, killing herself rather than running the risk of being seized and being forcibly converted to Islam upon her husband's death. Shah Jahan, on the other hand, is a 'tyrannical emperor' (*zulmi badshah*), a bigot who values his Muslim courtiers above 'the Hindu' Amar Singh, whom he and other Muslim courtiers view as a 'boor' (*ganwariar*) and unjustly murder.[141] 'Pirthi Singh of Jodhpur' tells the story of the above-mentioned Jaswant Singh's son and heir, who died suddenly in Delhi while his father was campaigning on Awrangzib's behalf in Kabul. Prithi Singh is shown to have much the same character as the above bard's Amar Singh, including the 'Hindu' religious credentials, characteristics that make Awrangzib wary of him to the point of viewing all Rajputs with 'great enmity' from then on, besides having Prithi Singh murdered on the same day on which they met.[142] Together, the above tales certainly suggest historical Rajput-Mughal rivalries, but in transcending ethnic and political divides to include religious difference as a source of individual character and political friction, they also imply that by the mid-19th century, when these tales were current, the concept of absolute Hindu-Muslim cultural hostility was not foreign to the masses of Punjab, the Rajputs and the Mughals being employed to represent larger 'opposing' communities.

Viewed as a whole, Temple's sample of Punjabi oral literature is sufficient to confirm that Muslims 'educated' in such tales were embedded in the 'local'. Strong clan, tribal and ethnic bonds are evident, as are ties to local linguistic and regional cultural traditions. 'Caste' affiliations are also prominent. Beyond these bonds, one can also consider a sense of 'belonging', willingly or unwillingly, to a local or imperial state. However, a broad spectrum of religious ideals, Hindu, Muslim and Sikh, reflected in the literature, obviously intersects the facets of identity mentioned above, in places adding another dimension to those facets,

---

[141] 'Raja Amar Singh...', pp. 249–51.
[142] 'Raja Pirthi Singh...', pp. 252–60.

as in the case of the Rajput-Mughal tales, while in others cutting across those facets, as in the case of the 'scavenger' caste Lal Beg. The most striking feature of religious influence, however, is not the Intoxicated Way, but the degree to which grades of the Sober Path are represented in these tales. Hinduism, Sikhism and a variety of local customs are certainly legitimated in the tales concerning Muslims, but the appreciation of pre- and post-Islamic historical periods, the preponderance of tales forwarding exclusively Hindu, Sikh or Islamic themes and the broad use of literary motifs common to the canons of larger literary traditions than that of the Punjab, confirm that embeddedness does not necessarily mean the sublimation of connectedness to a particular religious identity, whether Muslim, Hindu or Sikh. Yet, the same inclusion of custom also confirms that the 'new' Sober Path had not penetrated the illiterate classes of the Punjab by the late 19th century. Rather, the 'old' Sober Path of the variety promoted by the *shar'i*-minded reformers of the Chishtiyya, Qadiriyya and Suhrawardiyya is in ascendancy. Unless one is of the opinion that this had been the case for some centuries past, rather than a reflection of exposure to late indigenous movements, it is appropriate to conclude that even in the absence of the influence of British categories based on religious community, hospitality and/or hostility towards the social customs of Punjab in the late 19th century owed a great deal to 'new' trends in the articulation and dissemination of religious doctrine.

Conclusion: Out with the 'Old', In with the 'New'

The scholastic and literary worlds surveyed in this chapter confirm that regional particularities, class and gender-based distinctions, as well as the vagaries of time regarding British expansion, play pivotal parts in unravelling the cultural orientations of 19th century South Asian Muslims. Viewed through the lens of *madrasa*s, Bengal, Bihar and Orissa in the 1830s were places of declining Islamic learning, not merely in terms of the dwindling number of institutions, but also the quality of those that continued to function, none approaching instruction in the breadth of disciplines outlined in the *dar-i nizamiyya* a century earlier. Even narrowing the discussion to the few disciplines offered, no institution offered instruction by means of the full complement of works recommended in the *dar-i nizamiyya*. Sind in the 1850s, however, was worse off than the eastern areas—an intellectual wasteland, even in comparison with Orissa. No more than a handful of functioning *madrasa*s could be identified, and those offered even fewer disciplines than the eastern *madrasa*s. Relative to both of the above, Punjab in the 1880s was a vibrant centre of intellectual activity. In fact, the six Punjabi districts considered supported more *madrasa*s, *mawlana*s and students that all of those in Bengal, Bihar, Orissa and Sind combined. Given such variety, it is clear that a singular account of this state of affairs is implausible. Although some evidence has been presented that suggests the degradation of *madrasa*s began in the period prior to the East India Company's assumption of authority in Bengal, Bihar, Orissa and Sind, whether as a result of resumptions of endowments by local rulers or the usurpation of funds by grant holders, the extent of these factors requires further study. On the other hand, it is evident that wherever British rule spread, first by means of predations against the Muslim elite and intervention in endowments, and then as a diversion of state funds to English instruction as a result of the policy of Anglicisation, *madrasa*s were quite thoroughly degraded. The relatively healthy situation in Punjab, meanwhile, is best explained by the reconstitution of *madrasa*s funded in the manner of that at Deoband, i.e. by individual donations rather than large land endowments. Yet, there are a few areas in which the institutions of Punjab are no different than the rest, namely, the dearth of rational sciences and a concentration on law and *hadith*, to the exclusion of even theology and the principles of jurisprudence. Thus, despite the obviously varied circumstances noted, the consequences would be similar across the board. Such institutions could only produce scholars with a redacted approach to scriptural sources that echoed that of the 'new' Sober Path—a point confirmed by the writing of short-tract literature on *'aqa'id* and *fara'id*, rather than the voluminous treatises and commentaries of old—even if not directly imparted by the movements discussed in the previous chapter.

Apart from the financial pressures created by the rise of the colonial regime from region to region, the case of Punjab also illustrates the consequences of the need for instruction in colonial administrative norms in accounting for the exclusion of Islamic rational sciences in *madrasa*s under British rule. In short, colonial colleges, rather than *madrasa*s, now provided South Asian Muslims with the linguistic and administrative skills necessary for advancement in bureaucratic and judicial positions; thus, cash-strapped indigenous institutions had reason to limit their courses of instruction to religious sciences. The impact of European rational sciences on the Islamic is an additional factor worthy of consideration, and so taken up in the next chapter, but in this context it is worth noting that the study of Arabic and Persian continued unabated through *maktab*s and home-tutoring, despite the colonial turn towards English. In fact, with the exception of Sind, where paucity of *madrasa*s was echoed in the scarcity of *maktab*s, Bengal, Bihar, Orissa and Punjab supported a plethora of institutions catering to the capitalist and, to some extent, subaltern residents in the respective eras considered. The most striking difference between these places and times, however, is the changing patterns of study among non-Muslims. In the eastern provinces during the 1830s, Persian, in particular, was broadly studied by non-Muslim boys, while in Punjab, it and Arabic are restricted to Muslims, reflecting the effects of retiring Persian as the language of the state. The exact opposite is true for the study of vernacular languages. In the eastern provinces and Sind, vernacular languages were largely patronised by non-Muslims and broadly learned by Muslims only in areas where non-Muslims were economically or demographically dominant. In contrast, in Punjab, at a time when colonial policy promoted vernacular for bureaucratic reasons, Punjabi and Urdu were patronised by Muslims directly. The one aspect of education that does not bear the direct impact of colonial policy in the areas and times considered, however, is the education of girls and women. While these groups were largely restricted to home-tutoring and, therefore, the upper echelons of Muslim society in the eastern provinces, in Sind even before colonial rule took firm root, girls' *maktab*s were present. In the case of Punjab, however, it cannot be said that girls' *maktab*s were or were not patronised before the colonial discourse on gender began to take effect. In fact, all that can be said with any certainty is that prior to colonial intervention, the education of girls and women outside of the home seems to have depended on local customary attitudes.

The types of regional differences and apparently broader changes in the study of Arabic, Persian and vernacular languages that spread with British rule undoubtedly influenced the cultural milieu of each region, beginning with the fact that Persian—previously the intercommunal language of government—was converted into a 'Muslim' language. When added to the fact that vernacular languages were already patronised and taught by Muslims in the Arabic script and non-Muslims in a Sanskritic variant, it is clear to see how language became so important an element of 'religious' identity by the late 19th century. However, there is another factor to consider more directly related to literacy in Arabic, Persian and vernacular languages among

Muslims alone. In essence, such literacy, particularly among the capitalist and segments of the subaltern classes, meant that such groups were increasingly exposed to the short-tract literature on *'aqa'id* and *fara'id* written and printed by the *mawlawi*s and *mawlana*s 'graduating' from degraded or 'new' *madrasa*s. The proximity of this literature to the anti-customary 'new' Sober Path, not to mention the dissemination of the latter stream of thought as well, suggests that just as it is impossible to explain the rapidity and extent of 'colonial difference' based on colonial policies such as the Codification, so, too, is it far-fetched to assume that the rise of new cultural patterns is directly dependent on the policy of Anglicisation, without including changes in the intellectualism of indigenous peoples, as well as the convergence of indigenous trends and British designs. Given that British educational reforms, like legal reforms, did not begin to broadly impact Muslims until the late 19th and early 20th centuries, the rise of these indigenous corollaries and the decline of indigenous alternatives beginning in the early 19th century (at least wherever British rule spread), go a long way to explain how old cultural patterns were so thoroughly transformed in so short a time, rather than relying on the hegemony of the colonial discourse, particularly among the elite and capitalist classes, but also among subaltern groups. In fact, the best evidence of the impact of this general thrust is the fact that the antinomian influence of the Intoxicated Way is virtually absent in the oral, folk literature of Punjab's rural and urban subaltern groups as early as the 1870s, when Temple first began compiling his collection. In a cultural realm obviously outside of British legal and educational reforms at that time, one finds tropes mostly representative of the Sober Path, including historical periodisation and community boundaries often defined in religious terms, with local custom present, but acknowledged in ways circumscribed by no more than the latitudinarianism of 'old' modes in Islamic jurisprudence. Hence, by the early 20th century, the remnants of the 'Old Islam' still observed at shrines such as that of Pir Haji Mango became and remain the primary preserve of subaltern groups. A final variable that cements this point, in fact, is the discussion of the rise of a 'new' Intoxicated Way that follows in the next chapter.

CHAPTER FIVE

OBJECTIFICATION AND A 'NEW' INTOXICATED WAY

Despite the humble beginnings of Anglicisation under the watch of the East India Company, by the early 20th century, English schools and colleges had grown in number and begun to produce the first generations of elite and capitalist-class Muslims primarily educated in the European mould. In the midst of this transition, Anglicisation had received a boost from the Uprising of 1857, which provided the final pretext for government by the Crown to supplant Company rule in 1858. Continuity in educational policy since the 1830s hints at how little else to do with colonial policy actually changed with the onset of 'direct rule'. In the pattern of government, the Crown maintained 'subsidiary alliances' with more than 500 'Princely States' first negotiated by the Company, and continued to depend on South Asians in the lower ranks of all branches of state. The Codification process also continued to inform the state, together with Anglicisation shaping many of the governing institutions of 'British Raj' (1858–1947).

Another example of the continuity inherent in the governing institutions of the Company and the Raj, is the many censuses conducted, beginning in the late East India Company period with works like William Adam's previously considered 'Reports' in Bengal, Bihar and Orissa, but vastly expanded by the 1860s. While the nature of religious communities was moulded in various ways by Codification and Anglicisation, the induction of censuses emphasising religious community to aid in allocating quotas for government jobs, political representation and so on, encouraged the elite and capitalist classes educated in the former to ask and answer which demographic slot they fit in the latter. The result, according to Bernard Cohn and others who follow his lead, was a process of cultural 'objectification', such that by the 20th century:

> ...the whole Western educated class of Indians...have objectified their culture. They in some sense have made it into a 'thing'; they can stand back and look at themselves, their ideas, their symbols and culture and see it as an entity. What had previously been embedded in a whole matrix of custom, ritual, religious symbol, a textually transmitted tradition, has

now become something different. What had been unconscious now to some extent becomes conscious. Aspects of the tradition can be selected, polished and reformulated for conscious ends.[1]

Cohn restricts the predominance of Objectification to the 'Western educated class of Indians' because it is through a 'Western' lens that culture is objectified, the influence of the colonial discourse not able or intended to penetrate much further. Although such theses afford colonial subjects much agency in sculpting their own 'Modernity', the idea that the 'whole Western educated class of Indians' can be said to have 'objectified their culture' does not sit well with some. In fact, as early as the 1960s, before such theoretical perspectives became standard fare in the historiography of South Asia, Fazlur Rahman (d. 1988), a major 'Islamic Modernist' of the post-colonial period, commented that to 'many observers, the history of Islam in modern times is essentially the history of...a semi-inert mass receiving the destructive blows or the formative influences from the West'.[2]

The case can certainly be made that advocates of Objectification qualify as just such 'observers' of 'tradition' in general, particularly when it is acknowledged that Rahman's 'insider' critique has its echoes in the works of academic 'outsiders' who write the intellectual history of Muslims. Francis Robinson, for one, concurs with Rahman in asserting that so far as Muslim scholars are concerned, 'whether traditionalist [e.g. Deobandis] or modernist [i.e. "Western educated"]', it must be granted that they 'understood the world within an Islamic frame'.[3] Rahman and Robinson agree that apart from European thought and institutions, the 'Traditionalist' movements identified in this book as permutations of a 'new' Sober Path were 'directly bequeathed' to the 'Western' educated Muslims of the late 19th and early 20th centuries.[4] This contributes, in Rahman's thought and Robinson's words, to a progressive shift from 'other-worldly religion to this worldly religion', accounting for much of the communitarian social activism advocated by 'Traditionalists'

---

[1] See Bernard Cohn, 'The Census, Social Structure and Objectification in South Asia', *An Anthropologist among Historians and Other Essays* (New York: Oxford University Press, 1990), pp. 228–29.
[2] Fazlur Rahman, *Islam* (Chicago: University of Chicago Press, 1979), p. 212.
[3] Francis Robinson, 'Secularization, Weber and Islam', *Islam and Muslim History in South Asia* (Delhi: Oxford University Press, 2001), p. 128.
[4] Rahman, *Islam*, pp. 212–15.

and 'Modernists'.⁵ However, this is where Robinson the 'outsider' parts company with Rahman the 'insider', qualifying his 'Islamic frame' by paying closer attention to the manner in which European ideas were simultaneously adopted into and reshaped the Muslim 'Self' under colonial rule. For example, in Robinson's view an emphasis on history in Muslim works beginning in the late 19th century was driven by the impact of colonialism's Anglicising policy and the 'distancing effects of print', leading to 'an understanding of Islam as an object, which might be analysed, conceptualised and even presented as a system'.⁶ Rahman, on the other hand, does not deny the importance of European ideas, but views their integration from a more thoroughly internal perspective, thereby equating the process with the selective reading and legitimisation of Hellenic, etc. thought in the pre-colonial period. Thus, he argues that 'lay Muslims with a liberal education' must be split into three intellectual camps beginning in the colonial era. One gravitated towards 'pure Westernism', the second retreated into 'fundamentalism', but the third advocated 'an integration of modern ideas and institutions with the bases of Islam'.⁷ As for addressing the inversion of 'power' that is central to the thesis of Objectification—pre-colonial 'manipulations' having occurred while Muslims held the reins of the political authority—Rahman responds that the ultimate distinction between pre-colonial and colonial instances of 'crisis' is that 'political defeats and subjugation [absent in the former case] rendered the Muslim psychologically less capable of constructively rethinking his heritage' in the colonial era.⁸ This psychological impediment is reflected in the assumption among colonial era Muslims that 'reconstruction, if at all...will be done by influences from the West'.⁹

In this chapter, it is not my intention to weigh the scale of European influence over which Robinson quibbles with Rahman, but to add to

---

⁵ Francis Robinson, 'Religious Change and the Self in Muslim South Asia since 1800', *Islam and Muslim History in South Asia*, pp. 107.

⁶ Francis Robinson, 'Islam and the Impact of Print in South Asia', *Islam and Muslim History in South Asia*, p. 91.

⁷ Rahman explains that the 'integration of new social and cultural elements' won individual advocates, but did not create a 'new Islamic humanism'. Thus, 'liberalisation' veered into 'westernisation', while the 'disequilibrium in Western social life [e.g. World War I]', coupled with pressures applied by 'conservative and revivalist' elements, disenchanted others, leading them to 'fundamentalism' or 'integrationism'. Rahman, *Islam*, pp. 214–26, 232–33.

⁸ Ibid., p. 213.

⁹ Ibid., pp. 214–24.

their uniform cautions concerning the weight Cohn and others who depend on a dominant paradigm of doctrinal Islam as statically legalist and intrusive place on European influences and the colonial regime in accounting for cultural change. After all, it must be remembered that not only scholars, but even lay persons like Akbar and Awrangzib, were not 'unconscious' when manipulating the 'matrix of custom, ritual, religious symbol and textually transmitted tradition' to meet their own political ends. Furthermore, Rahman's own approach to 'Islamic Modernism'—which privileges *ijtihad*, legalism and theological transcendentalism—stands at the end of a number of 'Euro-Islamic' scholarly encounters reaching back to the 16th century, long before colonialism grasped the reins of power. Recall that by the 1580s, Akbar had invited Portuguese representatives of the Catholic Church to debate at the 'Idabat Khana and provide doctrinal writings for translation and study. By the late 17th century, members of the Mughal elite, such as Danishmand Khan, had already begun the translation of 'scientific' works as well. In the intervening period, Jahangir's court artists incorporated aspects of the Renaissance artistic tradition into their works, while European military advisors had found employment in Mughal service.

All of the above trends, including further translations of European sciences, continued into the 18th century. Among the philosophically inclined in the later period, authors such as Tafaz al-Husayn Khan (d. 1801)—a Madrasa-i Farangi Mahal student and, in the later years of his life, a reluctant officer of high-rank in the Nawabate of Oudh—picked up where the likes of Danishmand Khan had left off, learning Greek, Latin and English, and using them to produce Persian translations of Isaac Newton's *Philosophica Naturalis Principia Mathematica* and William Emerson's *Mechanics, or the Doctrine of Motion*, among other European works.[10] One of Tafaz al-Husayn's students, Khwaja Farid al-Din Ahmad (d. 1828)—*wazir* of the Mughal Sultan, Akbar II (r. 1806–1837), and ambassador to Iran and Burma for the East India Company—was also a noted mathematician and astronomer in his own right, who read and instructed students in European works.[11] Unlike

---

[10] S.A.A. Rizvi, *The Socio-Intellectual History of Isna-Ashari Shi'is in India* (Canberra: Ma'rifat Publishing House, 1986), p. 228. Also see Arif Abid, 'A Poisoned Chalice', 3 *Quarks Daily* (13 March 2006), available online at: <http://3quarksdaily.blog.com/3quarksdaily/2006/03/nawab_tafazzul_.html>

[11] Ibid., pp. 364–65.

Danishmand Khan, however, these men had not employed European secretaries to gain access to European ideas, but had worked in various capacities for, and benefited from close relations with, officers of the East India Company, ranging from Governor-Generals to administrator-scholars like William Jones. Their studies had also convinced both of Copernicus' mathematical proofs for heliocentrism, Newton's ideas about gravity, and so on, and at least in the case of Tafaz al-Husayn, a repudiation of Islamic geocentricism was publicly stated. Despite such individual initiatives, however, the general tendency of the period was to remain within the bounds of 16th and 17th century Islamic scholasticism, including a response to European thought confined to translation and study.

Even acknowledging that scholasticism was not greatly impacted by the translation and study of European works well into the 19th century, it is worth noting that a few scholars of the early 19th century, including Farid al-Din's contemporary, Mirza Abu Talib (d. 1818)—a *wazir* of Oudh and one of the earliest travellers from the region to Europe—did more forcefully attempt to convince his peers that European ideas and institutions differed significantly from the Islamic. Like his predecessors, Abu Talib also emphasised the veracity of Copernicus' heliocentric proofs and Newtonian mechanics.[12] In his travelogue, he heaps praise on the technological, industrial and scientific accomplishments of Europe, lauding the university system which sustained it. Yet, even Abu Talib had little to say about the philosophy of the time. Barely touching on the subject, he merely commented:

> The English have very peculiar opinions on the subject of perfection. They insist that it is merely an ideal quality, and depends entirely upon comparison; that mankind has risen, by degrees, from the state of savages to the exalted dignity of the great philosopher Newton; but that, so far from having yet attained perfection, it is possible that, in future ages, philosophers will look with as much contempt on the acquirements of Newton as we now do on the rude state of arts among savages. If this

---

[12] While in Britain, Abu Talib met up with another Muslim traveller, Saqi Din Muhammad of Patna, who also wrote a travelogue (1793–94). The latter work bears the distinction of being the earliest extant work by a Muslim in the English language, and its author is one of the first Muslims to settle in Britain, where he lived as an entrepreneur, opening perhaps the first 'Indian' restaurant in Europe, among other ventures. The work has recently been reprinted with a biographical essay of its author as *Dean Mahomet, The Travels of Dean Mahomet*, ed. Michael H. Fischer (Berkeley: University of California Press, 1997).

axiom of theirs be correct, man has yet much to learn, and all his boasted knowledge is but vanity.[13]

Abu Talib's opinion of the 'materialism' that informs this 'axiom' is only indirectly commented on in an assessment of British social institutions that he clearly bases on conversations with men in the classes aware of contemporary trends in the 'rational sciences'. He states that the 'first and greatest defect I observed in the English is their want of faith in religion, and their great inclination to philosophy'. This 'want of principle' has led to a society ordered by little more than the 'honour of the superior classes', the 'severity of the laws' and the 'fear of punishment', but 'totally devoid of honesty'. It is also a society unresponsive to the protestations of people burdened under the 'great increase of taxes and high price of provisions'. Insurrection is only averted by vigilant 'magistrates' and the deployment of 'soldiers to patrol the streets day and night, to disperse all persons whom they saw assembling together'.[14] Clearly, Abu Talib's praise of European sciences did not include its metaphysics or its political and legal philosophies, which he judged 'atheistic'.

Nevertheless, reflecting on the state of his corner of the Muslim World (the Persian/Urdu speaking elite of the Gangetic Basin), Abu Talib despaired that stagnation had set in. He complained that his account of the 'curiosities and wonders' and the 'manner and customs' of the places he visited would be in vain due to the 'want of energy and the indolent disposition' of the rich, the 'vanity' and 'limited knowledge' of the learned, and the 'difficulty of procuring a livelihood' for the rest.[15] He also hinted at a scholarly bias against European 'manners and customs', stating that the 'indolent' elite, too lazy to read a book requiring intellectual effort, would 'under the pretence of zeal for religion, entirely abstain and refrain from perusing it'.[16] Yet, when one considers Abu Talib's attitudes, it is quite apparent that his account of the European is as much edited by 'religion' as the attitudes of the Muslims he criticises. Indeed, his interest in no more than the technology and physical sciences of Europe reflects a decidedly Sober attitude.[17]

---

[13] Abu Talib Khan, *Travels of Mirza Abu Taleb Khan*, vol. 2, trans. C. Stewart (London: Longman et al., 1814), pp. 165–66.
[14] Ibid., pp. 128–31.
[15] Ibid., vol. 1, p. 1.
[16] Ibid., p. 6.
[17] A typical example of this attitude can be read in a letter to the Amir of Bukhara written by Shah 'Abd al-'Aziz on the legality of studying rational sciences. He wrote:

That a leading representative of the elite reflects this bias suggests just how far from Akbar's 'Ibadat Khana Muslim elites and scholarly classes had travelled in the intervening centuries. To confirm that Abu Talib is, in fact, not an isolated case, one need venture no further than the writings of a scholar of similar background from the next generation, Mawlana Karamat 'Ali (d. 1876).

Karamat 'Ali's *Risala fi Ma'akhidh al-'Ulum*, stands out as the first extent attempt to address a growing problem with philosophical writings among Muslims, first publicly commented on by the likes of Tafaz al-Husayn a century earlier. That is, neither the metaphysics of the philosophers, mystics or theologians appeared to match the findings of Muslim astronomers and mathematicians working under the influence of European contemporaries. Something of this problem, and Karamat 'Ali's response, can be gleaned from the following passage:

> The whole Qur'an is full of passages containing information on physical and mathematical sciences. If we would but spend a little reflection over it we should find wonderous meanings in every word it contains. The Qur'an has most satisfactorily confuted all the systems of ancient philosophy; it plucked up from the root the physical sciences as prevalent among the ancients. What a strange coincidence exists between the Qur'an and the philosophy of modern Europe.[18]

While this passage may prompt some contemporary commentators to laud Karamat 'Ali for forwarding the spirit of Islamic philosophy into the mid-19th century, the latter's work does not suggest that Karamat 'Ali went further than arguing that 'the philosophy of modern Europe' did not contradict the Qur'an. He did not offer an argument by which to assimilate (or rationally reject) a Copernican, rather than a geocentric cosmos, Newton's laws, or the soon-to-arise thesis of Darwinism, on Qur'anic grounds. No 'new' metaphysic issued from Karamat Ali's pen. Indeed, in this regard Karamat 'Ali is in the company of all the Muslim intellectuals of mid-19th century. Obviously, such shortfalls were not remedied by the decline of *madrasas* (and the virtual elimination of instruction in the 'rational sciences' they once provided) that followed the expansion of British rule, let alone the creeping rise of a

---

'The legality of an instrument depends on the purpose for which it is used... Should someone learn logic to support an untrue faith and confuse correct beliefs, the sin would lie in performing those unlawful acts and not in learning logic'. Cited in S.A.A. Rizvi, *Shah 'Abd al-'Aziz* (Canberra: Ma'rifat Publishing House, 1982), p. 241.

[18] Cited in Rizvi, *The Socio-Intellectual History of Isna-Ashari Shi'is in India*, p. 367.

'new' Sober Path which overtly rejected any learning that 'contradicted' its interpretation of the Qur'an and *hadith*, as illustrated in Chapter Three by the Deobandi founder Muhammad Qasim's insistence that any who challenged the idea of 'seven celestial stratum' were infidels and apostates. Yet, recognition of a problem and the statement of an accommodative hypothesis meant that an invitation to compose 'new' philosophical approaches was widely circulated among those dissatisfied with the prospect of deferring to European or 'new' Sober ideas.

Apart from the impact of internal scholastic decline and the spread of European thought among the philosophically inclined, it must also be acknowledged that the same thrusts were felt by mystics who advocated an Intoxicated Way. In the last two chapters, I mentioned that by the early 18th century, previously Intoxicated orders like the Chishtiyya turned their attention to law, and even writers of the 'new' Sober Path, who continued to defend a place for Sufism, altered its metaphysical and practical (e.g. shrine-based worship) tenets so as to limit antinomian and latitudinarian tendencies—the cultural effects of all the above being evident in the orally transmitted folk literature of Punjab by the mid- to late 19th century. Among the elite and capitalist classes with access to formal education, therefore, all of the above has already been argued to suggest that by the mid-19th century, the Intoxicated Way retained nothing of the cache it had once enjoyed. A cursory glance at the poetry of Asad Allah Khan Ghalib (d. 1869) or 'Inayat Khan's (d. 1927) Sufi writings, confirms that attitudes legitimated by the Intoxicated Way were not entirely absent, but that such figures increasingly competed for legitimacy with Sober rivals, from Khwaja Mir Dard, mentioned in Chapter Three as one of the 18th century's Naqshbandi authors of a 'new' Sober Path, to Ghalib's contemporary, Mu'min Khan Mu'min (d. 1852), who turned to Muhammad Isma'il's *Tariqa Muhammadiyya* in his later years.[19] Ghalib was relieved of

---

[19] Asad Allah Khan Ghalib needs no introduction to readers of Urdu poetry, being one of the originators of the 'modern' style in that language. Noted for his appetite for wine and gambling, most historians influenced by the dominant paradigm under question in this book, are often perplexed by his 'irreverence towards established religious norms', on the one hand, and 'sense of belonging to the community of Muslims'. Hence, although Jalal, whose juxtaposition is quoted above, mentions poems that outline Ghalib's concept of *fana'* (annihilation), she fails to attach his 'irreverence' to doctrinally conditioned antinomian and latitudinarian impulses, instead accounting for Ghalib's attitudes in terms of a general notion of the 'individual' (*fard*) predicated on 'the individual's right to an unmediated relationship with Allah', as opposed to the 'atonement of individual sins by the collectivity as in the Christian tradition'. In fact,

defending himself against the recriminations of alternatives by his own death, while 'Inayat Khan addressed the growing unpopularity of the Intoxicated Way among the elite and capitalist classes by travelling through Europe and the USA from 1910 to 1926, only returning to South Asia the year before he died. However, among those Sufis who remained, the choice was the same as that faced by the philosophically inclined: marginalisation or reform cognisant of European thought and/or the 'new' Sober Path.

The question that such continuous interest in, and acknowledgement of, European thought raises is whether the architects of the responses to that thought represent Objectification, or if their incorporation of European thought is accomplished within what Rahman, Robinson and others term an 'Islamic frame'? I seek the answer in the metaphysics, theology, legalism and actions of Sayyid Ahmad Khan (d. 1898), Mirza Ghulam Ahmad (d. 1908) and Muhammad Iqbal (d. 1938), the first and last of whom are to Fazlur Rahman's post-colonial 'Islamic Modernism' what the Wali Allahis, Deobandis and Ahl-i Hadith are to the various 'Jama'ats' mentioned in the last chapters. Meanwhile, Mirza Ghulam Ahmad was the founder of the *Ahmadiyya* 'sect' still active today. I find that although the 'Islam' of everyone from Ahmad Khan to Fazlur Rahman differs from that of the pre-colonial period and the 'new' Sober Path, among the above thinkers there remains continuity in the categories of thought and the general orientations of rational sciences and mysticism. Social historians, who consider such thinkers as 'new-fangled' within the rubric of Objectification, do not adequately take this continuity into account. Ironically, neither does Rahman. His stark differentiation between 'Fundamentalists/Traditionalists', 'Islamic Modernists' and 'pure Westernism' recognises the influence of 18th century reformist thought—i.e. the 'new' Sober Path—but by leaning in some respects towards the same himself, he fails to pay enough

---

betraying the role of the dominant paradigm in her assessment, she goes as far as to argue that Muslims as a whole reject 'God's immanence' in favour of a 'transcendental' divinity. When Ghalib's views on *fana'* are more thoroughly assimilated into his 'Islam', however, his perspective is immediately recognizable as specific to the Sufi conception of 'Intoxicated Way', one which can also be read in the works of 'Inayat Khan. For Jalal's views, see Jalal, *Self and Sovereignty*, pp. 1–9. Ghalib's, Dard's and Mu'min's poetry has been published in various forms, but for samples in the original Urdu with English translations, see K.C. Kanda, ed. and trans. *Masterpieces of Urdu Ghazal* (Lahore: Vanguard, 1990), pp. 42–71, 116–81, 182–215. For a sample of 'Inayat Khan's writings, see J. Wittenveed, ed. *The Heart of Sufism: The Essential Writings of Hazrat Inayat Khan* (London: Shambhala, 1999).

heed to the role of the 'old' Sober Path and the Intoxicated Way when defining the internal modes by which aspects of European thought were either legitimated or rejected by 'Islamic Modernists'. Consequently, Rahman's categories cannot accommodate Mirza Ghulam Ahmad. To do that, all of the above, from Ahmad Khan to Fazlur Rahman, must be acknowledged as part of a group whose ideas represent permutations of a 'new' Intoxicated Way; one that shares the spirit of *ijtihad*, legalism and metaphysical transcendentalism with the 'new' Sober Path, but rejects the latter's textualism in favour of the 'old' philosopher's and mystic's equation of Reason/Intuition with Revelation. All these Muslim thinkers employ time-honoured methodologies, rather than shaping new ones, to systematically legitimate or reject aspects of European thought within an 'Islamic frame'.

I. *Sayyid Ahmad Khan's 'Nature'*

The last Mughal Sultans, Akbar II and Bahadur Shah Zafar (r. 1837–1858), were politically impotent, but their courts remained lively centres of intellectual activity. The latter Sultan, an avid reader and noteworthy Persian/Urdu poet in his own right, insured that such luminaries as Ghalib and Mu'min were never far from his side. Nor were scholars of various Islamic sciences, religious and rational, as well as indigenous and British figures associated with the colonial Delhi College. This was the environment in which Sayyid Ahmad Khan was raised, and it is a sign of the place and times that although he is not among the earliest generations to have been exposed to European ideas, he is among the first whose career began as an employee of the East India Company's judiciary. It is equally a sign of the times that although he was the grandson of the aforementioned astronomer and mathematician, Farid al-Din, Ahmad Khan's literary career began as a staunch advocate of the 'new' Sober Path.[20] His first taste of formal education began with

---

[20] The earliest biographies of Sayyid Ahmad Khan were written by two of his contemporaries and remain the most detailed sources of Ahmad Khan's early life. The first, appearing during Ahmad Khan's lifetime (1885), was written by a colleague and Director of Public Education for the N.W. Provinces, G.F.I. Graham. The second, appearing shortly after Ahmad Khan's death, was the work of a friend and renowned Urdu poet, Altaf Husayn Hali (d. 1914). Both have been consulted here. G.F.I. Graham, *The Life and Work of Sir Sayyid Ahmad Khan* (Delhi: Idara-i Adabiyat-i Delli, 1974); A.H. Hali, *Hayat-i Javed*, trans K.H. Qadari & Matthews, D.J. (Delhi: Idara-i Adabiyat-i

reading the Qur'an at home under a woman teacher in Delhi. From there, he went on to a *maktab* to study Arabic, Persian and Urdu. He also studied mathematics and geometry under an uncle Zain al-'Abidin, a student of Farid al-Din, and *tibb* (medicine) under a leading *hakim* of the city.[21] Ahmad Khan's formal education, however, took a hiatus in 1835, when he reached 18. For the next three years, Ahmad Khan circulated among the poets and intellectuals resident in Delhi, attached to Delhi College and the Mughal court. He only returned to formal study in pursuit of qualifications to work when his father died in 1838 and his immediate family was left with no source of income other than his mother's pension from the impoverished Bahadur Shah Zafar. Another uncle, Khalil Allah Khan, a *sadr-amin* (judge) in the East India Company's Delhi court, took him on as a legal apprentice. In the process, Ahmad Khan was educated in English jurisprudence, civil and criminal. At the same time, he also studied *hadith* and Islamic jurisprudence under various well-known Delhi scholars.[22] While a clerk in his uncle's court, Ahmad Khan wrote the standard examination for the post of *munsif* (sub-judge) and was appointed to the post in 1841. Fourteen years later, just before the aged Sultan who paid his mother's pension lost his throne for raising his banner against the East India Company in the 1857 Uprising, Ahmad Khan had reached the rank of *sadr-amin*, the highest post available to a South Asian in the Company's judiciary.

Ahmad Khan's career confirms that he was exposed to European ideas and colonial institutions at a very young age. Even so, analysis of Ahmad Khan's early writings (largely short-tracts) reveals the influence of the 'new' Sober Path in two recurring themes: 'obedience to the prescriptions of the *shari'a*...and love and veneration for the Prophet as the living embodiment of this law on earth'.[23] Furthermore, Ahmad Khan's father was related to Khwaja Mir Dard, one of the writers of the

---

Delli, 1979). For a more contemporary and scholarly account of Ahmad Khan's place in 19th century British India, see David Lelyveld, *Aligarh's First Generation* (Princeton: Princeton University Press, 1977).

[21] On the maternal side of Ahmad Khan's family, his grandfather was Khwaja Farid al-Din, noted above for his works in mathematics and astronomy. Zain al-'Abidin, Farid al-Din's son and Ahmad Khan's uncle, was also a renowned mathematician.

[22] Hali lists the works of *fiqh* and *hadith* undertaken, as well as the instructors under whom Ahmad Khan studied. Hali, *Hayat-i Javed*, p. 33.

[23] Christian Troll, *Sayyid Ahmad Khan: A Reinterpretation of Muslim Theology* (Delhi: Vikas Publishing House, 1978), p. 42.

Tariqa Muhammadiyya movements, and both his parents were initiates of the Naqshbandiyya-Mujaddidiyya under Shah Ghulam 'Ali (d. 1824), one of Mir Dard's late successors. He also made pilgrimages to Ahmad Sirhindi's tomb until his dying day. More specifically, in keeping with Wali Allahi and *Tariqa Muhammadiyya* formulas, Ahmad Khan is well known to have criticised *taqlid* and advocated *ijtihad*, conceptualising the Prophet as the '*Pir* of *Pirs*', while writing approvingly of Shah Muhammad Isma'il.[24] Considering the totality of his works before 1858, therefore, it is not surprising that when faced with the idea of a heliocentric planetary system, Ahmad Khan viewed it as an assault on Qur'anic 'truth', responding in 1848 with a work in the vein of the Deobandi Muhammad Qasim's ideas, considered in Chapter Three.[25] As this work on a geocentric universe suggests, Ahmad Khan did have an interest in the rational sciences, but only as far as it did not transgress his 'new' Sober bounds.[26] Even after the 1857 Uprising, which he spent aiding the British, Ahmad Khan continued to write works in support of

---

[24] Ibid., pp. 42–57. Ahmad Khan addressed the same appeal for *ijtihad* to Deobandis in 1873. See 'Translation of Texts Related to Sayyid Ahmad's Creed', in Troll, *Sayyid Ahmad Khan: A Reinterpretation of Muslim Theology*, p. 275.

[25] Ahmad Khan's writing career began soon after 1838. His first works were manuals and compendiums of East India Company legal presidents and procedures, written between 1838 and 1841. In the same period, he also began writing on 'Islam'. Between 1841 and 1860, he produced six religious works. The first had to do with events in the life of the Prophet Muhammad and the 'proper' means to celebrate his birth. The second was a translation of an anti-Shi'a work from Persian. The third was an attack on the *pir*'s role in Sufism. The fourth was a defence of the groups the British referred to as 'Wahhabis'. The fifth is an exposition on the 'proper' role of the *pir* in Sufism. The last is a defence of a geocentric cosmos. In the order mentioned, these works are: *Jila al-Qulub Bizikr al-Mahbub* (1838); *Tuhfa-i Hasan* (1839); *Kalimat al-Haqq* (1849); *Rah-i Sunnat dar Radd-i Bid'at* (1850); and *Namiqa dar Bayan-i Masala-i Tasawwur-i Shaikh* (1852). The 'astronomical' work is the *Qaul-i Matin dar Ibtal-i Harkat-i Zamin* (1848). See Hali, *Hayat-i Javed*, pp. 31–32, 37–38. In the discipline of history, he published a work on the historical buildings and personalities of Delhi, then compiled a list of monarchs associated with Delhi beginning with Pandava rulers of the Hindu epics and ending with Queen Victoria, published in 1847 and 1852. He then wrote a history of Bijnor and produced a revised Persian edition of Abu al-Fadl's *A'in-i Akbari*, both appearing in 1855. In order of mention, these works are: *Asar al-Sanadid* (1847); *Silsilat al-Mulk* (1852); *Zila-i Bijnaur Tarikh* (1855). See Hali, *Hayat-i Javed*, pp. 32–41. For further consideration on these early historical works, see C.W. Troll, 'A Note on an Early Topographical Work of Sayyid Ahmad Khan: Asar al-Sanadid', *Journal of the Royal Asiatic Society* (1972): 135–46.

[26] These works are: *Tashil fi Jarr al-Saqil* (1844); and *Fawa'id al-Afkar fi 'Amal al-Farjar* (n.d.). Both are translations, the first a work of Ibn Sina's, and the second the work of his grandfather, Farid al-Din, into Urdu. See Hali, *Hayat-i Javed*, pp. 32–37.

Sober thought in general, and the 'new' Sober Path in particular.[27] Given the particularities of Ahmad Khan's class and intellectual background, however, as early as the 1860s, he would respond to three aspects of the new situation in which he found himself in a manner quite different to the advocates of the 'new' Sobriety.

Due in some part to his familial association with the likes of Farid al-Din, Zain al-'Abidin and intellectuals associated with Delhi College, including British civil servants, Ahmad Khan was first and foremost aware that European intellectuals had vastly furthered the fields of astronomy, mathematics and medicine, among others. In response, he formed an *anjuman* called the 'Scientific Society' in 1864, with a number of British and South Asian colleagues, funded by donations and membership subscriptions.[28] In the time the Scientific Society remained active (1864–89), it would expand to found an 'Institute' at Aligarh with its own library and press and, by 1866, publish the *Aligarh Institute Gazette*, a bilingual (English/Urdu) newspaper edited by Ahmad Khan that was issued weekly until his death in 1898.[29] The Society also translated and published various English works, 25 altogether, by 1885.[30] The predominance of mathematics fulfilled the

---

[27] His rebuttals of W.W. Hunter's *Indian Musalmans* (1872) and W. Muir's *Life of Mohamet* (1861) contain spirited explication and defence of the schools which Hunter, like other British authors, termed 'Wahhabi'. Also in this period, he translated into Urdu and added commentary to certain works by al-Ghazali, appearing in 1879. These would be followed in the 1880s by two works on *salat*, the first outlining Hanafi opinion on the object and conduct of daily prayer, the second a more theosophical treatise on the meaning of *salat*. Also, illustrating his public concerns in 1871, Ahmad Khan wrote a letter to the *Pioneer*—a leading newspaper of its day—expressing his concerns about the misconceptions held by the British about 'Wahhabism'. See *Pioneer* (31 March 1871) in Sayyid Ahmad Khan, *Writings and Speeches of Sir Syed Ahmad Khan*, ed. Shan Muhammad (Bombay: Nachiketa Publications, 1972), pp. 237–39; and for Ahmad Khan's views on Hunter, see Sayyid Ahmad Khan, *Review of Dr. Hunter's Indian Musalmans; are they bound by conscience to rebel against the Queen?* (Lahore: Premier Book House, n.d.).

[28] In the Bye-Laws of the society, the objectives are stated as: (1) the translation of English and other European language 'works on arts and sciences'; (2) to publish 'rare and valuable oriental works—No religious works will come under the notice of the Society'; (3) to publish newspapers, journals and magazines, 'which may be calculated to improve the native mind'; and, (4) to hold 'lectures on scientific or other useful subjects'. See 'Proceeding of the First Meeting of the Scientific Society', dated January 1864, in Yusuf Husain, ed. *Selected Documents from the Aligarh Archives* (Bombay: Asia Publishing House, 1966), p. 16. Note: the latter two points were added in 1867.

[29] Hali, *Hayat-i Javed*, pp. 91–94.

[30] Of these works, 15 are mathematical (including trigonometry, geometry, arithmetic and calculus), five are histories and two concern political philosophy. The remaining include a work on 'Modern Farming', one on electricity and another on geography.

Society's 'scientific' objective, pursuing the 'language' of the sciences before their direct study, but it also confirms that Ahmad Khan's translations did not transgress disciplines legitimated by Sober thought in general. The emphasis on history, second only to mathematics, is another instance in which Ahmad Khan continued a personal interest and a Sober staple. The choice of histories is also informative. Three of the five works are related to the Muslim World, one to Europe and one to East Asia, while works with alternative perspectives on Islam and Muslims, such as Hunter's *Indian Musalmans*, are not only scrupulously avoided, but are rebutted.[31] Lastly, the dearth of metaphysics, ethics and so on, again confirms a trend noted among earlier Sober thinkers: the restriction of interest in European learning to the 'physical' aspects of the 'rational sciences'. Thus, although the institutional vehicle of the *anjuman* reflects the colonial engagement, neither the translation of works nor the choice of works translated is ultimately representative of European intellectual frameworks.

This leads to the second manner in which Ahmad Khan responded differently compared with other advocates of the 'new' Sobriety. Due to his association with the aforementioned Delhi scholars, as well as his education and employment as an East India Company judicial officer, by 1858, Ahmad Khan would also have been aware that in Europe, institutions of higher learning were structured rather differently than *madrasas*. Thus, in the 1860s, Ahmad Khan began advocating for the establishment of an Urdu-medium 'university' about Delhi and/or an Urdu Department at the British Calcutta University.[32] By the end of the decade, Ahmad Khan's initiatives received the added spur of a visit to Cambridge, where his son, Sayyid Mahmud, had won a scholarship. In fact, Ahmad Khan had promoted travel to Europe as part of the agenda of the Scientific Society. The *Musafiran-i Landan*, recording his own impressions, would be the first of many future writings to draw marked criticism. Yet, Ahmad Khan does not say much more than Mirza Abu

---

See Graham, *The Life and Work of Sir Sayyid Ahmad Khan*, p. 83. The Society would also experiment with various European agricultural techniques on land made over by the state, and conduct a survey of techniques employed in the vicinity of Aligarh. See correspondence regarding these projects in, *Selected Documents*, pp. 1–139.

[31] Translations include: Charles Rollin's *Ancient History of Egypt and Ancient History of Greece* (1845); John Malcolm's *History of Persia* (1828); Mountstuart Elphinstone's *History of India* (1841); and Exoo's *History of China* (n.d.). See Graham, *The Life and Work of Sir Sayyid Ahmad Khan*, p. 83.

[32] Ibid., p. 97.

Talib had some 70 years earlier. Like his predecessor, Ahmad Khan writes approvingly of the Industrial Revolution, advances in the 'physical' sciences and the education of people. He even despaired that his words would fall on deaf ears, writing a stern warning of the disaster that would result from lack of heed.[33] However, there are also differences between the two travellers. Although Abu Talib only comments on the elite Muslims of the Gangetic Basin, finding them 'indolent' and 'decadent', Ahmad Khan's criticism of the same group adds a comparative dimension. Egypt and Turkey are found far 'advanced' (*taraqqi*) in manner and education, while Hindus and Parsis outshine his class of Muslims.[34] In terms of travel and study in Europe as well, Ahmad Khan laments that two Hindus from Bombay had arrived to study with his son, and four from Bengal had already graduated, while no Muslim had so far pursued such avenues of learning.[35] As well, Ahmad Khan's judgement of European institutions is far kinder then Abu Talib's. Whereas Abu Talib criticised the British political system and its wards as 'materialistic', Ahmad Khan had only praise for the system, finding that the aristocratic classes and members of parliament respected the 'rights' (*huquq*) of the 'masses' (*ra'ya*) like nowhere else.[36] Furthermore, he made a concerted effort to dispel the idea of the British as 'materialists' and 'atheists', beginning with a description of a Christian service on board the ship from Bombay to Aden.[37] Ahmad Khan's greatest problem with Europe was negative British perceptions of Islam and Muslims, to which he devoted a great deal of pages and thought.[38]

It is evident that Europe impressed Ahmad Khan greatly and that neither being shunned for it by his co-religionists, nor British misrepresentations about Islam and Muslims, dissuaded him of this conviction. In fact, the influence of European thought and institutions was magnified by his witnessing firsthand the material prosperity he

---

[33] Sayyid Ahmad Khan, *Musafiran-i Landan* (Lahore: Majlis-i Taraqqi-i Adab, 1961), pp. 288–89.
[34] Ibid., pp. 189–94.
[35] Ibid., p. 221.
[36] Ibid., pp. 228–29, 283–85.
[37] Ibid., p. 88.
[38] An encounter with an Englishman shipboard, who expressed the opinion that 'Hindustanis' were 'ungrateful and heartless', begins the discussion of the issue, leading Ahmad Khan to counter that this perception was wrought by lack of contact (pp. 119–20). The issue distresses him to the point that much of his time in London is spent researching a rebuttal to Muir's *Life of Mohamet*, and other 'Orientalists'. Ibid., pp. 119, 221–22.

perceived them to have delivered to England and France. In essence, everything he saw convinced him that Muslims could no longer afford to stand aloof from European thought and educational reform that reflected it. Thus, his first act on returning to Aligarh was to constitute a committee within the Scientific Society to study the root causes of Muslim distance from colonial schools and European sciences. 'The Committee for the Diffusion and Advancement of Learning among Muhammadans of India' solicited essays and awarded prizes to the most noteworthy two years later, in 1872. That June, Ahmad Khan wrote to colonial authorities informing them of the committee's activities and advising them that an English- or Urdu-medium version of Oxford or Cambridge funded by the state was not needed after all. Rather, Ahmad Khan and his Scientific Society associates would found their own institution, funded in much the same way as the reconstituted *madrasa*s considered in the previous chapter. As for the question of which language to employ for 'secular' instruction, two options were presented: English or Urdu. The letter also implies that the institution was to be named the 'Muhammadan Anglo-Oriental College', and that a fund-raising committee had been constituted.[39]

Although a decision does not appear to have been immediately made by the committee on language, it was a foregone conclusion that English would play a large part because, first, the necessary translations were not available, and second, it was the language of colonial administration. Thus, the college that opened its doors in 1875, at the same rural town of Aligarh where the Scientific Society had founded its 'Institute' in the 1860s, taught a mixed curriculum of 'European' rational sciences in English, and 'Islam' in Arabic, Persian and Urdu. Although Ahmad Khan's understanding of Islam is discussed further below, it should be noted that at Aligarh, his ideas were not taught. Rather, 'graduates' of Deobandi, Ahl-i Hadith and Ahl-i Sunnat *madrasa*s (including Ahmad Khan's most fervent critics) taught Arabic language and 'religious sciences' in keeping with their 'new' Sober outlooks.[40]

Ahmad Khan's deep involvement in the promotion of the English language and European thought leads to the third and last manner in

---

[39] 'Letter from Sayyid Ahmad Khan to C.A. Elliot [Secy. to Govn., NWP]', *Selected Documents*, pp. 149–51. Also 'Letter from Sayyid Ahmad Khan to the Muhammadan Chiefs of the Native States of India' (20th July 1872), *Selected Document*, pp. 162–64.

[40] Barbara Metcalfe, *Islamic Revival in British India* (Princeton: Princeton University Press, 1982), pp. 328–333; Rahman, *Islam*, p. 223.

which his intellectual pursuits differed from the 'new' Sobriety after 1858. All the translations and works in education with which Ahmad Khan was involved were exposing Muslims to ideas often in contravention of both branches ('old' and 'new') of the Sober Path and the 'old' Intoxicated Way. Ahmad Khan's post-1858 writings point out that he lost no time in addressing the above concern.[41] He would progressively come to these conclusions: (1) the only two attributes of God that humanity can know are that He is the 'First Cause' and the 'Creator'; (2) Heaven and Hell, like Satan, angels and *jinn*, are representations of pleasure and sorrow, or good and evil, rather than corporeal places and beings; (3) belief in miracles is due to lexicographical errors or metaphoric language, rather than their mention in the Qur'an; and, of course, (4) a geocentric cosmos is not upheld by the Qur'an. In fact, all of these ideas would ultimately be contained in Ahmad Khan's largest single exegetical writing, *Tafsir al-Qur'an*, published in six volumes between 1880 and 1898.

Evidently, the European thought that Ahmad Khan was so involved in translating and promoting did not fail to affect his ideas. In *Tafsir al-Qur'an*, he acknowledges this influence, referring to European thought as the 'new arts and sciences' (*'ulum wa funun jadida*).[42] He also declares that some European thought is in contravention of what the 'religious' say, whether Christian, Hindu or Muslim, and that they have, in turn, declared it 'wrong' (*ghalat*). Nevertheless, Ahmad Khan urges that this does not mean any contradiction between the 'new arts and sciences' and the Qur'an. The contradiction is between the 'new arts and sciences' and the 'Greek philosophers' (*falasifa Yunani*), whose ideas long ago became 'jumbled with *madhhabi* principles (*usul*) and tenets (*'aqa'id*)'.[43] Thus, Ahmad Khan not only approaches the Qur'an in the

---

[41] A number of exemplary works have been written on Ahmad Khan's religious thought, including the aforementioned by Christian Troll. Other works include J.M.S. Baljon, *The Reforms and Religious Ideas of Sir Sayyid Ahmad Khan* (Lahore: Shan Muhammad Ashraf, 1964); and Bashir A. Dar, *Religious Thought of Sir Syed Ahmad Khan* (Lahore: Institute of Islamic Culture, 1957). Pertinent articles from the *Aligarh Institute Gazette* and the *Tahdhib al-Akhlaq* by Ahmad Khan can be found in Sayyid Ahmad Khan, *Inthikhab-i Mazamin-i Aligarh Instiṭiyut Gazat* (Lucknow: Uttar Pradesh Akademi, 1982) and *Tazhib al-Akhlaq*, 2 vols. (Lahore: Tajiran Kutub Qawmi, n.d.). Also see Sayyid Ahmad Khan, *Maqalat-i Sar Sayyid*, 16 vols. (Lahore: Majlis-i Taraqqi-i Adab, 1962).

[42] Sayyid Ahmad Khan, 'Introduction', *Tafsir al-Qur'an* (Lahore: Dost Associates, 1998), p. 1.

[43] Ibid., p. 1.

light of the 'new arts and sciences', he also begins by establishing 'new' *usul*, which he claims issue from the Qur'an alone.⁴⁴ In other words, just as the 'new' Sober Path called for a return to the textual sources of Islam, Ahmad Khan follows the same lead. However, the principles (*usul*) upon which he built his interpretation often stem more roundly from 'Islam' (often of the same school) than those of the scholars whom he was opposing—principles 'hospitable' to European Naturalism, for example, rather than issuing from the latter.

In a series of correspondence between Ahmad Khan and an Aligarhi associate, the former defended his 15 principles by reducing them to 4 that he considers most crucial against his associate's criticism. The first principle is one which all 'Islamic' thought acknowledges, 'that God is true and the Qur'an is His Word'.⁴⁵ The rest, however, need to be spelled out before their intellectual origins can be identified. The second principle is that two things are apparent to humanity, one being 'God's Word' (*kalam*), implying the Qur'an, and the other being 'God's Work' (*kam*), implying the 'created' universe. This leads to the argument that God's Word and God's Work, or, the Qur'an and the created universe, cannot be 'contradictory' (*mukhtalif*). In fact, the test of any work's claims to be God's Word is its conformity to God's Work.⁴⁶ The third principle is that God's Work and 'Natural Laws' (*qanun qudrat*) 'are one practical contract', thus there can also be no contradiction between them.⁴⁷ The fourth principle is that humanity is distinguished from 'animals' by 'human reason' (*'aql insani*). Thus, 'in Islam and the Qur'an, there is no matter above human reason', whether concerned with God's Word, Work, or the Natural Laws by which all are joined to the Creator.⁴⁸

While most historians note the obvious influence of 19th century European thought on Ahmad Khan's 'naturalism', a minority have identified a strong affiliation between the Mu'tazila school of theology and the above metaphysics, some even calling him a 'Neo-Mu'tazili'.⁴⁹

---

⁴⁴ Ibid., p. 2.
⁴⁵ These letters are included in the edition of the *Tafsir al-Qur'an* consulted. See Ibid., p. 6.
⁴⁶ Ibid., p. 6.
⁴⁷ Ibid., p. 6.
⁴⁸ Ibid., p. 8.
⁴⁹ For example, Baljon concludes that as early as his *Tabyin al-Kalam* (1862), Ahmad Khan's notion of God resembled that of the Mu'tazila. See Baljon, *The Reforms and Religious Ideas of Sir Sayyid Ahmad Khan*, pp. 124–25. Also, for a focused account of

This is often based on the close relationship between Ahmad Khan's 15 *usul* and the Muʿtazila's 5 *usul*, sharing in particular an understanding on Reason, and the conception of God as uncompromisingly 'transcendent'.[50] However, Ahmad Khan differed with the latter insofar as he held there was no 'abrogation' (*nasikh*) and nothing has been 'abrogated' (*mansukh*) in the Qur'an, in keeping with the 'new' Sober Path, but contrary to the 'old' Muʿtazili and Ashaʿri theologians, as well as Hanafi jurists.[51] Specifically in contravention of the Muʿtazila, Ahmad Khan 'compromised' God's transcendence in that he argued the Qur'an was 'uncreated', like 'old' Ashʿari and 'new' Sober theologies.[52] Thus, it is interesting to note that Ahmad Khan did not attribute his ideas to any Muʿtazili, but often referenced Shah Wali Allah. In fact, the most prominent scholarly citation in his main discussion of *usul al-tafsir* is Wali Allah.[53] Pertaining to his concept of God, on such

---

Neo-Muʿtazilism, see Richard Martin and Mark Woodward w/ D. Atmaja, *Defenders of Reason in Islam: Muʿtazilism from Medieval School to Modern Symbol* (Oxford: One World Publications, 1997).

[50] For the Muʿtazila, see Chapter One.

[51] Ahmad Khan, *Tafsir al-Qur'an*, vol. 1, on 'abrogation' *usul* 12, pp. 28–29. Also see Sayyid Ahmad Khan, 'The Controversy over Abrogation (in the Qur'an)', trans. E. Hahn, *Muslim World* 64 (1974): 124–33.

[52] In *usul* 3, the author describes the Qur'an as an eternal 'portion' (*sahm*) of God, implying uncreatedness. See Ahmad Khan, *Tafsir al-Qur'an*, vol. 1, p. 19.

[53] Ibid., pp. 19–36. Shah Wali Allah is referred to in his introductory address (p. 2), as well as in the discussion of various *usul*, such as 7, 9, 11 and 13 (pp. 21, 26, 28, 29), always as a source of inspiration or doctrinal insight. The only exception is an instance in *usul* 7, in which Ahmad Khan disagrees with Wali Allah's argument that only the ideas of the Qur'an 'flowed from the unseen' to Muhammad, so that the words and language were the Prophet's. This argument has obvious bearing on Wali Allah's drive to translate the Qur'an into Muslim vernaculars. Ahmad Khan, however, writes that the above idea is in 'opposition to reason', for no idea can be expressed to or apprehended by a person without words. Thus, Ahmad Khan concludes that the Qur'an entered the Prophet's heart in the Arabic words contained in the written Qur'an (*mushaf*). In *usul* 10 and 11, Ahmad Khan goes on to say that the extant Qur'an is exactly as it was 'sent down', to the extent that even the arrangement of the verses of each Sura is 'authentic' (*mansus*) (p. 28.) Nothing in Ahmad Khan's life or work suggests that he took this position against Wali Allah because he was opposed to the translation of the Qur'an or its diffusion among laypersons. However, when added to *usul* 12's idea that there is no abrogation (*nasikh*) in the Qur'an (i.e. one verse cannot be said to over rule another), and *usul* 5's idea that the 'verity of the Qur'an' cannot be disproved by mention in it of things, beliefs or acts 'contrary to reality', it appears that Ahmad Khan could not allow for ideas alone to have been 'revealed' to Muhammad as this would not serve him in his polemics with, in particular, British Evangelicals, who dismissed the Qur'an's claims to revelation. As well, regarding Sober scholars, Ahmad Khan's position represents an intermediate position on the issue, one characteristic of his approach to other matters as well. (See *usul* 5, p. 20; and *usul* 12, pp. 28–29.)

central issues as the relationship between 'creative attributes' (*sifat bari*) and 'essence' (*dhat*), Ahmad Khan defers to Wali Allah.[54] Focusing on the Qur'an, Ahmad Khan attaches his views on the various aspects of Revelation—including those pertaining to his final conclusions about angels—to Wali Allah.[55] And most importantly, his idea that 'in the Qur'an there is no command that contradicts natural law'—even as it pertains to his final conclusions on miracles—is wholly attributed to Wali Allah's conception.[56]

This reference to Wali Allah can be explained by the influence and reputation of that scholar on Ahmad Khan personally, as well as on his opponents and intended audience. But the lack of reference to Mu'tazilism can just as securely be read as a reflection of the historical and contemporary biases of Sunni schools against Mu'tazilism, which forms the backbone of Imami Shi'i theology. Nevertheless, considering Ahmad Khan's deep personal background in Wali Allahi thought, this configuration of references also suggests how Ahmad Khan sincerely understood Wali Allah's thought and approximated Mu'tazili conclusions in the process, even though Wali Allah was a monist and Ahmad Khan a transcendentalist. Consider for example, Ahmad Khan's *usul* on the relationship between divine 'attributes' and 'essence'. In *usul* 7, he states that theologians hold that 'creative attributes (*sifat bari*) are neither identical to essence (*dhat*), nor other than it', while philosophers argue that these attributes are identical to essence and that 'their manifestation (*zuhur*) is necessarily required by the essence'.[57] He warns that these are matters of scholarly debate, but closes with a quote from Wali Allah that enunciates his own position:

> The dispute between the philosophers and the theologians over whether God creates voluntarily or positively is not a dispute over meaning, [given

---

[54] Ibid., p. 21.
[55] See *usul* 11 and 13, pp. 28–30.
[56] Ibid., pp. 25–28. That this is not just a polemical reference is supported by the fact that Ahmad Khan includes a quote from Wali Allah that implies miracles are not 'supernatural'—the type of quote we read in Chapter Three. As well, Ahmad Khan had begun arguing the point long before he wrote the *tafsir*, implying that it was not an idea recently concocted, but stemmed from education in Islam. As early as 1866, he had argued that 'no religious laws revealed to us by God can be at variance with rational laws'. See Shan Muhammad, ed. *The Aligarh Movement: Basic Documents*, vol. 1 (Delhi: Meenakshi Prakashan, 1978), p. 232.
[57] Ibid., p. 21.

that] for the theologians will is identical to essence and [the philosophers' concept of] origination is necessary causation.⁵⁸

In other words, he approximates the Mu'tazili position on essence and attributes—one in which God creates 'positively'—but approaches the issue from a synthetic Wali Allahi perspective.⁵⁹

As discussed in Chapter Three, Wali Allah was not a Mu'tazili. However, he did write theology, philosophy and mysticism with an eye to their reconciliation. If Deobandis are differentiated from Wali Allahis by increasingly ignoring this aspect of Wali Allah's thought, then Ahmad Khan can be distinguished from both by focusing, in particular, on aspects of Wali Allahi thought that echoes Mu'tazili conclusions. However, Ahmad Khan does not appear to have been directly inspired by Mu'tazilism itself. Thus, the opinion he attaches to the theologians referred to in the above context is generic, not differentiating between Mu'tazili and Ash'ari schools. This does not mean that Ahmad Khan remains a Wali Allahi. Indeed, the defining quality of his 'Neo-Mu'tazilism' is the lack of space he allows Intuition, a 'source' of knowledge upheld even by Deoband. Although he personally visited Sufi shrines all through his life, in his *tafsir* only 'human reason' is cited as a 'source' of knowledge beside Revelation. Thus, while Ahmad Khan quotes Wali Allah's opinion in *usul* 9 to make the point that the Qur'an 'makes no mention of miracles', in explaining instances that appear to be miraculous he does not in any way reflect the monism which the latter drew from Sufi and Ishraqi thought, and upon which he based his explanation of miracles. Ahmad Khan's 'causal relations' are not likened to the relation of all numbers to 'one'. Rather, Ahmad Khan's interpretation of Wali Allah stops at the idea that 'miracles conform to Natural Laws'.⁶⁰ In other words, Ahmad Khan maintained that the

---

⁵⁸ Ibid., p. 21. Also, in his *Sata'at*, Wali Allah wrote: 'God possesses a power other than the one which the *falasifa* term the very essence of Divinity, and also different from the power which the *mutakallimun* make out as equal to human faculties'. Shah Wali Allah, *Sata'at*, trans. G.N. Jalbani (Hyderabad: Shah Wali Allah Academy, 1970), p. 13.

⁵⁹ The proximity of Ahmad Khan's position to that of the Mu'tazila can also be gauged from *usul* 6. He states that the 'creative essence' (*dhat bari*), referring to what the Mu'tazila referred to as 'attributes of the essence', exists, but is beyond human reason. Thus, he concludes, all that can be known of these attributes is their 'infinitive sense (*ma'na masdari*): *'ilm* (knowing), *ijad* (creating)…'. In other words, all that can be known are the attributes the Mu'tazila referred to as 'attributes of the act'. See Ahmad Khan, *Tafsir al-Qur'an*, vol. 1, *usul* 6, pp. 20–21.

⁶⁰ Ibid., pp. 25–27.

causes of all acts may be apprehended through Reason, and that God 'absolutely transcends' the causal relations of the natural world, as in the writings of the Mu'tazila.

Furthermore, within the *tafsir* itself, Ahmad Khan's attitude towards *hadith*, for example, is also attached to Wali Allah, but employed to defend a different end. In Volume 6, Ahmad Khan tackles the topic of *isra'* and *mi'raj*, or Muhammad's journey to Jerusalem and ascension to Heaven. On his way to arguing that the entire event was a 'dream' (*khawab*), Ahmad Khan sets the scene of the event by first drawing from the works of noted theologians. He shows that there is a difference of opinion on every detail, from its duration to the relationship between episodes of the journey. This, he argues, is due to the scholars' approach to *hadith*, one that does not follow Wali Allah's maxim that one should 'depend on *hadith* until discrepancy (*tanaquz*) arises'.[61] He then goes on to show that *hadith* from all the major collections differ on such particulars as where Muhammad was when the event began, whether he was awake or asleep, whether Jibra'il was alone or with others, and so on.[62] This, he explains, is essentially due to the subjectivity of *hadith* literature, i.e. the role of the chain of transmitters, as well as the compiler's interpretation of events and choice of words.[63] Thus, although anchoring himself in a Wali Allahi approach to *hadith*, he dismisses the reliability of a genre of literature that is the cornerstone of the 'new' Sober Path. For those who would continue to employ *hadith* critically, however, he adds that when the events mentioned

---

[61] Ahmad Khan, *Tafsir al-Qur'an*, vol. 6, p. 11.
[62] Ibid., pp. 14–65.
[63] Ibid., pp. 65–66. Baljon, Dar and other authors largely accredit the influence of Orientalists, by the late 19th century differentiating into the field of 'Islamic Studies', for Ahmad Khan's questioning of *hadith*. In particular, the late 19th century works of Ignaz Goldziher forwarded the idea that the chains of transmission (*isnads*) of *hadith* and historical literature more generally, fell into two parts—'authentic' and 'fabricated'—thus casting doubt on the version of events recounted by virtually all the 'historical' genres. However, of late, intellectual historians have reassessed such perspectives, arguing that in the pre-colonial era, the science of *hadith* explicitly acknowledged the 'subjectivity' of the *hadith* collections to the point that less than a dozen individual reports were consider 'certain' (*mutawatir*), even if many more were considered 'sound' (*sahih*). In this light, Ahmad Khan's opinion appears as a reaffirmation of 'old' methods, based on the critical evaluation of *matn* and *isnad*, in the face of 'new' Sober thinkers like Wali Allah declaring whole collections authoritative on the basis of their categorisation as 'sound' rather than 'certain', and Orientalists questioning the very basis of an 'Islamic' understanding of the past. See I. Goldziher, *Muhammedanische Studien*, 2 vols. (Halle, 1890). For secondary discussions, see S. Humphreys, *Islamic History* (Princeton: University of Princeton Press, 1991), pp. 76–87.

are contradictory to Reason and scholars hold differing opinions, 'one takes heed of those verses that are not in contravention of reason'.[64] Ultimately, what the influence of Wali Allah's thought suggests is that education in the 'old' and 'new' Sober Path, as much as European thought, influenced Ahmad Khan's appeal to Reason as a source of knowledge. Further evidence is found in the manner in which his Sober opponents labelled his metaphysics.

Ahmad Khan's opponents arrived at their judgements of his metaphysics largely through the lens of Islamic thought, ruling him a 'naturalist' (*nechariyya*). Recall that al-Ghazali described 'naturalists' as those who acknowledge the 'Creator' through 'manifold researches into the world of nature'. His chief criticism was the inclination towards 'materialism' that this approach fostered by limiting the power of God over the 'natural', but al-Ghazali stopped short of declaring such thinkers 'apostates'. Given that Ahmad Khan's principles fit al-Ghazali's definition quite precisely, the condemnation of Muslim thinkers illustrates that they continued to view 'Islam' in terms of the categories of thought outlined at the beginning of this book, but with one important difference. Ahmad Khan's 'new' Sober critics did not hesitate to declare him an 'apostate'.[65] As Ahmad Rida of the Ahl-i Sunnat wrote, by denying the '*zaruriyat-i din*' (i.e. the corporeal existence of Heaven, Hell, angels, *jinn*, etc.), despite accepting the Qu'ran and Muhammad's prophethood, these '*nechariyya*' are '*murtadds*' and '*kafirs*'.[66] As well, accusations of apostasy were issued in *fatawa* from Mecca, and Jamal al-Din Afghani (d. 1897)—a leading 'Modernist' of the day active across the Muslim World—also weighed in on the side of the Sober, betraying his own 'Islam'. He not only accused Ahmad Khan of following the 'specious allegorical interpretations of the heretics of past Muslim centuries' by 'denying' angels, *jinn*, miracles, etc., but argued that Ahmad Khan's intent was to 'remove the beliefs of Muslims' so as to 'serve others [i.e. the British] and prepare the way for conversion to their religion'.[67] Given that even segments of 'new' Sober thinkers had legitimated British

---

[64] Ahmad Khan, *Tafsir al-Qur'an*, vol. 6, p. 91.
[65] Metcalfe, *Islamic Revival in British India*, pp. 325–29. Also see C.W. Troll, 'Sir Sayyid Ahmad Khan and his Theological Critics: the Accusations of 'Ali Bakhsh and Sir Sayyid's Rejoinder', *Islamic Culture* 52 (1978): 1–18.
[66] Ahmad Rida Khan, *Fatawa al-Haramayn bi-Rajf Nadwat al-Mayn* (Bareilly: Matba'-i Ahl-i Sunnat wa Jama'at, 1900), p. 29.
[67] Sayyid Jalal al-Din al-Afghani, 'Commentary on the Commentator', *An Islamic Response to Imperialism: Political and Religious Writings of Sayyid Jamal al-Din*

rule, and that Afghani was also an advocate of reform in the light of European ideas, it is clear that neither Ahmad Khan's politics nor his interest in European thought, sat at the root of such harsh and virtually hegemonic condemnation. Rather, it is his methodological bonds to the 'heretics of past Muslim centuries' that is at issue, illustrating just how deep into the scholarly classes the influence of the 'new' Sober Path had extended by the late 19th century. In fact, the only 'old' thinker read in this book to have collapsed the distinction between 'heretics' and 'apostates' to this extent is Ibn Taymiyya. In pointing out how closely Ahmad Khan's metaphysics resemble that of scholars previously judged 'heretical' by the Sober in al-Ghazali's day, Ahmad Khan's critics only lead the discussion back to his ties with the broader world of Reason, particularly of the Intoxicated variety.

Even the context in which Ahmad Khan wrote his *tafsir* illustrates that the schools of Intoxicated thought exerted an influence upon him. Of the three interrelated pursuits that consumed the last 40 years of his life—the translation of European works into Urdu, the founding of a school teaching European thought, and the writing of works that integrated European thought into an 'Islamic frame'—all have some precedent in the works of 'old' Intoxicated scholars. As noted previously, the translation of non-Muslim works into Persian, including European writings, began in earnest in the time of Akbar and continued through to the 19th century. Ahmad Khan focused this inclination on European works and substituted Urdu for Persian. Talk of reforming the education of at least the elite to include more 'physical' sciences in the 'mother tongue' had been a feature of Awrangzib's court. Ahmad Khan established a *'madrasa'* that accomplished this task, but drew all its 'physical' knowledge from European sources and employed the languages of his 'maternal' court: English and Urdu. And finally, Danishmand Khan, also from Awrangzib's regime and a supporter of educational reform, is the first instance cited here of comparative study between Islamic and European metaphysics, while Karamat 'Ali represents the first sign of movement towards integration. Ahmad Khan continued that comparative study and wrote the first attempt at integration. In other words, although Ahmad Khan's approach to Reason and the relationship he drew between God and His Work may reflect that of European

---

al-Afghani, ed. and trans. N.R. Keddie (Berkeley: University of California Press, 1968), pp. 123–29; and Metcalfe, *Islamic Revival in British India*, pp. 325–29.

Naturalism, it is rooted in principles particular to Wali Allahi and, given that Ahmad Khan makes no mention of any Mu'tazili or Shi'i thinker, not simply Mu'tazili theology, but the general milieu of the 'old' Intoxicated Way advocated by some theologians and all philosophers. This raises the question: Is Ahmad Khan's metaphysics the sign of a 'new' Intoxicated Way?

Insofar as Ahmad Khan's principles and many of the conclusions he derived on their basis are tied to 'old' ideas, he is more a 'revivalist' than the author of a 'new' Way. Apart from his 'Mu'tazilism', previous chapters have shown that the 'lay' assumption of the right to *ijtihad* was exercised in the Indo-Muslim context by Mughal rulers and courtiers. Thus, as previously mentioned, Ahmad Khan was already arguing for *ijtihad* before 1858. However, he also worked under the influence of the 'new' Sober Path, which not only insisted on *ijtihad*, but emphasised forms of transcendentalism, the need to return to the textual sources of Islam, and the idea that the Qur'an should be accessible to all without scholarly intercession—all four tenets central to his *tafsir*. The qualification of Ahmad Khan's ideas as indicative of a 'new' Intoxicated Way, therefore, rests on the fact that he wrote his metaphysics in an attempt to integrate European sciences, rather than Hellenic, Zoroastrian, Hindu or Buddhist thought, and did so by affecting a synthesis of certain strains of the 'new' Sober Path and 'old' Intoxicated Way. In particular, he emphasised lines of thought that promoted the concept of divinity's transcendence to the degree that divine intercession in the world was largely limited to the fixing of Natural Laws, and human interaction with the divine consisted of little more than applying Reason in the interpretation of Revelation and the natural world so those 'laws' may be known. The combination of influences, if not the idea, certainly implies a 'new' Intoxicated Way. But is this evidence of Objectification?

Although Ahmad Khan was not a *madrasa* 'graduate', it has been shown above that his social work and writings independently attest that he was deeply imbued with the doctrines and ideals of Islam. Furthermore, as is well known, Ahmad Khan was neither the first Muslim in history to integrate non-scriptural knowledge into his conception of Islam, nor was he the only Muslim of the day to attempt to assimilate aspects of European thought into an 'Islamic frame'. Most noteworthy among Ahmad Khan's 'Neo-Mu'tazili' contemporaries is the Egyptian scholar from al-Azhar *madrasa* in Cairo, Shaykh Muhammad 'Abdu (d. 1905), who separately echoed the former's calls for *ijtihad*, the reconciliation of European sciences and Islam by sidestepping past scholasticism to derive the principles (*usul*) of exegesis directly from the Qur'an, and to reform al-Azhar to teach European sciences along with religious sciences. Furthermore, comparing Ahmad Khan's *usul* with those that 'Abdu constructed in his unfinished *tafsir*, the same acceptance of causality in nature is affirmed to the point that 'Abdu forwards the concept of 'natural selection' in Darwinist terms.[68] Furthermore, others have followed the general approaches taken by Ahmad Khan and 'Abdu.[69] Although there are also differences between the two thinkers, such as 'Abdu's insistence on the 'createdness' of the Qur'an, can the congruence observed between a *madrasa* scholar from the peasantry of Egypt and a 'layman' from the aristocracy of Delhi be adequately explained by their shared exposure to European thought alone, when all that is truly 'new-fangled' in their metaphysics is the will to integrate European thought, at the expense of all other extra-Islamic intellectualism? Their works certainly attest to the 'power' imbued in European thought by colonial rule, as well as a certain lack of 'creativity' and evidence of a 'psychological impediment' blocking consideration of intellectual strains arising elsewhere in the world. However, neither individual's life nor work suggests that tradition is Objectified, so much as it attests that select bits and pieces of European thought were integrated through the lens of longstanding and systematically evolving strains of doctrinal Islam.

II. *Mirza Ghulam Ahmad's 'Messiah'*

Much the same conclusion can be drawn from Mirza Ghulam Ahmad's writings, though whereas Ahmad Khan put his eggs in the philosophical basket of Reason, Ghulam Ahmad tapped the mystical well of Intuition. From the petty landed class of the rural Punjabi town of Qadian, Ghulam Ahmad's family—once *jagirdar*s of the Mughals and officers in Ranajit Singh's 'successor' state—transferred their loyal-

---

[68] Although unfinished, much of 'Abdu's Qur'anic exegesis was published in his disciple Rashid Rida's (d. 1935) Cairo journal, *al-Manar*. For excerpts of Abdu's writings regarding the ideas presented here, see, Muhammad 'Abdu, 'Tafsir al-Qur'an al-Hakim', *Al-Manar* 8:24 (Feb. 1906), pp. 921–30; and 'Al-Islah al-Haqiqi wa al-Wajib li'l al-Azhar', *Al-Manar* 10:28 (Feb. 1906), pp. 758–65.

[69] An in-depth discussion of this topic can be read in R.C. Martin, M.R. Woodward w/ D. Atmaja, *Defenders of Reason in Islam*, pp. 128–36.

ties to the British and, like Ahmad Khan, fought on their side in the 1857 Uprising.[70] Soon after, having already provided Ghulam Ahmad a *maktab* education in Arabic, Persian and Urdu through various private tutors, his father sent him to be a clerk at the colonial courts in Syalkot, where he remained until 1868. It was during this period that Ghulam Ahmad first became embroiled in the ongoing polemics between Muslims, Hindus, Sikhs and Christians of various stripes raging around Punjab.[71] The impact of these debates on his ideas is taken up below, but it should be noted here that Ghulam Ahmad was as much a 'lay' Muslim as Ahmad Khan.

After 1868, Ghulam Ahmad's ideas began to veer from the Sober Path. He did not, however, move in the direction of Ahmad Khan. Although impressed with Ahmad Khan's polemical works, the publication of his *Tafsir-i Qur'an* in 1880 led Ghulam Ahmad's estimation of this thinker to diminish.[72] In both cases, whether the doctrines of the 'new' Sober Path or Ahmad Khan's 'new' Intoxicated Way, it is the lack of room allowed for the 'visions' which Ghulam Ahmad had begun receiving since the 1860s, that ultimately circumscribed his 'new' way, reflected in his assuming the title *mujaddid* (renewer) in 1882, and over the next two decades, those of *muhaddath, mahdi, masih* (messiah) and *avatar* (incarnation) of Krishna.[73] He would also refer to himself as *nabi*

---

[70] There are various 'official' biographies of Mirza Ghulam Ahmad, in a number of languages. For an early and most thorough work, see Abdur Rahman Dard, *Life of Ahmad*, vol. 1 (Lahore: Sultan Brothers, 1949). For a late and brief English version, see Iain Adamson, *Mirza Ghulam Ahmad of Qadian* (London: Elite International Publications, 1989). Although a number of scholarly works are also available, they are few in number relative to works on Ahmad Khan. Articles concerned with particular aspects of Ghulam Ahmad's thought or 'school' are noted in context below, but the two prime books on these subjects are: Yohanan Friedmann, *Prophecy Continuous: Aspects of Ahmadi Religious Thought and its Medieval Background* (Berkeley: University of California Press, 1989); and Spencer Lavan, *The Ahmadiyah Movement: A Historical Perspective* (Delhi: Manohar Book Service, 1974). Details of Ghulam Ahmad's biography are drawn from the above works.

[71] Lavan provides the most complete picture of these early years in Ghulam Ahmad's education and career. His tutors included Shi'is and Sunnis, and it is argued that he learned some English while working in the judiciary, for he claimed to receive revelations in English and refers to English works in his own writings, but his followers claim that he never learned the language. Lavan, *The Ahmadiyah Movement*, pp. 22–32.

[72] Ibid., pp. 31–32.

[73] The crux of Friedmann's well-documented thesis is that Ghulam Ahmad assumed all of these titles in an attempt to assert the supremacy of Islam above other faiths in the face of what he perceived as the Sufi and *'alim*'s failures before Christians. As Friedmann concludes, 'The situation had reached such proportions that only a divinely inspired leader could arrest the process of decline'. Friedmann, *Prophecy Continuous*, p. 106.

(prophet) and his 'visions' as *wahy* (revelation), as discussed below. Before turning to such particulars, however, it should be confirmed that by the 1890s, scholars associated with the schools of most of his contemporaries, including Ahmad Khan, found Ghulam Ahmad's claims tantamount to 'apostasy', based on the argument that they denied the 'finality' of Muhammad's prophetic mission.[74] One of the earliest *fatawa* stoked by these claims, issued in 1890, referred to Ghulam Ahmad as the 'Anti-Christ' (*dajjal*) or 'personification of all vices', an individual 'more astray than his playmate the devil', and the 'worst of apostates' (*ashadd al-murtaddin*).[75] A clash between Ghulam Ahmad and an Ahl-i Hadith adversary degenerated into such acrimony that even the District Magistrate's efforts to calm the situation failed.[76] Ahmad Rida of the Ahl-i Sunnat added his voice to the rising choir in 1906, and together with the jurists of Mecca and Medina, he also declared Ghulam Ahmad the 'Anti-Christ' (*dajjal*) and an 'apostate' (*murtadd*).[77] Nor did the controversy end with Ghulam Ahmad's death. In fact, it grew more heated, particularly in the 1920s and 1930s. As his followers continued to expand the 'missionary' zeal that Ghulam Ahmad had embarked upon, their efforts were met with similarly vehement opposition not only from Aligarhis, Deobandis, Ahl-i Hadith and Ahl-i Sunnat, but also from 'new' Sober players particularly active in Punjab, such as the *Tahrik-i Khaksar* (f. 1930) and *Majlis-i Ahrar-i Islam* (f. 1931).[78] Controversy also extended further outside of South Asia to the issuance of anti-Ahmadiyya *fatawa* in Cairo, Baghdad and Damascus, while the

---

[74] Ghulam Ahmad propagated his ideas though public speaking and the columns of local newspapers and journals to begin with, until his first book was published in 1880, followed by 65 more over the remainder of his life. As well, as he began gathering a small following, leading to the granting of *bay'a* as *mahdi* and *masih* by core members in 1889, the nascent movement launched its own journals. As the only form of *jihad* Ghulam Ahmad thought permissible for the propagation of the faith was 'verbal', missionary activities also took on great meaning, and the methods of Christian missionaries were adopted.

[75] Cited in Dard, *Life of Ahmad*, vol. 1, p. 426.

[76] Lavan, *The Ahmadiyah Movement*, pp. 50–57.

[77] See Ahmad Rida Khan, *Husam al-Haramayn 'ala Manhar al-Kufr wa al-Mayn* (Lahore: Maktaba Nabawiyya, 1985).

[78] For an example of an anti-Ahmadiyya work by an Ahl-i Hadith scholar, see Khadim 'Abd al-Amin Muhammad Ibrahim, *Nikamma Nabi Bama Tartali Dawe* (Lyallpur: Anjuman Ahl-i Hadith, 1937). Although neither the 'Khaksars' nor the 'Ahrars' were led by *madrasa*-bound scholars, their visions of Islam were strongly influenced by the 'new' Sober Path, as evinced by their polemical literature. For a Khaksar perspective, see Ghulam Muhammad Khan, *Muhammadi Gola* (Amritsar: n.p., 1930); and for an Ahrar tract, see Rahmat Allah Manzir, *Yad-i Raftgan* (Gurdaspur, n.p., 1938).

Ahmadiyya claimed their first 'martyrs' in Afghanistan when a number of missionaries were executed by the Durrani state, which officially declared affiliation with the movement a capital offence in 1924.[79] In the post-colonial context, the charge against the Ahmadiyya was furthered by all the Pakistani 'Jama'ats' mentioned in Chapter Three, as well as by the remnants of the Khaksars and Ahrars, leading to periodic riots from the 1950s and the state's declaration of Ahmadiyya 'non-Muslims' in the 1970s.[80] If the significance of the collapse of distinctions between 'heretics' and 'apostates' driven by 'new' Sober legalism was not evident in the context of Ahmad Khan, the reception of the Ahmadiyya by their co-religionists, not to mention the similar nature of the Ahmadiyya's retorts, should clarify the implications for sectarian and intra-sectarian relations in Muslim ranks, particularly when the political and economic interests of members clashed.

Despite the broad range of condemnatory *fatawa*, Ghulam Ahmad was exonerated by some members of the same groups and Muhammad Iqbal, whose ideas are taken up below. At least on a doctrinal level, such contrary opinions are best explained by the observation that all of Ghulam Ahmad's claims are rooted in long established mystical and philosophical thought. Although Ghulam Ahmad never joined a Sufi order and colonial influence is abundant, the influence of Ibn al-'Arabi, Shaykh Ahmad Sirhindi and Shah Wali Allah, as well as the Ishraqi, Mulla Sadr, and various Shi'i thinkers, is essential to explaining the metaphysical perspective and doctrinal bases of Ghulam Ahmad's claims.[81] This discussion, therefore, pays close attention to the particular interpretations of the above thinkers' ideas that Ghulam Ahmad upholds, in an effort to determine whether his approach can be said to represent Objectification.

Perhaps there is no better work to point out the difficulties with the idea of Objectification than Ghulam Ahmad's *Ta'lim-i Islam: Islami*

---

[79] Friedmann, *Prophecy Continuous*, pp. 22–31.

[80] Seyyid Vali Reza Nasr, *Mawdudi and the Making of Islamic Revivalism* (New York: Oxford University Press, 1996), pp. 43–44.

[81] Lavan mainly comments on the use of Sufi terminology and Sufi organizational structures, including *bay'a*, as well as the appointment of *khalifas* after Ghulam Ahmad's death, but Friedmann has delved deeply into the intellectual influences of the thinkers mentioned. The main point is Ghulam Ahmad's adoption of the doctrine of *wilayat*. Lavan, *The Ahmadiyah Movement*, pp. 36–38; Friedmann, *Prophecy Continuous*, pp. 49–93.

Usul ki Falasifi, first delivered as a lecture in 1896.[82] The venue was the second 'Conference of Great Religions', organised and moderated by a small group of Western-educated Punjabis from all religious communities. Five set questions were distributed and the lecturers were asked to address them specifically 'to know which religion is the one replete with truth'.[83] The conference was attended by various schools of Hindu thought, dominated by reformers from the Arya Samaj, as well as Sikhs, Christians and Theosophists. Islam was represented by the Ahmadiyya and representatives of the 'new' Sober Path. The organisers, venue, participants and format, therefore, provide reason to expect a sharp projection of Islam through the lens of Western education.

Ahmad Khan was invited to lecture, but declined with the words, 'I am not a preacher or a reformer or a *mawlawi*'.[84] Ghulam Ahmad, assuming no such barriers, was not able to attend in person, but a 'disciple' delivered his lengthy address, accompanied by a letter in which the author declared that his answers were the product of personal 'revelation'.[85] The admission of a source of knowledge other than Reason and Qur'anic Revelation immediately confirms the lasting influence of the 'old' and 'new' scholars mentioned above, despite the obvious references to Christianity and European Naturalism in

---

[82] The most complete exposition of Ghulam Ahmad's ideas can be read in his *Barahin-i Ahmadiyya*, published in five volumes in 1880–1905. It has been variously published since, including an English translation by Masum Beg, issued as *Barahin-i Ahmadiyya* (Lahore: Ahmadiyya Anjuman Isha'at-i Islam, 1955). Pertinent excerpts from this and various other works have also been published as Ghulam Ahmad, *The Essence of Islam*, 2 vols., trans. Muhammad Zafarullah Khan (London: Ahmadiyya Centenary Publications, 1978). The work discussed here is published as Ghulam Ahmad, *Ta'lim-i Islam: Islami Usul ki Falasifi* (Lahore: n.p., 1960); and *The Philosophy of the Teachings of Islam*, trans. Muhammad Zafarullah Khan (London: Islam International Publications, 1996).

[83] The quote is from the invitation to the conference issued by its chief organiser, Swami Sadhu Shugan Chandra, a Punjabi of Kshatriya caste. The points to be addressed according to the tenets of each faith, were: (1) The physical (*jismani*), moral (*akhlaqi*) and spiritual (*ruhani*) condition of humanity; (2) The condition of humanity in the 'afterlife'; (3) The object of life and the means of its attainment; (4) The role of the practical ordinances (*'amal*) in this life and the next; and, (5) The sources of 'knowledge' (*'ilm* and *ma'arifat*). The invitation is included in, *The Philosophy of the Teachings of Islam*, p. ii.

[84] Quoted in the Calcutta newspaper, *General aur Gohar Asifi* (24 January 1897). This report and others from the newspapers of the day are included in, Ibid., pp. vii–xii.

[85] Ghulam Ahmad publicly declared that his essay was 'revealed' in a letter issued before the conference, while also 'prophesying' that his words, being without 'human weakness', would prevail over others, Muslim and non-Muslim. For the letter, see Ibid., pp. v–vii.

his writings. Thus, for Ghulam Ahmad, God is the 'cause of all causes' and 'guardian' (*muhafiz*) of 'Creation', but is not subject to 'Natural Law'.[86] He also applies the metaphor of kingship in reference to God, quite specifically echoing Muhammad Isma'il's *Taqwiyat al-Iman*, that rulers are bound to the dictate of the good of the many above the few, while God is under no such compulsion.[87] That a particularly Sober Sufi notion of monism is inherent in these ideas, particularly Wali Allah's perspective, is confirmed in the statement that to place God's essence between 'similitude (*tashbih*) and purity (*tanziya*)' is the proper view.[88] As well, although Reason is acknowledged as a source of knowledge, its application is insufficient for humanity to gain ultimate 'knowledge'.[89] In other words, Revelation and/or Intuition are argued to be necessary to take the ultimate step.

To this point, most of Ghulam Ahmad's thought qualifies him as a follower of the 'new' Sober Path. However, his claim to have received 'revelation' (*wahy*) marks a sharp distinction between himself and all of the Muslim texts read in this work, including those of Ahmad Khan and the Deobandis. Ghulam Ahmad wrote:

> We cannot limit His Word (*kalam*) and Speech (*mukhatabat*) to any particular time. Now, as in the past, He is ready to enrich His seekers... However, all certainties concerning *shari'a* and *hudud* have been fulfilled. Also all prophethoods (*nubuwwatin*), having arrived at their climax in the person of our lord and master, the Holy Prophet, have been fulfilled.[90]

Given that it is on the basis of such statements that all of the aforementioned thinkers ultimately declared Ghulam Ahmad an 'apostate', one must be clear on his particular usage of terms like '*wahy*'. In the light of the Sufi/Shi'i concept of *wilayat* discussed in previous chapters, it should be apparent that Ghulam Ahmad is not claiming 'prophethood'

---

[86] By 'guardian', Ghulam Ahmad aims to suggest that the entire 'chain' of cause and effect, as well as the 'natural forces' by which the universe is ordered (i.e. gravity) are 'regulated' by God, such that they are manifestations of the 'Nature of God' (*qudrat-i Haqq*). Ghulam Ahmad, *Ta'lim-i Islam*, pp. 59–60.

[87] Ibid., pp. 64–65.

[88] This statement is made in the context of a discussion of God's 'essence' (*dhat*) and 'attributes' (*sifat bari*) that most broadly echo the Wali Allahi perspective. He writes that God's 'essence' is beyond human knowledge, and God's 'attributes' (e.g. knowledge) are 'perfect'. Ibid., pp. 62–68.

[89] Ibid., pp. 52–58.

[90] Ibid., pp. 56–57.

in the sense of delivering a new 'book'. Thus, he applies the term '*nabi*' (prophet), not '*rasul*' (apostle), to himself. Furthermore, as the above quote illustrates directly, he uses the term *wahy* to refer to what others term *kashf*, or Intuition. It is in consideration of *wahy* in the usual sense that the Qur'an and Muhammad are referred to as the fulfilment of the *shari'a*. On the other hand, it is in consideration of knowledge gained by *kashf* that he writes, 'millions of the virtuous have continuously received inspiration (*ilham*)', just as he has.[91] Adding that there are ranks of 'revelation' with prophetic revelation at the top, what he was doing, in essence, is nothing other than claiming to be '*insan al-kamil*' (perfect human).[92] Ghulam Ahmad even pointed out that Islam has always produced persons of the general ranks he claimed, but reflecting his particular metaphysical cues, he added that Islam is the only faith which can, given the finality of the *shari'a* delivered by Muhammad.[93]

Despite the congruence of Ghulam Ahmad, Wali Allahis and Deobandis on significant points from metaphysics to law, the import of his collapsing the distinction between *kashf* and *wahy*, at least in usage, cannot be overestimated. In essence, by explicitly 'equating' Intuition and Revelation (*kashf* and *wahy*), he is acknowledging the centrality of the *shari'a*, but leaving the door open for people like himself to claim exactly the authority that the 'new' Sober Path sought to deny Sufis, as well as the basis on which these same groups declared Shi'is 'apostates'. In this sense, his ideas are by definition Intoxicated, equating Intuition and Revelation. Acknowledging the doctrinal objections of philosophers like Ahmad Khan, however, one must add that Ghulam Ahmad's entire metaphysic, denying the 'absolute transcendence' of God upon which the former affirmed the fixity of 'Natural Law', would elicit a negative response from Aligarh. Thus, Ghulam Ahmad must also be placed among the advocates of Intuition, rather than Reason. However, it is without doubt the influence of the 'new' Sober Path—directly in terms of his theology and indirectly with regard to his defence of Intuition as the ultimate source of knowledge—rather than Western education or colonial paradigms, which sets Ghulam Ahmad's 'Islam' apart from the 'old'. But do his ideas represent another permutation of the 'new' Intoxicated Way?

---

[91] Ibid., p. 125.
[92] Also see Friedmann, *Prophecy Continuous*, pp. 142–44.
[93] Ghulam Ahmad, *Ta'lim-i Islam*, pp. 126–28.

Insofar as Ghulam Ahmad's principles and many of the conclusions he derives on their basis are tied to 'old' thought, he is more a 'revivalist' like Ahmad Khan than the author of a 'new' Way. The latter qualification is again earned by the fact that Ghulam Ahmad, like Ahmad Khan, effected a 'new' synthesis in response to 19th century European, rather than Hindu, Buddhist, Hellenic, etc. ideas. His ideas specifically reflect Wali Allah metaphysics, 'old' Shi'i and Sufi concepts of *wilayat*, and 'old' theological notions of *mujaddid*, *muhaddath*, *mahdi* and *masih* as a means to counter, rather than integrate, the ideals of the Arya Samajis, Christians and Theosophists with whom he debated. That this landed him in hot water with Muslims as well only confirms how dominant 'new' Sober ideas had become among the scholarly classes. It is a reflection of the influence of this latter group of Muslims, in fact, that explains why the 'absolute immanence' that was central to the 'old' Intoxicated Way, particularly of the Ishraqi and Sufi schools popular among earlier South Asian Muslim scholars, appears quite purposefully ignored by Ghulam Ahmad, as is the 'absolute transcendence' of Ahmad Khan's 'Neo-Mu'tazilism'. Again, the combination of influences, if not the idea, implies a 'new' Intuitive Way, but all that makes it Intoxicated is Ghulam Ahmad's claims to a grade of 'revelation' that contemporaries like the Deobandis sought to circumscribe, or others like the Ahl-i Hadith endeavoured to deny the 'old' Sufis. The clincher, however, is the intellectual parallels between the Ahmadiyya and contemporary movements outside South Asia, the *Babiyya* and *Baha'iyya*, which also enshrined 'prophetic' leaders based on 'old' ideas and suffered the consequences at the hands of those influenced by the 'new'.[94]

The implications of Ghulam Ahmad's ideas concerning the notion of Objectification can be further grasped through his views on the 'historical' Jesus ('Isa). Among contemporary scholars, Yohanan Friedmann

---

[94] These movements are related insofar as the leader of the Baha'iyya, Baha' Allah (d. 1892) was a member of the Babiyya founded by Sayyid 'Ali Muhammad al-Shirazi (d. 1850), until he began receiving revelations of his own in 1852–53 and schism began to take root. The chief differences between the Babiyya/Baha'iyya and the Ahmadiyya, are: (1) the formers' doctrinal rooting in Isma'ili thought and the latter's in Sufism; and, (2) the formers' repudiation of the *shari'a*, while upholding Muhammad's prophethood, and the latter's firm conviction concerning the necessity of the *shari'a*. For the Babiyya and Baha'iyya, see A. Basauni, *'Bab'; 'Baha'Allah';* and *'Baha'is', Encyclopaedia of Islam* (Leiden: E.J. Brill [CD ROM Ed.], 2004). For the parallels between the Ahmadiyya and the Babiyya/Baha'iyya, see Lavan, *The Ahmadiyya Movement*, pp. 73, 97, 173; Friedmann, *Prophecy Continuous*, p. 44.

has thoroughly discussed the manner in which Ghulam Ahmad's claims to be *mahdi* and *masih* are tied into his larger metaphysic, while Spencer Lavan most deeply roots these claims in Ghulam Ahmad's 'non-violent' theory of *jihad*.[95] However, they also point out that Ghulam Ahmad's view of Jesus differs from both Christian dogma and Muslim prophetology. Ghulam Ahmad presents his understanding of both views in such works as *'Isa Hindustan Mein*, written in 1899.[96] There are two essential differences between Christians and Muslims that Ghulam Ahmad was interested in. First, he writes that Muslims argue that Jesus was not crucified, while Christians hold that Jesus died on the cross. Second, he points out that Muslims hold the *mahdi* and *masih* to be distinct, while Christians only acknowledge the *masih* descending at the 'end of days'.[97] Ghulam Ahmad takes an intermediate position, arguing that Jesus was crucified, but did not die on the cross. He did not ascend to Heaven without bodily wounds before the crucifixion, as is the standard Muslim argument, nor was he 'resurrected' to ascend with bodily wounds, as in Christian salvation history. Ghulam Ahmad contends that rescued from the cross after approximately two hours, his wounds were healed and he travelled to 'India' and 'Tibet', where he preached until his natural death in Kashmir at 120 years of age. Furthermore, he reconciles distinctions on the *mahdi* and *masih* by arguing they are one: himself. Thus, as Friedman put it, although responding to Christian missionary attacks on Islam, Ghulam Ahmad was not only 'following classical Muslim tradition' in his response, but by claiming 'affinity with Jesus', he tried to 'deprive Christianity of

---

[95] Friedmann shows that in Ghulam Ahmad's 'prophetology', Jesus is to Moses, what Ghulam Ahmad is to Muhammad. Moses and Muhammad are 'law givers', while Jesus and he 'complete the divine scheme of things by terminating' the 'prophetic chains' by striving to 'implement the shari'a' promulgated by their predecessors. Friedmann, *Prophecy Continuous*, p. 121. Lavan makes a similar point, but concentrates more on the role of Ghulam Ahmad's theory of *jihad*, which allows no use of force to spread religion, enjoining '*tabligh*' (missionary work) instead, in making the connections between Ghulam Ahmad's mission and the 'Second Coming of Christ', which he claims to fulfill. Lavan, *The Ahmadiyah Movement*, pp. 49–50.

[96] This is no more than an example of Ghulam Ahmad's writings on Christianity, but it echoes the views he had begun to promote in the 1880s, discussed in previously mentioned works. For an alternative source on Christianity, see Mirza Ghulam Ahmad, *A Review of Christianity from a New Point of View* (Qadian: Nazir Dawat-o-Tabligh, 1973). For a comparison of Christian 'dogma', as stated by a Christian missionary, and Ghulam Ahmad's 'Islam', see Ghulam Ahmad, *Siraj al-Din 'Isai ke Char Sawalun ka Jawab* (Lahore: Sunrise, 1968). Both works were first published in the 1890s.

[97] Ghulam Ahmad, *'Isa Hindustan Mein* (Lahore: Nisar Art Press, 1962), pp. 7–13.

Jesus himself'.[98] It should be clarified, however, that Ghulam Ahmad attempted the above by turning the Gospels and Orientalist literature against his Christian adversaries. His entire argument for the 'short' crucifixion is based on a reading of the New Testament, including the insights of his own and others' 'kashf'.[99] Meanwhile, his 'life' of Jesus is substantiated by Orientalist arguments that Jewish tribes settled in Afghanistan in pre-Islamic times, as well as the idea that Buddhist and Christian tenets were not coincidentally complementary.[100] That is to say, in the case of Ghulam Ahmad, as in that of Ahmad Khan, 'Islam' is not exactly being Objectified by Western education, but the 'West' is being accessed and selectively assimilated/rejected through the lens of Islamic education. In Ahmad Khan's case, hospitality extended to European 'physical' sciences, but in Ghulam Ahmad's example, it ends at the assumption of 'Christian' and 'Hindu' titles.

III. *Muhammad Iqbal's 'Self'*

Muhammad Iqbal neither founded a college, like Ahmad Khan, nor a sect like Ghulam Ahmad. His influence was a function of his poetry and public addresses. Born in 1879 in the same part of Punjab in which Ghulam Ahmad was debating members of the Ahl-i Hadith and others, Iqbal was first *maktab*-educated in Arabic and Persian, and then passed into the colonial system, earning an MA in philosophy from Government College Lahore in 1898. Although he began writing Urdu verse while studying, his poetry would take a backseat to further study in 1905, when, upon the recommendation of Thomas Arnold, his thesis advisor at Government College, Iqbal began three years of study in Europe, earning a doctorate in philosophy in Germany and a

---

[98] Friedmann, *Prophecy Continuous*, p. 118.
[99] Ghulam Ahmad, *'Isa Hindustan Mein*, pp. 21–58.
[100] It is well known that the oral and written literature of Afghani (Pathan) tribes have long included genealogies that linked them to the 'Lost Tribes of Israel'. The idea entered Orientalist writings as early as the 16th century, being mentioned in Francois Bernier's *Travels*, read in Chapter 2. By the late 19th century this was so standard a feature of Orientalist historiography, that it is mentioned in the works of Edward Balfour and H.W. Bellows. The parallels between Christianity and Buddhism have been drawn by such eminent scholars of their day as Rhys Davids and H.T. Princep. The idea was taken furthest by the Russian Orientalist, Nicholas Notovich, who traveled to Tibet and claimed to have read *sutras* that confirmed Jesus sojourned in the region before his crucifixion. Excerpts from all these works and more are included in the appendices of Ghulam Ahmad, *'Isa Hindustan Mein*, pp. 116–43.

law degree from England.[101] While away, Iqbal was as deeply affected by all he saw and encountered as Ahmad Khan some three decades earlier, but unlike the latter, Iqbal did not come away feeling that his 'community' alone was in dire states. In his *Siqiliyya*, written while his ship passed the shores of Sicily in 1908, once the domain of Muslim rulers, he lamented that he must 'weep here' alone, but upon his return to India, he must also 'make others cry' with the news of the 'decline' of the Arabs.[102] Thus, when Iqbal began composing a response to the decay he perceived, he switched from Urdu to Persian and English in an effort to address a wider Muslim audience.

Iqbal's response, whether in Urdu, Persian or English, poetry, prose or speech, resembled Ahmad Khan's in various ways. Both argued that the 'contradictions' between Islamic metaphysics and European physics were due to 'Greek' influences, rather than a reflection of Qur'anic Truth. Apart from blaming Aristotle and Plato, in particular, for blunting the ethos of Islam, Iqbal also claimed that his metaphysics represented an interpretation of the Qur'an in light of the 'new arts and sciences'. In addition, like Ahmad Khan, although by a different intellectual route, Iqbal argued for 'freewill' and an allegorical interpretation of angels, *jinn*, the Day of Judgement, and Heaven and Hell. Most importantly, his entire metaphysical appraisal depended on his assumption of the right of *ijtihad*. Yet, Iqbal also differed from Ahmad Khan in important ways, including the fact that the later thinker included Reason and Intuition as equivalent sources of knowledge to Revelation. Indeed, Iqbal criticised al-Ghazali and his particular strain of Sufism for being led by Plato to find erroneously 'no hope in analytical thought', while Ibn Rushd and the Mu'tazila follow Aristotle in taking 'no notice of non-conceptual modes of approaching Reality'.[103] Thus, in Iqbal's final analysis, 'thought and intuition are organically related' and 'capable of reaching an immanent Infinite'.[104] Furthermore, the place of Sober

---

[101] Iqbal's Urdu poetry was published in various forms, but first collected in four major works: *Bang-i Dara* (1922), *Bal-i Jibra'il* (1936), *Armaghan-i Hijaz* (1936) and *Zarb-i Kalim* (1936). All these works are collected in Muhammad Iqbal, *Kulliyat-i Iqbal* (Lahore: Shaykh Ghulam 'Ali & Sons, 1973). A selection from all these works is also available in the Urdu original with an English translation: D.J. Matthews, ed. and trans. *Iqbal: A Selection of Urdu Verse* (New Delhi: Heritage Publishers, 1993).

[102] Muhammad Iqbal, 'Siqiliyya', *Bang-i Dara* (Lahore: Jahangir Book Depot, n.d.), pp. 100–01.

[103] Muhammad Iqbal, *The Reconstruction of Religious Thought in Islam* (Lahore: Sang-i Meel, 1996), pp. 12–13.

[104] Ibid., p. 13.

Sufism's 'transcendental monism', rather than Ahmad Khan's 'absolute transcendence', is central to Iqbal's thought.

In *Asrar-i Khudi*, the first of his major Persian poems published in 1915, he also began to outline the ideas on Islam he believed would remedy decay, beginning with the relationship between the human and the divine, holding that 'existence is an effect of the Self (*khudi*)', and 'a hundred words are hidden in its essence'.[105] That is to say, *khudi* is equivalent to God's 'essence' and the multiplicity of 'life' follows from the fact that 'the nature of the Self' is 'to manifest itself'. Representative of that multiplicity, humanity partakes in the Self, just as in 'every atom slumbers the might of the Self'.[106] Thus, human 'development', according to Iqbal, is driven by the same force from which 'proceeds the radiance of its being', i.e. 'Love' or 'Desire' (*ishq*) of the Self.[107] Most succinctly put, 'when the [individual] self is made strong by Love', it 'becomes God's hand'.[108] Iqbal describes the individual who achieves this 'state' as the '*insan al-kamil*' (perfect human) or the '*na'ib-i ilahi*' (divine vice-regent).[109] The route to the realisation of this state ultimately involves two primary 'acts': 'control' or 'command' over the individual's attachment to worldly fears and cares, and 'surrender' to the *shari'a*, while the purpose of those who achieve it is to 'execute the command of Allah in the world'.[110]

On the surface, *Asrar-i Khudi* is a reiteration of Sober Sufi notions of 'transcendental monism' and, in most respects, it is deeply imbued with that centuries old line of thought. However, Ayesha Jalal, following the lead of Annemarie Schimmel, points out that Iqbal's use of the term *khudi* is a break with past meaning, which she defines as 'selfishness or egotism'.[111] All past Sufis, including the 'shuhudi' Shaykh Ahmad Sirhindi, used the term when speaking of mystical experience requiring '*bi khudi*' (self-negation).[112] Iqbal, meanwhile, used the term in a 'purely positive sense', as Jalal puts it, arguing that only 'individual

---

[105] Muhammad Iqbal, *Asrar-i Khudi*, trans. R.A. Nicholson (Lahore: Shaykh Muhammad Ashraf, 1983), p. 16.
[106] Ibid., p. 19.
[107] Ibid., pp. 28–29.
[108] Ibid., p. 43.
[109] Ibid., pp. 79–84.
[110] Ibid., pp. 72–80.
[111] Ayesha Jalal, *Self and Sovereignty* (London: Routledge, 2000), p. 177. For Schimmel, see Annemarie Schimmel, *Gabriel's Wing* (Leiden: E.J. Brill, 1963), p. 42.
[112] Shaykh Ahmad Sirhindi, *Maktubat Imam Rabbani*, ed. Nur Muhammad (Lahore: Nur Muhammad, 1964), I:290, p. 740.

self-affirmation, *khudi*', would lead to 'purposeful collective action'.¹¹³ How then, is Iqbal's terminology reflective of a change in Sufi metaphysics, and what role does his 'Western education' play? The answer is not fully articulated in *Asrar-i Khudi*, but in his famous series of lectures delivered at Madras, Hyderabad and Aligarh and published in 1928 as *The Reconstruction of Religious Thought in Islam*. In the lecture titled, 'The Human Ego—His Freedom and Immortality', Iqbal used the terms 'ego', 'soul' and 'self' interchangeably. He explained that according to al-Ghazali and those of his intellectual leaning, 'the ego is a simple, indivisible and immutable soul-substance, entirely different from the group of our mental states and unaffected by time'.¹¹⁴ Juxtaposing this perspective with his understanding of ego in 'modern psychology', he suggested that in the latter group's estimation, the ego is 'part of the system of thought', such that every 'pulse of thought' is 'an indivisible unity' appropriated by the next in the act of knowing and recollecting. His point was to illustrate that both perspectives were lacking: the first because it failed to account for such phenomenon as 'multiple personalities' except by an appeal to 'evil spirits', and the second, as the lack of continuity between passing thoughts it upholds does not address the 'relatively permanent element in experience'. Thus, Iqbal's alternative, which he himself claimed came the closest to the Qur'anic Truth, was a concept of ego that reconciled 'multiplicity' and 'permanence' by positing an individual, specific, dynamic and free agent that is simultaneously embraced by the 'Ultimate Ego'. The nature of the latter is best outlined in other lectures. In the 'The Philosophical Tests of the Revelations of Religious Experience' and 'The Conception of God and the Meaning of Prayer', Iqbal defined the Ultimate Ego as a free actor capable of change as well, but whereas ego conceives of change in terms of 'serial duration', the Ultimate Ego 'exists in pure duration wherein the change ceases to be a succession of varying attitudes, and reveals its true character as continuous creation, untouched by weariness and unseizable [sic] by slumber or sleep'.¹¹⁵ Furthermore, 'Ultimate Reality' is the Ultimate Ego, and the 'world, in all its details, from the mechanical movement of what we call the atom of matter to the free

---

¹¹³ Jalal, *Self and Sovereignty*, pp. 177–78.
¹¹⁴ Iqbal, 'The Human Ego—His Freedom and Immortality', *Reconstruction*, pp. 87–109.
¹¹⁵ Iqbal, 'The Philosophical Test of the Revelations of Religious Experience', *Reconstruction*, p. 58.

movement of thought in the human ego, is the self-revelation of the "Great I am"'.[116] Therefore, the 'scientific observer of Nature is a kind of mystic seeker in the act of prayer', while formal prayer (i.e. *salat*) 'is intended to save the ego from the mechanising effects of business and sleep' by bringing 'it into closer touch with the ultimate source of life and freedom'.[117]

The above passage should illustrate that Iqbal's 'self' was intended to represent the synthesis of al-Ghazali's immutable, unmindful concept of 'soul' with 'modern psychology's' understanding of a dynamic, developing 'ego'. Yet, too much cannot be made of this synthesis. After all, did Iqbal not argue that 'prayer' is vital to 'save the ego' from 'business and sleep', and can the latter not be substituted in meaning with 'selfishness and egotism'? In other words, it is not the psychologist's approach to individuality that ultimately drove Iqbal's metaphysical conclusions. In fact, the change in terminology Iqbal affected is anchored in the fact that his monism is not that of Ibn al-'Arabi's *wahdat al-wujud*, but follows aspects of Shaykh Ahmad Sirhindi's and Shah Wali Allah's perspectives. Consider his vision of annihilation (*fana'*) and subsistence (*baqa'*) as a staring point. In his lectures, Iqbal confirmed that ego retains its individuality beside the Ultimate Ego. He explained:

> True infinity does not mean infinite extension which cannot be conceived without embracing all available finite extensions. Its nature consists in intensity and not extensity; and the moment we fix our gaze on intensity, we begin to see that the finite ego must be *distinct*, though not *isolated*, from the infinite. Extensively regarded I am absorbed by the spacio-temporal order to which I belong. Intensively regarded I consider the same socio-temporal order as a confronting 'other' wholly alien to me. I am distinct from and yet intimately related to that on which I depend for my life and sustenance.[118]

What ultimately qualifies this as a restatement of Sirhindi's *wahdat al-shuhud* is that nowhere along the line, not even at the end of time as in Wali Allah's reasoning, does the ego 'disappear into the One'. However, Iqbal did not follow Sirhindi's lead in concluding that the transcendentalism of the theologians must therefore be uncritically accepted. Focusing on Ash'ari doctrines of 'atomism', 'accidents' and 'time' in the work of 'creation', he was by no means dismissive, even

---

[116] Iqbal, 'The Conception of God and the Meaning of Prayer', *Reconstruction*, p. 68.
[117] Ibid., p. 84; and 'Human Ego', p. 98.
[118] Iqbal, 'Human Ego', p. 105.

pointing out parallels between Ash'ari atomism and 'Quantum Theory', but concluded that 'reconstruction in light of modern physics' is necessary.[119] Furthermore, he argued that both Ash'aris and modern physicists/philosophers have to draw 'psychological analysis' into their discussions of time, as 'conscious experience...alone reveals the true nature of time'.[120] The latter critique is clearly intended to strengthen Iqbal's views on the 'ego' and 'Ego', given that part of the ego's journey towards the Ego involves moving beyond the 'serial duration' born of discursive knowledge to experience 'pure duration'. In life, this can begin to be achieved by following Sirhindi's idea, referenced in Chapter One, that 'right belief' is insufficient; the individual has to engage in 'action', living and promoting the *shari'a* in the interests of self and community. As Iqbal put it, 'It is the deed that prepares the ego'.[121] Yet, as in his attitude towards theology, so in his approach to law, Iqbal did not merely defer to the jurists' definition of the *shari'a* in determining what 'deeds' are best suited to the task, an issue discussed below. At this juncture, however, it is important to note that Iqbal's concept of death is another place in which he abandoned the theologians/jurists, in this case to draw from Wali Allah's insights.

Like most theologians and Sober Sufis, Iqbal accepted the concept of an 'Intermediary World' (*barzakh*) between death and the Day of Judgement. His view of *barzakh*, however, is almost exactly that of Wali Allah's. It is 'a state of consciousness characterised by a change in the ego's attitude towards time and space'; it is not a 'passive state of expectation', but one in which 'the ego must continue to struggle'; the Day of Judgement is 'not an external event', it is the 'consummation of the life-process within the ego'; and finally, 'Heaven and Hell are states, not localities', the former being 'the joy of triumph over the forces of disintegration', the latter involving the 'painful realisation of one's failure'.[122] The only significant precept in which Iqbal deviated from Wali Allah, instead drawing from al-Farabi, is in the assertion that the ego/soul/self is dependent on effort to exist beyond life. 'Personal immortality', wrote Iqbal, 'is not ours by right; it is to be achieved by

---

[119] Iqbal, 'The Conception of God', pp. 65–72.
[120] Ibid., pp. 71–72. For a critique of time in Albert Einstein's 'Theory of Relativity', also see 'The Philosophical Test', pp. 40–43.
[121] Iqbal, 'Human Ego', p. 106.
[122] Ibid., pp. 107–09.

personal effort'.[123] In *toto*, therefore, *Asrar-i Khudi* and such lectures reflect the systematic development, rather than the Objectification of certain strains of 'transcendental monism', particularly that of Ahmad Sirhindi and Wali Allah, above those that posit an immutable 'self' and a passively omniscient 'Self'.

Expressed in terms of the law, the 'personal effort' expended in life that best prevents the 'self' from dissolving upon the death of the body is dependent on following the *shariʻa*. As in other realms of thought, here, too, Iqbal argued for *ijtihad*. That is to say, like the Wali Allahis, *Tariqa-i Muhammadiyya* and Ahmad Khan, Iqbal rejected past rulings to appeal directly to the 'sources' of the law in seeking, as he put it, to 'rebuild' the *shariʻa*. In contrast to the Wali Allahis and other advocates of transcendental monism in the 'new' Sober Path, however, Iqbal did not call for *ijtihad* to rid the *shariʻa* of the 'innovations' accrued since the death of Muhammad. Nor did he reject the four Sunni *madhhab*s in favour of a synthetic approach. He wished to 'reconstruct' Hanafi jurisprudence, as Ahmad Khan had sought to 'revive' theology, 'in light of modern thought and experience'.[124] Focusing on this motive, Farzana Shaikh illustrates that Iqbal shirked past precedent not only by claiming the right of *ijtihad* for lay persons and arguing that *hadith* was unreliable, but most importantly, by asserting that *ijmaʻ* (consensus) could include the legal findings of an elected legislative body.[125] Without debating Shaikh's points concerning Iqbal's break with the past, it must nevertheless be recognised that she does not adequately flush out the jurisprudential method that Iqbal proposed, a point on which Iqbal was quite explicit.

As he outlined in the lecture titled 'The Principle of Movement in the Structure of Islam', the primary function of the Qur'an, in Iqbal's estimation, was to 'awaken in man the higher consciousness of his relation with God and the universe'.[126] The Qur'an, he continued, 'is not a legal code, save for few general principles... relating to family'. Thus, the role of the Qur'an as part of the entire legal structure should be assessed 'from the point of view of the larger purpose which is being

---

[123] Ibid., p. 106.

[124] Iqbal, 'The Principle of Movement in the Structure of Islam', *Reconstruction*, p. 138.

[125] For Shaikh's complete argument, including her perspective on Ahmad Khan et al., see Farzana Shaikh, *Community and Consensus in Islam* (Cambridge: Cambridge University Press, 1989).

[126] Iqbal, 'The Principle of Movement', p. 145.

gradually worked out in the life of mankind as a whole'. That is to say, Iqbal invoked the concept of *istislah*, almost exactly as defined in the works of al-Ghazali.[127] With regard to the second textual source, *hadith*, although Iqbal mentioned the debate over the authenticity of collections raging among Orientalists, led by Ignaz Goldziher, he approached the issue through the perspectives of two specific Muslim thinkers: Wali Allah and Abu Hanifa. Iqbal wholeheartedly accepted Wali Allah's argument that the *shari'a* is no more than a 'modification' of Arabian 'custom'. Furthermore, he employed Wali Allah to affirm the critical methods of *'ilm al-hadith*, but like Ahmad Khan, broke with Wali Allah, the *Tariqa Muhammadiyya* and Deobandis to read this to mean that individual *hadith* should not be employed as a source of law in an 'indiscriminate' way. In addition, Iqbal ignored Wali Allah's influential contention that this modified Arabian custom is the *shari'a* of the age for all Muslims in the present time. Instead, he pointed out that Abu Hanifa employed the juristic tool of *istihsan*, 'which necessitates a careful study of actual conditions in legal thinking' as a response to the fact that Muhammad's legislation is 'specific to that [7th century Arab] people' and 'cannot be strictly enforced in the case of future generations'.[128] Thus, exactly as Ahmad Khan did in the interests of his metaphysics, Iqbal used Wali Allah as the springboard from which to dive into the argument that *hadith* can be overruled by Reason in the interests of the law, as also reaffirmed below by Iqbal's perspective on *ijma'* and *qiyas*, the third and fourth sources of the *shari'a* according to most 'old' schools of jurisprudence.

Regarding the Qur'an and *hadith*, it is apparent that Iqbal remained within the complex of debates and methodologies particular to Islamic jurisprudence, drawing mostly from the Hanafi school. The legitimisation of elected legislatures by means of *ijma'*, as most thoroughly discussed by Shaikh, is the first aspect of Iqbal's legal reasoning that adds something 'new' to doctrine. By not considering the jurisprudential method Iqbal wished his 'Muslim assemblies' to employ, however, many observers miss the fact that Iqbal wished to see *qiyas* form the methodological foundations of legislation—a method of analogical reasoning at the heart of 'old' juristic methodologies, but rejected by those of the 'new' Sober Path by the early 18th century. To Iqbal, lay Muslims

---

[127] Ibid., p. 148.
[128] Ibid., p. 150.

acting through a legislature did not mean that Utilitarian principles, or some other European legal attitude, should solely be employed in their legal reasoning. Rather, Iqbal was affirming what he perceived as the 'lay' Muslim's right to employ the very method of analogical reasoning and inductive logic developed by jurists of 'old'. Ultimately, this must be read, not only in the light of the fact that contemporary schools like Deoband denied lay Muslims this right but also that the 'new' Sober Path denied the practice of *ijma‘* and *qiyas* even to themselves, while applying a less than 'discriminate' appeal to *hadith*, and a decidedly 'codified' approach to *hadith*-based and Qur'anic edicts. Anticipating the objections of Deoband and company, Iqbal himself raised the problem of 'a modern Muslim assembly which must consist, at least for the present, mostly of men possessing no knowledge of the subtleties of Muhammadan Law'.[129] After considering and dismissing the idea of a supervisory 'ecclesiastical committee', as included in the 1906 Iranian constitution, the only remedy Iqbal proposed was 'to reform the present system of legal education in Muhammadan countries', such that Islamic jurisprudence and 'an intelligent study' of European jurisprudence is imparted. In the final analysis, the legislative structure to be adopted was European, but the process to be employed was quite specifically that of the 'old' Sober Path.

Academics often express the opinion that the problem with Iqbal is that he was not a 'systematic thinker'—a sentiment echoed in Jalal's statement that the 'many variations in his philosophical worldview were incomprehensible even to himself'.[130] I beg to differ. While it is true that Iqbal died before completing his work on legal reform and his socio-political perspective ebbed and flowed with the vagaries of time and place (as discussed further in the next chapter), his 'philosophical worldview' and its relationship with legalism was most systematically outlined by the 1920s. It involved little other than a synthesis of the Naqshbandiyya metaphysics of Ahmad Sirhindi and Wali Allah, and the 'revival' of Hanafi *usul al-fiqh*. Granted, Iqbal proposed a dynamic individual and divine 'self' as a means to legitimate aspects of European physics, biology, psychology and political philosophy, but his core ideas represent the systemic development of Wali Allah's 'evolutionary' vision, rather than the selection, polishing and reformulation of 'tradition'

---

[129] Ibid., p. 153.
[130] Jalal, *Self and Sovereignty*, p. 166.

through the lens of Western education for suddenly conscious ends. His perspective on Islam is not Objectification. Like the previous thinkers discussed in this chapter, Iqbal's thought represents a 'new' Intoxicated Way, dealing with a set of intellectual strains not previously integrated, Islamic and European. Regarding transformative influences, therefore, one must again say that although Western education and the colonial regime influenced Iqbal's views, he embraced aspects of both only insofar as they could be legitimated by expressions of the individual and community long established in the Sober Path.

Conclusion: A 'New' Intoxicated Way

When added to the previous chapters' survey of thought and institutions in the colonial period, the writings of these last 'lay' Muslims with scholarly leanings reveal that representatives of all categories of Islamic thought continued to define 'Islam' under British Raj. Moreover, as representatives of all categorical orientations have now been discussed, it can be added that some among them even echo al-Ghazali's classes of seekers exactly: *mutakallimun* (Ahl-i Hadith/Ahl-i Sunnat), *falasifa* (Ahmad Khan), *batiniyya* (Ghulam Ahmad) and *sufiyya* (Iqbal/Deobandis). Depending on categorical orientations, these thinkers and their 'schools' also exhibit varying degrees of hostility and hospitality towards non-scriptural knowledge and customs. Thus, for the 'new' Sober Path of the Deobandis, the use of print, administrative reforms to *madrasas*, and the legitimisation of a colonial state that theoretically allowed for autonomy in 'personal law', represented the extent of the school's hospitality towards British influence. In the 'new' Intoxicated Way of Aligarhis, Ahmadis and Iqbal, however, not only are the above types of influences legitimate, but so are European 'Naturalism' in the first case, the Christian 'Messiah' in the second, and the electoral and legislative capacity of the 'Self' in the last. Such thinkers' tendency to manipulate the 'whole matrix of custom, ritual, religious symbol and a textually transmitted tradition', for 'conscious ends', thus represents the latest of a long and continuous pattern in Islamic thought, rather than a novel urge to objectify unleashed by 'Western' education. Instead, it is the matrix of European thought and institutions that is manipulated for consciously Islamic ends.

Notwithstanding the above continuity and acknowledging that all Muslims who received a 'Western' education were not inclined to scholarship, it is also clear that the colonial regime played a pivotal role in determining the above formulations, its 'power' evident in the types of European knowledge and lack of non-European thought and institutions integrated, whether scientific/technological, religious or political. As discussed in the previous chapter, the rise of the 'new' Sober Path from a fringe movement in the 18th century to a central element of the Islamic discourse in the 19th century cannot be accounted for without the disintegration of indigenous education at British behest. On the other hand, the articulation of a 'new' Intoxicated Way is dependent on the influence of the colonial education system which replaced the former and, in the process, challenged or undermined the theology, metaphysics and other 'rational' and 'religious sciences' upon which the 'old' depended. Together, the above developments account for the lack of 'creativity' on which Rahman commented. However, there is more at play than the influence of European thought and institutions. That 'lay' Muslims stand at the forefront of the 'new' Intoxicated Way is an obvious consequence of the intellectual orientations of the reconstituted *madrasa*—one that abandoned the 'rational sciences' in keeping with the exigencies of the 'new' Sober Path. Furthermore, the 'new' Sober Path's own attacks on established intellectual authorities, its insistence on *ijtihad* and concerted efforts to directly expose 'lay' persons to scripture, cannot be discounted in leading the likes of Ahmad Khan et al., to engage textual sources, especially given the formative influence of the 'new' Path in each of their lives. In fact, it is the centrality of Wali Allahi 'transcendental monism', in particular, that leads Ahmad Khan to the 'absolute transcendence' of the Mu'tazila in seeking to integrate European Naturalism, while directly providing Ghulam Ahmad and Iqbal with the metaphysics that account for the former's claims to Revelation in adopting messianic titles and the latter's insistence on Islamic jurisprudence in adapting European modes of legislation. Thus, if Rahman views a concentration on European thought and institutions as a sign of such thinkers' lack of 'creativity', it must also be said that the heavy influence of Wali Allahi ideas is no less a 'psychological impediment' than political subjugation, entirely effacing the 'absolute immanence' that had previously formed the core of Islamic philosophy and mysticism.

Of course, Rahman would not agree, his own ideas carrying the same dependence on *ijtihad*, legalism and transcendentalism into the post-colonial period. Robinson might agree, although he would have to question his own characterisation of the shift from 'other-worldly to this-worldly religion' as equivalent to one from 'Persian' to 'Arab' Islam. If this work catches the attention of Cohn or Jalal, they would probably offer insightful retorts. Unless all of the above recognise that their visions share a dominant paradigm in defining doctrinal Islam as statically 'legalistic' and culturally 'intrusive', however, their approaches will not address the significance of the fact that transcendentalism (absolute or monistic), in past or present cases, has not precluded the equivalence of Reason, Intuition and Revelation, thus legitimating the inclusion of non-scriptural intellectualism and institutions within an 'Islamic frame'. Furthermore, the same transcendentalism, unlike 'absolute immanence', represents a theological/metaphysical bent that has and continues to roundly exclude antinomian and potentially inhibit latitudinarian tendencies by insisting on *shari'a* as the basis of legislation. Again, the governmental assumptions and structures of the Raj, which privileged religious constructs, as well as the local political and economic interests of the above authors, cannot be discounted among the influences manifest in the shift from absolute immanence to transcendentalism as the doctrinal bases of the 'new' Intoxicated Way. But the tilt of the relationship between the 'European' and 'Islamic' discourses of the period cannot be fully addressed until the former 'governmentality' is viewed in tandem with the doctrines of the 'new' Sober Path and the 'new' Intoxicated Way, when assessing the influences shaping the elite and capitalist Muslim 'self' under British Raj. Thus, the final task in this work, taken up in the next chapter, is spelled out by the above need.

CHAPTER SIX

NATIONALISM AND THE 'NEW ISLAM'

In 1931, during a series of 'Round Table Conferences' between South Asian and British politicians on the future of British Raj, Muhammad 'Ali Jawahar (d. 1931)—graduate of Aligarh and Oxford, associate of Gandhi and a towering political figure among Muslims—expressed the opinion that he and his co-religionists belonged to 'two circles of equal size... One is India, and the other is the Muslim World'.[1] Almost simultaneously, however, Muhammad Iqbal addressed segments of the Muslim political elite with the less 'composite' proposition that:

> Punjab, North-West Frontier Province, Sind and Baluchistan [be] amalgamated into a single State. Self-government within the British empire or without the British empire, the consolidated North-West Indian Muslim State appears to me the final destiny of Muslims, at least of North-West India.[2]

Although Iqbal's idea received a cold response in 1930, the period of British Raj ended less than two decades later with his vision acquiring 'national' borders in the form of Pakistan. Therefore, the leap from 'two circles' to 'one' for two-thirds of South Asia's Muslims is necessarily the crux of many studies concerned with the history of nationalism in the region.

Perhaps the most insightful and influential observations in contemporary writing on nationalism in general are those of Benedict Anderson. He breaks with Eric Hobsbawm's conception of nations as 'invented', to argue that they are 'imagined communities' arising in concert with 'print-capital' in Europe. This mode of collective imagining, Anderson continues, spread to South Asia and elsewhere through European influence and the reforms initiated by the colonial state.[3] While building

---

[1] For the entire speech, see Muhammad 'Ali Jawahar, *Selected Speeches and Writings of Maulana Mohamed Ali*, ed. Afzal Iqbal (Lahore: Muhammed Ashraf, 1944), vol. 2, pp. 350–61.
[2] For the entire speech, see Muhammad Iqbal, *Speeches and Statements of Iqbal*, ed. L.A. Sherwani (Lahore: Al-Manar Academy, 1948), pp. 3–36.
[3] See Benedict Anderson, *Imagined Communities* (London: Verso, 1983).

on this idea, Partha Chatterjee retorts that if the nation is imagined in Europe or by European colonists, as Anderson argues, what is left for the colonial subject to imagine? His answer is as astute as the question. Using the example of Bengal in the period of British Raj, Chatterjee makes the case that to understand nationalism in South Asia, one must first acknowledge that, reflecting British propensities to divide social space into 'Public' and 'Private' spheres, the urban 'bourgeoisie' (i.e. 'capitalist' classes) carved an 'Inner' domain of cultural sovereignty, including religion, gender, family, and so on, where they held the cards of reform, leaving only the 'Outer' domain, encompassing the state, economy, technology, etc., open to unfettered European direction. In other words, according to Chatterjee, there is no 'pure Westernism', as Rahman presumed, at least in the case of nationalism. This is an equally astute insight, leading Chatterjee to conclude that if 'the nation is an imagined community', then, considering the place of 'tradition' in South Asian imaginings, the 'Inner' domain 'is where it is brought into being'.[4]

Regarding nationalism among South Asian Muslims in particular, the range of contemporary opinion (outside of nationalist circles) can be addressed by focusing on two historians already encountered in this book: Farzana Shaikh and Ayesha Jalal. Shaikh approaches the issue by considering how legal concepts like *ijmaʿ* (consensus) and various aspects of Mughal political culture that had previously shaped notions of Muslim distinctiveness, were transformed by the 'lay' Muslim's engagement with the colonial regime into an overarching 'communalism', inclusive of a nationalised and separatist political identity, that achieved general acceptance among Muslims.[5] Jalal, however, replies that being based 'on a rationalisation of normative Islamic discourse, such an interpretation fails to make an analytical distinction between cultural identity informed by religion and the actual politics of Muslim identity'.[6] Thus, Jalal's work suggests that 'a religiously informed cultural identity', which she terms 'communitarianism', 'did not automatically translate into what came to be understood by the 1920s as communalism

---

[4] Partha Chatterjee, *Nation and its Fragments* (Princeton: Princeton University Press, 1994), p. 6.
[5] See Farzana Shaikh, *Community and Consensus in Islam* (Cambridge: Cambridge University Press, 1989).
[6] Ayesha Jalal, *Self and Sovereignty* (London: Routledge, 2000), p. 57.

and separatism'.[7] The steps involved after 1858 began with British 'perceptions of Indian society as an aggregate of religious communities', while 'Indian subjectivity, whether in its individual or communitarian colours, constituted an important dimension in the discourse on identity in the late 19th century'.[8] In the interests of the empire, the British viewed 'the Muslim landed elite' as 'natural allies', while Muslims like Sayyid Ahmad Khan enthusiastically took up colonial categories to their own advantage, as evinced by the reactionary concoction of 'two nations' (Hindu and Muslim) as a counterweight to the Indian National Congress' 'India'. The former ultimately resolved in the form of both official and Muslim sanction of 'separate electorates' by the first decade of the 20th century. However, Muslim political classes were not actually galvanised behind 'an all-India Muslim political organisation... until the last decade of British rule'.[9] In the interim, 'religious' identity was expressed through the rhetoric of *umma*, or a 'universal Muslim community', while political realities eschewed 'exclusively Muslim politics' in favour of the formation of 'alliances with other communities' on provincial and 'All-India' levels.[10] The shift from this 'composite nationalism' born of 'communitarianism', to that of 'separatism' based on 'communalism', occurred when Indian National Congress visions of a highly centralised 'India' lost the support of not only the elite and capitalist-class Muslims of North Western 'minority' provinces, who had led the charge against the Indian National Congress since the 1880s, but also key segments of the 'majority' Muslim provinces, most notably Punjab and Bengal. 'In the end', Jalal and Sugata Bose conclude, 'it was the particularisms of the Muslim provinces rather than a supra-local Islamic sentiment which provided the more important driving force in the making of Pakistan'.[11]

Despite obvious differences between Shaikh's and Jalal's perspectives, one constant remains: both accounts employ the same paradigmic approach to Islam that this work has found lacking, and so, both are tainted by the essentialisation of doctrinal Islam as statically 'legalistic' and culturally 'intrusive'. In Shaikh's terminology, 'Muslim politics' is 'exclusive', thus 'alliances' across religious divides somehow 'transgress'

---

[7] Sugata Bose and A. Jalal, *Modern South Asia* (London: Routledge, 1998), p. 168.
[8] Jalal, *Self and Sovereignty*, pp. 43–44.
[9] Bose and Jalal, *Modern South Asia*, p. 169.
[10] Ibid., pp. 169–70.
[11] Ibid., p. 188.

Islam. In Jalal's terms, 'supra-local Islamic sentiment', whether on the level of 'Muslim India' or *umma*, is explicitly opposed to the 'particularisms of the Muslim provinces'. Consequently, the Muslim 'imagination' is severely restricted by both authors. That 'subjectivity, whether in its individual or communitarian colours, [which] constituted an important dimension in the discourse on identity' is barely touched upon—a cardinal lapse in the light of Chatterjee's observation that if 'the nation is an imagined community', then the 'Inner' domain of elite and capitalist classes 'is where it is brought into being'. Thus, although drawing from the insights of both the above authors, I consider how the influence and/or deployment of the variety of 'Paths' and 'Ways' resident in the South Asian Muslim 'Inner' domain extended themselves into the 'Outer' when imagining India and Pakistan. The very recognition of a Sober Path and an Intoxicated Way, not to mention doctrinal permutations within each, 'old' and 'new', belies any attempt to approach Islam through a 'normative' gaze that privileges one or another of the above strains of thought. As each of these strains is also conceived to encourage a variety of cultural orientations, legitimating hostility and hospitality towards extra-scriptural thought and institutions, the temptation of any approach that fails to appreciate the multiplicity of possible relationships among Muslims, as well as between Muslims and non-Muslims, is nullified. Given that precisely this angle of approach is lacking in much of the contemporary historiography of South Asia, this is exactly the element of the discourse on nationalism that remains to be explored.

Shaikh merely illuminates the legal aspect of doctrinal Islam's influence on the Muslim imagination, while Jalal focuses on the socioeconomic and political underpinnings to avoid a rationalization of doctrine. Hence, the central question unanswered is the extent to which the hostility and hospitality Muslims exhibited towards European thought and institutions, as well as the divides between Muslims, was mediated by the 'old' and 'new' forms of Islam. I begin to answer this by clarifying what exactly defines the Islam of the elite and capitalist classes' 'Inner' domain, referencing attitudes towards gender and community in particular. Then, I reiterate in greater detail than presented above, the transformations in notions of community implicit in nationalised visions of the 'Outer' domain, paying close attention to the role of doctrinal Islam in conditioning individual participants, men and women, to promote or accept such shifts. I argue that although the politics of the 'Outer' domain is evidently influenced by European intellectual influences and directed by regional and class interests, the Islam of the 'Inner' domain legitimates or rejects aspects of the former by means of various doctrinal approaches representative of the 'new' Sober Path and 'new' Intoxicated Way. As this 'New Islam' in general embodies the ideal of strong allegiance to religious community, the literature under consideration once more suggests that British initiatives in the realm of Codification and Anglicisation, as well as such consequences as Objectification, are not acting alone in highlighting religious identity. Muslim subjectivity is an important factor in accepting colonial categories, not merely for the social and political advantages this accrued, but also because those categories echoed the 'Islamic' ideals of the late 19th and early 20th centuries. Resolving as an intermediate position between Shaikh and Jalal, I argue that the nationalisation of identities is as firmly driven by a change in doctrine from 'old' to 'new' as by the machinations of the colonial regime and the socio-political interests of Muslims. In this shift, however, the 'communitarian/communal' dichotomy is false. So-called 'composite nationalism' and outright 'separatism' are both forms of 'communalism'. That is to say, the leap from Jawahar's 'two circles' to Iqbal's 'self-government' was clearly prompted by elite and capitalist class contestations over the substance and leadership of the supra-community in a colonial setting, but was in both cases legitimated and promoted by the same doctrinal trends, i.e. the Sober and Intoxicated variants of the 'New Islam'.

I. *The 'Inner' Domain: The 'New Islam', Gender and Community*

I.i. *Gender*

The 'Old Islam' was obviously not equitable in the realm of gender roles and relations. A prime example is the fact that, in the context of the 'Great Mughals,' *purda* (seclusion) was the norm for elite women (Muslim and Hindu). However, it was also not a 'transgression' of doctrinal Islam, even in its legalistic form, for Muslim women to participate in various levels of public life, examples of which have been mentioned in Chapter Two, including positions as regents (*wakils*) and in the office of the *sadr*. Women scholars—mystics, historians, biographers and poets—were also commonplace and doctrinally sanctioned, though they were less prominent than their male counterparts. Although no Mughal sultans were women, there are examples, from South Asia and elsewhere, of female sultans (*sultanas*) who not only shirked the restrictions of *purda* for bureaucratic purposes, but also led armies into battle. Furthermore, beyond the elite, *purda* was not commonplace and, given the sweeping accommodations that the 'Old Islam' extended to customary laws, a dizzying array of local practices often determined the status of women, meaning anything from the lifting of *purda* to the disinheritance of daughters or even participation in *sati* (widow immolation).

Although evidence of 'Great Mughal' attempts to curb extreme customs like *sati* has already been discussed, it was not until the 18th century rise of 'capitalist' classes—steeped in local custom and vernacular cultures—that more widespread accommodations of custom became a concern. Not surprisingly, scholars of the 'new' Sober Path led the charge as part of their anti-customary agenda. A case in point is provided by a leading figure from the important Anjuman-i Punjab, Muhammad Husayn Azad (d. 1910), in his seminal and still widely read history of Urdu poetry, *Ab-i Hayat* (1880). According to the author, Khwaja Andalib—author of the *Tariqa Muhammadiyya*, Khwaja Mir Dard's father and head of the Naqshbandi-Mujaddidiyya of Delhi into the mid-18th century—regularly instructed female disciples, including 'dancing girls', in mixed company at his hospice. On one occasion, a youthful Shah 'Abd al-'Aziz—Wali Allah's son and successor—is said to have attended a gathering and was disapproving. Mir Dard explained, 'In the eyes of this *faqir* [i.e. his father], these are all mothers and sisters'. 'Abd al-'Aziz rebutted, 'Then how is it proper to bring mothers and sisters and seat them in the midst of a public gathering'.[12] Although the historical episodes related by Muhammad Husayn are well known to be unreliable (even fabricated at times), this anecdote is important for two reasons. First, it confirms that the 'new' Sober Path's attention to *purda* stood in sharp contrast with common practice, even among fellow scholarly travellers, let alone those on the 'old' Sober Path—a point well affirmed in 'Abd al-'Aziz's own *fatawa*. Second, Muhammad Husayn's historical perspective, accurate or not, provides much insight

---

[12] Muhammad Husayn Azad, *Ab-i Hayat* (Lucknow: U.P. Urdu Academy, 1982), p. 178. The translation is from Muhammad Husain Azad, *Ab-e Hayat*, ed. and trans. Frances Pritchett w/ Shamsur Rahman Faruqi (New Delhi: Oxford University Press, 2001), p. 176.

on the attitudes of his day and class. The fact that Muhammad Husayn's work ignores every woman who contributed to the development of Urdu literature, while lauding 'Abd al-'Aziz's attitude, says a great deal about his views on the subject of women in public life, as well as the source of his inspiration, i.e. the 'new' Sober Path. And, in this respect, Muhammad Husayn was not alone in the late 19th century.

Of all the socio-political issues confronted by the Muslim classes and locales of primary concern in this book, the question of appropriate gender roles is distinct in that its answer is the only one on which any semblance of consensus seems to have been present at the beginning of British Raj. Gender ideals, therefore, are the most appropriate place to begin this discussion of the Islam of the 'Inner' domain, and Ahmad Khan's attitudes and efforts confirm that Muhammad Husayn had company. As public, influential and otherwise Intoxicated a figure as Ahmad Khan was, he did not pay equal attention to, nor promote equal roles for, men and women. That he was also not alone is illustrated by the fact that 32 essays were submitted to the 'Committee for the Diffusion and Advancement of Learning among Muslims of India' from 1870 to 1872, and only two were concerned with women's education in English, and one of those was against it. However, pressure had been building to address women's education. Beginning in the 1860s, various *anjuman*s around South Asia considered the issue and girls' schools were opening, even in areas where none could be found in the early 19th century.[13] The problems facing these organisations would be brought to the fore when the Aligarhis promoted the formation of an umbrella organisation for these *anjuman*s and various segments of the scholarly classes in the 1880s. The 'Muslim Educational Conference', which would host annual meetings for decades to come, was intended to extend no further than the Muslims of the 'North-West Provinces', but would almost immediately expand to include the participation of Muslims from across British India.[14]

At the first meeting of the Educational Conference in 1886, reflecting the influence of various *anjuman*s already engaged in the issue of

---

[13] For examples of *anjuman*s involved in women's education, see Tahera Aftab, 'Reform Societies and Women's Education in Northern India', *Journal of the Pakistan Historical Society* 35:2 (April 1987): 121–35; and Gail Minault, *Secluded Scholars* (New York: Oxford University Press, 1998).

[14] *Aligarh Institute Gazette* (4 May 1886), *Aligarh Movement*, ed. Shan Muhammad (Delhi: Meenakshi Prakashan, 1978), vol. 2, pp. 767–69.

education for women, it was decided that the best means of redress was reform of the *maktab* system.[15] This, it was argued, would overcome the difficulty of *purda* making colonial schools unacceptable, while circumventing the lack of non-Christian missionary tutors. In other words, the *anjuman*s, like the advocates of the 'new' Sober Path, were in no way anti-*purda*. The immediate problem with the plan, discovered once numerous surveys had been conducted, has been discussed in Chapter Four: the 'Islamic' education system was in tatters, thanks to political decline and colonial intervention. The second difficulty revolved around the difference in objectives forwarded by *madrasa* and Western-educated participants in the Educational Conference. While the former promoted education in Urdu and Arabic, as was illustrated in Chapter Three's reading of the Deobandi Ashraf 'Ali Thanawi's *Bihishti Zewar*, the latter endorsed Urdu and English. As one core Aligarhi asserted in 1894, this alternative was necessary 'because our English-educated youth are desirous of marrying wives who may be instructed in the same language: and if this intention of theirs be overlooked, there is great fear of their taking wives from other communities'.[16] In addition, influential Aligarhis and others in favour of English, including Altaf Husayn Hali (d. 1914)—he was a noted academic and poet of the era, whose works include a poem specifically addressing the issue of gender, titled *Majalis al-Nisa* (1874)—was that while the *madrasa* educated thought of a woman's most public position as that of a *mawlawi* or *qadi*, promoters of Western education like Hali thought of them primarily as English teachers and practitioners of European medicine.[17]

Clearly, the issue of women's education was not merely promoted by the decline of indigenous educational institutions; colonialism played

---

[15] *Aligarh Institute Gazette* (1 January 1887), *Aligarh Movement*, vol. 2, pp. 772–23. At the second meeting, after a year-long census of *maktab*s, it was found that the infrastructure sought had crumbled, mostly due to the general poverty of Muslims. It was also argued that literacy rates were lower than ever among women. Thus, at the third meeting it was resolved that girls' *maktab*s must be revived—a course that would be pursued by the growing number of associated *anjuman*s in the remaining years of the 19th century. See *Pioneer* (29–30 December 1887), *Aligarh Movement*, vol. 2, pp. 774–77; and, *Aligarh Institute Gazette* (15 January 1889), *Aligarh Movement*, vol. 2, pp. 778–84.

[16] Haji Muhammad Isma'il Khan, 'On Female Education', *Aligarh Institute Gazette* (13 March 1894), *Aligarh Movement*, vol. 2, pp. 671–72.

[17] Altaf Husyan Hali, *Majalis-i Nisa* (New Delhi: Maktaba-i Jamia, 1971). Also Gail Minault, 'Hali's Majalis-i Nissa: Purdah and Woman Power in Nineteenth Century India', *Islamic Society and Culture*, M. Israel and N. Wagle, eds. (Delhi: Manoharlal, 1983), pp. 39–50.

a part. Indeed, the 'liberation' of South Asian women from the shackles of 'tradition', including *purda*, was a major element of the British 'Civilising Mission' employed to legitimate colonial rule, even when British women were denied the most basic property rights back at the metropole. Thus, Susie Tharu and Ke Lalita, like Partha Chatterjee, Sumit Sarkar and Lata Mani, not only insist that the colonial regime 'agitated debates' on women's education, but argue that the 'highly selective and dubious' use of 'tradition' in legal and other colonial reforms shaped such texts as the *Majalis-i Nisa*, explaining the entire discourse on gender as a 'complex and problematic' product of 'tradition' Objectified in light of 'Victorian norms of feminine propriety'.[18] While accepting the above differences between Aligarhis and Deobandis, however, Jalal astutely reads the similarities, particularly the concern for *purda*, as an attempt to avoid further conflict between Aligarhis and their opponents.[19] Taking a different tack from all of the above, Gail Minault explains Hali's attitudes, down to the idea that 'educated' women made better householders and could serve the needs of their own sex on a community level within the confines of *purda*, to the doctrinal influence of Deobandis and their 'new' Sober scholarly companions.[20] Minault's point is particularly telling, given that even if one acknowledges that British rule 'agitated debates' on women's education and Aligarhis had enough on their plate without further antagonising Deobandis, one cannot rest on these conclusions without also acknowledging that Muhammad Husayn's and Hali's attitudes towards *purda* independently lead the reader to the same source of 'Islamic' influence. The similarities between these authors' attitudes reflect the systematic development and influence of the 'new' Sober Path, even if postures are similar to Victorian values and colonial intervention and interests is obvious. The latter perspective can, in fact, be further substantiated by considering the broader 'rights' accorded or denied women by the above and other thinkers, rather than putting the spotlight on education alone.

It was shown in Chapter Three that one of the main features of the 'new' Sober Path was the exclusion of 'customary law' in the definition

---

[18] Susie Tharu and K. Lalita, eds., 'Literature of the Reform and Nationalist Movements', *Women Writing in India: 600 BC to Early Twentieth Century* (New York: Feminist Press, 1991), vol. 1, pp. 145–86.
[19] Jalal, *Self and Sovereignty*, p. 69.
[20] Minault, 'Hali's Majalis-i Nissa', pp. 41–42.

of the *shari'a*. In a polemical essay on the rights of women first published in 1871, Ahmad Khan began by pointing out that although 'England greatly favours the freedom of women, yet when its laws are examined, it is obvious that the English consider women quite insignificant, unintelligent and valueless'.[21] He substantiates his point by accurately outlining that in England, women cannot 'hold responsibility for any legal instrument' without a husband's consent, and that prior to a bill passed by Parliament in 1870, even property gained through inheritance and any profit it accrued belonged to the husband after marriage. In contrast, in Islamic law, he argued, adult women could independently enter into contracts, all property and profits belonged to her before or after marriage, she could bequeath or donate property freely, and a woman's consent to marriage was required. As for *purda*, he only stated that although there was 'excess' in India, in Europe there was excess of other kinds, so the 'limit set by the *shari'a* certainly seems to be perfectly correct'. Reading this article, Jalal assumes that Ahmad Khan was appealing to 'normative Islam', while downplaying 'Muslim practice', failing to recognise that customary practices such as disinheritance and so on, could be and were legitimated by the 'old' jurisprudence on any number of grounds.[22] However, in admitting that Western women enjoyed conditions 'many levels better than that of Muslim women', thus acknowledging Muslim practice, Ahmad Khan in fact indirectly confirmed the influence of the 'new' Sober Path, rather than an imaginary normative Islam or empowered Victorian values, concluding, 'People who associate these evils [i.e. lack of rights] with the religion of Islam are surely mistaken. To the extent that there is deterioration in the condition of women in India, it is due to the failure to observe the regulations of Islam fully'.[23] In other words, Ahmad Khan's 'regulations of Islam' were free of custom, as one only reads in the works (including *fatawa*) of 'new' Sober thinkers, from Wali Allah to Ashraf 'Ali.

When the issue of women's legal rights is added to that of education and *purda*, the congruence between works like those of Ashraf 'Ali's

---

[21] Sayyid Ahmad Khan, *Maqalat-i Sar Sayyid*, ed. Muhammad Isma'il Panipati (Lahore: *Majlis-i Taraqqi-i Abab*, 1962), vol. 6, pp. 201–05. The translation is by Kamran Talattof in Mansoor Moaddel and Talattof, eds., *Contemporary Debates in Islam* (New York: St. Martin's Press, 2000), pp. 159–62.

[22] Jalal, *Self and Sovereignty*, p. 73.

[23] Ahmad Khan, 'The Rights of Women', *Contemporary Debates in Islam*, pp. 160–61.

and Hali's on a range of issues confirms that by the mid- to late 19th century, the ideals of the 'new' Sober Path had been broadly internalised by the Muslim elite and capitalist classes. Having said this, the echo of 'new' Sober doctrines in the legalism of Ahmad Khan's 'new' Intoxicated Way, is not sufficient reason to conclude that all concurred. Recall that in Muhammad Iqbal's 'new' Intoxicated Way, 'old' legal doctrines are a cornerstone. In correspondence between Iqbal and his female 'friend', Attiya Faizi, in the early 1900s, Jalal argues that Iqbal echoed models ascribing women no more than domestic roles and arguing that subjects encouraging anything else should be avoided in women's education.[24] However, perhaps as a result of being taken to task by Faizi, herself an English-educated woman, but most definitely due to the development of his approach to jurisprudence, by the time Iqbal delivered his lectures of *The Reconstruction* in the late 1920s, his attitude had become less certain. By seeking to re-enliven the 'old' Hanafi jurisprudence, which allowed for concepts of public utility and juristic preference, while simultaneously casting aside past precedent, Iqbal came to invoke exactly such juristic tools as *istislah* (utility) and *istihsan* (preference) to leave open a reconsideration of whether such issues as 'the equality of man and woman...in point of divorce, separation and inheritance, is possible according to Muslim Law'.[25] In 1936, only two years before his death, the same uncertainty was also expressed in two poems—*Purda* and *Azadi-i Niswan*. In the first, he argued that more important than physical segregation is the fact that the 'self', male and female, 'sits in seclusion', while in the latter he admitted personal 'indecision' on the subject of women's liberation, but argued that it was ultimately up to women to lead the way.[26]

The 'Old Islam' also exerted itself through other avenues. For example, among the Khoja community, infamous for its disinheritance of daughters (see Chapter Three), there is evidence to suggest that *purda* was never practised. Thus, it was not so difficult for the Agha Khan III (d. 1957), leader of the Isma'ili segment of this community, to acquiesce to pressure from the colonial regime and his flock by declaring in the

---

[24] Jalal, *Self and Sovereignty*, p. 176.
[25] Muhammad Iqbal, *The Reconstruction of Religious Thought in Islam* (Lahore: Sang-i Meel, 1996), p. 148.
[26] Both poems are from the last collection of Urdu verse published in Iqbal's lifetime, titled *Zarb-i Kalim*. For Urdu originals and English translations, see D.J. Matthews, ed. and trans. *Iqbal: A Selection of Urdu Verse* (New Delhi: Heritage Publishers, 1993), pp. 138–41.

1890s, 'I have abolished it, nowadays you will never find an Isma'ili woman wearing veil'.²⁷ Further attesting to the diversity of past distinctions in present practice, it must be recalled that although Muhammad Husayn conveniently wrote women out of his 'history' of Urdu poetry, at least three other male authors each wrote literary anthologies (*tazkira*) devoted to women Urdu poets.²⁸ One of those mentioned in such works is Shah Jahan Begum (r. 1868–1901), whose pen-name was 'Shirin' and who, when not writing poetry, ruled as the third of four women to head the state of Bhopal.²⁹ From 1819 to 1926, these women staved off all male challengers to succession, even when the latter had the support of the 'Victorian' preference for male heirs formalised as policy in Governor-General Dalhousie's 'Doctrine of Lapse' (1848–1856). Shah Jahan Begum even bucked *purda* for a time, until convinced to return to the practice by her 'Rasputin', Siddiq Hasan Khan, one of the founders of the 'new' Sober Ahl-i Hadith. Her successor, Sultan Jahan Begum (r. 1901–1926), made no such concessions, even when touring her realm and mingling with the population. As well, Sultan Jahan Begum was a prime promoter of reform in her state and beyond, contributing to the creation of the 'All-India Muslim Ladies' Conference' (f. 1914) and the 'All-India Muslim Ladies' Association' (f. 1918).³⁰ In all of these actions, such rulers had the support of segments of the scholarly establishment, including such ranking, 'old' Hanafi jurists as Abbas Chiryakoti, who managed to have Siddiq Hasan expelled from Bhopal from 1857 to 1860, with the consent of Sikandar Begum (r. 1847–1868) after the latter questioned the former's religious credentials for smoking tobacco—another act already discussed as specifically detested by scholars of the 'new' Sober Path.

Although other cases can be cited regarding the continued influence of the 'Old Islam', the broad approval of *purda*, itself part of an anti-

---

²⁷ Cited in H. Papanek, 'Purdah: Separate Worlds and Symbolic Shelter', *Separate Worlds: Studies of Purdah in South Asia*, eds. H. Papanek and G. Minault (New Delhi: Chanakya Publishers, 1982).

²⁸ They appeared in 1864, 1878 and 1883. See Shamsur Rahman Faruqi, 'Constructing a Literary History, a Canon and a Theory of Poetry', *Ab-e Hayat*, ed. and trans. Pritchett w/ Faruqi, p. 40, fn. 46.

²⁹ For the history of Bhopal under these women, see Sharharyar M. Khan, *The Begums of Bhopal* (London: I.B. Tauris, 2000).

³⁰ S. Lambert-Hurley, 'British Colonial Domains in South Asia', *Encyclopedia of Women and Islamic Cultures*, eds. Saud Joseph and A. Najmabadi (Leiden: E.J. Brill, 2006), vol. 2, pp. 59–61.

customary legal initiative that extended to 'new' Intoxicated thinkers like Ahmad Khan, together with congruence between Aligarhi and Deobandi attitudes concerning the ultimately 'domestic' goals of women's education, can only lead to one conclusion: the 'New Islam', particularly its Sober Path, ruled supreme in defining gender ideals during the period of British Raj. The final piece of evidence necessary to drive home the point, in fact, comes from the attention that capitalist class women inspired by Western education were required to pay the issue of *purda*. Consider the example of Rokiya Sakhawat Husayn (d. 1932), who parlayed home-tutoring of the fashion described in Chapter Four, as well as the latitude afforded her by a Western-educated brother and husband, into a strident advocacy of women's education through the All-India Muslim Ladies' Conference and the non-sectarian 'All-India Women's Conference' (f. 1927), also establishing two girls' schools in Bengal along the way. Her long literary career, which included the publication of essays, a novel in Bengali, and a short story in English, could not pass without taking on the issue of *purda*. Of particular note is the latter short story, a satire of *purda* set in a dream world in which men are restricted to the home, and women are masters of the public domain.[31] Nazar Sajjad Hyder (d. 1967)—born to a supply agent in the British Army then posted in Kohat (NWFP), but originally from Lucknow—is another case in point. She wrote essays and novels in Urdu, contributing to various magazines. She also numbered among the women who proposed the All-India Muslim Ladies' Conference, and opened a number of girls' schools around Lucknow. Her general disposition can also be gauged from the fact that she socially boycotted bigamous men and gave up *purda* in 1923, because such 'social confinement causes...social and national waste' for no reason other than to satisfy a man's 'controlling vision'. Yet, in deference to women who did observe *purda*, Hyder is also credited with designing and popularising the form of *burqa* still worn in contemporary South Asia, one much less cumbersome than that worn by elite women in the past, thus intended to allow women whatever level of access to public life guaranteed by the 'new' Sober Path.[32]

---

[31] For the story titled 'Sultana's Dream' and a short biography of this author's life and work, see Tharu and Lalita, eds. *Women Writing in India*, vol. 1, pp. 340–52.
[32] For the article mentioned and a short biography, see Ibid., pp. 391–93.

To these two women toiling under the pressures of Victorian norms, the customary attitudes legitimated by the 'old' Path and Way, and the 'purifying' drive of the 'new', one can add such authors and activists as Rashid Jahan (d. 1952), Ismat Chugtai (d. 1992), Radia Sajjad Zahir (d. 1979), Fatima Jinnah (d. 1967) and Siddiqa Begum Sewharwi, among others who carried the struggle into the post-colonial context.[33] Although most historians attribute the abuses hurled at each of these women for venturing beyond 'normative' Islamic ideals, when the dominant paradigm is cast aside, the dominance of the 'New Islam' in the 'Inner' domain—particularly the 'new' Sober Path—must actually be accredited with thrusting the twin stigmas of 'ornamentation' or 'prostitution' on women seeking public roles.[34] The recognition that the 'New Islam' is at issue, rather than some ahistorical and essentialising 'norm', is obviously of great significance to discussions of gender. However, its import also extends beyond gender because the 'New Islam' includes particular attitudes towards definitions of community in general.

I.ii. *Community*

Notions of community in the 'Great Mughal' context encompassed a vast array of often intersecting options. Even for paragons of the 'old' Sober Path, like Awrangzib, the primacy of the '*umma*', or universal Muslim community, was legitimately mediated by sect, gender, ethnicity, class, polity and geographic locale. In general, the same can be said for the elite and capitalist class Muslims under British Raj. In Ahmad Khan's *Musafiran-i Landan*, the author identifies a variety of 'communities' based on various social criteria. 'India' (*'Hind'/'tamam Hindustan'*) is equated with 'Europe', both made up of many 'communities', or '*qawms*', for whom these 'continental' spaces are their 'homeland', or '*watan*'.[35] Among the groups that Ahmad Khan identifies as '*qawms*', such supra-local groupings as 'Europeans', 'Arabs' or 'Indians' ('Hindus'/'Hindustanis') are included. There are also religious *qawms*, the two largest of 'India' being the 'Muslim Indians (*Hindu Musalmans*) and our compatriot (*ham watan*) Hindu brothers'.[36]

---

[33] Ibid., vol. 2, pp. 117–21, 126–37, 144–53, 197–204.
[34] Jalal, *Self and Sovereignty*, pp. 69–72.
[35] Sayyid Ahmad Khan, *Musafiran-i Landan* (Lahore: Majlis-i Taraqqi-i Adab, 1961), pp. 183–90.
[36] Ibid., p. 160.

Sectarian/tribal *qawm*s like the Memons of Gujarat are noted as well. Ethno-linguistic groups are also referred to as *qawm*s, including the English, French, Egyptians, Somalis and Bengalis. And finally, capping all of the intersecting ethno-linguistic, religious and sectarian *qawm*s and geographic *watan*s, Ahmad Khan acknowledges membership in the '*umma*', or a universal Muslim community.

That Ahmad Khan was not alone in viewing his world through such multiple lenses is confirmed by a variety of contemporaneous and latter-day sources. Hali reflected the same ethos of *umma*, *qawm* and *watan* in such poems as *Hubb-i Watan* (1874), which implored 'love of the homeland', i.e. 'India', irrespective of religious community, while his epic *Musaddas-i Madd-o Jazr-i Islam* (1879) focused on the state of the *umma* and his 'Muslim Indian' *qawm*.[37] In the early 20th century, Iqbal followed suit with such works as *Tarana-i Hindi*, first published in 1904, declaring, 'We are Indian (*Hindi*); our homeland (*watan*) is India', while in the same period adding his *Tarana-i Milli*, appealing for unity on the level of *umma*.[38] When noting terminology and mapping intersections, in fact, there is very little to differentiate between the period of British Raj and those that preceded it, not merely in South Asia, but elsewhere in the Muslim World. However, notions of community begin to provide clues to change in the Islam of the 'Inner' domain over time—again highlighting the inordinate influence of the 'new' Sober Path—when a closer examination of the perceived state and hierarchical relationship drawn between each level of community is engaged.

Whether speaking of Ahmad Khan, Hali, Iqbal and other 'new' Intoxicated thinkers, turning to the works of any number on the 'new' Sober Path, or recalling the writing of 'Old Islam' represented in the works of such poets as Asad Allah Khan Ghalib, there is no escaping the sense that members of the Muslim Indian *qawm* felt that their communities, including the *umma*, were in decline. Writing on Delhi in particular, in the wake of the 1857 Uprising, Ghalib, himself a pauper at the time, lamented in one of his letters:

---

[37] There are various published versions of these works. '*Hubb-i Watan*' can be found in Altaf Husayn Hali, *Jawahar-i Hali* (Lahore: Karavan Adab, 1989), p. 204. Two original Urdu editions (1879/1886) of the *Musaddas* have recently been published in their original Urdu with an English translation as C. Shackle and J. Majeed, ed. and trans. *Hali's Musaddas* (Delhi: Oxford University Press, 1997).

[38] Muhammad Iqbal, '*Tarana-i Hindi*' and '*Tarana-i Milli*', *Bang-i Dara* (Lahore: Jahangir Book Depot, n.d.), pp. 57, 122.

> Delhi is now a military base. The only Muslims left in the city are either common labourers or else menial servants employed by [British] government officials. All the rest are Hindus. The male children of the deposed Bahadur Shah who have escaped execution receive pensions of a measly five rupees a month. As for the Muslim women of the city, the older ones have been reduced to pimping and the younger ones to prostitution. Count the deaths of the noblemen of the Muslim community… In short, the [Mughal] fort, [the states of] Jhajjar, Bahadur Garh and Faruq Nagar, all these princedoms, yielding revenues to the tune of some three million rupees, are all wiped out. How can you find accomplished people anymore? What I wrote to you before about the dearth of competent physicians is absolutely true. You may also take as the unvarnished truth what I mentioned about the paucity of the pious and saintly.[39]

Evidently, the connection between political, economic and intellectual decline, as already illustrated in the previous chapters' discussions of the motivations leading so many to begin articulating 'new' Paths and Ways as early as the 18th century, was not lost on men like Ghalib. As discussed in Chapter Three, for 'new' Sober thinkers the source of decline was pointedly argued to be the result of a lack of unity on the level of *qawm* and *umma* generated by the vast variety of Reasoned and Intuited doctrine included in the 'Old Islam', and the solution posited was to declare all but their own approach to scripture *bida'* (innovation) and *shirk* (polytheism). Naturally, followers of the 'new' Intoxicated Way did not share this approach to scripture, but so far as lack of unity is considered problematic, even the 'new' Intoxicated perspective of community in the period of British Raj, reflects little more than the influence of the 'new' Sober Path. For example, in his *Shikwa* and *Jawab-i Shikwa*, published in 1912, Iqbal echoes Hali's *Musaddas-i Madd-o Jazr-i Islam*, which in turn rehashes Shah Wali Allah's outlook, portraying the *umma* and his particular *qawm* as fallen and unconscious, the antithesis of the world of *Rashidun* Caliphs, Shi'i Imams and such 'true Muslims' as al-Ghazali. Iqbal also echoes Hali, who ventures little further than Wali Allah, in calling for the abandonment of 'India's garish idols' and 'Christian' lifestyles, to 'return' to the 'example of the Chosen Messenger' as a means of accommodating the 'new age'.[40] Simultaneously illustrating the lived pre-eminence of

---

[39] Mirza Asad Allah Khan Ghalib, *Urdu Letters of Asadu'llah Khan Ghalib*, trans. Daud Rahbar (Albany: State University of New York Press, 1987), pp. 27–28.
[40] See Muhammad Iqbal, '*Shikwa*' and '*Jawab-i Shikwa*', *Bang-i Dara*, pp. 126–32, 154–61.

ethnic *qawm*s versus the Sober ideal of placing religious communities above all, no one shirks the task of lessening ethnic divides. As Iqbal put it in *Khidr-i Rah* (1922), 'If race takes precedence over the religion of Muslims, you have flown from the world like the dust of the highway'.[41] And finally, all of the above intellectuals make no attempt to incorporate the antinomianism and latitudinarianism of the past into their solutions for the present and future. Hindus, Christians and Muslims are self-evidently distinct communities and each has their own solutions to the problems all may face.

The individual Muslim's responsibility to find solutions to the problems of their communities, particularly the *umma* and Muslim Indian *qawm*, is another indication of the influence of the 'new' Sober Path. Ahmad Khan's whole life and works as a '*nechari*' and promoter of Western education, as much as Deoband and company's drive to propagate a 'purified' Islam, is predicated on the idea of the individual Muslim as an active participant in shaping the destiny of his or her community. Thus, in her consideration of the relationship Iqbal drew between the individual and community—one whose essence is an extension of all the above thinkers' activism—Jalal correctly concludes that by '[p]utting a premium on individual self-realisation as a means to reaching God, Iqbal departed from the more esoteric aspects of Islamic mystical tradition by stressing the importance of associating with others in collective social action'.[42] What Jalal and others fail to adequately consider in presenting this shift as primarily a response to 'inglorious [Muslim] passivity under colonial subjugation', is that collective social action is not a departure from schools of 'mystical tradition' whose metaphysics revolved about transcendentalism, which has always sought to balance the esoteric and exoteric.[43] That Iqbal was particularly focused on Wali Allah's metaphysics only confirms the import of this transcendentalism, itself a mirror image of the Sober Path. That it is a reflection of the 'new' Sober Path in particular, however, is confirmed by its connection with calls for *ijtihad* (independent reasoning) as a means to addressing the problems of the 'new age'.

In previous chapters, it has been repeatedly illustrated that 'new' Sober thinkers—from Wali Allah and 'Abd al-Wahhab to late schools

---

[41] Muhammad Iqbal, *Khidr-i Rah*, *Iqbal: A Selection of Urdu Verse*, pp. 66–70.
[42] Jalal, *Self and Sovereignty*, p. 177.
[43] Ibid., p. 166.

like the Ahl-i Hadith and Jama'at-i Islami—employ the juristic tool of *ijtihad* (independent reasoning) as a means to legitimate the theological, mystical and, most particularly, the legal changes they seek. The influence of such thinkers and schools on 'new' Intoxicated thinkers, from Ahmad Khan to Fazlur Rahman, has also been shown in accounting for their own dependence on *ijtihad*. Thus, the influence of the 'new' Sober Path, directly or indirectly, can also be gauged in the more widespread ethos of change within an 'Islamic frame' that permeates the era of British Raj, at least in so far as it provides doctrinal legitimisation for new avenues of thought. Take, for example, Muhammad Husayn Azad's *Ab-i Hayat*, which not only charts the history of Urdu poetry in a manner reflecting European methods, but further advocates the adoption of post-Enlightenment European forms of history and poetics. Francis Pritchett and Shamsur Rahman Faruqi, among others steeped in a dominant paradigm that views doctrinal Islam as static and exclusivistic, describe such developments as 'a triumph of British techniques of management and control in India', leading to 'an inferiority complex' that gave Muhammad Husayn and 'the Urdu literary community' the gumption to 'write off most of its heritage as harmful, or false, or both'.[44] Yet, the problem with this view is revealed in the correspondence between Muhammad Husayn and Ahmad Khan, which includes hints of the manner in which such far-reaching change was legitimated, although none of the above historians take this into account. Ahmad Khan encouraged Muhammad Husayn to bring writing 'even closer to nature', arguing that the 'extent to which a work comes closer to nature is the extent to which it gives pleasure'.[45] The point is important for it calls into question the commonly held assumption that 'British techniques of management and control' alone led Muhammad Husayn to revisions in keeping with the 'new kinds' of history and poetics so far 'shut up in the storage trunks of English'.[46] As the

---

[44] The 'heritage' to which such authors refer is predicated on the idea widely held among 'Islamic' thinkers that poetry was 'timeless'—a perspective rooted in the vision of the Qur'an's 'eternality'. See Faruqi, 'Constructing a Literary History, a Canon and a Theory of Poetry', pp. 21–31.

[45] Aslam Faruqi, *Muhammad Husayn Azad* (Karachi: Anjuman Taraqqi-i Adab, 1965), vol. 1, 279–82. Cited in Francis Pritchett, 'Everybody Knows This Much...', *Ab-e Hayat*, p. 4.

[46] Muhammad Husayn Azad, *Nazm-i Azad*, ed. Tabassum Kashmiri (Lahore: Maktaba Jami'a, 1987), p. 46. Cited in Ibid., p. 4.

last chapter's discussion of Ahmad Khan suggests, this thinker's ideas are as strongly shaped by his education in the 'new' Sober Path, which independently challenged past authority by means of the principle of *ijtihad*. In considering the inspirational realm acting on authors like Muhammad Husayn, therefore, one must give stock to the fact that the 'Islamic' spirit of the age, from its peripheral beginnings in the works of the Wali Allahis, Khwaja Mir Dard and others, through to the central ideals of the Ahl-i Hadith and Ahmad Khan, was *ijtihad*. It has to be considered that it is *taqlid*, or the 'imitation' of past precedent, against which Muhammad Husayn is primarily arguing when he derides 'fixed things' and laments being 'ensnared in the toils of a few trifling ideas'.[47] The relationship between Muhammad Husayn's vision and that of European thought is dialectical in the manner of movements outlined in the pre-colonial context, even if one acknowledges the late 'power' of European thought and the 'psychological impediments' constricting Islamic 'knowledge'. It is not merely the adoption, but the doctrinally legitimised espousal of the European 'hall of sciences and arts'.[48] Standing on its own, this brief discussion hardly cements the point, but taken in the context of this book's other considerations, which include a historically conscious approach to the Qur'an as early as Wali Allah's writing and as far away as West Africa, there certainly appears to be room for further consideration of such questions, particularly given that all of this was engaged in the interests of communities also defined by the 'new' Sober Path, and not solitary individuals 'concerned to have the strength to cope with the challenge of Europe'.

Read together, notions of community, the hierarchies and relationships drawn between *umma*, *qawm*, *watan* and non-Muslim communities, encouragement of individual action in the interests of community, as well as the drive to revise these communities' historical, literary and other intellectual approaches in the interests of positive change, simply cannot be read as mere extensions of British initiatives and exigencies. When there exist 'Islamic' doctrines legitimising the same, and it has already been shown through various avenues that these doctrines, particularly as encompassed by the 'new' Sober Path, were being articulated throughout the 18th century and had risen to prominence

---

[47] Muhammad Husayn Azad, *Ab-i Hayat*, pp. 77–79; *Ab-e Hayat*, ed. and trans. Pritchett w/ Faruqi, pp. 103–05.
[48] Azad, *Ab-i Hayat*, p. 77; *Ab-e Hayat*, p. 103.

by the mid-19th century, duel influences must be considered. In fact, the discussion of *ijtihad* should also have illustrated that even within the 'Islamic frame', more than one form of influence must be considered. On the 'new' Sober Path, *ijtihad* was employed to narrow the field of vision provided by the exercise of Reason and Intuition, even in relation to the 'Old Islam', let alone the 'new' Intoxicated Way. But, when speaking of the 'Old Islam' and the 'new' Intoxicated Way, the capacity for intellectual borrowings and adaptations, particularly concerning non-scriptural knowledge gained through the study of European thought and institutions, must be taken into account, rather than deferring to the idea that Islamic doctrine renders Muslims incapable of such movement. With regard to the notion of religious community, however, it is most clear that the overwhelming influence of the 'new' Sober Path had the effect of instilling forms of rigidity that were not present in early times, even when considering such Sober individuals as Awrangzib. This rigidity and, therefore, a last example of the influence of the 'new' Sober Path that becomes evident through a discussion of community, is evinced by the forms of sectarianism rampant during the era of British Raj.

As early as 1858, at the tail end of the Uprising, Ghalib despaired that 'if scattered, separated friends are ever to be reunited, it won't be before Judgement Day. And what will be the point of a reunion even then if the Sunnis congregate in one place and the Shi'as, segregated from them, in another...'.[49] And who did Ghalib blame for this? The answer is stated in another letter that rebuts the charges of a 'new' Sober critic who rejected Ibn al-'Arabi's docrine of *wahdat al-wujud* and admonished the poet for his Shi'ism and like of alcohol. Ghalib curtly responded:

> This is how we're given to drink. To earn the title of *mawlawi* by instructing the Hindu grocers of Dariba and their sons, dipping into questions of menstruation and the condition of women after parturition, is one thing. And implanting in the heart the truth of the doctrine of the Unity of Being [*wahdat al-wujud*] is another...Now I, for my part, am a true believer in the Divine Unity (*muwahhid*).[50]

---

[49] Ghalib, *Urdu Letters*, p. 114.
[50] Ibid., pp. 34–35.

The writings of 'new' Intoxicated thinkers like Hali and Iqbal continue in a similar vein, replete with cautions against sectarianism as a source of decline. In other words, the tone these authors take is that sectarianism has progressively scaled new heights of discord; Hali, in particular, lays the blame squarely on the shoulders of 'new' Sober thinkers. In his *Musaddas-i Madd-o Jazr-i Islam*, Hali's most stinging attacks on the 'new' Sober Path's approach to the 'example of the Chosen Messenger', include labelling such thinkers 'bigots' (*ta'asib*), whose only intellectual strategy is to 'Think of everything in the opposite way to your opponent. Think of whatever he calls night as day'.[51] That Hali was primarily speaking of advocates of Deoband and company, is reflected in such lines as, they 'make speeches through which hate may be enflamed'; they 'brand their Muslim brother infidels'; they over-stress 'external commandments'; and, 'The whole basis of their practice lies in *fatawa*/Their every opinion an excellent substitute for the Qur'an'.[52] The result is that it has become 'impossible to find 10 Muslims who will be happy to see one another'.[53] That little had changed with the turn of the 20th century is confirmed by Iqbal's warning, 'You, caught up in Abu Bakr and 'Ali, become aware!'[54]

Unfortunately, there is no need to doubt Ghalib's, Hali's or Iqbal's assessments. One of Wali Allah's best-circulated works declared Shi'as 'apostates', and libraries can be filled with the anti-Shi'a writings of Deobandi and Ahl-i Hadith authors. More telling yet was the example of Shah Muhammad Isma'il's *Taqwiyat al-Iman*, read in Chapter Three. Here, not only non-Sunnis, but fellow Sunni theologians, mystics and legists who did not tread the author's 'new' Sober Path, were declared 'infidels' (*kafir*s). It is no wonder then that, in the era of British Raj, the Ahl-i Sunnat declared Deobandis and Ahl-i Hadith thinkers apostates, the latter declared the former the same, all declared Ahmad Khan and other Aligarhis apostates, and even Ahmad Khan chimed in to declare the Ahmadiyya beyond Islam, which responded in kind. Furthermore, later groups and individuals, inspired by the doctrinal approaches of

---

[51] Although the versions of this poem read are taken from Shackle and Majeed's edition, verses mentioned are repeated in both versions consulted, so only verse numbers are cited when reference to the *Musaddas* is made. See verse 201.
[52] Ibid., verses 187–95.
[53] Ibid., verse 210.
[54] Muhammad Iqbal, *Khidr-i Rah*, Iqbal: A Selection of Urdu Verse, pp. 66–70.

'new' Sober schools, did not shy away from this intolerance, to the point that in Urdu alone, the number of tracts making such charges is beyond collation.[55] The most important distinction between earlier polemics and this barrage, pin-pointing 'new' Sober inspiration, is not merely the participation of the prominent schools representing this doctrinal bent, but the fact that the concept of 'heresy' is virtually absent. All opponents are declared apostates and infidels. This does not mean that alliances could not be forged across sectarian and inter-faith divides, but recalling that the doctrine of *jihad* includes various provisions dependent on classification as 'People of the Book,' polytheists, heretics and apostates, the essentialisation of apostasy, no doubt, legitimated sectarian and inter-faith violence on a whole new level as well.

The irony of the sectarianism rife in the 'new' Sober Path is that it began with thinkers like Wali Allah seeking 'reconciliation' and 'agreement'. Such ironies were also not lost on Hali. Thus, using both the Qur'an and *hadith* to bolster his point, Hali offered an accommodative alternative that reflected the longstanding ethos of the 'old' Sober Path, as well as the 'new' Intoxicated Way under construction in his day, stating:

> Let those who so please turn the Prophet into God.
> Let them exalt the Imams above the Prophet in rank.
> Let them make offerings day and night at the shrines.
> Let them keep going to offer their prayers to the martyrs.
> Not the slightest injury will result to the belief in God's oneness.
> Their Islam will not be spoiled nor will their faith leave them.[56]

Clearly, Hali aimed to promote a united *umma, qawm* and *watan*, but one that neither sought nor required singularity in doctrine, practice or extra-communitarian affiliations. The fact that he felt the need to point this out as early as the 1870s, however, confirms that notions of community in the period of British Raj reflect the growing hegemony of the 'new' Sober Path in the 'Inner' domain of South Asia's elite and capitalist class Muslims.

---

[55] A large sample of such works held in the India Office Library and the British Library, in Urdu and other vernaculars, has been proscribed by the government of India. For the catalogue, see Graham Shaw and M. Lloyd, eds. *Publications Proscribed by the Government of India* (London: British Library, 1985).

[56] Hali, *Musaddas*, verse 197.

II. *The 'Outer' Domain:* Umma, Qawm *and Nation*

II.i. *From Shariʿa to Caliphate and Sultanate to Separate Electorates: 1858–1909*

From about the lifetime of al-Ghazali to the extinction of the Mughal state and its 'successors' in 1858, Muslim statecraft was guided by the political philosophy of Caliphate and Sultanate. In other words, the establishment of British Raj was not merely the final nail in the coffin of Muslim political power, its structural weight and intellectual orientation crushed the very foundations of 'Islamic' statehood. How, then, were the pieces picked up? Recalling that what remained of Islamic thought on the subject of state was tinted by a 'New Islam' that placed a premium on notions of *umma* and *qawm*, it is not surprising that one of the first steps taken towards reconstituting legitimacy under British Raj was how membership in the *umma*, previously symbolised by the Mughal Sultan's adoption of Caliphal heirs, could be acknowledged in a political environment defined by colonialism. The second was whether the concept of a Muslim Indian *qawm*, forged by Mughal expansion, but granted nominal authority by latter-day, largely independent *nawab*s and *nizam*s, would play any further political role. The reaction of Muslim intellectuals to these issues is crucial to any discussion of the later adoption of nationalism within the framework of the 'New Islam', and is addressed here with an eye to noting how the 'New Islam' shaped the earliest response.

II.i.a. *Umma and Caliphate*

After East India Company forces entered Delhi in 1803, thus rendering any pretence of Mughal authority a sham, many mosques around South Asia began dropping the incumbent Mughal Sultan's name from the *khutba*—inclusion depending on the exercise of the functions vested in Caliphal titles and powers. Instead, as Ahmad Khan recalls in one of his later essays, a statement to the following effect was offered: 'O God, help the Muslim with a just ruler, help them to be virtuous and obedient to thyself, and to follow the example of the Prophet, the Sayyid of the Universe'.[57] Nevertheless, the tradition of Caliphate having being

---

[57] A series of Ahmad Khan's articles from the *Aligarh Institute Gazette* of the late 1890s, and two articles from *Tahdhib al-Akhlaq* in the 1880s, address the issue of

carried forward by the Mughals to the extent that even 'new' Sober thinkers like Wali Allah included the institution as part of his revised political philosophy, implied that the absence of a Caliph was almost as problematic as the lack of a sultan or his *nawab*s and *nizam*s. The problem, however, was not merely the fact that Muslim political power was in serious decline across the world, but that 'new' Sober thinkers like Wali Allah, who sought the reconstitution of the institution, made it plain that the holder of the title must hail from the Quraysh tribe of Muhammad, if 'universal' authority were claimed. This disqualified the 'Turkic' Ottoman Sultans, the last remaining Muslim state of any consequence in the 19th century. Thus, although Muhammad Isma'il had prophesied that *'Shah Gharbi'* ('The Western King') would come to the aid of South Asian Muslims in their *jihad* against the British in the 1820s, Shah Muhammad Ishaq (d. 1846)—a relative and teacher at the Madrasa-i Rahimiyya in Delhi—had left his post to secure Ottoman aid in the 1840s, and the rhetoric of *Shah Gharbi* also played a part in the 1857 Uprising, there is very little suggestion that the Ottomans were acknowledged as rightful Caliphs by 'new' Sober stalwarts.[58] As the title 'Shah' implies, these initiatives were not acknowledgements of an *'ajami* Sultan's claims to universal Caliphate, but appeals for aid from the most powerful Muslim 'king' still remaining; that, too, a misplaced hope, given that this period was a highpoint in Anglo-Ottoman relations.

Caliphate and were compiled in 1916, at the height of pro-Caliphate agitation, by Qadi Shiraj al-Din Ahmad. The work is published as Sayyid Ahmad Khan, *Haqiqat-i Khilafat/The Truth about the Khilafat* (Lahore: Ripon Press, 1916). The present article is originally from the *Tahdhib al-Akhlaq*, and is found in the latter compilation on pp. 18–21.

[58] In all the South Asian versions of this 'prophecy', the author is said to be the Persian poet, Ni'mat Allah Wali (d. 1430). Ni'mat Allah did, in fact, compose a *divan* bemoaning the state of the world and prophesying the coming of the *mahdi*, but the events of the South Asian versions—including that of Shah Muhammad Isma'il in his *Al-Araba'in fi Ahwal al-Mahdiyin*—bear little resemblance to Ni'mat Allah's work. By the 1857 Uprising, it is significant to note that Muhammad Isma'il's is one of many versions in circulation, his even having appeared in print by 1851. For a brief discussion of the above background, two versions of the poem circulating in 1857 and various official British correspondence on the significance of these poems and the identity of '*Shah Gharbi*', see Salim al-Din Quraishi, ed. *Cry for Freedom: Proclamations of Muslim Revolutionaries of 1857* (Lahore: Sang-i Meel, 1997), pp. xvi–xvii, 86–108. Also, there is mention of the prophecy in one of the proclamations issued by the army at Delhi in 1857. See Ibid., pp. 2, 28. For Muhammad Ishaq's mission, see Shafi Ali Khan, 'The Nationalist 'Ulama's Interpretation of Shah Wali Allah's Thought and Movement: The Post-Jihad Period', *Journal of the Pakistan Historical Society* 38:1 (1990), 38–39.

If the rhetoric of Caliphate was not necessary to legitimate anti-colonial activities, it was also not vital to pro-colonial initiatives, even when involving the Ottomans. Consider this example from the Crimean War (1854–56), in which the Ottomans and British squared off against the Russians. By this time, vernacular papers (however limited their circulation) and literature began exhibiting a vociferously pro-Ottoman stance, large public rallies were held, relief funds were collected, and volunteers (medical and military) were dispatched from urban centres across South Asia to the Russo-Ottoman front, without any overtly anti-colonial intent.[59] Rather, a discussion between a British officer and a group of South Muslims during the Crimean War is most illustrative of how Anglo-Ottoman and Anglo-Indian relations were legitimated. Published in the *London Times*, this letter to the editor relays that its author was approached by a group of Muslim men smoking on a veranda in an unnamed South Asian city, and asked to relate how the war in the Crimea was proceeding. The British officer informed them that proceedings were on course, and pointed out 'the obligation they were under to our country [i.e. England] for having aided the head of the Muslim faith in the hour of peril'.[60] To his surprise, the Muslims were not particularly grateful, stating that 'England engaged in the war because she was summoned by the Sultan to his standard as one of his vassals'.[61] The British author was certainly not pleased to hear this rationalisation, but he should have been. He missed the point that by conceiving of the British as the 'vassals' of Ottoman Sultans, according to Islamic political philosophy, British possessions became *dar al-Islam* and the Muslims of South Asia could view the British as their legitimate rulers, while also salvaging some pride.

After the failure of the 1857 Uprising, the drive to endow the British with greater legitimacy only grew, employing every method at hand. 'New' Sober thinkers responded to Britain's assumption of 'direct rule' in 1858, with accepting *fatawa* based on similar criterion as that outlined by Shah 'Abd al-'Aziz in 1803, applying the legal provisions

---

[59] See N.M. Qureishi, *Pan-Islam in British Indian Politics: A Study of the Khilafat Movement* (Leiden: E.J. Brill, 1999): Azmi Ozcan, *Pan-Islamism, Indian Muslims, the Ottomans and British* (Leiden: E.J. Brill, 1997); and Gail Minault, *The Khilafat Movement: Religious Symbolism and Political Mobilization in India* (New York: Columbia University Press, 1982). For consideration in a broader context than South Asia, see Jacob Landau, *The Politics of Pan-Islam* (Oxford: Clarendon Press, 1994).
[60] *London Times* (19 September 1876), p. 9.
[61] Ibid., p. 9.

for personal law afforded to *dhimmis* under Muslim rule to Muslims under British ('Christian') rule. Deobandis, in fact, echoed 'Abd al-'Aziz exactly. For example, Rashid Ahmad's *fatawa* retained the idea that British India is '*dar al-harb*', but *jihad* is not necessary as 'personal law' is guaranteed, while education in English, employment by Christians and the use of colonial institutions is permitted.[62] Similarly, the Ahl-i Hadith scholar, Nazir Husayn, issued *fatawa* to the effect that *jihad* was '*haram*' (forbidden).[63] The Ahl-i Sunnat leader, Ahmad Rida, went a step further, arguing that as 'personal law' was upheld, British India was '*dar al-Islam*'.[64]

Meanwhile, Ahmad Khan and other Aligarhis trod an equally accepting, but alternative path. In *Sarkashi-i Zila Bijnor*, published in 1858, Ahmad Khan provides the first detailed account of political unrest in the town to which he was posted as *sadr-amin* during that time, emphasising the 'loyalism' of Muslims such as himself, while *Asbab-i Baghawat-i Hind*, presented to the colonial government in 1859, deflects blame for the Uprising from Muslims to lay it squarely on the shoulders of the East India Company.[65] Had the East India Company followed 'the custom of the Muslims in countries that they subjected to their rule', Ahmad Khan contends, British officers would have been aware of grievances and been able to avert the need for revolt.[66] By their haughtiness and distance, they allowed grievances to fester. To avoid future disturbance, therefore, colonial laws must be adapted to the 'thought and...custom'

---

[62] Rashid Ahmad Gangohi, *Fatawa-i Rashidiyya* (Karachi: Saeed Company, 1967), vol. 1, pp. 76, 81, 90; vol. 3, p. 20.

[63] Nazir Husayn, *Fatawa-i Naziriyya*, 4 vols. (Delhi: Printing Works, 1915), vol. 4, p. 472.

[64] See Ahmad Rida Khan, *Do Ahamm Fatwe* (Lahore: Maktaba Rizwiyya, 1977).

[65] See Sayyid Ahmad Khan, *Sarkashi-i Zila Bijnor* (Karachi: Salman Akademi, 1962); *Asbab-i Baghawat-i Hind* (Delhi: Kutub Khana-i Anjuman-i Taraqqi, 1971). A third work in this vein appeared in 1861, titled the 'An Account of the Loyal Mohamedans [sic] of India'. This was a series of three pamphlets, the first and second providing accounts of Muslims who had been killed by the 'rebels' or aided the British, the second and third using the Qur'an, *hadith* and *fiqh* to counter the general perceptions which he feared the British and Muslims held of each other. See Sayyid Ahmad Khan, 'An Account of the Loyal Mohamedans of India', in *Political Profile of Sir Syed Ahmad Khan: A Documentary Record*, ed. Hafeez Malik (Islamabad: Islamic University, 1982), pp. 193–268. Also, Siddiq Hasan Khan of the Ahl-i Hadith wrote a work similar to those of Sayyid Ahmad Khan arguing for Muslim 'loyalty', titled *Tarjuman-i Wahhabiyya* (Lahore: n.p., 1895).

[66] Ahmad Khan, 'An Account of the Loyal Mohamedans of India', p. 158.

of the ruled, for the ruled 'cannot be adapted to the laws'.[67] Despite the criticism and call for redress which Ahmad Khan directs at the British, however, he insisted that the East India Company's government did not interfere with the Muslims' religious practices, this perception being a misunderstanding blamed on the injudicious acts of certain officers, rather than Company policy.[68] This position is substantiated by reference to none other than Muhammad Isma'il. According to Ahmad Khan, the *jihad* in which Muhammad Isma'il lost his life in 1831, was directed at the Sikhs alone and its leaders explicitly excluded British-governed regions from action.[69] He does not deny calls for *jihad* against the East India Company regime in 1857, but argues that they offer no evidence of the legality of *jihad* against the British. Rather, Ahmad Khan proposes that cooperative action was and remains overwhelmingly the 'Muslim custom' of government.

All the above concerns led Ahmad Khan and his Aligarhi affiliates to found the 'British Indian Association' in 1866, convened to serve the interests of the 'North-West Provinces', Muslim and Hindu. It is noteworthy that in his first address to members, Ahmad Khan reaffirmed the legitimisation of British Raj by offering the following to his mixed British and South Asian audience:

> It was ordained by a higher power than any on earth, that the destinies of India should be placed in the hands of an enlightened nation, whose principles of government were in accordance with those of intellect, justice and reason. Yes, my friends, the great God above, He who is equally the God of the Jew, the Hindu, the Christian, and the Muslim, placed the British over the people of India.[70]

---

[67] Ibid., p. 142. Numbering among the various 'customs' that Ahmad Khan accuses the British of transgressing, one finds all the issues raised in the *fatawa* and proclamations issued against the East India Company by the *mujahidin* before and during the 1857 Uprising and discussed in other chapters. This includes the 'offensive and irritating way' in which Christian missionaries conducted themselves, as well as the close association between certain colonial officers and missionaries; the late neglect of Islamic disciplines in 'Oriental Colleges'; and land reforms that had favoured 'moneylenders' and ruined *zamindars*, particularly Muslims. Ibid., pp. 146–48.
[68] Ibid., p. 146–47.
[69] Ibid., p. 138. As discussed in Chapter Three, letters penned by the leader of this movement, Sayyid Ahmad Barelwi, as well as the activities of members in British India, suggest a rather different perspective.
[70] Sayyid Ahmad Khan, 'Speech' (Aligarh, 10 May 1866), *Aligarh Movement*, vol. 1, p. 232.

In particular, Ahmad Khan went on to explain, he was referring to the 'direct rule' of the British Government, which had removed the prime 'obstacle' between the people and Parliament, i.e. the 'merchant princes' of the East India Company.[71] He points out that what this means is that 'it is necessary that the requirements and wishes of that portion of mankind on whose behalf they [members of parliament] are to exert themselves, be made clearly known to them'.[72] For this purpose, an association with a branch in London (i.e. the British Indian Association) was organised. However, his only reference to British political philosophy is a quote from the Utilitarian philosopher and East India Company civil servant, John Stuart Mill, employed as an echo of 'Muslim custom':

> Quote: 'The rights and interests of every or of any person are only secure from being disregarded when the person interested is himself able and habitually disposed to stand up for them. The second is that the general propensity attains a greater height, and is more widely diffused, in proportion to the personal energies enlisted in promoting it'. These principles, my friends, are as applicable to the people of India as they are to those of any other nation.[73]

Thus, to his South Asian audience, Ahmad Khan offered an 'Islamic' or 'Hindu' government that promised to serve their interests, while to the British he pointed out that his organisation was sanctioned and would abide by the English 'book'. No doubt Ahmad Khan's attempts to prove Muslim 'loyalism', like the *fatawa* of 'new' Sober thinkers, had as much to do with the horrors British authorities unleashed on South Asian Muslims in the wake of the 1857 Uprising, than representing the only doctrinal perspective, but their net effect, when added to the *fatawa* of so many prominent *'ulama'*, was undoubtedly the legitimisation of British Raj in the eyes of many peers.

When the 'Outer' domain's need to legitimate or de-legitimate British rule was fulfilled by Islamic political and legal philosophy, not to mention 'Islamic' interpretations of Utilitarianism, while the 'Inner' domain's push to identify on the level of *umma* could be achieved by heralding the unity of *shari'a*, it is clear that the symbolic value of Caliphate would be on the wane throughout the 19th century. Yet, a

---

[71] Ibid., p. 232.
[72] Ibid., p. 232.
[73] Ibid., p. 232.

change of heart concerning Ottoman candidacy for universal Caliphate would also arise by the 1870s, not as a sign of 'a gradual trend towards substituting a foreign loyalty for commitment to India',[74] as some historians argue, but as a means to forward the entire structure of authority in Islam in a British Indian context.[75] An initial factor leading South Asian Muslims in this direction is the fact that interest in Ottoman affairs, already mentioned to have begun with early 19th century attempts by anti-colonial Wali Allahis to garner aid, burgeoned by the latter half of the century, even among those with no anti-colonial sentiments, as an expression of *umma* consciousness. As in the 1850s, not only were vernacular presses key, but rallies were organised and funds raised even at Deoband, the scholars at the *madrasa* encouraging their students to defer the cost of their book-prizes to a fund for Ottoman soldiers wounded in the latest round of Russo-Ottoman wars.[76] The reinvigoration of Caliphate as a symbol of the *umma*, meanwhile, was at least in part a reflection of change in Istanbul. In 1876, Sultan 'Abd al-Hamid II (r. 1876–1909) ascended the throne and, unlike his immediate predecessors—who had forwarded the Westernising reforms known as '*Tanzimat*', initiated a constitutional period and granted 'Ottoman' citizenship to all irrespective of religion and race in an effort to counter regional nationalisms—recognised the failure of 'Ottomanism' to stem local uprisings and sought to shore the state by emphasising Ottoman claims to universal Caliphate. The pivotal factor leading to broad South Asian Muslim acceptance of Ottoman claims to universal Caliphate, however, even by 'new' Sober thinkers who had previously insisted that Quraysh lineage was a prerequisite, is the fact that British relations with the Ottomans had cooled at exactly the moment South Asian Muslim attitudes towards British rule were turning to renewed resentment.

Letters to the *London Times* in the 1870s reflect the change in British attitudes by arguing against attaching British-Ottoman relations to the sentiments of British India's Muslims. As one author quipped, drawing the 1857 Uprising into the equation, 'Surely, if such ingratitude be a return for our support of the Sultan of Rum, we may rather expect favour than dislike for pursuing a contrary course!'[77] In fact,

---

[74] Landau, *The Politics of Pan-Islam*, p. 185.
[75] Minault, *The Khilafat Movement*, p. 5.
[76] S.M. Rizvi, *Tarikh-i Dar ul-'Ulum Deoband* (Delhi: Idara-i Ihtemam, 1980), p. 144.
[77] *London Times* (20 September 1876), p. 6.

such opinions, along with a decidedly anti-Ottoman rhetoric emphasising atrocities committed by Ottoman troops, were daily fare in such newspapers as the *London Times* by the 1870s. Illustrating that these were not just the random ravings of *London Times* readers, an 1875 work by James Long—missionary, linguist and official 'reporter' on the indigenous vernacular presses of Bengal after the 1857 Uprising—went so far as to say that the time had come for Britain to stop propping up the Muslim 'sick man' of Europe, and allow the 'Christian' Russians to take Istanbul, helping the 'despotic' Ottomans to go the way of the Mughals.[78] He argued that this served British interests by allowing Russia to expand towards the Mediterranean, rather than through Central Asia towards South Asia. Furthermore, he pointed out that since Britain had recently acquired the Khedive of Egypt's shares in the Suez Canal, British-Ottoman relations need not be dependent on Ottoman control of land routes towards South Asia. As for his consideration of South Asian Muslims, like others arguing against paying them heed, this author pointed out that 'sectarian bitterness' isolates the 'Indian Moslems [sic] from the Turks', as much as it does from each other, and that the majority of South Asia's population is Hindu, thus unconcerned with the Ottomans, but impressed by Russia's growing prestige.[79] And finally, he echoed others in arguing that 'Moslem [sic] pride and fanaticism' has been the greatest barrier before the 'advancement of European civilisation', and that the only remedy is to 'teach them…that the shadow of the Kaliphate [sic] is going down, as the shadow of the Great Mogul [sic] has gone down in Delhi'.[80] He adds a telling quote from a Russian general to cap his point: 'Their pride must first be humbled before the light of Christianity and civilisation can penetrate'.[81] So, British observers had fallen into two camps: one still seeing cordial relations with the Ottomans as important to British interests in South Asia, as had been the case in the 1850s, and the other arguing that British foreign policy need not concern itself with the activities mentioned above.[82] From the vantage of point of the

---

[78] James Long, *The Position of Turkey in Relation to British Interests in India*, pp. 5–12.
[79] Ibid., p. 9. Also see S. (An Indian Civil Service Officer), *Turkey and India or Our Indian Muslims* (London: East India Association, 1876), pp. 19–30.
[80] Ibid., p. 9.
[81] Ibid., p. 9.
[82] For the British view of Muslims as a homogeneously antagonistic entity by virtue of their religion, see James Long, *The Position of Turkey in Relation to British Interests*

South Asian Muslim classes concerned with such matters, that meant that the British 'vassal' was no longer standing solidly by the Ottoman Sultan's side.

The extent to which all of the above factors, but particularly renewed anti-colonial sentiment, fuelled the recognition of the Ottomans as universal Caliphs can be judged by the urgency arch loyalist Ahmad Khan and other Aligarhis devoted to debunking such claims. In a series of articles published in the 1880s and 1890s, Ahmad Khan, among others, sought to resolve the issue of *umma* and Caliphate by reminding readers that the unity of the *shari'a* was the sole institution, or ultimate symbol, of universal Muslim bonds. Of course, there was nothing novel about this, the *shari'a* ideally binding Muslims in the works of legalistic thinkers through the ages. However, the deep roots of Caliphal rhetoric required a more vigorous response. Thus, Ahmad Khan drew together 'old' and 'new' political philosophers, from Ibn Taymiyya to Wali Allah, to de-legitimate Caliphate, primarily arguing that the Ottomans were not Qurayshi Arabs, and so not qualified, while also making it clear that the juristic foundations of universal Caliphate had been challenged since the 11th century. As well, Ahmad Khan's efforts and influence did not act alone to drive home the point. Poets of Hali's popularity were echoing him in verse. In his *Musaddas-i Madd-o Jazr-i Islam*, Hali nowhere suggests that Caliphate is incumbent on the *umma*, let alone his *qawm*. Interestingly, Hali's views on the status of Caliphs in history implicitly echo those of Wali Allah's *khass, amm* and *jabir* classifications. The only Caliphs Hali associates with the *khass* are those who followed the death of Muhammad, representing an idyllic time devoid of social divisions, when the entire community was 'drunk with the intoxicating wine of truth'.[83] He names no names nor mentions any specific events, except to say that although there was dispute, 'there was no viciousness in their disputes'—a clear reference to disputes over succession, yet obviously muted to subsume Sunni-Shi'a divides among his contemporaries. The

---

in India; and A.K. Connell, *Discontent and Danger in India* (London: C. Kegan Paul, 1880). For the emphasis on a 'fanatical' element, see S. (An Indian Civil Service Officer), *Turkey and India or Our Indian Muslims* (London: W. Ridgeway, 1876). For further examples of British opinion on the so-called 'Eastern Question' in general, see T. Sinclair, *A Defence of Russia and the Christians of Turkey* (London: Chapman & Hall, 1877); M. Maccoll, *Three Years of the 'Eastern Question'* (London: Chatto & Wyndus, 1878); and G.D.C. Argyll, *The Eastern Question from the Treaty of Paris 1856 to the Treaty of Berlin 1878* (London: n.p., 1879).

[83] Hali, *Musaddas*, verse 55.

only other context in which Caliphate is mentioned is in terms of the rulers of Andalus and Baghdad, placed in an era definitively distanced from the idyllic, *khass* 'Age of the Caliphate'. Here again, it is interesting to note that the Umayyads of Damascus are not referenced, another attempt to defuse Shi'i-Sunni sensibilities. Instead, Arab rule is raised above all, the *umma* itself being described as 'the garden of the Arabs'.[84] Yet, the praise paid to the latter Caliphs is less for otherworldly 'piety' than for the 'worldly' spread of *tawhid* and *shari'a*, the 'revival' of Hellenic learning, advances in astronomy and medicine, the development of art and architecture, the promotion of economic prosperity, and so on.[85] The only point of convergence when considering these varieties of Caliph is that both sets were Arabs and that their day is done. As Hali puts it in one verse, the Umayyad Caliphs of Spain represent 'the token of the Arabs in that land'.[86] Three verses later he laments that 'the Tartar's flood washed away' Abbasid Baghdad.[87] In essence, Hali informs his reader that only the *Rashidun* of the earliest Muslim community could live up to *khass* Caliphal ideals, while even the Arab Umayyads and Abbasids represented the heads of *amm* governments ruling only portions of the *umma*, no matter their pedigree or accomplishments. Identifying the non-Arab Ottomans as Caliphs in any ideal sense is thus delegitimated, their rank reduced to that of one among many *amm* or *jabir* 'Tartar' governments claiming Caliphal authority. Thus, like Ahmad Khan, in place of the religio-political Caliphate as the symbol of *umma*, Hali offered the purely legalistic *shari'a*.

Given the immense popularity Hali enjoyed, it is significant that even he was swimming against the tide, as far as Caliphate was concerned. After the Russo-Ottoman conflict of the 1870s, the vernacular press had begun translating articles directly from Turkish and Arabic newspapers.[88] In the 1880s, the Ottomans pursued the support of South Asian Muslims by establishing an Istanbul-based Urdu journal, the *Paik-i Islam*, while the pro-Ottoman *Anjuman-i Islam*, with offices in London, British India and elsewhere, began operating in 1886. By the 1890s, despite the efforts of Ahmad Khan and Hali, the Ottoman bug had even begun to infect Aligarh's inner core. As prominent an

---

[84] Ibid., verse 104.
[85] Ibid., verses 69–85.
[86] Ibid., verse 82.
[87] Ibid., verse 85.
[88] Qureishi, *The Khilafat Movement*, pp. 40–50.

Aligarh professor as Shibli Numani (d. 1914), founder of the Nadwat al-'Ulama' (f. 1894) as a compromise between Ahmad Khan's and Deoband's religious and political ideals, was also among the number that visited Istanbul and contributed to the pro-Ottoman literature of the 1890s.[89] Such continuous activities meant that the Armenian Uprising of the 1890s was followed with concern by Urdu-speaking Muslims with access to such journals as Lahore's *Paisa Akhbar*, Delhi's *Akmal al-Akhbar* or Amritsar's *Vakil*. In addition, Ottoman military 'success' in the Greco-Ottoman War of 1897–98 was met with great enthusiasm. One vernacular newspaper declared: 'Once more on the soil of Christian Europe the sword of Islam has smitten the unbelievers and has been sheathed in victory', expressing a widespread sentiment among the literate classes.[90] Furthermore, as a report from the Lieutenant-Governor of the North West Province to the central government in 1897 attests:

> There is no doubt that there is great sympathy with Turkey, and that the prevalent feeling partakes of the nature of an Islamic revival. It is, I believe, partly due to incitements from outside India and partly spontaneous, and I think it has been growing for some time, and is fostered in Muslim schools. The Commissioner of Agra tells me that many more people than formerly have taken to wearing the Turkish Fez; and this is perhaps a straw indicating how the wind is beginning to blow.[91]

Secondary studies of pro-Ottoman activity in the period conclude that this effusive support for the Ottomans among many South Asian Muslims was at least partially informed by the perception 'that their prestige in India was dependent on the maintenance of Ottoman Turkey' and 'if that Empire ceased to exist', as a Muslim journal had feared almost a year before the war, 'the Muslims will at once fall into insignificance'.[92]

---

[89] Shibli Numani, *Safar Nama-i Rum wa Misr wa Sham* (Lahore: M. Sana Allah Khan, 1961). Another core member of the Aligarh coterie with pro-Ottoman views was Mahdi 'Ali Khan. See Muhsin al-Mulk Mahdi 'Ali Khan, *Tahdhib al-Akhlaq* (Lahore: Allah Vale ki Qaumi Dukan, 1934). It should also be recalled that the Ottoman fez had been a part of the uniform of Aligarh College since its founding for precisely 'pan-Islamic' reasons, a discussion of which is included in Graham's biography of Ahmad Khan.

[90] Cited in Qureishi, *The Khilafat Movement*, p. 44.

[91] Ibid., p. 45. For other British perspectives, see G.H. Perris, *The Eastern Crisis of 1897 and British Policy in the Near East* (London: n.p., 1897); H.W. Nevison, *Scenes in the Thirty Days War between Greece and Turkey* (London: J.M. Dent, 1898); and A.R. Colquhoun, *Russia Against India* (London: Harper & Brothers, 1900).

[92] Qureishi, *The Khilafat Movement*, pp. 34–35.

While such warnings were issuing from South Asia, however, British journalists and parliamentarians set aside debate to take a decidedly anti-Ottoman stance by the late 19th century. In a last-ditch effort to quell this rising tide, even Ahmad Khan wrote negatively of these two institutions:

> In my opinion much of the outcry raised by the Muslims was solely due to the tone of the British Press. Mr. Gladstone and the English newspapers denounced Muslims and strongly condemned the Turks. This was very irritating and painful to the Muslims in general and particularly to the Turks...Now after the Turkish victory the Muslims, as a reaction from that state of annoyance, have indulged in excessive rejoicing.[93]

That is to say, by the last decade of the 19th century, Caliphal rhetoric had acquired more meaning than in the 1870s, and objections to the Ottoman's Turkic, rather than Quraysh, lineage, were conveniently being pushed aside, even by those who had insisted on them only a few years earlier. The reason is clear. Although universal Caliphate was not yet an openly anti-colonial tool, when promoted by the only major Muslim state still on the world stage, it was recognised as an effective vehicle by which to press South Asian Muslim grievances against an 'Outer' domain defined by British Raj, while remaining within the basic framework of their 'Inner' domain's 'New Islam'.

II.i.b: Qawm *and Separate Electorates*
Although the loyalism of Ahmad Khan and Hali to British Raj separated them from a growing segment of Muslims enamoured with the adoption of Ottoman Caliphs as symbols of the *umma*, that loyalism did not sour their efforts to politicise the Muslim Indian *qawm*. The reason for this is that differences on the issue of the *umma*'s appropriate representative and convergence on the politicisation of the *qawm* were both the result of the British Raj's control over the 'Outer' domain and the 'New Islam's' definition of the 'Inner.'

From 1858 to the mid-1880s, the idea of a Muslim Indian community was expressed, among other notions of community, in various writings such as Ahmad Khan's *Musafir-i Landan* and Hali's *Musaddas-i Madd-o Jazr-i Islam*. Both works, however, illustrate that this level of community had lost its political meaning with the fall of the Mughals,

---

[93] Ahmad Khan, *Haqiqat-i Khilafat*, pp. 6–7.

representing no more than a segment of the *umma*, based on geography, and simultaneously a portion of the Indian *watan*, defined by religion. Nonetheless, in the mid-1880s, an issue would arise that immediately re-endowed the Muslim Indian *qawm* with political implications—in 1885, 72 men of the same classes as those Muslims so far considered, but from a predominantly Bengali cultural milieu, assembled in Bombay for the first session of the Indian National Congress.[94] Only two of the delegates were Muslim (3%). By the fourth Congress, the number had risen to 219 of 1,248 delegates (17.5%).[95] Early Muslim members, like the non-Muslims, were products of Western education, thus establishing that some Muslims were becoming acquainted with parliamentary systems of government and quite accepting of the basic agenda of the Indian nationalism. However, the absence of large numbers of Muslims in Congress ranks also confirms that the scholars of 'Islam', Sober and Intoxicated, as well as lay Muslim elites and capitalists, at least perceived economic and political reasons to hold back support. In a series of now-famous speeches delivered in the 1880s, Ahmad Khan best illustrates the parameters of the latter factors, particularly among Muslims of his class and locale, by declaring that 'India' is not a 'nation' in the European sense. Instead, he reminds his audience of the number of '*qawms*' one must acknowledge:

> Consider the Hindus alone. The Hindus of our province, the Bengalis of the east, and the Marattas of the Deccan, do not form one nation.[96]

---

[94] The Indian National Congress was founded in 1885 by a group of English and South Asian men seeking political reform in South Asia. Until the turn of the century, the organisation would be led by individuals who remained emphatically 'loyal' to the colonial state, but lobbied for a say in the running of affairs. These pro-British participants were called the 'Moderates' by the British. By the turn of the century, however, more strident calls for reforms, leading to early calls for self-rule when rebuffed, as well as the introduction of Hindu nationalist elements under the leadership of such men as B. Tilak (d. 1920), Socialist elements under Jawaharlal Nehru (d. 1964), and M.K. Gandhi's particular brand of political thought, changed the complexion of the party, as well as British appellations. The British dubbed this brand of participants 'Extremists'. For an introduction to the history the Indian National Congress through excerpts of the writings of its leadership, Moderate and Extremist, see Stephen Hay, ed. *Sources of Indian Tradition*, vol. 2 (New York: Columbia University Press, 1988), pp. 84–172. For a more comprehensive account, see D.A. Low, ed. *Congress and the Raj* (London: Arnold-Heinemann, 1977).

[95] Sharif al-Mujahid, ed. *Muslim League Documents* (Karachi: Quaid-i Azam Academy, 1990), p. 456.

[96] These speeches were delivered at the Muhammad Educational Conference (1886), the largest single gathering of Muslims at the time, and at the meeting of an *anjuman*

Furthermore, not all the *qawm*s of India are equal in education, temperament or demographics. The Indian National Congress, in Ahmad Khan's opinion, was the work of the more 'advanced' Bengali Hindus, and represented only their interests. For non-Bengalis, therefore, the agenda of Congress was argued to be less than beneficial. For Ahmad Khan, in particular, the point being made was that any electoral system implied the certainty of being entirely shut out of political office, 'Muslim India' out-voted by Hindus 4:1 on an 'All-India' level—a realisation obviously following from British censuses, and further fuelled by the prospect of a 'Hindu' majority government in a local environment already rife with Hindu communal activity, including 'cow protection', *shuddhi* ('re-conversion' of Muslims to Hinduism), and Hindi advocacy. Thus, Ahmad Khan concluded that for all but Bengali Hindus, pursuing education and cooperation with the British government was the best course of action. The alternative, should the British be dislodged from power, is that the leading two *qawm*s—Hindu and Muslim—would descend upon each other, while the French or Germans or Russians would replace the British without any means of defence available to the warring *qawm*s of South Asia.[97]

These speeches caused a great stir, initiating a flurry of polemics between Aligarhis and Congress leadership, particularly between Ahmad Khan and the leading Muslim member in that era, Badr al-Din Tyabji (d. 1909), a Bombay lawyer of the Gujarati Bohra community. In an open letter first published in the English language *Pioneer* (1888), Tyabji argued that the Indian National Congress only intended to forward demands in the 'general public interest' and on which there was 'absolute or partial unanimity on the part of Hindus and Muslims'.[98] Ahmad Khan's ultimate retort was the formation of the 'United Indian Patriotic Association' in 1888. Although Ahmad Khan had previously advocated provincial politics through the British Indian Association, the Patriotic Association's objectives included publishing information for the parliament and people of Britain to show that all of 'Muslim India'

---

in Meerut (1888). English translations were first published in 1888, in Sayyid Ahmad Khan, *The Present State of Indian Politics: Speeches and Letters*, ed. Theodore Beck (Lahore: Sang-i Meel, 1982), pp. 2–23, 54–74.

[97] Ibid., p. 61.
[98] *Pioneer* (April 1888) in *Present State of Indian Politics*, pp. 78–86. For more on Tyabji, see L. Futehally, *Badruddin Tyabji* (New Delhi: National Book Trust, 1994).

and the other *qawm*s of India were not represented by the Congress agenda, without bar of race or creed.[99] Nevertheless, of the 102 founding members named, 86 were Muslim. Of these, the descendents of the former Nawabs of Oudh and the incumbent Nizam of Hyderabad accounted for 4 members, and officials ranking as *wazir*s another 6. The vast majority, accounting for all Hindu and 60 Muslims, were petty landlords from the North-West Provinces. The remainder, numbering 16 individuals, comprised scholars, journalists and members of the colonial bureaucracy. In other words, the agenda of the Patriotic Association was not only forwarded by the Urdu-speaking Muslim elite and 'capitalists' of the 'minority' provinces, this was the only *qawm* to which it appealed, despite its 'Indian' agenda. That is not to say that the same sort of agenda, driven by the same or alternative kinds of economic and political concerns, had not spawned parallel movements in 'majority' provinces. One organisation with similar anxieties was the Central Muslim Association (f. 1883) in Bengal. Adding to the complexity, there were others who argued that such fears were altogether unfounded, such as Punjab's *Anjuman-i Islami* (f. 1869), which even had close ties with Ahmad Khan.[100] In fact, the import of the Patriotic Association and its anti-Congress stance is that there was no consensus among Muslims, let alone among 'Indians', and that such movements were ultimately predicated on locally perceived class interests, rather than religious affiliations or divides.

Yet, such organisations did re-enliven the idea of a politicised 'Muslim Indian' *qawm* and played a role in equipping Muslims more generally to participate in the politics of British Raj on that level. The strategy adopted by core members of the Patriotic Association was not restricted to the types of publications mentioned above, but also involved a pro-active campaign to 'educate' all segments of the population in its ideology. A circular was issued to numerous Muslim *anjuman*s, professional, literary and scholarly, highlighting the Association's arguments against Congress, and winning the affiliation of 17 Muslim *anjuman*s in Lahore, Karachi, Bombay, Bangalore, Madras, Calcutta, Dacca, Patna, Lucknow and Delhi, and 36 in rural towns from Punjab

---

[99] The official 'Rules and Objectives', as well as lists of founding members, donors, and affiliated *anjuman*s, etc., noted below, can be found in, *Present State of Indian Politics*, pp. 227–34.
[100] Jalal, *Self and Sovereignty*, pp. 88–89.

to Bengal.[101] Various schools of Sober thought were also contacted and elements of Ahl-i Hadith and Madrasa-i Farangi Mahal, as well as the scholarly segment later associated with the Ahl-i Sunnat, lent their support to the Patriotic Association. Public meetings chaired by scholars, regardless of school or sect, were held in various cities and were attended by thousands, significant mosques and Sufi shrines often providing the venue.[102] From 102 founding members, therefore, those sharing the Patriotic Association's ideals grew, more thoroughly including the same Urdu-speaking Muslim classes, while expanding its support among urban segments of the Muslim population in areas to the East and South. This proved sufficient to stem the steady increase in Muslim attendance of Congress annual moots noted before 1888, peaking at 17.5% of delegates. By the mid-1890s, Muslim attendance had plummeted to its lowest in colonial history—less than 1%.[103] As large Patriotic Association rallies and an 1895 petition signed by 50,000 'literate Muslims' and 'presented to the House of Commons' would prove, the core concern of the movement was the implication for the Muslim 'minority' of 'governing India on democratic principles'.[104]

Despite such successes in keeping Muslims from Congress, the fact that the Patriotic Association's 'loyalism' had not addressed broader Muslim grievances against or sentiments about British Raj—including some championed by the Indian National Congress, whose activism had begun to bear the promise of political reform along 'democratic' lines—meant that those involved in the former organisation recognised that preparations had to be made for the inevitable introduction of electoral politics. Hence, a 'small meeting' of Aligarhis had already been convened at Ahmad Khan's house in December 1894—a meeting that would prove significant in long-term consequences. The meeting was intended to draft a petition and form a new political organisation to be named 'The Muslim Anglo-Oriental Defence Association of Upper India'. The need for another organisation, rather than developing the

---

[101] See *The Present State of Indian Politics*, pp. 227–34.

[102] For example, a meeting of 4,000 persons was held at the shrine of Mu'in al-Din Chishti at Ajmer (Rajputana), presided over by a *qadi* and *sajjada nashin* (descendent) of the revered Chishtiyya *pir*. The same scene was enacted at the tomb of 'Ala' al-Din Sabir in Roorkee (Hindustan) before a crowd of 15,000. See *The Present State of Indian Politics*, pp. 227–34.

[103] *Muslim League Documents*, p. 456.

[104] *Pioneer* (January 1895), *Aligarh Movement*, vol. 3, pp. 1033–43.

agenda of the Patriotic Association, was, in the words of Theodore Beck, principal of Aligarh College, that the latter 'did not definitely represent Muslim interests, though it was mainly Muslim', and employed 'popular agitation'.[105] The political options discussed were to either join the 'Hindu' agitations, set up counter agitations, do nothing or adopt a 'modified line of political activity'.[106] The 'modifications' implied and evident in the latest organisation's rules were to represent only the interests of Muslims of the North-West Provinces, an obvious acceptance of the primary base of support identified during the Patriotic Association's activities, but without popular agitation, an equally transparent wink to British authorities not to be alarmed.[107] Thus, interests would be pursued, as suggested by the First Resolution passed by the organisation at its first general meeting in December 1894, by petitioning the government for 'adequate representation and protection of Muslims in Upper India' at all council levels with a scheme by which the previously derided electoral system could be employed.[108]

At a meeting of the Defence Association in December 1895, the issue of representation was again discussed by 12 men, mostly Aligarhis and Western-educated lawyers. Theodore Beck and Sayyid Mahmud (Ahmad Khan's son) had previously been charged with researching the scheme. To date, their work had established, in Beck's words, 'All authorities on Representative Government agree that adequate representation ought to be secured for minorities'.[109] This obviously strengthened their case. One of the difficulties identified, however, was that the same authorities did not recognise the 'Muslim community' as a 'political unit, with its own interests and sentiments'.[110] By the following year, the Defence Association completed its scheme and published it through the press, the *Pioneer* referring to it as 'A Muslim Manifesto'.[111] The document itself warrants close consideration. It begins by stating that the time to agitate against 'elective principles' has passed, the opposition of 'enfranchised Hindus' and sentiment in England being overwhelming.

---

[105] *Aligarh Movement*, vol. 3, p. 1038.
[106] Ibid., p. 1033.
[107] Ibid., p. 1042.
[108] MAO Defense Association's 'Resolution I', *Aligarh Movement*, vol. 3, pp. 1044–46.
[109] *Aligarh Movement*, vol. 3, p. 1059.
[110] Ibid., p. 1059.
[111] *Pioneer* (December 1896), *Aligarh Movement*, vol. 3, pp. 1063–66.

This being the case, in the interests of fulfilling the principle of 'securing the representation of minorities', it goes on to consider the pitfall of the 'tyranny of the majority' and the manner in which Muslims fall victim to the amplification of this tendency in the 'Indian' context. The essential difficulty identified was that as the electors were majority Hindu, even if Muslims were elected, 'the essence of representation is that the man elected should represent the electors'.[112] The argument continued:

> Consequently, if they [Hindus] were compelled by law to elect Muslims, these Muslims would represent not Muslim but Hindu constituencies and the Muslim community would remain almost as much underrepresented as before, in fact there is more likelihood they will be misrepresented, for inasmuch as so large a body of Muslims will necessarily contain persons holding a variety of opinions, the Hindu electors will, if they are intelligent, choose persons whose views approximate to their own and who are not in agreement with the majority of the Muslims... The case was illustrated a hundred times over in the National Congress agitations, in which the favourite devise was adopted of choosing a Muslim as chairman of a meeting, even if he were the only one in the room...[113]

The solution most in accord with the '[e]lementary principles of representative institutions', the 'Manifesto' surmised, was that the 'electors of the Muslim members should consist of Muslims and the electors of the Hindu members of Hindus', at all levels of government.[114] The Muslim 'right' to 'separate electorates', therefore, was pressed on the basis of the argument that 'Muslims are for political purposes a community with separate traditions, interests, political convictions and religion', more distinct than the Liberals and Conservatives of England, or the Catholics and Protestants of Ireland.[115] Whether acknowledged as a 'nation' or not, the 'Manifesto' closed with the appeal:

> It is not a question whether Muslims are right or wrong... The point is they have different views [from Congress], and any rational system of representation should provide for their expression.[116]

That the British government eventually adopted 'separate electorates' as part of the Government of India Act of 1909, while also sanctioning

---

[112] Ibid., p. 1065.
[113] Ibid., p. 1065.
[114] Ibid., p. 1065.
[115] Ibid., p. 1066.
[116] Ibid., p. 1066.

the formation of the first 'All-India' Muslim organisation to contest elections, evinces the efficacy of a strategy that did not raise British suspicions or, at least in government circles, appear to challenge British interests. Given that this 'All-India Muslim League', founded in 1906 and presided over by figures such as the Agha Khan, was largely headed by the same characters who had formed the core of the 'Patriotic' and 'Defence' associations, both intended to protect the interests of the elite and capitalist Muslims of 'Upper India', illustrates the manner in which the regional and class-based interests of mostly 'Upper Indian' Muslims, contributed to the rise of separate electorates for 'Muslim' and 'Hindu India' in general. Consequently, the governmental structures of British Raj, both directly by means of censuses and indirectly through the agenda of the Indian National Congress, played an important role in transforming 'religiously informed' cultural identities into politicised ones. Even the names of the organisations that preceded the Muslim League illustrate that distress at a Hindu *qawm* simultaneously politicised and declared the 'majority' played a great part in contorting the Muslim 'minority's' posture from 'Patriotic' to 'Defensive'. A focus on the influence of British Raj, therefore, sheds much light on the politicisation of religious identity, whether referred to as 'communitarianism' or 'communalism'.

However, there are some factors a focus on British Raj does not take into account and some questions it even fails to raise. Not taken into account is the fact that although the Muslim Indian *qawm* had been depoliticised since 1858, prior to that year, it had included a political aspect symbolised by the Mughal state and even deployed, however unsuccessfully, in the 1857 Uprising. The 'Muslim Indian' *qawm* was not created out of thin air, therefore, but re-enlivened, in the absence of the Mughals, as a religio-political electorate with a political party as its new institutional representative. Acknowledging this connection to the past also raises the question of whether the 'history' lived by early Aligarhis, etc., contributed to the architects of, and participants in, all of the organisations mentioned, culminating in the Muslim League, not swinging some other way entirely to press, for example, some form of 'secularism' as the solution to their socio-economic and political dilemmas, thus relegating 'religion' to the 'private' sphere. In essence, this 'history' begs the question: Why would a man like Ahmad Khan, who dedicated his life to educating his co-religionists in European 'arts and sciences', not venture further in the case of European political philosophy than the 'composite provincialism' of the British Indian Association, the 'composite Indianism' of the Patriotic Association, and the 'provincial separatism' of the Defence Association, before turning to separate electorates? Granted, the socio-economic and political pressures of British Raj, particularly being declared a 'minority', played an important role in dissuading many like Ahmad Khan from pursuing the truly 'secular' alternative. However, it should be recalled that the 'secular' track was exactly the one followed by non-Muslim minorities in other contemporary contexts, as in the construction of Arab nationalism. Thus, even being a 'minority' is not sufficient cause to have dissuaded men like Ahmad Khan so thoroughly. Nor is the fact that Ahmad Khan was a Muslim, for men like him were well placed to employ the tried and tested antinomian and latitudinarian aspects of the 'Old Islam' to offer some form of legitimisation to 'secular' action. The answer, therefore, rests in the type of Muslims under discussion. Men of Ahmad Khan's class and locale were firmly committed to pursuing their interests within an 'Islamic frame', and by that time, not the 'old' but the 'New Islam'—transcendental, legalistic and so intent on asserting Islam's political character—defined the doctrine of the 'Inner' domain. For Ahmad Khan and like minds who shirked the expression of politicism through Caliphal rhetoric not to offend the British, Islamic doctrine's political implications were left in need of an alternative mode of articulation. Thus, the re-politicisation of the Muslim *qawm*, whether on a provincial or an 'All-India' level, best satisfied the requirements of the 'Outer' domain, while also remaining cognisant of the 'Inner' domain's doctrinal promotion of the idea, included in the Muslim Manifesto, that South Asian Muslims, like their local constituents and their global brethren, were 'for political purposes' a community with 'separate traditions, interests and convictions' from non-Muslims. This did not mean that Muslims could not or would not promote cooperation with non-Muslim communities, whether British or South Asian, as the activities of the British Indian and Patriotic Association has already proven. But, for some, that cooperation would come from the socio-economically, politically, religiously and historically defensible position of the *qawm*, just as for others it was already being pursued through the rhetoric of *umma*. The best proof is in the political developments of the early to mid-20th century covered in the next section, developments that also offer a definitive discussion of 'communitarian' versus 'communal' identities.

II.ii. *From Caliphate and Separate Electorates to India and Pakistan: 1909–1947*

In less than a single lifetime, from 1858 to 1909, the elite and capitalist class Muslims of 'Upper India' had travelled from the utter devastation and humiliation following the 1857 Uprising to renegotiate their position as a social and political force in British India. As much as their journey had been shaped by specifically colonial pressures, it was also guided by a 'New Islam' that put great stock in religious community and defined its parameters in a particular manner. The rhetoric of Caliphate emerged as the prime means by which to employ the *umma* consciousness so central to current doctrine in a manner suited to forwarding more local interests. The re-politicisation of the Muslim Indian *qawm* once represented by the Mughal state and the provision for 'personal law' in the colonial apparatus, now institutionalised as a 'separate electorate', added another institutional means by which the individual Muslim could pursue his/her local interests. But, the most outstanding of all feats was that neither option seriously 'transgressed' the 'Islamic frame' of the day. Without doctrinal prohibitions to contend with, the efficacies of alleviating 'minority' status by attaching oneself to a far larger collective through the institution of Caliphate, while simultaneously creating a separate legal space under a colonial cloak from which to negotiate with local competitors for power, insured that a convergence of advocates and ideologies could easily arise, if the socio-economic and political interests so far retarding that process also came together. The same conditions additionally implied that a separate legal space could transform into the call for a sovereign political space should interests later diverge. And, that is precisely what occurred.

II.ii.a. *The Khilafat Movement: 1909–1930*
After the euphoria that followed Ottoman victories in the late 1890s, as well as the modicum of respite from anti-colonial sentiment offered by the inclusion of 'separate electorates' in the Government of India Act of 1909, anxiety returned with the reversal of Ottoman fortunes in the Balkan Wars of 1911–12. The diminishing world of the Ottomans coincided with the rise of such local factors as a so-called 'extremist' faction in the Indian National Congress that forwarded a more resolutely independent course for 'India' than earlier 'moderates', and employed a decidedly 'Brahmanical' rhetoric in its justifications and activities. One

issue such elements had opposed was the British 'partition' of Bengal along 'communal' lines in 1905. Bengali Muslims, on the other hand, had been quite pleased with this administrative division, allowing them less competition for local resources, greater access to government jobs, and other advantages. The reversal of the Bengal partition in 1911, therefore, largely as an act of supplication before the strikes, boycotts and calls for 'Swaraj' (self-rule) arranged by anti-partition 'Hindu' activists, sent shivers down many a Muslim spine and lent to further cold-shoulders in the direction of the British. Feeling alienated from both the British and their non-Muslim neighbours, the perceived need to cement pacts with sympathetic outside powers that could provide some local leverage only grew, bringing the clerical classes and Muslim Leaguers together for the first time.

The first notable institution to arise and embody a convergence of forces was the *Anjuman-i Khuddam-i Ka'ba* in 1913. This organisation was the first step in the 'Khilafat Movement', whose significance to the future of South Asian Muslim polity is apparent even in the identities of its founders. The three principal actors were a leading Madrasa-i Farangi Mahal scholar, 'Abd al-Bari (d. 1926), and the Muslim Leaguers and Aligarh graduates, Muhammad 'Ali Jawahar, and his brother, Shawkat 'Ali (d. 1938). The *anjuman*'s ostensible purpose was support for Ottoman 'Caliphs' and protection of the sacred cities of Mecca and Medina.[117] That is to say, with the support of a leading scholar from a surviving bastion of the 'Old Islam', clerical debate over the permissibility of acknowledging the non-Quraysh Ottoman Sultans as universal Caliphs was emphatically curtailed in favour of recognition. As well, 'Abd al-Bari's association with Aligarhis and Muslim League members provided clerical legitimisation for the scholastic movement, the political party and the hand its founders played in the argument for separate electorates. Meanwhile, the advocacy of Aligarhis and Muslim Leaguers sent a clear signal to the growing ranks of young and frustrated 'Western-educated' classes—the era of Ahmad Khan's and Hali's 'loyalism' was over, with the new leaders of the *qawm* preferring to stand up against the coloniser by expressing their *umma* consciousness in the increasingly adversarial terms of Caliphate, rather than the politically quietist *shari'a*. The overarching result was the creation of a broader network of supporters among Western- and *madrasa*-educated

---

[117] Minault, *The Khilafat Movement*, pp. 33–36.

Muslim men and women than witnessed during any earlier movement, including the 1857 Uprising.

The British government played its part in further stoking the Khilafat Movement, no more than a year after the *anjuman* was formed. In 1914, Britain and the Ottomans were among the hosts of World War I, and British India (or more accurately, its resources and 'native' army men) was pressed into participation without consulting its leading political parties, including the Muslim League and the Indian National Congress. Ottoman leaders and their allies also extended an invitation to South Asian Muslims, but by further cultivating their image as Caliphs and employing the rhetoric of *jihad* in their anti-British propaganda. The message was published in Urdu and couched in descriptions of British atrocities in the theatre of war, as well as the latter's stoking of communal disharmony and exploitation of the economy in South Asia—all of which would be ended if South Asian Muslims deserted to fight alongside the Ottomans and their allies.[118] As the message itself suggests, such tracts and leaflets were not merely circulated in South Asia; they were also dropped among South Asian Muslim soldiers who were deployed against the Ottomans in West Asia. In addition, Urdu-language newspapers, such as *Jihan-i Islam*, sprang up in Istanbul to complement those already following the war closely in South Asia, adding to the anti-British chorus available. Nor were the Germans silent, publishing Urdu-language newsletters, such as the Berlin-based *Jangi Akhbar*, besides a multitude of tracts that included comparisons of German and British economic and industrial might, arguing that one of Britain's aims in the war was to destroy Germany's potential as a powerful European ally of an independent 'India'.[119]

Ultimately, both invites were heard, but enthusiasm for the Ottoman party was more broadly heeded. By the time the 'Arab Revolt'

---

[118] For example, see the writings of Muhammad Jamal, *Angrezon ka Zulm aur 'Iraqi Maqtal* (1916); *Hindi Bhaion ko Ek Mushfiqana Nasibat* (1917); *Al-Jihad fi Sabil al-Haqq* (1917); *Muhibban-i Watan se Iltija* (1917); and *Rasul-i Allah ke Rawza-i Mubarak par Gola-Bari aur Sada'e Intiqam* (1917). All were published in Istanbul. No publisher is provided, but the works are available through *Documents Proscribed by the Government of India*.

[119] For samples of the Ottoman *Jihan-i Islam* from 1915, see *Documents Proscribed by the Government of India*, #1501. For German propaganda, see *Jangi Akhbar* 15 (Berlin: n.p., 1915); Anon., *Jarman ka Tamaddun aur Jang* (Berlin: Mashriqi Akhbari Daftar, 1914); Anon., *Hindustani Sipahiyon* (Berlin: n.p., 1915); Anon., *Dunya ki Jang ka Pahla Sal* (Berlin: n.p., 1915). All works are available through *Documents Proscribed by the Government of India*.

of 1915–16 further threatened Ottoman authority over the holy cities, Istanbul began issuing accounts of British atrocities in the sacred city, and leading Deobandis such as Mahmud Hasan (d. 1920) and 'Ubaid Allah Sindhi (d. 1944) not only abandoned the argument made by all Wali Allahis, beginning with Wali Allah himself, that universal Caliphate required a Qurayshi candidate, they also cast aside the *fatawa* issued by the Deobandi founder, Rashid Ahmad, who legitimated British Raj, to echo Ottoman calls for *jihad* against the British. The danger to British interests inherent in these developments was taken seriously enough that Mahmud Hasan was arrested in Mecca and interned on Malta, while 'Ubaid Allah was forced to seek asylum in Afghanistan. However, this only opened the door for the less radical Anjuman-i Khuddam-i Ka'ba to expand its agenda and gain greater support. Thus, by the end of the war, which culminated in an Ottoman defeat, their state's looming dismemberment and European proposals for an émigré Jewish state in the former province of Palestine, Bari and like-minded agitators were able to effect a coup against the politically quietest old-guard of the Muslim League. The year 1919, therefore, began with Bari issuing a *fatwa* urging the victorious British to uphold the Ottoman Caliph's authority over the holy cities under threat of South Asian Muslim mobilisation. By the next annual Muslim League conference in September 1919, two groups reflecting this agenda would be constituted: an 'All-India Khilafat Committee', including *madrasa* and Western-educated intellectuals and activists, and the 'Jama'at-i 'Ulama'-i Hind', initially conceived as an umbrella group for various religious schools, but progressively coming under the sway of the Deobandis like Husayn Ahmad Madani (d. 1957), Mahmud Hasan's student and successor as head of the *madrasa*. As all observers agree, by the end of 1919, South Asian Muslims were 'displaying an unusual degree of unanimity'.[120] That is to say, in the rhetoric of Caliphate, the 'New Islam's' strident advocacy of *umma* consciousness had found an institutional outlet that suited the socio-economic and political aspirations of South Asia's elite and capitalist classes. But, what of *qawm* and *watan*?

Much of the anti-colonial activity during World War I can be explained by the fact that the alienation, which so many Muslim leaders had felt from their Hindu compatriots, was alleviated by new developments in the relationship between the Muslim League and the Indian

---

[120] Jalal, *Self and Sovereignty*, pp. 198–210.

National Congress. In 1913, the same year that the Anjuman-i Khuddam-i Ka'ba had kicked off the Khilafat movement, the Indian National Congress urged one of its young Muslim luminaries, Muhammad 'Ali Jinnah (d. 1948), to join the Muslim League with the explicit intent of forging closer ties between these parties. The move bore fruit while the war still raged in the form of the 'Lucknow Pact' of 1916, which agreed on the maintenance of separate electorates in future constitutional provisions. As always, colonial authorities were also on hand to spur mass involvement. Not only was the British government intransigent on the issue of the Ottomans, Mecca and Medina, it also set forth on the task of colonising the Ottoman's West Asian provinces, as agreed upon under the secretive 'Sykes-Picot' Agreement of 1916, and pursued in the wake of the war under League of Nations 'mandate'. As well, those who had participated in the war on the British side with promises of significant political reform in South Asia upon its conclusion were disappointed by the limited content of the 'Montagu-Chelmsford' reforms of 1918. Meanwhile, the authorities responded to South Asian objections by extending repressive wartime emergency measures into peacetime under the Rowlatt Act, and followed that with the massacre of about 1,000 demonstrators at Amritsar, both in 1919. It was under the influence of these political circumstances that Gandhi attended the November 1919 'Khilafat Conference' that brought together all concerned *anjuman*s and parties, and in the following month, the Indian National Congress, the Muslim League, Jama'at-i 'Ulama'-i Hind and the Khilafat Committee coordinated their meetings, essentially merging the 'Khilafat' and 'Non-Cooperation' movements. The key to it all, however, at least for those groups at the centre of this rapprochement, was the institution of separate electorates, allowing Muslims to overcome the fears outlined by Ahmad Khan, so that what Muhammad 'Ali Jawahar had termed a 'Federation of Faiths' as early as 1904, could begin to be negotiated.[121] So began a return from 'Defence' to 'Patriotism', an indication that *umma*, *qawm* and *watan* had been reconciled in the form of Caliphate, separate electorates and composite Indian nationalism.

The extant literature confirming the reconciliation of parties and objectives is vast, including newspapers, journals, party pamphlets, poetry and song. A hint of the popular chords at which such literature pulled is well expressed by the cover illustration of one collection of

---

[121] Muhammad 'Ali Jawahar, *Select Writings and Speeches*, vol. 2, pp. 117–18.

Urdu songs, penned by a Muslim and titled *Khawab-i Pareshan* ('Dream of the Distressed'). It depicts a tall Englishman—sword in his right hand, pistol in his left—shooting a child before the eyes of its fallen, wailing mother, as an impish, subservient South Asian man clutches the coloniser's coat-tails.[122] As well, the *fatawa* issued by members of the Jama'at-i 'Ulama'-i Hind were shorn of their original scholarly format and pomposity to be reproduced in simple language and point form for print and widespread distribution. A seminal example, issued in 1920 and signed by all the organisation's leaders, including the Farangi Mahali scholar 'Abd al-Bari and the Deobandi Husayn Ahmad Madani, declared it '*haram*' to participate in any colonial council, join or remain in the colonial army or police force, hold any colonial rank or title, attend schools funded by the colonial government or use colonial courts.[123] The full-fledged legitimation of 'non-cooperation' is clearly evident, but a Qur'anic quote is also added to confirm the pro-Ottoman component of the movement by pointing out that 'whoever intentionally kills a believer, their reward is an eternity in Hell'.[124] Such works were also supplemented by its signatories' other writings and speeches. Among the letters and speeches of the period, in fact, were some even written and delivered by Mahmud Hasan, who only a few years earlier had declared *jihad* against the British incumbent on all Muslims seeking to avoid Hell.[125] The effect of such broad and accessible legitimisation was that the combined Non-Cooperation-Khilafat Movement grew into the largest anti-colonial mobilisation of South Asians, Hindu and Muslim, even surpassing the 1857 Uprising in scale. Women such as Sultan Jahan Begum of Bhopal, among others associated with the 'All-India Muslim Ladies' Conference' and the 'All-India Muslim Ladies' Association', also ensured that the movement's leadership and participants in the rallies and demonstrations organised, were not all-male affairs, even including women observing *purda*. Thus, this movement truly heralded the era of populist politics, involving people

---

[122] See, Muhammad Husayn, *Khawab-i Pareshan* (Sardhana: Istifa Husayn, n.d.), in *Documents Proscribed by the Government of India*, #1471.

[123] This and other *fatawa* were broadly published in the early 1920s. Various editions are available through *Documents Proscribed by the Government of India*, #1491–98.

[124] See *'Ulama'-i Hind ka Muttafiqa Fatwa* (Dehra Dun: Khilafat Committee, 1921).

[125] See Mahmud Hasan, *Hazrat Shaykh al-Hind Mawlana Mahmud al-Hasan Sahib ka Ek Zaruri Khatt* (Azamgarh: Khilafat Committee, 1921); and *Khutba-i Sadarat aur Fatwa Tark-i Muwalat* (Deoband: Matba'-i Qasimi, 1920).

of various classes and locales, men and women, in the singular cause of the *umma, qawm* and *watan*.

Of course, all were not necessarily swayed by such tactics. The Ahmadiyya movement brooked no allegiance to Caliphate and remained steadfastly loyal to British Raj, arguing that the former institution had no role in the post-messianic world ushered in by the appearance of its founder, Mirza Ghulam Ahmad. Among the 'new' Sober clerics, Ahmad Rida Khan of the Ahl-i Sunnat also dissuaded followers from anti-colonial activities in the name of Caliphate. He did not object to the support extended to Muslims abroad, but had three problems with the Khilafat Movement: recognising the Ottoman Sultan as Universal Caliph as he was not of Qurayshi descent, joining groups that included advocates of lines of thought he had already declared 'apostates', and making joint cause with Hindu '*kafirs*' against British 'People of the Book'.[126] Yet, such objectors were not sufficient in number to dent the movement's popularity, given the legitimacy lent by Aligarhis, Deobandis and Farangi Mahalis, not to mention the Indian National Congress under Gandhi in conjunction with the Muslim League. For that to happen, internal fissures had to appear and widen. Thus, it may be that 'unanimity' was a chimera from the start, given that the first effective blow from within was delivered by none other than Gandhi, who unilaterally suspended the Non-Cooperation Movement when violence erupted in Bihar, leading to the deaths of 17 policemen and 172 farmers in 1922. This led to great resentment, not only among Muslim leaders, but also Indian National Congress leadership, who were dismayed at the fact that so large and effective a mobilisation could be suspended by one man over violence in one village alone. Though severely weakened, the Khilafat Movement vowed to soldier on alone, only to have the rug pulled entirely from under its feet by Turkish nationalists, who abolished the Ottoman Sultanate in 1924. And finally, even the goodwill that had built up between Muslim Leaguers and the Indian National Congress was smashed when the latter's 'Nehru Report' (1928) repudiated the Lucknow Pact's agreement on separate electorates and rejected Jinnah's counter-proposal of weighted representation at the centre in

---

[126] In fact, there were even some Deobandis who made such arguments, but their voices were not represented through the Jama'at-i 'Ulama'-i Hind, the issue eventually contributing to the formation of the pro-Pakistan Jama'at-i 'Ulama'-i Islam. See Usha Sanyal, *Ahmad Riza Khan Barelwi* (Oxford: One World Publications, 2005), pp. 77–81, 109–10; and I.H. Qureshi, *Ulema in Politics* (Karachi: Ma'aref, 1974), pp. 270–71.

any future constitutional provisions.[127] Therefore, a decade that began with the greatest 'degree of unanimity' ended with Jinnah resigning from the Indian National Congress and retiring from politics, Muhammad 'Ali Jawahar denouncing Gandhi as a tool of the Right-Wing 'Hindu Mahasabha' (f. 1915), and Iqbal addressing the Muslim League with his proposal for a separate 'North-West Muslim State'.[128]

Of course, neither the ideal of a universal Caliph nor the doctrinal necessity of *umma* consciousness died with the Ottoman state and the Khilafat Movement. For those on the 'new' Sober Path, in particular, it may have been doctrinally feasible to forego the qualification of Qurayshi lineage, but the institution of universal Caliphate itself had been an integral part of this scholarly line's agenda since its inception about the early 18th century. Thus, most argued that the problem was a lack of qualified candidates in the present and recommended that followers pray that an appropriate individual would arise in the future, much as had been the strategy a century earlier. Others, however, including Iqbal, fell back on the type of argument made by Ahmad Khan, drawn from pre-colonial sources ranging from al-Ghazali to Ibn Taymiyya, that the institution of Caliphate was not incumbent on Muslims. As Iqbal put it in one of his late 1920s lectures, citing the Mu'tazila school as his source, universal Caliphate is no more than a 'matter of expediency'. However, in line with the polymath scholar Ibn Khaldun (d. 1406), he added that the institution's historical role had been to serve as the 'first dim vision of an International Islam'.[129] Thus, Iqbal ultimately moved beyond most of his day to argue:

---

[127] Jalal, *Self and Sovereignty*, pp. 300–03.

[128] Although Hindi particularism, cow protection and *shuddi* found some voice in the Indian National Congress' 'Extremist' wing, the later group's growing cooperation with Muslim parties about and in the wake of World War I, not to mention Gandhi's 'non-violent' strategy, led many Hindus raised in the traditions of the Brahmo Samaj, Arya Samaj and such later 'revivalist' groups as the Rama Krishna Mission (led by Swami Vivekananda (d. 1902)), to establish a party of their own. The first expression of this urge was the Hindu Mahasabha, soon to be led by V.D. Savarkar (d. 1966), author of the influential '*Hindutva*', and K.B. Hedgewar, later the founder of the Rashtriya Swayamsevak Sangh (f. 1925). Such parties and their affiliates would play a major role in the violence that preceded, accompanied and has followed 'Partition', including the murder of Gandhi. Virtually all contemporary 'Hindu nationalist' parties, including the Bharatiya Janata Party that has held state and federal-level offices since the 1980's have issued from these organisations. For an excellent account of all these movements, see Peter van der Veer, *Religious Nationalism* (Berkeley: University of California Press, 1994).

[129] Iqbal, *Reconstruction*, pp. 138–39.

For the present every Muslim nation must sink into her own deeper self, temporarily focus her vision on herself alone, until all are strong and powerful enough to form a living family of republics. A true and living unity, according to the nationalist thinkers, is not so easy as to be achieved by a merely symbolic overlordship. It is truly manifested in a multiplicity of free independent units whose racial rivalries are adjusted and harmonised by the unifying bond of a common spiritual aspiration. It seems to me that God is slowly bringing home to us the truth that Islam is neither Nationalism nor Imperialism, but a League of [Muslim] Nations which recognises artificial boundaries and racial distinctions for facility of reference only, and not for restricting the social horizon of its members.[130]

The question remaining for South Asian Muslims, therefore, was: To which 'nation' would they belong?

II.ii.b. *India and Pakistan: 1930–1947*
From the perspective of Muslim leaders like Muhammad 'Ali Jawahar, who had tied their political careers to the institutions of Caliphate and separate electorates, the 1930s clearly began as a decade in which the *umma* had lost its Caliph and the Muslim Indian *qawm* could not depend on its 'Hindu' partners. A void had manifested itself, one pried open by the realisation of just how disconnected South Asian Muslims had become from the pulse of other members of the *umma*. The call for unity was exposed as unreal and, in the process, the very real leverage provided South Asian Muslim leadership by the threat of Muslim support from beyond the borders of British India, deployed since the early 19th century to further local interests against the colonial regime and, since the 1880s, to counter Indian National Congress designs, was no more. Reliance on separate electorates to maintain some degree of autonomy, therefore, could only grow when the Indian National Congress was distancing itself from the institution. Yet, for the majority of politically active Muslims who had followed such leaders as the Jawahar brothers, the Indian National Congress and a nationalist rhetoric that emphasised the *watan* to which all belonged could not easily be delegitimised, particularly when such stalwarts of the Khilafat Movement as Husayn Ahmad Madani and most of the Jama'at-i 'Ulama'-i Hind, as well as Abu al-Kalam Azad (d. 1958), a founding member of the Khilafat Committee and rising star in the Indian National Congress,

---

[130] Ibid., p. 140.

remained loyal to Gandhi. Thus, although the British began the 1930s confident enough in its sovereignty to invite all parties to the 'Round Table Conferences' in London, only to yield nothing, the decade truly belonged to the Indian National Congress.

The Indian National Congress boycotted the first round of talks in 1930, instead backing Gandhi's latest 'Civil Disobedience Movement', which began with the famous Salt March early that year. Even without the Khilafat cause, Muslim participation continued, drawing from classes and areas previously untapped, such as the Pathans of the North-West Frontier Province under the leadership of 'Abd al-Ghaffar Khan (d. 1988), from then on known as the 'Frontier Gandhi'. And, although various considerations led the Indian National Congress to suspend the new movement to attend the second round of talks in 1931, one of the deal breakers, leading to the resumption of the Civil Disobedience Movement with a patented Gandhi 'fast unto death', was the insistence on separate electorates by the Muslims in attendance, including Jawahar and Iqbal, in concert with 'depressed' Hindu castes. Thus, with the exception of Madani, Azad and their followers, Muslim elites and capitalists were conspicuous in their relative absence from the latter round of the Civil Disobedience Movement (1932–34). Nevertheless, Gandhi's movement did win the support of Muslims of another class, thanks to the increasing consolidation and activism of 'Leftist' politics. The latter included factions of the Indian National Congress, the Communist Party of India and other, smaller socialist parties whose ranks were filled by great resentment among rural and urban working classes against British and indigenous capitalists (landed and industrialist). In the end, this convergence of Gandhi and the Left proved broad-based enough to press the British into offering a new Government of India Act in 1935, largely to put an end to the Civil Disobedience Movement. Meanwhile, the influence in the Indian National Congress of the very landed and industrialist classes, against which the working classes had been rallying since the 1920s, led the party to accept the new dispensation, despite its limitations. Although the 1935 Act firmed central authority by various means, the increased powers it vested in provincial legislatures, as well as the limited expansion of the electorate from six to thirty million, suited the interests of the capitalist classes well. As the elections of 1937 went on to illustrate, Gandhi and the Leftists' promise of fiscal, land and labour reforms was the deciding force in the Indian National Congress' winning control of

6 of the 11 provincial legislatures (the other four held by representatives of local, ethno-linguistic groupings). However, the running of these legislatures proved that in government, the industrialist/landed backers of the 'Hindu' Right would trump the combined Left. Cabinet posts were flooded with the former types and campaign promises not only remained unfulfilled, but draconian laws promulgated by the British to quell the Civil Disobedience Movement were now employed by Indian National Congress ministries to drown out the growing frustration among the working class in the provinces. A thoroughly discredited Indian National Congress, therefore, was relieved when British authorities responded to the start of World War II by declaring British India at war without consulting indigenous leadership (again), providing the party the pretext to resign from government in 1939.

During this entire period of 'Congress Raj', it is clear that Leftist agendas added to the factors that won the party many Muslim votes. When coupled with the rhetoric of 'Hindu-Muslim unity' established since Khilafat-Non-Cooperation days and still sung by the Jama'at-i 'Ulama'-i Hind and Gandhi, such support for the Indian National Congress left the Muslim League out in the cold. Of course, that does not imply that among elite and capitalist classes the vision of a politicised *qawm* had been replaced by 'secular' forms of Indian nationalism, socialist or liberal. Rather, it suggests just how heavily the relationship between the *qawm*s of South Asia rested on the institutions of personal law and separate electorates. As long as one or both of these institutions was in place, 'Muslims Indians' of various classes were willing to consider the possibility of life without the latter. Having witnessed the rule of Congress ministries in the late 1930s, however, the reasoning underlying separate electorates, i.e. constitutional safeguards for 'Muslim India' and other 'minorities', became painfully apparent. For at least one person, Iqbal, as early as the late 1920s, the paradox of depending on the *qawm* to be at one with the *watan* could not be solved without stepping out of its variables to create new ones, i.e. to call for a *watan* of its own for the *qawm*.

If Leftist rhetoric had been significant to 'Congress Raj', Marxist doctrines had made their way into Iqbal's 'new' Intoxicated Way. In fact, as many of Iqbal's verses from the period illustrate, socialism did not contradict 'Islam'. In three poems first published in the 1930s, *Lenin*, *Karl Marx ki Awaz* and *Bolshevik Rus*, Iqbal acknowledges all as serving God, though professing atheism, for exposing the greed, hypocrisy and 'old ideas' that rest behind European Christianity, i.e. imperialism and capitalism. On the latter, he wrote:

> The democratic (*jamhuri*) system of the West is the same old instrument, in whose frets lies naught but songs of Caesars...
> Ethnicity (*nasl*), nationalism (*qawmiyyat*), the Church, kingship (*sultanat*), civilization (*tahdhib*), race (*rang*)
> 'Imperialism' (*khwajagi*) has chosen its narcotics well.[131]

Nevertheless, Iqbal was no more a Marxist than a Liberal. He insisted that the metaphysics and jurisprudential methodology of his 'new' Intoxicated Way was necessary to guide the revolutionary drive of Marx and Lenin. Without this knowledge, the realisation of the Ego/Self is impossible and without that even Marxists become addicted to the old 'narcotics' of Liberals. In one of his lectures, he makes the distinction most succinctly:

> The idealism of Europe never became a living factor in her life, and the result is a perverted ego seeking itself through mutually intolerant democracies whose sole function is to exploit the poor in the interest of the rich. Believe me, Europe today is the greatest hindrance in the way of man's ethical advancement. The Muslim, on the other hand, is in possession of these ultimate ideas on the basis of revelation, which, speaking from the inmost depths of life, internalises its own apparent externality...Early Muslims emerging out of the spiritual slavery of pre-Islamic Arabia were not in a position to realise the true significance of this basic idea. Let the Muslim of today appreciate his position, reconstruct his social life in light of ultimate principles, and evolve, out of the hitherto partially revealed purpose of Islam, that spiritual democracy which is the ultimate aim of Islam.[132]

South Asian Muslims having been identified as a religious 'minority' thanks to British censuses, however, implied that 'a non-Muslim legislature' would have to 'exercise the power of *ijtihad*', and this he concluded was 'doubtful'.[133] Thus, in 1930, only a couple of years after his lectures were first delivered, Iqbal sought to resolve this dilemma along with the broader issue of constitutional safeguards by arguing for a separate Muslim state, whether federated with 'India', or not.

Was Iqbal alone in perceiving the *qawm*'s 'need' for a *watan* of its own? As suggested by the cold shoulder the Muslim League threw his

---

[131] Iqbal, *Iqbal: A Selection of Urdu Verse*, pp. 109–11, 140–41, 144.
[132] Iqbal, *Reconstruction*, pp. 156–57.
[133] Ibid., p. 152.

call in 1930, let alone the subsequent growth of Congress Raj, Iqbal was certainly not in the company of all and sundry. More in keeping with Iqbal's company is a group of Punjabi Muslim students at Cambridge, led by Chaudhary Rahmat 'Ali (d. 1951), who in 1933 even coined a name for that *watan*: 'Pakistan', or 'Land of the Pure'.[134] As a map published by this group in 1940 depicts, Pakistan was to be one among 10 South Asian Muslim states, comprising every Muslim majority British province, every Muslim majority Princely State, whether ruled by a Muslim 'prince' or not, and every Hindu majority Princely State ruled by a Muslim. That is to say, Iqbal shared the company of idealists and dreamers. For such intellectual calls for the 'territorialisation' of the *qawm* to extend further, the idea would require more practical purposes and borders. And that is what it acquired when the unanimity and security of the Khilafat Movement collapsed and Congress Raj proved that Indian nationalism required a cautionary approach.

By 1935, Iqbal and others from the party heeded the call of caution by convincing Jinnah to return from retirement to lead the Muslim League on the basis of this ideology of separatism.[135] The resounding defeat of the 1937 elections even with Jinnah at the helm, followed by the rejection of a Muslim League proposal for a coalition government where it had won seats (in the heartland of 'Upper India'), do not suggest that the ideology had garnered broad support by that time. In fact, the Muslim League's poor showing at the polls reconfirms the ideology of separatism as a 'top-down' and 'Upper Indian' undertaking. However, just as the onset of World War II had provided relief to the beleaguered Indian National Congress, it provided hope to the Muslim League, allowing room to negotiate its own deal with the British. That came in the form of support for the British war effort, in return for which British authorities would have to accept the Muslim League as *the* representative of the Muslim Indian *qawm*. And so, in 1940, at the annual meeting of the revived Muslim League, Iqbal's territorialised *qawm* was posthumously given voice in the 'Lahore Resolution', which stated that 'the areas in which Muslims are numerically in a majority... should be

---

[134] For Rahmat 'Ali's account, see Stephen Hays, ed. *Sources of Indian Tradition*, vol. 2 (New York: Columbia University Press, 1988), pp. 234–36. For his map, see Akbar S. Ahmed, *Jinnah, Pakistan and Islamic Identity: The Search for Saladin* (London: Routledge, 1997), p. xxvii.
[135] See Muhammad Iqbal, *Letters of Iqbal to Jinnah* (Lahore: Muhammad Ashraf, n.d.).

grouped to constitute "Independent States" in which the constituent units shall be autonomous and sovereign'.[136] In the absence of Indian National Congress guarantees of separate electorates or weighted representation in any future 'Indian' constitution, the Bengali and Punjabi joined hands with 'Upper Indian', and the politics of 'Defence' once more overtook that of 'Patriotism'.

Obviously, the 'spiritual democracy' for which Iqbal had sought a *watan* was not the goal of those who passed or supported the Lahore Resolution. Apart from other more 'this-worldly' pursuits, even the idealistic had other visions. In his address to the very session of the Muslim League at which the Resolution was passed, Jinnah acknowledged that the crux of the 'problem in India' was to 'adequately and effectively safeguard the rights and interests of Muslims and various other minorities', rather than to make room for the 'spiritual democracy' that Iqbal believed was 'the ultimate aim of Islam'.[137] Furthermore, Jinnah's vision of any future state or states that might arise, should the Indian National Congress continue to resist constitutional safeguards for the Muslim Indian *qawm*, was clearly a secular, liberal democracy of exactly the type that Iqbal considered the undesirable 'song of Caesars'. As well, although support was provided to the idea of territorialising the *qawm* by a host of individual members of the Ahmadiyya, Sufi *pirs, sajjada nashins*, and *madrasa*-educated *mawlanas, mawlawis* and *mullas* (Sunni and Shi'a) scattered through cities, towns and villages from Peshawar to Dacca, it is clear that few of them were advocates of either Iqbal's 'spiritual democracy' or Jinnah's 'secular' state.[138] Particularly in the case of Deobandis like Shabbir Ahmad 'Uthmani (d. 1949), who broke with the Jama'at-i 'Ulama'-i Hind to band together with prominent members of the Ahl-i Sunnat to form the pro-Pakistan Jama'at-i 'Ulama'-i Islam in 1945, the territorialised *qawm* would be the realm of a 'new' Sober *shar'i*-state. 'Supra-local Islamic sentiment' this is not—each proponent, let alone supporters, had socio-economic and political ground to gain. However, it is representative of the entire gamut of thought and institutions included in the 'New Islam'. That is to say, the successful transformation of separatism from the academic ideal of a few into a practical possibility for the many depended on its

---
[136] See *Sources of Indian Tradition*, vol. 2, p. 228.
[137] Ibid., p. 229.
[138] For an important account of the popular dimension of the Pakistan Movement, see Ian Talbot, *Freedom's Cry* (Karachi: Oxford University Press, 1996).

doctrinal legitimacy for the broadest spectrum of the 'Inner' domain's influential individuals and schools, as much as its socio-economic merits. Only with broad-based doctrinal legitimacy could the Pakistan Movement re-ignite that part of the imagination that had been banished to the void since the demise of the Khilafat Movement: a political platform in the primary interests of the *umma, qawm* and *watan*, one on which representatives of all doctrinal perspectives could agree, even if their visions for the future were opposed. This doctrinal, political and socio-economic convergence is the difference between the Muslim League's virtually total rejection by the Muslim electorate of 1937, and its near-complete sweep in the elections of 1946.

Further reflecting the 'Inner' domain's 'New Islam' quite perfectly in the 'Outer' world of nationalism, the place women would enjoy was shaped by the very range of gender ideals discussed earlier. An eloquent example, encompassing the divisions and convergences involved, is furnished by the life and works of Fatima Jinnah (d. 1967), younger sister of Muhammad 'Ali Jinnah. From the Gujarati Khoja community, the female Jinnah was not, at least, restricted to the 'old' customary or 'new' puritan strictures on *purda*, and was encouraged by her Western-educated brother to pursue an English education, resulting in her own dental clinic in Bombay by 1923. As the political scene grew heated, she began attending Muslim League sessions in 1937, and by 1938, was involved in establishing the 'Muslim League Women's Central Committee', which was instrumental in drawing women into the Pakistan Movement's rallies, etc., as well as to the polls. After the creation of Pakistan and her brother's death, her political involvement continued with her speaking out against corruption and the rise of military rule. Finally, as head of a large coalition of secular and Islamist parties, she ran for head of state in the 1965 elections, winning 37% of the national vote and 47% of the vote in 'East Pakistan'. Had she and her supporters been allowed even a share of the power mandated by the popular vote, the Pakistan of today may have looked rather different than it does, but the US-backed military strongman of her day vetoed all such hopes by fixing the electoral colleges. Through all this hardened politics, however, Fatima Jinnah was cast in the 'domestic' role as '*Madr-i Millat*' (Mother of the Nation). This domestication of a woman whose reality is shaped by a complex, multi-pronged relationship between her self and the public sphere, extended into her choice of attire. Until her death in 1967, she sported a look acquired during the colonial days of her political career. Seeking to establish a median position between the variety of approaches to *purda* enshrined in the 'New Islam', Fatima appeared neither in *burqa* nor in her previously 'uncovered' attire. She always draped a *dupatta* (a light scarf) over her hair in the fashion of many subaltern groups and roughly approximating the Deobandi scholar Mumtaz 'Ali's conception of *hijab*, leaving a legacy of propriety among the classes she represents that became widespread and even appropriated by Benazir Bhutto (d. 2007), elected Prime Minister of Pakistan for parts of the 1980s and 1990s.[139]

Of course, there is a flip side to this coin. The broadest spectrum of perspectives can also lead to the greatest capacity for clashes. Anyone familiar with the post-colonial history of Pakistan will attest that 'clashes' have occurred, even within a given school of thought. The same Islamist parties that had issued *fatawa* confirming the legitimacy of a woman head-of-state in the case of Fatima Jinnah, issued decrees renouncing Benazir Bhutto's bid for the same office on the basis of gender. Debates over the nature of the state and the public roles it should afford women obviously continue in Pakistan and India, but the debate in the wake of Lahore Resolution has since subsided, i.e. the debate over whether territorialising the *qawm* was legitimate in any shape or form. Four modes of anti-separatist, pro-Indian nationalist thought were already available to be voiced after 1940. The first and most obvious response—sired on the 'Hindu Revivalism' of 19th century thinkers, and raised on the 20th century rhetoric of the Hindu Mahasabha—was that of 'Hindu nationalists'. In the view of the 'Rashtriya Swayamsevak Sangh' (f. 1925), for example, 'India' was a 'nation' first and foremost defined by 'Hinduism', which was remoulded to include Brahmanism, Buddhism, Jainism and Sikhism as 'sects', but to exclude Islam, Christianity and Judaism. Thus, Muslims in 'Mother India' could or could not constitute a nation, but were unanimously depicted as a foreign and hostile force that needed to be fought as much as the British. At its most extreme, leaders like M.S. Golwalkar (d. 1973) even argued that Nazi Germany's 'solution' for the 'Jewish problem' provided a model for dealing with South Asia's

---

[139] Most works on Fatima Jinnah are in Urdu and hagiographical in approach. For example, see Sayyid Kawash Ridwi, *Mohtarma Fatima Jinnah* (Karachi: Pakistan People's Forum, 1970). A selection of her own writings and speeches have been collected as Salah al-Din Khan, *Speeches, Messages and Statements of Madr-i Millat Mohtarma Fatima Jinnah, 1948–57* (Lahore: Research Society of Pakistan, 1976). Some important insights (as well as the electoral statistics mentioned) can also be gained from works concerned with Muhammad 'Ali Jinnah, particularly, Akbar Ahmed, *Jinnah, Pakistan and Islamic Identity* (London: Routledge, 1997).

Muslims.¹⁴⁰ The second mode, also born of Hindu Revivalism, but by no means as chauvinistic a variety, was 'Gandhian nationalism'. It, too, held that 'India' was a 'nation', but unlike the Hindu nationalists, argued that all Indians were bound by a religious 'universalism' that subsumed Islam and Muslims as one of 'Mother India's' many castes or sects.¹⁴¹ In comparison with Hindu nationalism, the Gandhian variety managed to garner the support of some Muslims, but the Vedantic/Sanskritic theosophy that underwrote it always made the majority wary. The third mode, being 'secular' in nature, was far more popular, particularly among Western-educated Muslim classes, including Indian National Congress leaders like Abu al-Kalam Azad. From this perspective, 'India' was a 'nation' based on shared territory and history, irrespective of its linguistic and religious diversity. By enshrining liberal, democratic institutions in its future constitution, the 'public' domain would operate through secular political parties, with linguistic concerns addressed at the provincial level and religion relegated to the 'private' domain.¹⁴² The merits, flaws and courses pursued then and now by representatives of all the above modes has been the subject of various works, but most important to this discussion is the conclusion reached by many that the lines between them were and remain frequently blurred beyond distinction. This observation alone provides great insight to why there is a persistent return to the politics of 'Defence' among Muslims. However, the fourth and final mode of anti-separatist, pro-Indian nationalist thought had a great advantage over the former. The fourth mode alone fell within an 'Islamic frame'.

Of all the Muslim authors and works that made a case for Indian nationalism after the Lahore Resolution, that with the most widespread appeal was and remains Husayn Ahmad Madani's *'Muttahida Qawmiyyat aur Islam'* ('Composite Nationalism and Islam').¹⁴³ Although contemporary in its choice of quotes from the Qur'an and *hadith* when defining *umma, qawm* and *watan*, while historically grounded in the example of the Prophet's multi-faith Madinan state when arguing against separatism, the gist of Madani's argument is less contemporary

---

¹⁴⁰ See fn. 128.
¹⁴¹ These views are best laid out in M.K. Gandhi, *Hind Swaraj*, ed. J. Parel (New York: Cambridge University Press, 1997).
¹⁴² For his own account of the entire debate, see Abu al-Kalam Azad, *Hamari Azadi* (Bombay: Orient Longmans, 1961).
¹⁴³ Husayn Ahmad Madani, *Muttahida Qawmiyyat aur Islam* (Deoband: Majlis-i Qasim al-Ma'arif, 1941).

or historical than doctrinaire. '*Muttahida Qawmiyyat*', or literally 'united communities', is little more than a restatement of the terms upon which the rapprochement of the Khilafat and Non-Cooperation movements had been based, but with one important exception: no mention of separate electorates. Instead, as one might expect from a 'new' Sober Deobandi jurist and head of the Jama'at-i 'Ulama'-i Hindu, Madani's Muslim Indian *qawm* is maintained within a united Indian *watan* by an Indian National Congress guarantee that the legal space the colonial state provided for *shari'a* in the realm of personal law, would be sanctioned as 'permanent law' in a future Indian constitution.[144] That is to say, Madani employs a strategy whose legitimacy had been affirmed as far back as 1803, when Shah 'Abd al-'Aziz had issued *fatawa* discouraging *jihad* against the colonial state, and was reaffirmed by every 'new' Sober school of thought to arise after the 1857 Uprising, but before World War I. Viewed from the perspective of a 'secular' ideal, Peter Hardy and other contemporary scholars, though not the 'secularists' of the Indian National Congress who needed Muslim support, characterise Madani's formula for 'composite nationalism' as akin to 'juristic apartheid'.[145] Put within an 'Islamic frame,' however, such Muslim supporters of Congress were merely seeking to extend the legal provisions of *dhimmi* status applied to non-Muslims under Muslim rule and (in a manner) to Muslims under British Raj, to themselves under 'Hindu' rule.

Beyond placing Indian nationalism within an 'Islamic frame,' Madani's work also reveals a strong urge to separate the Lahore Resolution from doctrinal Islam. Thus, it is important to mention that Madani places Iqbal at the centre of his treatise, in the process acknowledging the legitimisation that the latter's 'Islamic' credentials provided pro-separatist politicians. However, claiming to have been an avid reader of Iqbal from an early point in his literary career, Madani argues that those who associate Iqbal with separatism 'do not properly understand...his philosophical mind'. Madani argues that separatism is, in fact, based on exactly that 'Greek or European' philosophy which Iqbal dissuaded his readers from following.[146] As for European notions of nationalism, Madani concedes that it may have benefited Europeans, but points

---

[144] Ibid., pp. 53–55.
[145] Cited in Annemarie Schimmel, *Islam in the Indian Subcontinent* (Leiden: E.J. Brill, 1980), p. 220.
[146] Madani, *Muttahida Qawmiyyat aur Islam*, p. 77.

out that one cannot assume that the same situation and ingredients exist in India, and that one should not blindly adopt a form of political organisation that is 'haram and prohibited' in Islam.[147] The only explanation that Madani offers for separatism, therefore, is that it is a plot by the enemies of Islam—the British and their self-serving Muslim lackeys—and is followed by others out of ignorance and fear.[148]

Whether by direct influence or as an echo of Madani's sentiments, other Muslim authors and works—besides those of the Jama'at-i 'Ulama'-i Hind, who saw in Madani's formula an authoritative place for themselves in the future of South Asian Muslims—leapt on the same bandwagon. These included Abu al-Kalam Azad, whose 'secularism' depended, much like Madani's composite nationalism, on the idea that the autonomy in personal law granted under colonial rule would continue in an independent India. Similar exhortations issued from Sayyid Abu al-'Ala' Mawdudi's (d. 1979) recently formed Jama'at-i Islami, as well as the Khaksars and Ahrars. And finally, the influential 'All-India Shi'a Political Conference' also sided with the Indian National Congress on similar grounds. That is to say, with the exception of individual scholars and the renegades of the Ahl-i Sunnat and Deoband who founded the Jama'at-i 'Ulama'-i Islam, as well as abstainers such as the Isma'ili community under Agha Khan III and the 'new' Sober Tablighi Jama'at, the influence of the 'new' Sober Path on the 'Inner' domain manifested itself in the 'Outer' as firmly pro-Indian nationalism. It was only after 'Partition' that 'new' Sober scholars such as Mawdudi took it upon themselves to migrate and 'Islamise' Pakistan. Given the authority vested in this category of thought by the elite and capitalist classes by the 1940s, this was serious opposition for the Pakistan movement. Muslims whose socio-economic and political interests coincided with 'new' Sober scholars in the colonial era, therefore, were free to lambaste separatism and its leadership with 'Islamic' sanction. Yet, as in the case of Madani's writing, their ire was not directed at Iqbal. Instead, the entire movement was represented as Jinnah's personal scheme. The depth of the divisions this sowed among Muslims is amply illustrated by the distance between pro-separatist reference to Jinnah as *qa'id-i 'azam* ('great leader') and one of the pro-Indian Ahrar leaders famously dubbing him *kafir-i 'azam* ('great infidel'), a representation

---

[147] Ibid., pp. 58–59.
[148] Ibid., pp. 34–37.

that continues to haunt his memory and the historiography of India and Pakistan.

Evidently, the issue of 'India' or 'Pakistan' set off a fresh round of doctrinal battles once publicly raised in 1940. Having outlined all of these divides and others (regional, class-based, etc.) in her work, Jalal cannot be faulted for arguing that Muslim 'consensus' is as far from the reality of the late British Raj as the earth is from the sun. Yet, the irony is that compared with the doctrinal and practical complexity of the Mughal era, the above reality renders the Muslims of late British Raj at least as close to each other as the earth and the moon. No matter their political differences, all of the groups and parties involved agreed on forms of transcendentalism, types of legalism and degrees of *ijtihad*. Thus, it is imprudent to dismiss Shaikh's approach so completely, at least insofar as she emphasises the need to pay closer attention to Islamic doctrine than Jalal. I do not mean to imply that 'the contradiction between regional majorities and religious minorities' was not a factor in shaping the judgement of this 'Punjabi' or that 'Delhi-wala' on any issue, as Jalal so ably illustrates. Nor do I mean to suggest that Iqbal or any other figure who deployed 'Islamic' legitimatisation for political separatism failed to outline how sectarian, ethno-linguistic and other differences would be resolved in a sovereign Muslim state. My central point is that it is the 'this-worldly' orientation of the 'New Islam', Sober and Intoxicated, of which Jalal and Shaikh inadvertently speak, rather than the imagined influence of a 'normative' form, which defines the religious dimension of the 'Inner' domain that Chatterjee identifies as the birthplace of nationalism in South Asia.

The doctrinal distinction between the 'Old' and 'New Islam' is overwhelmingly pertinent to the rise of communalism and the legitimisation of nationalism, composite and separatist. In both cases, this 'newness', though by no means untouched by 'the colonial state's social engineering', was primarily shaped by calls for *ijtihad*, transcendentalism and the dominance of particular forms of legalism, all of which promoted the primacy of religious identity, rather than merely 'religious informed' identities. This 'new' packet of doctrine did not mean that alliances between Muslims of different sects, or Muslims and non-Muslims, were impossible on local or pan-Indian levels. However, shooting for a singularly Islamic identity by means of the 'New Islam' depended on the construction of non-Muslims as absolute cultural 'others', in all cases no longer accepting Hindus in particular as 'People of the

Book'. The difference between the Jama'at-i 'Ulama'-i Hind's composite nationalism, and the Jama'at-i 'Ulama'-i Islam's separatist nationalism, therefore, is not a distinction between 'communitarian' and 'communal' identities. Madani's legitimisation of Indian nationalism, it should be recalled, depended on the creation of a defined legal space for Islamic 'personal law' within India, based on explicitly juristic doctrines and not on the recognition of shared customs, language, history, and so on. The difference between Madani's 'India' and his Deobandi colleague 'Uthmani's Pakistan is ultimately no more than the former's invocation of the minimum doctrinally required for the *qawm*'s participation in a state dominated by 'apostates' and/or 'infidels', versus the latter's idealistic pursuit of the maximum political and legislative scope possible under the circumstances. Even in Iqbal's 'new' Intoxicated line, the legitimacy of Muslims living as *dhimmi*s in a 'Hindu' or 'secular' state is nowhere questioned. Rather, the desire to do so is challenged by the potential to make room for Islamic jurisprudence to legislate more extensively, though in a mode altogether different from that envisioned down the 'new' Sober Path.

That the Muslim League's territorial nationalism averted *dhimmi* status for those Muslims included in Pakistan (or later Bangladesh) cannot be denied. However, 60 years of debate over, and periodic application of, separate electorates for Muslims and non-Muslims in the 'Islamic Republic', primarily championed by advocates of the 'new' Sober Path, rather than Liberals or Socialists, only add credence to the need for further explorations of the 'Islamic frame' into which European ideas were selectively included or rejected in the pressure-cooker of British Raj. As well, when expressed in terms specific to the 'new' Sober Path, consequences for intra-Muslim harmony were as severely threatened as those for the inter-communal. In effect, the 'new' Sober scholar could, did and does explicitly turn scholarly and sectarian differences among Muslims into grounds for charges of 'apostasy', both in India and Pakistan. The slinging of *fatawa* charging alternative interpretations with apostasy is not new. What is novel is the lack of reference to 'heresy' and the fact that almost every group, including scholars and laypersons, was and is doing it. Although first widely employed in an environment charged by colonial intervention, this cannot be entirely explained by the colonial state's contributions to Codification, Anglicisation, Objectification and Nationalism; it can only be fully resolved when the direct influence of the polemical modes of the 'new' Sober

Path are added. As for advocates of the 'new' Intoxicated Way, the same *ijtihad*, transcendentalism and legalism shows that charges of apostasy, etc., ultimately depended on the particular ethos of individual Sober movements and schools, Hali, Ahmad Khan and Iqbal showing great tolerance towards doctrinal variety, despite strong perspectives of their own. What the latter always shared with the former, however, was an approach to Islamic identity that avoided most forms of customary law and latitudinarianism, and all forms of antinomianism. In the absence of the 'old' Intoxicated Way, whose 'absolute immanence', in particular, legitimated customary law, antinomian perspectives and latitudinarian attitudes without compromising doctrinal Islam, the 'Inner' domain's 'New Islam', Intoxicated and Sober, provided greater impetus to reform and engage in religiously collective political activity, but lost most of the 'old' mechanisms by which to accommodate the regional, sectarian and other divides that shaped the 'Outer'.

Conclusion: From Sultanates to Nations

Approaching the post-colonial 'nation' as an 'imagined community' born in an 'Inner' domain of cultural sovereignty, while the 'Outer' is dominated by the assumptions and interests of an alien authority, has resounding value for the closing chapter of a history of Islam in the transition from Mughal to post-colonial South Asia.

A close examination of the 'Inner' domain, focused on gender and community ideals, reveals that although the 'old' Sober Path continued to have some influence in the era of British Raj, it is the 'New Islam', Sober and Intoxicated, that plays the largest role in igniting the imaginations of South Asia's Muslim elite and capitalist classes. That is to say, the almost hegemonic inclination towards transcendentalism, legalism and *ijtihad* is reflected in both the emphasis on 'this-worldly' bonds between the individual and his/her distinct religious community, and the absolute forfeiture of the antinomianism and curtailing of the latitudinarianism promoted by the 'absolute immanence' and 'other-worldly' orientation of the 'old' Intoxicated Way. In Francis Robinson's words, the 'new Muslim self is a doing self'.[149] The 'New Muslim' is

---

[149] Francis Robinson, 'Religious Change and the Self in Muslim South Asia Since 1800', *Islam and Muslim History in South Asia*, pp. 105–21.

one who seeks 'agreement', as most emphatically represented by consensus on some form of *purda* and 'domesticity' in the definition of a woman's place. The 'New Muslim' is one who seeks 'unity', as suggested by consensus on the primacy of religious community, irrespective of acknowledged class and regional distinctions. And finally, the 'New Muslim' is one who 'acts', as confirmed by consensus on the need for individual and collective endeavour in everything from reforming literature to developing the Ego/Self.

When the ideals of the 'Inner' domain's 'New Islam' are read alongside the political options pursued in the 'Outer', the influence of the former on the latter is quite apparent. The individual, from Hali to Madani and from the Sultanas of Bhopal to Fatima Jinnah, are collective, though not identical, 'actors' in the 'this-worldly' interests of the *umma* and *qawm*. The class and regional distinctions of the *watan* undoubtedly influence individual courses pursued, but the 'unity' of Muslims is always the first call accompanying activity, and there is broad 'agreement' on the idea that eschewing past precedent and local custom is the route to betterment. And finally, as long as the legal distinctiveness of the Muslim community, whether at the level of *umma* or *qawm*, is guaranteed, political cooperation ranging from partnered activism to composite nationhood is open to negotiation. Of course, the influence of colonial Codification, Anglicisation and Objectification cannot be discounted in explaining the political options pursued in the 'Outer' domain. Indeed, the political trajectory pursued by the Urdu-speaking Muslim elite and capitalist classes reveals that the initiatives and pressures of British Raj were major contributors in the rise of 'communalism', and that 'the particularisms of the Muslim provinces rather than a supra-local Islamic sentiment…provided the more important driving force' in the formation of Pakistan. However, the best evidence to suggest that there is more at play than the internalisation of European ideas while reacting to colonial pressures is that the above 'consensus' on ideals is accompanied by spectacular discord in practice—discord that cannot be accurately accounted for through the lens of a dominant paradigm on Islam that paints doctrine as statically legalistic and culturally intrusive.

The fact is that despite consensus on 'this worldly-ness', transcendentalism, legalism and *ijtihad*, the 'New Islam' was also variegated, not merely in terms of Sober and Intoxicated approaches, but also permutations under each umbrella. The particulars of that transcendentalism (monistic, monotheistic or absolute), legalism ('old' or 'new') and *ijtihad* (subject to Revelation or Reason/Intuition) legitimated varying degrees of hospitality or hostility towards extra-Islamic influences (intellectual, cultural, socio-economic and political). This variegation, not an ill-conceived disconnect between the 'pragmatic' interests of the 'Western' educated and innate exclusivity of the 'normative' Muslim, illuminates Hali's acceptance of one who turns the 'Prophet into God' as a member of the *umma* and *qawm*, at the same moment that Deobandis, Ahl-i Hadith and others declared all such persons 'apostates', flaming a level of sectarian strife previously unheralded. This diversity, not an assumed tension between 'supra-local ideals' and 'local particularisms', illustrates how members of the Jama'at-i 'Ulama'-i Hind and the Muslim League could join each other and the Indian National Congress to rally behind the symbolism of Caliphate, while the Ahl-i Sunnat and Ahmadiyya could justify sitting on the sidelines. And most importantly with regard to nationalism, this multiplicity, not a false dichotomy between 'communitarianism' and 'communalism', explains why Madani could remain bound to 'composite nationalism', while Iqbal progressively pushed for 'separatism'.

In short and by way of conclusion, the propensity of a history conditioned by the dominant paradigm on Islam to attribute transformation to European influence does shed light on some aspects of the rise of communalism and nationalism, but fails to illumine the relationship between the ideal of Islamic unity and the reality of Muslim discord without falling back on the assumption of inherent bigotry and pragmatic transgression. Only when that paradigm is replaced with one that acknowledges doctrinal Islam as dynamic, multidisciplinary and, depending on the individual subscriber's orientation, ultimately hospitable and/or hostile towards extraneous influences, can an integration of pre-colonial thought and institutions, colonial initiatives and pressures, and the socio-economic and political interests of all the segments of Muslim society be realised, reflecting the manner in which the people who lived this history so obviously saw themselves and their actions. It is in this sense that the 'Muslim' or 'Hindu' nations 'imagined' by the mid-20th century, India and Pakistan, were from the 'Islamic' perspective equally legitimate. Living as *dhimmi*s in India, or exercising full legislative authority in Pakistan, were in the final analysis two sides of the same doctrinal coin, leaving individual Muslims to call one or the other depending on disparate interests rooted in the particularisms of Muslim provinces. What was missing from this 'New Islam', however—an omission indisputably rooted in the decline of Muslim power and the destruction of institutions that followed, rather than British 'perceptions of Indian society as an aggregate of religious communities'—was the 'old' option of collapsing the distinction between the '72 sects of Islam and Hinduism'. Thus, although Iqbal proposed a separate state, even Muhammad 'Ali Jawahar, who had almost simultaneously spoken of belonging to 'two circles'—India and the Muslim World—did not fail to remind his audience that these circles 'are not concentric'.[150]

---

[150] Muhammad 'Ali Jawahar, *Selected Speeches and Writings*, vol. 2, pp. 350–61.

CONCLUSION

TOWARDS A 'POST-ORIENTALIST' HISTORY

Despite concerted efforts to remove the bullet of Orientalism's assumptions and essentialisms from the study of Islam and Muslims, shards remain lodged in the body of scholarship. Here, I am not referring to overt examples such as the thesis of a 'clash of civilisations', but to many works that themselves seek to move beyond the terms set by 18th and 19th century Orientalists, as well as by 20th century Nationalists. Common to all the above works, no residue of the Orientalist discourse is more deforming than the essentialisation of doctrinal Islam as statically legalistic and the assumption that this legalism is always culturally intrusive. This dated paradigm is evident in histories of South Asia that portray Sultan Akbar's intellectual and institutional mediationism as a 'transgression' of doctrinal Islam, while casting Sultan Awrangzib's legalism as not only a sign of 'pristine' Islam, but also necessarily 'exclusivistic', if not 'bigoted'. The same paradigm is also apparently influential in works that present the doctrinal changes initiated by the early 18th century, as well as the decline of the *madrasa* and its reconstitution in the 19th century, as more of the same in comparison with the effects of British policy leading to Codification, Anglicisation and Objectification. The identical problem looms in works that view the influence of 'Western' education as further 'transgression' where acknowledged by Muslims, and when not, as more signs of Islamic 'exclusivity' and/or 'bigotry'. And finally, the dominant paradigm is no less evident in works that interpret the newness of communalism and nationalism as nothing other than an extension of colonial initiatives and exigencies, whether forwarded by the authorities or adopted by their subjects.

When that shard is extracted, a rather different history takes shape, beginning with the fact that doctrinal Islam is multidisciplinary and variable within disciplines. Theology includes concepts of immanent monism, transcendental monism, monotheism and absolute transcendentalism. Jurisprudence is rooted in four Sunni and two Shi'a schools, most accepting concepts of independent reasoning, analogical reasoning and consensus, some extending to notions of public utility, equity and the virtual inclusion of customary law as an additional source of the *shariʿa*. Mysticism ranges from concepts included in theology and jurisprudence to the addition of antinomian and latitudinarian doctrines, while also exploring the ethical and psychological aspects of the human experience. In addition, philosophy inserts further perspective on theological, mystical and legal discourses, extends discussions of politics, economics, ethics and psychology, and ventures into various fields of rational scientific inquiry. Considering only these general interests and formulations, it is clear that the views of theologians, jurists, mystics and philosophers acknowledge Reason and Intuition as alternative sources of knowledge to Revelation. Philosophers, Muʿtazili theologians and extreme 'wujudi' mystics go further, routinely declaring Reason and/or Intuition sources of knowledge 'equivalent' to Revelation, while the jurists, Ashʿari theologians, some 'wujudi' and all 'shuhudi' mystics profess in theory, if not in practice, the primacy of Revelation over Reason and/or Intuition. Therefore, non-scriptural knowledge and local customary practice are almost always accorded space in the definition of the 'Islamic', depending on one or the other of the two relationships drawn between Reason/Intuition and Revelation, each forwarding particular socio-ethical worldviews that I refer to as the 'Sober Path' and the 'Intoxicated Way'. These two Paths and Ways are themselves subject to forks. Although all on the Sober Path divide the world into two religious groups, 'Muslims' and 'non-Muslims', each fork leads to a particular blend of hospitality and hostility towards the people, objects, institutions and intellectualism active in any locality. The 'Intoxicated Way' is also forked, some branches intersecting with the Path, others leading to antinomian and/or latitudinarian potentialities that chart alternative ground. Unless a value judgement is imposed on such multiplicity, essentialising one or another Path or Way as 'orthodox', any valid conception of doctrinal Islam must include them all and their particular brands of hostility and hospitality.

Practice may not match theory, but Akbar and his supporters clearly acknowledged and espoused the Intoxicated Way, while Awrangzib and his cadre obviously propagated the Sober Path. Thus, when confronted with governing a region defined by multiple traditions and identities, Akbar deployed Sufi, Ishraqi and other philosophies as a means to forward his and his supporters political and socio-economic interests. All of the above branches of the Intoxicated Way promoted the equivalence of Islamic and pre-Islamic thought and institutions, i.e. the end of the '72 sects of Islam and the Hindus', in exchange for the relatively free reign of class, vocational, tribal and ethnic 'customs'. When bequeathed the same multiplicity, though aligned in rather different ways, Awrangzib apparently believed that alternative forms of Sufism, philosophy, etc., were the order of the day. Doctrines reflective of the Sober Path promoted cultures that reign in class, vocational, tribal and ethnic customs by drawing firm borders between individual sects among the '72'. Akbar and Awrangzib could afford these tactics because neither Paths and Ways were 'transgressions' of the complex of thought that is doctrinal Islam, but both allowed the legitimisation of important aspects of the local environment in which they lived and sought to rule. Akbar's and Awrangzib's intellectual and institutional proclivities, therefore, illustrate that 'embeddedness' in 'India' is a function of 'connectedness' to the broader 'Muslim World'.

This raises another level of complexity, with the Sober Path and Intoxicated Way not merely being variegated in a given space and time, but free to systematically chart alternative avenues when new spaces and times are encountered. Thus, the late 17th and early 18th century's capitalisation of the economy, regionalisation of culture, and decentralisation of political authority led to the mapping of a 'new' Sober Path that responded to capitalisation and regionalism by accommodating vernacular languages and regional polities, while promoting a textual, codified and anti-customary perspective through those languages and polities in an effort to establish religious uniformity. As long as political authority (even in decentralised form) remained in Muslim hands, this new branch remained peripheral, with the institutions supporting the entire complex of Paths and Ways continuing to function. Once colonial authority began to displace Muslim rule, however, supporting institutions crumbled, leaving only those directly or indirectly representative of the 'new' Sober Path to lead reconstitution. In other words, the 'Old Islam', with its multiple hospitable/hostile Paths and Ways to local thought and institutions, was left in ruin. As if losing the structure of learning was not sufficiently devastating, the simultaneous introduction of 'Western' education's challenge to the 'Old Islam's' theology, metaphysics and other rational sciences, left little room for a healthy recovery. The majority of those on the 'new' Sober Path, already doctrinally reductionist and scholastically handicapped by the ongoing destruction of supportive institutions, could only respond by further distancing the rational sciences from doctrine. Subsequently, by the late 19th century, barely a sliver of the 'Old Islam' remained, the effect of which is evident today: Reason, Intuition, the disciplines that employed them and the socio-ethical worldviews they engendered are broadly discredited as 'un-Islamic' by large segments of the contemporary '*ulama*'.

In these desperate straits, a few thinkers activated those branches of the 'old' Intoxicated Way that intersected with 'new' Sober Path, to replace the lamp of ancient systems with the bulb of modern European thought, thus mapping the branches of a 'new' Intoxicated Way. Being intimately connected, the 'new' Sober Path and the 'new' Intoxicated Way shared such pivotal doctrines as transcendentalism, legalism and *ijtihad* (independent reasoning), forsaking absolute immanence and its antinomian and latitudinarian potentiality. Thus, the socio-ethical worldview of the 'New Islam', including the 'new' Intoxicated Way, was substantively different from the 'Old', particularly with regard to notions of community. In fact, British perceptions of Muslims and Hindus as primary and distinct communities in South Asia had been amplified in Muslim ears even before the effects of Codification, Anglicisation and Objectification could transfer British assumptions and essentialisms to their subjects. This is a pivotal factor in explaining the rapidity of the rise of 'communalism' among the elite and capitalist Muslim classes, even if the particularisms of localities remained dominant in reality. That is not to imply that the particulars of transcendentalism (monistic, monotheistic or absolute), legalism ('old' or 'new') and *ijtihad* (subject to Revelation or Reason/Intuition) did not afford varying degrees of hospitality or hostility towards extra-scriptural influences (intellectual, cultural, socio-economic and political), extending to alliances with other religious communities. In fact, responses to the intellectual, cultural, socio-economic and political conditions of the colonial era exhibit multiple examples of the legitimisation of non-scriptural knowledge, sectarian variety and local customary practice. Pro- and anti-colonial positions, as well as the option of composite and separatist attitudes towards South Asia's non-Muslims in the imagining of nations, further illustrate the 'New Islam's' capacity for hospitality. However, the singular and constant difference between the 'Old' and 'New Islam' is that, in the latter case, all affiliations were between sectarian and/or religious communities. Nowhere in the colonial period can an urge, let alone an effort, to dissolve sectarian/religious boundaries in the manner of the 'Great Mughal' era be observed.

Of course, colonial initiatives and interests cannot be discounted in explaining the lack of antinomian and/or latitudinarian doctrines in the 'New Islam'. Aside from the destruction of doctrinal Islam's institutional base along with Muslim polities, the erection of colonial institutions that categorised Muslims as a religio-political 'minority' and depicted them as cohesively antagonistic to the Hindu 'majority' rendered antinomian and latitudinarian doctrines a threat to the socio-economic well-being of the Muslim elite and capitalist classes. That the 'New Islam' excluded antinomian/latitudinarian tendencies, therefore, is less related to European intellectual influence, than to the structure of colonial intervention, including the hostility of the Hindu 'majority' it simultaneously constructed. In a colonial environment, the exclusion of antinomian and curtailment of latitudinarian doctrines carried a number of advantages: first, it fulfilled the will to work within an 'Islamic frame'; second, it considered the desire to access and assimilate aspects of European thought; and third, it factored in the need to safeguard political and socio-economic interests. That is to say, the 'New Islam', Sober and Intoxicated, is a series of choices made by its authors, not unlike those made by Muslims in the Mughal context or elsewhere, albeit under the pressure of specifically colonial circumstances that were rife with psychological impediments. These choices, particularly the muting of antinomian and latitudinarian doctrines, not only made it possible for a Muslim 'minority' to politically, socio-economically and culturally ally with the Hindu 'majority' in the making of an Indian 'nation', they also added the option of Pakistan to which so many eventually flocked.

When choice is part of the equation, an understanding of doctrinal Islam as dynamic and variegated, and of Muslim practice as hospitable and hostile to aspects of local time and space, broadens the scope of historical discussion to include consideration of thought and institutions otherwise only mentioned in passing. It also illuminates otherwise obscured insights on the post-colonial context. Most obviously, variety and choice expose the *'shari'as'* of states like Saudi Arabia, the Islamic Republic of Iran and the Islamic Republic of Pakistan as products of 18th century capitalisation, etc., colonialism and post-colonial realities, rather than representing the 'normative' ideals of Islam and Muslims. The same can be said for non-state actors, like Al-Qa'ida and the Taliban Movement. The differences between these states as well as between state and non-state actors further reveals variety in political philosophy and social ideals, while difference of opinion on issues ranging from nationalism to the use of violence as a valid means to an end illustrate that although all of these groups represent the 'new' Sober Path, dynamism and variegation within that complex of thought and institutions is by no means absent. And finally, any attempt to equate the 'new' Sober Path with doctrinal Islam is itself belayed by the fact that an Intoxicated Way, 'old' and 'new', has in the past and continues into the present to play a role in the definition of doctrine and the socio-ethical worldview of Muslims.

Dynamism and variety in the composition of Islamic doctrine also exposes the fact that the choices available to Muslims are not relegated to some form of the 'new' Sober Path, on the one hand, or some 'Western' model on the other. There is also the 'new' Intoxicated Way and the entire intellectual and institutional gamut of the 'Old Islam', which are no less 'Islamic', yet historically proven to repose an extraordinary capacity to systematically bridge not only Islamic and European thought and institutions, but also those of other traditions, past and present. The merit in revitalising the 'old' theory of *jihad* that explicitly forbade attacks on non-combatants—rather than adopting the disregard for civilian life characteristic of 'modern' warfare—is only the most obvious change possible. Consider, further, that one of the noteworthy features of the 'new' Sober Path that differentiates it from the 'old' is the effacement of the distinction between 'heretics' and 'apostates', as well as between 'People of the Book' and 'infidels'. In essence, not only has the capacity for antinomianism and latitudinarianism across faith lines been forfeited, but 'new' Sober thinkers even actively bar passage to Muslim 'others' on their own portion of the Path. Thus, as Hali so eloquently put it as early as the 1870s, it has even become 'impossible to find 10 Muslims who will be happy to see one another'. Since that acute notion of the 'other' is ultimately related to the manner in which late thinkers responded and continue to respond to the political, socio-economic and intellectual conditions unleashed by capitalisation and colonialism, restoring 'old' Paths and Ways so 'new' extensions can be constructed in response to contemporary realities resolves as an important component of a 'happier' future. Sayyid Ahmad Khan thought it possible, seeking to revive aspects of 'old' theology, in the process opening the door to assimilating and rejecting aspects of Europe's 'new arts and sciences', while remaining politically committed to the interests of his Muslim *qawm* under British rule. Muhammad Iqbal felt the same, ignoring the 'new' jurisprudence, while beginning to reconstruct the 'old', with its concepts of analogical reasoning, consensus, public utility and equity, when pondering the workability of Europe's political institutions within an 'Islamic frame,' without compromising a firmly anti-colonial political stance. These are just two drops in an ocean of alternatives. It remains to be seen whether contemporary Muslims—currently shackled by the authority invested in the 'new' Sober Path and European thought and institutions, both of which conceive of Islamic doctrine as rigid and Muslim practice as set—can break these bonds to better address the issues confronting them today.

SELECTED BIBLIOGRAPHY

Primary Sources

Books

Adam, William. *Second Report on the State of Education in Bengal*. Calcutta: G.H. Huttman, 1836.
—— *Third Report of the State of Education in Bengal*. Calcutta: G.H. Huttman, 1838.
Ahmad, Mirza Ghulam. *Ta'lim-i Islam: Islami Usul ki Falasifi*. Lahore: n.p., 1960.
—— *A Review of Christianity from a New Point of View*. Qadian: Nazir Dawat-o-Tabligh, 1973.
—— *Siraj al-Din 'Isai ke Char Sawalun ka Jawab*. Lahore: Sunrise, 1968.
—— *'Isa Hindustan Main*. Lahore: Nisar Art Press, 1962.
Ahmad, Nizam al-Din. *Tabaqat-i Akbari*. 3 vols. Trans. Brajendranath De. Calcutta: Royal Asiatic Society, 1939.
'Ali, Sayyid Mumtaz. *Huquq al-Niswan*. Lahore: Dar al-Isha'at-i Punjab, 1898.
Annand, *A Brief Outline of the Existing System for the Government of India*. London: Saunders & Benning, 1832.
Argyll, G.D.C. *The Eastern Question from the Treaty of Paris 1856 to the Treaty of Berlin 1878*. London: n.p., 1879.
Arnold, Edwin. *Education in India*. London: Bell & Daldy, 1860.
Awliya', Nizam al-Din. *Fawa'id al-Fuad*. Ed. and trans. B.B. Lawrence, *Morals of the Heart*. New York: Paulist Press, 1992.
Azad, Muhammad Husayn. *Ab-i Hayat*. Lucknow: U.P. Urdu Academy, 1982.
al-Bada'uni, 'Abd al-Qadir. *Muntakhab al-Tawarikh*. 3 vols. Trans. G.S.A. Ranking [I], W.H. Lowe [II], W. Haig [III]. Delhi: Idara-i Adabiyat-i Delli, 1973.
Bahadur, Hamid al-Din Khan. *Ahkam-i 'Alamgiri*. Trans. Jadunath Sarkar, *Anecdotes of Aurangzeb*. Calcutta: Sarkar & Sons, 1963.
Barani, Diya' al-Din. *Fatawa-i Jahandari*. Trans. Afsar Khan & ed. Habib, Muhammad, *The Political Theory of the Delhi Sultanate*. Delhi: Kitab Mahal, 1962.
—— *Tarikh-i Firoz Shahi*. Trans. H.M. Elliot, *History of India III*. Delhi: Kitab Mahal, 1964.
Barelwi, Sayyid Ahmad. *Makatib-i Sayyid Ahmad*. Lahore: Photolitho., n.d.
Bernier, Francois. *Travels in the Mughal Empire*. Trans. Archibald Constable. Delhi: S. Chand & Co., 1972.
Buckingham, J.S. *Plan for the Future Government of India of India*. London: Partridge & Oakey, 1853.
Burton, Richard. 'Muslim Education at Schools and Colleges under the Native Rulers and Our Government', in *Education in Sind Before the British Conquest and the Educational Policies of the British Government*. Hyderabad: University of Sind, 1971.
Colquhoun, A.R. *Russia Against India*. London: Harper & Brothers, 1900.
Connell, K. *Discontent and Danger in India*. London: C. Kegan Paul, 1880.
Dehlawi, Shah 'Abd al-'Aziz. *Fatawa-i Shah 'Abd al-'Aziz*. 2 vols. Delhi: n.p., 1893–94.
Dehlawi, Shah Wali Allah, *Fawz al-Kabir fi Usul al-Tafsir*. Trans. G.N. Jalbani. Islamabad: National Hijra Council, 1985.
—— *Hujjat Allah al-Baligha*. Trans. M.K. Hermansen. Leiden: E.J. Brill, 1996.
—— *Lamahat*. Trans. G.N. Jalbani. Hyderabad: Shah Wali Allah Academy, 1970.
—— *Sata'at*. Trans. G.N. Jalbani. Hyderabad: Shah Wali Allah Academy, 1970.

—— *Ta'wil al-Ahadith.* Trans. G.N. Jalbani. Lahore: Shan Muhammad Ashraf, 1973.
Fatawa al-'Alamgiriyya. 10 vols. Karachi: Qadimi Kutub Khana, n.d.
Frere, H.B.E. 'Education in Sind', in *Education in Sind Before the British Conquest and the Educational Policies of the British Government.* Hyderabad: University of Sind, 1971.
Gangohi, Rashid Ahmad. *Tafsir-i Rashidi.* Bijnur: Madni Dar al-Talif, 1970.
—— *Hidayat al-Shi'a.* Karachi: Kutub Khana-i Haqqaniyya, 1963.
—— *Fatawa-i Rashidiyya.* Karachi: Saeed Company, 1967.
al-Ghazali, Abu Hamid Muhammad. *Munqidh min al-Dalal.* Ed. and trans. W. Montgomery Watt, *The Faith and Practice of al-Ghazali.* Lahore: Shan Muhammad Ashraf, 1963.
—— *Ihya 'Ulum al-Din.* 3 vols. Trans. Fazl al-Karim. Karachi: Dar al-Isha'at, 1993.
Graham, G.F.I. *The Life and Work of Sir Sayyid Ahmad Khan.* Delhi: Idara-i Adabiyat-i Delli, 1974.
Grant, R. *A Sketch of the History of the East India Company from its Formation to the Regulation Act of 1773.* London: Black, Parry & Co., 1813.
Hali, Altaf Husayn. *Madd-o-Jazr-i Islam.* Ed. and trans. C. Shackle and J. Majeed, *Hali's Musaddas.* Delhi: Oxford University Press, 1997.
—— *Hayat-i Javed*, Trans K.H. Qadari & D.J. Matthews. Delhi: Idara-i Adabiyat-i Delli, 1979.
—— *Majalis-i Nisa.* New Delhi: Maktaba-i Jamia, 1971.
Hasan, Mahmud. *Hazrat Shaykh al-Hind Mawlana Mahmud al-Hasan Sahib ka Ek Zaruri Khatt.* Azamgarh: Khilafat Committee, 1921.
—— *Khutba-i Sadarat aur Fatwa Tark-i Muwalat.* Deoband: Matba'-i Qasimi, 1920.
al-Hujwiri, 'Ali ibn 'Uthman. *Kashf al-Mahjub.* Trans. Renold A. Nicholson. Karachi: Dar al-Isha'at, 1990.
Husain, Rokeya. *Sultana's Dream and Selections from the Secluded Ones.* Ed. and trans. R. Jahan. New York: Feminist Press, 1981.
Husayn, Sayyid Nazir. *Fatawa-i Naziriyya.* 4 vols. Delhi: Printing Works, 1915.
Ibn 'Abd al-Wahhab, Muhammad. *Kitab al-Tawhid.* Trans. A.M. Mujahid. Riyadh: Dar al-Salam Publications, 1996.
Ibn al-'Arabi, Muhi al-Din. *Fusus al-Hikam.* Ed. and trans. R.W.J. Austin, *The Bezels of Wisdom.* New Pork: Paulist Press, 1980.
Ibn Mubarak, Abu al-Fadl. *Mukatabat-i 'Allami, daftar I.* Ed. and trans. Mansura Haidar. Delhi: Munshiram Manoharlal Publishers, 1998.
—— *Akbar Nama.* 3 vols. Trans. H. Beveridge. Calcutta: Asiatic Society, 1907.
—— *A'in-i Akbari.* 3 vols. Trans. H. Blochmann. Calcutta: Asiatic Society of Bengal, 1927.
Ibn al-Muqaffa'. *Risala fi 'l-Sahaba.* Ed. and trans. Charles Pellat. Paris: Maisonneuve et Larose, 1976.
Ibn Rushd, Abu al-Walid Muhammad. *Bidayat al-Mujtahid.* Trans. Rudolph Peters. Leiden: E.J. Brill, 1977.
Ibn Taymiyya, Taqi al-Din Ahmad. *Risala fi 'l-Siyasa al-Shar'iyya.* Ed. and trans. Omar Farrukh, *Ibn Taymiyya on Public and Private Law in Islam.* Beirut: Khayat Book & Publishing Co., 1966.
—— *Al-Hisba fi 'l-Islam.* Trans. M. Holland. Leicester: The Islamic Foundation, 1985.
Iqbal, Muhammad. *Kulliyat-i Iqbal.* Lahore: Shaykh Ghulam 'Ali & Sons, 1973.
—— *Iqbal: A Selection of Urdu Verse.* Ed. and trans. D.J. Matthews. New Delhi: Heritage Publishers, 1993.
—— *Bang-i Dara.* Lahore: Jahangir Book Depot, n.d.
—— *The Reconstruction of Religious Thought in Islam.* Lahore: Sang-i Meel, 1996.
—— *Asrar-i Khudi.* Trans. R.A. Nicholson. Lahore: Shaykh Muhammad Ashraf, 1983.
—— *Speeches and Statements of Iqbal.* ed. L.A. Sherwani. Lahore: Al-Manar Academy, 1948.
—— *Letters of Iqbal to Jinnah.* Lahore: Muhammad Ashraf, n.d.
Jawahar, Muhammad 'Ali. *Selected Speeches and Writings of Maulana Mohamed Ali.* Ed. Afzal Iqbal. Lahore: Muhammad Ashraf, 1944.

Jayasi, Malik Muhammad. *The Padumawati of Malik Muhammad Jayasi*. Ed. and trans. G.A. Grierson. Calcutta: Asiatic Society, 1911.
The Judicial System of British India. London: Pelham Richardson, 1852.
Jurjani, Minhaj al-Siraj. *Tabaqat-i Nasir*. Trans. H. Raverty. Delhi: Oriental Books Reprint Corp., 1970.
Khan, Abu Talib. *Travels of Mirza Abu Taleb Khan*. 2 vols. Trans. C. Stewart. London: Longman, 1814.
Khan, Ahmad Rida. *Al-Ataya li-Nabawiyya fi'l Fatawa al-Rizwiyya*. 6 vols. Mubarakpur: Sunni Dar al-Isha'at, 1981.
—— *Malfuzat-i 'Ala' Hazrat*. 4 vols. Gujarat: Fazl-i Academy, n.d.
—— *Fatwa al-Haramain bi-Rajf Nadwat al-Main*. Bareilly: Matba'-i Ahl-i Sunnat wa Jama'at, 1900.
—— *Do Ahamm Fatwe*. Lahore: Maktaba Rizwiyya, 1977.
—— *Husam al-Haramayn 'ala Manhar al-Kufr wa al-Mayn*. Lahore: Maktaba Nabawiyya, 1985.
Khan, Ghulam Husein. *Siyar al-Muta'kharin*. Trans. Haji Mustapha. Calcutta: J. White, 1790.
Khan, Muhammad Khafi. *Muntakhab al-Lubab*. Ed. and trans., S. Moinul Haq, *Khafi Khan's History of Alamgir*. Karachi: Pakistan Historical Society Journal, 1975.
Khan, Saqi Musta'id. *Ma'athir-i Alamgiri*. Trans. J.N. Sarkar. Calcutta: Royal Asiatic Society, 1947.
Khan, Sayyid Ahmad. *Haqiqat-i Khilafat*. Lahore: Ripon Press, 1916.
—— *The Present State of Indian Politics: Speeches and Letters*. Ed. Theodore Beck. Lahore: Sang-i Meel Publications, 1982.
—— *Sarkashi-i Zila Bijnor*. Karachi: Salman Akademi, 1962.
—— *Asbab Baghawat-i Hind*. Delhi: Kutub Khana-i Anjuman-i Taraqqi, 1971.
—— *Inthikhab-i Mazamin-i Aligarh Institiyut Gazat*. Lucknow: Uttar Pradesh Akademi, 1982.
—— *Tahdhib al-Akhlaq*. 2 vols. Lahore: Tajiran Kutub Qawmi, n.d.
—— *Maqalat-i Sar Sayyid*. 16 vols. Lahore: Majlis-i Taraqqi-i Adab, 1962.
—— *Tafsir al-Quran*. 6 vols. Lahore: Dost Associates, 1998.
—— *Musafiran-i Landan*. Lahore: Majlis-i Taraqqi-i Adab, 1961.
—— *Review of Dr. Hunter's Indian Musalmans; are they bound by conscience to rebel against the Queen?* Lahore: Premier Book House, n.d.
—— *Writings and Speeches of Sir Sayyid Ahmad Khan*. Ed. S. Muhammad. Bombay: Nachiketa Publications, 1972.
Khan, Shah Nawaz. *Ma'athir al-Umara'*. Trans. H. Beveridge. Patna: Janaki Prakashan, 1979.
Khan, Siddiq Hasan. *Tarjuman-i Wahhabiyya*. Lahore: n.p., 1895.
Leitner, G.W. *History of Indigenous Education in the Punjab*. Calcutta: Government Printing Press, 1883.
Long, James. *The Position of Turkey in Relation to British Interests in India*. London: East India Association, 1876.
Maccoll, M. *Three Years of the 'Eastern Question'*. London: Chatto & Wyndus, 1878.
Madani, Husayn Ahmad. *Muttahida Qawmiyyat aur Islam*. Deoband: Majlis-i Qasim al-Ma'arif, 1941.
Mahomet, Dean. *The Travels of Dean Mahomet*. Ed. Michael H. Fischer. Berkeley: University of California Press, 1997.
Maneri, Sharaf al-Din ibn Yahya. *Maktubat al-Sadi*. Ed. and trans. Syed Hasan Askari. New York: Paulist Press, 1980.
Manucci, Niccolao. *Storia do Mogor*. 3 vols. Trans. W. Irvine. Calcutta: Editions Indian, 1966.
Al-Mawardi, Abu al-Hasan. *Al-Ahkam al Sultaniyya w' al-Wilayat al-Diniyya*. Ed. and trans. W.H. Wahba, *The Ordinances of Government*. Reading: Garnet Publishers, 1996.
Mill, J.S. *Memorandum of the Improvements in the Administration of India During the Last 30 Years*. London: W.H. Allen, 1858.

Monserrate, Antonious. *The Commentary of Father Monserrate*. Trans. J.S. Hoyland. Calcutta: Oxford University Press, 1922.
Nagar, Ishwardas. *Futuhat-i 'Alamgiri*. Trans. Tasneem Ahmad. Delhi: Idara-i Adabiyat-i Delli, 1978.
Nanawtawi, Muhammad Qasim. *Qibla Numa*. Deoband: Majlis Ma'arif al-Quran, 1969.
—— *Tahdhir al-Nass*. Delhi: Matba' Mujtaba'i, 1891.
—— *Manazara-i Ajibat*. Muradabad: Matba' Gulzar-i Ibrahim, 1890.
—— *Tafsiyat al-Aqa'id*. Delhi: Matba'-i Mujtaba'i, 1934.
Nanawtawi, Muhammad Yaqub. *Sawahn-i Qasimi*. Delhi: Mujtaba-i Press, 1894.
Nevison, H.W. *Scenes in the Thirty Days War between Greece and Turkey*. London: J.M. Dent, 1898.
Nizam ul-Mulk. *Siyasat Nama*. Trans. H. Darke. London: Routledge & Kegan Paul, 1978.
Numani, Shibli. *Safar Nama-i Rum wa Misr wa Sham*. Lahore: M. Sana Allah Khan, 1961.
—— *Sirat al Nabi*. Karachi: Dar al-Isha'at, 1984.
Perris, G.H. *The Eastern Crisis of 1897 and British Policy in the Near East*. London: n.p., 1897.
Perry, Erskine. *Cases Illustrative of Oriental Life: the Application of English Law to India*. New Delhi: Asian Educational Services, 1988.
Proposal of a Plan for Remodeling the Government of India. London: Smith, Elder & Co., 1853.
Al-Qandahari, Muhammad 'Arif. *Tarikh-i Akbari*. Trans. Tasneem Ahmad. Delhi: Pragati Publishers, 1993.
S. (An Indian Civil Service Officer), *Turkey and India or Our Indian Muslims*. London: W. Ridgeway, 1876.
Shahid, Shah Muhammad Isma'il. *Taqwiyat al-Iman*. Karachi: Nur Muhammad Asah al-Matabi' wa Karkhana Tijarat Kutub, 1958.
—— *Sirat al-Mustaqim*. Deoband: Kutab Khana-i Ashrafiyya Rashid Co., 1960.
—— *Darajat-i Imamat*. Delhi: Farangi Press, 1899.
—— *Abaqat*. Hyderabad: Al-Lajanat al-'Ilmiyya, 1960.
Sinclair, T. *A Defence of Russia and the Christians of Turkey*. London: Chapman & Hall, 1877.
Sirhindi, Shaykh Ahmad. *Maktubat Imam Rabbani*. Ed. Nur Muhammad. Lahore: Nur Muhammad, 1964.
Sutherland, J. *Sketches of the Relations Subsisting Between the British Government in India and the Different Native States*. Calcutta: Military Orphan Press, 1837.
Thanawi, Ashraf 'Ali. *Bihishti Zewar*. Karachi: Karkhana-i Tirajat-i Kutub, 1914.
—— *Hayat al-Muslimin*. Delhi: 'Ilmi Kitab Khana, 1962.
Thanawi, Imdad Allah. *Tahqiq-i Wahdat al-Wujud wa al-Shuhud*. Karachi: Pak-i Akademi, 1963.
—— *Diya' al-Qulub*. Delhi: Matba'-i Mujtaba'i, 1877.
—— *Kulliyat-i Imdadiyya*. Kanpur: Matba'-i Qayyumi, 1943.
—— *Marqumat-i Imdadiyya*. Delhi: Maktaba-i Burhan, 1979.
—— *Faisala-i Haft Mas'ala*. Kanpur: Matba'-i Majidi, 1960.
Trevelyan, C.E. *On the Education of the People of India*. London: Longman, 1838.
Tytler, Alexander F. *Considerations on the Present Political State of India*. London: Black, Parry & Co., 1815.

Documentary Anthologies/Microfilm Collections

The Aligarh Movement: Basic Documents, 3 vols. Ed. Shan Muhammad. Delhi: Meenakshi Prakashan, 1978.
The Great Indian Education Debate. Eds. Lynn Zastoupil and M. Moir. Richmond: Curzon Press, 1999.
Imperialism and Orientalism: A Documentary Source Book. Eds. B. Harlow and M. Carter. Massachussets: Blackwell, 1999.
Jinnah on Pakistan. Ed. Syed Sharifuddin Peerzada. Bombay: Kitab Publishing House, 1943.
The Legends of the Punjab. 3 vols. Ed. and trans. R.C. Temple. Islamabad: Institute of Folk Heritage, 1981.
Letters from the Mughal Court: 1580–1583. Ed and trans. John Correia-Afonso. Anand: Gujarat Sahitya Prakash, 1980.
Muslim League Documents. Ed. Sharif al-Mujahid. Karachi: Quaid-i Azam Academy, 1990.
One Teacher, One School. Ed. J. DiBona. New Delhi: Biblia Impex Ltd., 1983.
Publications Proscribed by the Government of India. Eds. Graham Shaw and Mary Lloyd. London: British Library, 1985.
Selected Documents from the Aligarh Archives. Ed. Yusuf Husain. Bombay: Asia Publishing House, 1966.
Selections from Bengal Government Records on Wahhabi Trials (1863–1870). Ed. Muinuddin Ahmad Khan. Dacca: Asiatic Society of Pakistan, 1961.
Sources of Indian Tradition II. Ed. Stephen Hay. New York: Columbia University Press, 1988.

Newspapers

Allen's India Mail (1857–58)
The British Indian Advocate (1857)
The British Standard (1857)
The Colonial Gazette (1857)
The Guardian (1857)
The London Times (1857–58; 1876–77; 1897–98)

Secondary Sources

Articles

Abd al-Kadir, Ali. 'Land, Property and Land Tenure in Islam.' *Islamic Quarterly* 5 (1959).
Aftab, Tahera. 'Reform Societies and Women's Education in Northern India.' *Journal of the Pakistan Historical Society* 35:2 (Apr. 1987).
Ahmad, S.G. 'A Typological Study of State Functionaries Under the Mughals.' *Asian Profile* 10 (1982).
Alam, Muzaffar. 'State Building Under the Mughals: Religion, Culture and Politics.' *Cahiers d'asie centrale* 3–4 (1997).
Ali, Muhammad A. 'A Critical Evaluation of Shah Wali Allah's Attitude to Ijtihad vis-à- vis the Views of other Jurists.' *Hamdard Islamicus* 20:1 (1997).
Anderson, M.R. 'Islamic Law and the Colonial Encounter in British India', *Institutions and Ideologies.* Eds. D. Arnold and P. Robb. London: Curzon Press, 1993.
Antoun, Richard. 'The Islamic Court, the Islamic Judge, and the Accommodation of Tradition.' *International Journal of Middle East Studies* 12 (1980).

Arnold, David. 'Gramsci and Peasant Subalternality in India.' *Subaltern Studies I*. Ed. R. Guha. Delhi: Oxford University Press, 1982.

Al-Awa, M. 'The Place of Custom in Islamic Legal Theory.' *Islamic Quarterly* 17 (1973).

Al-Azmeh, Aziz. 'Islamic Legal Theory and the Appropriation of Reality.' *Islamic Law: Social and Historical Context*. Ed. A. al-Azmeh. London: Routledge, 1988.

Baer, G. 'The Waqf as a Prop for the Social System (16th–20th Centuries).' *Islamic Law and Society* 4:3 (1997).

Bayly, C.A. 'The Pre-History of Communalism? Religious Conflict in India, 1700–1860.' *Modern Asian Studies* 19:2 (1985).

Behl, Aditya. 'The Landscape of Paradise: Malik Muhammad Jayasi and the Embodied City.' Paper delivered at the 9th Annual South Asia Conference. Berkeley: University of California, 1995.

Bhadra, Gautam. 'Four Rebels of 1857.' *Selected Subaltern Studies*. Eds. R. Guha and G. Spivak. New York: Oxford University Press, 1988.

—— 'The Mentality of Subalternity: Kantanama and Rajdharma', *Subaltern Studies VI*. Delhi: Oxford University Press, 1989.

Bilgrami, Rafat. 'Women Grantees in the Mughal Empire.' *Journal of the Pakistan Historical Society* 36:3 (1988).

Blake, S.P. 'The Patrimonial-Bureaucratic Empire of the Mughals.' *Journal of Asian Studies* 39 (1997).

Bonouvrie, Netty. 'Female Sufi Saints on the Indian Subcontinent.' *Religious Traditions*. Eds. R. Kloppenborg and W. Hanegraaf. Leiden: E.J. Brill, 1995.

Brenner, Louis. 'Muslim Thought in Eighteenth century West Africa.' *Eighteenth Century Muslim Renewal and Revivalist Movements*. Eds. N. Levitzion and J. Voll. Syracuse: University Press, 1987.

Brett, Michael 'The Way of the Peasant.' *Bulletin of the School of Oriental and African Studies XLVII* (1984).

Chakrabarty, Dipesh. 'Conditions for Knowledge of Working Class Conditions: Employers, Government and the Jute Workers of Calcutta, 1890–1940.' *Subaltern Studies II*. Ed. R. Guha Delhi: Oxford University Press, 1983.

—— 'Trade Unions in a Hierarchical Culture: The Jute Workers of Calcutta, 1920–50.' *Subaltern Studies III*. Ed. R. Guha. Delhi: Oxford University Press, 1984.

—— 'Invitation to Dialogue.' *Subaltern Studies IV*. Ed. R. Guha Delhi: Oxford University Press, 1985.

Chatterjee, Partha. 'Agrarian relations and Communalism in Bengal, 1926–35.' *Subaltern Studies I*. Ed. R. Guha. Delhi: Oxford University Press, 1982.

—— 'More on Modes of Power and the Peasantry.' *Subaltern Studies II*. Ed. R. Guha Delhi: Oxford University Press, 1983.

Chittick, W.C. 'Notes on Ibn al-'Arabi's Influence in India.' *Muslim World* 82 (1992).

Cohn, Bernard. 'The Command of Language and the Language of Command.' *Subaltern Studies IV*. Ed. R. Guha Delhi: Oxford University Press, 1985.

—— 'The Census, Social Structure and Objectification in South Asia.' *An Anthropologist among Historians and Other Essays*. New York: Oxford University Press, 1990.

Cook, M. 'On the Origins of Wahhabism.' *Journal of the Royal Asiatic Society* 2:2 (1992).

Crompton, Louis. 'Male Love and Islamic Law in Arab Spain.' *Islamic Homosexualities*. Eds. S.O. Murray and W. Roscoe. New York: University Press, 1997.

Crooke, W. 'Notes on Some Muhammadan Saints and Shrines in the United Provinces.' *Indian Antiquary* (May 1924).

Cuno, Kenneth. 'The Origins of Private Ownership of Land in Egypt: A Reappraisal.' *International Journal of Middle East Studies* 12 (1980).

Al-Farangi, M.S. 'La Notion de Propriete en Islam.' *L'Egypt contemporaire* 59:331 (1968).

Al-Ghazali, Muhammad. 'Universal Social Culture: An Empirico-Revelational Paradigm of Shah Wali Allah.' *American Journal of Islamic Social Sciences* 11:1 (1994).
Gilmartin, David. 'Religious Leadership and the Pakistan Movement in Punjab.' *Modern Asian Studies* 13: 3 (1979).
Guha, Ranajit. 'On Some Aspects of the Historiography of Colonial India.' *Subaltern Studies I*. Ed. R. Guha. Delhi: Oxford University Press, 1982.
—— 'Dominance without Hegemony and its Historiography.' *Subaltern Studies VI*. Ed. R. Guha Delhi: Oxford University Press, 1989.
—— 'Discipline and Mobilize.' *Subaltern Studies VII*. Ed. R. Guha. Delhi: Oxford University Press, 1993.
Hardiman, David. 'Subaltern Studies at Crossroads.' *Economic and Political Weekly* (Feb. 1986).
Hassan, Ahmad. 'The Principle of Istihsan in Islamic Jurisprudence.' *Islamic Studies* 16 (1977).
Hermansen, M.K. 'Shah Wali Allah of Delhi's Hujjat Allah al-Baligha: Tension Between the Universal and the Particular in an 18th Century Islamic Theory of Religious Revelation.' *Studia Islamica* 63 (1986).
Humphreys, Sally. 'Law as Discourse.' *History and Anthropology* 1 (1985).
Imamuddin, S.M. 'Education Under the Mughals in India.' *Islamic Quarterly* 26 (1982).
Inalcik, Halil. 'The Rise of the Ottoman Empire.' *The Cambridge History of Islam* 1A. Eds. P.M. Holt, A.K.S. Lambton and B. Lewis. Cambridge: University Press, 1995.
Islaha, Abdul Azim. 'Shah Wali Allah's Concept of al-Irtifaqat.' *Journal of Objective Studies* 2:1 (1990).
Kassim, Husain. 'Sarakhsi's Doctrine of Juristic Preference as a Methodological Approach to World Affairs.' *American Journal of Islamic Social Sciences* 5 (1989).
Khan, A.S. 'A Critical Appraisal of Dar ul-Ulum Deoband and its Leadership.' *Journal of the Research Society of Pakistan* 31:4 (1994).
Khan, S. Ali. 'The Nationalist Ulama's Interpretation Of Shah Wali Allah's Thought and Movement: The Post-Jihad Period.' *Journal of the Pakistan Historical Society* 38:1 (Jan. 1990).
Kugle, Scott Alan. 'Framed, Blamed and Renamed: The Recasting of Islamic Jurisprudence in Colonial South Asia.' *Modern Asian Studies* 35:2 (Jan. 2001).
Lambton, A.K.S. 'The Internal Structure of the Saljuq Period', *Cambridge History of Islam* 5. Cambridge: University Press, 1968.
Lapidus, Ira. 'The Separation of State and religion in the development of Early Islamic Society.' *International Journal of Middle East Studies* 6 (1975).
Layish, Aharon. 'The Maliki Waqf According to Wills and Waqfiyyat.' *Bulletin of the School of Oriental and African Studies XLVI* (1983).
Leonard, Karen. 'The 'Great Firm' Theory of the Decline of the Mughal Empire.' *Comparative Studies in Sociology and History* 21:3 (Jan. 1979).
Little, Donald P. 'Does Ibn Taymiyya have a Screw Loose?' *Studia Islamica* 41 (1975): 93–111.
Makdisi, George. 'Ash'ari and the Ash'arites in Islam Religious History.' *Studia Islamica* 17 (1962); 18 (1963).
Makdisi, John. 'Legal Logic and Equity in Islamic Law.' *American Journal of Comparative Law* 33 (1985).
Malik, Z.U. 'Religious Perceptions and Attitudes of Later Mughals.' *Journal of Objective Studies* 6:2 (1994).
Masud, M.K. 'Trends in the Interpretation of Islamic Law in the Fatawa Literature of Deoband School.' MA Thesis: Institute of Islamic Studies, McGill, 1969.
Metcalfe, B.D. 'Islamic Reform and Islamic Woman: Maulana Thanawi's Jewelry of Paradise.' *Moral Conduct and Moral Authority in South Asian Islam*. Berkeley University of California Press, 1984.

—— 'Presidential Address: Too Much, Too Little: Reflections on Muslims in the History of India.' *Journal of Asian Studies* 54:4 (1995).

Muhammad, Miraj. 'Shah Wali Allah's Concept of the Shari'ah.' *Islamic Perspectives*. Eds. Khurshid Ahmad and Z.I. Ansari. Jeddah: Saudi Publishing House, 1980.

Nadvi, S.H.H. 'The Role of Resurgent Ulama and Sufi-Sheikhs in the Reconstruction of Islamic Education.' *Muslim Education Quarterly* 3:2 (1986).

Nehemia Levitzion, 'The Eighteenth Century Background to the Islamic Revolutions in West Africa.' *Eighteenth Century Renewal and Reform in Islam*. Eds. N. Levitzion and J. Voll. Syracuse: University Press, 1987.

Nasr, Seyyed Hossein. 'Oral Transmission and the Book in Islamic Education', *The Book in the Islamic World*. Ed. George Atiyah. Albany: SUNY, 1995.

O'Connell, J.T. 'Vaishnava Perceptions of Muslims in 16th Century Bengal.' *Islamic Society and Culture*. Eds. Milton Israel and N.K. Wagle. New Delhi: Manohar Publishers, 1983.

Othman, Muhammad Z. 'The Status of 'Urf in Islamic Law.' *IIUM Law Journal* 3:2 (1993).

Pandey, Gayanendra. 'The Colonial Construction of 'Communalism': British Writing on Banares in the 19th Century.' *Subaltern Studies VI*. Ed. R. Guha Delhi: Oxford University Press, 1989.

Pearson, M.N. 'The Mughals and the Hajj.' *Journal of the Oriental Society of Australia* 18–19 (1986–87).

Prakash, Gyan. 'Writing Post-Orientalist Histories of the Third World.' *Comparative Journal of Society and History* (1990).

Sarkar, Sumit. 'Orientalism Revisited: Saidian Frameworks in the Writing of Modern Indian History.' *Mapping Subaltern Studies and the Post-Colonial*. Ed. V. Chaturvedi. London: Verso, 2000.

Siddiqi, I.H. 'Muslim Educational Movements in North India.' *Journal of the Institute of Islamic Studies* 9 (1972).

Siddiqqi, Z. 'The Institution of Qazi Under the Mughals.' *Medieval India* 1 (1969).

Al-Tayob, Abdul Kader. 'The Transformation of a Historical Tradition: From Khabar to Tarikh.' *American Journal of Islamic Social Sciences* 5:2 (1988).

Tibawi, A.L. 'Philosophy of Muslim Education.' *Islamic Quarterly* 4 (1957).

J. Voll, 'Linking Groups in the Networks of 18th Century Revivalist Schools: The Mizjaji Family in Yemen.' *Eighteenth Century Renewal and Reform in Islam*. Eds. N. Levitzion and J. Voll. Syracuse: University Press, 1987.

Wagle, N.K. 'Hindu-Muslim Interaction in Medieval Maharashtra.' *Hinduism Reconsidered*. Eds. Gunther-Dietz Sontheimer and J. Kuke. New Delhi: Manohar Publishers, 1997.

Washbrook, David. 'South Asia, the World System and World Capitalism.' *South Asia and World Capitalism*. Ed. S. Bose Delhi: Oxford University Press, 1990.

Books

Agrawal, C.M. *Wazirs of Aurangzeb*. Bodh-Gaya: Kauchan Publications, 1978.

Ahmad, A.S. *Jinnah, Pakistan and Islamic Identity: The Search for Saladin*. London: Routledge, 1997.

Ahmad, Aziz. *An Intellectual History of Islam in India*. Edinburgh: Edinburgh University Press, 1969.

Ahmad, Laiq. *The Prime Ministers of Aurangzeb*. Allahabad: Chugh Publications, 1976.

Alam, Muzaffar. *The Crisis of Empire in Mughal North India, 1707–48*. Delhi: Oxford University Press, 1993.

Anderson, Benedict. *Imagined Communities*. London: Verso, 1995.

Ansari, Sara. *Sufi Saints and State Power*. Lahore: Vanguard Books, 1992.

Ali, M. Athar. *The Mughal Nobility Under Aurangzeb*. London: Asia House Publishing, 1966.

Arberry, A.J. *Sufism: An Account of the Mystics of Islam*. New York: Harper & Row, 1970.
Asher, Catherine. *Architecture of Mughal India*. Cambridge: Cambridge University Press, 1992.
Awan, Muhammad Tariq *The History of India and Pakistan*. 3 vols. Lahore: Ferozesons, 1991.
Baldick, V. *Mystical Islam: An Introduction to Sufism*. London: I.B. Taurus, 1989.
Baljon, J.M.S. *The Reforms and Religious Ideas of Sir Sayyid Ahmad Khan*. Lahore: Sh. Muhammad Ashraf, 1964.
—— *Religion and Thought of Shah Wali Allah Dihlawi*. Leiden: E.J. Brill, 1986.
Banerjee, A.C. *English Law in India*. Delhi: Abhinav Publications, 1984.
Barnett, Richard. *North India Between Empires: Awadh, the Mughals and the British*. Berkeley: University of California Press, 1980.
Bayly, C.A. *Rulers, Townsmen and Bazaars: North Indian Society in the Age of British Expansion, 1770–1870*. Cambridge: Cambridge University Press, 1983.
—— *Indian Society and the Making of the British Empire*. Cambridge: Cambridge University Press, 1988.
Bayly, C.A., ed. *The Peasant Armed: Indian Revolt of 1857*. Oxford: Clarendon, 1986.
Bhatia, M.L. *Administrative History of Medieval India*. Delhi: Radha Publications, 1992.
Blair, Sheila and Jonathan Bloom. *The Art and Architecture of Islam 1250–1800*. New Haven: Yale University Press, 1995.
Bose, S., ed. *South Asia and World Capitalism*. Delhi: Oxford University Press, 1990.
Brand, Michael and Glenn Lowry. *Fatehpur Sikri: A Source-Book*. Cambridge, MA: Harvard University Press, 1985.
Brass, Paul. *Language, Religion and Politics in North India*. Cambridge: Cambridge University Press, 1974.
Brown, Peter. *The Cult of Saints: Its Rise and Function in Latin Christianity*. Chicago: University of Chicago Press, 1981.
Chakrabarty, Dipesh. *Habitations of Modernity: Essays in the Wake of Subaltern Studies*. Chicago: University of Chicago Press, 2002.
Chanda, S.N. *1857: Some Untold Stories*. Delhi: Sterling Publishers, 1976.
Chandra, Satish. *Parties and Politics at the Mughal Court, 1707–1740*. Aligarh: Muslim University Press, 1959.
Chatterjee, Partha. *The Nation and its Fragments*. Princeton: Princeton University Press, 1994.
Chaturvedi, Vinayak, ed. *Mapping Subaltern Studies and the Post-Colonial*. London: Verso, 2000.
Chaudhuri, S.B. *Theories of Indian Mutiny*. Calcutta: World Press, 1965.
Chaudhuri, S.H. *Civil Disturbances during British Rule in India, 1765–1857*. Calcutta: World Press, 1955.
Chittick, William C. *The Sufi Path to Knowledge: Ibn al-Arabi's Metaphysics of Imagination*. Albany: SUNY Press, 1989.
Cook, M.A. *Muhammad*. Oxford: Oxford University Press, 1983.
Corbin, Henri. *History of Islamic Philosophy*. Trans. L. Sherrard. London: Kegan Paul, 1993.
—— *L'Imagination creatrice dans le soufisms de Ibn Arabi*. Paris: Falumarion, 1988.
Cornell, V. et al., eds. *Religion, Society and the Other: Hostility, Hospitality and the Hope of Human Flourishing*. Sevilla: Elijah Interfaith Academy Think Tank, 2003.
Coulson, N.J. *A History of Islamic Law*. Edinburgh: Edinburgh University Press, 1964.
Crone, Patricia. *Meccan Trade and the Rise of Islam*. Princeton: Princeton University Press, 1987.
Crone, Patricia and M. Hinds. *God's Caliph: Religious Authority in the First Centuries of Islam*. Cambridge: Cambridge University Press, 1986.
Datta, K.K. *Anti-British Plots and Movements Before 1857*. Meerut: Meenakshi Prakashan, 1970.

Davies, C.C. *An Historical Atlas of the Indian Peninsula.* Delhi: Oxford University Press, 1979.

Davis, Richard. *Images, Miracles and Authority in Asian Religious Traditions.* Boulder: West View Press, 1998.

Dodge, Bayard. *Muslim Education in Medieval Times.* Baltimore: Garamond Press, 1962.

Donner, F.M. *The Early Islamic Conquests.* Princeton: Princeton University Press, 1981.

Dutta, S.C. *History of Adult Education in India.* New Delhi: Indian Adult Education Association, 1986.

Eaton, R., ed. *India's Islamic Traditions, 711–1750.* New Delhi: Oxford University Press, 2005.

Endress, G. and J. Aertsen. *Averroes and the Aristotelian Tradition.* Leiden: E.J. Brill, 1999.

Engineer, Asghar Ali. *The Muslim Communities of Gujarat: An Exploration of the* Bohras, Khojas and Memons. Delhi: Ajanta Publishers, 1898.

Fakhry, Majid. *A History of Islamic Philosophy.* New York: Columbia University Press, 1983.

Farooqi, N.R. *Mughal-Ottoman Relations, 1556–1748.* Delhi: Idara-i Adabiyat-i Delli, 1989.

Faruqi, Z. *Aurangzeb and His Times.* Delhi: Idara-i Adabiyat-i Delli, 1972.

Frank, F.M. *Al-Ghazali and the Ash'arite School.* Durham: Duke University Press, 1994.

Frank, Richard. *Beings and their Attributes: The Teachings of the Basrian School of the Mu'tazila in the Classical Period.* Albany: SUNY Press, 1978.

Freitag, Sandria B. *Collective Action and Community: Public Arenas and the Emergence of Communalism in North India.* Berkeley: University of California Press, 1989.

Friedmann, Yohanan. *Prophecy Continuous: Aspects of Ahmadi Religious Thought and its Medieval Background.* Berkeley: University of California Press, 1989.

—— *Shaykh Ahmad Sirhindi.* Montreal: McGill-Queen's University Press, 1971.

Geertz, Clifford. *The Interpretation of Cultures: Selected Essays.* New York: Basic Books, 1973.

—— *Islam Observed: Religious Development in Morocco and Indonesia.* Chicago: University of Chicago Press, 1975.

Gellner, Ernest. *Muslim Society.* Cambridge: Cambridge University Press, 1984.

Gerber, Haim. *State, Society and Law in Islam: Ottoman Law in Comparative Perspective.* Albany: SUNY Press, 1994.

Gordon, Stewart. *Marathas, Marauders and State Formation in 18th Century India.* Delhi: Oxford University Press, 1994.

Greaves, M.A. *Education in British India, 1698–1947.* London: University of London, 1967.

Guha, Ranajit. *Dominance without Hegemony: History and Power in Colonial India.* Cambridge, MA: Harvard University Press, 1997.

—— *Elementary Aspects of Peasant Insurgency in Colonial India.* Delhi: Oxford University Press, 1983.

Guha, Ranajit and Gayatri Spivak, eds. *Selected Subaltern Studies.* Delhi: Oxford University Press, 1988.

Guha, Ranajit, ed. *A Subaltern Studies Reader.* Minneapolis: University of Minnesota, 1997.

Gutas, D. *Avicenna and the Aristotelian Tradition.* Leiden: E.J. Brill, 1988.

Hallaq, W.B. *Law and Legal Theory in Classical and Medieval Islam.* Brookfield: Varorium, 1995.

Hallisey, R.C. *The Rajput Rebellion Under Aurangzeb.* Columbia: University of Missouri Press, 1977.

Hamid, Abdul. *A Chronicle of British Indian Legal History.* Jaipur: RBSA Publishers, 1991.

Hardy, Peter. *The Muslims of British India*. Cambridge: Cambridge University Press, 1972.
Hedayetullah, Muhammad. *Sayyid Ahmad*. Lahore: Shan Muhammad Ashraf, 1970.
Hintze, A. *The Mughal Empire and its Decline*. Aldershot: Ashgate, 1997.
Hiskett, Mervyn. *The Sword of Truth*. Evanston: Northwestern University Press, 1994.
Hodgson, Marshall G.S. *The Venture of Islam*, 3 vols. Chicago: University of Chicago Press, 1977.
Humphreys, S. *Islamic History: A Framework for Inquiry*. Princeton: Princeton University Press, 1991.
Hunter, Shireen, ed. *The Politics of Islamic Revivalism: Diversity and Unity*. Bloomington: Indiana University Press, 1988.
Husain, Iqbal. *The Rise and Decline of the Ruhela Chieftaincies in 18th Century India*. Delhi: Oxford University Press, 1994.
Ibrahim, Mahmood. *Merchant Capital and Islam*. Austin: University of Texas Press, 1990.
Irwin, Robert. *The Middle East in the Middle Ages: The Early Mamluk Sultanate, 1250–1382*. London: Croom Helm, 1986.
Israel, Milton and N.K. Wagle, eds. *Islamic Society and Culture*. New Delhi: Manohar Publishers, 1983.
Izutsu, T. *A Comparative Study of the Key Philosophical Concepts in Sufism and Taoism*, 2 vols. Tokyo: KICLS, 1966–67.
Jaffar, S.M. *Education in Muslim India*. Delhi: Idara-i Adabiyat-i Delli, 1973.
Jafri, S.H.M. *The Origins and Early Development of Shi'a Islam*. London: Longman, 1979.
Jalal, Ayesha. *Self and Sovereignty: Individual and Community in South Asian Islam since 1850*. London: Routledge, 2000.
—— *The Sole Spokesman: Jinnah, the Muslim League and the Demand for Pakistan*. Cambridge: Cambridge University Press, 1985.
Jalal, Ayesha and S. Bose. *Modern South Asia*. London: Routledge, 1999.
Johansen, Baber. *The Islamic Law on Land Tax and Rent: The Peasants' Loss of Property Rights as Interpreted in the Hanafite Legal Literature of the Mamluk and Ottoman Periods*. London: Groom Helm, 1988.
Kanda, K.C., ed. and trans. *Masterpieces of Urdu Ghazal*. Lahore: Vanguard, 1990.
Kaur, Kuldip. *Madrasa Education in India*. Chandigarh: CRRID, 1990.
Keay, John. *The Honorable Company*. London: Harper & Collins, 1991.
Kennedy, Hugh. *The Prophet and the Age of the Caliphates: The Islamic Near East from the 6th to the 11th Century*. London: Longman, 1986.
—— *The Early Abbasid Caliphate: A Political History*. New Jersey: Barnes & Noble, 1981.
Kozlowski, G.C. *Muslim Endowments and Society in British India*. Cambridge: Cambridge University Press, 1986.
Khadduri, Majid. *The Islamic Conception of Justice*. Baltimore: Johns Hopkins University Press, 1984.
Khan, Hamiuddin. *History of Muslim Education*, 2 vols. Karachi: All Pakistan Education Conference, 1967.
Knysh, Alexander. *Ibn al-'Arabi in the Later Islamic Tradition*. Albany: SUNY Press, 1999.
Kulshreshtha, S.S. *The Development of Trade and Industry Under the Mughals*. Allahabad: Kitab Mahal, 1964.
Lameer, J. *Al-Farabi and Aristotelian Syllogistics*. Leiden: E.J. Brill, 1994.
Lambton, A.K.S. *State and Government in Medieval Islam: An Introduction to the Study of Islamic Political Theory, the Jurists*. Oxford: Oxford University Press, 1981.
Lapidus, Ira. *A History of Islamic Societies*. Cambridge: Cambridge University Press, 1988.

Last, Murray. *The Sokoto Caliphate*. London: Londmans, Green & Co., 1967.
Lavan, Spencer. *The Ahmadiyah Movement: A Historical Perspective*. Delhi: Manohar Book Service, 1974.
Lev, Yaocov. *State and Society in Fatimid Egypt*. Leiden: E.J. Brill, 1990.
Lewis, Bernard. *The Origins of Isma'ilism*. Cambridge: W. Heffer, 1940.
Libson, Gideon. *Jewish and Islamic Law: A Comparative Study of Custom During the Geonic Period*. Cambridge, MA: Harvard University Press, 2003.
Lings, Martin. *Muhammad: His Life Based on the Earliest Sources*. New York: Inner Traditions Intl., 1983.
Ludden, David, ed. *Reading Subaltern Studies: Critical History, Contested Meaning and the Globalization of South Asia*. London: Anthem, 2002.
Madelung, Wilferd. *The Succession to Muhammad: A History of Early Islam*. Cambridge: Cambridge University Press, 1996.
Makdisi, George. *The Rise of Colleges: Institutions and Learning in Islam and the West*. Edinburgh: Edinburgh University Press, 1981.
Marcus, Abraham. *The Middle East on the Eve Of Modernity*. New York: Columbia University Press, 1989.
Marmura, M.E., ed. *Islamic Theology and Philosophy*. Albany: SUNY Press, 1984.
Marshall, P.J. *Bengal: The British Bridgehead—Eastern India, 1740-1828*. Cambridge: Cambridge University Press, 1988.
Martin, R.C. and M.R. Woodward w/D.S. Atmaja. *Defenders of Reason in Islam: Mu'tazilism from Medieval School to Modern Symbol*. Oxford: One World, 1997.
Massignon, L. *La Passion de Hosayn b. Hallaj*. 4 vols. Paris: Gallimard, 1975.
Metcalfe, B.D. *Islamic Revival in British India: Deoband, 1860-1900*. Princeton: Princeton University Press, 1982.
Minault, Gail. *The Khilafat Movement: Religious Symbolism and Political Mobilization in India*. New York: Columbia University Press, 1982.
—— *Secluded Scholars: Women's Education and Muslim Social Reform in Colonial India*. Delhi: Oxford University Press, 1998.
Mohanrajan, P. A. *Glimpses of early Printing and Publishing in India*. Madras: Mohanaralli Publishers, 1990.
Momen, Majid. *An Introduction to Shi'a Islam*. New Haven: Yale University Press, 1985.
Moosvi, Shireen, ed. and trans. *Episodes in the Life of Akbar: Contemporary Records and Reminiscences*. New Delhi: National Book Trust, 1994.
Morimoto, Kosei. *The Fiscal Administration of Egypt in the Early Islamic Period*. Kyoto: Dohosha Publishers, 1981.
Morris, James W. *The Wisdom of the Throne: An Introduction to the Philosophy of Mulla Sadra*. Princeton: Princeton University Press, 1981.
Mottahedeh, Roy. *Loyalty and Leadership in Early Islamic Society*. Princeton: Princeton University Press, 1980.
Mukhia, H. *The Mughals of India*. Oxford: Blackwell, 2004.
Naqvi, Hamida. *Agricultural, Industrial and Urban Dynamism under the Sultans of Delhi, 1206-1555*. Delhi: Munshiram Manoharlal Publishers, 1986.
Nasr, Sayyid Husain. *Science and Civilization in Islam*. Lahore: Suhail Academy, 1999.
Nasr, Seyyid Vali Reza. *Mawdudi and the Making of Islamic Revivalism*. New York: Oxford University Press, 1996.
Netton, I.R. *Muslim Neo-Platonists: An Introduction to the Thought of the Brethren of Purity*. London: Allen & Unwin, 1982.
New Cambridge History of India. Cambridge: Cambridge University Press, 1986-2000.
Ozcan, Azmi. *Pan-Islamism, Indian Muslims, the Ottomans and British*. Leiden: E.J. Brill, 1997.
Pandey, G. *Hindus and Others: The Question of Identity in India Today*. New Delhi: Viking Press, 1993.
—— *The Construction of Colonialism in Colonial India*. Delhi: Oxford University Press, 1990.

Patton, W.M. *Ahmad ibn Hanbal and the Mihna*. Leiden: 1897.
Pearson, M.N. *The Portuguese in India*. Cambridge: Cambridge University Press, 1987.
Peters, Rudolph. *Islam and Colonialism: The Doctrine of Jihad in Modern History*. Paris: Mouton, 1979.
—— *Jihad in Medieval and Modern Islam*. Leiden: E.J. Brill, 1977.
Prakash, Gyan. *The World of the Rural Labourer in Rural India*. Delhi: Oxford University Press, 1992.
Quraishi, Mansooruddin. *Muslim Education and Learning in Gujarat*. Baroda: MSU, 1972.
Qureishi, N.M. *Pan-Islam in British Indian Politics: A Study of the Khilafat Movement*. Leiden: E.J. Brill, 1999.
Rahman, Fazlur. *Major Themes of the Quran*. Minneapolis: Bibliotheca Islamica, 1994.
—— *Islam*. Chicago: University Press, 1979.
Rahman, Mujibur. *History of Madrasa Education*. Calcutta: Rais Anwar Rahman, 1977.
Ray, Krishna Lal. *Education in Muslim India*. Delhi: B.R. Publishing Corp., 1984.
Richards, John F. *The Mughal Empire*. Cambridge: Cambridge University Press, 1996.
Rizvi, S.A.A. *Muslim Revivalist Movements in Northern India*. Agra: Agra University Press, 1965.
—— *A History of Sufism in India*. 2 vols. Delhi: Munshiram Manoharlal, 1983.
—— *The Socio-Intellectual History of Isna-Ashari Shi'is in India*. Canberra: Ma'rifat Publishing House, 1986.
—— *Shah Wali Allah and his Times*. Canberra: Ma'rifat Publishing, 1980.
—— *Shah 'Abd al-'Aziz*. Canberra: Ma'rifat Publishing House, 1982.
Rizvi, Sayyid Mahbub. *Tarikh-i Dar al-Ulum Deoband*. Delhi: Idarah-i Ihtemam, 1980.
Roberts, I.E. *History of British India under the Company and the Crown*. London: Oxford University Press, 1983.
Robinson, Francis. *Separatism Among Indian Muslims: The Politics of the United Provinces' Muslims 1860–1923*. Cambridge: Cambridge University Press, 1974.
—— *The 'Ulama of Farangi Mahall*. Delhi: Permanent Black, 2001.
—— *Islam and Muslim History in South Asia*. Delhi: Oxford University Press, 2001.
Rosenthal, E.I.J. *Political Thought in Medieval Islam*. Cambridge: Cambridge University Press, 1958.
Said, Edward. *Orientalism*. New York: Vintage Books, 1979.
Said, Halil Ibrahim. *Revolution and Reaction*. Ann Arbor: University Microfilms International, 1978.
Saksena, K.P. *Muslim Law as Administered in India and Pakistan*. Lucknow: Eastern Book Co., 1963.
Sankhdher, B.M. *Ram Moham Roy: The Apostle of Indian Awakening*. New Delhi: Navarang Press, 1989.
Sanyal, Usha. *Devotional Islam and Politics in British India*. New York: Oxford University Press, 1996.
Sato, Tsugitaka. *State and Rural Society in Medieval Islam*. Leiden: E.J. Brill, 1997.
Schacht, J. *An Introduction to Islamic Law*. Oxford: Oxford University Press, 1962.
Schimmel, Annemarie. *Mystical Dimensions of Islam*. Chapel Hill: University of North Carolina Press, 1975.
—— *Islam in the Indian Subcontinent*. Leiden: E.J. Brill, 1980.
Sekhon, Sant Singh. *A History of Punjabi Literature*, 2 vols. Patiala: Punjab University Publishing Bureau, 1996.
Sen, S.N. *Scientific and Technical Education in India, 1781–1900*. New Delhi: Indian National Scientific Academy, 1991.
Shaban, M.A. *The Abbasid Revolution*. Cambridge: Cambridge University Press, 1970.
—— *Islamic History: A New Interpretation I, 600–750*. Cambridge: Cambridge University Press, 1976.
Shaikh, Farzana. *Community and Consensus in Islam: Muslim Representation in Colonial India 1860–1947*. Cambridge: Cambridge University Press, 1989.

Sharib, Z.H. *The History and Prospects of Rural Education in India*. Bombay: All-India Institute of Local Self-Governance, 1982.
Siddiqqi, Noman Ahmad. *Land Revenue Administration under the Mughals, 1700–50*. Aligarh: Asia Publishing House, 1970.
Simonsen, J.B. *Studies in the Genesis and Early Development of the Caliphal Taxation System*. Copenhagen: Akademisk Forlag, 1988.
Smith, W.C. *Islam in Modern History*. New York: Mentor Books, 1963.
Sontheimer, Gunther-Dietz and H. Kuke, eds. *Hinduism Reconsidered*. New Delhi: Manohar Publishers, 1997.
Stein, B. *A History of India*. Oxford: Blackwell, 1998.
Stern, S.M. *Studies in Early Isma'ilism*. Leiden: E.J. Brill, 1983.
Streusand, D.E. *The Formation of the Mughal Empire*. Delhi: Oxford University Press, 1989.
Stokes, Eric. *The English Utilitarians and India*. Oxford: Clarendon Press, 1959.
—— *The Peasant and the Raj: Studies in Agrarian Society and Peasant Rebellion in Colonial India*. Cambridge: Cambridge University Press, 1978.
—— *The Peasant and the Raj*. Cambridge: Cambridge University Press, 1978.
Subaltern Studies: Writings on South Asian History and Society. 10 vols. Delhi: Oxford University Press, 1982–2000.
Sulaiman, Ibrahim. *A Revolution in History*. London: Mansell Publishing, 1986.
Tabataba'i, H.M. *An Introduction to Shi'i Law: A Bibliographical Study*. London: Ithaca Press, 1984.
Takeshita, Masataka. *Ibn al-Arabi's Theory of the Perfect Man and its Place in the History of Islamic Thought*. Tokyo: ISCAA, 1987.
Tharu, Susie and K. Lalita, eds. *Women Writing in India: 600BC to Early Twentieth Century*. New York: The Feminist Press, 1991.
Trimingham, J.S. *The Sufi Orders in Islam*. London: Oxford University Press, 1971.
Tritton, A.S. *The Caliphs and their Non-Muslim Subjects*. London: Milford, Oxford University & Cass, 1930.
Troll, Christian W. *Sayyid Ahmad Khan: A Reinterpretation of Muslim Theology*. Delhi: Vikas Publishing House, 1978.
Umar, Muhammad. *Islam in Northern India*. Delhi: Munshiram Manoharlal Publishers, 1993.
van der Veer, Peter. *Religious Nationalism*. Berkeley: University of California Press, 1994.
Vrijhof, Pieter and Jacques Waardenburg, eds. *Religion and Society*. Le Hague: W. de Gruyter, 1979.
Wansborough, J. *Quranic Studies*. Oxford: Oxford University Press, 1977.
Watt, W. Montgomery. *The Faith and Practice of al-Ghazali*. Lahore: Sh. Muhammad Ashraf, 1963.
—— *The Formative Period of Islamic Thought*. Edinburgh: Edinburgh University Press, 1973.
—— *Muhammad: Prophet and Statesman*. Oxford: Oxford University Press, 1962.
Wolfson, H.A. *The Philosophy of the Kalam*. Cambridge, MA: Harvard University Press, 1976.
Zaehner, Z.C. *Hindu and Muslim Mysticism*. Oxford: One World, 1994.

GLOSSARY

Note: Unless otherwise indicated, all terms are common to Arabic, Persian and Urdu, but are given in the Arabic form.

'āda: 'custom'
ahl al-kitāb: 'People of the Book'; followers of the Abrahamic tradition
'ālim (pl. 'ulamā'): 'learned' in the religious sciences
amīr (pl. umarā'): 'governor' or 'ruler'
anjūmān: Urdu term for 'society' or 'organisation'
'aql: 'reason'
baqā': 'abiding' or 'subsisting' in God
bāṭin: 'inner' or 'esoteric' meaning of scripture/doctrine
bay'a: 'consent', as in the 'oath of allegiance' to a Caliph
bid'a: 'innovation', usually implying heresy, although there are also positive types (bid'a ḥasana)
dār al-Islām: 'Land of Islam'; areas under Muslim governance
dār al-ḥarb: 'Land of War'; areas under non-Muslim governance
dhikr: 'mentioning' God, as in a meditative exercise
dhimmī: 'protected'; non-Muslim subject of Muslim governance granted certain rights in exchange for payment of taxes. Dhimmī status is generally extended to the ahl al-kitāb, but in the South Asian context has included Zoroastrians, Hindus, Buddhists, Jains and Sikhs, although not necessarily recognising the latter as 'People of the Book'
falsafa: 'philosophy'
fanā': 'annihilation' in God
faqīh (pl. fuqahā'): an expert in fiqh; a jurist
faqīr: 'mendicant'
fatwa (pl. fatāwa): the legal opinion of a muftī (jurisconsult)
fiqh: 'jurisprudence'
firmān (pl. farāmīn): Persian/Urdu term for official 'edict' of state
ḥadīth (pl. aḥādīth): 'report', particularly of the sayings of the Prophet Muhammad
ḥakīm (pl. ḥukamā'): 'physician' or 'philosopher'
ijmā': 'consensus'; one of the sources of the sharī'a according to fiqh
istiḥsān: 'juristic preference' in fiqh
ijtihād: 'independent legal reasoning' in fiqh
'ilm (pl. 'ulūm): 'knowledge' or 'science'
imām: 'leader', usually in congregational prayer; teacher. In Shī'ism, the sinless head of the community/in Sunnism, often used interchangeably with khalīfa.
insān al-kāmil: 'Perfect Human'; Ṣūfī concept of one at the apex of the hierarchy of gnostic knowledge
iqṭā': grant of land revenue. The holder is an iqṭā'i. Also, see jagīr
jagīr: Persian/Urdu term for iqṭā'. The holder of the grant is a jagīrdār
jihād: 'struggle' or 'striving' for religion. In fiqh, this includes the jihād al-akbar ('great struggle') for personal purification, and the jihād al-asghar ('little struggle') in favour of spreading or maintaining the sharī'a.
jizya: 'poll-tax' on adult, male dhimmīs
kāfir: 'infidel' or 'unbeliever'
kalām: 'theology'

kashf: 'intuition'
khanqah: 'hospice' for *Ṣūfīs*
khuṭba: 'sermon' delivered at congregational prayers
madhhab (pl. *madhāhib*): 'school', particularly employed in regard of *fiqh*
madrasa: 'college'; formal institution of higher Islamic learning
maktab: 'school'; formal institution of primary Islamic learning, often associated with a mosque
mawlawī: 'preacher' or 'teacher' of religious subjects, especially the *Qurʾān*
muftī: 'jurisconsult' empowered to issue *fatāwa*
mujāhid (pl. *mujāhidīn*): participant in *jihād*
mutakallim (pl. *mutakallimūn*): an expert in *kalām*: a theologian
nawāb: Urdu term for a state official of high rank, derived from the Arabic *nāʾib*/'deputy'
pīr: Persian/Urdu term for a *Ṣūfī* 'saint'
qāḍī: 'judge'
qawm: 'community'
qibla: the direction towards which Muslims orient themselves during *ṣalāṭ* (i.e. the Kaʿba in Mecca).
qiyās: legal argumentation based on 'analogy'; one of the 'sources' of the *sharīʿa* according to *fiqh*
ṣalāṭ: formal prayer performed five times daily
samāʿ: ecstatic music recital in *Ṣūfism*
sharīʿa: 'Law', usually in reference to the legal corpus of the *fuqahāʾ*
shirk: 'association' of partners with God; polytheism
sunna: 'custom', usually of Prophet Muhammad, transmitted by means of *ḥadīth*; one of the 'sources' of the *sharīʿa* according to *fiqh*
tafsīr: 'exegesis' of the *Qurʾān*
taqlīd: 'imitation', as in the acceptance of a legal position without independent consideration
ṭarīqa: the 'way'; a *Ṣūfī* order, or the method of a particular adept
tawḥīd: God's 'Unity'
umma: the Muslim 'community'
uṣūl (sing. *aṣl*): 'roots' or 'principles', as in *uṣūl al-fiqh* (principles of jurisprudence)
ʿurf: 'customary law'
waḥdat al-shuhūd: 'Unity of Witness'; Aḥmad Sirhindī's doctrinal expression of *Ṣūfī* notions of God's ultimate 'transcendence'
waḥdat al-wujūd: 'Unity of Being'; Ibn al-ʿArabī's doctrinal expression of *Ṣūfī* notions of God's ultimate 'immanence'
waḥy: 'inspiration' or 'revelation'
waqf (pl. *awqāf*): 'trust' or 'endowment'
wazīr (pl. *wuzarāʾ*): 'minister' in government
ẓāhir: 'outer' or 'exoteric' meaning of scripture or doctrine
zakāt: obligatory alms tax, calculated on basis of personal holdings
zamīndār: Urdu term for 'landlord', including various classes of larger landholdings

INDEX OF PERSONS

'Abd al-'Aziz, Shah   132, 151, 152, 205, 228n17, 274, 293, 328
'Abd al-Bari, Mawlana   312, 316
'Abd al-Ghani, Shah   152, 162
'Abd al-Nabi, Shaykh   74, 75n14, 76, 76n19
'Abd al-Qadir, Shah   151
'Abd al-Rahim, Shaykh   133–134, 142, 144, 148, 151, 174
'Abd al-Rida, Shaykh   133
'Abdu, Shaykh Muhammad   247
Abu Talib, Mirza   227, 227n12, 228, 229, 237
Abu Yusuf   42
Adam, William   186–189, 192–194, 199, 203, 223
al-'Adawiya, Rabi'a   54
Afghani, Sayyid Jalal al-Din   245, 245n67, 246
Agha Khan I–III   128, 129n34, 130, 279, 309, 329
Ahmad, Khwaja Farid al-Din   226, 233n21
Ahmad, Mirza Ghulam   viii, 14, 231–232, 248, 249–257, 267, 317
Ahmad, Nizam al-Din   77, 80n26
Akbar, (Sultan) Jalal al-Din   vii, xviii, 6–7, 13, 65, 67–91, 93–100, 105–107, 111–115, 226, 229, 246, 337–339
'Ali, Chaudhary Rahmat   323
'Ali, Mawlana Karamat   229, 246
'Ali, Mawlana Mamluk   162
'Ali, Sayyid Mumtaz   133, 170
'Ali, Shah Ghulam   234
Andalib, Khwaja   149, 274
Arnold, Edwin   190
al-Ash'ari, Abu al-Hasan   31
Awliya', Nizam al-Din   21, 49, 72
Awrangzib, (Sultan) Muhi al-Din   vii, xix, 6–7, 13, 65, 67–68, 70, 91–115, 119–121, 131–133, 143–144, 216–217, 226, 246, 282, 288, 337–339
Azad, Abu al-Kalam   319, 327, 329
Azad, Muhammad Husayn   274–275, 277, 280, 286–287

Babar, (Sultan) Zahir al-Din   xviii, 69n2, 75n14, 79n25
Bada'uni, 'Abd al-Qadir   71–80, 85–87, 89
Barani, Diya' al-Din   21, 45–46, 78, 88n60
Barelwi, Ahmad Rida   170–171, 245, 250, 294, 317
Barelwi, Sayyid Ahmad   157, 170, 205, 295n69
al-Basri, Hasan   54
Beck, Theodore   307
Begum, Shah Jahan   280
Begum, Sikandar   280
Begum, Sultan Jahan   280, 316
Bernier, Francois   109–110, 112
Bhonsle, Shivaji   xviii, 96, 113
Bhutto, Benazir   326
al-Bistami, Abu Yazid   26n26, 54–55
Burton, Richard   182, 190, 196–197

Chishti, Mawdud   212
Chishti, Shaykh Salim   82
Chugtai, Ismat   282
Copernicus   166n161, 179, 227

Dard, Khwaja Mir   149, 230, 233, 274, 287
Dayananda, Swami   165
Descartes, Rene   109

Fakhr al-Din, Mawlana   148
al-Farabi, Muhammad ibn Muhammad   23n8, 24, 50, 52, 86, 262
Frere, Henry Bartle Edward   181–182, 196–197

Gandhi, Mohandas K.   xxi, 119, 269, 303n94, 315, 317–318, 320–321, 327
Gangohi, Rashid Ahmad   133, 161–163, 165–168, 294, 314
Ganj-i Shakar, Shaykh Farid al-Din   212
Gassendi, Pierre   109
Ghalib, Asad Allad Khan   230, 232, 283–284, 288–289
al-Ghazali, Abu Hamid Muhammad   vii, 19–30, 42, 44, 47, 49–52, 54–55,

362 INDEX OF PERSONS

59, 62–63, 88, 109–110, 235n27, 245–246, 258, 260–261, 264, 266, 284, 291, 318

al-Hallaj, Husayn ibn Mansur 26n26, 26n27, 54–55, 210
Hali, Altaf Husayn 276–277, 279, 283–284, 289–290, 299–300, 302, 312, 332–334, 342
Hasan, Mahmud 314, 316
Hastings, Warren 124, 126n27
al-Hujwiri, 'Ali ibn 'Uthman vii, 20–22, 27–30, 45, 47, 50–51, 53, 55, 60, 62–63, 109–110
Humayun, (Sultan) Nasir al-Din xviii, 79n25
Husayn, Rokeya Sakhawat 281
Husayn, Sayyid Nazir 172, 294
Hyder, Nazar Sajjad 281

Ibn 'Abd al-Wahhab, Muhammad 150–152, 188, 285
Ibn al-'Arabi, Shaykh Muhyi al-Din 21, 51, 53, 55–61, 82, 115, 135, 137, 251, 261, 288
Ibn 'Ata', Wasil 30
Ibn Battuta 21
Ibn Khaldun 318
Ibn Mubarak, Abu al-Fadl 77, 79n26, 81–86, 89–90, 191n44, 234n25
Ibn Mubarak, Abu al-Faydi 84, 86
Ibn al-Muqaffa', 'Abd Allah 21, 44
Ibn Qasim, Muhammad 73
Ibn Rushd, Abu al-Walid Muhammad 21, 24n12, 37–39, 50–51, 64, 258
Ibn Taymiyya, Taqi al-Din Ahmad 21, 36, 38, 43–44, 46, 64, 76, 88n60, 137, 246, 299, 318
Ibn Sina, Abu 'Ali al-Husayn 24, 86, 109, 145, 234n26
Iqbal, Muhammad viii, xxi, 9, 14, 231, 251, 257–269, 273, 279, 283–285, 289, 318, 320–324, 328–332, 334–335, 342
Isma'il, Shah Muhammad vii, 132, 148, 152–155, 157–158, 160, 165, 167, 171, 174, 188, 201, 205, 230, 234, 253, 289, 292, 295

Jahan, Rashid 282
Jahangir, (Sultan) Nur al-Din xix, 80n26, 93–96, 98, 106, 108, 111, 226
Jawahar, Muhammad 'Ali 269, 312, 315, 318–319, 335
Jawahar, Shawkat 'Ali 312

Jesus (Christ) 84, 214, 255–257
Al-Jilani, 'Abd al-Qadir 213
Jinnah, Fatima 282, 325–326, 333
Jinnah, Muhammad 'Ali 315, 317–318, 323–325, 326n139, 329
Jones, William 125, 179, 227
al-Junayd, Abu al-Qasim 55

Kalim Allah, Shah 148
Khan, 'Abd al-Ghaffar 320
Khan, Hakim al-Mulk Danishmand 109, 110n135, 226–227, 246
Khan, 'Inayat 230–231
Khan, Muhammad Khafi 91, 98–101, 103, 107, 111, 113
Khan, Sayyid Ahmad viii, 9, 14, 158n131, 231–255, 257–259, 263–264, 266–267, 271, 275, 278–279, 281–283, 285–287, 289, 291, 294–296, 299–307, 309–310, 312, 315, 318, 332, 342
Khan, Siddiq Hasan 158n131, 172, 280, 294n65
Khan, Tafaz al-Husayn 226–227, 229
Khidr, Khwaja 149, 208–209, 214

Leitner, Gottlieb William 197–203

Macaulay, Thomas Babington 180–181, 189
Madani, Husayn Ahmad 314, 316, 319–320, 327–329, 331, 333–334
Mahmud, Sayyid 236, 307
Maneri, Sharaf al-Din 21, 49
Mango, Pir Haji 177, 185, 221
Manucci, Niccolao 98, 109–110, 112
al-Mawardi, Abu al-Hasan 21, 36–38, 64, 88n60, 100n96
Mawdudi, Sayyid Abu 'Ala' 329
Monserrate, Antonius 84–85, 87, 89, 107, 112
Moses (Prophet) 210, 256n95
Muhammad (Prophet) xvii, 22, 25, 29, 34, 50, 54, 57, 75, 80, 84, 141, 149, 210, 214, 244–245, 250, 254, 263–264, 293, 299
Murdoch, John 180

Nanawtawi, Muhammad Qasim 133, 161–166, 230, 234
Newton, Isaac 227
Nizam al-Din, Mulla 184
Numani, Shibli 301

INDEX OF PERSONS

Perry, Erskine   128–130, 174

Qandahari, Muhammad 'Arif   71–74, 77, 80–83
al-Qazwini, Asad Beg   90–91
al-Qunawi, Sadr al-Din   137

Rafi' al-Din, Shah   151, 162
Rahman, Fazlur   224, 231–232, 286
al-Razi, Abu Bakr Muhammad   50
Roy, Ram Mohan   180, 181n14

al-Sarakhsi, Muhammad   42
Sewharwi, Saddiqa Begum   282
Shah Jahan, (Sultan) Shihab al-Din   xix, 68, 70, 92–98, 107–108, 111, 186, 216–217
al-Shirazi, Fath Allah   86
al-Shirazi, Rafi' al-Din   77
al-Shirazi, Sadr al-Din (a.k.a. Mulla Sadr)   52, 87
Shukoh, Dara   7, 68, 92
Al-Simnani, 'Ala' al-Dawlah   59

Sindhi, 'Ubaid Allah   314
Sirhindi, Shaykh Ahmad   7, 21, 53, 55n148, 137, 234, 251, 259, 261, 263, 265
al-Suhrawardi, Shihab al-Din   87

Temple, R.C.   184, 206–207, 211, 213–214, 217, 221
Timur (Amir)   69n2, 70, 80
Trevelyan, Charles Edward   179–182, 190
Tyabji, Badr al-Din   304

'Uthmani, Shabbir Ahmad   324, 331

Wali Allah, Shah   132, 134–147, 151, 164–165, 167, 172, 174, 188, 241–244, 251, 255, 262–265, 278, 284–285, 290, 292, 299, 314
Wilson, Horace Hayman   179, 181, 189

Zahir, Radi Sajjad   282

INDEX OF SUBJECTS

'ada 11, 47, 58–59, 153. *See also* custom/customary law
'adl 31
Afghanistan 21, 69n2, 158, 172, 251, 257, 314
Agra 181, 301
Ahl-i Hadith 133, 172–173, 177, 231, 238, 250, 255, 257, 266, 280, 286–287, 289, 294, 306, 334
ahl al-kitab 38, 64. *See also* People of the Book
Ahl-i Sunnat 133, 170–173, 177, 234, 238, 245, 250, 266, 289, 294, 306, 317, 324, 329, 334
Ahmadi(s)/Ahmadiyya 231, 251–252, 255, 289, 317, 324, 334
Ahmadnagar xviii, xix, 90, 94, 95n76, 96. *See also* People of the Book
Ahrar(s) 250, 251, 329
Ajmir 72
Aligarh/Aligarhi(s) 235, 236n30, 238, 240, 250, 254, 260, 266, 269, 275–277, 281, 289, 294–295, 299, 301, 304, 306–307, 309, 312, 317
All-India Khilafat Committee 314–15, 319
All-India Muslim Ladies' Association 280, 316
All-India Muslim Ladies' Conference 280–281, 316
All-India Muslim League. *See* Muslim League
All-India Shi'a Conference 329
All-India Women's Conference 281
Anglo-Muhammadan Law 125–126, 156, 174
anjuman(s) 198n78, 202, 235–236, 275–276, 305, 312–313, 315
Anjuman-i Khuddam-i Ka'ba 312, 314–315
Anjuman-i Islami 305
Anjuman-i Punjab 197, 274
antinomian/antinomianism 12, 14, 22, 27, 61, 64, 80n26, 112, 178, 185, 213, 221, 230, 268, 285, 310, 332, 338, 340–342

'aqa'id 143, 185, 191, 193, 196, 201, 203, 205, 219, 221, 239
'aql 12, 20, 25, 153. *See also* Reason
Arab(s)/Arabic 11–13, 22, 30, 63, 73n10, 74n13, 110, 125–126, 128, 132, 134n44, 140, 143, 169, 171, 174, 181–182, 184n25, 185–187, 190n43, 191–204, 208, 212, 220, 233, 238, 241n53, 249, 257–258, 276, 282, 299–300
Arya Samaj 165, 252, 318n128
Ash'ari(s) 23, 29, 32–34, 52, 63, 241, 243, 261–262
al-Azhar 247–248

Babiyya 255
Baghdad 19, 30, 36, 62, 69, 212–213, 250, 300
Baha'iyya 255
Bahmanid(s) xvii–xviii, 95n77
Balkan War(s) 311
Baluch/Baluchi(s)/Baluchistan 22, 82, 158, 182n20, 269
Bangladesh 331
barzakh 138–139, 262
Basra 21
batin/batiniyya 19, 22, 24, 30, 51, 266
baqa' 26, 28, 55, 59, 164, 261
bay'a 146, 159, 250n74, 251n81
Bengal 11, 14, 71, 80n26, 93, 124, 127n30, 158–159, 171–172, 178, 184–188, 191, 193–199, 201–204, 218–220, 223, 237, 270–271, 281, 298, 305–306, 312
Berar xviii
bid'a 102, 115, 152–155, 168–169, 171, 213, 284
Bidar xviii
Bihar 11, 14, 124, 184–188, 193, 195–199, 202–204, 218–220, 223, 317
Bijapur xviii–xix, 90, 94–96
Bohra 128nn33–34, 304
Brahmo Samaj 180, 195, 318n128
Britain 13, 122, 173, 181n14, 227n12, 293, 298, 304, 313
British Indian Association 295–296, 304, 310

British Raj 13, 119, 133, 161, 170, 172, 223, 266, 268–270, 275, 281–284, 286, 288–291, 295–296, 302, 305–306, 309–310, 314, 317, 328, 330–333
Buddhist(s)/Buddhism 10n28, 26n26, 30, 48, 50, 61, 73, 128n34, 247, 255, 257, 326
burqa 170, 281, 326

Cairo 21, 36, 247–248, 250
Caliph(s)/Caliphal/Caliphate(s) 33, 34n55, 44, 73n10, 74n13, 77–78, 89, 96, 98, 114, 146–147, 156, 158–160, 201, 210, 284, 291–293, 296–297, 299–300, 302, 310–315, 317–319, 334
Capitalist(s)/Capitalism 120–123, 131–133, 143–144, 171–173, 175, 178, 183, 185, 192–193, 196, 201, 204–206, 220–221, 223, 230–231, 268, 270–274, 279, 281–282, 290, 303, 305, 309, 311, 314, 320–322, 329, 332–333, 340–341
Central Muslim Association 305
Chishti(s)/Chishtiyya 47–49, 70, 72, 82, 148, 177, 212, 218, 230, 306n102
Christian(s)/Christianity 1, 10n28, 38–39, 64, 67, 82–83, 85, 90, 94, 131, 155, 181, 195, 237, 239, 249, 252, 255–257, 266, 284–285, 294–295, 298, 326
Civil Disobedience Movement 320–321
Civilising Mission 2, 277
communalism 270, 330, 334, 337
Cordova 21–22
cow protection 318n128
Crimean War 293
custom/customary law 5, 7–8, 11–13, 22, 30, 41–42, 46–47, 52, 58, 63–65, 71, 74n14, 76n19, 85, 89, 91, 107–108, 112–115, 127–131, 133–134, 140–142, 144, 151–155, 167–168, 170–171, 173, 177, 205, 208, 211, 213, 218, 221, 223, 226, 264, 266, 274, 277–278, 294, 331–333, 338–339

dajjal 250
Damascus 19, 21, 36, 69, 250, 300
dar al-harb 37, 38, 43n99, 156, 294
dar al-Islam 37, 43n99, 73, 293–294
dars-i nizamiyya 123, 163, 184–188, 196, 202, 204
dawabit 45–46, 68, 73, 105
Deccan 80n26, 95n76, 111, 303

Deoband/Deobandi(s) 9, 120, 130–133, 161–165, 167–168, 170–173, 177, 185, 204, 219, 230–231, 238, 243, 250, 253–255, 264–266, 276–277, 281, 285, 289, 294, 297, 301, 314, 316–317, 324, 326, 329, 331, 334
Delhi 11, 13, 21, 69n2, 92, 101, 103, 109, 120, 132–133, 135, 148, 151, 155, 161, 163–164, 170, 181, 183, 217, 233, 234n25, 236, 248, 274, 283–284, 291–292, 298, 301, 305
dharmashastra(s) 9
dhawq 25, 83
dhikr 47n121, 48, 54, 167
dhimmi(s) 39–40, 64, 73–74, 156, 294, 328, 331, 334
dupatta 326
Dutch East India Company xix, 93n71

Egypt/Egyptian(s) 22, 69n2, 95n77, 144n88, 237, 247–248, 283, 298
England 238, 258, 278, 293, 307–308
English East India Company xviii–xxi, 93n71, 119, 122–125, 127, 129–130, 142, 155–157, 161, 174–175, 178, 179, 180–185, 189–190, 195–196, 204–205, 216n136, 219, 223, 226–227, 232–233, 234n25, 236, 291, 294–296
Enlightenment 1
Ethiopia/Ethiopian(s) 22, 95
Europe/Europeans 1–2, 4, 13–14, 71, 83n41, 90–91, 93–94, 110n135, 112–113, 116, 126, 156, 164, 166, 168n169, 179–183, 186, 194–195, 204–205, 219, 223–233, 235–240, 245–248, 252, 255, 257–258, 265–270, 272–273, 276, 278, 286–288, 298, 301, 303, 309, 313–314, 322, 328, 331, 333–334, 340–343
Evangelical(s) 179–180

fana' 25–26, 28, 54–55, 59, 164, 230n19, 261
fara'id 49, 134, 143, 185, 191–194, 196, 201, 203, 205, 219, 221
Fara'idi Movement 171
farangi(s) 90, 216
farman (pl. *faramin*) 77, 124
Fatehpur Sikri 72, 82, 83n41, 84, 87
fatwa (pl. *fatawa*) 71–72, 99–100, 113, 126n27, 127n30, 134n48, 151, 152n113, 155–157, 166–167, 171, 175, 205, 245, 250–251, 274, 278, 289,

293–294, 295n67, 296, 314, 316, 326, 328, 331
Firdawsi/Firdawsiyya 49, 191
fiqh 9, 27, 34, 35n56, 41, 86, 100, 126, 127n30, 134, 167–168, 171, 187, 213, 233n22, 294n65
French East India Company xviii–xx

German(s)/Germany 257, 304, 313, 326
Ghazna/Ghaznawid(s) xvii, 21, 27, 119, 129n34, 158
Ghuri/Ghurid(s) xvii, 119, 128n34
Goa 83–84
Golconda xviii–xix, 74n13, 90, 93n71, 94–96, 111
Greek(s) 11, 22, 51, 87, 226, 239, 258, 328
Gujarat 11, 84, 90, 128, 177, 283

hadith(s) 10, 23, 34, 35n55, 37n69, 42, 43n99, 73, 75, 86, 98, 103, 123, 131, 135, 141–142, 149–155, 161–162, 166–168, 171–172, 174, 187, 191n49, 193, 196, 202–203, 219, 230, 233, 244, 263–265, 290, 294n65, 327
hajj 72, 76, 78, 80, 135, 158
Hanafi(s) 21, 34, 38–42, 48, 64, 73, 75, 99, 107n123, 131, 133–134, 141–142, 167–168, 171, 174, 235n27, 241, 263–265, 279–280
Hanbali(s) 21, 34, 36, 38, 142, 150
Hellenic 20, 26n26, 61, 63–64, 166, 225, 247, 255, 300
hijab 170, 326
hikma 23, 187. *See also* philosophy
Hikmat-i Ilahi 52, 87
Hindu(s)/Hinduism 2–3, 5–9, 10n28, 26n26, 30, 39, 48, 50, 64, 67, 70, 73–76, 79, 82, 84–85, 87, 95, 97, 99–100, 103–109, 115, 119, 123n14, 124, 128, 149, 157, 159–160, 165, 166n161, 168, 180, 181n14, 182, 189–190, 195, 205–208, 211–212, 214, 216–218, 234n25, 237, 239, 247, 249, 252, 255, 257, 271, 273, 282, 284–285, 288, 295–296, 298, 303–305, 307–309, 312, 314, 316–321, 323, 326–328, 330–331, 334–335, 339–341
Hindu Mahasabha 318, 326
hudud 36, 44, 253
Hyderabad 104, 260, 305

'Ibadat Khana 67, 72, 82, 85, 226, 229
Iberia 21, 63
ijtihad 13–14, 35, 81, 89, 99–100, 139–141, 149–150, 167, 171–172, 226, 232, 234, 247, 258, 263, 267, 285–288, 322, 330, 332–334, 340
ikhtilaf 134
Imam(s)/Imamate(s) 19, 34n55, 39, 47n121, 128, 129n34, 146–147, 154–156, 158, 160, 162, 210, 284, 290
India/Indian(s) 3–9, 12–14, 63, 89, 112, 114, 116, 119, 122, 124, 128, 162, 172, 178, 206, 208, 223–224, 227n12, 256, 258, 269, 271–272, 275, 278, 282–283, 286, 290n55, 295–297, 301, 303–306, 308–311, 313–315, 318, 320–324, 326–331, 334–335, 339, 341
Indian National Congress 119, 271, 303–304, 306, 309, 311, 313, 315, 317–321, 323–324, 327–329, 334
Indic/Indicism 5, 8, 20, 22, 63–64, 70–71, 114, 116, 207
Indologist(s) 125, 179, 181, 206
insan al-kamil 57, 254, 259
Intoxicated Way 13–14, 65, 81, 87, 89, 97, 112, 114–116, 149, 177–178, 183, 185, 207, 210, 213–214, 218, 221, 230–232, 239, 247, 249, 254–255, 266–268, 272–273, 279, 284, 288, 290, 321–322, 332, 338–340, 342
Intuition 12, 20, 25, 27, 30, 51–52, 59–60, 62–63, 81, 154–155, 167, 232, 248, 253–254, 258, 268, 288, 334, 338, 340
Iran/Irani(s) 19, 21, 46, 47n121, 61, 80n26, 87n55, 100, 109, 111, 129n34, 226
Ishraqi(s)/Ishraqism 11, 70, 86–87, 114, 135, 243, 251, 255, 338
irtifaqat 144–145
Islamicate 10
Iraq/Iraqi(s) 21, 73n10
Isma'ili(s)/Isma'ilism 8, 128, 129n34, 132, 209, 255n94, 279–280, 329
istihsan 42, 141–142, 264, 279
istislah 42, 141–142, 264, 279

jagir(s)/*jagirdar*(s) 80n28, 96, 102, 121, 215, 248
Jain(s)/Jainism 67, 73, 82, 87, 97, 106, 326
Jama'at-i Islami 119, 172–173, 286, 329

Jama'at-i 'Ulama'-i Hind   9, 119, 172–173, 314–316, 317n126, 319, 321, 324, 328–329, 331, 334
Jama'at-i 'Ulama'-i Islam   119, 172–173, 317n126, 324, 329, 331
Jerusalem   19, 166n159, 244
Jesuit(s)   83n41, 84–85, 90, 94
jihad   37–38, 40, 64, 88n60, 90, 100, 146–147, 156–161, 171, 205, 250n74, 256, 290, 292, 294–295, 313–314, 316, 328, 342
jinn(s)   83, 239, 245, 258
jizya   37–40, 67, 74, 78, 89, 97, 103–104
jurisprudence   9, 11, 27, 34–35, 41, 47, 63, 73, 81, 100, 103, 110, 125, 127, 129–131, 135, 139–140, 142, 146, 149–150, 155, 165–167, 171, 174, 179, 185, 187, 196, 203, 219, 221, 233, 263–265, 267, 278–279, 331, 337–338, 343

Ka'ba   72, 80, 98, 154, 312, 314–315
Kabul   69n2, 71, 80n26, 111, 217
kafir(s)   31, 50, 64, 72–73, 86, 90, 94, 99, 160, 166, 245, 289, 317
kalam   9–10, 23n6, 187, 240, 253
kashf   12, 20, 25, 27, 60, 254, 257. See also Intuition
Kashmir   xxi, 47n121, 108, 256
Khaksar(s)   250, 251, 329
Khalji(s)   xvii, 45n113, 216
Khandesh   xvii, xix
Khilafat Movement   312–313, 315–319, 323, 325
Khoja(s)   8, 128, 129n34, 279, 325
khudi   259–260
khutba   291
Kufa   21

Lahore   11, 20–22, 27, 100–101, 108n127, 133, 183, 197–202, 257, 301, 305
Lahore Resolution   323–324, 326–328
latitudinarian(s)/latitudinarianism   12, 14, 22, 64, 80n26, 112, 178, 185, 213, 221, 230, 268, 285, 310, 332, 338, 340–342
Lodhi(s)   xvii, xix, 45n113, 74n13
Lucknow   11, 80n26, 183–184, 281, 305
Lucknow Pact   315, 317

madrasa(s)   1, 14, 19, 44, 62, 120, 123, 161–164, 175, 178, 182–196, 199, 201–205, 218–221, 229, 236, 238, 246–248, 266–267, 276, 297, 312, 314, 324, 337

Madrasa-i Farangi Mahal   183–184, 226, 306, 312
Madrasa al-Nizamiyya   19, 44
Madrasa-i Rahimiyya   135, 157, 162, 292
Mahabharata   67, 71, 81, 208
Mahdi   69, 79, 184n25, 249, 250n74, 255–256, 292n58
Majlis-i Ahrar Islam. See Ahrar(s)
maktab(s)   14, 123, 175, 178, 182, 185, 190–201, 204, 210, 220, 233, 249, 257, 276
Malamati(s)/Malamatiyya   61
Maliki(s)   21, 34, 38–39, 41–42, 64, 75, 171
Malwa   xvii, xix–xx, 81
Mamluk   xvii, 45n113, 69n2, 95n76
Maratha(s)   95–96, 100
ma'rifa   55
Marxist   321–322
masih   249, 250n74, 255–256
mawlana(s)   192–193, 195, 199, 219, 221, 324
mawlawi(s)   159–160, 161n141, 169, 192–194, 199, 221, 252, 276, 288, 234
Mecca   19, 72, 76, 79, 86, 90, 135, 162–163, 166n159, 171, 209–211, 214, 245, 250, 312, 314–315
Medina   19, 72, 90, 135, 171, 209–211, 250, 312, 315
Memon(s)   128, 130, 283
mi'raj   244
monism   136–139, 243, 253, 259, 261, 263, 267, 337
monotheism   137, 139, 207, 337
mufti(s)   74n14, 79n25, 99, 115, 124, 175
Mughal(s)   vii, xvii–xxi, 2–4, 7–8, 11–12, 19, 35, 40, 42, 47, 48n122, 52, 55, 68–71, 72n7, 73, 74n13, 78n24, 82n38, 83, 86, 88n60, 89–90, 93–98, 107n123, 111n142, 114, 120–121, 131, 134–135, 144, 146–147, 155–156, 172, 174, 215–217, 226, 233, 247–248, 270, 274, 284, 291–292, 298, 302, 309, 311, 330, 332, 341
Muhammadan Anglo-Oriental College   238
mujtahid(s)   35, 44, 76–78, 81–82, 99, 113, 154, 171, 199
mulla(s)   75, 110, 192–193, 199, 324
Multan   209, 212
murtadd(s)   245, 250
Muslim Educational Conference   275
Muslim League   309, 312–315, 317–318, 321–325, 331, 334

INDEX OF SUBJECTS 369

Muslim Anglo-Oriental Defence
  Association 306–307, 309–310
Mu'tazili (pl. Mu'tazila)/Mu'tazilism 4,
  28–34, 52, 63, 240–243, 247, 258, 318,
  338
mysticism 9–10, 21, 47–48, 54, 63, 81,
  92, 135, 139, 142, 164, 193, 231, 243,
  267, 338

nabi 249
Nadwat al-'Ulama' 301
Nationalism 2, 14–15, 120, 162, 173,
  269–273, 291, 297, 303, 310, 319, 322,
  325, 328–331, 334, 337, 342
Naqshbandi(s)/Naqshbandiyya 7,
  47–49, 61, 113, 165, 230, 265
Naqshbandi-Mujaddidiyya 274
nechari/nechariyya 245, 285
Non-Cooperation Movement 315, 317,
  328
Nuqtawi(s) 87

Orientalist(s)/Orientalism 3–4, 85, 87,
  89, 205, 207, 257, 264, 337
Orissa 11, 14, 124, 184–186, 188, 193,
  195–199, 202–204, 218–220, 223
Ottoman(s) 131, 144, 146–147,
  292–293, 297–302, 311–315
Oudh 226–227, 305

Pakistan(s) 3, 13–14, 20, 119, 172, 177,
  251, 269, 271–272, 311, 319, 323–326,
  329–331, 333–334, 341
People of the Book 38–39, 50, 64,
  73n10, 290, 317, 342
Persian(s) 11–13, 20, 22, 30, 44, 46, 51,
  63, 67, 71, 87, 116, 123, 126, 128, 132,
  143, 169, 174, 181–183, 186, 188–192,
  194–201, 203–205, 208, 220, 226, 228,
  232–233, 238, 246, 249, 257–259,
  268
philosophy 9–11, 23, 29, 39, 43–44,
  51–53, 55, 63, 73, 86–87, 104–105,
  109–110, 114, 135, 139, 142, 146,
  150, 156, 158, 162, 165–167, 185,
  202, 227–229, 243, 257, 265, 267,
  291–293, 296, 310, 328, 338–339,
  342
pir(s) 102, 113, 128, 154, 158, 177, 185,
  209, 211–212, 221, 234
Portuguese 83, 90, 93–94, 112, 226
Princely States 223, 323
Purana(s) 208, 214
purda 168–170, 273–274, 276–281,
  316, 325–326, 333

qadi(s) 8, 47–49, 71, 73–75, 78, 81, 87,
  92, 99–102, 113, 115, 124, 169, 175,
  199, 210, 211–212, 276
Qadiri(s)/Qadiriyya 47–48, 148–150,
  158, 170–171, 213, 218
al-Qa'ida 1, 341
Qalandari(s)/Qalandariyya 61
Qandahar 71–74, 77, 80–83, 94–95, 158
qanun 68, 240
qawm(s) 282–285, 287, 290–291, 299,
  302–305, 309–312, 315, 317 319,
  321–328, 331, 333–334, 342
qisas 101
qiyas 35, 37, 42, 46, 52, 141–142, 172,
  264–265
Qur'an 7, 10, 23, 29, 31–36, 40, 43,
  46–47, 50, 54, 58, 76, 80–81, 115,
  128–130, 140–144, 149, 151–155, 163,
  167–168, 171, 174, 191–193, 197–198,
  201, 208, 229–230, 233, 239–243,
  247–249, 252, 254, 258, 263–264, 287,
  289–290, 316, 327

Rajput(s) 73, 76, 84, 89, 96, 105,
  216–218
Ramayana 211, 214
Rashtriya Swayamsevak Sangh 326
Reason 12, 19–20, 23, 25–33, 44, 46,
  50–52, 55, 60, 62–64, 72, 81, 85–88,
  109–111, 130, 141, 144, 154–156, 165,
  167, 169, 173, 182, 219, 232, 240–241,
  243–248, 252–254, 258, 264, 268, 279,
  281, 288, 295, 302, 334, 338, 340
Revelation 7, 12, 20, 25, 27, 29, 32,
  50–52, 57, 59–60, 62–63, 81, 129, 143,
  154, 232, 242–243, 247, 250, 252–255,
  258, 260–261, 267–268, 322, 334, 338,
  340

Safawid(s) xviii–xx, 87n55, 94–95,
  128n34
sahw 28, 53
sama' 48, 98, 113, 149
sati 84, 107–108, 274
separate electorates 271, 291, 302,
  308–312, 315, 317, 319–321, 324, 328,
  331
Shafi'i(s) 21, 34, 36–38, 109, 140, 142,
  171, 174
shar'i/shari'a 11, 27, 34, 35–37, 39–43,
  45–50, 52–53, 58–61, 62, 64, 68–70,
  72–73, 76, 85, 98, 100, 103, 107, 110,
  114–115, 125, 131, 133–134, 139–142,
  146, 149, 154, 157, 159, 165, 167–169,
  173, 213, 218, 233, 253–254, 259,

262–264, 268, 278, 291, 296, 299–300, 312, 324, 328, 338
Shattariyya 47–48
shirk (pl. mushrik) 31, 115, 150, 152–155, 168, 171, 263, 274, 284–285, 310
Shi'a(s)/Shi'i(s)/Shi'ism 33–34, 40, 62, 67–68, 71, 73, 79, 94–97, 99, 104, 123, 150, 168, 172, 188, 199, 201–202, 210, 242, 247, 251, 253, 255, 284, 288–289, 300, 324, 329, 337
shuddhi 304
Shuhudi(s) 62–63, 115, 149, 164, 259, 338
Sikh(s)/Sikhism 8, 159, 205–206–207, 211, 216–218, 241, 249, 252, 295, 326
Sind/Sindhi(s) 11, 14, 22, 73, 82, 119, 123, 158, 177, 181–182, 184–185, 190, 196–199, 202–204, 207, 218–220, 269, 314
Sober Path 12–14, 21, 63–65, 72–74, 81, 89, 97, 104–105, 107, 109, 112, 114–116, 119, 126, 130, 132–133, 147, 149, 157, 160–161, 164–165, 168–174, 183, 185, 188, 196, 201, 205–207, 210–211, 213, 218–219, 221, 224, 230–233, 235, 239–241, 244–247, 249, 252–254, 263–268, 272–290, 318, 329, 331–332, 338–340, 342–343
Suhrawardi(s)/Suhrawardiyya 47–48, 177, 209, 212–213, 218
sukr 28, 53
sunna 34–35, 37, 40, 42–43, 46, 58, 134, 140–141, 149, 153, 155, 160
Sunni(s)/Sunnism 33–34, 39–40, 62, 71, 73, 95, 99, 123, 128, 130, 139–140, 146, 166, 188, 199, 202, 242, 263, 288–289, 300, 324, 337

Tablighi Jama'at 119, 172–173, 329
tafsir 86, 98, 143, 187, 201–202, 239, 241, 243–244, 246–249
Tahrik-i Khasar. See Khaksar(s)
talfiq 139–140
Taliban Movement 1, 341
taqlid 23, 35, 40, 46, 81, 139, 167–168, 171, 234, 287
Tarikh-i Ilahi 67–68, 78, 80, 87, 89, 92, 96, 109
tariqa 25, 115, 165, 167
Tariqa Muhammadiyya 149–150, 152, 157, 167, 169, 171–173, 230, 234, 264, 274

tasawwuf 10, 92, 164
Tavernier, Jean Baptiste 108, 112
tawhid 31, 53, 55, 67, 153, 155, 300
Tawhid-i Ilahi 67–68, 81–82, 85, 87–89, 92, 109
Timurid(s) 69–70

'ulama' 43, 158, 296, 340
Umayyad(s) xvii, 73, 78n24, 79n25 146, 300
umma 43–44, 58, 147, 212, 214, 271–272, 282–285, 287, 290–291, 296–297, 299–300, 302–303, 310–312, 314–315, 317–319, 325, 327, 333–334
United Indian Patriotic Association 304–307, 310
Upanishad(s) 7
Urdu 11, 13–14, 49, 67, 123, 132–133, 151–152, 164, 171, 174, 199–201, 204, 207–208, 220, 228, 232–233, 235–326, 328, 246, 249, 257–258, 274–276, 280–281, 286, 290, 300–301, 305–306, 313, 316, 333
'urf 11, 47, 140, 142, 213
'urs 103, 168, 177
Utilitarian(s)/Utilitarianism 179–180, 201, 203, 265, 296

wahdat al-shuhud 59, 61, 135, 137, 261
wahdat al-wujud 55, 60–61, 87, 135, 137, 149, 164, 261, 288
Wahhabi(s)/Wahhabiyya 133, 161, 170–172, 177
wahy 12, 20, 27, 60, 154, 250, 253–254
Wali Allahi(s) 13, 132–133, 147–148, 152–159, 161–163, 168, 170–174, 196, 231, 234, 243–244, 247, 254, 263, 267, 287, 297, 314
waqf(s) 41, 106, 163
watan(s) 282–283, 287, 290, 303, 314–315, 317, 319, 321–325, 237–328, 333
wazir(s)/wazirat 39, 44, 71, 88, 101, 103–104, 216, 226–227, 305
World War I 313–314, 328
World War II 321, 323
Wujudi(s) 62–64, 114–115, 164, 338

zahir 51, 282
zakat 38, 48, 103–104
Zoroastrian(s)/Zoroastrianism 67, 82, 85, 87, 106, 247